Frommer's®
Costa Rica 2012

by Eliot Greenspan

John Wiley & Sons, Inc.

Published by:
John Wiley & Sons, Inc.
111 River St.
Hoboken, NJ 07030-5774

ISBN 978-1-118-02752-3 (paper); 978-1-118-07691-0 (paper); 978-1-118-11437-7 (ebk); 978-1-118-11440-7 (ebk); 978-1-118-11444-5 (ebk)

Editor: Melinda Quintero with Jennifer Reilly
Production Editor: Jana M. Stefanciosa
Cartographer: Roberta Stockwell
Photo Editors: Richard Fox, Alden Gewirtz
Design and Layout by Vertigo Design
Graphics and Prepress by Wiley Indianapolis Composition Services

Front cover photo: Rincon de la Vieja ©Patrick Di Fruscia / SuperStock, Inc.
Back cover photos: *Left:* A Bananaquit in the Central Valley ©Rolf Nussbaumer Photography / Alamy Images. *Middle:* Guanacaste beach ©Jaime Kowal / Workbook Stock / Getty Images. *Right:* Man biking in Puerto Viejo ©Alberto Coto / Getty Images

CONTENTS

LIST OF MAPS

ABOUT THE AUTHOR

Eliot Greenspan is a poet, journalist, musician, and travel writer who took his backpack and typewriter the length of Mesoamerica before settling in Costa Rica in 1992. Since then, he has worked steadily as a travel writer, food critic, freelance journalist, and translator, and continued his travels in the region. He is the author of *Frommer's Belize, Frommer's Ecuador, Frommer's Guatemala, Costa Rica for Dummies,* and *Costa Rica Day By Day,* as well as the chapter on Venezuela in *Frommer's South America.*

DEDICATION

I'd like to dedicate this edition, with love, appreciation and gratitude, to Warren Greenspan, November 26, 1932—January 11, 2011.

—Eliot Greenspan

ACKNOWLEDGMENTS

I say this every year, but I continue to be eternally grateful to Anne Becher and Joe Richey, who were instrumental in getting me this gig—*muchas gracias.* I'd also like to thank my parents, Marilyn and Warren Greenspan, who showed unwavering love, support, and encouragement (well, one out of three ain't bad) when I chose words and world-wandering over becoming a lawyer or a doctor. Jody and Ted Ejnes (my sister and brother-in-law) deserve a mention; they risked life and limb—literally—leading to two important tips that may help you save yours. (I now believe Ted, and he may have actually almost stepped on a crocodile.) Chrissie Long and Derek Marin did some excellent phone, fax, and fact-checking work on this edition. And a big tip of my hat to Jennifer Reilly for her editorial diligence and patience.

—Eliot Greenspan

HOW TO CONTACT US

In researching this book, we discovered many wonderful places—hotels, restaurants, shops, and more. We're sure you'll find others. Please tell us about them, so we can share the information with your fellow travelers in upcoming editions. If you were disappointed with a recommendation, we'd love to know that, too. Please write to:

Frommer's Costa Rica 2012
John Wiley & Sons, Inc. • 111 River St. • Hoboken, NJ 07030-5774

ADVISORY & DISCLAIMER

Travel information can change quickly and unexpectedly, and we strongly advise you to confirm important details locally before traveling, including information on visas, health and safety, traffic and transport, accommodations, shopping, and eating out. We also encourage you to stay alert while traveling and to remain aware of your surroundings. Avoid civil disturbances, and keep a close eye on cameras, purses, wallets, and other valuables.

While we have endeavored to ensure that the information contained within this guide is accurate and up-to-date at the time of publication, we make no representations or warranties with respect to the accuracy or completeness of the contents of this work and specifically disclaim all warranties, including without limitation warranties of fitness for a particular purpose. We accept no responsibility or liability for any inaccuracy or errors or omissions, or for any inconvenience, loss, damage, costs, or expenses of any nature whatsoever incurred or suffered by anyone as a result of any advice or information contained in this guide.

The inclusion of a company, organization, or website in this guide as a service provider and/or potential source of further information does not mean that we endorse them or the information they provide. Be aware that information provided through some websites may be unreliable and can change without notice. Neither the publisher nor author shall be liable for any damages arising herefrom.

FROMMER'S STAR RATINGS, ICONS & ABBREVIATIONS

Every hotel, restaurant, and attraction listing in this guide has been ranked for quality, value, service, amenities, and special features using a **star-rating system.** In country, state, and regional guides, we also rate towns and regions to help you narrow down your choices and budget your time accordingly. Hotels and restaurants are rated on a scale of zero (recommended) to three stars (exceptional). Attractions, shopping, nightlife, towns, and regions are rated according to the following scale: zero stars (recommended), one star (highly recommended), two stars (very highly recommended), and three stars (must-see).

In addition to the star-rating system, we also use **seven feature icons** that point you to the great deals, in-the-know advice, and unique experiences that separate travelers from tourists. Throughout the book, look for:

special finds—those places only insiders know about

fun facts—details that make travelers more informed and their trips more fun

kids—best bets for kids and advice for the whole family

special moments—those experiences that memories are made of

overrated—places or experiences not worth your time or money

insider tips—great ways to save time and money

great values—where to get the best deals

The following abbreviations are used for credit cards:

AE	American Express	**DISC**	Discover	**V**	Visa
DC	Diners Club	**MC**	MasterCard		

TRAVEL RESOURCES AT FROMMERS.COM

Frommer's travel resources don't end with this guide. Frommer's website, **www.frommers. com**, has travel information on more than 4,000 destinations. We update features regularly, giving you access to the most current trip-planning information and the best airfare, lodging, and car-rental bargains. You can also listen to podcasts, connect with other Frommers.com members through our active-reader forums, share your travel photos, read blogs from guidebook editors and fellow travelers, and much more.

THE BEST OF COSTA RICA

With more than two million visitors each year, Costa Rica is currently—and consistently—one of the hottest vacation and adventure-travel destinations in Latin America. Despite its popularity and mass appeal, Costa Rica remains a place rich in natural wonders and biodiversity, where you can still find yourself far from the maddening crowds. The country boasts a wealth of unsullied beaches that stretch for miles, small lodgings that haven't attracted hordes of tourists, jungle rivers for rafting and kayaking, and spectacular cloud forests and rainforests with ample opportunities for bird-watching and hiking. In addition to the country's trademark eco- and adventure-tourism offerings, you will also find luxury resorts and golf courses, plush spas, and some truly spectacular boutique hotels and lodges.

Having lived in Costa Rica for more than 20 years, I continue to explore and discover new spots, adventures, restaurants, and lodgings—and my "best of" experiences keep on coming. In this chapter, I've selected the very best of what this unique country has to offer. This chapter is meant to give you an overview of the highlights so that you can start planning your own adventure.

THE best OF NATURAL COSTA RICA

- **Rincón de la Vieja National Park** (northeast of Liberia, in Guanacaste): This is an area of rugged beauty and high volcanic activity. The Rincón de la Vieja Volcano rises to 1,848m (6,061 ft.), but the thermal activity is spread out along its flanks, where numerous geysers, vents, and fumaroles let off its heat and steam. This is a great place to hire a guide and a horse for a day, with waterfalls and mud baths, hot springs, and cool jungle swimming holes to explore. You'll pass through pastureland, scrub savanna, and moist secondary forest; the bird-watching is excellent. See p. 196.
- **The Río Sarapiquí Region** (north of San José btw. Guanacaste in the west and the Caribbean coast in the east): This region is a prime place for an ecolodge experience. Protected tropical forests climb from the Caribbean coastal lowlands up into the central mountains, affording you a glimpse of a plethora of life zones and ecosystems. **Braulio Carrillo National Park** borders several other private reserves here, and a variety of ecolodges will suit any budget. See "Puerto Viejo de Sarapiquí," in chapter 9.

PREVIOUS PAGE: **A red-eyed tree frog in Tortuguero.**

Tabacón Hot Springs.

o **Arenal Volcano/Tabacón Hot Springs** (near La Fortuna, northwest of San José): When the skies are clear and the lava is flowing, Arenal Volcano offers a thrilling light show accompanied by an earthshaking rumble that defies description. You can even see the show while soaking in a natural hot spring and having a drink at the swim-up bar at **Tabacón Grand Spa Thermal Resort** (www.tabacon.com; ✆ **877/277-8291** in the U.S. and Canada, or 2519-1999 in Costa Rica). If the rushing torrent of volcano-heated spring water isn't therapeutic enough, you can get an incredibly inexpensive massage here. See "Arenal Volcano & La Fortuna," in chapter 9.

o **Monteverde Cloud Forest Biological Reserve** (in the mountains northwest of San José): There's something both eerie and majestic about walking around in the early morning mist surrounded by bird calls and towering trees hung heavy in broad bromeliads, flowering orchids, and hanging moss and vines. The reserve has a well-maintained network of trails, and the community is truly involved in conservation. Not only that, but in and around

Monteverde Cloud Forest Biological Reserve.

THE BEST OF NATURAL COSTA RICA

THE BEST BEACHES

THE BEST ADVENTURES

THE BEST BIRD-WATCHING

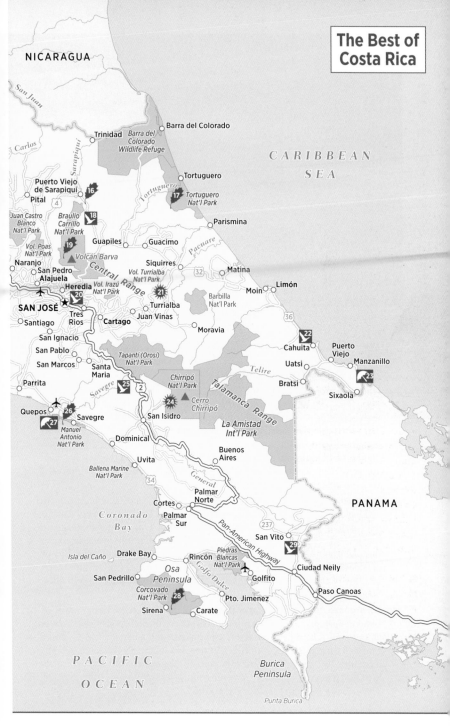

The Best of
Costa Rica

Manuel Antonio National Park.

Monteverde and Santa Elena, you'll find a whole slew of related activities and attractions, including canopy tours that allow you to swing from treetop to treetop while hanging from a skinny cable. See p. 330.

o **Manuel Antonio** (near Quepos on the central Pacific coast): The reason this place is so popular and renowned? Monkeys! The national park here is full of them, even the endangered squirrel monkeys. But you'll also find plenty to see and do outside the park. The road into Manuel Antonio has many lookouts that consistently offer postcard-perfect snapshots of steep jungle hills meeting the sea. Uninhabited islands lie just off the coast, and the beaches here are perfect crescents of soft, white sand. See "Manuel Antonio National Park," in chapter 10.

o **Osa Peninsula** (in southern Costa Rica): This is Costa Rica's most remote and biologically rich region. **Corcovado National Park,** the largest remaining patch of virgin lowland tropical rainforest in Central America, takes up much of the Osa Peninsula. Jaguars, crocodiles, and scarlet macaws all call this place home. Whether you stay in a luxury nature lodge in **Drake Bay** or outside of **Puerto Jiménez,** or camp in the park itself, you will be surrounded by some of the most lush and most intense jungle this country has to offer. See chapter 11.

o **Tortuguero Village & Jungle Canals** (on the Caribbean coast, north of Limón): Tortuguero Village is a small collection of rustic wooden shacks on a narrow spit of land between the Caribbean Sea and a dense maze of jungle canals. It's been called Costa Rica's Venice, but it actually has more in common with the South American Amazon. As you explore the narrow canals here, you'll see a wide variety of herons and other water birds, three types of monkeys, three-toed sloths, and caimans. If you come between June and October, you might be treated to the awe-inspiring spectacle of a green turtle nesting—the small stretch of Tortuguero beach is the last remaining major nesting site of this endangered animal. See "Tortuguero National Park," in chapter 12.

THE best BEACHES

With more than 1,200km (750 miles) of shoreline on its Pacific and Caribbean coasts, Costa Rica offers beachgoers an embarrassment of riches.

○ **Santa Rosa National Park:** If you really want to get away from it all, the beaches here in the northwest corner of Costa Rica are a good bet. You'll have to four-wheel-drive or hike 13km (8 miles) from the central ranger station to reach them. And once there, you'll find only the most basic of camping facilities: outhouse latrines and cold-water showers. But you'll probably have the place almost to yourself. In fact, the only time it gets crowded is in October, when thousands of olive ridley sea turtles nest in one of their yearly *arribadas* (arrivals). See p. 202.

○ **Playa Nacascolo:** With silky soft white sand, this is the best stretch of beach on the Papagayo Peninsula. The waters here are protected from ocean swells and great for swimming. See "Playa Hermosa, Playa Panamá & Papagayo," in chapter 7.

○ **Playa Avellanas:** Just south of Tamarindo, this long, white-sand beach has long been a favorite haunt for surfers, locals, and those in-the-know. Playa Avellanas stretches on for miles, backed largely by protected mangrove forests. On the verge of "being discovered," there's still very little going on here—aside from the nearby JW Marriott resort and Lola's, perhaps my favorite beachfront restaurant in the country. See p. 247.

○ **The Beaches around Playa Sámara:** Playa Sámara itself is nice enough, but if you venture just slightly farther afield, you'll find some of the nicest and least developed beaches along the entire Guanacaste coast. **Playa Carrillo** is a long, almost always deserted crescent of palm-backed white sand located just south of Sámara, while **Playa Barrigona** and **Playa Buena Vista** are two hidden gems tucked down a couple of dirt roads to the north. See "Playa Sámara," in chapter 8.

○ **Playa Montezuma:** This tiny beach town at the southern tip of the Nicoya Peninsula has weathered fame and infamy, but retains a funky sense of individuality. European backpackers, vegetarian yoga enthusiasts, and UFO seekers choose Montezuma's beach over any other in Costa Rica. The waterfalls are what set it apart from the competition, but the beach stretches for miles, with plenty of isolated spots to plop down your towel or mat. Nearby are the **Cabo Blanco** and **Curú** wildlife preserves. See "Playa Montezuma," in chapter 8.

○ **Malpaís & Santa Teresa:** While the secret is certainly out, there's still some time to visit Costa Rica's fastest growing hot spot before the throngs and large resorts arrive. With just a smattering of luxury lodges, surf camps, and assorted hotels and cabinas, Malpaís is the place to come if you're looking for miles of

A Santa Teresa surfer.

Punta Uva.

deserted beaches and great surf. If you find Malpaís is too crowded, head farther on down the road to Santa Teresa and beyond, to Playa Hermosa and Manzanillo. See "Malpaís & Santa Teresa," in chapter 8.

o **Manuel Antonio:** The first beach destination to become popular in Costa Rica, Manuel Antonio retains its charms despite burgeoning crowds and mushrooming hotels. The beaches inside the national park are idyllic, and the views from the hills approaching the park are enchanting. This is one of the few remaining habitats for the endangered squirrel monkey. Rooms with views tend to be a bit expensive, but many a satisfied guest will tell you they're worth it. See "Manuel Antonio National Park," in chapter 10.

o **Punta Uva & Manzanillo:** Below Puerto Viejo, the beaches of Costa Rica's eastern coast take on true Caribbean splendor, with turquoise waters, coral reefs, and palm-lined stretches of nearly deserted white-sand beach. Punta Uva and Manzanillo are the two most sparkling gems of this coastline. Tall coconut palms line the shore, providing shady respite for those who like to spend a full day on the sand, and the water is usually quite calm and good for swimming. See "Puerto Viejo," in chapter 12.

THE best ADVENTURES

o **Mountain-Biking the Back Roads of Costa Rica:** The lack of infrastructure and paved roads here that most folks bemoan is a huge boon for mountain bikers. The country has endless back roads and cattle paths to explore. Tours of differing lengths and all difficulty levels are available. Contact **Coast to Coast Adventures** (© **2280-8054;** www.ctocadventures.com). See p. 80.

o **Swinging through the Treetops on a Canopy Tour:** This unique adventure has become ubiquitous in Costa Rica. You'll find zip-line canopy tours all over the country. In most cases, after a strenuous climb using ascenders, you strap on a harness and zip from treetop to treetop while dangling from a cable.

Check chapter 4, "The Active Vacation Planner," and the various destination chapters to find a canopy tour operation near you.

o **Rafting the Upper Reventazón River** (near Turrialba): The Class V Guayabo section of this popular river is serious white water. Only experienced and gutsy river runners need apply. If you're not quite up to that, try a 2-day Pacuare River trip, which passes through primary and secondary forests and a beautiful steep gorge. Plans to build a dam here have thankfully been rejected, or at least stalled, for the time being. **Costa Rica Nature Adventures** (© **800/321-8410** in the U.S., or 2225-3939; www.toenjoynature.com) can arrange these tours. See p. 91.

o **Surfing & Four-Wheeling Guanacaste Province:** This northwestern province has dozens of respectable beach and reef breaks, from Witch's Rock at Playa Naranjo near the Nicaraguan border to Playa Nosara more than 100km (62 miles) away. In addition to these two prime spots, try a turn at Playa Grande, Punta Langosta, and playas Negra, Avellanas, and Junquillal. Or find your own secret spot. Rent a four-by-four with a roof rack, pile on the boards, and explore. See chapter 7.

o **Trying the Adventure Sport of Canyoning:** While far from standardized, canyoning usually involves hiking along and through the rivers and creeks of steep mountain canyons, with periodic breaks to rappel down the face of a waterfall, jump off a rock into a jungle pool, or float down a small rapid. **Pure Trek Canyoning** (© **866/569-5723** in the U.S. and Canada, or 2479-1313; www.puretrekcostarica.com), **Desafío Adventure Company** (© **866/210-0052** in the U.S. and Canada, or **2479-9464**; www.desafiocostarica.com) in La Fortuna, and **Psycho Tours** (© **8353-8619**; www.psychotours.com), near Puerto Jiménez, are the prime operators. See chapters 9 and 11.

A tourist riding a canopy tour.   A canyoning tour.

○ **Windsurfing or Kitesurfing on Lake Arenal:** With steady gale-force winds (at certain times of the year) and stunning scenery, the northern end of Lake Arenal has become a major international windsurfing and kitesurfing hot spot. See chapter 9.

○ **Diving off the Shores of Isla del Coco** (off the Pacific coast): Legendary among treasure seekers, pirate buffs, and scuba divers, this small island is consistently rated one of the 10 best dive sites in the world. A protected national park, Isla del Coco is surrounded by clear Pacific waters, and its reefs are teeming with life (divers regularly encounter

Windsurfing on Lake Arenal.

large schools of hammerhead sharks, curious manta rays, and docile whale sharks). Because the island is so remote and has no overnight facilities for visitors, the most popular way to visit is on 10-day excursions on a live-aboard boat, where guests live, eat, and sleep onboard—with nights anchored in the harbor. See p. 256.

○ **Hiking Mount Chirripó** (near San Isidro de El General on the central Pacific coast): The highest mountain in Costa Rica, Mount Chirripó is one of the few places in the world where (on a clear day) you can see both the Caribbean Sea and the Pacific Ocean at the same time. Hiking to Chirripó's 3,724m (12,215-ft.) summit takes you through a number of distinct bioregions, ranging from lowland pastures and a cloud forest to a high-altitude páramo, a tundralike landscape with stunted trees and morning frosts. See "San Isidro de El General: A Base for Exploring Chirripó National Park," in chapter 10.

THE best DAY HIKES & NATURE WALKS

○ **Lankester Gardens:** If you want a really pleasant but not overly challenging day hike, consider a walk among the hundreds of distinct species of flora on display here. **Lankester Gardens** (✆ **2511-7939;** www.jbl.ucr.ac.cr) is just 27km (17 miles) from San José and makes a wonderful day's expedition. The trails meander from areas of well-tended open garden to shady natural forest. See p. 180.

○ **Rincón de la Vieja National Park:** This park has a number of beautiful trails through a variety of ecosystems and natural wonders. My favorite hike is down to the Blue Lake and Cangrejo Falls. It's 5.1km (3¼ miles) each way, and you'll want to spend some time at the base of this amazing lake;

plan on at least 5 hours for the outing, and bring along lunch and plenty of water. You can also hike up to two craters and a crater lake here, and the Las Pailas loop is ideal for those seeking a less strenuous hike. This remote volcanic national park is about an hour north of Liberia (it's only 25km/16 miles, but the road is quite rough), or about 5 hours from San José. See p. 196.

○ **La Selva Biological Station:** This combination research facility and rustic nature lodge has an extensive and well-marked network of trails. You'll have to reserve in advance (www.threepaths.co.cr; *C* **2524-0607**) and take the guided tour if you aren't a guest at the lodge. But the hikes are led by very informed naturalists, so you might not mind the company. The Biological Station is located north-northeast on the Caribbean slope of Costa Rica's central mountain range. It'll take you about 1½ hours to drive from San José via the Guápiles Highway. See p. 348.

○ **Arenal National Park & Environs:** This area has great hiking. The national park itself has several excellent trails that visit a variety of ecosystems, including rainforest, secondary forest, savanna, and, my favorite, old lava flows. Most of them are on the relatively flat flanks of the volcano, so there's not too much climbing involved. The Arenal Observatory Lodge also has great trails, and the trek down to the base of the La Fortuna Waterfall is a fun scramble. It's about a 3½-hour drive from San José to La Fortuna and Arenal National Park. See "Arenal Volcano & La Fortuna," in chapter 9.

○ **Monteverde Cloud Forest Biological Reserve:** In the morning rush of high season, when groups and tours line up to enter the reserve, you'd think the park was named "Crowd Forest." Still, the guides here are some of the most

Rincón de la Vieja National Park.

La Selva Biological Station.

professional and knowledgeable in the country. Take a tour in the morning to familiarize yourself with the forest, and then spend the late morning or afternoon (your entrance ticket is good for the entire day) exploring the reserve. Off the main thoroughfares, Monteverde reveals its rich mysteries with stunning regularity. Walk through the gray mist and look up at the dense tangle of epiphytes and vines. The only noises are the rustlings of birds or monkeys and the occasional distant rumble of Arenal Volcano. The trails are well marked and regularly tended. It's about 3½ hours by bus or car to Monteverde from San José. See p. 330.

o **Corcovado National Park:** This large swath of dense lowland rainforest is home to Costa Rica's second-largest population of scarlet macaws. The park has a well-designed network of trails, ranger stations, and camping facilities. Most of the lodges in Drake Bay and Puerto Jiménez offer day hikes through the park, but if you really want to experience it, you should hike in and stay at one or more of the campgrounds. This is strenuous hiking, and you will have to pack in some gear and food, but the reward is some of Costa Rica's most spectacular and unspoiled scenery. Because strict limits are placed on the number of visitors allowed into the park, you'll always be far from the crowds. See "Puerto Jiménez: Gateway to Corcovado National Park," in chapter 11.

o **Cahuita National Park:** Fronted by the Caribbean and a picture-perfect white-sand beach, the trails here are flat, well-maintained paths through thick lowland forest. Most of the way they parallel the beach, which is usually no more than 90m (295 ft.) away, so you can hike out on the trail and back along the beach, or vice versa. White-faced and howler monkeys are common, as are brightly colored land crabs. See p. 479.

THE best BIRD-WATCHING

o **Observing Oropendola & Blue-Crowned Motmot at Parque del Este:** A boon for city bird-watchers, this San José park rambles through a collection of lawns, planted gardens, and harvested forest, but it also includes second-growth scrub and dense woodland. Oropendola and blue-crowned motmot are common species here. See p. 132.

o **Spotting Hundreds of Marsh & Stream Birds along the Río Tempisque Basin:** Hike around the Palo Verde Biological Station, or take a boat trip down the Bebedero River with **Ríos Tropicales** (© **2233-6455;** www.riostropicales.com). This area is an important breeding ground for gallinules, jacanas, and limpkins, and is a common habitat for numerous heron and kingfisher species. Palo Verde is about a 3½-hour drive from San José. See p. 194.

o **Looking for 300-plus Species of Birds in La Selva Biological Station:** With an excellent trail system through a variety of habitats, from dense primary rainforest to open pasturelands and cacao plantations, this is one of the finest places for bird-watching in Costa Rica. With such a variety of habitats, the number of species spotted runs to well over 300. La Selva is located just a few miles south of Puerto Viejo. See p. 348.

o **Sizing up a Jabiru Stork at Caño Negro National Wildlife Refuge:** Caño Negro Lake and the Río Frío that feeds it are incredibly rich in wildlife and a major nesting and gathering site for aquatic bird species. These massive birds are getting less common in Costa Rica, but this is still one of the best places

A Red-lored parrot.

to spot one. **Caño Negro Natural Lodge** (www.canonegro lodge.com; ☎ **2265-3302**) sits right on the edge of the refuge and makes a great base for exploring this region to the north of La Fortuna. See p. 306.

○ **Catching a Scarlet Macaw in Flight over Carara National Park:** Home to Costa Rica's largest population of scarlet macaws, Carara Biological Reserve is a special place for devoted bird-watchers and recent converts. Macaws are noisy and colorful birds that spend their days in the park but choose to roost in the evenings near the coast. They arrive like clockwork every morning and then head for the coastal mangroves around dusk. These daily migrations give birders a great chance to see these magnificent

Blue-crowned motmots.

birds in flight. The reserve is located about 2 hours from San José along the central Pacific coast. See p. 358.

○ **Looking for a Resplendent Quetzal in the Cerro de la Muerte:** Don't let the name (Mountain of Death) scare you away from the opportunity to see this spectacular bird, revered by the ancient Aztecs and Mayas. Serious bird-watchers won't want to leave Costa Rica without crossing this bird off their lists, and neophytes might be hooked for life after seeing one of these iridescent green wonders fly overhead, flashing its brilliant red breast and trailing 2-foot-long tail feathers. **Trogon Lodge** (www.grupomawamba.com; ☎ **2293-8181**) can almost guarantee a sighting. The Cerro de la Muerte is a high mountain pass along the way to San Isidro de El General about 1½ hours from San José. See "Cerro de la Muerte & San Gerardo de Dota: Where to See Quetzals in the Wild," in chapter 10.

○ **Spotting Hundreds of Species at Wilson Botanical Gardens:** With more than 7,000 species of tropical plants and flowers, the well-tended trails and grounds of this beautiful research facility are fabulous for bird-watching. Hummingbirds and tanagers are particularly plentiful, but the bounty doesn't end there—more than 360 different species of birds have been recorded here. **Wilson Gardens** (☎ **2773-4004;** www.threepaths.co.cr) is located about an hour outside the town of Golfito. See "Golfito: Gateway to the Golfo Dulce," in chapter 11.

○ **Taking Advantage of the Caribbean's Best Birding at Aviarios Sloth Sanctuary of Costa Rica:** Aviarios Sloth Sanctuary of Costa Rica (☎ **2750-0775;** www.slothrescue.org) has established itself as a prime bird-watching resort on the Caribbean. If it flies along this coast, chances are good that you'll spot it here; more than 330 species of birds have been spotted so far. In the afternoon, large flocks of several heron species nest here, including white, cattle, and boat-billed herons. Located on the Caribbean coast, Aviarios is about a 3½-hour drive from San José. See p. 482.

THE best DESTINATIONS FOR FAMILIES

○ **San José:** If you're spending any time in San José, you'll probably want to be outside the rough-and-tumble downtown area. The best place to experience Costa Rica's capital city (and still get a decent night's sleep) is the **Doubletree Cariari By Hilton** (www.cariarisanjose.doubletree.com; ✆ **800/222-8733** in the U.S. and Canada). With facilities that include several large pools, a gym, a casino, and a game room (not to mention a babysitting service), there's something here for everyone. If you're traveling with teens, they'll feel right at home at the nearby Mall Cariari, which has a multiplex theater, an indoor skating rink, and, of course, a food court. Just 15 minutes from downtown, it's well situated for exploring all of the city's sights and attractions. See p. 165.

○ **La Paz Waterfall Gardens** (✆ **2482-2100;** www.waterfallgardens.com): This multifaceted attraction features paths and suspended walkways alongside a series of impressive jungle waterfalls. Kids love the variety and vibrancy of the various attractions, from the buzzing hummingbirds to the impressive power of the waterfalls. The rooms at the **Peace Lodge** here are some of the best in the country. See p. 164.

San José Children's Museum.

La Paz Waterfall Gardens.

o **Playa Hermosa:** The protected waters of this Pacific beach make it a family favorite. However, just because the waters are calm doesn't mean it's boring. I recommend staying at the beachfront **Hotel Playa Hermosa Bosque del Mar** (www.hotelplayahermosa.com; ✆ 2672-0046) and checking in at **Aqua Sport** (✆ 2672-0050), where you can rent sea kayaks, sailboards, paddleboats, beach umbrellas, and bicycles. See "Playa Hermosa, Playa Panamá & Papagayo," in chapter 7.

o **Playa Tamarindo:** This lively surf town has a bit of something for everyone. This is a great spot for teens to learn how to surf or boogie-board, and there are a host of tours and activities to please the entire family. **Hotel Capitán Suizo** (www.hotelcapitansuizo.com; ✆ 2653-0075; p. 242) has an excellent location on a calm section of beach, spacious rooms, and a great pool for kids and adults alike. See "Playa Tamarindo & Playa Langosta," in chapter 7.

o **Monteverde:** Located about 160km (99 miles) northwest of San José, this area not only boasts the country's most famous cloud forest, but also sports a wide variety of related attractions and activities. After hiking through the reserve, you should be able to keep most kids happy and occupied riding horses; squirming at the local serpentarium; or visiting the butterfly farm, frog pond, bat jungle, and hummingbird gallery. More adventurous families can take a horseback ride or one of the local zip-line canopy tours. See "Monteverde," in chapter 9.

o **Playa de Jacó:** On the central Pacific coast, this is Costa Rica's liveliest and most developed beach town. The streets are lined with souvenir shops, ice-cream stands, and inexpensive eateries. Older kids can rent a surf- or boogie board, although everyone should be careful with the rough surf. The **Club del Mar Condominiums & Resort** (www.clubdelmarcostarica.com;

℗ **866/978-5669** in the U.S. and Canada; p. 367) is situated at the calm southern end of the beach and is accommodating to families with small children. See "Playa de Jacó," in chapter 10.

○ **Manuel Antonio:** Manuel Antonio has a little bit of everything: miles of gorgeous beaches, tons of wildlife (with almost guaranteed monkey sightings), and plenty of active-tour options. Of the load of lodging options, **Hotel Sí Como No** (www.sicomono.com; ℗ **2777-0777**), with its large suites, two pools, water slide, and nightly movies, is probably your best bet. See "Manuel Antonio National Park," in chapter 10.

THE best LUXURY HOTELS & RESORTS

○ **Hotel Grano de Oro** (San José; www.hotelgranodeoro.com; ℗ **2255-3322**): San José has dozens of old homes that have been converted into hotels, but few offer the luxurious accommodations or professional service found at the Grano de Oro. All the guest rooms have attractive hardwood furniture, including old-fashioned wardrobes in some rooms. When it's time to relax, you can soak in a hot tub or have a drink in the rooftop lounge while taking in San José's commanding view. See p. 118.

○ **Marriott Costa Rica Hotel** (San Antonio de Belén, San José area; www.marriott.com; ℗ **888/236-2427** in the U.S. and Canada): Of all the contenders in the upscale urban market, the Marriott seems to be doing the best job. Everything is in great shape, the service is bend-over-backward, the restaurants are excellent, and the hotel offers all the facilities and amenities you could want. See p. 165.

○ **Peace Lodge** (north of Varablanca; www.waterfallgardens.com; ℗ **954/727-3997** in the U.S., or 2482-2720 in Costa Rica): While the bathrooms of the deluxe units are the most luxurious and unique in the country, everything else is done in grand style as well. Each room comes with at least one custom-tiled Jacuzzi on a private balcony. The hotel adjoins the popular La Paz Waterfall Gardens. See p. 164.

○ **Four Seasons Resort Costa Rica** (Papagayo Peninsula; www.fourseasons.com/costarica; ℗ **800/332-3442** in the U.S. and Canada): This was the first large resort to cater to the high-end luxury market in Costa Rica, and it's still the best. A beautiful setting, wonderful installations, a world-class golf course, and stellar service continue to make this the current king of the hill in the upscale market. See p. 211.

○ **JW Marriott Guanacaste Resort & Spa** (Hacienda Pinilla; www.marriott.com; ℗ **888/236-2427** in the U.S. and Canada, or 2681-2000 in Costa Rica): This large, beachfront resort features fabulous rooms, a massive pool, stellar service, excellent restaurants, and a stunning setting on a beautiful and mostly underdeveloped stretch of coastline. See p. 246.

○ **Florblanca Resort** (Playa Santa Teresa; www.florblanca.com; ℗ **2640-0232**): The individual villas at this intimate resort are some of the largest and most luxurious in the country. The service and food are outstanding, and the

Villa Caletas.

location is breathtaking, spread over a lushly planted hillside steps away from Playa Santa Teresa. See p. 275.

o **Hotel Punta Islita** (on the Pacific coast, north end of Nicoya Peninsula; www. hotelpuntaislita.com; © **866/446-4053** in the U.S. and Canada, or 2656-3036 in Costa Rica): This great getaway is perched on a high, flat bluff overlooking the Pacific Ocean. The rooms are large and comfortable, the food is excellent, and the setting is stunning. If you venture beyond your room and the hotel's inviting hillside pool, there's a long, almost always deserted beach for you to explore, as well as a wealth of activities for the more adventurous. See p. 285.

o **The Springs Resort & Spa** (near Arenal Volcano; www.thespringscostarica. com; © **954/727-8333** in the U.S. and Canada, or 2401-3313 in Costa Rica): Opulent rooms with extravagant bathrooms, a series of sculpted hot-spring pools, excellent restaurants, extensive facilities, and fabulous views make this the top luxury hotel near Arenal Volcano. See p. 311.

o **Villa Caletas** (north of Jacó; www.hotelvillacaletas.com; © **2630-0505**): Spread out over a steep hillside high above the Pacific, these individual villas have a Mediterranean feel. The Greek Doric amphitheater follows the same motif. Carved into the hillside, the theater frequently features evening concerts of jazz or classical music. The "infinity pool" here was one of the first in Costa Rica and is still my favorite. Sitting in a lounge chair at the pool's infinity edge, you'll swear that it joins the sea beyond. See p. 360.

o **Arenas del Mar** (Manuel Antonio; www.arenasdelmar.com; ©/fax **2777-2777**): With large and ample rooms, excellent service and amenities, a beautiful little spa, and the best beach access and location in Manuel Antonio, this hotel has a lot to offer. See p. 386.

THE best MODERATELY PRICED HOTELS

- **Hôtel Le Bergerac** (San José; www.bergerachotel.com; © **2234-7850**): This classy little hotel has been pleasing diplomats, dignitaries, and other discerning travelers for years. Ask for one of the garden rooms or get the old master bedroom with its small private balcony. See p. 120.

- **Villa del Sueño Hotel** (Playa Hermosa; www.villadelsueno.com; © **800/378-8599** in the U.S. and Canada): It's not right on the beach (you'll have to walk about 90m/295 ft.), but everything else here is right on the money: clean, comfortable rooms; a nice pool; and an excellent restaurant. You can't do better in Playa Hermosa. See p. 213.

- **Samara Tree House Inn** (Playa Samara; www.samaratreehouse.com; © **2656-0733**): The beachfront studio apartments, set on raised stilts, are just steps from the sand. The whole complex is centrally located and well-run, making this the best hotel option in Playa Sámara at any price. See p. 284.

- **Arco Iris Lodge** (Monteverde; www.arcoirislodge.com; © **2645-5067**): This small lodge is right in Santa Elena, and it's the best deal in the Monteverde area. The owners are extremely knowledgeable and helpful. See p. 341.

- **Hotel Verde Mar** (Manuel Antonio; www.verdemar.com; © **2777-1805**): Manuel Antonio has very few "beachfront" hotels and just one is in this price range. This intimate place enjoys a lush setting, just a short walk through thick trees to the beach. See p. 390.

- **Cabinas Jiménez** (Puerto Jiménez; www.cabinasjimenez.com; © **2735-5090**): This is the best hotel you'll find right in Puerto Jiménez. Set right on the edge of the Golfo Dulce, several of the rooms here feature private balconies overlooking the water. See p. 437.

- **Cabinas Sol y Mar** (Playa Zancudo; www.zancudo.com; © **2776-0014**): These beachfront rooms are a real bargain. In fact, they fall into this book's "inexpensive" category. No matter, they feel out of that price range with a prime location just steps from the surf, surrounded by lush gardens and shady palm trees. The bar and restaurant here are excellent, lively, and justifiably popular. See p. 451.

- **Playa Negra Guesthouse** (Cahuita; www.playanegra.cr; © **2755-0127**): Located just across a dirt road from a long desolate section of Playa Negra, the individual Caribbean-style bungalows here are cozy and beautifully done. The grounds are lushly planted, and the whole operation has a refined ambiance. See p. 485.

- **Cariblue Bungalows** (Playa Cocles; www.cariblue.com; © **2750-0035**): Try to get one of the private wooden bungalows here. If you do, you might be so happy and comfortable that you won't want to leave. Just 90m (295 ft.) or so away, however, are the warm waves of the Caribbean Sea. See p. 504.

THE best ECOLODGES & WILDERNESS RESORTS

Ecolodge options in Costa Rica range from tent camps with no electricity, cold-water showers, and communal buffet-style meals to some of the most luxurious accommodations in the country. Generally, outstanding ecolodges and wilderness resorts are set apart by an ongoing commitment (financial or otherwise) to minimizing their effect on surrounding ecosystems and to supporting both conservation efforts and the residents of local communities. They should also be able to provide naturalist guides and plentiful information. All of the following do.

See "Responsible Tourism" on p. 56 for more info on sustainable travel to Costa Rica.

o **Arenal Observatory Lodge** (near La Fortuna; www.arenalobservatorylodge. com; ⓒ **2290-7011**): Originally a research facility, this lodge has upgraded over the years and features comfortable rooms with impressive views of Arenal Volcano. Excellent trails lead to nearby lava flows and a nice waterfall. Toucans frequent the trees near the lodge, and howler monkeys provide the wake-up calls. See p. 313.

o **Monteverde Lodge & Gardens** (Monteverde; www.monteverdelodge.com; ⓒ **2257-0766**): One of the original ecolodges in Monteverde, this place has only improved over the years, with great guides, updated rooms, and lush gardens. The operation is run by the very dependable and experienced Costa Rica Expeditions. See p. 341.

o **La Paloma Lodge** (Drake Bay; www.lapalomalodge.com; ⓒ **2293-7502**): If your idea of the perfect nature lodge is one where your front porch provides some prime-time viewing of flora and fauna, this place is for you. If you decide to leave the comfort of your porch, the Osa Peninsula's lowland rainforests are just outside your door. See p. 425.

o **Bosque del Cabo Rainforest Lodge** (Osa Peninsula; www.bosquedelcabo. com; ⓒ **2735-5206**): Large, comfortable private cabins perched on the edge of a cliff overlooking the Pacific Ocean and surrounded by lush rainforest make this one of my favorite spots in the country. There's plenty to do and great guides here. See p. 439.

o **Playa Nicuesa Rainforest Lodge** (Golfo Dulce; www.nicuesalodge.com; ⓒ **866/504-8116** in the U.S. and Canada, or 2258-8250 in Costa Rica): This lodge is by far the best option on the Golfo Dulce. Set in deep forest, the individual bungalows here are a perfect blend of rusticity and luxury. See p. 447.

o **Tortuga Lodge** (Tortuguero; www.costaricaexpeditions.com; ⓒ **800/886-2609** in the U.S. and Canada, or 2257-0766 in Costa Rica): The canals of Tortuguero snake through a maze of lowland primary rainforest. The beaches here are major sea-turtle nesting sites. This is not only the most comfortable option in the area, but also another of the excellent ecolodges run by Costa Rica Expeditions. See p. 470.

Tortuga Lodge.

o **Selva Bananito Lodge** (in the Talamanca Mountains south of Limón; www.selvabananito.com; © **2253-8118**): This is one of the few lodges providing direct access to the southern Caribbean lowland rainforests. There's no electricity here, but that doesn't mean it's not plush. Hike along a riverbed, ride horses through the rainforest, climb 30m (100 ft.) up a ceiba tree, or rappel down a jungle waterfall. The area has fabulous bird-watching and nearby Caribbean beaches. See p. 476.

THE best BED & BREAKFASTS & SMALL INNS

o **Finca Rosa Blanca Coffee Plantation & Inn** (Heredia; www.fincarosablanca.com; © **2269-9392**): If the cookie-cutter rooms of international resorts leave you cold, then perhaps the unique rooms of this unusual inn will be more your style. Square corners seem to have been prohibited here in favor of turrets and curving walls of glass, arched windows, and a semicircular built-in couch. It's set into the lush hillsides just 20 minutes from San José. See p. 170.

o **Vista del Valle Plantation Inn** (near Grecia; www.vistadelvalle.com; © **2450-0800**): This is a great choice if you want something close to the airport but have no need for San José. The separate cabins are influenced by traditional Japanese architecture, with lots of polished woodwork and plenty of light. The gardens are meticulously tended, and the restaurant is excellent. A nice tile pool and Jacuzzi overlook a deep river canyon. See p. 166.

- **Hidden Canopy Tree Houses** (Monteverde; www.hiddencanopy.com; ✆ **2645-5447**): The individual cabins here are set on high stilts and nestled into the surrounding cloud forest canopy. All abound in brightly, varnished local hardwoods. A refined, yet convivial, vibe presides over afternoon tea or cocktails, when guests enjoy the main lodge's sunset view. See p. 339.

- **Monte Azul** (Rivas; www.monteazulcr.com; ✆ **2742-5222**): Intimate, artsy, remote and lush, this place offers personalized attention and oozes charm. If the birds, gardens, river and Mount Chirripó ever start to bore you, this working artists' retreat always has paintings and sculptures on display. See p. 411.

- **Cabinas Los Cocos** (Playa Zancudo; www.loscocos.com; ✆/fax **2776-0012**): If you've ever dreamed about chucking it all and setting up shop in a simple house right on the beach, give it a trial run here first. See p. 451.

- **Casa Verde Lodge** (Puerto Viejo; www.cabinascasaverde.com; ✆ **2750-0015**): This is my favorite budget lodging along the Caribbean coast. The rooms are clean and airy and have comfortable beds with mosquito nets. The owners are friendly and always doing some work in the gardens or around the grounds. See p. 495.

- **Tree House Lodge** (Punta Uva; www.costaricatreehouse.com; ✆ **2750-0706**): The collection of private houses at this small beachfront property are the most creative and luxurious accommodations to be found on the Caribbean coast. I like the namesake Tree House, although the Beach House Suite is quite spectacular as well. See p. 503.

THE best RESTAURANTS

- **Grano de Oro Restaurant** (San José; ✆ **2255-3322**): This elegant little hotel has an elegant restaurant serving delicious Continental dishes and decadent desserts. The open-air seating in the lushly planted central courtyard is delightful, especially for lunch. See p. 124.

- **Park Café** (San José; ✆ **2290-6324**): A former Michelin two-star chef has set up shop in the interior patio garden of an old downtown mansion. The results are predictably fabulous. The regularly changing menu here is always varied, creative, and fairly priced. See p. 124.

- **Product-C** (Santa Ana; ✆ **2282-7767**): This is just about my favorite seafood restaurant in Costa Rica, and it's not even on the coast. Fresh fish is bought at the Puntarenas docks around dawn every morning, and these folks even raise and harvest their own oysters. See p. 278.

- **Ginger** (Playa Hermosa; ✆ **2672-0041**; www.gingercostarica.com): Serving an eclectic mix of traditional and Pan Asian–influenced tapas, this sophisticated little joint is taking this part of Guanacaste by storm. They've got a list of creative cocktails to match the inventive dishes. See p. 214.

- **Mar y Sol** (Playa Flamingo; ✆ **2654-4151**; www.marysolflamingo.com): In a beautiful open-air dining room on a high hilltop with great views, the Catalan chef here serves top-notch international fare. See p. 232.

Mar y Sol.

o **Dragonfly Bar & Grill** (Tamarindo; ℂ **2653-1506;** www.dragonflybarand grill.com): Southwestern American and Pacific Rim fusion cuisines are the primary culinary influences at this popular restaurant. Portions are large, service excellent, and prices fair. See p. 245.

o **Lola's** (Playa Avellanas; ℂ **2652-9097**): With a perfect setting on the sand and excellent hearty fare, this is one of the best beachfront restaurants in the country. See p. 247.

o **Nectar** (at Florblanca Resort, Santa Teresa; ℂ **2640-0232**): Guanacaste's best boutique resort also has one of its best restaurants. The menu changes nightly but always has a heavy Pan-Asian fusion flavor to it. The setting is romantic and subdued, in an open-air space just steps from the sand. See p. 278.

o **Playa de los Artistas** (Montezuma; ℂ **2642-0920**): This place has the perfect blend of refined cuisine and beachside funkiness. There are only a few tables, so make sure you get here early. Fresh, grilled seafood is served in oversize ceramic bowls and on large wooden slabs lined with banana leaves. See p. 271.

o **El Lagarto** (Playa Sámara; ℂ **2656-0750;** www.ellagartobbq.com): Witnessing the giant grill stations being fed with fresh coals from a raging fire overhead is worth the price of admission here, but the food and ambience are also fabulous. The menu is large, and the fresh seafood and massive steaks are all expertly prepared. See p. 286.

- **Sofia** (Monteverde; ✆ **2645-7017**): Sofia serves excellent New Latin–fusion fare at a small space about halfway along the rough dirt road between Santa Elena and the Monteverde Cloud Forest Preserve. Their sister restaurants, **Chimera** (✆ **2645-6081**), which specializes in creative tapas, and **Trio** (✆ **2645-7254**), which is a hip, bistro style joint right in town, are also excellent. See p. 343.

- **Lemon Zest** (Playa de Jacó; ✆ **2643-2591**): Set unpromisingly on the second-floor of a small shopping complex, this place serves up the best and most creative meals in Jacó. A wide range of world cuisines influence the adventurous menu here, which is complemented by a good wine list, and topped off with stellar desserts. See p. 370.

- **El Patio Bistro Latino** (Manuel Antonio; ✆ **2777-0794;** www.elpatio bistrolatino.com): A casually elegant little place, El Patio Bistro Latino has made a name for itself in the Manuel Antonio area. The chef's creative concoctions take full advantage of fresh local ingredients. See p. 392.

- **La Pecora Nera** (Puerto Viejo; ✆ **2750-0490**): I'm not sure that a tiny surfer town on the remote Caribbean coast deserves such fine Italian food, but it's got it. Your best bet here is to allow yourself to be taken on a culinary roller-coaster ride with a mixed feast of the chef's nightly specials and suggestions. See p. 506.

THE best VIEWS

- **The Summit of Irazú Volcano** (near San José): On a very clear day, you can see both the Pacific Ocean and the Caribbean Sea from this vantage point. Even if visibility is low and this experience eludes you, you can view the volcano's spectacular landscape, the Meseta Central, and the Orosi Valley. See p. 179.

- **Iguanazul Hotel** (Playa Junquillal; www.iguanazul.com; ✆ **2658-8123**): On a high bluff above Playa Junquillal, this hotel has a wonderful view of the Pacific and the windswept coastline in either direction. It gets best around sunset and is better yet if you can commandeer one of the hammocks set in a little palapa on the hillside itself. See p. 249.

- **Brisas del Mar** (Malpaís; ✆ **2640-0941**): It's a steep hike or drive up from the beach to this hilltop restaurant, but both the food and view are worth it. Enjoy a sunset drink while taking in the panoramic views of Malpaís, Playa Carmen, and the Pacific Ocean. See p. 278.

- **Tabacón Grand Spa Thermal Resort** (near Arenal Volcano; www.tabacon. com; **877/277-8291** in the U.S. and Canada, or 2519-1999 in Costa Rica): Arenal Volcano seems so close, you'll swear you can reach out and touch it. Unlike Irazú Volcano (see above), when *this* volcano rumbles and spews, you may feel the urge to seek cover. Most rooms have spectacular views from sheltered private patios or balconies. See p. 308.

- **Villa Caletas** (Playa Hermosa de Jacó; www.hotelvillacaletas.com; ✆ **2630-0505**): You'll have a view over the Golfo de Nicoya and the Pacific Ocean beyond. Sunsets at the hotel's outdoor amphitheater are legendary, but it's beautiful here during the day as well. See p. 360.

The summit of Mount Chirripó.

- **Agua Azul** (Manuel Antonio; ✆ **2777-5280**): With a high perch and perfect views, not to mention good food and drinks, this is a popular spot in Manuel Antonio. Front-row tables and bar seating here offer up spectacular views over the rainforest and out to the Pacific Ocean and offshore islands beyond. See p. 391.

- **The Summit of Mount Chirripó** (near San Isidro): What more can one say? At 3,724m (12,215 ft.), this is the highest spot in Costa Rica. On a clear day, you can see both the Pacific Ocean and the Caribbean Sea from here. Even if it isn't clear, you can catch some pretty amazing views and scenery. See "San Isidro de El General: A Base for Exploring Chirripó National Park," in chapter 10.

THE best AFTER-DARK FUN

- **Night Tours** (countrywide): Most Neotropical forest dwellers are nocturnal. Animal and insect calls fill the air, and the rustling on the ground all around takes on new meaning. Night tours are offered at most rainforest and cloud forest destinations throughout the country. Many use high-powered flashlights to catch glimpses of various animals. Some of the better spots for night tours are **Monteverde, Tortuguero,** and the **Osa Peninsula.** Volcano viewing in **Arenal** is another not-to-miss nighttime activity.

- **El Cuartel de la Boca del Monte** (San José; ✆ **2221-0327;** www.el cuartel.net): From Wednesday to Saturday, San José's young, restless, and beautiful pack it in here. Originally a gay and bohemian hangout, it is now decidedly mixed and leaning toward yuppie. There's frequently live music. See p. 143.

o **San Pedro** (San José): This is San José's university district, and at night its streets are filled with students strolling among a variety of bars and cafes. If you'd like to join them, keep in mind that **Terra U** caters to the college crowd, **Omar Khayyam** is a great place to grab an outdoor table and watch the crowds walk by, and the **Jazz Café,** as its name indicates, is a hip live-music venue that often features local jazz and rock outfits. See "San José After Dark," in chapter 5.

o **Tamarindo** (Guanacaste): The most developed and popular destination on Guanacaste's Gold Coast, Tamarindo also has the area's best nightlife scene. **Bar 1** and **El Garito** are my top choices. But I also like the open-mic nights at **Dragonfly**

TOP: **San Pedro at night.** RIGHT: **San Clemente Bar & Grill.**

Bar & Grill, and the clubby dance vibe at **Aqua.** See "Playa Tamarindo & Playa Langosta" and "Playa Grande," in chapter 7.

o **Mata 'e Caña** (Santa Elena; © **2645-5883**): After the night tours are done, and the monkeys are all asleep in the treetops, this is the place to be in the

Monteverde area. The crowd is a friendly mix of locals, tourists, guides and more. See p. 344.

o **Jacó** (Central Pacific coast): While some of the late-night scene here can be seedy—you'll find a few strip clubs and brothels—plenty of respectable places are around for those looking for after-hours fun. My top spot is the laid-back beach front **Ganesha Lounge.** I also like to shoot pool and toss down a few at **Tabacón.** See "Playa de Jacó After Dark," in chapter 10.

o **San Clemente Bar & Grill** (Dominical; ✆ **2787-0055**): This is a quintes-sential surfers' joint, but whether you hang ten or not, this is where you'll want to hang out in Dominical at night. The fresh seafood and Tex-Mex specialties are hearty, tasty, and inexpensive. And there are pool, Ping-Pong, and foosball tables, as well as televised sporting events and surf videos. See "Dominical," in chapter 10.

o **Puerto Viejo:** This small beach town on the southern end of Costa Rica's Caribbean coast is one of the most active after-dark scenes in the country. **Johnny's Place** and the **Lazy Mon @ Stanford's** take turns as the major dance-and-party spot, but there are several other happening places, as well as a few after-hours beach bonfires and jam sessions, to be found. See "Puerto Viejo," in chapter 12.

THE best WEBSITES ABOUT COSTA RICA

o **The Tico Times** (www.ticotimes.net): The English-language *Tico Times* makes it easy for *norteamericanos* (and other English speakers) to see what's happening in Costa Rica. It features the top story from its weekly print edi-tion, as well as a daily update of news briefs, a business article, regional news, a fishing column, and travel reviews. There's also a link to current currency-exchange rates.

o **Latin American Network Information Center** (http://lanic.utexas.edu/la/ ca/cr): This site houses a vast collection of information about Costa Rica, and is hands-down the best one-stop shop for browsing, with helpful links to a diverse range of tourism and general information sites.

o **Costa Rica Maps** (www.mapcr.com): In addition to selling a wonderful waterproof map to the country, this site features several excellent down-loadable nationwide, regional, and city maps, and a host of other useful information.

o **The U.S. Embassy in Costa Rica** (www.usembassy.or.cr): The official site of the U.S. Embassy in Costa Rica has a good base of information and regular updates of concern to U.S. citizens abroad, as well as about Costa Rica in general.

o **CostaRicaLiving E-Board** (www.crl-eboard.info): This is an information clearinghouse site put together by the folks at Costa Rica Living newsgroup. The site is chock-full of useful information, suggestions, reviews, and tips. If you want more information, feel free to join the newsgroup. The active newsgroup deals with a wide range of issues, and its membership includes many longtime residents and bona fide experts.

o **La Nación Digital** (www.nacion.com): If you can read Spanish, this is an excellent site to read regularly or simply browse. The entire content of the country's paper of record is placed online daily, and there's also an extensive searchable archive. It does maintain a small summary of major news items in English, although this section tends to run about a week behind current events.

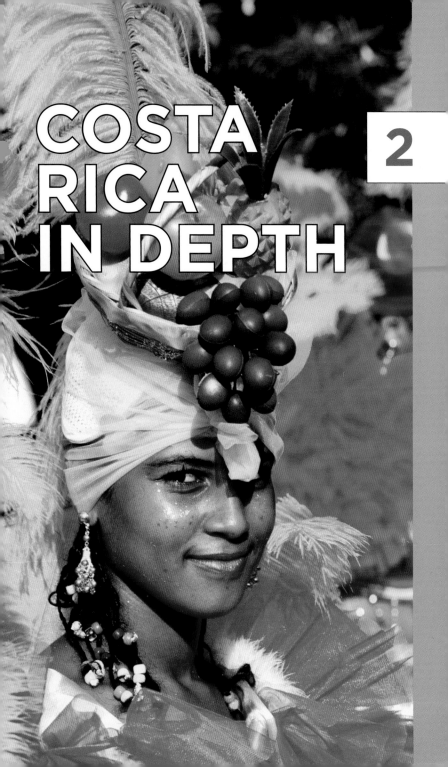

COSTA
RICA
IN DEPTH

2

*P*ura Vida! (Pure Life!) is Costa Rica's unofficial national slogan, and in many ways it defines the country. You'll hear it exclaimed, proclaimed, and simply stated by Ticos from all walks of life, from children to octogenarians. It can be used as a cheer after your favorite soccer team scores a goal, or as a descriptive response when someone asks you, "How are you?" *("¿Como estas?")*. It is symbolic of the easygoing nature of this country's people, politics, and personality.

Costa Rica itself is a mostly rural country with vast areas of protected tropical forests. It is one of the biologically richest places on earth, with a wealth of flora and fauna that attracts and captivates biologists, photographers, ecotourists, and casual visitors alike.

Often called the "Switzerland of Central America," Costa Rica is, and historically has been, a sea of tranquillity in a region that has been troubled by turmoil for centuries. For over 100 years, it has enjoyed a stable democracy and a relatively high standard of living for Latin America. The literacy rate is high, as are medical standards and facilities. Perhaps most significant, at least for proud and peace-loving Costa Ricans, is that this country does not have an army.

COSTA RICA TODAY

Costa Rica has a population of around five million, more than half of whom live in the Central Valley and are considered as urban. Some 94% of the population is of Spanish or otherwise European descent, and it is not at all unusual to see fair-skinned and blond Costa Ricans. This is largely because the indigenous population in place when the first Spaniards arrived was small and thereafter was quickly reduced to even more of a minority by wars and disease. Some indigenous populations still remain, primarily on reservations around the country; the principal tribes include the Bribri, Cabécar, Boruca, and Guaymí. In addition, on the Caribbean coast and in the big cities is a substantial population of English-speaking black Creoles who came over from the Antilles to work on building the railroad and on the banana plantations. Racial tension isn't palpable, but it exists, perhaps more out of standard ignorance and fear rather than an organized or articulated prejudice.

In general, Costa Ricans are a friendly and outgoing people. While interacting with visitors, Ticos are very open and helpful. Time has relative meaning to Ticos. Although most tour companies and other establishments operate efficiently, don't expect punctuality, in general.

In a region historically plagued by internal strife and civil wars, Costa Ricans are proud of their peaceful history, political stability, and relatively high

PREVIOUS PAGE: **A Carnaval celebrant in Limón.**

Bananas at one of Costa Rica's many banana plantations.

level of development. However, this can also translate into arrogance and prejudice toward immigrants from neighboring countries, particularly Nicaraguans, who make up a large percentage of the workforce on the banana and coffee plantations.

Roman Catholicism is the official religion of Costa Rica, although freedom to practice any religion is guaranteed by the country's constitution. More than 75% of the population identifies itself as Roman Catholic, while another 14% are part of a number of evangelical Christian congregations. There is a small but visible Jewish community as well. By and large, a large section of Ticos are religiously observant, if not fervent, though it seems that just as many lead quite secular lives.

Costa Rica is the most politically stable nation in Central America, and it has the largest middle class. Even the smallest towns have electricity, the water is mostly safe to drink, and the phone system is relatively good and very widespread. Still, the gap between rich and poor is wide, and there are glaring infrastructure needs. The roads, hospitals, and school systems have been in a slow but steady state of decay for decades, with no immediate signs that these matters will improve anytime soon. Several "Free Zones" and some high-tech investments and production facilities have dramatically changed the face of Costa Rica's economy. Intel, which opened two side-by-side assembly plants in Costa Rica, currently accounts for more than 20% of the country's exports, compared with traditional exports such as **bananas** (8%) and **coffee** (3%). Although Intel and other international companies often trumpet a growing gross domestic product, very little of the profits actually make their way into the Costa Rican economy.

Tourism is the nation's true principal source of income, surpassing cattle ranching, textiles, and exports of coffee, pineapples, bananas, and Intel microchips. Over two million tourists visit Costa Rica each year, and over half the working population is employed in the tourism and service industries. Ticos whose fathers and grandfathers were farmers and ranchers find themselves hotel

---

 Where There Is a Tico, There Is Freedom

In 1989, on a visit to Costa Rica, Uruguayan President Julio María Sanguinetti famously declared: *"Donde hay un costarricense, esté donde esté, hay libertad,"* which is roughly translated in the title above.

Personally, I get a kick out of the version co-opted by a local condiment company in their advertising campaign, which states, "Where there is a Tico, there is Salsa Lizano." I find it to be equally true.

31

The Little Drummer Boy

Costa Rica's national hero is Juan Santamaría. The legend goes that young Juan enlisted as a drummer boy in the campaign against William Walker (p. 34). On April 11, 1865, when Costa Rican troops had a band of Walker's men cornered in a downtown hostel in Rivas, Nicaragua, Santamaría volunteered for a nearly certain suicide mission to set the building on fire. Although he was mortally wounded, Santamaría was successful in torching the building and driving Walker's men out, where they were swiftly routed. Today, April 11 is a national holiday.

owners, tour guides, and waiters. Although most have adapted gracefully and regard the industry as a source of new jobs and opportunities for economic advancement, restaurant and hotel staff can seem gruff and uninterested at times, especially in rural areas. And, unfortunately, an increase in the number of visitors has led to an increase in crime, prostitution, and drug trafficking. Common sense and street savvy are required in San José and in many of the more popular tourist destinations.

The global economic crisis has definitely hit Costa Rica. Tourism was noticeably down, but is bouncing back. Moreover, because credit has historically been so tight, there was no major mortgage or banking crisis in the country. And it seems that Costa Rica dodged a bullet and will recover nicely.

LOOKING BACK AT COSTA RICA
Early History

Little is known of Costa Rica's history before its colonization by Spanish settlers. The pre-Columbian Indians who made their home in this region of Central America never developed the large cities or advanced culture that flowered farther north in what would become Guatemala, Belize, and Mexico. However, ancient artifacts indicating a strong sense of aesthetics have been unearthed from scattered excavations around the country. Beautiful gold and jade jewelry, intricately carved grinding stones, and artistically painted terra-cotta objects point to a small but highly skilled population.

Spain Settles Costa Rica

In 1502, on his fourth and last voyage to the New World, Christopher Columbus anchored just offshore from present-day Limón. Whether he actually gave the country its name—"the rich coast"—is open to debate, but the Spaniards never did find much gold or minerals to exploit here.

The earliest Spanish settlers found that, unlike settlements to the north, the native population of Costa Rica was unwilling to submit to slavery. Despite their small numbers, scattered villages, and tribal differences, they fought back against the Spanish until they were overcome by superior firepower and European diseases. When the fighting ended, the European settlers in Costa Rica found that very few Indians were left to force into servitude. The settlers were thus forced to till their own lands, a situation unheard of in other parts of Central America. Few pioneers headed this way because they could settle in Guatemala, with its

Cartago's Basilica.

large native workforce. Costa Rica was nearly forgotten, as the Spanish crown looked elsewhere for riches to plunder and souls to convert.

It didn't take long for Costa Rica's few Spanish settlers to head for the hills, where they found rich volcanic soil and a climate that was less oppressive than in the lowlands. **Cartago,** the colony's first capital, was founded in 1563, but it was not until the 1700s that additional cities were established in this agriculturally rich region. In the late 18th century, the first coffee plants were introduced, and because these plants thrived in the highlands, Costa Rica began to develop its first cash crop. Unfortunately, it was a long and difficult journey transporting the coffee to the Caribbean coast and then onward to Europe, where the demand for coffee was growing.

From Independence to the Present

In 1821, Spain granted independence to its colonies in Central America. Costa Rica joined with its neighbors to form the Central American Federation; but in 1838, it withdrew to form a new nation and pursue its own interests. By the mid-1800s, coffee was the country's main export. Free land was given to anyone willing to plant coffee on it, and plantation owners soon grew wealthy and powerful, creating Costa Rica's first elite class. Coffee plantation owners were powerful enough to elect their own representatives to the presidency.

 The Last Costa Rican Warrior

"Military victories, by themselves, are not worth much. It's what are built from them that matters."

—Jose "Pepe" Figueres

This was a stormy period in Costa Rican history. In 1856, the country was invaded by **William Walker,** a soldier of fortune from Tennessee who, with the backing of U.S. President James Buchanan, was attempting to fulfill his grandiose dreams of presiding over a slave state in Central America (before his invasion of Costa Rica, he had invaded Nicaragua and Baja, California). The people of Costa Rica, led by their own president, Juan Rafael Mora, marched against Walker and chased him back to Nicaragua. Walker eventually surrendered to a U.S. warship in 1857, but, in 1860, he attacked Honduras, claiming to be the president of that country. The Hondurans, who had had enough of Walker's shenanigans, promptly executed him.

Until 1890, coffee growers had to transport their coffee either by oxcart to the Pacific port of Puntarenas or by boat down the Río Sarapiquí to the Caribbean. In the 1870s, a progressive president proposed a railway from San José to the Caribbean coast to facilitate the transport of coffee to European markets. It took nearly 20 years for this plan to reach fruition, and more than 4,000 workers lost their lives constructing the railway, which passed through dense jungles and rugged mountains on its journey from the Central Valley to the coast. Partway through the project, as funds were dwindling, the second chief engineer, Minor Keith, proposed an idea that not only enhanced his fortunes but also changed the course of Central American history. Banana plantations would be developed along the railway right of way (land on either side of the tracks). The export of this crop would help to finance the railway, and, in exchange, Keith would get a 99-year lease on 1,976,000 hectares (800,000 acres) of land with a 20-year tax deferment. The Costa Rican government gave its consent, and in 1878 the first bananas were shipped from the country. In 1899, Keith and a partner formed the **United Fruit Company,** a business that eventually became the largest landholder in Central America and caused political disputes and wars throughout the region.

In 1889, Costa Rica held what is considered the first free election in Central American history. The opposition candidate won the election, and the control of the government passed from the hands of one political party to those of another without bloodshed or hostilities. Thus, Costa Rica established itself as the region's only true democracy. In 1948, this democratic process was challenged by **Rafael Angel Calderón,** who had served as the country's president from 1940 to 1944. After losing by a narrow margin, Calderón, who had the backing of the communist labor unions and the Catholic Church, refused to concede the country's leadership to the rightfully elected president, **Otillio Ulate,** and a civil war ensued. Calderón was eventually defeated by José "Pepe" Figueres. In the wake of this crisis, a new constitution was drafted; among other changes, it abolished Costa Rica's army so that such a revolution could never happen again.

In 1994, history seemed to repeat itself—peacefully this time—when **José María Figueres** took

Presidential Welcome

President John F. Kennedy visited Costa Rica in March 1963. Upon his arrival, the Irazú Volcano woke up and erupted, after more than 2 decades of dormancy. Soot and ash reached as far as San José, where the soon-to-be-assassinated leader addressed students and political figures.

> "Peace is the most honorable form of exhaustion, and the most exhausting form of honor."
>
> —Oscar Arias

the reins of government from the son of his father's adversary, Rafael Angel Calderón. In 2001, Otton Solís and his new Citizen's Action Party (PAC) forced the presidential elections into a second round, opening a crack in a two-party system that had become seemingly entrenched for good. Although Solís himself finished third and didn't make it to the runoff, his upstart Citizen's Action Party won quite a few deputy slots.

The battered traditional two-party system was further threatened in 2004, when major corruption scandals became public. Two former presidents were arrested (Miguel Angel Rodríguez and Rafael Angel Calderón), and another (José María Figueres) is in Switzerland refusing a legislative call to return and testify, as well as avoiding an Interpol warrant for his capture and arrest. All were implicated, as well as a long list of high-level government employees and deputies, in various financial scandals or bribery cases. As of press time, both Calderón and Rodríguez were convicted and sentenced to jail time, but are out pending an appeals process.

In 2010, Costa Rica elected its first female president, **Laura Chinchilla,** who was a vice-president in the outgoing Arias administration. So far, Chinchilla's presidency has been largely uneventful, aside from a minor, currently ongoing border dispute with Nicaragua, in which Nicaraguan military forces, using a flawed Google Earth map as part of their justification, have taken possession of a remote, previously uninhabited jungle island along their common border. The case is making its slow way through international courts.

ART & ARCHITECTURE

Since it's a small and provincial country, you'll find Costa Rica's culture somewhat similarly limited in size and scope. That said, the culture does have vibrant current scenes in all the major arts—music, literature, architecture, dance, and even film.

Architecture

Costa Rica lacks the large-scale pre-Columbian ceremonial ruins found throughout much of the rest of Mesoamerica. The only notable early archaeological site is **Guayabo** (p. 184). However, only the foundations of a few dwellings, a handful of carved petroglyphs, and some road and water infrastructure are still visible here.

Similarly, Costa Rica lacks the large and well-preserved colonial-era cities found throughout much of the rest of Latin America. The original capital of **Cartago** (p. 175) has some old ruins and a few colonial-era buildings, as well as the country's grandest church, **La Basílica de Nuestra Señora de los Angeles (Basílica of Our Lady of the Angels) ★** (p. 178), which was built in honor of the country's patron saint, La Negrita, or the Virgin of Guadalupe.

In downtown San José, Barrio Amón and Barrio Otoya are two side-by-side upscale neighborhoods replete with a stately mix of architectural stylings, with everything from colonial-era residential mansions, to Art Deco apartment buildings, and modern high-rise skyscrapers. One of the standout buildings here is the

Guayabo National Park.

Metal School (Escuela Metalica), which dates to the 1880s, and was shipped over piece-by-piece from France, and erected in place.

On much of the Caribbean coast, you will find mostly wooden houses, built on raised stilts to rise above the wet ground and occasional flooding. Some of these houses feature ornate gingerbread trim. Much of the rest of the country's architecture is pretty plain. Most residential houses are simple concrete-block affairs, with zinc roofs.

A few modern architects are creating names for themselves. **Ronald Zurcher,** who designed the Four Seasons Resort (p. 211) and several other large hotel projects, is one of the shining lights of contemporary Costa Rican architecture.

Art

Unlike Guatemala, Mexico, or even Nicaragua, Costa Rica does not have a strong tradition of local or indigenous arts and crafts. The strong suit of Costa Rican art is European and Western influenced, ranging from neoclassical to modern in style.

 Colonial-Era Remnant or Crime Deterrent?

Most Costa Rican homes feature steel or iron grating over the doors and windows. I've heard more than one tour guide say this can be traced back to colonial-era architecture and design. However, I'm fairly convinced it is a relatively modern adaptation to the local crime scene.

Early painters to look out for include **Max Jimenez, Francisco Amighetti, Manuel de la Cruz,** and **Teodorico Quiros.** Deceased and living legends of the art world include **Rafa Fernández, Lola Fernández,** and **Cesar Valverde.** Contemporary artists making waves and names for themselves include **Fernando Carballo, Rodolfo Stanley, Lionel Gonzalez, Manuel Zumbado,** and **Karla Solano.**

Sculpture is perhaps one of the strongest aspects of the Costa Rican art scene, with the large bronze works of **Francisco "Paco" Zuñiga** among the best of the genre. Meanwhile, the artists **José Sancho, Edgar Zuñiga,** and **Jiménez Deredia** are all producing internationally acclaimed pieces, many of monumental proportions. You can see examples by all of these sculptors around the country, as well as at San José's downtown **Museo de Arte Costarricense** ★★ (p. 127). I also enjoy the whimsical works of **Leda Astorga,** who sculpts and then paints a pantheon of plump and voluptuous figures in interesting, and at times, compromising, poses.

You'll find several excellent museums and galleries in San José (p. 127), as well as in some of the country's larger and more popular tourist destinations.

Wood artwork at Original Grand Gallery in La Fortuna.

COSTA RICA IN POPULAR CULTURE

Books

Though Costa Rica's literary output is sparsely translated and little known outside of Costa Rica, there are some notable authors to look out for, especially if you can read in Spanish.

Some of the books mentioned below might be difficult to track down in U.S. bookstores, but you'll find them all in abundance in Costa Rica. A good place to check for most of these titles is **Seventh Street Books,** on Calle 7 between avenidas 1 and Central in San José (✆ **2256-8251**).

GENERAL INTEREST For a straightforward, albeit somewhat dry, historical overview, there's *The History of Costa Rica,* by **Ivan Molina** and **Steven Palmer.** For a more readable look into Costa Rican society, pick up *The Ticos: Culture and Social Change* by **Richard, Karen,** and **Mavis Biesanz,** an examination of the country's politics and culture, by the authors of the out-of-print *The Costa Ricans.* Another work worth checking out is *The Costa Rica Reader: History, Culture, Politics* ★, a broad selection of stories, essays, and excerpts edited by Steven Palmer and Ivan Molina, the authors of the history book mentioned above.

To learn more about the life and culture of Costa Rica's Talamanca coast, an area populated by Afro-Caribbean people whose forebears emigrated from Caribbean islands in the early 19th century, look for *What*

Happen: A Folk-History of Costa Rica's Talamanca Coast ★ by **Paula Palmer.** This book is a collection of oral histories taken from a wide range of local characters.

FICTION & POETRY *Costa Rica: A Traveler's Literary Companion* ★★, edited by **Barbara Ras** and with a foreword by **Oscar Arias Sánchez,** is a collection of short stories by Costa Rican writers, organized by region of the country. If you're lucky, you might find a copy of *Stories of Tatamundo,* by **Fabian Dobles,** or *Lo Peor/The Worst,* by **Fernando Contreras.**

Young adults will enjoy **Kristin Joy Pratt**'s *A Walk in the Rainforest,* while younger children will like the beautifully illustrated *The Forest in the Clouds,* by **Sneed Collard** and **Michael Rothman,** and *The Umbrella.* Pachanga Kids ★ (www.pachangakids.com) has published several illustrated bilingual children's books with delightful illustrations by **Ruth Angulo,** including *Mar Azucarada/Sugar Sea* by **Roberto Boccanera** and *El Coyote y la Luciernaga/The Coyote and the Firefly* by **Yazmin Ross,** which (full disclosure) I translated, and which includes a musical CD that features your humble author's singing. Another bilingual children's book worth checking out is *Zari & Marinita: Adventures in a Costa Rican Rainforest.*

One of the most important pieces in the Costa Rican canon, **Carlos Luis Fallas**'s 1941 tome *Mamita Yunai* is a stark look at the impact of the large banana giant United Fruit on the country. More recently, **Fernando Contreras** takes up where his predecessor left off in *Unico Mirando al Mar,* which describes the conditions of the poor, predominantly children, who scavenge Costa Rica's garbage dumps.

In the field of poetry, **Eunice Odio, Juaquín Gutiérrez,** and **Jorge Debravo** are early poets who set the gold standard. Their more modern successors include **Alfonso Chase, Virginia Grutter, Laureano Alban, Ana Istaru, Osvaldo Sauma,** and **Luis Chavez.**

NATURAL HISTORY I think that everyone coming to Costa Rica should read *Tropical Nature* ★★★ by **Adrian Forsyth** and **Ken Miyata.** My all-time favorite book on tropical biology, this is a wonderfully written and lively collection of tales and adventures by two Neotropical biologists who spent quite some time in the forests of Costa Rica.

Mario A. Boza's beautiful *Costa Rica National Parks* has been reissued in an elegant coffee-table edition. Other worthwhile coffee-table books include *Rainforests: Costa Rica and Beyond* ★ by **Adrian Forsyth,** with photographs by **Michael** and **Patricia Fogden,** *Costa Rica: A Journey Through Nature* ★ by **Adrian Hepworth,** and *Osa: Where the Rainforest Meets the Sea* ★★ by **Roy Toft** (photographer) and **Trond Larsen** (author).

For an introduction to a wide range of Costa Rican fauna, there's *The Wildlife of Costa Rica: A Field Guide* ★★ by **Fiona Reid, Jim Zook, Twan Leenders,** and **Robert Dean,** or *Costa Rica: Traveller's Wildlife Guides* ★, by **Les Beletsky.** Both pack a lot of useful information into a concise package and make great field guides for amateur naturalists and inquisitive tourists.

A Guide to the Birds of Costa Rica ★, by **F. Gary Stiles** and **Alexander Skutch,** is an invaluable guide to identifying the many birds you'll see during your stay. Most guides and nature lodges have a copy of this book on hand. This classic faces competition from the more recent ***Birds of Costa Rica*** ★, by **Richard Garrigues** and **Robert Dean.** Bird-watchers might want a copy of *A Bird-Finding Guide to Costa Rica* ★ by **Barrett Lawson,** which details each country's bird-watching bounty by site and region.

Other interesting natural-history books that will give you a look at the plants and animals of Costa Rica include **Costa Rica Natural History,** by **Daniel Janzen;** *A Guide to Tropical Plants of Costa Rica,* by **Willow Zuchowsky;** *The Natural History of Costa Rican Mammals,* by **Mark Wainwright;** *A Guide to the Amphibians and Reptiles of Costa Rica,* by **Twan Leenders;** and the classic *A Neotropical Companion,* by **John C. Kricher,** reissued in an expanded edition with color photos.

For a rather complete list of field guides, check out **www.zona tropical.net**.

Film

Costa Rica has a budding and promising young film industry. Local feature films like **Tropix, Caribe,** and **Passport** are all out on subtitled DVD. **El Camino (The Path)** by Costa Rican filmmaker **Ishtar Yasin Gutiérrez** was screened at the Berlin Film Festival, while **Gestación (Gestation),** by **Esteban Ramírez,** was widely played around the country and is awaiting a DVD release. Both released in 2010, **Hilda Hidalgo**'s *Del Amor y Otros Demonios (Of Love and Other Demons)* is a compelling treatment of Gabriel García Márquez's novel of the same name, while **Paz Fabrega**'s *Agua Fría de Mar (Cold Sea)* is a touching story set on a remote Costa Rican beach that has picked up a few prizes at international festivals.

If you want to see Costa Rica used simply as a backdrop, the major motion picture productions of **1492,** by **Ridley Scott** and starring Gerard Depardieu and Sigourney Weaver; **Congo,** featuring Laura Linney and Ernie Hudson; and **The Blue Butterfly,** with William Hurt, all feature sets and scenery from around the country.

The small **Costa Rican Film and Video festival** (www.centrodecine. go.cr) is each November in San José.

Music

Several musical traditions and styles meet and mingle in Costa Rica. The northern Guanacaste region is a hotbed of folk music that is strongly influenced by the *marimba* (wooden xylophone) traditions of Guatemala and Nicaragua, while also featuring guitars, maracas, and the occasional harp. On the Caribbean coast you can hear traditional calypso sung by descendants of the original black workers brought over to build the railroads and tend the banana plantations. Roving bands play a mix of guitar, banjo, washtub bass, and percussion in the bars and restaurants of Cahuita and Puerto Viejo.

Tamarindo musicians playing folk music.

Costa Rica also has a healthy contemporary music scene. The jazz-fusion trio **Editus** has won two Grammy awards for its work with Panamanian salsa giant (and movie star and Tourism Minister) **Rubén Blades.** Meanwhile, **Malpaís,** the closest thing Costa Rica has to a super-group, is a pop-rock outfit that is tearing it up in Costa Rica and around Central America.

You should also seek out discs by **Cantoamérica,** which plays upbeat dance music ranging from salsa to calypso to merengue. Jazz pianist **Manuel Obregón** (a member of Malpaís) has several excellent solo albums out, including *Simbiosis,* on which he improvises along with the sounds of Costa Rica's wildlife, waterfalls, and weather; as well as his work with the *Papaya Orchestra,* a collaboration and gathering of musicians from around Central America.

Local label **Papaya Music ★** (www.papayamusic.com) has done an excellent job promoting and producing albums by Costa Rican musicians in a range of styles and genres. Their offerings range from the Guanacasteca folk songs of **Max Goldemberg,** to the boleros of **Ray Tico,** to the original calypso of **Walter "Gavitt" Ferguson.** You can find their discs at gift shops and record stores around the country, as well as at airport souvenir stores.

Classical music lovers will want to head to San José, which has a symphony orchestra, youth symphony, opera company, and choir. The local symphony sometimes features the works of local composers like **Benjamin Guitiérrez** and **Eddie Mora.** On occasion, small-scale music festivals will bring classical offerings to some of the beach and inland tourist destinations around the country.

Bars and discos around the country spin salsa, merengue, and cumbia, as well as more modern grooves that include house, electronic, trip-hop, and reggaeton.

TICO etiquette & CUSTOMS

In general, Costa Ricans are easygoing, friendly, and informal. That said, Ticos tend to be conservative and try to treat everyone very respectfully. Moreover, in conversation, Ticos are relatively formal. When addressing someone, they use the formal *usted* in most instances, reserving the familiar *vos* for close friends, family, and children or teenagers.

Upon greeting or saying goodbye, both sexes shake hands, although across genders, a light kiss on one cheek is common.

Proud of their neutrality and lack of armed forces, everyday Costa Ricans are uncomfortable with confrontation. What may seem like playful banter or justified outrage to a foreign tourist may be taken very badly by a Tico.

In some cases, especially in the service industry, a Tico may tell you what he or she thinks you want to hear, just to avoid a confrontation—even if he or she knows there's little chance of follow-through or ultimate customer satisfaction. I've also had, on more than one occasion, a Tico give me wrong directions, instead of telling me they didn't know the way.

The two words mentioned at the start of this chapter—*pura vida*—will go a long way to endearing you to most Ticos. In conversation, *pura vida* is used as a greeting, exclamation, adjective, and general space filler. Feel free to sprinkle a *pura vida* or two into your conversations with locals. I'm sure it will be well received. For more tips on talking like a Tico, see "Some Typical Tico Words & Phrases" on p. 550.

Tico men dress conservatively. It is very rare to see Costa Rican men wear short pants except at the beach. In most towns and cities, while accepted, tourists will stand out when wearing short pants, sandals, and other typical beach, golf, or vacation wear. Costa Rican women, on the other hand, especially young women, do tend to show some skin in everyday, and even business, situations. Still, be respectful in your dress, especially if you plan on visiting churches, small towns, or local families.

Women, no matter how they dress, may find themselves on the receiving end of whistles, honks, hoots, hisses, and catcalls. For more information on this manifestation of Costa Rican machismo, see "Women Travelers," on p. 528.

Punctuality is not a Costa Rican strong suit. Ticos often show up anywhere from 15 minutes to an hour or more late to meetings and appointments—this is known as *la hora tica,* or "Tico time." That said, buses and local airlines, tour operators, movie theaters, and most businesses do tend to run on a relatively timely schedule.

EATING & DRINKING

Costa Rican food is not especially memorable. Although some of the exotic fruits and vegetables served up, certainly are. Moreover, creative chefs using fresh local ingredients have livened up the dining scene in San José and at most of the major tourist destinations. A few are even serving up creative takes on traditional Costa Rican classics.

Outside of the capital and the major tourist destinations, your options get very limited very fast. In fact, many destinations are so remote that you have no choice but to eat in the hotel's restaurant. At remote jungle lodges, the food is usually served buffet- or family-style and can range from bland to inspired, depending on who's doing the cooking, and turnover is high.

If you see a restaurant billing itself as a *mirador,* it means it has a view. If you are driving around the country, don't miss an opportunity to dine with a view at some little roadside restaurant. The food might not be all that great, but the view and scenery will be.

At even the more expensive restaurants, it's hard to spend more than $50 per person unless you really splurge on drinks. It gets even cheaper outside the city and high-end hotels. However, if you really want to save money, Costa Rican, or *típico,* food is always the cheapest nourishment available. It's primarily served in *sodas,* Costa Rica's equivalent of diners. At a *soda,* you'll have lots of choices: rice and beans with steak, rice and beans with fish, rice and beans with chicken, or, for vegetarians, rice and beans. You get the picture.

I have separated restaurant listings throughout this book into three price categories, based on the average cost of a meal per person, including tax and service charge. The categories are **Expensive,** more than $25; **Moderate,** $10 to $25; and **Inexpensive,** less than $10. (Note, however, that individual items in the listings—entrees, for instance—do not include the sales or service taxes.) Keep in mind that an additional 13% sales tax applies, as well as a 10% service charge. Ticos rarely tip, but that doesn't mean that you shouldn't. If the service was particularly good and attentive, you should probably leave a little extra.

Meals & Dining Customs

Rice and beans are the bases of Costa Rican meals—all three of them. At breakfast, they're called *gallo pinto* and come with everything from eggs to steak to seafood. At lunch or dinner, rice and beans are an integral part of a *casado* (which

A typical *casado.*

A waiter at a *soda* in Puerto Viejo.

translates as "married" and is the name for the local version of a blue-plate special). A *casado* usually consists of cabbage-and-tomato salad, fried plantains (a starchy, banana-like fruit), and a chicken, fish, or meat dish of some sort. On the Caribbean coast, rice and beans are called "rice 'n' beans," and are cooked in coconut milk.

Dining hours in Costa Rica are flexible but generally follow North American customs. Some downtown restaurants in San José are open 24 hours; however, expensive restaurants tend to be open for lunch between 11am and 3pm and for dinner between 6 and 11pm.

APPETIZERS Known as *bocas* in Costa Rica, appetizers are served with drinks in most bars. Often the *bocas* are free, but even if they aren't, they're very inexpensive. Popular *bocas* include *gallos* (tortillas piled with meat, chicken, cheese, or beans), *ceviche* (a marinated seafood salad), tamales (stuffed cornmeal patties wrapped and steamed inside banana leaves), *patacones* (fried green plantain chips), and fried yuca.

SANDWICHES & SNACKS Ticos love to snack, and a large variety of tasty little sandwiches and snacks are available on the street, at snack bars, and in *sodas*. *Arreglados* are little meat-filled sandwiches, as are *tortas*, which are served on little rolls with a bit of salad tucked into them. Tacos, tamales, *gallos* (see above), and *empanadas* (turnovers) also are quite common.

MEAT Costa Rica is beef country, having converted much of its rainforest land to pastures for raising beef cattle. Consequently, beef is cheap and plentiful, although it might be a bit tougher—and cut and served thinner—than it is back home. One typical local dish is called *olla de carne,* a bowl of beef broth with large chunks of meat, local tubers, and corn. Spit-roasted chicken is also very popular here and is surprisingly tender.

SEAFOOD   Costa Rica has two coasts, and, as you'd expect, plenty of seafood is available everywhere in the country. *Corvina* (sea bass) is the most commonly served fish and is prepared innumerable ways, including as *ceviche.* (***Be careful:*** In many cheaper restaurants, particularly in San José, shark meat is often sold as *corvina.*) You should also come across *pargo* (red snapper), *dorado* (mahimahi), and tuna on some menus, especially along the coasts. Although Costa Rica is a major exporter of shrimp and lobster, both are relatively expensive and in short supply here.

VEGETABLES   On the whole, you'll find vegetables surprisingly lacking in the meals you're served in Costa Rica—usually nothing more than a little pile of shredded cabbage topped with a slice or two of tomato. For a much more satisfying and filling salad, order *palmito* (hearts of palm salad). The heart (actually the stalk or trunk of these small palms) is first boiled and then chopped into circular pieces and served with other fresh vegetables, with salad dressing on top. If you want something more than this, you'll have to order a side dish such as *picadillo,* a stew or purée of vegetables with a bit of meat in it.

Though they are giant relatives of bananas and are technically considered a fruit, *plátanos* (plantains) are really more like vegetables and require cooking before they can be eaten. Green plantains have a very starchy flavor and consistency, but they become as sweet as candy as they ripen. Fried *plátanos* are one of my favorite dishes. Yuca (manioc root or cassava in English) is another starchy staple root vegetable in Costa Rica.

One more vegetable worth mentioning is the *pejibaye,* a form of palm fruit that looks like a miniature orange coconut. Boiled *pejibayes* are frequently sold from carts on the streets of San José. When cut in half, a *pejibaye* reveals a large seed surrounded by soft, fibrous flesh. You can eat it plain, but it's usually topped with a dollop of mayonnaise.

FRUITS   Costa Rica has a wealth of delicious tropical fruits. The most common are mangoes (the season begins in May), papayas, pineapples, melons, and bananas. Other fruits include *marañón,* which is the fruit of the cashew tree and has orange or yellow glossy skin; *granadilla* or *maracuyá* (passion fruit); *mamón chino,* which Asian travelers will immediately recognize as rambutan; and *carambola* (star fruit).

DESSERTS   *Queque seco,* literally "dry cake," is the same as pound cake. *Tres leches* cake, on the other hand, is so moist that you almost need to eat it with a spoon. Flan is a typical custard dessert. It often comes as either

Papaya, star fruit, and passion fruit.

Coconut, Straight Up

Throughout Costa Rica (particularly on the coastal road btw. Limón and Cahuita), keep your eye out for roadside stands selling fresh, green coconuts, or *pipas* in Spanish. Green coconuts have very little meat, but are filled with copious amounts of a slightly sweet, clear liquid that is amazingly refreshing.

According to local legend, this liquid is pure enough to be used as plasma in an emergency situation. Armed with a machete, the *pipa* seller will cut out the top and stick in a straw. In the best of cases, the *pipa* will have been cooled over ice. The entire thing should cost $1 or less.

---

flan de caramelo (caramel) or *flan de coco* (coconut). Numerous other sweets are available, many of which are made with condensed milk and raw sugar. *Cajetas* are popular handmade candies, made from sugar and various mixes of evaporated, condensed, and powdered milk. They are sold in differing-size bits and chunks at most *pulperías* (general stores) and streetside food stands.

Beverages

Frescos, refrescos, and *jugos naturales* are my favorite drinks in Costa Rica. They are usually made with fresh fruit and milk or water. Among the more common fruits used are mangoes, papayas, blackberries, and pineapples. You'll also come across *maracuyá* (passion fruit) and *carambola* (star fruit). Some of the more unusual frescos are *horchata* (made with rice flour and a lot of cinnamon) and *chan* (made with the seed of a plant found mostly in Guanacaste—definitely an acquired taste). The former is wonderful; the latter requires an open mind (it's reputed to be good for the digestive system). Order *un fresco con leche sin hielo* (a *fresco* with milk but without ice) if you're avoiding untreated water.

If you're a coffee drinker, you might be disappointed here. Most of the best coffee has traditionally been targeted for export, and Ticos tend to prefer theirs weak and sugary. Better hotels and restaurants are starting to cater to gringo and European tastes and are serving up superior blends. If you want black coffee, ask for *café negro;* if you want it with milk, order *café con leche.*

For something different for your morning beverage, ask for *agua dulce,* a warm drink made from melted sugar cane and served either with milk or lemon, or straight.

WATER Although water in most of Costa Rica is safe to drink, bottled water is readily available and is a good option if you're worried about an upset stomach. *Agua mineral,* or simply soda, is sparkling water in Costa Rica. If you like your water without bubbles, request *aqua mineral sin gas,* or *agua en botella.*

BEER, WINE & LIQUOR The German presence in Costa Rica over the years has produced several fine beers, which are fairly inexpensive. Most Costa Rican beers are light pilsners. The most popular brands are Bavaria, Imperial, and Pilsen. I personally can't tell much of a difference between any of them. Licensed local versions of Heineken and Rock Ice are also available.

You can find imported wines at reasonable prices in the better restaurants throughout the country. You can usually save money by ordering a Chilean wine over a Californian or European one.

Costa Rica distills a wide variety of liquors, and you'll save money by ordering these over imported brands. The national liquor is *guaro*, a crude cane liquor that's often combined with a soft drink or tonic. When drinking it straight, it's customary to follow a shot with a bite into a fresh lime covered in salt. If you want to try *guaro*, stick to the Cacique brand.

Several brands and styles of coffee-based liqueurs are also produced in Costa Rica. **Café Rica** is similar to Kahlúa, and you can find several types of coffee cream liqueurs. The folks at **Café Britt** produce their own line of coffee liqueurs which are quite good and available in most supermarkets, liquor stores, and tourist shops.

Costa Ricans also drink a lot of rum. The premier Costa Rican rum is **Centenario,** but I recommend that you opt for the Nicaraguan **Flor de Caña ★** or Cuban **Havana Club ★**, both of which are far superior rums. *Note:* Because of the trade embargo, it is illegal to bring Havana Club into the United States.

TIPS ON SHOPPING IN COSTA RICA

Costa Rica is not known for shopping. Most of what you'll find for sale is pretty run-of-the-mill. The country is not known for its handicrafts. So scant are its offerings that most tourist shops sell Guatemalan clothing, Panamanian appliquéd textiles, El Salvadoran painted wood souvenirs, and Nicaraguan rocking chairs. Still, Costa Rica does have a few locally produced arts and handicrafts to look out for, and a couple of towns and villages with well-deserved reputations for their unique works.

Perhaps the most famous of all towns is **Sarchí ★** (p. 172), a Central Valley town filled with handicraft shops. Sarchí is best known as the citadel of the colorfully painted Costa Rican **oxcart,** reproductions of which are manufactured in various scaled-down sizes. These make excellent gifts. (Larger oxcarts can be easily disassembled and shipped to your home.) A lot of furniture is also made in Sarchí.

Up in Guanacaste, the small town of **Guaitíl** (p. 241) is famous for its pottery. A host of small workshops, studios, and storefronts ring the town's central park (which is actually a soccer field). Many of the low-fired ceramic wares here carry ancient local indigenous motifs, while others get quirky modern

A detail of an oxcart.

Stop! Be Careful of What You Buy!

International laws prohibit trade in endangered wildlife, so don't buy any plants or animals, even if they're readily for sale. Do not buy any kind of sea-turtle products (including jewelry); wild birds; lizards, snakes, or cat skins; corals; or orchids (except those grown commercially). No matter how unique, beautiful, insignificant, or inexpensive it might seem, your purchase will directly contribute to the further hunting of these species.

In addition, be careful when buying wood products. Costa Rica's rainforest hardwoods are a finite and rapidly disappearing resource. Try to buy sustainably harvested woods, if at all possible.

treatments. You can find examples of this low-fired simple ceramic work in many gift shops around the country, and even at roadside stands all across Guanacaste.

You might also run across **carved masks ★★★** made by the indigenous **Boruca** people of southern Costa Rica. The small Boruca villages where these masks are carved are off the beaten path, but you will find them for sale at some of the better gift shops around the country. These full-size wood masks come in a variety of styles, both painted and unpainted, and run anywhere from $20 to $150, depending on the quality of workmanship. *Tip:* Don't be fooled. You'll see scores of mass-produced wooden masks at souvenir and gift shops around Costa Rica. Many are imported from Mexico, Guatemala, and Indonesia. Real Boruca masks are unique indigenous art works, and the better ones are signed by their carver.

In addition to the masks, quite a bit of Costa Rican woodwork is for sale, but it is, for the most part mass-produced wooden bowls, napkin holders, placemats, and the like. A couple of notable exceptions include the work of **Barry Biensanz ★★** (p. 154), whose excellent hardwood creations are sold at better gift shops around the country, and the unique, large-scale sculptures created and sold at the **Original Grand Gallery** (p. 307), in La Fortuna.

Coffee remains my favorite gift item. It's a great deal, it's readily available, and Costa Rican coffee is some of the best in the world. See the "Joe to Go" box on p. 135 for tips on buying **coffee** in Costa Rica.

A few other items worth keeping an eye out for include reproductions of **pre-Columbian gold jewelry** and **carved-stone figurines.** The former are available as either solid gold, silver, or gold-plated. The latter, although interesting, can be extremely heavy.

Across the country you'll find hammocks for sale. I personally find the Costa Rican **hammocks** a little crude and unstable. The same vendors usually have single-person hanging chairs, which are strung similarly to the full-size hammocks and are a better bet.

It's especially hard to capture the subtle shades and colors of the rainforests and cloud forests, and many a traveler has gone home thinking that his or her digital camera contained the full beauty of the jungle, only to see dozens of bright-green and random blurs when viewing the photos on a larger screen. To avoid this heartache, you might want to pick up a good **coffee-table book** or at least some **postcards** of the sights you want to remember forever and send them to yourself. For recommendations of coffee-table books, see "Costa Rica in Popular Culture," above.

Contemporary and **classic Costa Rican art** is another great option, both for discerning collectors and those looking for a unique reminder of their time in the country. San José has the greatest number of galleries and shops, but you will find good, well-stocked galleries in some of the more booming tourist destinations, including Liberia, Manuel Antonio, Jacó, and Monteverde. Throughout the book, I list my favorite galleries, and you can check out "Art & Architecture," above, for a list of some of the country's more prominent artists.

Finally, one item that you'll see at gift shops around the country is **Cuban cigars.** Although these are illegal to bring into the United States, they are perfectly legal and readily available in Costa Rica.

Woven baskets on sale at Galería Namu (p. 137).

WHEN TO GO

Costa Rica's high season for tourism runs from late November to late April, which coincides almost perfectly with the chill of winter in the United States, Canada, and Great Britain, and includes Christmas, New Year's, Easter, and most school spring breaks. The high season is also the dry season. If you want some unadulterated time on a tropical beach and a little less rain during your rainforest experience, this is the time to come. During this period (and especially around the Christmas holiday), the tourism industry operates at full tilt—prices are higher, attractions are more crowded, and reservations need to be made in advance.

Local tourism operators often call the tropical rainy season (May through mid-Nov) the "green season." The adjective is appropriate. At this time of year, even brown and barren Guanacaste province becomes lush and verdant. I personally love traveling around Costa Rica during the rainy season (but then again, I'm not trying to flee cold snaps in Canada). It's easy to find or at least negotiate reduced rates, there are far fewer fellow travelers, and the rain is often limited to a few hours each afternoon (although you can occasionally get socked in for a week at a time). *A **drawback:*** Some of the country's rugged roads become downright impassable without four-wheel-drive during the rainy season.

Weather

Costa Rica is a tropical country and has distinct wet and dry seasons. However, some regions are rainy all year, and others are very dry and sunny for most of the year. Temperatures vary primarily with elevations, not with seasons: On the coasts it's hot all year; in the mountains it can be cool at night any time of year. Frost is common at the highest elevations (3,000–3,600m/9,840–11,808 ft.).

Average Daytime High Temperatures & Rainfall in San José

	JAN	FEB	MAR	APR	MAY	JUNE	JULY	AUG	SEPT	OCT	NOV	DEC
TEMP (°F)	75	76	79	79	80	79	77	78	79	77	77	75
TEMP (°C)	24	24	26	26	27	26	25	26	26	25	25	24
DAYS OF RAIN	1.3	1.5	2.2	4.2	11.5	14.5	13.7	14.5	18.1	17.9	8.6	2.3

Generally, the **rainy season** (or "green season") is from May to mid-November. Costa Ricans call this wet time of year their winter. The **dry season,** considered summer by Costa Ricans, is from mid-November to April. In Guanacaste, the dry northwestern province, the dry season lasts several weeks longer than in other places. Even in the rainy season, days often start sunny, with rain falling in the afternoon and evening. On the Caribbean coast, especially south of Limón, you can count on rain year-round, although this area gets less rain in September and October than the rest of the country.

In general, the best time of year to visit weatherwise is in December and January, when everything is still green from the rains but the sky is clear.

Holidays

Because Costa Rica is a Roman Catholic country, most of its holidays are church-related. The biggies are Christmas, New Year's, and Easter, which are all celebrated for several days. Keep in mind that Holy Week (Easter week) is the biggest holiday time in Costa Rica, and many families head for the beach. (This is the last holiday before school starts.) Also, there is no public transportation on Holy Thursday or Good Friday. Government offices and banks are closed on official holidays, transportation services are reduced, and stores and markets might also close.

Official holidays in Costa Rica include **January 1** (New Year's Day), **March 19** (St. Joseph's Day), Thursday and Friday of Holy Week, **April 11** (Juan Santamaría's Day), **May 1** (Labor Day), **June 29** (St. Peter and St. Paul Day), **July 25** (annexation of the province of Guanacaste), **August 2** (Virgin of Los Angeles's Day), **August 15** (Mother's Day), **September 15** (Independence Day), **October 12** (Discovery of America/Día de la Raza), **December 8** (Immaculate Conception of the Virgin Mary), **December 24** and **25** (Christmas), and **December 31** (New Year's Eve).

Calendar of Events

Some of the events listed here might be considered more of a *happening* than an event—there's not, for instance, a Virgin of Los Angeles PR Committee that readily dispenses information. If I haven't listed a contact number, your best bet is to call the **Costa Rican Tourist Board (ICT)** at ☏ **866/COSTA RICA** in the U.S. and Canada, or 2223-1733 in Costa Rica, or visit **www.visitcostarica.com**.

For an exhaustive list of events beyond those listed here, check http://events.frommers.com, where you'll find a searchable, up-to-the-minute roster of what's happening in cities all over the world.

JANUARY

Copa del Café (Coffee Cup), San José. Matches for this international event on the junior tennis tour are held at the Costa Rica Country Club (☏ **2228-9333;** www.copacafe.com). First week in January.

Fiestas of Palmares, Palmares. Perhaps the largest and best organized of the traditional *fiestas,* it includes bullfights, a horseback parade *(tope),* and many concerts, carnival rides, and food booths (www.fiestaspalmares.com). First 2 weeks in January.

Fiestas of Santa Cruz, Santa Cruz, Guanacaste. This religious celebration honors the Black Christ of Esquipulas (a famous Guatemalan statue), featuring folk dancing, marimba music, and bullfights. Mid-January.

Fiesta of the Diablitos, Rey Curré village near San Isidro de El General. Boruca Indians wearing wooden devil and bull masks perform dances representative of the Spanish conquest of Central America; there are fireworks displays and an Indian handicrafts market. Late January.

MARCH

Día del Boyero (Oxcart Drivers' Day), San Antonio de Escazú. Colorfully painted oxcarts parade through this suburb of San José, and local priests bless the oxen. Second Sunday in March.

National Orchid Show, San José. Orchid growers throughout the world gather to show their wares, trade tales and secrets, and admire the hundreds of species on display. Contact the Costa Rican Tourist Board for the location and dates in 2012. Mid-March.

APRIL

Holy Week. Religious processions are held in cities and towns throughout the country. Week before Easter.

Juan Santamaría Day, Alajuela. Costa Rica's national hero is honored with parades, concerts, and dances. April 11.

MAY

Carrera de San Juan. The country's biggest marathon runs through the mountains, from the outskirts of Cartago to the outskirts of San José. May 17.

JULY

Fiesta of the Virgin of the Sea, Puntarenas. A regatta of colorfully decorated boats carrying a statue of Puntarenas's patron saint marks this festival. A similar event is held at Playa de Coco. Saturday closest to July 16.

Annexation of Guanacaste Day, Liberia. Tico-style bullfights, folk dancing, horseback parades, rodeos, concerts, and other events celebrate the day when this region became part of Costa Rica. July 25.

AUGUST

Fiesta of the Virgin of Los Angeles, Cartago. This is the annual pilgrimage day of the patron saint of Costa Rica. Many people walk from San José 24km (15 miles) to the basilica in Cartago. August 2.

Día de San Ramón, San Ramón. More than two dozen statues of saints from various towns are brought to San Ramón, where they are paraded through the streets. August 31.

Costa Rica's Independence Day, celebrated all over the country. One of the most distinctive aspects of this festival is the nighttime marching band parades of children in their school uniforms, who play the national anthem on steel xylophones. September 15.

International Beach Clean-Up Day. This is a good excuse to chip in and help clean up the beleaguered shoreline of your favorite beach. Third Saturday in September.

Fiesta del Maíz, Upala. At this celebration of corn, local beauty queens wear outfits made from corn plants. October 12.

Limón Carnival/Día de la Raza, Limón. A smaller version of Mardi Gras, complete with floats and dancing in the streets, commemorates Columbus's discovery of Costa Rica. Week of October 12.

All Souls' Day/Día de los Muertos, celebrated countrywide. Although it is not as elaborate or ritualized as in Mexico, most Costa Ricans take some time this day to remember the dead with flowers and trips to cemeteries. November 2.

Fiesta de los Negritos, Boruca. Boruca Indians celebrate the feast day of their patron saint, the Virgin of the Immaculate Conception, with costumed dances and traditional music. December 8.

Día de la Pólvora, San Antonio de Belén and Jesús María de San Mateo. Fireworks honor Our Lady of the Immaculate Conception. December 8.

Las Posadas. Countrywide, children and carolers go door-to-door seeking lodging in a reenactment of Joseph and Mary's search for a place to stay. Begins December 15.

El Tope and Carnival, San José. The streets of downtown belong to horses and their riders in a proud recognition of the country's important agricultural heritage. The next day, those same streets are taken over by carnival floats, marching bands, and street dancers. December 26 and 27.

Festejos Populares, San José. Bullfights and a pretty respectable bunch of carnival rides, games of chance, and fast-food stands are set up at the fairgrounds in Zapote. (www.festejospopulares.com). Last week of December.

THE LAY OF THE LAND

Costa Rica occupies a central spot in the isthmus that joins North and South America. For millennia, this land bridge served as a migratory thoroughfare and mating ground for species native to the once-separate continents. It was also where the Mesoamerican and Andean pre-Columbian indigenous cultures met.

The country comprises only .01% of the earth's landmass, yet it is home to 5% of the planet's biodiversity. More than 10,000 identified species of plants, 880 species of birds, 9,000 species of butterflies and moths, and 500 species of mammals, reptiles, and amphibians are found here.

The key to this biological richness lies in the many distinct life zones and ecosystems found in Costa Rica. It might all seem like one big mass of green to the untrained eye, but the differences are profound.

In any one spot in Costa Rica, temperatures remain relatively constant year-round. However, as seen above, they vary dramatically according to altitude, from tropically hot and steamy along the coasts to below freezing at the highest elevations.

For more information on Costa Rican flora and fauna, see chapter 14. For information on sustainable issues in the country, see "Responsible Tourism," below.

Costa Rica's Ecosystems

RAINFORESTS

Costa Rica's **rainforests** are classic tropical jungles. Some receive more than 508cm (200 in.) of rainfall per year, and their climate is typically hot and humid, especially in the lowland rainforests. Trees grow tall and fast, fighting for sunlight in the upper reaches. In fact, life and foliage on the forest floor are surprisingly sparse. The action is typically 30m (98 ft.) up, in the canopy, where long vines stream down, lianas climb up, and bromeliads grow on the branches and trunks of towering hardwood trees.

Some of the more indicative rainforest tree species include the parasitic strangler fig and the towering ceiba, which can reach some 60m (196 ft.). Mammal species that call the Costa Rican rainforests home include the jaguar, three-toed sloth, all four native monkey species, and Baird's Tapir, while some of the more prominent birds you might spot are the Harpy eagle, Scarlet Macaw and the Chestnut-mandibled toucan.

You can find these lowland rainforests along the southern Pacific coast and Osa Peninsula, as well as along the Caribbean coast. **Corcovado, Cahuita,** and **Manuel Antonio** national parks, as well as the **Manzanillo-Gandoca Wildlife Refuge,** are fine examples of lowland rainforests. Examples of mid-elevation rainforests include the **Braulio Carillo National Park** and the forests around **La Selva** and the **Puerto Viejo de Sarapiquí** region, and those around **Arenal volcano** and **Lake Arenal** area.

TROPICAL DRY FORESTS

In a few protected areas of Guanacaste (chapter 7), you will still find examples of the otherwise vanishing **tropical dry forest.** During the long and pronounced dry season (late Nov to late Apr), no rain relieves the unabated heat. In an effort to conserve much-needed water, the trees drop their leaves but bloom in a riot of color: Purple jacaranda, scarlet *poró,* and brilliant orange flame-of-the-forest are just a few examples. Then during the rainy season, this deciduous forest is transformed into a lush and verdant landscape.

Other common dry forest trees include the Guanacaste, with its broad, shade canopy, and distinctive pochote, whose trunk is covered with thick, broad thorns.

Because the foliage is less dense than that found in cloud forests and rainforests, dry forests are excellent places to view a variety of wildlife. Howler monkeys are commonly seen in the trees, and coatimundi, puma, and coyote roam the ground. Costa Rica's remaining dry forests are most prominently found in **Santa Rosa, Guanacaste, Rincón de la Vieja,** and **Palo Verde** national parks.

CLOUD FORESTS

At higher altitudes you'll find Costa Rica's famed **cloud forests.** Here the steady flow of moist air meets the mountains and creates a nearly constant mist. Epiphytes—resourceful plants that live cooperatively on the branches and trunks of other trees—grow abundantly in the cloud forests, where they must extract moisture and nutrients from the air. Because cloud forests are found in generally steep, mountainous terrain, the canopy here is lower and less uniform than in lowland rainforests, providing better chances for viewing elusive fauna.

The remarkable **Resplendent Quetzal** is perhaps the most famous and sought-after denizen of Costa Rica's cloud forests, but you'll also find a broad and immense variety of flora and fauna, including a dozen or more hummingbird species, wild cats, monkeys, reptiles, and amphibians. **Orchids,** many of them epiphytic, thrive in cloud forests, as do mosses, ferns, and a host of other plants, many of which are cultivated and sold as common household plants throughout the rest of the world.

A Guaria Morada, the national flower.

Costa Rica's most spectacular cloud forest is the **Monteverde Cloud Forest Biological Reserve** (p. 330), but you can also explore Monteverde's neighbor, the **Santa Elena Cloud Forest Reserve** (p. 333), or, much closer to San José, the **Los Angeles Cloud Forest Reserve** (p. 317).

MANGROVES & WETLANDS

Along the coasts, primarily where river mouths meet the ocean, you will find extensive **mangrove forests, wetlands** and **swamps.** Mangroves, in particular, are an immensely important ecological phenomenon. Around the intricate tangle of mangrove roots exists one of the most diverse and rich ecosystems on the planet. All sorts of fish and crustaceans live in the brackish tidal waters. Many larger salt water and open-ocean fish species begin life in the nutrient rich, and relatively safe and protected environment of a mangrove swamp.

Mangrove swamps and wetlands are havens for and home to scores of water birds: **cormorants, magnificent frigate birds, pelicans, kingfishers, egrets, ibises,** and **herons.** The larger birds tend to nest up high in the canopy, while the smaller ones nestle in the underbrush. And in the waters, **caimans** and **crocodiles** cruise the maze of rivers and unmarked canals.

A Hot Lips flower.

Mangrove forests, swamps, and wetlands exist all along both of Costa Rica's coasts. Some of the prime areas that can be explored by tourists include the areas around the **Sierpe river mouth** and **Diquis delta** near **Drake Bay** (p. 416), the **Golfo Dulce** (p. 441) in the southern zone, **Palo Verde National Park** and the **Tempisque river** basin in Guanacaste (chapter 7), and the **Manzanillo-Gandoca Wildlife Refuge** on the Caribbean coast (chapter 12).

PÁRAMO

At the highest reaches, the cloud forests give way to **elfin forests** and **páramos.** More commonly associated with the South American Andes, a páramo is characterized by a variety of tundralike shrubs and grasses, with a scattering of twisted, windblown trees. Reptiles, rodents, and raptors are the most common residents here, and since the vegetation is so sparse, they're often easier to spot. **Mount Chirripó, Chirripó National Park** (p. 407), and the **Cerro de la Muerte** (**Mountain of Death;** p. 406) are the principal areas of páramo in Costa Rica.

VOLCANOES

Costa Rica is a land of high volcanic and seismic activity. The country has three major **volcanic mountain ranges,** and many of the volcanoes are still active, allowing visitors to experience the awe-inspiring sight of steaming **fumaroles,** sky-lighting **eruptions,** and intense **lava flows** during their stay. In ecological terms, cooled-off lava flows are fascinating laboratories, where you can watch pioneering lichen and mosses eventually give way to plants and shrubs, and eventually trees and forests.

The top spot to see volcanic activity is, hands-down, the **Arenal volcano** (chapter 9). Another reliable place to see steady volcanic activity, in the form of mud pots, fumaroles, and hot springs is in the **Rincón de la Vieja National Park** (p. 196). Closer to San José, the **Poás** (p. 163) and **Irazú volcanoes** (p. 179) are both currently active, although relatively quiet.

Searching for Wildlife

Animals in the forests are predominantly nocturnal. When they are active in the daytime, they are usually elusive and on the watch for predators. Birds are easier to spot in clearings or secondary forests than they are in primary forests. Unless you have lots of experience in the Tropics, your best hope for enjoying a walk through the jungle lies in employing a trained and knowledgeable guide. (By the way, if it's been raining a lot and the trails are muddy, a good pair of rubber boots comes in handy. These are usually provided by the lodges or at the sites, where necessary.)

Here are a few helpful hints:

- **Listen.** Pay attention to rustling in the leaves; whether it's monkeys up above or *pizotes* on the ground, you're most likely to hear an animal before seeing one.

- **Keep quiet.** Noise will scare off animals and prevent you from hearing their movements and calls.

- **Don't try too hard.** Soften your focus and allow your peripheral vision to take over. This way you can catch glimpses of motion and then focus in on the prey.

- **Bring binoculars.** It's also a good idea to practice a little first to get the hang of them. It would be a shame to be fiddling around and staring into space while everyone else in your group oohs and aahs over a quetzal.

- **Dress appropriately.** You'll have a hard time focusing your binoculars if you're busy swatting mosquitoes. Light, long pants and long-sleeved shirts are your best bet. Comfortable hiking boots are a real boon, except

A jaguar.

where heavy rubber boots are necessary. Avoid loud colors; the better you blend in with your surroundings, the better your chances are of spotting wildlife.

o **Be patient.** The jungle isn't on a schedule. However, your best shots at seeing forest fauna are in the very early morning and late afternoon hours.

o **Read up.** Familiarize yourself with what you're most likely to see. Most lodges and hotels have a copy of *A Guide to the Birds of Costa Rica* and other wildlife field guides, although it's always best to have your own. A good all-around book to use is Carrol Henderson's *The Field Guide to the Wildlife of Costa Rica.*

RESPONSIBLE TOURISM

Costa Rica is one of the planet's prime ecotourism destinations. Many of the hotels, isolated nature lodges, and tour operators around the country are pioneers and dedicated professionals in the sustainable tourism field. Many other hotels, lodges, and tour operators are honestly and earnestly jumping on the bandwagon and improving their practices, while still others are simply "green-washing," using the terms "eco," "green," and "sustainable" in their promo materials, but doing little real good in their daily operations.

In 2010, Costa Rica was ranked third globally in the Environmental Performance Index (EPI; http://epi.yale.edu). Despite its reputation, the substantial amounts of good work being done, and ongoing advances being made in the field, Costa Rica is by no means an ecological paradise free from environmental and social threats. Untreated sewage is dumped into rivers, bays, oceans, and watersheds at an alarming rate. Child labor and sexual exploitation are rampant, and certain sectors of the tourism trade only make these matters worse.

Over the last decade or so, Costa Rica has taken great strides toward protecting its rich biodiversity, however. Thirty years ago it was difficult to find a protected area anywhere, but now more than 11% of the country is protected within the national park system. Another 10% to 15% of the land enjoys moderately effective preservation as part of private and public reserves, Indian reserves, and wildlife refuges and corridors. Still, Costa Rica's precious tropical hardwoods continue to be harvested at an alarming rate, often illegally, while other primary forests are clear-cut for short-term agricultural gain. Many experts predict that Costa Rica's unprotected forests could be gone within the early part of this century.

Recycling is beginning to gather momentum in Costa Rica. More and more you will see separate bins for plastics, glass, and paper on town and city streets, at national parks, and at the country's more sustainable hotels and restaurants. Your hotel will be your best bet for finding a place to deposit recyclable waste, especially if you choose a hotel that has instituted sustainable practices.

While you can find hotels and tour operators using comprehensive sustainable practices all across Costa Rica—even in the San José metropolitan area—a few prime destinations are particular hot spots for sustainable tourism practices. Of note are the remote and wild Osa Peninsula and Golfo Dulce area of southern Costa Rica, the rural northern zone that includes both Monteverde and the Arenal Volcano and Lake Arenal attractions, and the underdeveloped Caribbean coast, with the rainforest canals of Tortuguero, Cahuita National Park, and the Manzanillo-Gandoca Wildlife Refuge.

In addition to focusing on wildlife viewing and adventure activities in the wild, ecolodges in these areas tend to be smaller, often lacking televisions, air-conditioning, and other typical luxury amenities. The more remote lodges usually depend largely or entirely on small solar and hydro plants for their power consumption. That said, some of these hotels and lodges provide levels of comfort and service that are quite luxurious.

In Costa Rica, the government-run tourism institute (ICT) provides a sustainability rating of a host of hotels and tour agencies under its **Certificate of Sustainable Tourism Program (CST).** You can look up the ratings at the website www.turismo-sostenible.co.cr.

Bear in mind that this program is still relatively new and the list is far from comprehensive. Many hotels and tour operators in the country haven't completed the extensive review and rating process. Moreover, die-hard ecologists find some of these listings somewhat suspect. Still, this list and rating system is a good start, and is improving and evolving constantly.

A parallel program, **"The Blue Flag,"** is used to rate specific beaches and communities in terms of their environmental condition and practices. The Blue Flags are reviewed and handed out annually. Current listings of Blue Flag approved beaches and communities can be found at www.visitcostarica.com.

See individual chapters for recommendations on the hotels and lodges that I consider leaders in sustainable tourism practices in Costa Rica. As I've said earlier, more and more hotels are continuing to adopt sustainable and ethical tourism practices. Please supplement my recommendations with your own research via the web, and sites such as the CST site mentioned above.

While sustainable tourism options are widespread in Costa Rica, organic and sustainably grown fruits and vegetables (as well as coffee) are just beginning to become available. Very few restaurants feature organic produce, although that is starting to change.

If you're not booking your hotel, tours, and transportation by yourself, you might want to consider using a tour agency that has earned high marks in this area. In Costa Rica, **Horizontes ★★**, Calle 32 between avenidas 3 and 5 (☏ **2222-2022;** www.horizontes.com), has garnered particularly high marks from several rating agencies and organizations. Other exemplary operators include **Costa Rica Expeditions ★★** (☏ **2257-0766;** www.costaricaexpeditions.com), **Costa Rica Sun Tours ★** (☏ **2296-7757;** www.crsuntours.com), and **Swiss Travel Service** (☏ **2282-4898;** www.swisstravelcr.com).

In addition to the agencies listed above, those looking for a taste of what many consider "the real" Costa Rica should consider booking through **ACTUAR ★★** (☏ **866/393-5889** in the U.S., or 2248-9470 in Costa Rica; www.actuarcostarica.com). This organization groups together a network of small, rural lodges and tour operators. In many cases, accommodations are quite rustic. Bunk beds and thin foam mattresses are common. However, all of the hotels, lodges, and tour operators are small-scale and local. In many cases, they are family operations. If you want a true taste of typical, rural Costa Rica, traveling with ACTUAR is a great way to go.

Finally, another great way to make your tourism experience more sustainable is to volunteer. For specific information on volunteer options in Costa Rica, see "Volunteer & Study Programs," in chapter 4, "The Active Vacation Planner."

Beyond the country's hotels, tour operators, and volunteer options, it's worth noting here that the local commuter airline **Nature Air** (𝒞 **800/235-9272** in the U.S. and Canada, or 2299-6000; www.natureair.com) has been a pioneer in the field. In 2004, Nature Air became the first certified carbon-neutral airline on the planet, and they continue to supplement their own sustainable practices with contributions to reforestation and conservation programs.

SUGGESTED COSTA RICA ITINERARIES

3

C osta Rica is a compact, yet varied, destination with numerous natural attractions and a broad selection of exciting sights, scenery, adventure activities, and ecosystems. On a trip to Costa Rica you can visit rainforests, cloud forests, and active volcanoes, and walk along miles of beautiful beaches on both the Pacific and Caribbean coasts. Adventure hounds will have their fill choosing from an exciting array of activities, and those looking for some rest and relaxation can grab a chaise longue and a good book. Costa Rica is also a relatively compact country, which makes visiting several destinations during a single vacation both easy and enjoyable.

The fastest and easiest way to get around the country is by small commuter aircraft. Most major destinations are serviced by regular commuter or charter airline companies. However, this does imply using San José or Liberia as periodic transfer hubs. If your connections don't line up, you may end up having to tack on nights in either of these cities in the middle of your trip. Luckily, sufficient flights and internal connections make this an infrequent inconvenience.

Getting around Costa Rica by car is another excellent option. Most major destinations are between 2 and 5 hours from San José by car, and many can be linked together in a well-planned and convenient loop. For example, one popular loop links Arenal Volcano, Monteverde, and Manuel Antonio. However, be forewarned that the roads here are often in terrible shape, many major roads and intersections are unmarked, and Tico drivers can be reckless and rude. See "By Car" under "Getting Around Costa Rica," in chapter 13 for more information on driving in Costa Rica.

The following itineraries are specific blueprints for fabulous vacations, and you can follow them to the letter. You might also decide to use one or more of them as an outline and then fill in some blanks with other destinations, activities, and attractions that strike your fancy from the rest of this book.

COSTA RICA REGIONS IN BRIEF

Costa Rica rightfully should be called "Costas Ricas" because it has two coasts: one on the Pacific Ocean and one on the Caribbean Sea. These two coasts are as different from each other as are the Atlantic and Pacific coasts of North America.

Costa Rica's **Pacific coast** is the most extensive, and is characterized by a rugged (although mostly accessible) coastline where forested mountains often meet the sea. It can be divided into four distinct regions—Guanacaste, the

PREVIOUS PAGE: **A green turtle in Tortuguero.**

Costa Rica Regions in Brief

Nicoya Peninsula, the Central Coast, and the Southern Coast. There are some spectacular stretches of coastline, and most of the country's top beaches are here. This coast varies from the dry, sunny climate of the northwest to the hot, humid rainforests of the south.

The **Caribbean coast** can be divided into two roughly equal stretches. The remote northeast coastline is a vast flat plain laced with rivers and covered with rainforest; it is accessible only by boat or small plane. Farther south, along the stretch of coast accessible by car, are uncrowded beaches and even a bit of coral reef.

Bordered by Nicaragua in the north and Panama in the southeast, Costa Rica is only slightly larger than Vermont and New Hampshire combined. Much of the country is mountainous, with three major ranges running northwest to southeast. Among these mountains are several volcanic peaks, some of which are still active. Between the mountain ranges are fertile valleys, the largest and most populated of which is the Central Valley. With the exception of the dry Guanacaste region, much of Costa Rica's coastal area is hot and humid and covered with dense rainforests.

See the map above for a visual of the regions detailed below.

SAN JOSÉ   San José is Costa Rica's capital and its primary business, cultural and social center—it sits fairly close the country's geographical center, in the heart of its Central Valley (see below). It's a sprawling, urban area, with a population of around 1 million. Its streets are narrow, in poor repair, poorly marked and often chocked full with traffic. However, a few notable parks, like the Parque La Sabana and Parque del Este, do serve to lessen the urban blight. San José is home to the country's greatest collection of museums, fine restaurants and stores, galleries, and shopping centers.

THE CENTRAL VALLEY The Central Valley is characterized by rolling green hills that rise to heights between 900 and 1,200m (2,952–3,936 ft.) above sea level. The climate here is mild and springlike year-round. It's Costa Rica's primary agricultural region, with coffee farms making up the majority of landholdings. The rich volcanic soil of this region makes it ideal for farming. The country's earliest settlements were in this area, and today the Central Valley (which includes San José) is densely populated, crisscrossed by decent roads, and dotted with small towns. Surrounding the Central Valley are high mountains, among which are four volcanic peaks. Two of these, **Poás** and **Irazú,** are still active and have caused extensive damage during cycles of activity in the past 2 centuries. Many of the mountainous regions to the north and to the south of the capital of San José have been declared national parks (Tapantí, Juan Castro, and Braulio Carrillo) to protect their virgin rainforests against logging.

GUANACASTE The northwestern corner of the country near the Nicaraguan border is the site of many of Costa Rica's sunniest and most popular **beaches,** including **Playa del Coco, Playa Hermosa, Playa Flamingo, Playa Conchal, Tamarindo,** and the **Papagayo Peninsula.** Scores of beach destinations, towns, and resorts are along this long string of coastline. Because many foreigners have chosen to build beach houses and retirement homes here, Guanacaste has experienced considerable development over the years. You won't find a glut of Cancún–style high-rise hotels, but condos, luxury resorts, and golf courses have sprung up all up and down the coastline here. Still, you won't be towel-to-towel with thousands of strangers. On the contrary, you can still find long stretches of deserted sands. However, more and more travelers are using Liberia as their gateway to Costa Rica, bypassing San José and the central and southern parts of the country entirely.

Tamarindo.

With about 165cm (65 in.) of rain a year, this region is by far the driest in the country and has been likened to west Texas. Guanacaste province is named after the shady trees that still shelter the herds of cattle roaming the dusty savanna here. In addition to cattle ranches, Guanacaste has semiactive volcanoes, several lakes, and one of the last remnants of tropical dry forest left in Central America. (Dry forest once stretched all the way from Costa Rica up to the Mexican state of Chiapas.)

PUNTARENAS & THE NICOYA PENINSULA   Just south of Guanacaste lies the Nicoya peninsula. Similar to Guanacaste in many ways, the Nicoya peninsula is nonetheless somewhat more inaccessible, and thus much less developed and crowded. However, this is already starting to change. The neighboring beaches of **Malpaís** and **Santa Teresa** are perhaps the fastest growing hot spots anywhere along the Costa Rican coast.

While similar in terms of geography, climate, and ecosystems, as you head south from Guanacaste, the region begins to get more humid and moist. The forests are taller and lusher than those found in Guanacaste. The Nicoya peninsula itself juts out to form the Golfo de Nicoya (Nicoya Gulf), a large, protected body of water. **Puntarenas,** a small fishing city, is the main port found inside this gulf, and one of the main commercial ports in all of Costa Rica. Puntarenas is also the departure point for the regular ferries that connect the Nicoya peninsula to San José and most of mainland Costa Rica.

THE NORTHERN ZONE   This inland region lies to the north of San José and includes rainforests, cloud forests, hot springs, the country's two most active volcanoes (**Arenal** and **Rincón de la Vieja**), **Braulio Carrillo National Park,** and numerous remote lodges. Because this is one of the few regions of Costa Rica without any beaches, it primarily attracts people interested in nature and active sports. **Lake Arenal** boasts some of the best windsurfing and kitesurfing in the world, as well as several good mountain-biking trails along its shores. The **Monteverde Cloud Forest,** perhaps Costa Rica's most internationally recognized attraction, is another top draw in this region.

THE CENTRAL PACIFIC COAST   Because it's the most easily accessible coastline in Costa Rica, the central Pacific coast has a vast variety of beach resorts and hotels. **Playa de Jacó,** a beach just an hour or so drive from San José, attracts many sunbirds, charter groups, and a mad rush of Tico tourists every weekend. It is also very popular with young surfers, and has a distinct party vibe to it. **Manuel Antonio,** one of the most emblematic destinations in Costa Rica, is built up around a popular coastal national park, and caters to people looking to blend beach time and fabulous panoramic views with some wildlife viewing and active adventures. This region is also home to the highest peak in Costa Rica—**Mount Chirripó**—a beautiful summit, where frost is common.

THE SOUTHERN ZONE   This hot, humid region is one of Costa Rica's most remote and undeveloped. It is characterized by dense rainforests, large national parks and protected areas, and rugged coastlines. Much of the area is uninhabited and protected in **Corcovado, Piedras Blancas,** and **La**

Amistad national parks. A number of wonderful nature lodges are spread around the shores of the **Golfo Dulce** and along the **Osa Peninsula.** There's a lot of solitude to be found here, due in no small part to the fact that it's hard to get here and hard to get around. But if you like your ecotourism authentic and challenging, you'll find the southern zone to your liking.

THE CARIBBEAN COAST   Most of the Caribbean coast is a wide, steamy lowland laced with rivers and blanketed with rainforests and banana plantations. The culture here is predominantly Afro-Caribbean, with many residents speaking an English or Caribbean patois. The northern section of this coast is accessible only by

Corcovado National Park.

boat or small plane and is the site of **Tortuguero National Park,** which is known for its nesting sea turtles and riverboat trips. The towns of **Cahuita, Puerto Viejo,** and **Manzanillo,** on the southern half of the Caribbean coast, are increasingly popular destinations. The beautiful beaches and coastline here, as yet, have few large hotels. This area can be rainy, especially between December and April.

COSTA RICA IN 1 WEEK

The timing is tight, but this itinerary packs a lot into a weeklong vacation. This route takes you to a trifecta of Costa Rica's primary tourist attractions: Arenal Volcano, Monteverde, and Manuel Antonio. You can explore and enjoy tropical nature, take in some beach time, and experience a few high-adrenaline adventures to boot.

DAY 1: ARRIVE & SETTLE INTO SAN JOSÉ

Arrive and get settled in **San José.** If your flight gets in early enough and you have time, head downtown and tour the **Museos del Banco Central de Costa Rica (Gold Museum)** ★★ (p. 130).

FRESH FRUIT

As you walk around town, stop at one of the roadside stands or kiosks selling small bags of precut and prepared fruit. Depending on the season, you might find mango, pineapple, or papaya on offer. If you're lucky they'll have *mamon chino,* an odd-looking golf ball–size fruit you might also know as rambutan or litchi nut.

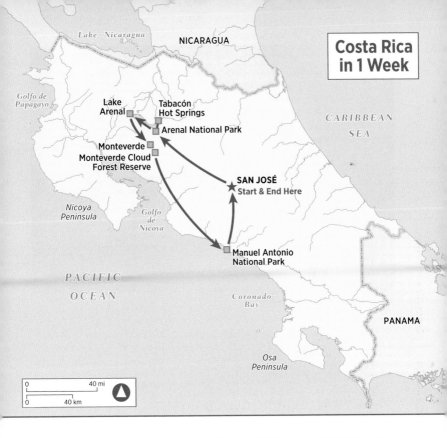

Head over to the **Teatro Nacional** (National Theater; p. 140). If anything is playing that night, buy tickets for the show. For an elegant and delicious dinner, I recommend **Grano de Oro Restaurant ★★★** (p. 124), a refined restaurant with seating in and around an open-air central courtyard in a beautiful downtown hotel.

DAY 2: HOT ROCKS ★★

Rent a car and head to the Arenal National Park to see **Arenal Volcano ★★**. Settle into your hotel and spend the afternoon at the **Tabacón Grand Spa Thermal Resort ★★★** (p. 308), working out the kinks from the road. In the evening either sign up for a volcano-watching tour or take one on your own by driving the road to **Arenal National Park** and finding a quiet spot to pull over and wait for the sparks to fly.

DAY 3: ADVENTURES AROUND ARENAL, ENDING UP IN MONTEVERDE ★★

Spend the morning doing something adventurous around Arenal National Park. Your options range from white-water rafting to mountain biking to horseback riding and then hiking to the Río Fortuna Waterfall. My favorite is the **canyoning** adventure offered by **Desafío Expeditions ★★** (p. 304).

Tabacón Grand Spa Thermal Resort.

Allow at least 4 hours of daylight to drive around **Lake Arenal** to **Monteverde.** Stop for a break at the **Lucky Bug Gallery ★★** (p. 323), along the road between Tabacón and Nuevo Arenal, and an excellent place to shop for gifts, artwork, and souvenirs. Once you get to Monteverde, settle into your hotel and head for a drink and dinner at **Sofía ★★★** (p. 343).

DAY 4: MONTEVERDE CLOUD FOREST BIOLOGICAL RESERVE ★★★

Wake up early and take a guided tour of the **Monteverde Cloud Forest Biological Reserve ★★★** (p. 330). Be sure to stop in at the **Hummingbird Gallery ★** (p. 338) next door to the entrance after your tour. The scores of brilliant hummingbirds buzzing around your head at this attraction are always fascinating. Spend the afternoon visiting several of the area's attractions, which might include any combination of the following: the **Butterfly Garden ★**, **Orchid Garden ★★**, **Monteverde Serpentarium ★**, **Frog Pond of Monteverde ★**, the **Bat Jungle,** and the **World of Insects** (p. 336).

DAY 5: FROM THE TREETOPS TO THE COAST ★★★

Use the morning to take one of the **zip-line canopy tours** here. I recommend **Selvatura Park ★★** (p. 334), which has a wonderful canopy tour, as well as other interesting exhibits. Be sure to schedule the tour early enough so that you can hit the road by noon for your drive to **Manuel Antonio National Park.** Settle into your hotel and head for a **sunset drink** at **Agua Azul ★** (p. 391), which offers up spectacular views over the rainforest to the sea. You can drop your car off at any point now and just rely on taxis and tours.

A canopy tour at Selvatura.

DAY 6: MANUEL ANTONIO ★★

In the morning take a boat tour of the **Damas Island estuary** (p. 381) with Jorge Cruz, and then reward yourself for all the hard touring so far with an afternoon lazing on one of the beautiful beaches inside **Manuel Antonio National Park** ★★ (p. 379). If you just can't lie still, be sure to hike the loop trail through the rainforest here and around **Cathedral Point** ★★. Make reservations at the **El Patio Bistro Latino** ★★★ (p. 392) for an intimate and relaxed final dinner in Costa Rica.

DAY 7: SAYING ADIÓS

Fly back to **San José** in time to connect with your departing flight home. If you have extra time, feel free to head back into Manuel Antonio National Park, do some souvenir shopping, or simply laze around your hotel pool. You've earned it.

COSTA RICA IN 2 WEEKS

If you have 2 weeks, you'll be able to hit all the highlights mentioned above, as well as some others, and at a slightly more relaxed pace to boot. The first part of this itinerary is very similar to the 1-week itinerary laid out above. It's a real judgment call, but you might want to substitute a 2- to 3-day trip to Tortuguero for either the Guanacaste or the southern zone section listed below, or whittle down a day here or there along the way in order to squeeze in Tortuguero.

DAYS 1 & 2: SAN JOSÉ

Follow the options listed under **DAYS 1 AND 2** in "Costa Rica in 1 Week," above. Another excellent option for dinner on your second night is **Café Mundo** ★ (p. 122), a lively restaurant and nightspot set in a wonderfully restored old colonial home in the heart of downtown.

DAY 3: ACTIVE IN ARENAL

Spend the morning doing something adventurous in **Arenal National Park** ★★, as recommended in **DAY 3** in "Costa Rica in 1 Week," above. If you're really active, you can schedule a second adventure for the afternoon or take time to visit the town of **La Fortuna.** In the evening, return to the **Tabacón Grand Spa Thermal Resort** ★★★ (p. 308). If you were smart, you'll have already booked yourself a **spa treatment.**

A butterfly at the Monteverde Butterfly Garden.   Relaxing in a hammock in Guanacaste.

DAY 4: DRIVING (& SHOPPING) YOUR WAY AROUND THE LAKE TO MONTEVERDE

Give yourself at least 4 hours of daylight to drive around **Lake Arenal** to **Monteverde.** But you can take even longer. During your drive, be sure to stop at the **Lucky Bug Gallery ★★** (p. 323), where you can shop for gifts, artwork, and souvenirs. Once you're in Monteverde, settle into your hotel and head for a drink and dinner at **Chimera ★★** (p. 343).

DAY 5: MONTEVERDE CLOUD FOREST BIOLOGICAL RESERVE

Spend **DAY 5** as described for **DAY 4** of "Costa Rica in 1 Week," above; however, head to **Sofía ★★★** (p. 343) for dinner and grab a window table fronting its well-lighted and lush gardens.

DAY 6: MORE MONTEVERDE

There's just no way you can hit all the local **Monteverde** attractions in a day. Use today to visit a few that you missed. Also be sure to stop in at several of the local **art galleries** and **crafts shops.** Monteverde has one of the country's most vibrant arts scenes and several worthwhile galleries, including **Casa de Arte ★** (p. 339). In the evening, be sure to try **Café Caburé ★★** (p. 343), a low-key restaurant serving eclectic international fare and a wide range of homemade organic chocolate creations.

DAY 7: MONTEVERDE TO MANUEL ANTONIO

Spend this day as in **DAY 5** of "Costa Rica in 1 Week," above. However, after your sunset drink, head down into the town of Quepos for dinner at **El Patio Bistro Latino ★★★** (p. 392), a cozy little spot serving some of the best food in the area.

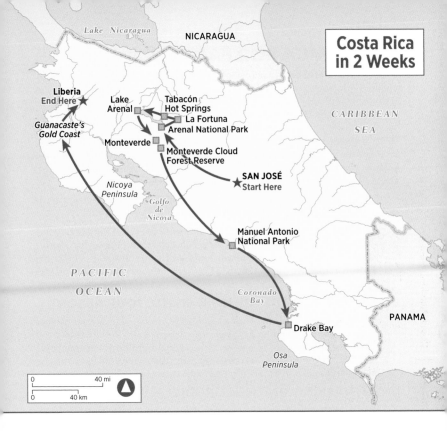

DAY 8: MANUEL ANTONIO ★★

Spend this day as in **DAY 6** of "Costa Rica in 1 Week," above.

DAYS 9, 10 & 11: SOUTHERN COSTA RICA

Fly from Quepos and Manuel Antonio to **Drake Bay** and settle into a remote **ecolodge,** such as **La Paloma Lodge ★★★** (p. 425). You'll need 3 days to experience the many natural wonders of this southern zone. Aside from hiking in the rainforest, you'll be able to take scuba or snorkel outings, sportfishing trips, kayak adventures, and surfing lessons.

DAYS 12, 13 & 14: GUANACASTE'S GOLD COAST

You've had enough nature and adventure; it's time to enjoy some pure R & R. From the southern zone, fly up to **Guanacaste** and spend your final days enjoying the pleasures of one of Costa Rica's **Gold Coast** beaches. If you can afford it and rooms are available, I recommend the **Four Seasons Resort ★★★** (p. 211). Alternatively, you might enjoy a smaller boutique hotel such as **Hotel Playa Hermosa Bosque del Mar ★★** (p. 213).

If just lying on the beach or poolside is too mellow, you have scores of tour and activity options. If you're not feeling that active or adventurous, simply break out that novel you've been too busy to open and enjoy. On your last day, fly home from **Liberia** or **San José**.

COSTA RICA FOR FAMILIES

Costa Rica is a terrific destination for families. If you're traveling with very small children, you might want to stick close to the beaches, or consider a large resort with a children's program and babysitting services. But for slightly older kids and teens, particularly those with an adventurous streak, Costa Rica is a lot of fun. Youngsters and teens, especially those with strong adventurous and inquisitive traits, will do great here. The biggest challenges to families traveling with children are travel distances and the logistical trials of moving around within the country, which is why I recommend flying in and out of Liberia and basing yourself in Guanacaste.

DAY 1: ARRIVE IN GUANACASTE

Fly directly into **Liberia.** From here it's a drive of 30 to 45 minutes to any of the area's many beach resorts, especially around the **Papagayo Peninsula.** I recommend either the **Four Seasons Resort ★★★** (p. 211) or the **Hilton Papagayo Resort ★** (p. 213). Both have excellent children's programs and tons of activity and tour options.

DAY 2: GET YOUR BEARINGS & ENJOY YOUR RESORT

Get to know and enjoy the facilities and activities offered up at your hotel or resort. Spend some time on the beach or at the pool. Enjoy the resort's on-hand watersports equipment and activities. Check out the **children's program** and any scheduled **activities** or **tours** that particularly appeal to anyone in the family. Feel free to adapt the following days' suggestions accordingly.

DAY 3: RAFTING ON THE COROBICÍ RIVER

The whole family will enjoy a **rafting tour** on the gentle Corobicí River. **Rios Tropicales ★★** (p. 194) offers leisurely trips that are appropriate for

A sailboat cruise.

all ages, except infants. In addition to the slow float and occasional mellow rapids, there'll be plenty of opportunities to watch birds and other wildlife along the way. If you're here between late September and late February, book a **turtle tour** (p. 233) at nearby **Playa Grande** for the evening. The whole family will be awe-struck by the amazing spectacle of a giant leather-back turtle digging a nest and laying its eggs.

DAY 4: PARENT'S DAY OFF

Drop the kids off with the children's program for at least 1 full day and treat yourselves to a **sailboat cruise.** You'll spend some time cruising the coast, take a break or two to snorkel, and probably stop for lunch at a deserted beach. If you really want to pamper yourself, also schedule some **spa services.**

DAY 5: HACIENDA GUACHIPELIN ★

It's time to head for the hills, which are mostly volcanoes in this neck of the woods. Book a full-day outing to **Hacienda Guachipelin ★** (p. 199), near the Rincón de la Vieja National Park. Older and more adventurous children can sign up for a **horseback ride** or **canopy tour.** Younger children should get a kick out of visiting this working farm and cattle ranch.

Learning to surf.

DAY 6: LEARN TO SURF

Head to **Tamarindo ★** (p. 243) and arrange for the whole family to take **surf** or **boogie-board lessons.** Hopefully you will have already booked a class with **Tamarindo Surf School** or **Witch's Rock Surf Camp** (p. 241). Be sure to rent your boards for a full day, so that you can practice after the lesson is over.

DAY 7: LEAVING LIBERIA

Use any spare time you have before your flight out of **Liberia** to buy last-minute souvenirs and gifts, or just laze on the beach or by the pool. Your best bet for shopping is probably the **Kaltak Arts & Craft Market** (*℃* **2667-0696**), which is conveniently located on the way to the airport.

A WEEK OF ADVENTURES IN COSTA RICA

Costa Rica is a major adventure-tourism destination. The following basic itinerary packs a lot of adventure into a single week; if you want to do some mountain biking or kayaking, just schedule that time in. If you're into windsurfing or kiteboarding, you'll definitely want to visit Lake Arenal between December and March.

DAY 1: ARRIVE & SETTLE INTO SAN JOSÉ

Arrive and get settled in **San José.** If your flight gets in early enough and you have time, head downtown and tour the **Museos del Banco Central de Costa Rica ★★** (p. 130) and the **Teatro Nacional** (p. 140). Take a break for an afternoon coffee at **Cafeteria 1930** (p. 122). Be sure to grab

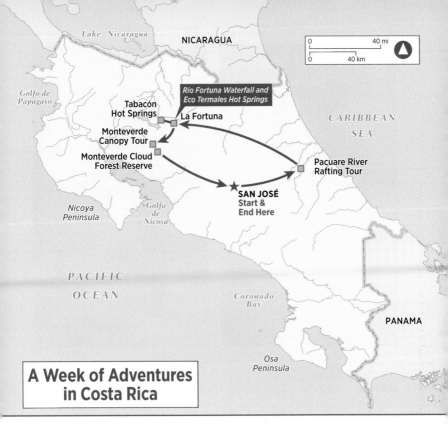

an outdoor table and enjoy some people-watching. For a delicious dinner with a spectacular view, head to **La Cava Grill ★** (p. 158), which is in the hills above Escazú.

DAYS 2 & 3: GET WET & WILD

Take a 2-day white-water rafting expedition on the **Pacuare River** with **Exploradores Outdoors ★** (p. 148). Camp out at their rustic tent camp on the river's edge. When you finish running the Pacuare, have them arrange for a transfer to **La Fortuna** at the end of your rafting trip. Settle into your hotel and head to the **Tabacón Grand Spa Thermal Resort ★★★** (p. 308) to have a soothing soak and to watch the volcano.

DAY 4: WATERFALLS TWO WAYS

Go canyoning with **Desafío Expeditions ★★** (p. 304) in the morning, and then hop on a horse or a mountain bike in the afternoon and be sure to stop at the **Río Fortuna Waterfall ★** (p. 305). Take the short hike down to the base of the falls and take a dip in one of the pools there. In the evening, check out the hot springs at **Eco Termales ★★** (p. 309).

Pacuare River rafting.

Biking in Costa Rica.

DAY 5: GETTING THERE IS PART OF THE FUN & ADVENTURE

Arrange a **taxi-to-boat-to-horse** transfer over to **Monteverde** with **Desafío Expeditions ★★** (p. 304). Settle in quickly at your hotel and take a zip-line **canopy tour** in the afternoon. I recommend the **Original Canopy Tour ★** (p. 335) in Monteverde. Finally, if you've got the energy, take a **night tour** through the Monteverde Cloud Forest Reserve.

DAY 6: MONTEVERDE CLOUD FOREST BIOLOGICAL RESERVE ★★★

Wake up early and head back to take a daytime guided tour of the **Monteverde Cloud Forest Biological Reserve ★★★**. Be sure to bring a packed lunch. After the guided tour, spend the next few hours continuing to explore the trails through the cloud forest here. See if you can spot a **quetzal** (p. 85) on your own. Then transfer back to San José.

DAY 7: SQUEEZE IN A SOCCER GAME BEFORE SPLITTING

Unfortunately, you'll most likely be on an early flight home from **San José.** If you have a few hours to kill, head for a **hike** or **jog** around Parque La Sabana or, better yet, try to join a **pickup soccer game** (p. 131) here.

SAN JOSÉ & ENVIRONS IN 3 DAYS

While most tourists seek to almost immediately get out of San José for greener pastures, Costa Rica's vibrant capital still has plenty to see and do. If you have even more days, take a white-water rafting trip on the Pacuare River, or head out to the Irazú Volcano, Orosi Valley, and Cartago area.

DAY 1: GETTING TO KNOW THE CITY

Start your day on the **Plaza de la Cultura.** Visit the **Museos del Banco Central de Costa Rica ★★** (p. 130), and see if you can get tickets for a performance that night at the Teatro Nacional (p. 140). From the Plaza de la Cultura, stroll up Avenida Central to the **Museo Nacional de Costa Rica (National Museum) ★★** (p. 129).

☕ Kalú Café ★★

Once you've toured the museum, have lunch at **Kalú,** at Calle 7 and Avenida 11, a lovely cafe and artsy boutique. See p. 123.

After lunch, head over to the nearby **Centro Nacional de Arte y Cultura (National Center of Art and Culture) ★** (p. 127). As soon as you're finished taking in all this culture, some shopping at the open-air stalls at the **Plaza de la Democracia** (p. 134) is in order.

☕ Café Mundo ★

Try dinner at the trendy local hangout **Café Mundo,** at Calle 15 and Avenida 9, 3 blocks east and 1 block north of the INS building. See p. 122.

Museo Nacional de Costa Rica.

San José in 3 Days

Day 1

1 Plaza de la Cultura
2 Museos del Banco Central de Costa Rica
3 Museo Nacional de Costa Rica
4 Kalú Café
5 Centro Nacional de Arte y Cultura
6 Plaza de la Democracia
7 Café Mundo
8 Teatro Nacional

Day 3

9 Museo de Arte Costarricense
10 Parque La Sabana
11 Mercado Central
12 Restaurante Nuestra Tierra
13 Salsa 54
14 Castro's

Day 2 Itinerary attractions are outside San José

After dinner, head to the **Teatro Nacional** for the night's performance.

DAY 2: ENJOYING SOME NEARBY ATTRACTIONS

Get an early start for the **Poás Volcano ★★** (p. 163), before the clouds sock the main crater in. After visiting the volcano, head to the **La Paz Waterfall Gardens ★★** (p. 162). Take a walk on the waterfall trail, and also enjoy the immense butterfly garden and lively hummingbird garden. This is a good place to have lunch. On your way back to San José, you'll be making a loop through the hills of **Heredia,** with a stop at **INBio Park ★★** (p. 169). In addition to being a fascinating natural-history museum, INBio Park also has a wonderful collection of intriguing animal sculptures by Costa Rican artist José Sancho.

A San José street scene.

DAY 3: MORE CITY SIGHTS & SHOPPING

Spend your third day further exploring the capital. Start by heading out on Paseo Colón to the **Museo de Arte Costarricense (Costa Rican Art Museum)** ★★ (p. 127). Be sure to spend some time in their continually growing open-air sculpture garden. After visiting the museum, take a stroll around the beautiful and expansive downtown **Parque La Sabana** (p. 131). Intrepid travelers can also do some shopping at the **Mercado Central** ★ (p. 138), or take a late-night turn on the dance floor at **Castro's** ★ (p. 142) or **Salsa 54** (p. 142).

☕ Restaurante Nuestra Tierra

For a final taste of local culture, head for dinner at **Restaurante Nuestra Tierra,** located right downtown, across from the Plaza de la Democracia. See p. 123.

3

SUGGESTED COSTA RICA ITINERARIES

San José & Environs in 3 Days

4

THE
ACTIVE
VACATION
PLANNER

Active and adventure travelers will have their hands full and hearts pumping in Costa Rica. While it's possible to stay clean and dry, most visitors want to spend at least some time getting their hair wet, their feet muddy, and their adrenaline flowing. Opportunities range from bird-watching to scuba diving to kiteboarding, and beyond.

This chapter lays out your options, from tour operators who run multiactivity package tours that often include stays at ecolodges, to the best places in Costa Rica to pursue active endeavors (with listings of tour operators, guides, and outfitters that specialize in each), to an overview of the country's national parks and bioreserves. I also list some educational and volunteer travel options for those of you who desire to actively contribute to the country's social welfare, or assist Costa Rica in the maintenance and preservation of its natural wonders.

ORGANIZED ADVENTURE TRIPS

Because many travelers have limited time and resources, organized ecotourism or adventure-travel packages, arranged by tour operators in either Costa Rica or the United States, are a popular way of combining several activities. Bird-watching, horseback riding, rafting, and hiking can be teamed with, say, visits to Monteverde Cloud Forest Biological Reserve and Manuel Antonio National Park.

Traveling with a group has several advantages over traveling independently: Your accommodations and transportation are arranged, and most (if not all) meals are included in the package cost. If your tour operator has a reasonable amount of experience and a decent track record, you should proceed to each of your destinations quickly without snags and long delays. You'll also have the opportunity to meet like-minded souls who are interested in nature and active sports. Of course, you'll pay more for the convenience of having all your arrangements handled in advance.

In the best cases, group size is kept small (10–20 people), and tours are escorted by knowledgeable guides who are either naturalists or biologists. Be sure to ask about difficulty levels when you're choosing a tour. Most companies offer "soft adventure" packages that those in moderately good, but not phenomenal, shape can handle; others focus on more hard-core activities geared toward only seasoned athletes or adventure travelers.

Costa Rican Tour Agencies

Because many U.S.-based companies subcontract portions of their tours to established Costa Rican companies, some travelers like to cut out the middleman and set up their tours directly with these companies. That means that these packages are often less expensive than those offered by U.S. companies, but it doesn't mean they are cheap. You're still paying for the convenience of having your arrangements handled for you.

Scores of agencies in San José offer a plethora of options. These agencies can arrange everything from white-water rafting to sightseeing at one of the nearby volcanoes or a visit to a butterfly farm. Although it's generally quite easy to arrange a day trip at the last minute, other tours are offered only on set dates or when enough people are interested. Contact a few of the companies before you leave home and find out what they might be doing when you arrive. These local operators tend to be a fair share less expensive than their international counterparts, with 10-day tours generally costing in the neighborhood of $1,500 to $3,500 per person, not including airfare to Costa Rica.

Coast to Coast Adventures ★ (© 2280-8054; www.ctocadventures. com) has a unique excursion involving no motor vehicles. The company's namesake 12-day trip spans the country, with participants traveling on rafts, by mountain bike, and on foot. Custom-designed trips (with a minimum of motorized transport) of shorter duration are also available.

Costa Rica Expeditions ★★ (© 2257-0766; www.costaricaexpeditions. com) offers everything from 10-day tours covering the entire country to 3-day/2-night and 2-day/1-night tours of Monteverde Cloud Forest Biological Reserve and Tortuguero National Park, where they run their own lodges. It also offers 1- to 2-day white-water rafting trips and other excursions. All tours and excursions include transportation, meals, and lodging. Its tours are some of the most expensive in the country, but it is the most consistently reliable outfitter as well (and its customer service is excellent). If you want to go out on your own, Costa Rica Expeditions can supply you with just transportation from place to place.

Costa Rica Sun Tours ★ (© 866/271-6263 in the U.S. and Canada, or 2296-7757 in Costa Rica; www.crsuntours.com) offers a wide range of tours and adventures and specializes in multiday tours that include stays at small country lodges for travelers interested in experiencing nature.

Horizontes ★★ (© 2222-2022; www.horizontes.com) is not a specifically adventure-oriented operator, but it offers a wide range of individual, group, and package tours, including those geared toward active and adventure travelers, as well families and even honeymooners. The company hires responsible and knowledgeable guides, and is a local leader in sustainable tourism practices.

Serendipity Adventures ★ (© 888/226-5050 in the U.S. and Canada, or 2558-1000; www.serendipityadventures.com), an adventure-travel operator, offers everything from ballooning to mountain biking, and sea kayaking to canyoning, as well as most of the popular white-water rafting trips.

International Adventure Tour Operators

These agencies and operators specialize in well-organized and coordinated tours. Many travelers prefer to have everything arranged and confirmed before arriving in Costa Rica, and this is a good idea for first-timers and during the high season. **Be warned:** Most of these operators are not cheap, with 10-day tours generally costing in the neighborhood of $2,500 to $5,000 per person, not including airfare to Costa Rica.

Abercrombie & Kent ★★ (© 800/554-7016; www.abercrombiekent. com) is a luxury-tour company that offers upscale trips around the globe, and it has several tours of Costa Rica on its menu. It specializes in 8-day highlight tours

PLANNING A COSTA RICAN wedding

Getting married in Costa Rica is simple and straightforward. In most cases, all you need are current passports. You'll have to provide some basic information, including a copy of each passport, your dates of birth, your occupations, your current address, and the names and addresses of your parents. Two witnesses are required to be present at the ceremony. If you're traveling alone, your hotel or wedding consultant will provide the required witnesses.

Things are slightly more complicated if one or more of the partners was previously married. In such a case, the previously married partner must provide an official copy of the divorce decree.

Most travelers who get married in Costa Rica do so in a civil ceremony officiated by a local lawyer. After the ceremony, the lawyer records the marriage with Costa Rica's National Registry, which issues an official marriage certificate. This process generally takes between 4 and 6 weeks. Most lawyers or wedding coordinators then have the document translated and certified by the Costa Rican Foreign Ministry and at the embassy or consulate of your home country within Costa Rica before mailing it to you. From here, it's a matter of bringing this document to your local civil or religious authorities, if necessary.

Because Costa Rica is more than 90% Roman Catholic, arranging for a church wedding is usually easy in all but the most isolated and remote locations. To a lesser extent, a variety of denominational Christian churches and priests are often available to perform or host the ceremony. If you're Jewish, Muslim, Buddhist, or a follower of some other religion, bringing your own officiant is a good idea.

Tip: Officially, the lawyer must read all or parts of the Costa Rican civil code on marriage during your ceremony. This is a rather uninspired and somewhat dated legal code that, at some weddings, can take as much as 20 minutes to slog through. Most lawyers and wedding coordinators are quite flexible and can work with you to design a ceremony and text that fits your needs and desires. Insist on this.

Most of the higher-end and romantic hotels in Costa Rica have ample experience in hosting weddings. Many have an in-house wedding planner. Narrowing the list is tough, but I'd say the top choices include Hotel Punta Islita (p. 285), Villa Caletas (p. 360), Makanda by the Sea (p. 388), Florblanca Resort (p. 275), and the Four Seasons Resort (p. 211). If you want a remote, yet luxurious, rainforest lodge to serve as host and backdrop, try La Paloma Lodge (p. 425), Bosque del Cabo Rainforest Lodge (p. 439), or Lapa Ríos (p. 440).

If you're looking for service beyond what your hotel can offer, or if you want to do it yourself, check out www.weddings.co.cr, www.weddingscostarica.net, www.liquidweddings.com, or www.tropicaloccasions.com.

hitting Monteverde, Arenal, and Tortuguero, and also has an excellent family tour. Service is personalized and the guides are top-notch.

Aventouras ★ (© **800/930-2846;** www.aventouras.com) this small-scale adventure tour operator specializes in off-the-beaten track destinations, using local guides, and staying in small environmentally conscious and sustainable hotels and lodges.

Costa Rica Experts ★ (✆ **800/827-9046** or 773/935-1009; www.costa ricaexperts.com) offers a large menu of a la carte and scheduled departures, as well as day trips and adventure packages, and has decades of experience organizing tours to the country.

Nature Expeditions International ★ (✆ **800/869-0639**; www.naturexp. com) specializes in educational and "low intensity adventure" trips tailored to independent travelers and small groups. These folks have a steady stream of programmed departures or can customize a trip to your needs.

Overseas Adventure Travel ★★ (✆ **800/493-6824**; www.oattravel.com) offers good-value natural-history and "soft adventure" itineraries with optional add-on excursions. Tours are limited to 16 people and are guided by naturalists. All accommodations are in small hotels, lodges, or tent camps, and they offer up very good bang for your buck.

Southern Explorations ★ (✆ **877/784-5400**; www.southernexplorations. com) has a range of nature and adventure oriented guided excursions, as well as set itinerary self-guided tours, for individuals, groups, and families.

In addition to these companies, many environmental organizations, including the **Sierra Club** (✆ **415/977-5522**; www.sierraclub.org) and the **Smithsonian Institute** (✆ **877/338-8687**; www.smithsonianjourneys.org), regularly offer organized trips to Costa Rica.

ACTIVITIES A TO Z

Each listing in this section describes the best places to practice a particular sport or activity and lists tour operators and outfitters. If you want to focus on only one active sport during your Costa Rican stay, these companies are your best bets for quality equipment and knowledgeable service.

Adventure activities and tourism, by their very nature, carry certain risks and dangers. Over the years, there have been several deaths and dozens of minor injuries in activities ranging from mountain biking to white-water rafting to canopy tours. I've tried to list only the most reputable and safest of companies. However, if you ever have any doubt as to the safety of the guide, equipment, or activity, it's better to be safe than sorry. Moreover, know your limits and abilities, and don't try to exceed them.

See "A Week of Adventures in Costa Rica," in chapter 3, for additional tour ideas.

Biking

Costa Rica has several significant regional and international touring races each year, but as a general rule the major roads are dangerous and inhospitable for cyclists. Roads are narrow and without a shoulder, and most drivers show little care or consideration for those on two wheels. The options are much more appealing for mountain bikers and off-track riders. If you plan to do a lot of biking and are very attached to your rig, bring your own. However, several companies in San José and elsewhere rent bikes, and the quality of the equipment is improving all the time. I list rental shops in each of the regional chapters that follow.

The area around **Lake Arenal** and **Arenal Volcano** wins my vote as the best place for mountain biking in Costa Rica. The scenery's great, with primary forests, waterfalls, and plenty of trails. And the hot springs at nearby Tabacón

Ruta de los Conquistadores

Each year, Costa Rica hosts what many consider to be the most challenging and grueling mountain-bike race on the planet. La Ruta de los Conquistadores (the Route of the Conquerors; www.adventurerace.com) retraces the path of the 16th-century Spanish conquistadores from the Pacific Coast to the Caribbean Sea—all in 4 days. The race usually takes place in mid-November, and draws hundreds of competitors from around the world.

Grand Spa Thermal Resort are a perfect place for those with aching muscles to unwind at the end of the day. See chapter 9 for full details.

TOUR OPERATORS & OUTFITTERS

Bike Arenal ★ (℃ 866/465-4114 in U.S. and Canada, or 2479-7150 in Costa Rica; www.bikearenal.com) is based in La Fortuna and specializes in 1-day and multiday trips around the Arenal area.

Coast to Coast Adventures ★ (℃ 2280-8054; www.ctocadventures.com) offers mountain-biking itineraries among its many tour options.

ExperiencePlus! Specialty Tours ★★ (℃ 800/685-4565; www.experienceplus.com) offers guided group bike tours around the country. This is the only company I know of that uses touring bikes. It also offers guided group hiking tours, and multisport adventure itineraries.

Lava Tours (℃ 888/862-2424 in the U.S. and Canada, or 2281-2458 in Costa Rica; www.lava-tours.com) conducts a variety of fixed-date-departure and custom mountain-bike tours all over Costa Rica.

Serendipity Adventures ★ (℃ 888/226-5050 in the U.S. and Canada, or 2558-1000; www.serendipityadventures.com) offers several mountain-biking trips among its many other expeditions.

Bird-Watching

With more than 850 species of resident and migrant birds identified throughout the country, Costa Rica abounds with great bird-watching sites. Lodges with the best bird-watching include **Savegre Lodge,** in Cerro de la Muerte, off the road to San Isidro de El General (quetzal sightings are almost guaranteed); **La Paloma Lodge** in Drake Bay, where you can sit on the porch of your cabin as the avian parade goes by; **Arenal Observatory Lodge,** on the flanks of Arenal Volcano; **La Selva Biological Station,** in Puerto Viejo de Sarapiquí; **Aviarios del Caribe** and **Selva Bananito Lodge,** both just north of Cahuita; **Lapa Ríos** and **Bosque del Cabo,** on the Osa Peninsula; **Playa Nicuesa Rainforest Lodge,** along the Golfo Dulce; **La Laguna del Lagarto Lodge,** up by the Nicaraguan border; and **Tiskita Lodge,** down by the Panamanian border.

Some of the best parks and preserves for serious birders are **Monteverde Cloud Forest Biological Reserve** (for Resplendent Quetzals and humming-birds); **Corcovado National Park** (for scarlet macaws); **Caño Negro Wildlife Refuge** (for wading birds, including jabiru storks); **Wilson Botanical Gardens** and the **Las Cruces Biological Station,** near San Vito (the thousands of flowering plants here are bird magnets); **Guayabo, Negritos,** and **Pájaros Islands biological reserves** in the Gulf of Nicoya (for magnificent frigate birds and brown boobies); **Palo Verde National Park** (for ibises, jaca-nas, storks, and roseate spoonbills); **Tortuguero National Park** (for great green macaws); and **Rincón de la Vieja National Park** (for parakeets and curas-sows). Rafting trips down the Corobicí and Bebedero rivers near Liberia, boat trips to or at Tortuguero National Park, and hikes in any cloud forest also provide good bird-watching opportunities.

In San José, your best bets are to head toward the lush grounds and gardens of the **University of Costa Rica,** or to **Parque del Este,** a little farther east in the foothills just outside of town.

COSTA RICAN TOUR AGENCIES

Costa Rica Expeditions ★★ (© **2257-0766;** www.costaricaexpeditions.com) and **Costa Rica Sun Tours ★** (© **866/271-6263** in the U.S. and Can-ada, or 2296-7757 in Costa Rica; www.crsuntours.com) are well-established companies with very competent and experienced guides who offer a variety of tours to some of the better birding spots in Costa Rica.

INTERNATIONAL TOUR OPERATORS

Costa Rican Bird Route ★★ (© **608/698-3448** in the U.S.; www.costaricanbirdroute.com) is a bird-watching and conservation effort that has created several bird-watching specific itineraries, which they offer up as guided tours, or self-guided adventures.

Field Guides (© **800/728-4953** in the U.S. and Canada; www.fieldguides.com) is a specialty bird-watching travel operator. Its 16-day tour of Costa Rica covers a lot of ground, and group size is limited to 14 participants.

Tropical Birding ★ (© **800/348-5941** in the U.S. and Canada; www.tropicalbirding.com) specializes in birding tours around the world, which happens to be based in Ecuador. These folks excel at small group tours, with highly skilled guides, and run periodic trips to Costa Rica.

Victor Emanuel Nature Tours ★★ (© **800/328-8368** in the U.S. and Canada; www.ventbird.com) is a well-respected, longstanding small-group tour operator specializing in bird-watching trips in Latin America.

WINGS ★ (© **888/293-6443** in the U.S. and Canada; www.wingsbirds.com) is a specialty bird-watching travel operator with more than 30 years of field experience. Group size is usually between 6 and 14 people.

Bungee Jumping

Pacific Bungee (p. 364) and **Tropical Bungee ★** (p. 89) offer bungee jumps. I prefer Tropical Bungee, as its operations are set up on an old steel bridge, high over a river, surrounded by forests, whereas Pacific Bungee conducts their jumps from large steel towers.

Camping

Heavy rains, difficult access, and limited facilities make camping a challenge in Costa Rica. Nevertheless, a backpack and tent will get you far from the crowds and into some of the most pristine and undeveloped nooks and crannies of the country. Camping is forbidden in some national parks, so read the descriptions for each park carefully before you pack a tent.

WHERE TO SEE THE resplendent quetzal

Revered by pre-Columbian cultures throughout Central America, the Resplendent Quetzal has been called the most beautiful bird on earth. Ancient Aztec and Maya Indians believed that the robin-size quetzal protected them in battle. The males of this species have brilliant red breasts; iridescent emerald green heads, backs, and wings; and white tail feathers complemented by a pair of iridescent green tail feathers that are more than .5m (1¾ ft.) long.

The belief that these endangered birds live only in the dense cloud forests cloaking the higher slopes of Central America's mountains was instrumental in bringing many areas of cloud forest under protection as quetzal habitats. (Since then, researchers have discovered that the birds do not, in fact, spend their entire lives here.) After nesting between March and July, Resplendent Quetzals migrate down to lower slopes in search of food. These lower slopes have not been preserved in most cases, and now conservationists are trying to salvage enough lower-elevation forests to help the quetzals survive.

Although for many years **Monteverde Cloud Forest Biological Reserve** was *the* place to see quetzals, throngs of people crowding the reserve's trails now make the pursuit more difficult. Other places where you can see quetzals are in the **Los Angeles Cloud Forest Reserve** near San Ramón, in **Tapantí National Wildlife Refuge,** and in **Chirripó National Park.** Perhaps the best place to spot a quetzal is at one of the specialized lodges located along the **Cerro de la Muerte** between San José and San Isidro de El General.

If you'd like to participate in an organized camping trip, contact **Coast to Coast Adventures** (☎ 2280-8054; www.ctocadventures.com) or **Serendipity Adventures** (☎ 888/226-5050 in the U.S. and Canada, or 2558-1000; www.serendipityadventures.com).

In my opinion, the best place to pop up a tent on the beach is in **Santa Rosa National Park.** The best camping trek is, without a doubt, a hike through **Corcovado National Park** or a climb up **Mount Chirripó.**

Canopy Tours

Canopy tours are all the rage in Costa Rica, largely because they are such an exciting and unique way to experience tropical rainforests. It's estimated that some two-thirds of a typical rainforest's species live in the canopy (the uppermost, branching layer of the forest). From the relative luxury of Rain Forest Aerial Tram's high-tech funicular to the rope-and-climbing-gear rigs of zip-line operations, a trip into the canopy will give you a bird's-eye view of a Neotropical forest. There are now canopy-tour operations in or close to nearly every major tourist destination in the country, including Monteverde, Manuel Antonio, La Fortuna, Tabacón, Montezuma, Punta Islita, Villablanca, and Rincón de la Vieja, as well as on Tortuga Island and around Guanacaste and the Osa Peninsula. See the individual destination chapters for specific recommendations on canopy tours around the country.

Arenal Hanging Bridges, Arenal volcano area (p. 302)	**Rainforest Aerial Tram Atlantic,** en route to Puerto Viejo de Sarapiquí (p. 146)
Canopy Safari, Manuel Antonio (p. 383)	**Selvatura Park,** Monteverde area (p. 334)
Cartagena Canopy Tour, Northern beach area, Guanacaste (p. 241)	**Sky Tram,** Arenal volcano area (p. 303)
Chiclets Tree Tour, Playa Hermosa (p. 365)	**Vista Los Sueños Canopy Tour,** Playa Herradura (p. 358)
Hacienda Guachipelin, Rincón de la Vieja, Guanacaste (p. 199)	**Waterfall Canopy Tour,** Montezuma (p. 266)
Hacienda Pozo Azul, Puerto Viejo de Sarapiquí (p. 346)	**Witch's Rock Canopy Tour,** Papagayo Peninsula, Guanacaste (p. 211)

Most canopy tours involve strapping yourself into a climbing harness and being winched up to a platform some 30m (100 ft.) above the forest floor, or doing the work yourself. Many of these operations have a series of treetop platforms connected by taut cables. Once up on the first platform, you click your harness into a pulley and glide across the cable to the next (slightly lower) platform, using your hand (protected by a thick leather glove) as a brake. When you reach the last platform, you usually rappel down to the ground. (Don't worry—they'll teach even the most nervous neophyte.)

Although this can be a lot of fun, do be careful because these tours are popping up all over the place and there is precious little regulation of the activity. Some of the tours are set up by fly-by-night operators (obviously, I don't list any of those). Be especially sure that you feel comfortable and confident with the safety standards, guides, and equipment before embarking. Before you sign on to any tour, ask whether you have to hoist yourself to the top under your own steam, and then make your decision accordingly. Most canopy tours run between $45 and $65 per person.

Canyoning Tours

Canyoning tours are even more adventurous than canopy tours. Hardly standardized, most involve hiking down along a mountain stream, river, and/or canyon, with periodic breaks to rappel down the face of a waterfall, or swim in a jungle pool. The best canyoning operations in Costa Rica are offered by **Pure Trek Canyoning** ★★ (p. 304) and **Desafío Adventure Company** ★★ (p. 304), both in La Fortuna; and **Psycho Tours** ★★★ (p. 431), which operates outside of Puerto Jiménez. The latter is arguably my favorite adventure tour in the country.

Diving & Snorkeling

Many islands, reefs, caves, and rocks lie off the coast of Costa Rica, providing excellent spots for underwater exploration. Visibility varies with season and location. Generally, heavy rainfall tends to swell the rivers and muddy the waters, even well offshore. Rates run from $70 to $150 per person for a two-tank dive, including equipment, and $35 to $75 per person for snorkelers. Most of the dedicated dive operators listed throughout this book also offer certification classes.

Banana plantations and their runoff have destroyed most of the Caribbean reefs, although **Isla Uvita,** just off the coast of Limón, and **Manzanillo,** down near the Panamanian border, still have good diving. Most divers choose Pacific dive spots such as **Isla del Caño, Bat Island,** and the **Catalina Islands,** where you're likely to spot manta rays, moray eels, white-tipped sharks, and plenty of smaller fish and coral species. But the ultimate in Costa Rican dive experiences is 7 to 10 days on a chartered boat, diving off the coast of **Isla del Coco** (see "Diving Trips to Isla del Coco [Cocos Island]," on p. 256).

Snorkeling is not incredibly common or rewarding in Costa Rica. The rain, runoff, and wave conditions that drive scuba divers well offshore tend to make coastal and shallow-water conditions less than optimal. If the weather is calm and the water is clear, you might just get lucky. Ask at your hotel or check the different beach listings in this book to find snorkeling options and operators up and down Costa Rica's coasts. The best snorkeling experience to be had in Costa Rica is on the reefs off **Manzanillo Beach** in the southern Caribbean coast, particularly in the calm months of September and October.

DIVING OUTFITTERS & OPERATORS

In addition to the companies listed below, check the listings at specific beach and port destinations in the regional chapters.

Aggressor Fleet Limited ★★ (*©* **800/348-2628** in the U.S. and Canada; www.aggressor.com) runs the 36m (118-ft.) *Okeanos Aggressor* on regular trips out to Isla del Coco.

Diving Safaris de Costa Rica ★★ (*©* **2672-1260;** www.costarica diving.net) is perhaps the largest, most professional, and best-established dive operation in the country. Based out of Playa Hermosa, this outfitter is also a local pioneer in Nitrox diving.

Undersea Hunter ★★ (*©* **800/203-2120** in the U.S., or 2228-6613; www.underseahunter.com) offers the *Undersea Hunter* and its sister ship, the *Sea Hunter,* two pioneers of the live-aboard diving excursions to Isla del Coco.

Fishing

Anglers in Costa Rican waters have landed over 100 world-record catches, including blue marlin, Pacific sailfish, dolphin, wahoo, yellowfin tuna, *guapote,* and snook. Whether you want to head offshore looking for a big sail, wrestle a tarpon near a Caribbean river mouth, or choose a quiet spot on Arenal Lake to cast for *guapote,* you'll find it here. You can raise a marlin anywhere along the Pacific coast, while feisty snook can be found in mangrove estuaries along both coasts.

Many of the Pacific port and beach towns—Quepos, Puntarenas, Playa del Coco, Tamarindo, Flamingo, Golfito, Drake Bay, Zancudo—support large charter fleets and have hotels that cater to anglers; see chapters 7 and 9 to 12 for recommended boats, captains, and lodges. Fishing trips usually range between $400 and $2,500 per day (depending on boat size) for boat, captain, tackle, drinks, and lunch, so the cost per person depends on the size of the group.

Costa Rican law requires all fishermen to purchase a license. The cost is $24, and the license is good for 1 year from the date of purchase. All boats, captains, and fishing lodges listed here and throughout the book will help you with the technicalities of buying your license.

Costa Rica Outdoors ★ (☏ **800/308-3394** in the U.S. and Canada or 2231-0306 in Costa Rica; www.costaricaoutdoors.com) is a well-established operation founded by local fishing legend and outdoor writer Jerry Ruhlow, specializing in booking fishing trips around the country.

Golfing

Costa Rica is not one of the world's great golfing destinations. Currently, seven regulation 18-hole courses are open to the public and visitors. Still, these courses offer some stunning scenery, and almost no crowds. However, be prepared—strong seasonal winds make playing most of the Guanacaste courses very challenging from December through March.

The most spectacular course in Costa Rica is at **Four Seasons Resort ★★★** (p. 211), but it is open only to hotel guests. Greens fees run around $250.

Another very lovely option is the **Reserva Conchal** course **★★** at the **Westin Playa Conchal Resort & Spa** (p. 225) up in Guanacaste. Greens fees here are $150, including a cart. With advance notice and depending on available tee times, this course is currently open to guests at other hotels in the region.

Hacienda Pinilla ★★ (p. 239) is an 18-hole links-style course located south of Tamarindo. This might just be the most challenging course in the country, and the facilities, though limited, are top-notch. Currently, the course is open to golfers staying at hotels around the area, with advance reservations. Greens fees run around $185 for 18 holes, including a cart.

The **Papagayo Golf & Country Club ★** (p. 218), on the outskirts of Playa del Coco, offers up a full 18-hole course, with a pro shop, driving range, and rental equipment. It costs $95 in greens fees, including a cart.

Another major resort course is at the **Los Sueños Marriott Ocean & Golf Resort ★★** in Playa Herradura (p. 360). Greens fees, including a cart, run around $160 for the general public, and guests pay slightly less.

Currently, the best option for golfers staying in and around San José is **Parque Valle del Sol ★** (☏ **2282-9222;** www.vallesol.com), an 18-hole course in the western suburb of Santa Ana. Greens fees are $94, including a cart.

Golfers who want the most up-to-date information, or those who are interested in a package deal that includes play on a variety of courses, should contact **Costa Rica Golf Adventures ★** (☏ **888/672-2057** in the U.S. and Canada; www.golfcr.com) or **Tee Times Costa Rica** (☏ **866/448-3182** in the U.S. and Canada; www.teetimescostarica.com).

Hang Gliding, Paragliding & Ballooning

Based out of Jacó, **Hang Glide Costa Rica** (☏ **8353-5514;** www.hangglidecr. com) offers a half-hour of gentle hang gliding in a tandem rig, which begins with a tow by an ultralight, for $99 to $149 per person.

Paragliding is taking off (pardon the pun) in the cliff areas around Caldera, just south of Puntarenas, as well as other spots around the Central Pacific coast. If you're looking to paraglide, check in with the folks at **Grandpa Ninja's B&B** (www.paraglidecostarica.com; ☏ **2664-6833**). These folks cater to paragliders, and offer lessons or tandem flights. Lessons run around $110 per day, including equipment, while a 30 to 45 minute tandem flight with an experienced pilot will run you around $75.

Serendipity Adventures (☏ **888/226-5050** in the U.S. and Canada, or 2558-1000; www.serendipityadventures.com) will take you up, up, and away in a hot-air balloon near Arenal Volcano. A basic flight costs around $345 per passenger, with a two-person minimum, and a five-person or 800-pound maximum.

Horseback Riding

Costa Rica's rural roots are evident in the continued use of horses for real work and transportation throughout the country. Visitors will find that horses are easily available for riding, whether you want to take a sunset trot along the beach, ride through the cloud forest, or take a multiday trek through the northern zone.

Most travelers simply saddle up for a couple of hours, but those looking for a more specifically equestrian-based visit should check in with the following folks. Rates run between $15 to $30 per hour, depending upon group size and the length of the ride.

Nature Lodge Finca Los Caballos ★ (☏ **2642-0124;** www.naturelodge.net) specializes in horse tours and has the healthiest and best kept horses in the Montezuma area.

Serendipity Adventures (☏ **888/226-5050** in the U.S. and Canada, or 2558-1000; www.serendipityadventures.com) offers horseback treks and tours around the country, but their main stable is just outside La Fortuna.

Motorcycling

Visiting bikers can either cruise the highways or try some off-road biking around Costa Rica. All the caveats about driving conditions and driving customs in Costa Rica apply equally for bikers. If you want to rent a Harley-Davidson for cruising around the country, **María Alexandra Tours** (☏ **2289-5552;** www.mariaalexandra.com) conducts guided bike tours and rents well-equipped late-model Harleys by the day or the week. If your tastes run to off-road riding, **MotoAdventures** (☏ **440/256-8508** in the U.S., or 2228-8494 in Costa Rica; www.motoadventuring.com) runs guided multiday tours on Honda dirt bikes. Bike rental rates run between $70 and $150 per day. To rent a street bike, you will need a Costa Rican motorcycle license or foreign equivalent; no special motorcycle license is required for the off-road bikes. In both instances, the rental company will want you to show sufficient experience and proficiency before letting you take off on their bike.

Rock Climbing

Although this is a nascent sport in Costa Rica, the possibilities are promising, with several challenging rock formations close to San José and along the Cerro de la Muerte, as well as great climbing opportunities on Mount Chirripó. The folks at **Tropical Bungee** (☏ **2248-2212;** www.bungee.co.cr) are the most dependable operators in this field, and they regularly organize climbing outings. Alternatively, you could visit **Mundo Aventura** (© **2221-6934;** www.maventura.com), an adventure- and climbing-gear store with an indoor climbing wall and in-house tour company. A full-day guided climbing trip should cost you around $70 to $90, including equipment and lunch.

Spas & Yoga Retreats

Overall, prices for spa treatments in Costa Rica are generally less expensive than those in the United States or Europe, although some of the fancier options, like the Four Seasons or Tabacón Grand Spa Thermal Resort, rival the services, facilities, and prices found anywhere on the planet.

The **Four Seasons Resort** ★★★ (p. 211) on the Papagayo Peninsula has ample and luxurious facilities and treatment options, as well as scheduled classes in yoga, aerobics, and other disciplines.

Florblanca Resort ★★★ (p. 275) in Santa Teresa, has some of the most beautiful boutique spa facilities that I have ever seen. Two large treatment rooms are set over a flowing water feature.

Luna Lodge ★★ (p. 440) is a gorgeous lodge located on a hillside overlooking Playa Carate, on the border with Corcovado National Park. These folks run a fairly full schedule of dedicated yoga and wellness programs and have a good little spa on-site.

Pranamar Villas & Yoga Retreat ★★★, Santa Teresa (p. 276), is a new, upscale, beachfront resort, with a beautiful, open air-yoga space. A range of daily classes are offered, and a steady stream of visiting teachers and groups use the spot for longer retreats and seminars.

Samasati ★, Puerto Viejo de Talamanca (p. 492), is a lovely yoga retreat in some dense forest on a hillside above the Caribbean. Accommodations here range from budget to rustically luxurious.

Serenity Spa ★ (p. 366) started out with a little storefront spa in Jacó but now contracts out the spa services at several large resorts up and down the Pacific coast. At last count, it was running the spas at Villa Caletas (p. 360), Hotel Sí Como No (p. 388), and Villa Blanca (p. 317).

Tabacón Grand Spa Thermal Resort ★★★, Tabacón (p. 308), is a top-notch spa with spectacular hot springs, lush gardens, and a volcano view. A complete range of spa services and treatments is available at reasonable prices.

Xandari Resort & Spa ★★, Alajuela (p. 164), is a unique and distinctive little luxury hotel that has some top-notch spa facilities and services. This is a good choice if you're looking for a day or two of pampering, or for day treatments while staying in San José.

Surfing

Endless Summer II, the sequel to the all-time surf classic, was filmed in Costa Rica. Point and beach breaks that work year-round are located all along Costa Rica's immense coastline. **Playas Hermosa, Jacó,** and **Dominical,** on the central Pacific coast, and **Tamarindo** and **Playa Guiones,** in Guanacaste, are mini surf meccas. **Salsa Brava** in Puerto Viejo is a steep and fast wave that peels off both right and left over shallow coral. It has a habit of breaking boards, but the daredevils keep coming back for more. Beginners and folks looking to learn should stick to the mellower sections of **Jacó** and **Tamarindo**—surf lessons are offered at both beaches. Crowds are starting to gather at the more popular breaks, but you can still stumble onto secret spots on the **Osa** and **Nicoya peninsulas** and along the northern **Guanacaste** coast. Costa Rica's signature wave is still found at **Playa Pavones,** which is reputed to have one of the longest lefts in the world. The cognoscenti, however, also swear by places such as **Playa Grande, Playa Negra, Matapalo, Malpaís,** and **Witch's Rock.** An avid surfer's best bet is to rent a dependable four-wheel-drive vehicle with a rack and take a surfin' safari around Guanacaste.

If you're looking for an organized surf vacation, contact **Tico Travel** (**©** **800/493-8426** in the U.S. and Canada, or 2257-7118 in Costa Rica; www.ticotravel.com), or check out **www.crsurf.com**. For swell reports, general surf information, live wave-cams, and great links pages, point your browser to **www.surfline.com**. Although killer sets are possible at any particular spot at any time of the year, depending upon swell direction, local winds, and distant storms, in broad terms, the northern coast of Guanacaste works best from December to April; the central and southern Pacific coasts work best from April to November; and the Caribbean coast's short big-wave season is December through March. Surf lessons, usually private or in a small group, will run you anywhere from $20 to $40 per hour, including the board.

White-Water Rafting, Kayaking & Canoeing

Whether you're a first-time rafter or a world-class kayaker, Costa Rica's got some white water suited to your abilities. Rivers rise and fall with the rainfall, but you can get wet and wild here even in the dry season. Full-day rafting trips run between $75 and $90 per person.

The best white-water rafting ride is still the scenic **Pacuare River;** although there has been talk about damming it to build a hydroelectric plant, the project has thankfully failed to materialize. If you're just experimenting with river rafting, stick to Class II and III rivers, such as **Reventazón, Sarapiquí, Peñas Blancas,** and **Savegre.** If you already know which end of the paddle goes in the water, you'll have plenty of Class IV and V sections to run.

Die-hard river rats should get *Chasing Jaguars: The Complete Guide to Costa Rican Whitewater,* by Lee Eudy, a book loaded with photos, technical data, and route tips on almost every rideable river in the country.

Canoe Costa Rica (**©**/fax **732/736-6586** in the U.S., or 2282-3579; www.canoecostarica.com) is the only outfit I know of that specializes in canoe trips; it works primarily with custom-designed tours and itineraries, although it does have several set departure trips each year.

Costa Rica Nature Adventures ★★ (**©** **800/321-8410** in the U.S., or 2225-3939; www.toenjoynature.com) is a major rafting operator that runs daily trips on the most popular rivers in Costa Rica. Its **Pacuare Jungle Lodge** ★★★ (www.junglelodgecostarica.com; **©** **800/963-1195** is very plush, and a great place to spend the night on one of its 2-day rafting trips.

Exploradores Outdoors ★ (**©** **2222-6262;** www.exploradoresoutdoors.com) is another good company run by a longtime and well-respected river guide. They run the Pacuare, Reventazón, and Sarapiquí rivers, and even combine a 1-day river trip with onward transportation to or from the Caribbean coast, or the Arenal volcano area, for no extra cost.

IN SEARCH OF turtles

Few places in the world have as many sea-turtle nesting sites as Costa Rica. Along both coasts, five species of these huge marine reptiles come ashore at specific times of the year to dig nests in the sand and lay their eggs. Sea turtles are endangered throughout the world due to over-hunting, accidental deaths in fishing nets, development on beaches that once served as nesting areas, and the collection and sale (often illegally) of their eggs. International trade in sea-turtle products is already prohibited by most countries (including the U.S.), but sea-turtle numbers continue to dwindle.

Among the species of sea turtles that nest on Costa Rica's beaches are the **olive ridley** (known for their mass egg-laying migrations, or *arribadas*), **leatherback, hawksbill, green,** and **Pacific green turtle.** Excursions to see nesting turtles have become common, and they are fascinating, but please make sure that you and/or your guide do not disturb the turtles. Any light source (other than red-tinted flashlights) can confuse female turtles and cause them to return to the sea without laying their eggs. In fact, as more development takes place on the Costa Rican coast, hotel lighting may cause the number of nesting turtles to drop. Luckily, many of the nesting beaches have been protected as national parks.

Here are the main places to see nesting sea turtles: **Santa Rosa National Park** (near Liberia, olive ridleys nest here from July–Dec, and to a lesser extent from Jan–June), **Las Baulas National Marine Park** (near Tamarindo, leatherbacks nest here from early Oct through mid-Feb), **Ostional National Wildlife Refuge** (near Playa Nosara, olive ridleys nest from July–Dec, and to a lesser extent from Jan–June), and **Tortuguero National Park** (on the northern Caribbean coast, green turtles nest here from July through mid-Oct, with Aug–Sept their peak period. In lesser numbers, leatherback turtles nest here from Feb–June, peaking during the months of Mar and Apr).

See the regional chapters for descriptions of the resident turtles and their respective nesting seasons, as well as listings of local tour operators and companies that arrange trips to see sea turtles nesting.

Rio Locos (© **2556-6035;** www.whiteh2o.com) is a small company based in Turrialba. These folks are a good option for hard-core kayakers, small custom group tours, and folks who find themselves in Turrialba.

Ríos Tropicales ★★ (© **866/722-8273** in the U.S. and Canada, or 2233-6455 in Costa Rica; www.riostropicales.com) is one of the major operators in Costa Rica, with tours on most of the country's popular rivers. Accommodations options include a very comfortable lodge on the banks of the Río Pacuare for the 2-day trips.

Windsurfing & Kiteboarding

Windsurfing is not very popular on the high seas here, where winds are fickle and rental options are limited, even at beach hotels. However, **Lake Arenal** is considered one of the top spots in the world for high-wind boardsailing. During the winter months, many of the regulars from Washington's Columbia River Gorge take up residence around the nearby town of Tilarán. Small boards, water starts, and fancy gibes are the norm. The best time for windsurfing on Lake Arenal is between December and March. The same winds that buffet Lake Arenal make their way down to **Bahía Salinas** (also known as Bolaños Bay), near La Cruz, Guanacaste, where you can get in some good windsurfing. Both spots also have operations offering lessons and equipment rentals in the high-action sport of kiteboarding. Board rentals run around $55 to $85 per day, while lessons can cost between $50 to $100 for a half-day private lesson. See "La Cruz & Bahía Salinas," in chapter 7, and "Along the Shores of Lake Arenal," in chapter 9, for details.

COSTA RICA'S TOP NATIONAL PARKS & BIORESERVES

Costa Rica has 28 national parks, protecting more than 12% of the country. They range in size from the 212-hectare (524-acre) Guayabo National Monument to the 189,696-hectare (468,549-acre) La Amistad National Park. Many of these national parks are undeveloped tropical forests, with few services or facilities available for visitors. Others, however, offer easier access to their wealth of natural wonders.

Most of the national parks charge a $10 per-person per-day fee for any foreigner, although Chirripó National Park costs $15 per day. Costa Ricans and foreign residents continue to pay just $1. At parks where camping is allowed, an additional charge of around $2 per person per day usually applies.

This section is not a complete listing of all of Costa Rica's national parks and protected areas, but rather a selective list of those parks that are of greatest interest and accessibility. They're popular, but they're also among the best. You'll find detailed information about food and lodging options near some of the individual parks in the regional chapters that follow. As you'll see from the descriptions, Costa Rica's national parks vary greatly in terms of attractions, facilities, and accessibility.

If you're looking for a camping adventure or an extended stay in one of the national parks, I recommend **Santa Rosa, Rincón de la Vieja, Chirripó,** or **Corcovado.** Any of the others are better suited for day trips or guided hikes, or in combination with your travels around the country.

For more information, call the national parks information line at ⓒ **1192,** or the main office at ⓒ 2283-8004. You can also stop by the **National Parks Foundation office** (ⓒ **2257-2239**) in San José, located between Calle 23 and Avenida 15. Both offices are open Monday through Friday from 8am to 5pm.

The Central Valley

GUAYABO NATIONAL MONUMENT This is the country's only significant pre-Columbian archaeological site. It's believed that Guayabo supported a population of about 10,000 people some 3,000 years ago. The park is set in a forested area rich in flora and fauna, although the ruins are quite small and limited when compared to sites in Mexico, Guatemala, and South America. **Location:** 19km (12 miles) northeast of Turrialba, which is 53km (33 miles) east of San José. See p. 183.

IRAZÚ VOLCANO NATIONAL PARK ★ Irazú Volcano is the highest (3,378m/ 11,080 ft.) of Costa Rica's four active volcanoes and a popular day trip from San José. A paved road leads right up to the crater, and the lookout also has a view of both the Pacific and the Caribbean on a clear day. The volcano last erupted in 1963 on the same day U.S. President John F. Kennedy visited the country. There are picnic tables, restrooms, an information center, and a parking area here. **Location:** 55km (34 miles) east of San José. See p. 179.

POÁS VOLCANO NATIONAL PARK ★★ Poás is the other active volcano close to San José. The main crater is more than 1.6km (1 mile) wide, and it is constantly active with fumaroles and hot geysers. I slightly prefer Poás to Irazú because it is surrounded by dense cloud forests and has some nice gentle trails to hike. Although the area around the volcano is lush, much of the growth is stunted due to the gases and acid rain. On January 8, 2009, a 6.1 magnitude earthquake struck Costa Rica, with its epicenter very close to Poás. The park was closed for several days, and an uptick in volcanic activity was noted. The park still sometimes closes when the gases get too feisty. There are picnic tables, restrooms, and an information center. **Location:** 37km (23 miles) northwest of San José. See p. 163.

Guanacaste & the Nicoya Peninsula

PALO VERDE NATIONAL PARK A must for bird-watchers, Palo Verde National Park is one of Costa Rica's best-kept secrets. This part of the Tempisque River lowlands supports a population of more than 50,000 waterfowl and forest bird species. Various ecosystems here include mangroves, savanna brush lands, and evergreen forests. There are camping facilities, an information center, and some nice accommodations at the Organization for Tropical Studies (OTS) research station here. **Location:** 200km (124 miles) northwest of San José. Be warned that the park entrance is 28km (17 miles) off the highway down a very rugged dirt road; it's another 9km (5½ miles) to the OTS station and campsites. For more information, call the OTS (© **2524-0607;** www.threepaths.co.cr). See "Liberia," in chapter 7.

RINCON DE LA VIEJA NATIONAL PARK ★★ This large tract of parkland experiences high volcanic activity, with numerous fumaroles and geysers, as well as hot springs, cold pools, and mud pots. You'll find excellent hikes to the upper craters and to several waterfalls. You should hire a guide for any hot-spring or mud-bath expeditions; inexperienced visitors have been burned. Camping is permitted at two sites, each with an information center, a picnic area, and restrooms. **Location:** 266km (165 miles) northwest of San José. See p. 196.

SANTA ROSA NATIONAL PARK ★ Occupying a large section of Costa Rica's northwestern Guanacaste province, Santa Rosa has the country's largest area of tropical dry forest, important turtle-nesting sites, and the historically significant La Casona monument. The beaches are pristine and have basic camping facilities, and the waves make them quite popular with surfers. An information center, a picnic area, and restrooms are at the main campsite and entrance. Additional campsites are located on pristine and undeveloped beaches here. **Location:** 258km (160 miles) northwest of San José. For more information, you can call the park office at *℃* **2666-5051.** See p. 202.

The Nicoya Peninsula

BARRA HONDA NATIONAL PARK Costa Rica's only underground national park, Barra Honda features a series of limestone caves that were once part of a coral reef some 60 million years ago. Today the caves are home to millions of bats and impressive stalactite and stalagmite formations. Only Terciopelo Cave is open to the public. A camping area, restrooms, and an information center are here, as well as trails through the surrounding tropical dry forest. **Location:** 335km (208 miles) northwest of San José. See p. 283.

The Northern Zone

ARENAL NATIONAL PARK ★★ This park, created to protect the ecosystem that surrounds Arenal Volcano, has a couple of good trails, and a prominent lookout point that is extremely close to the volcano. The main trail here will take you through a mix of transitional forest, rainforest, and open savannah, before an invigorating scramble over a massive rock field formed by a cooled-off lava flow. **Location:** 129km (80 miles) northwest of San José. See p. 300.

CAÑO NEGRO NATIONAL WILDLIFE REFUGE ★ A lowland swamp and drainage basin for several northern rivers, Caño Negro is excellent for birdwatching. A few basic cabinas and lodges are in this area, but the most popular way to visit is on a combined van and boat trip from the La Fortuna/ Arenal area. **Location:** 20km (12 miles) south of Los Chiles, near the Nicaraguan border. See "Arenal Volcano & La Fortuna," in chapter 9.

MONTEVERDE CLOUD FOREST BIOLOGICAL RESERVE ★★★ This private reserve might be the most famous patch of forest in Costa Rica. It covers some 10,520 hectares (26,000 acres) of primary forest, mostly mid-elevation cloud forest, with a rich variety of flora and fauna. Epiphytes thrive in the cool, misty climate. The most famous resident is the spectacular Resplendent Quetzal. There is a well-maintained trail system, as well as some of the best-trained and experienced guides in the country. Nearby you can visit both the Santa Elena and Sendero Tranquilo reserves. **Location:** 167km (104 miles) northwest of San José. See p. 330.

Central Pacific Coast

CARARA NATIONAL PARK ★★ Located just off the highway near the Pacific coast, on the road to Jacó, this is one of the best places in Costa Rica to see scarlet macaws. Several trails run through the park, including one that is wheelchair accessible. The park is comprised of various ecosystems, ranging from rainforests to transitional forests to mangroves. **Location:** 102km (63 miles) west of San José. See p. 358.

CHIRRIPÓ NATIONAL PARK ★★ Home to Costa Rica's tallest peak, 3,761m (12,336-ft.) Mount Chirripó, Chirripó National Park is a hike, but on a clear day you can see both the Pacific Ocean and the Caribbean Sea from its summit. A number of interesting climbing trails are here, and camping is allowed. **Location:** 151km (94 miles) southeast of San José. See p. 407.

MANUEL ANTONIO NATIONAL PARK ★★ Though relatively small, Manuel Antonio is the most popular national park and supports the largest number of hotels and resorts. This lowland rainforest is home to a healthy monkey population, including the endangered squirrel monkey. The park is best known for its splendid beaches. **Location:** 129km (80 miles) south of San José. See p. 374.

The Southern Zone

CORCOVADO NATIONAL PARK ★★★ The largest single block of virgin lowland rainforest in Central America, Corcovado National Park receives more than 508cm (200 in.) of rain per year. It's increasingly popular but still very remote. (It has no roads; only dirt tracks lead into it.) Scarlet macaws live here, as do countless other Neotropical species, including two of the country's largest cats, the puma and the endangered jaguar. Camping facilities and trails are throughout the park. **Location:** 335km (208 miles) south of San José, on the Osa Peninsula. See p. 426.

The Caribbean Coast

CAHUITA NATIONAL PARK ★★ A combination land and marine park, Cahuita National Park protects one of the few remaining living coral reefs in the country. The topography here is lush lowland tropical rainforest. Monkeys and numerous bird species are common. **Location:** On the Caribbean coast, 42km (26 miles) south of Limón. See p. 479.

TORTUGUERO NATIONAL PARK ★★ Tortuguero National Park has been called the Venice of Costa Rica due to its maze of jungle canals that meander through a dense lowland rainforest. Small boats, launches, and canoes carry visitors through these waterways, where caimans, manatees, and numerous bird and mammal species are common. The extremely endangered great green macaw lives here. On the beaches green sea turtles nest here every year between June and October. The park has a small but helpful information office and some well-marked trails. **Location:** 258km (160 miles) northeast of San José. See p. 462.

TIPS ON HEALTH, SAFETY & ETIQUETTE IN THE WILDERNESS

Much of what is discussed here is common sense. For more detailed information, see "Health," in chapter 13. Although most tours and activities are safe, risks are involved in any adventure activity. Know and respect your own physical limits before undertaking any strenuous activity. Be prepared for extremes in temperature and rainfall and for wide fluctuations in weather. A sunny morning hike can quickly become a cold and wet ordeal, so it's usually a good idea to carry along some form of rain gear when hiking in the rainforest, or to have a dry change of clothing waiting at the end of the trail. Be sure to bring along plenty of sunscreen when you're not going to be covered by the forest canopy.

monkey **BUSINESS**

No trip to Costa Rica would be complete without at least one monkey sighting. Home to four distinct species of primates, Costa Rica offers the opportunity for one of the world's most gratifying wildlife-viewing experiences. Just listen for the deep guttural call of a howler or the rustling of leaves overhead—telltale signs that monkeys are in your vicinity.

Costa Rica's most commonly spotted monkey is the white-faced or **capuchin monkey** (*mono cara blanca* in Spanish), which you might recognize as the infamous culprit from the film *Outbreak*. Contrary to that film's plot, however, capuchins are native to the New World tropics and do not exist in Africa. Capuchins are agile, medium-size monkeys that make good use of their long, prehensile tails. They inhabit a diverse collection of habitats, ranging from the high-altitude cloud forests of the central region to the lowland mangroves of the Osa Peninsula. It's almost impossible not to spot capuchins at Manuel Antonio (see chapter 10), where they have become a little too dependent on fruit and junk-food feedings by tourists. Please do not feed wild monkeys (and try to keep your food away from them—they're notorious thieves), and boycott establishments that try to attract both monkeys and tourists with daily feedings.

Howler monkeys (*mono congo* in Spanish) are named for their distinct and eerie call. Large and mostly black, these monkeys can seem ferocious because of their physical appearance and deep, resonant howls that can carry for more than a mile, even in dense rainforest. Biologists believe that male howlers mark the bounds of their territories with these deep, guttural sounds. In the presence of humans, however, howlers are actually a little timid and tend to stay higher up in the canopy than their white-faced cousins. Howlers are fairly common and easy to spot in the dry tropical forests of coastal Guanacaste and the Nicoya Peninsula (see chapter 7).

Even more elusive are **spider monkeys** (*mono araña* in Spanish). These long, slender monkeys are dark brown to black and prefer the high canopies of primary rainforests. Spiders are very adept with their prehensile tails but actually travel through the canopy with a hand-over-hand motion frequently imitated by their less graceful human cousins on playground monkey bars around the world. I've had my best luck spotting spider monkeys along the edges of Tortuguero's jungle canals (see chapter 12), where howlers are also quite common.

The rarest and most endangered of Costa Rica's monkeys is the tiny **squirrel monkey** (*mono titi* in Spanish). These small, brown monkeys have dark eyes surrounded by large white rings, white ears, white chests, and very long tails. In Costa Rica, squirrel monkeys can be found only at Manuel Antonio (see chapter 10) and the Osa Peninsula (see chapter 11). These seemingly hyperactive monkeys are predominantly fruit eaters and often feed on bananas and other fruit trees near hotels in both of the above-mentioned regions. Squirrel monkeys usually travel in large bands, so if you do see them, you'll likely see quite a few.

If you do any backcountry packing or camping, remember that it really *is* a jungle out there. Don't go poking under rocks or fallen branches. Snakebites are very rare, but don't do anything to increase the odds. If you encounter a snake, stay calm, don't make any sudden movements, and *do not* try to handle it. Also avoid swimming in major rivers unless a guide or local operator can vouch for their safety. Although white-water sections and stretches in mountainous areas are generally safe, most mangrove canals and river mouths in Costa Rica support healthy crocodile and caiman populations.

Bugs and bug bites will probably be your greatest health concern in the Costa Rican wilderness, and even they aren't as big of a problem as you might expect. Mostly, bugs are an inconvenience, although mosquitoes can carry malaria or dengue (see "Health," in chapter 13, for more information). A strong repellent and proper clothing minimize both the danger and the inconvenience; you might also want to bring along some cortisone or Benadryl cream to soothe itching. **And remember:** Whenever you enter and enjoy nature, you should tread lightly and try not to disturb the natural environment. The popular slogan well known to most campers certainly applies here: "Leave nothing but footprints; take nothing but memories." If you must take home a souvenir, take photos. Do not cut or uproot plants or flowers. Pack out everything you pack in, and *please* do not litter.

STUDY & VOLUNTEER PROGRAMS
Language Immersion

As more people travel to Costa Rica with the intention of learning Spanish, the number of options for Spanish immersion vacations increases. You can find courses of varying lengths and degrees of intensiveness, and many that include cultural activities and day excursions. Many of these schools have reciprocal relationships with U.S. universities, so, in some cases, you can even arrange for college credit. Most Spanish schools can arrange for homestays with a middle-class Tico family for a total-immersion experience. Classes are often small, or even one-on-one, and can last anywhere from 2 to 8 hours a day. Listed below are some of the larger and more established Spanish-language schools, with approximate costs. Most are in San José, but schools are also in Monteverde, Manuel Antonio, Playa Flamingo, Malpaís, Playa Nosara, and Tamarindo. A 1-week class with 4 hours of class per day, including a homestay, tends to cost between $350 to $500. (I'd certainly rather spend 2 weeks or a month in one of these spots than in San José.) Contact the schools for the most current price information.

Adventure Education Center (AEC) Spanish Institute ★ (© 800/ 237-2730 in the U.S. and Canada, or 2258-5111 in Costa Rica; www.adventure spanishschool.com) has branches in Dominical, and Turrialba, and specializes in combining language learning with adventure activities.

Centro Lingüístico Conversa ★ (© 888/669-1664 in the U.S. and Canada, or 2203-2071; www.conversa.net) has classes in both San José and Santa Ana (a suburb of the capital city).

Centro Panamericano de Idiomas (CPI) ★ (© 877/373-3116 in the U.S., or 2265-6306; www.cpi-edu.com) has three campuses: one in the quiet suburban town of Heredia, another in Monteverde, and one at the beach in Playa Flamingo.

Costa Rican Language Academy ★ in San José (② **866/230-6361** in the U.S., or 2280-1685; www.spanishandmore.com) has intensive programs with classes held Monday to Thursday to give students a chance for longer weekend excursions. The academy also integrates Latin dance and Costa Rican cooking classes into the program.

Escuela D'Amore ★ (② **800/261-3203** in the U.S. and Canada, or ②/fax 2777-1143; www.escueladamore.com) is situated in the lush surroundings of Manuel Antonio.

Wayra Instituto de Español (② **2653-0359;** www.spanish-wayra.co.cr) is a long-standing operation located in the beach town of Tamarindo.

Alternative Educational Travel

Costa Rica Rainforest Outward Bound School (② **800/676-2018** in the U.S., or 2278-6062; www.crrobs.org) is the local branch of this well-respected international adventure-based outdoor-education organization. Courses range from 2 weeks to a full semester, and offerings include surfing, kayaking, tree climbing, and learning Spanish.

Eco Teach (② **800/626-8992** in the U.S. and Canada; www.ecoteach. com) works primarily in facilitating educational trips for high school and college student groups. Trips focus on Costa Rican ecology and culture. Costs run around $1,500 to $2,000 per person for a 10-day trip, including lodging, meals, classes, and travel within the country. Airfare to Costa Rica is extra.

The **Institute for Central American Development Studies ★** (② **2225-0508;** www.icads.org) offers internship and research opportunities in the areas of environment, agriculture, human rights, and women's studies. An intensive Spanish-language program can be combined with work-study or volunteer opportunities.

The **Monteverde Institute** (② **2645-5053;** www.mvinstitute.org) offers study programs in Monteverde and also has a volunteer center that helps in placement and training of volunteers.

The **Organization for Tropical Studies ★** (② **919/684-5774** in the U.S., or 2524-0607 in Costa Rica; www.threepaths.co.cr) represents several Costa Rican and U.S. universities. This organization's mission is to promote research, education, and the wise use of natural resources in the Tropics. Research facilities include La Selva Biological Station near Braulio Carrillo National Park and Palo Verde, and the Wilson Botanical Gardens near San Vito. Housing is provided at one of the research facilities. The wide variety of programs range from full-semester undergraduate programs to specific graduate courses (of varying duration) to its tourist programs. (These are generally sponsored/run by established operators such as Costa Rica Expeditions or Elderhostel.) Programs range in duration from 3 to 10 days, and costs vary greatly. Entrance requirements and competition for some of these courses can be demanding.

Sustainable Volunteer Projects

Below are some institutions and organizations that are working on ecology and sustainable development projects in Costa Rica.

APREFLOFAS (Association for the Preservation of the Wild Flora and Fauna; ② **2240-6087;** www.apreflofas.or.cr) is a pioneering local conservation organization that accepts volunteers and runs environmentally sound educational tours around the country.

Asociación de Voluntarios para el Servicio en las Areas Protegidas (ASVO) ★ (☏ **2258-4430;** www.asvocr.org) organizes volunteers to work in Costa Rican national parks. A 2-week minimum commitment is required, as is a basic ability to converse in Spanish. Housing is provided at a basic ranger station; a $20 daily fee covers food, which is basic Tico fare.

Caribbean Conservation Corporation (☏ **800/678-7853** in the U.S. and Canada, or 2278-6058 in Costa Rica; www.cccturtle.org) is a nonprofit organization dedicated to sea turtle research, protection, and advocacy. Their main operation in Costa Rica is headquartered in Tortuguero, where volunteers can aid in various scientific studies, as well as nightly patrols of the beach during nesting seasons to prevent poaching.

Global Volunteers (☏ **800/487-1074** in the U.S. and Canada; www.globalvolunteers.org) is a U.S.-based organization that offers a unique opportunity to travelers who've always wanted a Peace Corps–like experience but can't make a 2-year commitment. For 2 to 3 weeks, you can join one of its working vacations in Costa Rica. A certain set of skills, such as engineering or agricultural knowledge, is helpful but by no means necessary. Each trip is undertaken at a particular community's request, to complete a specific project. However, be warned: These "volunteer" experiences do not come cheap. You must pay for your transportation as well as a hefty program fee, around $2,500 for a 2-week program.

Habitat for Humanity International (☏ **2296-3436;** www.habitatcostarica.org) has several chapters in Costa Rica and sometimes runs organized Global Village programs here.

Vida (☏ **2221-8367;** www.vida.org) is a local nongovernmental organization working on sustainable development and conservation issues; it can often place volunteers.

5

SAN JOSÉ

F ounded in 1737, San José was a forgotten backwater of the Spanish empire until the late 19th century, when it boomed with the coffee business. Sure, the city has its issues: gridlock traffic, poorly maintained sidewalks, and street crime. But, at 1,125m (3,690 ft.) above sea level, San José enjoys springlike temperatures year-round and its location in the Central Valley—the lush Talamanca Mountains rise to the south, the Poás, Barva, and Irazú volcanoes to the north—makes it both stunning and convenient as a base of exploration.

Things to Do　San José boasts some of the finest museums in Central America, including the shining **Gold Museum** with its extensive collection of pre-Columbian gold and the **Jade Museum** with its unique focus on functional and decorative relics made of this translucent stone. Art lovers will enjoy the **Costa Rican Art Museum,** featuring a lovely open-air sculpture garden.

Shopping　For local craft items and cheap souvenirs, head to the **Mercado Central,** or the open-air market on the **Plaza de la Democracia.** Be sure to check out the extensive and impressive collection of indigenous art and craftworks on offer at **Galería Namu.** And don't forget to pick up some signature, shade-grown Costa Rican **coffee** and a bottle or two of **Salsa Lizano,** the ubiquitous vinegar and tamarind-based sauce spread on dishes across the country.

Eating & Drinking　Imagine yourself drifting back in time to the days of the coffee barons in the elegant **Grano de Oro Restaurant,** or sample the contemporary fusion cuisine of Michelin two-star chef Richard Neat at the intimate and romantic **Park Café.** For a taste of traditional Costa Rican cuisine and culture, head to **Restaurante Nuestra Tierra.**

 San José's Top Sustainable Hotels

Crowne Plaza Corobicí (p. 118)
Hotel Grano de Oro (p. 118)
Hotel Parque del Lago (p. 119)

Nightlife & Entertainment The city's nightlife is lively and varied. The hip and bohemian crowds have several haunts, including the **Cuartel de la Boca del Monte, El Observatorio, Rayeula,** and the whole **University district,** while those looking for live music can head to the **Jazz Café.** Adventurous souls should shake their booties at a classic salsa joint like **Castro's** or **Salsa 54,** and those wanting a contemporary club vibe can head to **Rhapsodia** or **Vertigo.**

PREVIOUS PAGE: **The Teatro Nacional.**

For as long as I've written this book, my stock advice to tourists has been to get in and out of San José as quickly as possible. In most cases, this remains good counsel. Still, San José is the country's only major urban center, with varied and active restaurant and night-life scenes, several museums and galleries worth visiting, and a steady stream of theater, concerts, and other cultural events that you won't find elsewhere in the country.

ORIENTATION
Arriving
BY PLANE

Juan Santamaría International Airport (© 2437-2626 for 24-hr. airport information; airport code SJO) is near the city of Alajuela, about 20 minutes from downtown San José. A taxi into town costs between $22 and $32, and a bus is only C450. The Alajuela–San José buses run frequently and will drop you off anywhere along Paseo Colón or at a station near the Parque de la Merced (downtown, btw. calles 12 and 14 and avs. 2 and 4). There are two separate lines: **Tuasa** (© 2442-6900) buses are red; **Station Wagon** (© 8388-9263) buses are beige/yellow. At the airport, the bus stop is directly in front of the main terminal, beyond the parking structure. Be sure to ask whether the bus is going to San José, or you'll end up in Alajuela. If you have a lot of luggage, you probably should take a cab.

Most car-rental agencies have desks and offices at the airport, although if you're planning to spend a few days in San José itself, I personally think a car is a liability. (If you're heading off immediately to the beach, though, it's much easier to pick up your car here than at a downtown office.)

Tip: Chaos and confusion greet arriving passengers the second they step out of the terminal. You must abandon your luggage carts just before exiting the building and then face a gauntlet of aggressive taxi drivers, shuttle drivers waving signs, and people offering to carry your bags. Fortunately, the official airport taxi service (see below) has a booth inside the calm area just before the terminal exit. And official airport porters also hang out in this area. Still, there's often really nowhere for them to have to carry your bags because the line of waiting taxis and shuttles is just steps away. Keep a very watchful eye on your bags: Thieves have historically preyed on newly arrived passengers and their luggage. You should tip porters about 50¢ per bag.

In terms of taxis, you should stick with the official airport taxi service, **Taxis Unidos Aeropuerto** (© 2221-6865; www.taxiaeropuerto.com), which operates a fleet of orange vans and sedans. These folks have a kiosk in the no man's land just outside the exit door for arriving passengers. Here they will assign you a cab. These taxis now use meters, and fares to most downtown hotels should run $22 to $32. Despite the fact that Taxis Unidos has an official monopoly at the airport, you will usually find a handful of regular cabs (in traditional red sedans) and "pirate" cabs, driven by freelancers using their own vehicles. You could use either of these latter options, and "pirate" cabs tend to charge a dollar or two less, but I recommend the official service for safety and standardized prices.

You have several options for **exchanging money** when you arrive at the airport. An ATM in the baggage claim area is connected to both the PLUS and Cirrus networks. There's also a **Global Exchange** (© 2431-0686; www.global exchange.co.cr) money exchange booth just as you clear Customs and Immigration. It's open whenever there are arriving flights; however, these folks exchange at more than 10% below the official rate. A branch of the **Banco de San José** is inside the main terminal, on the second floor across from the airline check-in counters, as well as a couple of more ATMs up there. The taxi company and rental-car agencies accept U.S. dollars. See "Money & Costs," in chapter 13, for more details.

Tip: There's really no pressing need to exchange money the minute you arrive. Taxis Unidos accepts dollars. You can wait until after you settle into your hotel, and see if the hotel will give you a good rate of exchange, or use one of the many downtown banks or ATMs.

If you arrive in San José via Nature Air, private aircraft, or another small commuter or charter airline, you might find yourself at the **Tobías Bolaños International Airport** in Pavas (© 2232-2820; airport code SYQ). This small airport is on the western side of downtown San José, about 10 minutes by car from the center. There are no car-rental desks here, so unless you have a car or a driver waiting for you here, you will have to take a cab into town, which should cost between $10 and $20.

BY BUS

If you're coming to San José by bus, where you disembark depends on where you're coming from. (The different bus companies have their offices, and thus their drop-off points, all over downtown San José. When you buy your ticket, ask where you'll be let off.) Buses arriving from Panama pass first through Cartago

A panoramic view of San José.

"I KNOW THERE'S GOT TO BE A number HERE SOMEWHERE . . ."

This is one of the most confusing aspects of visiting Costa Rica in general, and San José in particular. Although downtown San José often has street addresses and building numbers for locations, they are almost never used. Addresses are given as a set of coordinates such as "Calle 3 between avenidas Central and 1." It's then up to you to locate the building within that block, keeping in mind that the building could be on either side of the street. Many addresses include additional information, such as the number of meters from a specified intersection or some other well-known landmark. (These "meter measurements" are not precise but are a good way to give directions to a taxi driver. In basic terms, 100m = 1 block, 200m = 2 blocks, and so on.) These landmarks are what become truly confusing for visitors to the city because they are often simply restaurants, bars, and shops that would be familiar only to locals.

Things get even more confusing when the landmark in question no longer exists. The classic example of this is "the Coca-Cola," one of the most common landmarks used in addresses in the blocks surrounding San José's main market. The trouble is, the Coca-Cola bottling plant that it refers to is no longer there; the edifice is long gone, and one of the principal downtown bus depots stands in its place. Old habits die hard, though, and the address description remains. You might also try to find someplace near the *antiguo higuerón* ("old fig tree") in San Pedro. This tree was felled over a decade ago. In outlying neighborhoods, addresses can become long directions such as "50m (½ block) south of the old church, then 100m (1 block) east, then 20m (two buildings) south." Luckily for visitors, most downtown addresses are more straightforward.

Oh, and if you're wondering how letter carriers manage, well, welcome to the club. Some folks actually get their mail delivered this way, but most people and businesses in San José use a post office box. This is called an *apartado* and is abbreviated "Apdo." or "A.P." in mailing addresses.

and San Pedro before letting passengers off in downtown San José; buses arriving from Nicaragua generally enter the city on the west end of town, on Paseo Colón. If you're staying here, you can ask to be let off before the final stop.

BY CAR

For those of you intrepid readers arriving by car, you'll enter San José via the Interamerican Highway. If you arrive **from Nicaragua and the north,** the highway brings you first past the airport and the city of Alajuela, to the western edge of downtown, right at the end of Paseo Colón, where it hits Parque La Sabana (La Sabana Park). The area is well marked with large road signs that direct you either to downtown (CENTRO) or to the western suburbs of Rohrmoser, Pavas, and Escazú. If you're heading toward downtown, follow the flow of traffic and turn left on Paseo Colón.

For those of you entering **from Panama and the south,** things get a little more complicated. The Interamerican Highway first passes through the city of Cartago and then through the San José suburbs of Curridabat and San Pedro before reaching downtown. This route is relatively well marked, and if you stick with the major flow of traffic, you should find San José without any problem.

Visitor Information

The **Instituto Costarricense de Turismo** (**ICT;** ℭ **2443-1535;** www.visit costarica.com) desk at the Juan Santamaría International Airport is in the baggage claims area, just before Customs. You can pick up maps and browse brochures, and they might even lend you a phone to make or confirm a reservation. It's open daily from 9am to 5pm.

City Layout

Downtown San José is laid out on a grid. *Avenidas* (avenues) run east and west, while *calles* (streets) run north and south. The center of the city is at **Avenida Central** and **Calle Central.** To the north of Avenida Central, the avenidas have odd numbers beginning with Avenida 1; to the south, they have even numbers beginning with Avenida 2. Likewise, calles to the east of Calle Central have odd numbers, and those to the west have even numbers. The main downtown artery is **Avenida 2,** which merges with Avenida Central on either side of downtown. West of downtown, Avenida Central becomes **Paseo Colón,** which ends at Parque La Sabana and feeds into the highway to Alajuela, the airport, Guanacaste, and the Pacific coast. East of downtown, Avenida Central leads to San Pedro and then to Cartago and the Interamerican Highway heading south. **Calle 3** takes you out of town to the north, onto the Guápiles Highway that leads to the Caribbean coast.

The Neighborhoods in Brief

San José is divided into dozens of neighborhoods, known as *barrios.* Most of the listings in this chapter fall within the main downtown area, but there are a few outlying neighborhoods you'll need to know about.

DOWNTOWN   In San José's busy downtown, you'll find most of the city's museums, as well as a handful of small urban parks and open-air plazas, and the city's main cathedral. Many tour companies, restaurants, and hotels are located here. Unfortunately, traffic noise and exhaust fumes make this one of the least pleasant parts of the city. Streets and avenues are usually bustling and crowded with pedestrians and vehicular traffic, and street crime is most rampant here. Still, the sections of Avenida Central between calles 6 and 7, as well as Avenida 4 between calles 9 and 14, have been converted into pedestrian malls, greatly improving things on these stretches.

A colonial-era building in San José.

Parque La Sabana.

BARRIO AMÓN/BARRIO OTOYA   These two picturesque neighborhoods, just north and east of downtown, are the site of the greatest concentration of historic buildings in San José. Some of these have been renovated and turned into boutique hotels and atmospheric restaurants. If you're looking for character and don't mind the noise and exhaust fumes from passing cars and buses, this neighborhood makes a good base for exploring the city.

LA SABANA/PASEO COLÓN   Paseo Colón, a wide boulevard west of downtown, is an extension of Avenida Central and ends at Parque La Sabana. It has several good, small hotels and numerous restaurants. This is also where several of the city's car-rental agencies have their in-town offices. Once the site of the city's main airport, the Parque La Sabana (La Sabana Park) is San José's largest public park, with ample green areas, sport and recreation facilities, the new National Stadium, and the Museo de Arte Costarricense (Costa Rican Art Museum).

SAN PEDRO/LOS YOSES   Located east of downtown San José, Los Yoses is an upper-middle-class neighborhood that is home to many diplomatic missions and embassies. San Pedro is a little farther east and is the site of the University of Costa Rica. Numerous college-type bars and restaurants are all around the edge of the campus, and several good restaurants and small hotels can be found in both neighborhoods.

GETTING AROUND
By Bus

Bus transportation around San José is cheap—the fare is usually somewhere around ₡115 to ₡375—although the Alajuela/San José buses that run in from the airport cost ₡450. The most important buses are those running east along

A bus stop in San José.

Avenida 2 and west along Avenida 3. The **Sabana/Cementerio** bus runs from Parque La Sabana to downtown and is one of the most convenient buses to use. You'll find a bus stop for the outbound Sabana/Cementerio bus near the main post office on Avenida 3 near the corner of Calle 2, and another one on Calle 11 between avenidas Central and 1. This bus also has stops all along Avenida 2. **San Pedro** buses leave from the end of the pedestrian walk on Avenida Central between calles 9 and 11, and take you out of downtown heading east.

The city's bus drivers can make change, although they don't like to receive large bills. Be especially mindful of your wallet, purse, or other valuables, because pickpockets often work the crowded buses.

By Taxi

Although taxis in San José have meters (*marías*), the drivers sometimes refuse to use them, particularly with foreigners, so you'll occasionally have to negotiate the price. Always try to get them to use the meter first (say *"ponga la maría, por favor"*). The official rate at press time is C545 for the first kilometer (½ mile) and C15 every 4 seconds. If you have a rough idea of how far it is to your destination, you can estimate how much it should cost from these figures. After 10pm taxis are legally allowed to add a 20% surcharge. Some of the meters are programmed to include the extra charge automatically, but be careful: Some drivers will use the evening setting during the daytime or (at night) to charge an extra 20% on top of the higher meter setting.

Depending on your location, the time of day, and the weather (rain places taxis at a premium), it's relatively easy to hail a cab downtown. You'll always find taxis in front of the Teatro Nacional (albeit at high prices) and around the Parque

Central at Avenida Central and Calle Central. Taxis in front of hotels and the El Pueblo tourist complex usually charge more than others, although this is technically illegal. Most hotels will gladly call you a cab, either for a downtown excursion or for a trip back out to the airport. You can also get a cab by calling **Coopetaxi**(✆**2235-9966**), **Coopeirazu**(✆**2254-3211**), **Coopetico**(✆**2224-7979**), or **Coopeguaria** (✆ **2226-1366**). **Cinco Estrellas Taxi** (✆ **2228-3159**) is based in Escazú but services the entire metropolitan area and airport, and claims to always have an English-speaking operator on call.

On Foot

Downtown San José is very compact. Nearly every place you might want to go is within a 15-by-4-block area. Because of traffic congestion, you'll often find it faster to walk than to take a bus or taxi. Be careful when walking the streets any time of day or night. Flashy jewelry, loosely held handbags or backpacks, and expensive camera equipment tend to attract thieves. **Avenida Central** is a pedestrian-only street from calles 6 to 7, and has been redone with interesting paving stones and the occasional fountain in an attempt to create a comfortable pedestrian mall. A similar pedestrian-only walkway runs along **Avenida 4,** between calles 9 and 14.

Pedestrians walking along Avenida Central.

By Train

San José has very sporadic and minimal urban commuter train service. One line connecting the western neighborhood of Pavas with the eastern suburb of San Pedro passes right through the downtown, with prominent stops at, or near, the U.S. Embassy, Parque La Sabana, the downtown court area, and the Universidad de Costa Rica (University of Costa Rica) and Universidad Latina (Latin University). The train runs commuter hours roughly every 1½ hours between 5 and 8:30am and 4:10 and 8pm. Another line runs between downtown San José and Heredia. This train runs roughly every 15 minutes between 5:30 and 8:30am, and again between 4:30 and 7:30pm, with much less frequent service during non-commuter hours. Fares range from C200 to C400, depending on the length of your ride.

By Car

It will cost you between $45 and $150 per day to rent a car in Costa Rica (the higher prices are for 4WD vehicles). Many car-rental agencies have offices at the airport. If not, they will usually either pick you up or deliver the car to any San

If you plan to rent a car, I recommend reserving it in advance from home. All the major international agencies and many local companies have toll-free numbers and websites. Sometimes you can even save a bit on the cost by reserving in advance. Costa Rica's car-rental fleet is not sufficient to meet demand during the high season when rental cars run at a premium. Sometimes this allows agencies here to gouge last-minute car-rental shoppers.

José hotel. If you decide to pick up your rental car in downtown San José, be prepared for some very congested streets.

The following companies have desks at Juan Santamaría International Airport, as well as offices downtown: **Alamo** (𝄢 **2242-7733** for central reservations; www.alamocostarica.com), **Adobe Rent A Car** (𝄢 **2442-2422** at the airport, or 2258-4242 in San José; www.adobecar.com), **Avis** (𝄢 **800/331-1084** in the U.S., or 2293-2222 central reservation number in Costa Rica; www.avis.co.cr), **Budget** (𝄢 **800/527-0700** in the U.S., 2440-4412 at the airport, or 2255-4750 in San José; www.budget.co.cr), **Dollar** (𝄢 **2443-2736** at the airport, or 2257-1585 in San José; www.dollarcostarica.com), **Hertz** (𝄢 **888/437-8927** in the U.S., 2430-7707 at the airport, or 2221-1818 in San José; www.costaricarentacar.com), **National Car Rental** (𝄢 **877/862-8227** toll-free in the U.S. and Canada, 2440-0084 at the airport, or 2242-7878 in San José; www.natcar.com), **Payless Rent A Car** (𝄢 **2256-0101** main reservations office in San José, 2432-4747 at the airport; www.paylesscar.com), **Thrifty** (𝄢 **800/847-4389** in the U.S., 2442-8585 at the airport, or 2257-3434 in San José; www.thrifty.com), and **Toyota Rent A Car** (𝄢 **2441-1411** at the airport, or 2258-5797 in San José; www.toyotarent.com).

Dozens of other car-rental agencies are in San José, and most will arrange for airport or hotel pickup or delivery. One of the more dependable agencies is **Hola! Rent A Car,** across the street from (west of) Denny's, La Uruca (𝄢 **2520-0100;** www.hola.net). For more advice on renting cars, see "Getting Around: By Car," in chapter 13.

As part of the highway to Caldera project, the Prospero Fernandez highway (CR27) has been greatly improved between San José and the western suburbs of Escazú, Santa Ana, and Ciudad Colón. This improvement comes at a cost, however; drivers will pay C290 each way between San José and Escazú. The toll station is just beyond the main exit to Escazú, if you are coming from San José.

[FastFACTS] SAN JOSÉ

American Express American Express Travel Services is represented in Costa Rica by **ASV Olympia,** Oficentro La Sabana, Sabana Sur (𝄢 **2242-8585;** www.asvolympia.com), which can issue traveler's checks and replacement cards and provide other standard services. To report lost or stolen Amex traveler's checks within Costa Rica, call the number above or 𝄢 **0800-011-0826,** or call collect to 800/011-0826 in the U.S.

Area Code See "Telephones," in chapter 13. There are no city or area codes to dial from within Costa Rica; use the country code, 506, only when dialing a San José number from outside Costa Rica. (To call San José from the U.S., dial the international access code 011, then 506, and then the eight-digit number.)

Dentists Call your embassy, which will have a list of recommended dentists. Many bilingual dentists also advertise in the *Tico Times.* Because treatments are so inexpensive in Costa Rica, dental tourism has become a popular option for people needing extensive work.

Doctors Contact your embassy for information on doctors in San José, or see "Hospitals," below.

Drugstores San José has countless pharmacies and drugstores. Many of them deliver at little or no extra cost. The pharmacy at the **Hospital Clínica Bíblica,** Avenida 14 between calles Central and 1 (✆ **2522-1000**), is open daily 24 hours. The pharmacy (✆ **2208-1080**) at the **Hospital CIMA** in Escazú is also open 24 hours daily. **Farmacia Fischel** (✆ **2519-0000**; www.fischel.co.cr) has numerous branches around the metropolitan area.

Embassies & Consulates See chapter 13.

Emergencies In case of any emergency, dial ✆ **911** (which should have an English-speaking operator); for an ambulance, call ✆ **1028;** and to report a fire, call ✆ **1118.**

Express Mail Services Many international courier and express-mail services have offices in San José, including **DHL,** on Paseo Colón between calles 30 and 32 (✆ **2209-0000;** www.dhl.co.cr); **EMS Courier,** with desks at the principal metropolitan post offices (✆ **800/900-2000** in Costa Rica; www.correos.go.cr); **FedEx,** which is based in Heredia but will arrange pickup anywhere in the metropolitan area (✆ **800/463-3339;** www.fedex.com); and **United Parcel Service,** in Pavas (✆ **2290-2828;** www.ups.com).

Hospitals **Clínica Bíblica,** Avenida 14 between calles Central and 1 (✆ **2522-1000;** www.clinicabiblica.com), is conveniently close to downtown and has several English-speaking doctors. The **Hospital CIMA** (✆ **2208-1000;** www.hospitalcima.com), located in Escazú on the Próspero Fernández Highway, which connects San José and the western suburb of Santa Ana, has the most modern facilities in the country.

Internet Access Internet cafes are all over San José. Rates run between

C300 and C2,000 per hour. Many hotels have their own Internet cafe or allow guests to send and receive e-mail. And many have added wireless access, either for free or a small charge. You can also try **Racsa,** Avenida 5 and Calle 1 (✆ **2287-0087;** www.racsa.co.cr), the state Internet monopoly, which sells prepaid cards in 5-, 10-, and 15-hour denominations for connecting your laptop to the Web via a local phone call. Some knowledge of configuring your computer's dial-up connection is necessary, and you'll want to factor in the phone call charge if calling from a hotel.

Laundry & Dry Cleaning Self-service laundromats are uncommon in Costa Rica, and hotel services can be expensive. **Aqua Matic** (✆ **2291-2847**) and **Tyson** (✆ **2215-2362**) are two dependable laundry and dry-cleaning chains with outlets all over town. The latter will even pick up and deliver your clothes free of charge.

Maps The Costa Rican Tourist Board (ICT; p. 50) can usually provide you with decent maps of both Costa Rica and San José. Also try **Seventh Street Books,** Calle 7 between avenidas Central and 1 (✆ **2256-8251**); **Librería Lehmann,** Avenida Central between calles 1 and 3 (✆ **2522-4848**); and **Librería Universal,**

Avenida Central and calles Central and 1 (☎ **2222-2222**).

Police   Dial ☎ **911** or 2295-3272 for the police. They should have someone available who speaks English.

Post Office   The main post office (correo) is on Calle 2 between avenidas 1 and 3 (☎ **2202-2900;** www.correos.go.cr). See "Mail," on p. 521, for more information.

Restrooms   Public restrooms are rare to nonexistent, but most big hotels and public restaurants will let you use their restrooms. Downtown, you can find public restrooms at the entrance to the Museos del Banco Central de Costa Rica (p. 130).

Safety   Pickpockets and purse slashers are rife in San José, especially on public buses, in the markets, on crowded sidewalks, near hospitals, and lurking outside of bank offices and ATMs. Leave most of your money and other valuables in your hotel safe, and carry only as much as you really need when you go out. If you do carry anything valuable with you, keep it in a money belt or special passport bag around your neck. Day packs are a prime target of brazen pickpockets throughout the city. One common scam involves someone dousing you or your pack with mustard or ice cream. Another scamster (or two) will then quickly come to your aid—they are usually much more interested in cleaning you out than cleaning you up.

Stay away from the red-light district northwest of the Central Market. Also be advised that the Parque Nacional is not a safe place for a late-night stroll. Other precautions include walking around corner vendors, not between the vendor and the building. The tight space between the vendor and the building is a favorite spot for pickpockets. Never park a car on the street, and never leave anything of value in a car, even if it's in a guarded parking lot. Don't even leave your car unattended by the curb in front of a hotel while you dash in to check on your reservation. With these precautions in mind, you should have a safe visit to San José. Also, see "Safety," in chapter 13.

Time Zone   San José is on Central Standard Time (same as Chicago and St. Louis), 6 hours behind Greenwich Mean Time. For the exact time (in Spanish), call ☎ **1112.**

Useful Telephone Numbers   For directory assistance, call ☎ **1113;** for international directory assistance, call ☎ **1024.**

Weather   The weather in San José (including the Central Valley) is usually temperate, never getting extremely hot or cold. May through November is the rainy season, although the rain usually falls only in the afternoon and evening.

WHERE TO STAY

San José offers up a wide range of hotel choices, from plush boutique hotels to budget pensions and backpacker hangouts. Many downtown hotels and small inns are housed in beautifully converted and restored old mansions. The vast majority of accommodations—and the best deals—are in the moderate price range, where you can find everything from elegant little inns to contemporary business-class chains. Staying in San José puts you in the center of the action, and close to all of the city's museums, restaurants, and nightlife venues. However, it also exposes you to many urban pitfalls, including noise, traffic, pollution, and street crime.

   The prices quoted here are for hotels' rack rate, the maximum that it charges; it is, however, not always necessary to pay that rate. You can typically find discounts of up to 20% for rooms when booking directly, or through websites such as hotels.com or expedia.com (see "Tips on Accommodations," p. 517, for more tips). **Note:** Quoted discount rates almost never include breakfast, local taxes, or other applicable hotel fees.

Downtown San José/Barrio Amón

The urban center of San José is the city's heart and soul, with a wide range of hotels and restaurants and easy access to museums and attractions. It also has several popular public parks and plazas, and the atmospheric Barrio Amón, a charming neighborhood home to the city's greatest concentration of colonial-era architecture. The neighborhood's biggest drawbacks are the street noise, bus fumes, gridlock traffic, and petty crime.

EXPENSIVE

Aurola Holiday Inn ★ Situated directly across the street from the attractive downtown Parque Morazán, this is downtown San José's only high-rise business-class hotel. The rooms are quite well kept and cozy. Service can be somewhat hit-or-miss, and the restaurants here leave lots to be desired. Still, the location is great for exploring downtown on foot (although be careful at night, as this borders one of the city's red-light districts), and if you get one of the upper-floor rooms on the north side, you'll have one of the best views in the city.

Av. 5 and Calle 5, San José. www.holiday-inn.com. ✆ **800/465-4329** in the U.S. and Canada, or 2523-1000. Fax 2248-3101. 200 units. $160 double; $230 junior suite; $300 suite. Rates include breakfast. Discounts for reservations made online. AE, MC, V. Free parking. **Amenities:** 2 restaurants; bar; poolside snack bar; executive-level rooms; exercise room; Jacuzzi; indoor pool; room service; sauna; smoke-free rooms. *In room:* A/C, TV, hair dryer, minibar, Wi-Fi.

Clarion Amón Plaza ★ On the north edge of the historic Barrio Amón neighborhood, this hotel is a reliable business-class option. Though the property or rooms are nothing distinctive, in terms of service, location, and price, it gets my nod over the nearby Holiday Inn. The rooms are good sized, well kept, and come with plenty of amenities. And you are close to all the downtown action. I recommend paying the upgrade for one of the executive-floor rooms, which get you free happy-hour food and drinks, and a separate lounge area. While the food is merely average, the ambience of their little outdoor, sidewalk cafe, El Cafetal de la Luz, is delightful. A fairly swanky casino is on-site. You can usually do a bit better than the rack rates listed below if you book through www.choicehotels.com.

Av. 11 and Calle 3 bis, San José. www.hotelamonplaza.com. ✆ **877/424-6423** in the U.S. and Canada, or 2523-4600 in Costa Rica. Fax 2523-4614. 87 units. $140 double; $230 suite. AE, DC, MC, V. Free parking. **Amenities:** Restaurant; bar; lounge; casino; babysitting; executive-level rooms; small exercise room; Jacuzzi; sauna; smoke-free rooms. *In room:* A/C, TV, hair dryer, Wi-Fi.

MODERATE

In addition to the hotels listed below, the **Sleep Inn,** Av. 3 between calles 9 and 11 (www.sleepinnsanjose.com; ✆ **2222-0101**), is a modern, American-style chain hotel in the heart of downtown, while **Hotel Doña Inés** (www.donaines. com; ✆ **2222-7443**), on Calle 11 between avenidas 2 and 6; **Hotel Rincón de San José** (www.hotelrincondesanjose.com; ✆ **2221-9702**), on the corner of Avenida 9 and Calle 15; **Mansion del Parque Bolivar ★** (www.hotelparque bolivar.com; ✆ 2222-3636), on Avenida 9 between calles 11 and 13; and

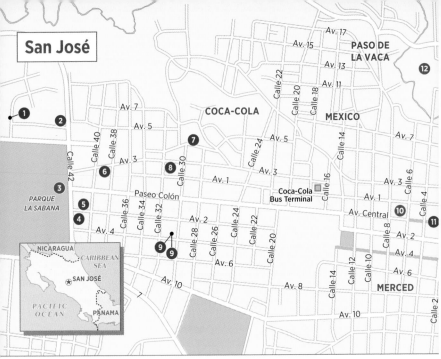

San José

HOTELS

Aurola Holiday Inn **27**
Clarion Amón Plaza **16**
Costa Rica Backpackers **46**
Crowne Plaza Corobicí **2**
Days Hotel **6**
Gran Hotel Costa Rica **32**
Hostel Pangea **13**
Hotel Aranjuez **52**
Hotel Britannia **14**
Hotel Cacts **7**
Hotel Colonial **39**
Hotel Del Rey **36**

Hotel Don Carlos **24**
Hotel Doña Inés **40**
Hotel Grano de Oro **9**
Hôtel Le Bergerac **49**
Hotel Parque del Lago **5**
Hotel Presidente **35**
Hotel Rincón de San José **22**
Hotel Santo Tomás **28**
Kap's Place **51**
Mansion del Parque Bolivar **23**
Sleep Inn **37**
Taylor's Inn **15**
Tranquilo Backpackers **19**

Taylor's Inn (www.taylorinn.com; ☎ **2257-4333**), on Avenida 13 Calle 3, are all little boutique properties that are also good options.

Gran Hotel Costa Rica   The Gran Hotel Costa Rica oozes historic charm and has arguably the best location of any downtown hotel (bordering the Teatro Nacional and the Plaza de la Cultura). A major remodeling has finally brought the rooms and amenities almost up to snuff. However, rooms still feel a bit spartan and dated, and some guests find the street noise a problem here. The **Cafeteria 1930** (p. 122) is perhaps the hotel's greatest attribute. It's memorable not so much for its food as for its atmosphere—it's an open-air patio that overlooks the Teatro Nacional, street musicians, and all the activity of the Plaza de la Cultura.

ATTRACTIONS

Catedral Metropolitano **30**
Centro Nacional de Arte y Cultura **38**
Mercado Central **10**
Museo de Arte Costarricense **3**
Museo de Jade Marco Fidel Tristán **25**
Museo de Los Niños **12**
Museo Nacional de Costa Rica **45**
Museos del Banco Central de Costa Rica **34**
Parque Zoológico Simón Bolívar **20**
Spirogyra Butterfly Garden **17**
Teatro Melíco Salazar **31**
Teatro Naciónal **33**

DINING

Aya Sofya **48**
Café del Teatro Nacional **33**
Café Mundo **21**
Cafeteria 1930 **32**
Caracas Arepas & Juice Bar **26**
Grano de Oro Restaurant **9**
Kalu Café **18**
La Esquina de Buenos Aires **41**
Machu Picchu **8**
Olio **47**
Park Café **1**
Q'Café **11**
Restaurante Nuestra Tierra **44**
Soda Tapia **4**
Tin Jo **43**
Vishnu **29, 42**
Whappin' **50**

Av. 2, btw. calles 1 and 3, San José. www.grandhotelcostarica.com. ☏ **800/949-0592** in the U.S., or 2221-4000. Fax 2221-3501. 103 units. $89 double; $185 suite. Rates include breakfast buffet. AE, DC, MC, V. Parking nearby. **Amenities:** 2 restaurants; bar; small gym; room service. *In room:* TV, minibar, Wi-Fi.

Hotel Britannia   Built in 1910, the large, low main building, with its wrap-around veranda, is one of the most attractive in the neighborhood. In the lobby, tile floors, large stained-glass picture windows, a brass chandelier, and reproduction Victorian decor all help set a tone of tropical opulence. There's also a four-story addition, which is separated from the original building by a narrow atrium. Rooms in the original home have hardwood floors and furniture; high ceilings and fans help keep them cool. Although the streetside rooms have double glass, light sleepers will still want to avoid them. The quietest rooms are those toward the back of the addition. The hotel's breakfast, along with afternoon tea and happy-hour drinks, is served in a sky-lit room adjacent to the restaurant.

Calle 3 and Av. 11, San José. www.hotelbritanniacostarica.com. ℂ **800/263-2618** in the U.S. or 2223-6667. Fax 2223-6411. 24 units. $89–$105 double; $117 junior suite. AE, MC, V. Parking nearby. **Amenities:** Restaurant; bar; room service; all rooms smoke-free. *In room:* A/C (in suites), TV, hair dryer, minibar (in suites), Wi-Fi.

Hotel Del Rey You can't miss the Del Rey: It's a massive pink corner building with vaguely colonial styling. The lobby continues the facade's theme with pink-tile floors and stone columns. Inside, a carved hardwood door marks every guest room. The rooms vary in size and comfort: Quiet interior rooms have no windows, and larger rooms with windows have street noise. Try for a sixth-floor room with a balcony. The hotel's main restaurant is across the street in an old restored home, with plenty of stained glass. Much of the first floor is taken up with a bustling casino and the neighboring Blue Marlin Bar, which is very popular with tourists, expatriates, and prostitutes. The hotel's owners also manage the popular Key Largo Bar, just across the street.

Av. 1 and Calle 9, San José. www.hoteldelrey.com. ℂ **866/765-8037** in the U.S. and Canada, or 2257-7800. Fax 2221-0096. 104 units. $118–$135 double; $340 suite. AE, MC, V. Parking nearby. **Amenities:** Restaurant; bar; room service. *In room:* A/C, TV, hair dryer, minibar, Wi-Fi.

Hotel Don Carlos ★★ If you're looking for a small downtown hotel that is unmistakably Costa Rican and hints at the days of the planters and coffee barons, this is the place for you. Located in an old residential neighborhood, only blocks from the business district, the Don Carlos was a former president's mansion. Inside you'll find a slew of arts-and-crafts works and archaeological reproductions, as well as orchids, ferns, palms, and parrots. The rooms are all distinct and vary greatly in size, so be specific when you reserve, or ask if it's possible to see a few when you check in. Breakfast is served in an outdoor orchid garden and atrium. The gift shop here is one of the largest in the country.

779 Calle 9, btw. avs. 7 and 9, San José. www.doncarloshotel.com. ℂ **2221-6707.** Fax 2258-1152. 33 units. $80–$90 double. Rates include continental breakfast. AE, MC, V. Free parking. **Amenities:** Restaurant; bar; Jacuzzi; room service. *In room:* TV, hair dryer, Wi-Fi.

Hotel Presidente This business-class hotel is a good midrange option in the heart of downtown. Although the hotel's eight stories practically qualify it for skyscraper status, few of the rooms have any view to speak of; those with north-facing windows are your best bet. Rooms are all well-kept and feature the amenities you'd expect; upgrades have updated both furnishings and decor. If you want more space, opt for one of the junior suites. Rooms and suites with a "spa" designation come with a private Jacuzzi. The master suite is a massive two-bedroom affair, featuring a private eight-person Jacuzzi. A very popular casual cafe-style restaurant is just off the street. While similar in style and vibe, the Presidente is more tranquil and subdued than the Del Rey (see above), especially after dark.

Av. Central and Calle 7, San José. www.hotel-presidente.com. ℂ **2010-0000.** Fax 2221-1205. 100 units. $101–$111 double; $135–$175 junior or spa suite; $390 master suite. Rates include full breakfast buffet. AE, MC, V. Free parking. **Amenities:** Restaurant; bar; casino; small gym; rooftop Jacuzzi and sauna; room service. *In room:* A/C, TV, hair dryer, minibar, Wi-Fi.

INEXPENSIVE

In addition to the places listed below, **Kap's Place** (www.kapsplace.com; ℰ **2221-1169**), across from the Hotel Aranjuez on Calle 19 between avenidas 11 and 13, is another good choice, while real budget hounds might want to try **Tranquilo Backpackers** (www.tranquilobackpackers.com; ℰ **2222-2493**), on Calle 7 between avenidas 9 and 11; **Hostel Pangea ★** (www.hostelpangea.com; ℰ **2221-1992**), on Avenida 7 and Calle 3; or **Costa Rica Backpackers** (www.costaricabackpackers.com; ℰ **2221-6191**), on Avenida 6 between calles 21 and 23.

Hotel Colonial ★, Calle 11 between avenidas 4 and 6 (www.hotelcolonial cr.com; ℰ **2223-0109**), is a good boutique hotel in a restored Victorian-style home a couple of blocks south of the city center, with rooms that fall into the upper end of this price range.

Hotel Aranjuez ★ ✐   This is probably the best and deservedly most popular budget option close to downtown. On a quiet and safe street in the Barrio Amón neighborhood, this humble hotel is made up of five contiguous houses. All rooms are simple and clean, and some are a little dark. Rooms and bathrooms vary greatly in size, so ask when reserving, or try to see a few rooms when you arrive. The nicest features here, aside from the convivial hostel-like atmosphere, are the lush and shady gardens; the hanging orchids, bromeliads, and ferns decorating the hallways and nooks; and the numerous open lounge areas furnished with chairs, tables, and couches—great for lazing around and sharing travel tales with your fellow guests. The hotel has a couple of computers, as well as a free Wi-Fi network, and provides free local calling.

Calle 19, btw. avs. 11 and 13, San José. www.hotelaranjuez.com. ℰ **2256-1825.** Fax 2223-3528. 35 units, 6 with shared bathroom. $27 double with shared bathroom; $49 double with private bathroom. Rates include breakfast buffet and taxes. MC, V. Free parking. **Amenities:** Several lounges. *In room:* TV, Wi-Fi.

Hotel Santo Tomás ★ ✐   Even though it's on a busy downtown street, this converted mansion is a quiet oasis inside. Built more than 100 years ago by a coffee baron, the house has been lovingly restored and maintained by its owner, Thomas Douglas. Throughout the hotel you'll enjoy the deep, dark tones of well-aged and well-worked wood, and various interior courtyards, open-air terraces, and garden nooks. The rooms vary in size, but most are fairly spacious and have a small table and chairs. A small outdoor pool with a Jacuzzi is above it; the two are solar heated and connected by a tiny water slide. The staff and management are extremely helpful, and the restaurant here is excellent. This neighborhood is a little bit sketchy after dark, so you'd be advised to take a taxi to and from the hotel for any evening excursions.

Av. 7, btw. calles 3 and 5, San José. www.hotelsantotomas.com. ℰ **2255-0448.** Fax 2222-3950. 30 units. $48–$66 double. Rates include breakfast buffet. MC, V. Parking nearby. **Amenities:** Restaurant; bar; lounge; exercise room; Jacuzzi; small outdoor pool; all rooms smoke-free. *In room:* TV, hair dryer, Wi-Fi.

La Sabana/Paseo Colón

Located on the western edge of downtown, the La Sabana Park is San José's largest city park, and Paseo Colón is a broad commercial avenue heading straight into the heart of the city. Stay in this neighborhood if you're looking for fast, easy access to the highways heading to Escazú, Santa Ana, the Pacific coast, and the airport and northern zone. As you're on the edge of town, the area can be pretty dead at night.

EXPENSIVE

In addition to the place mentioned below, **Days Hotel** ★ (www.dayshotelsan jose.com; 🕾 **2547-2323**), inside the Centro Colón building on Avenida 3, between calles 38 and 40, is a new, well-located business-class hotel, with a great restaurant and excellent amenities.

Crowne Plaza Corobicí ★   Just past the end of Paseo Colón and on the edge of Parque La Sabana, the Corobicí is a dependable business-class option. The lobby is a vast expanse of marble floor faced by blank walls, although the Art Deco furnishings lend a bit of character. Guest rooms are contemporary and comfortable, with firm beds and walls of glass through which, on most floors, you get good views of the valley and surrounding mountains. The Corobicí has a large, modern spa, where you will find a well-equipped gym featuring a large exercise room, on-staff trainers, and regular classes. The Fuji restaurant here is one of the better Japanese and sushi restaurants in San José.

Autopista General Cañas, Sabana Norte, San José. www.crowneplaza.com. 🕾 **800/227-6963** in the U.S., or 2232-8122. Fax 2231-5834. 213 units. $175 double; $215 suite; $500 presidential suite. AE, MC, V. Free parking. **Amenities:** 2 restaurants; bar; lounge; casino; extensive health club and spa; Jacuzzi; midsize outdoor pool; room service; sauna; all rooms smoke-free. *In room:* A/C, TV, hair dryer, minibar, Wi-Fi (for a small fee).

Hotel Grano de Oro ★★★ 📖   San José boasts dozens of old homes that have been converted into hotels, but the Grano de Oro tops them all in terms of design, comfort, and service. I favor the patio rooms, which have French doors

The terrace at the Hotel Grano de Oro.

opening onto private patios. Throughout all the guest rooms, you'll find attractive hardwood furniture. The Vista de Oro suite is the hotel's crown jewel, with its own private staircase and wonderful views of the city and surrounding mountains. If you don't grab one of the suites (which have whirlpool tubs), you still have access to the hotel's two rooftop Jacuzzis. The top-notch restaurant (p. 124) serves some of the city's best desserts. The hotel owners support a noble shelter for young, unwed mothers, Casa Luz. Feel free to inquire as to how you can help.

Calle 30, no. 251, btw. avs. 2 and 4, 150m (1½ blocks) south of Paseo Colón, San José. www.hotel granodeoro.com. © **2255-3322.** Fax 2221-2782. 40 units. $130–$155 double; $180–$335 suite. AE, MC, V. Free parking. **Amenities:** Restaurant (p. 124); bar; lounge; concierge; 2 rooftop Jacuzzis; room service; all rooms smoke-free; spa services. *In room:* TV, minibar, Wi-Fi.

MODERATE

Hotel Parque del Lago ★   This midsize business-class hotel is located on the western edge of busy Paseo Colón, right near the Costa Rican Art Museum and Parque La Sabana. Rooms are large and modern, but have a somewhat sober decor. The junior suites are especially spacious, with a comfortable couch, sitting area, wet bar, and microwave. The hotel has Wi-Fi and an elegant little restaurant and bar area just off the lobby. This hotel is convenient to both downtown and the western suburbs of Escazú and Santa Ana, with easy access to the country's major highways.

Calle 40, btw. Av. 2 and Paseo Colón, San José. www.parquedellago.com. © **2257-8787.** Fax 2223-1617. 40 units. $85 double; $105 junior suite; $185 penthouse. Rates include buffet breakfast. AE, MC, V. Free parking. **Amenities:** Restaurant; bar; lounge; small exercise room and spa; room service; sauna; smoke-free rooms. *In room:* A/C, TV, hair dryer, minibar, Wi-Fi.

INEXPENSIVE

Hotel Cacts 🏠   Housed in a contemporary home on a business and residential street, this is one of the more interesting and unusual budget hotels in San José. The seemingly constantly expanding complex is a maze of rooms and hallways on several levels. Rooms vary considerably in size, so it's always best to check out a few first if possible. The deluxe rooms here come with televisions and telephones, whereas the standard rooms lack both of these amenities. A small pool and separate Jacuzzi are in a lush garden patio. The third-floor open terrace serves as the breakfast area. The staff here is very helpful, and the hotel will receive mail and faxes, change money, and store baggage for guests.

Av. 3 bis, no. 2845, btw. calles 28 and 30, San José. www.hotelcacts.com. © **2221-2928** or 2221-6546. Fax 2222-9708. 26 units. $59–$69 double. Rates include breakfast buffet. MC, V. Free parking. **Amenities:** Lounge; Jacuzzi; small outdoor pool; all rooms smoke-free. *In room:* TV, no phone (in standard rooms), Wi-Fi.

San Pedro/Los Yoses

Located just east of downtown, Los Yoses is home to numerous foreign embassies and consulates, and was one of the city's early upper-class outposts, while San Pedro is home to the University of Costa Rica, and offers up a distinct college town vibe. Staying here, you'll be close to much of the city's action but still enjoy some peace and quiet. If you've rented a car, be sure your hotel provides secure parking or you'll have to find (and pay for) a nearby lot.

If you plan to be in town for a while or are traveling with family or several friends, you might want to consider staying in an *apartotel,* a cross between an apartment complex and a hotel. You can rent by the day, week, or month, and you get a furnished apartment with a full kitchen, plus housekeeping. Options include **Apartotel El Sesteo** ★ (www.sesteo.com; ✆ **2296-1805;**

fax 2296-1865), **Apartotel La Sabana** ★ (www.apartotel-lasabana.com; ✆ **877/ 722-2621** in the U.S. and Canada, or 2220-2422; fax 2231-7386), **Apartotel María Alexandra** (www.mariaalexandra. com; ✆ **2228-1507;** fax 2289-5192), and **Apartotel Los Yoses** (www.apartotel. com; ✆ **888/790-5264** in the U.S. and Canada, or 2225-0033; fax 2225-5595).

MODERATE

Hôtel Le Bergerac ★★ ▓ With charm and sophistication, the Hôtel Le Bergerac has ingratiated itself over the years with business travelers and members of various diplomatic missions. Still, you don't have to be a diplomat or business traveler to enjoy this hotel's charms. Le Bergerac is composed of three houses with courtyard gardens in between. Almost all the rooms are fairly large, and each is a little different. I favor those with private patio gardens. In the evenings, candlelight and classical music set a relaxing and romantic mood.

Calle 35 no. 50, San José. www.bergerachotel.com. ✆ **2234-7850.** Fax 2225-9103. 25 units. $90–$145 double. Rates include full breakfast. AE, DC, MC, V. Free parking. **Amenities:** Restaurant; lounge; concierge. *In room:* TV, hair dryer.

Hotel Milvia ★ ▓ Art lovers should definitely look into this offbeat little hotel. This old converted home is chock-full of paintings and sculptures by a wide range of contemporary Costa Rican artists. One of the owners, Florencia Urbina, is one of these artists. But you'll also find works by Mario Maffioli and Fabio Herrera, among others. My favorite pieces are the large-scale sculptures by Leda Astorga, including two functional and funny chairs. The rooms are bright and airy, and most are plenty spacious. The hotel has a mix of courtyards and gardens that seem to beckon one to linger with a book or sketch pad in hand.

1 block north and 2 blocks east of the Muñoz y Nanne Supermarket, San Pedro. www.hotel milvia.com. ✆ **2225-4543.** Fax 2225-7801. 9 units. $69 double. Rates include continental breakfast. AE, MC, V. **Amenities:** Lounge. *In room:* TV, Wi-Fi.

WHERE TO EAT

San José has an excellent variety of restaurants serving cuisines from all over the world. You can find superb French, Italian, and contemporary fusion restaurants around the city, as well as Peruvian, Japanese, Swiss, and Spanish spots. If you're looking for cheap eats, you'll find them all across the city in little restaurants known as **sodas,** which are the equivalent of diners in the United States.

Fruit vendors stake out spots on almost every street corner in downtown San José. If you're lucky enough to be in town between April and June, you can sample more varieties of mangoes than you ever knew existed. I like buying them already cut up in a little bag; they cost a little more this way, but you don't get

A vendor *selling* pejibaye.

nearly as messy. Be sure to try a green mango with salt and chili peppers—it's guaranteed to wake up your taste buds. Another common street food is *pejibaye,* a bright orange palm nut about the size of a plum. They're boiled in big pots on carts; you eat them in much the same way you eat an avocado, and they taste a bit like squash.

San José has quite a few 24-hour restaurants. The best place to get some local late-night color is **Chelles,** on Avenida Central and Calle 9 (see "San José After Dark," later in this chapter). Then there's **Del Mar,** which belongs to and is across from the Hotel Del Rey (p. 116); with stained-glass windows and efficient service. Finally, you'll find a **Denny's** (© **2431-5050;** www.dennyscosta rica.com), at the Best Western Irazú, on the highway out to the airport. Another is beside the Hampton Inn at the airport).

Downtown San José

EXPENSIVE

La Esquina de Buenos Aires ★★ 📷 ARGENTINE Excellent Argentine cooking and authentic decor transport you almost immediately to this restaurant's namesake city. At once a neighborhood tango tavern and true steakhouse, this place has a lively and welcoming vibe. Grilled meats are the specialty here, but the long menu also features excellent pastas, and a range of fish, poultry, and steak. Start things off with some *empanadas,* which can be ordered with any number of fillings, or some thinly sliced beef carpaccio. The grill throws out some exotic blood sausages, tripe, and sweetbreads, but I recommend the *bife de chorizo,* or strip steak. This place fills up fast, especially on weekends, so be sure to have a reservation.

Calle 11 and Av. 4. © **2223-1909.** www.laesquinadebuenosaires.com. Reservations recommended. Main courses C7,000–C13,000. AE, MC, V. Mon–Fri 11:30am–3pm and 6–10:30pm; Sat–Sun noon to 10pm.

MODERATE

Café Mundo ★ INTERNATIONAL   This popular place mixes contemporary cuisine with a casually elegant ambience. Wood tables and Art Deco wrought-iron chairs are spread spaciously around several rooms in this former colonial mansion. Additional seating is on the open-air veranda and in the small gardens. Appetizers include vegetable tempura, crab cakes, and chicken satay alongside more traditional Tico standards such as *patacones* (fried plantain chips) and fried yuca. There's a long list of pastas and pizzas, as well as more substantial main courses, nightly specials, and delicious desserts. One room here has colorful murals by Costa Rican artist Miguel Casafont. This place is almost always packed with a broad mix of San José's gay, bohemian, theater, arts, and university crowds.

Calle 15 and Av. 9, 200m (2 blocks) east and 100m (1 block) north of the INS building. ✆ **2222-6190.** Reservations recommended. Main courses C4,500–C15,000. AE, MC, V. Mon–Thurs 11am–10:30pm; Fri 11am–11:30pm; Sat 5–11:30pm.

Cafeteria 1930 📷 INTERNATIONAL   With veranda and patio seating directly fronting the Plaza de la Cultura, this is one of the most atmospheric spots for a casual bite and some good people-watching. A wrought-iron railing, white columns, and arches create an old-world atmosphere; on the plaza in front of the cafe, a marimba band performs and vendors sell handicrafts. Stop by for the breakfast and watch the plaza vendors set up their booths, or peruse the *Tico Times* over coffee while you have your shoes polished. The menu covers a lot of ground, and the food is respectable, if unspectacular, but there isn't a better place downtown to bask in the tropical sunshine while you sip a beer or have a light lunch, and it's a great place to come before or after a show at the Teatro Nacional.

The Plaza de la Cultura.

At the Gran Hotel Costa Rica, Av. 2, btw. calles 1 and 3. ✆ **2221-4011.** Sandwiches C6,800–C7,800; main courses C6,800–C9,200. AE, DC, MC, V. Daily 6am–11pm.

Kalú Café ★★ 📷 CAFE/BAKERY   This hip restaurant and cafe is casual and chic. The best seats are on a covered outdoor back patio. The menu features soups, salads, panini, pizzas, and a handful of main courses. The daily lunch specials are a great deal, and are very popular with downtown workers. The Kalú burger features a grilled portobello mushroom instead of a beef patty, but it's not vegetarian, as it's topped with caramelized onions, a sundried tomato pesto, and bacon. The desserts here are astounding. I especially like the dark cherry and almond cream tart. Just off the cafe is Boutique Kiosko (p. 137).

Calle 7 and Av. 11. ✆ **2221-2081.** www.kalu.co.cr. Reservations recommended. Main courses C5,800–C8,650. AE, MC, V. Mon 11:30am–6pm; Tues–Sat 11:30am–9:30pm.

Restaurante Nuestra Tierra 📷 COSTA RICAN   Sure it's touristy, but if you want a *casado* or some *gallo pinto,* anytime of the day or night, this is the place to come. The decor seeks to imitate a humble country ranch kitchen, with heavy wooden tables, chairs, and paneling, and strings of fresh onions and bunches of bananas hung from the rafters and columns. Service is friendly and efficient; dressed in typical *campesino* outfits, servers periodically break out into traditional folkloric dances. The biggest downside here is that the restaurant fronts the very busy Avenida 2, so head for a second-floor table away from the traffic.

Av. 2 and Calle 15. ✆ **2258-6500.** Main courses C6,000–C15,000. MC, V. Daily 24 hr.

Tin Jo ★★★ CHINESE/PAN-ASIAN   San José has hundreds of Chinese restaurants, but most simply serve up tired takes on chop suey, chow mein, and fried rice. In contrast, Tin Jo has a wide and varied menu, with an assortment of Cantonese and Szechuan staples, as well as a range of Thai, Japanese, and Malaysian dishes, and even some Indian food. Some of the dishes are served in edible rice-noodle bowls, and the pineapple shrimp in coconut-milk curry is served in the hollowed-out half of a fresh pineapple. Dishes not to miss include the salt-and-pepper shrimp, beef teriyaki, and Thai curries. For dessert, try the sticky rice with mango, or banana tempura. The cozy decor features artwork and textiles from across Asia. Tin Jo is also a great option for vegetarians, and even vegans.

Calle 11, btw. avs. 6 and 8. ✆ **2221-7605** or 2257-3622. www.tinjo.com. Reservations recommended. Main courses C5,500–C9,000. AE, MC, V. Mon–Sat 11:30am–3pm and 5:30–10pm (Fri–Sat kitchen open 'til 11pm); Sun 11:30am–10pm.

INEXPENSIVE

In addition to the places listed below, the **Q'Café** (✆ **2221-0707;** www.quecafe.com) is a delightful little European-style cafe with a pretty perch above the busy corner of Avenida Central and Calle 2. Try to grab a seat overlooking the action on the street below.

Caracas Arepas & Juice Bar ★ VENEZUELAN/COSTA RICAN   A brightly lit lunch joint in the heart of the tourist district, this little Latin restaurant is a great stop between museums. Serving up a fusion of Costa Rican and Venezuelan plates, the specialty here is the *arepa,* a Venezuelan corn meal sandwich filled with shredded meats and local cheeses. Try the *Caraqueño,* a pulled beefsteak sandwich, mixed with beans and Turrialba cheese. The menu features a long list of creative smoothies, such as the Mango Tango, a blend of orange and mango juices; and the Bala Fria, a chocolate, ice cream and coffee concoction.

Av. 7, btw. Calles 7 and 9, 1 block north of Parque Morazan. ☎ **2258-6565.** www.caracasarepas. com. *Arepas* C1,100–C2,900; main dishes C2,000–C3,000. AE, MC, V. Mon–Thurs 6am–7pm; Fri 6am–9pm; Sat 11am–9pm.

Café del Teatro Nacional ★ CAFE/COFFEEHOUSE   Even if there's no show on during your visit, you can enjoy a light meal, sandwich, dessert, or a cup of coffee here, while soaking up the neoclassical atmosphere. The theater was built in the 1890s from the designs of European architects, and the Art Nouveau chandeliers, ceiling murals, and marble floors and tables are pure Parisian. The ambience is French-cafe chic, but the marimba music drifting in from outside the open window and the changing art exhibits by local artists will remind you that you're still in Costa Rica. In addition to the regular hours of operation listed below, the cafe is open until 8pm any evening that there is a performance in the theater.

In the Teatro Nacional, Av. 2, btw. calles 3 and 5. ☎ **2221-1329.** Sandwiches C2,000–C4,400; main courses C4,000–C4,500. AE, MC, V. Mon–Sat 9am–4:30pm.

Vishnu VEGETARIAN   Vegetarians will likely find their way to this Vishnu restaurant or one of its many sister outlets around the city. The vibe's a little too plastic, too loud, and too brightly lit for my tastes in a vegetarian joint. However, most people just come for the filling *plato del día* that includes soup, salad, veggies, an entree, and dessert for under $4. The menu also offers bean burgers and cheese sandwiches on whole-wheat bread. At the cashier's counter you can buy natural cosmetics, honey, and bags of granola. Another Vishnu (☎ **2223-3095**) is on the north side of Avenida 8, between calles 11 and 9.

Av. 1, btw. calles 1 and 3. ☎ **2256-6063.** Main courses C3,150–C3,450. AE, MC, V. Mon–Sat 7am–9pm; Sun 9am–7:30pm.

La Sabana/Paseo Colón

VERY EXPENSIVE

Park Café ★★★ 🍴 FUSION   Having opened and run a Michelin two-star restaurant in London and another one-star joint in Cannes, Richard Neat now finds himself in San José. The intimate restaurant spreads around the interior patio courtyard of a stately old downtown mansion, which also doubles as an antiques and imported furniture store. The menu changes regularly but might feature roasted scallops with ricotta tortellini in a pumpkin jus, or some expertly grilled quail on a vegetable purée bed, topped with poached quail egg. Presentations are artfully done, and often served in such a way as to encourage sharing. The well-thought-out and fairly priced wine list is a perfect complement to the cuisine.

Sabana Norte, 1 block north of Rostipollos. ☎ **2290-6324.** www.parkcafecostarica.blogspot. com. Reservations recommended. Main courses C12,500–C15,500. V. Tues–Sat noon to 2pm and 7–10pm.

EXPENSIVE

Grano de Oro Restaurant ★★★ INTERNATIONAL   Set around the lovely interior courtyard of the wonderful Hotel Grano de Oro (p. 118), this restaurant manages to have an atmosphere that's intimate, relaxed, and refined all at the same time. The French chef here has created a wide-ranging and eclectic menu.

Main courses run from the local sea bass encrusted in macadamia nuts, to elaborate lamb, rabbit, and duck dishes. Be sure to save room for the "Grano de Oro pie," a decadent dessert with various layers of chocolate and coffee mousses and creams. This place also has a good wine list, including a range of options by the glass.

Calle 30, no. 251, btw. avs. 2 and 4, 150m (1½ blocks) south of Paseo Colón. ☎ **2255-3322.** Reservations recommended. Main courses C9,700–C19,600. AE, MC, V. Daily 7am–10pm.

MODERATE

Machu Picchu ★ PERUVIAN/INTERNATIONAL   Machu Picchu is an unpretentious little restaurant that is perennially one of the most popular places in San José. The menu is classic Peruvian. One of my favorite entrees is the *causa limeña*, lemon-flavored mashed potatoes stuffed with shrimp. The *ceviche* here is excellent, as is the *ají de gallina*, a dish of shredded chicken in a fragrant cream sauce, and octopus with garlic butter. For main dishes, I recommend *corvina a lo macho*, sea bass in a slightly spicy tomato-based seafood sauce. Be sure to ask for a pisco sour, a classic Peruvian drink made from pisco, a grape liquor. These folks have a sister restaurant over in San Pedro (☎ **2283-3679**).

Calle 32, btw. avs. 1 and 3, 150m (1½ blocks) north of the KFC on Paseo Colón. ☎ **2222-7384.** www.restaurantemachupicchu.com. Reservations recommended. Main courses C5,550–C10,560. AE, DC, MC, V. Mon–Sat 11am–10pm, Sun 11am–6pm.

INEXPENSIVE

Soda Tapia ✦ COSTA RICAN   The food is unspectacular, but dependable and quite inexpensive at this very popular local diner. Seating is inside the brightly lit dining room, as well as on the sidewalk-style patio fronting the parking area. Dour but efficient waitstaff take the order you mark down on your combination menu/bill. This is a great place for late-night eats or for before or after a visit to Parque La Sabana or the Museo de Arte Costarricense. These folks also have another site in a small strip mall in Santa Ana (☎ **2203-7174**).

Calle 42 and Av. 2, across from the Museo de Arte Costarricense. ☎ **2222-6734.** Sandwiches C1,800–C3,850; main dishes C2,200–C4,400. AE, MC, V. Mon–Thurs 6am–1am; Fri–Sat 24 hr.; Sun 6am–11:45pm.

San Pedro/Los Yoses

In addition to the restaurants listed below, local and visiting vegetarians swear by the little **Comida Para Sentir Restaurante Vegetariano San Pedro** (☎ **2224-1163**), located 125m (1¼ blocks) north of the San Pedro Church. Despite the massive size and popularity of the nearby **Il Pomodoro** (☎ **2224-0966**), I prefer **Pane E Vino** (☎ **2280-2869;** www.paneevino.co.cr), an excellent pasta-and-pizza joint on the eastern edge of San Pedro, with other outlets around town, as well.

For Peruvian cuisine, try the branch of **Machu Picchu** (☎ **2283-3679;** p. 125) in San Pedro. Finally, if you're hankering for sushi, try **Ichiban** ★ (☎ **2253-8012;** www.ichibanrestaurante.com) in San Pedro, or **Matsuri** ★ (☎ **2280-5522**), a little farther east in Curridabat. Both of these sushi places have outlets on the west side of town as well. Finally, for good Middle-Eastern fare, I recommend **Aya Sofya** (☎ **2224-5050**), located in Los Yoses, 2 blocks north of Bagleman's.

EXPENSIVE

Donde Carlos ★★ ARGENTINE/STEAK   Bold architectural touches abound in this stylish restaurant, yet the food is built primarily around simple, expertly grilled meats and fresh fish. You pass the wood-burning Argentine-style charcoal grill as you enter. I like the outdoor tables on the second-floor balcony when the weather permits. Most folks stick to the hearty steak options, but you can also order a wide range of sausages and offal meats, as well as fresh tuna. Don't pass on the apple pancake dessert—it's delicious. All portions are huge, and this place has a good and reasonably priced wine list to boot.

1 block north of the Fatima Church in Los Yoses. © **2225-0819.** www.dondecarlos.com. Main courses C11,000–C14,000. AE, MC, V. Mon–Thurs noon–3pm and 6:30–10:30pm; Fri noon–3pm and 6:30–11pm; Sat noon–11pm; Sun noon–7pm.

MODERATE

Olio ★ 🍴 MEDITERRANEAN   Exposed brick walls, dark wood wainscoting, and stained-glass lamps imbue this place with character and romance. The extensive tapas menu features traditional Spanish fare, as well as bruschetta, antipasti, and a Greek *mezza* plate. For a main dish, I recommend the chicken Vesuvio, which is marinated first in a balsamic vinegar reduction and finished with a creamy herb sauce; or the *arrollado siciliano,* which is a thin filet of steak rolled around spinach, sun-dried tomatoes, and mozzarella cheese and topped with a pomodoro sauce. The midsize wine list features very reasonably priced wines from Italy, France, Spain, Germany, Chile, Greece, and even Bulgaria. Nonsmokers be warned: The bar and dining areas here are often tightly packed and smoke-filled.

Barrio California, 200m (2 blocks) north of Bagelman's. © **2281-0541.** Reservations recommended. Main courses $5–$12. AE, DC, MC, V. Mon–Wed noon–11pm; Thurs–Fri noon–midnight; Sat 6pm–midnight.

Whappin' ★ COSTA RICAN/CARIBBEAN   You don't have to go to Limón or Cahuita to get good home-cooked Caribbean food. In addition to *rondon,* a coconut milk–based stew or soup (see "That Run-down Feeling," on p. 496), you can also get the classic rice and beans cooked in coconut milk, as well as a range of fish and chicken dishes from the coastal region. I like the whole red snapper covered in a spicy sauce of sautéed onions. A small bar is at the entrance and some simple tables are spread around the restaurant, with an alcove here and there. Everything is very simple, and prices are quite reasonable. After a dinner of fresh fish, with rice, beans, and *patacones,* the only letdown is that the beach is some 4 hours away.

Barrio Escalante, 200m (2 blocks) east of El Farolito. © **2283-1480.** www.whapin.com. Main courses C4,900–C11,000. AE, MC, V. Mon–Sat 11:30am–2:30pm and 6–10pm.

WHAT TO SEE & DO

Most visitors to Costa Rica try to get out of the city as fast as possible so they can spend more time on the beach or off in the rainforests. But San José has a few attractions to keep you busy. Some of the best and most modern museums in Central America are here, with a wealth of fascinating pre-Columbian artifacts. Standouts include the Museo de Jade Marco Fidel Tristán (Jade Museum) and the Museo de Arte Costarricense (Costa Rican Art Museum), featuring a top-notch collection of Costa Rican art, and a beautiful, open-air sculpture garden.

Just outside San José in the Central Valley are also several great things to see and do. With day trips out of the city, you can spend quite a few days in this region. See "San José & Environs in 3 Days," in chapter 3, for additional touring ideas.

ORGANIZED TOURS   San José is so compact that you can easily visit all the major sights on your own. However, if you want to take a city tour, which will run you between $20 and $50, here are some companies you can use: **Horizontes Travel ★★**, Calle 28 between avenidas 1 and 3 (ⓒ **2222-2022;** www.horizontes.com); **Gray Line Tours,** Avenida 7 between calles 6 and 8, with additional offices at the Hampton Inn and Best Western Irazú (ⓒ **2220-2126;** www.graylinecostarica.com); and **Swiss Travel Service** (ⓒ **2282-4898;** www.swisstravelcr.com). These same companies also offer a complete range of day trips out of San José (see "Side Trips from San José," later in this chapter, as well as the "What to See & Do" sections of chapter 6). Almost all of the major hotels have tour desks, and most of the smaller hotels will also help arrange tours and day trips.

The Top Attractions

Catedral Metropolitano (Metropolitan Cathedral) ★   San José's principal Catholic cathedral was built in 1871. Rather plain from the outside, the large neoclassical church features a pretty mix of stained glass works, tile floors, and assorted sculptures and bas-reliefs. It also boasts a wonderfully restored 19th-century pipe organ. A well-tended little garden surrounds the church and features a massive marble statue of Pope Juan Pablo II, with a woman and child, carved by celebrated Costa Rican sculptor Jorge Jiménez Deredia. Deredia also has a work at the Vatican. The cathedral is just across from the downtown Parque Central (Central Park).
Av. 2 and Calle Central. ⓒ **2221-3820.** Free admission. Mon–Sat 6am–6pm; Sun 6am–9pm.

Centro Nacional de Arte y Cultura (National Center of Art and Culture) ★   Occupying a full city block, this was once the National Liquor Factory (FANAL). Now it houses the offices of the Cultural Ministry, several performing-arts centers, and the Museum of

A sculpture at Museo de Arte Costarricense.

Art displays at Museo de Jade Marco Fidel Tristán.

Contemporary Art and Design. The latter has done an excellent job of promoting cutting-edge Costa Rican and Central American artists, while also featuring impressive traveling international exhibits, including large retrospectives by prominent Latin American and international art stars. If you're looking for modern dance, experimental theater, or a lecture on Costa Rican video, this is a good place to start. Allow around 2 hours to take in all the exhibits here.

Calle 13, btw. avs. 3 and 5. ✆ **2255-3376** or 2221-2022. Free admission. Mon–Fri 7am–3pm.

Museo de Arte Costarricense (Costa Rican Art Museum) ★★ This small museum at the end of Paseo Colón in Parque La Sabana was originally the country's principal airport terminal. Today it houses a collection of works in all media by Costa Rica's most celebrated artists. On display are some exceptionally beautiful pieces in a wide range of styles, demonstrating how Costa Rican artists have interpreted and imitated the major European movements over the years. In addition to the permanent collection of sculptures, paintings, and prints are rotating temporary exhibits. Be sure to visit the outdoor sculpture garden, which features works by José Sancho, Jorge Jiménez Deredia, Max Jiménez, Edgar Zuñiga, and Francisco Zuñiga. Moreover, the outdoor setting is lovely. You can easily spend an hour or two at this museum—more if you take a stroll through the neighboring Parque La Sabana (p. 131).

Calle 42 and Paseo Colón, Parque La Sabana Este. ✆ **2256-1281.** www.musarco.go.cr. Free admission. Tues–Sun 9am–4pm.

Museo de Jade Marco Fidel Tristán (Jade Museum) ★ Jade was the most valuable commodity among the pre-Columbian cultures of Mexico and Central America, worth more than gold. Located on the first floor of the INS (National Insurance Company) building, this popular museum houses a huge collection of jade artifacts dating from 500 B.C. to A.D. 800. Most are large pendants that were parts of necklaces and are primarily human and animal figures. A fascinating display illustrates how the primitive peoples of this region carved this extremely hard stone.

The museum also possesses an extensive collection of pre-Columbian polychrome terra-cotta vases, bowls, and figurines. Some of these pieces are amazingly modern in design and exhibit a surprisingly advanced technique. Particularly fascinating is a vase that incorporates real human teeth, and a display that shows how jade was embedded in human teeth merely for decorative reasons. All of the explanations are in English and Spanish. Allot at least an hour to tour this museum.

Av. 7, btw. calles 9 and 9B, INS Building. ℂ **2287-6034.** Admission $8, free for children 11 and under. Mon–Fri 8:30am–3:30pm; Sat 9am–1pm.

Museo de Los Niños (Children's Museum) ☺   If you're traveling with children, you'll definitely want to come here, and you might want to visit even if you aren't. A former barracks and then a prison, this museum houses an extensive collection of exhibits designed to edify and entertain children of all ages. Experience a simulated earthquake or make music by dancing across the floor. Many exhibits encourage hands-on play. The museum sometimes features limited shows of "serious" art and is also the home of the National Auditorium. You can spend anywhere from 1 to 4 hours here. Be careful, though: The museum is large and spread out; it's easy to lose track of a family member or friend.

This museum is a few blocks north of downtown, on Calle 4. It's within easy walking distance, but you might want to take a cab because you'll have to walk right through the worst part of the red-light district.

Calle 4 and Av. 9. ℂ **2258-4929.** www.museocr.org. Admission C1,100 adults, C800 students and children 17 and under. Daily 9am–5pm.

Museo Nacional de Costa Rica (National Museum) ★★   Costa Rica's most important historical museum is housed in a former army barracks that was the scene of fighting during the civil war of 1948. As you approach the building, or walk around it, you can still see hundreds of bullet holes on the turrets at its

Museo Nacional de Costa Rica.

corners. Inside this traditional Spanish-style courtyard building, you will find displays on Costa Rican history and culture from pre-Columbian times to the present. In the pre-Columbian rooms, you'll see a 2,500-year-old jade carving that is shaped like a seashell and etched with an image of a hand holding a small animal.

Among the most fascinating objects unearthed at Costa Rica's numerous archaeological sites are many *metates,* or grinding stones. This type of grinding stone is still in use today throughout Central America; however, the ones on display here are more ornately decorated and some are the size of a small bed and are believed to have been part of funeral rites. A separate vault houses the museum's collection of pre-Columbian gold jewelry and figurines, while two adjoining homes have been restored to their 19th-century grandeur. The newest addition here is a massive butterfly garden, with over 25 species of butterflies, and exhibits of the insects fascinating life cycle. It takes about 2 hours to take in the lion's share of the collection here.

Calle 17, btw. avs. Central and 2, on the Plaza de la Democracia. ✆ **2257-1433.** www.museocosta rica.go.cr. Admission $8 adults, $4 students and children 11 and under. Tues–Sat 8:30am–4:30pm. Sun 9am–4:30pm. Closed Jan 1, May 1, Dec 25, and Holy Thursday, Good Friday, and Easter Sunday.

Museos del Banco Central de Costa Rica (Gold Museum) ★★

Located directly beneath the Plaza de la Cultura, this unusual underground museum houses one of the largest collections of pre-Columbian gold in the Americas. On display are more than 20,000 troy ounces of gold in more than 2,000 objects, spread over three floors. The sheer number of pieces can be overwhelming and seem redundant, but the unusual display cases and complex lighting systems show off every piece to its utmost. This complex also includes separate numismatic and philatelic museums (coins and stamps, for us regular folks), and a modest gift shop.

Calle 5, btw. avs. Central and 2, underneath the Plaza de la Cultura. ✆ **2243-4202.** www.museosdelbancocentral.org. Admission C5,500 adults, C3,500 students, free for children 11 and under. Daily 9am–4:30pm.

Parque Zoológico Simón Bolívar ☺

This zoo no longer suffers from the overwhelming sense of neglect and despair that once plagued it, though it's still pretty lackluster and depressing. Why spend time here when you could head out into the forests and jungles? You won't see the great concentrations of wildlife available in one stop here at the zoo, but you'll see the animals in their natural habitats, not yours. The zoo is really geared toward locals and school groups, with Asian, African, and Costa Rican animals. There's a children's discovery area, a snake-and-reptile house, and a gift shop. You can easily spend a couple of hours here.

Av. 11 and Calle 7, in Barrio Amón. ✆ **2256-0012.** www. fundazoo.org. Admission C2,100 adults, C1,400 children 3–12, free for children 2 and under. Daily 9am–4:30pm.

A gold artifact at the Museos del Banco Central.

A butterfly at the Spirogyra Butterfly Garden.

Spirogyra Butterfly Garden   This butterfly garden is smaller and less elaborate than the Butterfly Farm (p. 162), but it provides a good introduction to the life cycle of butterflies. It's also a calm and quiet oasis in a noisy and crowded city, quite close to downtown. Plan on a half-hour to several hours here, depending on whether they have lunch or refreshments at the small coffee shop and gallery. You'll be given a self-guided-tour booklet when you arrive, and an 18-minute video runs continuously throughout the day. Spirogyra is near El Pueblo, a short taxi ride from San José's center.

100m (1 block) east and 150m (1½ blocks) south of El Pueblo Shopping Center. ℂ/fax **2222-2937.** www.butterflygardencr.com. Admission $7 adults, $6 students and $5 children 11 and under. Daily 8am–4pm.

OUTDOOR ACTIVITIES & SPECTATOR SPORTS

Due to the chaos and pollution, you'll probably want to get out of the city before undertaking anything too strenuous. But if you want to brave the elements, there are a few outdoor activities in and around San José. For information on horseback riding, hiking, and white-water rafting trips from San José, see "Side Trips from San José," later in this chapter.

Parque La Sabana ★★ (La Sabana Park, at the western end of Paseo Colón), formerly San José's international airport, is the city's center for active sports and recreation. Here you'll find everything from jogging trails, soccer fields, and a few public tennis courts to the impressive new National Stadium. Aside from events at the National Stadium, all the facilities are free and open to the public. On weekends, you'll usually find free, public aerobic, yoga or dancercise classes taking place. Families gather for picnics, people fly kites, pony rides are available for the kids, and there's even an outdoor sculpture garden. If you

Parque La Sabana.

A Costa Rican bullfight.

really want to experience the local culture, try getting into a pickup soccer game here. However, be careful in this park, especially at dusk or after dark, when it becomes a favorite haunt for youth gangs and muggers.

BIRD-WATCHING   Serious birders will certainly want to head out of San José, but it is still possible to see quite a few species in the metropolitan area. Two of the best spots for urban bird-watching are the campus at the **University of Costa Rica,** in the eastern suburb of San Pedro, and **Parque del Este ★,** located a little farther east on the road to San Ramón de Tres Ríos. You'll see a mix of urban species, and if you're lucky, you might spy a couple of hummingbirds or even a blue-crowned motmot. To get to the university campus, take any San Pedro bus from Avenida Central between calles 9 and 11. To get to Parque del Este, take the San Ramón/Parque del Este bus from Calle 9 between avenidas Central and 1.

BULLFIGHTING   Although I hesitate to call it a sport, **Las Corridas a la Tica (Costa Rican bullfighting)** is a popular and frequently comic stadium event. Instead of the blood-and-gore/life-and-death confrontation of traditional bullfighting, Ticos just like to tease the bull. In a typical *corrida* (bullfight), anywhere from 50 to 150 *toreadores improvisados* (literally, "improvised bullfighters") stand in the ring waiting for the bull. What follows is a slapstick scramble to safety whenever the bull heads toward a crowd of bullfighters. The braver bullfighters try to slap the bull's backside as the beast chases down one of his buddies.

You can see a bullfight during the various Festejos Populares (City Fairs) around the country. The country's largest Festejos Populares are in Zapote, a suburb east of San José, during Christmas week and the first week in January. Admission is C5,000 to C10,000. This is a purely seasonal activity and occurs in San José only during the Festejos. However, nearly every little town around the country has yearly *festejos*. These are spread out throughout the year. Ask at your hotel; if your timing's right, you might be able to take in one of these.

HOTEL SPAS & WORKOUT FACILITIES   Most of the city's higher-end hotels have some sort of pool and exercise facilities. You'll find the best of these at the Marriott Costa Rica Hotel (p. 165) and Crowne Plaza Corobicí (p. 118). If you're looking for a good, serious workout, I recommend the **Multispa ★** (*©* **2231-5542;** www.multispa.net), in the Tryp Corobicí. Even if you're not a guest at the hotel, you can use the facilities here and join in any class for $20 per day. Multispa has five other locations around the Central Valley.

JOGGING   Try **Parque La Sabana,** mentioned above, or head to **Parque del Este,** which is east of town in the foothills above San Pedro. Take the San Ramón/Parque del Este bus from Calle 9 between avenidas Central and 1. It's never a good idea to jog at night, on busy streets, or alone. Women should be particularly careful about jogging alone. And remember, Tico drivers are not accustomed to joggers on residential streets, so don't expect drivers to give you much berth.

SOCCER (FÚTBOL)   Ticos take their *fútbol* seriously. Costa Rican professional soccer is some of the best in Central America, and the national team, or *Sele* (*selección nacional*), qualified for the World Cup in 2002 and 2006, although they failed to qualify for the 2010 World Cup in South Africa. The soccer season runs from September to June, with the finals over several weeks in late June and early July.

Fans at a fútbol *match.*

The main San José team is Saprissa (affectionately called El Monstruo, or "The Monster"). **Saprissa's stadium** is in Tibás (☎ **2240-4034;** www. saprissa.co.cr; take any Tibás bus from Calle 2 and Av. 5). Games are often held on Sunday at 11am, but occasionally they are scheduled for Saturday afternoon or Wednesday evening. Check the local newspapers for game times and locations.

International and other important matches are held in the new **National Stadium** on the north eastern corner of Parque La Sabana.

You don't need to buy tickets in advance. Tickets generally run between C1,000 and C7,500. It's worth paying a little extra for *sombra numerado* (reserved seats in the shade). This will protect you from both the sun and the more rowdy aficionados. Costa Rican soccer fans take the sport seriously, and periodic violent incidents, both inside and outside the stadiums, have marred the sport here, so be careful. Other options include *sombra* (general admission in the shade), *palco* and *palco numerado* (general admission and reserved mezzanine), and *sol general* (general admission in full sun).

SWIMMING If you aren't going to get to the beach anytime soon and your hotel doesn't have a pool, you can use the pool at the Multispa facility at the hotel **Crowne Plaza Corobicí** (p. 118) for $20.

SHOPPING

Serious shoppers will be disappointed in Costa Rica. Aside from coffee and oxcarts, there isn't much that's distinctly Costa Rican. To compensate for its own relative lack of goods, Costa Rica does a brisk business in selling crafts and clothes imported from Guatemala, Panama, and Ecuador.

THE SHOPPING SCENE San José's central shopping corridor is bounded by avenidas 1 and 2, from about Calle 14 in the west to Calle 13 in the east. For several blocks west of the Plaza de la Cultura, **Avenida Central** is a pedestrian-only street mall where you'll find store after store of inexpensive clothes for men, women, and children. Depending on the mood of the police that day, you might find a lot of street vendors as well. Most shops in the downtown district are open Monday through Saturday from about 8am to 6pm. Some shops close for lunch, while others remain open (it's just the luck of the draw for shoppers). You'll be happy to find that the sales and import taxes have already been figured into the display price.

MARKETS Several markets are near downtown, but by far the largest is the **Mercado Central ★** (see below), located between avenidas Central and 1 and calles 6 and 8.

A daily street market is on the west side of the **Plaza de la Democracia ★★**. Two long rows of outdoor stalls sell T-shirts, Guatemalan and Ecuadorian handicrafts and clothing, small ceramic *ocarinas* (a small musical wind instrument), and handmade jewelry. The atmosphere here is much more open than at the Mercado Central, which I find just a bit too claustrophobic. You might be able to bargain prices down a little bit, but bargaining is not a traditional part of the vendor culture here, so you'll have to work hard to save a few dollars.

joe **TO GO**

Two words of advice: Buy coffee. Lots of it.

Coffee is the best shopping deal in all of Costa Rica. Although the best Costa Rican coffee is allegedly shipped off to North American and European markets, it's hard to beat the coffee that's roasted right in front of you here. Best of all is the price: One pound of coffee sells for around $3 to $6. It makes a great gift and truly is a local product.

Café Britt is the big name in Costa Rican coffee. These folks have the largest export business in the country, and, although high-priced, their blends are very dependable. Café Britt is widely available at gift shops around the country, and at the souvenir concessions at both international airports. My favorites, however, are the coffees roasted and packaged in Manuel Antonio and Monteverde, by **Café Milagro** and **Café Monteverde,** respectively. If you visit either of these places, definitely pick up their beans.

In general, the best place to buy coffee is in any supermarket. Why pay more at a gift or specialty shop? You can also try **Café Trébol,** on Calle 8 between avenidas Central and 1 (on the western side of the Central Market; (✆ **2221-8363**). It's open Monday through Saturday from 7am to 6:30pm and Sunday from 9am to 1pm.

Be sure to ask for whole beans; Costa Rican grinds are often too fine for standard coffee filters. The store will pack beans for you in whatever size bag you want. If you buy prepackaged coffee in a supermarket in Costa Rica, the whole beans will be marked either *grano* (grain) or *grano entero* (whole bean). If you opt for ground varieties *(molido),* be sure the package is marked *puro;* otherwise, it will likely be mixed with a good amount of sugar, the way Ticos like it.

One good coffee-related gift to bring home is a coffee sock and stand. This is the most common mechanism for brewing coffee beans in Costa Rica. It consists of a simple circular stand, made out of wood or wire, which holds a sock. Put the ground beans in the sock, place a pot or cup below it, and pour boiling water through. You can find the socks and stands at most supermarkets and in the Mercado Central. In fancier crafts shops, you'll find them made out of ceramic. Depending on its construction, a stand will cost you between $1.50 and $15; socks run around 30¢, so buy a few spares.

MODERN MALLS With globalization and modernization taking hold in Costa Rica, much of the local shopping scene has shifted to large megamalls. Modern multilevel affairs with cineplexes, food courts, and international brand-name stores are becoming ubiquitous. The biggest and most modern of these malls include the **Mall San Pedro, Multiplaza** (one each in

A vendor at the Plaza de la Democracia market.

Escazú and the eastern suburb of Zapote), and **Terra Mall** (on the outskirts of downtown on the road to Cartago). Although they lack the charm of small shops found around San José, they are a reasonable option for one-stop shopping; most contain at least one or two local galleries and crafts shops, along with a large supermarket, which is always the best place to stock up on local coffee, hot sauces, liquors, and other nonperishable foodstuffs.

Shopping A to Z

ART GALLERIES

Arte Latino   This gallery carries original artwork in a variety of media, featuring predominantly Central American themes. Some of it is pretty gaudy, but this is generally a good place to find Nicaraguan and Costa Rican "primitive" paintings. El Pueblo Shopping Center, 15. ℂ 2258-7083.

Galería Jacobo Karpio   This excellent gallery handles some of the more adventurous modern art to be found in Costa Rica. Karpio has a steady stable of prominent Mexican, Cuban, and Argentine artists, as well as some local talent. Av. 1, casa no. 1352, btw. calles 13 and 15. 50m (164 ft.) west of the Legislative Assembly. ℂ 2257-7963.

Galería Kandinsky   Owned by the daughter of one of Costa Rica's most prominent modern painters, Rafa Fernández, this small gallery usually has a good selection of high-end contemporary Costa Rican paintings, be it the house collection or a specific temporary exhibit. Centro Comercial Calle Real, San Pedro. ℂ 2234-0478.

TEORetica ★★   This small downtown gallery was founded by one of the more adventurous and internationally respected collectors and curators in Costa Rica, the late Virginia Pérez-Ratton. It's still one of the best galleries in the country, and you'll usually find very interesting and cutting-edge exhibitions here. Calle 7, btw. avs. 9 and 11. © 2233-4881. www.teoretica.org.

BOOKS

Librería Internacional   This is the closest Costa Rica has to a major book retailer. Most of the books here are in Spanish, but they do have a small-to-modest selection of English-language contemporary fiction, nonfiction, and natural history texts. Librería Internacional has various outlets around San José, including in most of the major modern malls. Av. Central, ¾ block west of the Plaza de la Cultura. © 2257-2563. www.libreriainternacional.com.

Seventh Street Books ★★   There's no better bookstore in San José for English-language books. They are especially strong in the realm of field guides and natural history books, publishing quite a few titles in this category themselves. But you can also find a range of fiction, coffee-table books, general guidebooks, and even good English-language and bilingual children's books. Calle 7, btw. avs. 1 and Central. © 2256-8251.

HANDICRAFTS

Notable exceptions to the city's generally meager crafts offerings include the fine wooden creations of **Barry Biesanz** ★★ (© **2289-4337;** www.biesanz.com). His work is sold in many of the finer gift shops around and at his own shop (p. 154), but beware: Biesanz's work is often imitated, so make sure that what you buy is the real deal (he generally burns his signature into the bottom of the piece). **Lil Mena** is a local artist who specializes in working with and painting on handmade papers and rough fibers. You'll find her work in a number of shops around San José.

   Cecilia "Pefi" Figueres ★★ makes practical ceramic wares that are lively and fun. Look for her brightly colored abstract and figurative bowls, pitchers, coffee mugs, and more at some of the better gift shops around the city.

Boutique Annemarie ★   Occupying two floors at the Hotel Don Carlos (p. 116), this shop has an amazing array of wood products, leather goods, papier-mâché figurines, paintings, books, cards, posters, and jewelry. You'll see most of this stuff at the other shops, but not in such quantities or in such a relaxed and pressure-free environment. At the Hotel Don Carlos, Calle 9, btw. avs. 7 and 9. © 2233-5343.

Boutique Kiosco ★★ 🎒   This place features a range of original and one-off pieces of functional, wearable, and practical pieces made by contemporary Costa Rican and regional artists and designers. While the offerings are regularly changing, you'll usually find a mix of jewelry, handbags, shoes, dolls, furniture, and knickknacks. Often the pieces are made with recycled or sustainable materials. Calle 7 and Av. 11, Barrio Amón. © 2258-1829. www.kioscosjo.com.

Galería Namu ★★   Galeria Namu has some very high-quality arts and crafts, specializing in truly high-end indigenous works, including excellent Boruca and Huetar carved masks and "primitive" paintings. It also carries a good selection of more modern arts and craft pieces, including the ceramic work of Cecilia "Pefi" Figueres. This place organizes tours to visit various indigenous tribes and artisans as well. Av. 7, btw. calles 5 and 7. ✆ 2256-3412. www.galerianamu.com.

La Casona Just off Avenida Central, in the heart of downtown, La Casona is a 3-story warren of crafts and souvenir stalls. The various stalls sell similar craft and souvenir works imported from Guatemala, Ecuador, Panama, and even China. On a rainy day, this is a great alternative to the outdoor market on the Plaza de la Democracia (see above). Calle Central btw. avs. Central and 1. ✆ 2222-7999.

Mercado Central ★ 📷 Although this tight maze of stalls is primarily a food market, vendors also sell souvenirs, leather goods, musical instruments, and many other items. Be especially careful with your wallet, purse, and prominent jewelry, as skilled pickpockets frequent the area. All the streets surrounding the Mercado Central are jammed with produce vendors selling from small carts or loading and unloading trucks. It's always a hive of activity, with crowds of people jostling for space on the streets. Your best bet is to visit on Sunday or a weekday; Saturday is particularly busy. Btw. avs. Central and 1 and calles 6 and 8, San José. No phone.

JEWELRY

Studio Metallo ★★ The outgrowth of a jewelry-making school and studio, this shop has some excellent handcrafted jewelry made in a range of styles, using everything from 18-karat white and yellow gold and pure silver, to some less exotic and expensive alloys. Some works integrate gemstones, while many others focus on the metalwork. 6½ blocks east of the Iglesia Santa Teresita, Barrio Escalante. ✆ 2281-3207. www.studiometallo.com.

Galería Namu wares.

A stall at the Mercado Central.

LEATHER GOODS

In general, Costa Rican leather products are not of the highest grade or quality, and prices are not particularly low. **Del Río** (© **2262-1415**) is a local leather goods manufacturer, with stores in most of the city's modern malls. It also offers free hotel pickup and transfer to its factory outlet in Heredia (p. 167).

LIQUOR

The best prices I've seen for liquor are at the city's large supermarkets, such as **Más × Menos.** A Más × Menos store is on Paseo Colón and Calle 26 and another is on Avenida Central at the east end of town, just below the Museo Nacional de Costa Rica.

SAN JOSÉ AFTER DARK

Catering to a mix of tourists, college students, and just generally party-loving Ticos, San José has a host of options to meet the nocturnal needs of visitors and residents alike. You'll find plenty of interesting clubs and bars, a wide range of theaters, and some very lively discos and dance salons.

To find out what's going on in San José while you're in town, pick up the **Tico Times** (English) or **La Nación** (Spanish). The former is a good place to find out where local expatriates are hanging out; the latter's "Viva" and "Tiempo Libre" sections have extensive listings of discos, movie theaters, and live music.

Tip: Several very popular nightlife venues are located in the upscale suburbs of Escazú and Santa Ana, as well as in Heredia (a college town) and Alajuela. See "The Central Valley" chapter for more details on nightlife in these areas.

The Teatro Nacional.

The Performing Arts

Theater is very popular in Costa Rica, and downtown San José is studded with small theaters. However, tastes tend toward the burlesque, and the crowd pleasers are almost always simplistic sexual comedies. The **National Theater Company** (© 2221-1273) is an exception, tackling works from Lope de Vega to Lorca to Mamet. Similarly, the small independent group **Abya Yala** (© 2240-6071; www.teatro-abyayala.org) also puts on several cutting-edge avant-garde shows each year. Almost all of the theater offerings are in Spanish, although the **Little Theater Group** (© 8858-1446; www.littletheatregroup.org), a long-standing amateur group, periodically stages works in English. Check the *Tico Times* to see if anything is running during your stay.

Costa Rica has a strong modern-dance scene. Both the **University of Costa Rica** and the **National University** have modern-dance companies that perform regularly in various venues in San José. In addition to the university-sponsored companies, a host of smaller independent companies are worth catching; check local papers for details.

The **National Symphony Orchestra** is respectable by regional standards, although its repertoire tends to be rather conservative. Symphony season runs March through November, with concerts roughly every other weekend at the **Teatro Nacional,** Avenida 2 between calles 3 and 5 (© 2221-5341; www.teatronacional.go.cr), and the **Auditorio Nacional** (© 2256-5876) at the Museo de Los Niños (p. 129). Tickets cost between $3 and $30 and can be purchased at the box office.

Visiting artists stop in Costa Rica on a regular basis. Recent concerts have featured hard rockers Aerosmith, Metallica, and Green Day, teen idols the Jonas Brothers, Colombian sensation Shakira, and Spanish heartthrob Julio Iglesias. Many of these performances take place in San José's two historic theaters, the **Teatro Nacional** (see above) and the **Teatro Melico Salazar,** Avenida 2 between calles Central and 2 (☏ **2233-5424** or 2257-6005; www.teatromelico. go.cr), as well as at the **Auditorio Nacional** (see above). Really large shows are held at soccer stadiums or natural amphitheaters.

Costa Rica's cultural panorama changes drastically every November when the country hosts large arts festivals. In odd-numbered years, **El Festival Nacional de las Artes** reigns supreme, featuring purely local talent. In even-numbered years, the month-long fete is **El Festival Internacional de las Artes,** with a nightly smorgasbord of dance, theater, and music from around the world. Most nights of the festival offer between 4 and 10 shows. Many are free, and the most expensive ticket is usually around $5. For exact dates and details, you can contact the **Ministry of Youth and Culture** (☏ **2221-1022;** www.mcjdcr. go.cr), although information is in Spanish.

The Club, Music & Dance Scene

You'll find plenty of places to hit the dance floor in San José. Salsa and merengue are the main beats that move people here, and many of the dance clubs, discos, and salons feature live music on the weekends. You'll find a pretty limited selection, though, if you're looking to catch some small-club jazz, rock, or blues.

The daily "Viva" and Friday's "Tiempo Libre" sections of *La Nación* newspaper have weekly performance schedules. Some dance bands to watch for are Gaviota, Chocolate, Son de Tikizia, Taboga Band, and La Orquestra Son Mayor. While Ghandi, Akasha, El Parque, and Malpaís are popular local rock groups, Marfil is a good cover band, and the Blues Devils, Chepe Blues, and the Las Tortugas are outfits that play American-style hard driving rock and blues. If you're

Salsa dancing at a San José club.

looking for jazz, check out Editus, El Sexteto de Jazz Latino, or pianist and Minister of Culture Manuel Obregón. For a taste of something eclectic, look for Santos y Zurdo, Sonámbulo Psicotrópical, or Amarillo, Cyan y Magenta.

Most of the places listed below charge a nominal cover charge; sometimes it includes a drink or two.

Castro's ★   This is a classic Costa Rican dance club. The music varies throughout the night, from salsa and merengue to reggaeton and occasionally electronic trance. The rooms and various types of environments include some intimate and quiet corners, spread over a couple of floors. It's open daily from noon to anytime between 3 and 6am. Av. 13 and Calle 22, Barrio Mexico. ✆ 2256-8789.

Salsa 54   This is the place to watch expert salsa dancers and to try some steps yourself. You can take Latin dance classes here, or you might learn something just by watching. This place is popular with Ticos, and tourists are a rare commodity here—tourists who can really dance salsa, even more so. It's open on weekends 'til 4am. Calle 3, btw. avs. 1 and 3. ✆ 2233-3814.

Vértigo   Tucked inside a nondescript office building and commercial center on Paseo Colón, this club remains one of the more popular places for rave-style late-night dancing and partying. The dance floor is huge and the ceilings are high, and electronic music rules the roost. It's open Friday and Saturday 'til 6am. Edificio Colón, Paseo Colón. ✆ 2257-8424. www.vertigocr.com.

The Bar Scene

San José has something for every taste. Lounge lizards will be happy in most hotel bars downtown, while students and the young at heart will have no problem mixing in at the livelier spots around town. Sports fans have plenty of places to catch the most important games of the day, and a couple of brewpubs are drastically improving the quality and selection of the local suds.

The best part of the varied bar scene in San José is something called a *boca*, the equivalent of a tapa in Spain: a little dish of snacks that arrives at your table when you order a drink. Although this is a somewhat dying tradition, especially in the younger, hipper bars, you will still find *bocas* alive and well in the older, more traditional San José drinking establishments. In most, the *bocas* are free, but in some, where the dishes are more sophisticated, you'll have to pay for the treats. You'll find drinks reasonably priced, with beer costing around $2 to $3 a bottle, and mixed drinks costing $4 to $10.

Chelles   This classic downtown bar and restaurant makes up for its lack of ambience with plenty of tradition and a diverse and colorful clientele. The lights are bright, the chairs surround simple Formica-topped card tables, and mirrors adorn most of the walls. Simple sandwiches and meals are served, and pretty good *bocas* come with the drinks. It's open daily, round-the-clock. Av. Central and Calle 9. ✆ 2221-1369.

El 13 ★   Little more than a hole-in-the-wall, this new spot has been packing in a wide ranging crowd of punks, bohos, artists, and assorted revelers. A humble cafe and sandwich shop during the day, it really gets going at night. Thursday through Saturday nights folks are literally hanging out the windows, and spread out onto the street. This place is proudly LGBT friendly. Av. 8, btw. calles 11 and 13. ✆ 2221-7228. http://el13cafebar.com.

El Cuartel de la Boca del Monte ★★ This popular bar, one of San José's best, began life as an artist-and-bohemian hangout, and has evolved into a massive melting pot, attracting everyone from the city's young and well-heeled, to foreign exchange students and visitors. Artists still come, too. Live music is usually Monday, Wednesday, and Friday nights, and when there is, the place is packed shoulder to shoulder. From Monday to Friday it's open for lunch and again in the evenings; on weekends it opens at 6pm. On most nights it's open 'til about 1am, although the revelry might continue 'til about 3am on Friday or Saturday. One corner has been separated into a more bohemian-style bar or pub called La Esquina. Av. 1, btw. calles 21 and 23 (50m/½ block west of the Cine Magaly). ✆ 2221-0327. www.elcuartel.net.

El Observatorio ★★ 🎒 It's easy to miss the narrow entrance to this hot spot across from the Cine Magaly. Owned by a local filmmaker, its decor includes a heavy dose of cinema motifs. The space is large, with high ceilings, and one of the best (perhaps only) smoke extraction systems of any popular bar, making the place bearable, even though most of the clientele are chain-smoking. There's occasional live music and movie screenings and a decent menu of appetizers and main dishes drawn from various world cuisines. It's open 10:30am to 2pm and 6pm to 2am daily. Calle 23, btw. avs. Central and 1. ✆ 2223-0725. www.el observatorio.tv.

Key Largo ★ This meticulously restored downtown mansion is also one of San José's top prostitute pickup bars. Housed in a beautiful old building just off Parque Morazán in the heart of downtown, Key Largo is worth a visit if only to take in the scene and admire the dark-stained carved wood ceilings. There are a couple of pool tables, usually a live band, and always working women—however, this is still an acceptable place for visiting couples and those not actively shopping the wares. It's open 8pm to 2:30am daily. Calle 7, btw. avs. 1 and 3. ✆ 2257-7800.

Rayuela ★★ Named after a classic Julio Cortazar novel, this small, dark, cozy bar oozes boho charm. Poets and folk singers often hold court, and a simple menu of drinks and light bites is offered. If this place is too mellow or artsy for you, their sister spot next door, **El Lobo Estepario,** is larger and has a livelier club feel, with dance music and regular concerts. Av. Central, btw calles 13 and 15. ✆ 8383-7098. http://enrayuela.blogspot.com.

HANGING OUT IN SAN PEDRO

The funky 2-block stretch of **San Pedro** ★★ just south of the University of Costa Rica has been dubbed La Calle de Amargura, or the "Street of Bitterness," and it's the heart and soul of this eastern suburb and college town. Bars and cafes are mixed in with bookstores and copy shops. After dark the streets are packed with teens, punks, students, and professors barhopping and just hanging around. You can walk the strip until someplace strikes your fancy—you don't need a travel guide to find **Omar Khayyam** (✆ **2253-8455**), **Tavarua Surf & Skate Bar** (✆ **2225-7249**), or **Caccio's** (✆ **2224-3261**), which lie at the heart of this district—or you can try one of the places listed below. **Note:** La Calle de Amargura attracts a certain unsavory element. Use caution here. Try to visit with a group, and try not to carry large amounts of cash or wear flashy jewelry.

One of the many bars on La Calle Amargura in San Pedro.

You can get here by heading out (east) on Avenida 2, and following the flow of traffic. You will first pass through the neighborhood of Los Yoses before you reach a large traffic circle with a big fountain in the center (La Fuente de la Hispanidad). The Mall San Pedro is located on this traffic circle. Heading straight through the circle, you'll come to the Church of San Pedro, about 4 blocks east of the circle. The church is the major landmark in San Pedro. You can also take a bus here from downtown.

Jazz Café ★ The Jazz Café is consistently a great spot to find live music and one of the more happening spots in San Pedro. It remains one of my favorites, although low ceilings and poor air circulation make it almost unbearably smoky most nights. Wrought-iron chairs, sculpted busts of famous jazz artists, and creative lighting give the place ambience. There's live music here most nights. It's open daily 'til about 2am. There's a sister **Jazz Café Escazú** (✆ **2288-4740**) on the western end of town. Next to the Banco Popular on Av. Central. ✆ 2253-8933. www.jazzcafecostarica.com.

Terra U Set on a busy corner in the heart of the university district, this two-story joint is one of the most popular bars in the area. Part of this is due to the inviting open-air street-front patio area, which provides a nice alternative to the all-too-common smoke-filled rooms found at most other trendy spots. It's open daily 'til 2am. 200m (2 blocks) east and 150m (1½ blocks) north of the church in San Pedro. ✆ 2225-4261. www.terrau.com.

The Gay & Lesbian Scene

Because Costa Rica is such a conservative Catholic country, the gay and lesbian communities here are rather discreet. Homosexuality is not generally under attack, but many gay and lesbian organizations guard their privacy, and the club scene is changeable and not well publicized.

The most established and happening gay and lesbian bar and dance club in San José is **La Avispa** ★, Calle 1 between avenidas 8 and 10 (✆ **2223-5343;** www.laavispa.co.cr). It is popular with both men and women, although it sometimes sets aside certain nights for specific persuasions. There's also **Club Oh** ★ (✆ **2221-9341**), on Calle 2 between avenidas 14 and 16; **Pucho's Bar** (✆ **2256-1147**), on Calle 11 and Avenida 8; and **El Bochinche** (✆ **2221-0500;** www.bochinchesanjose.com), on Calle 11 between avenidas 10 and 12. For a more casual and mixed scene, check out **El 13** (see above).

Casinos

Gambling is legal in Costa Rica, with casinos at virtually every major hotel. However, as with Tico bullfighting, some idiosyncrasies are involved in gambling *a la Tica.*

If blackjack is your game, you'll want to play "rummy." The rules are almost identical, except that the house doesn't pay 1½ times on blackjack—instead, it pays double on any three of a kind or three-card straight flush.

If you're looking for roulette, what you'll find here is a bingolike spinning cage of numbered balls. The betting is the same, but some of the glamour is lost.

You'll also find a version of five-card-draw poker, but the rule differences are so complex that I advise you to sit down and watch for a while and then ask questions before joining in. That's about all you'll find. There are no craps tables or baccarat.

There's some controversy over slot machines—one-armed bandits are currently outlawed—but you will be able to play electronic slots and poker games. Most casinos here are casual and small by international standards. You may have to dress up slightly at some of the fancier hotels, but most are accustomed to tropical vacation attire.

SIDE TRIPS FROM SAN JOSÉ

San José makes an excellent base for exploring the beautiful Central Valley. For first-time visitors, the best way to make the most of these excursions is usually to take a guided tour, but if you rent a car, you'll have greater independence. Some day trips also can be done by public bus.

Tip: Virtually every attraction, tour, and activity described in "The Central Valley" chapter makes for an easy day trip out of San José.

Guided Tours & Adventures

A number of companies offer a wide variety of primarily nature-related day tours out of San José. The most reputable include **Costa Rica Expeditions** ★★ (✆ **2257-0766;** www.costaricaexpeditions.com), **Costa Rica Sun Tours** ★ (✆ **2296-7757;** www.crsuntours.com), **Horizontes Tours** ★★ (✆ **2222-2022;** www.horizontes.com), and **Swiss Travel Service** (✆ **2282-4898;** www.swisstravelcr.com). Prices range from around $30 to $60 for a half-day trip, and from $70 to $150 for a full-day trip.

Before signing on for a tour of any sort, find out how many fellow travelers will be accompanying you, how much time will be spent in transit and eating lunch, and how much time will actually be spent doing the primary activity. I've had complaints about tours that were rushed, that spent too much time in a bus or on secondary activities, or that had a cattle-car, assembly-line feel to them. The tours below are arranged by type of activity. In addition to these, you'll find many other tours that combine two or three different activities or destinations.

BUNGEE JUMPING There's nothing unique about bungee jumping in Costa Rica, but the site here is quite beautiful. If you've always had the bug, **Tropical Bungee ★** (© **2248-2212;** www.bungee. co.cr) will let you jump off an 80m (262-ft.) bridge for $65; two jumps cost $95. Transportation is provided free from San José twice daily. Someone should be there from 9am to 3pm every day. They

The Rain Forest Aerial Tram Atlantic.

prefer for you to have a reservation, but if you show up on your own, they'll probably let you jump, unless huge groups are booked ahead of you. These folks also offer paragliding tours.

CANOPY TOURS & AERIAL TRAMS Getting up into the treetops is a big trend in Costa Rican tourism, and scores of such tours are around the country. You have several options relatively close to San José.

Perhaps the most popular canopy-style day trip destination from San José is the **Rain Forest Aerial Tram Atlantic ★** (© **866/759-8726** in the U.S. and Canada, or 2257-5961 in Costa Rica; www.rainforesttram. com), built on a private reserve bordering Braulio Carrillo National Park. This pioneering tramway is the brainchild of rainforest researcher Dr. Donald Perry, whose cable-car system through the forest canopy at Rara Avis helped establish him as an early expert on rainforest canopies. On the 90-minute tram ride through the treetops, visitors have the chance to glimpse the complex web of life that makes these forests unique. Additional attractions include a butterfly garden, serpentarium, and frog collection. They also have their own zip-line canopy tour, and the grounds feature well-groomed trails through the rainforest and a restaurant—with all this on offer, a trip here can easily take up a full day. If you want to spend the night, 10 simple but clean and comfortable bungalows cost $150 per person per day (double occupancy), including three meals, three guided tours, taxes, two tram rides, and unlimited use of the rest of the facilities.

The cost for a full-day tour, including both the aerial tram and canopy tour, all the park's other attractions, and transportation from San José and either breakfast or lunch, is $139. Alternatively, you can drive or take one of the frequent Guápiles buses—they leave every half-hour throughout the day and cost C1,140—from the Caribbean bus terminal (Gran Terminal del Caribe) on Calle Central, 1 block north of Avenida 11. Ask the driver to let you off in front of the *teleférico*. If you're driving, head out on the Guápiles Highway as if driving to the Caribbean coast. Watch for the tram's roadside welcome center—it's hard to miss. For walk-ins, the entrance fee is $116; students and anyone under 18 pay $92. Because this is a popular tour for groups, I highly recommend that you get an advance reservation in the high season and, if possible, a ticket; otherwise you could wait a long time for your tram ride or even be shut out. The tram handles only about 80 passengers per hour, so scheduling is tight; the folks here try to schedule as much as possible in advance.

For a zip-line style tour, the folks at **Original Canopy Tour ★** (*©* **2291-4465;** www.canopytour.com) have their **Mahogany Park** operation, located about 1 hour outside of San José. The tour here features 9 platforms, and at the end you have the choice of taking a cable to a ground station or doing an 18m (60-ft.) rappel down to finish off. The tour takes about 2 hours and costs $45. Package tours with transportation from San José are also available.

DAY CRUISES   Several companies offer cruises to lovely Tortuga Island in the Gulf of Nicoya. These full-day tours generally entail an early departure for the 1½-hour chartered bus ride to Puntarenas, where you board your vessel

A cruise to Tortuga Island.

Rafting on the Pacuare River.

for a 1½-hour cruise to Tortuga Island. Then you get several hours on the uninhabited island, where you can swim, lie on the beach, play volleyball, or try a canopy tour, followed by the return journey.

The original and most dependable company running these trips is **Calypso Tours ★** (② **2256-2727;** www.calypsotours.com). The tour costs $119 per person and includes round-trip transportation from San José, a basic continental breakfast during the bus ride to the boat, all drinks on the cruise, and an excellent buffet lunch on the beach at the island. The Calypso Tours main vessel is a massive motor-powered catamaran. They also run a separate tour to a private nature reserve at **Punta Coral ★**. The beach is much nicer at Tortuga Island, but the tour to Punta Coral is more intimate, and the restaurant, hiking, and kayaking are all superior here. These folks provide daily pickups from San José, Manuel Antonio, Jacó, and Monteverde, and you can use the day trip on the boat as your transfer or transportation option between any of these towns and destinations.

HIKING   Most of the tour agencies listed above offer 1-day guided hikes to a variety of destinations. In general, I recommend taking guided hikes to really see and learn about the local flora and fauna.

RAFTING, KAYAKING & RIVER TRIPS   Cascading down Costa Rica's mountain ranges are dozens of tumultuous rivers, several of which are very popular for white-water rafting and kayaking. If I had to choose just one day trip out of San José, it would be a white-water rafting trip. For between $75 and $120, you can spend a day rafting through lush tropical forests; multiday trips are also available. Some of the most reliable rafting companies are **Costa Rica Nature Adventures ★★** (② **800/321-8410** in the U.S., or 2225-3939; www.toenjoynature.com), **Exploradores Outdoors ★** (② **2222-6262;**

www.exploradoresoutdoors.com), and **Ríos Tropicales ★★ (© 866/ 722-8273** in the U.S. and Canada, or 2233-6455 in Costa Rica; www.rios tropicales.com). These companies all ply a number of rivers of varying difficulties, including the popular Pacuare and Reventazón rivers. For details, see "White-Water Rafting, Kayaking & Canoeing," in chapter 4.

VOLCANO VISITS   The **Poás, Irazú** (see chapter 6 for more details), and **Arenal** volcanoes are three of Costa Rica's most popular destinations, and the first two are easy day trips from San José. Although numerous companies offer day trips to Arenal, I don't recommend them because travel time is at least 3½ hours in each direction. You usually arrive when the volcano is hidden by clouds and leave before the night's darkness shows off its glowing eruptions. For more information on Arenal Volcano, see chapter 9.

6

THE CENTRAL VALLEY

nown locally as La Meseta Central or El Valle Central, the long, thin, doglegging Central Valley is Costa Rica's most densely populated region. In addition to San José, it is home to both Alajuela and Heredia, numerous smaller cities, suburbs and towns, and the country's principal international airport. Most visitors start and end their Costa Rican vacations in the Central Valley.

The hills, mountains, and volcanoes that ring the Central Valley are an agricultural wonderland, planted with a wide range of crops, most prominently coffee. These towns, cities, hillsides, and volcanoes are home to a wide range of compelling attractions, from volcanic national parks and La Paz Waterfall Gardens, to the country's premier natural history museum, INBio Park. And this is a perfect place to tour a working coffee farm. Although technically one valley over, the colonial-era capital city of Cartago is included in this chapter, because of its general geographic location and proximity to San José. With its ornate and locally revered Basilica, earthquake-damaged Central Park ruins, and the lovely, neighboring Orosi Valley, this is an area well worth exploring.

> ### The Central Valley's Top Sustainable Hotels
>
> **Casa Turire** (p. 185)
> **Finca Rosa Blanca** (p. 170)
> **Hotel Bougainvillea** (p. 171)
> **Xandari Resort & Spa** (p. 164)

ESCAZÚ & SANTA ANA

Escazú: 5.5km (3.4 miles) W of San José; Santa Ana: 13km (8 miles) W of San José

Located just west of San José, these affluent suburbs have boomed in recent years, as the metropolitan area continues to grow and expand. Both Escazú and Santa Ana are popular with the Costa Rican professional class, as well as North American retirees and expatriates. Quite a few hotels have sprung up to cater to their needs. Both have large modern malls, endless little strip malls, and important business parks. It's easy to commute between Escazú or Santa Ana and downtown San José via car, bus, or taxi. And the area is about the same distance from the airport as downtown San José.

Essentials

GETTING THERE & DEPARTING   By Car: Head west out of San José along Paseo Colón. Turn left when you hit La Sabana Park, and turn right a few blocks later, at the start of the Próspero Fernández Highway (CR27). You will see well-marked exits for both Escazú and Santa Ana along this highway.

    By Bus: **Escazú-** and **Santa Ana–bound** buses leave from the Coca-Cola bus station, as well as from Avenida 1 between calles 24 and 28. Alternatively, you can pick up both the Escazú and Santa Ana buses from a busy bus stop at the start of the Próspero Fernández Highway (CR27) on the southeast corner of the Parque La Sabana, next to the Gimnasio Nacional. Buses leave roughly every 5 to 10 minutes from 5am until 8pm, and less frequently during off hours. A bus costs between C255 and C300.

By Taxi: Taxi fare should run around $8 to $15, each way between San José and Escazú, and another $10 to $15 or so between Escazú and Santa Ana.

ORIENTATION Both Escazú and Santa Ana are old farming towns that have been swallowed up by metro San José's urban sprawl. Each has a small downtown core built around an old church, with ever expanding rings of residential and commercial development radiating off this core. Both also have numerous little satellite towns, such as San Antonio de Escazú, San Rafael de Escazú, and Pozos de Santa Ana.

FAST FACTS You'll find banks, ATMs, and Internet cafes all over Escazú and Santa Ana, especially in the many malls and shopping centers.

What to See & Do

Escazú and Santa Ana have few traditional tourism attractions, but both offer easy access to the attractions and activities offered up in San José and elsewhere around the Central Valley.

However, if you are in downtown Santa Ana, do take a few minutes to visit the town's main **cathedral,** a lovely old stone church, with thick wooden beams, colorful stained glass windows, and a red-clay tile roof.

And while most folks don't come to Costa Rica to see movies, if you do decide to go, head for the **Nova Cinemas** (✆ **2299-7485;** www.imax.costa. rica.cr) multiplex, with the country's only IMAX theater and several other VIP salas, in the Avenida Escazú shopping complex.

GOLF & TENNIS Some of the best Central Valley facilities for visiting golfers and tennis players can be found at **Parque Valle del Sol ★** (✆ **2282-9222;** www.vallesol.com), in Santa Ana. The 18-hole course here is open to the general public. Greens fees are $94 per golfer per day, including the cart and unlimited playing both on the course and driving range. The tennis courts here cost C3,500 per hour weekdays and C7,000 per hour weekends. Reservations are essential. The golf course at the Cariari Country Club is not open to the general public.

Santa Ana cathedral.

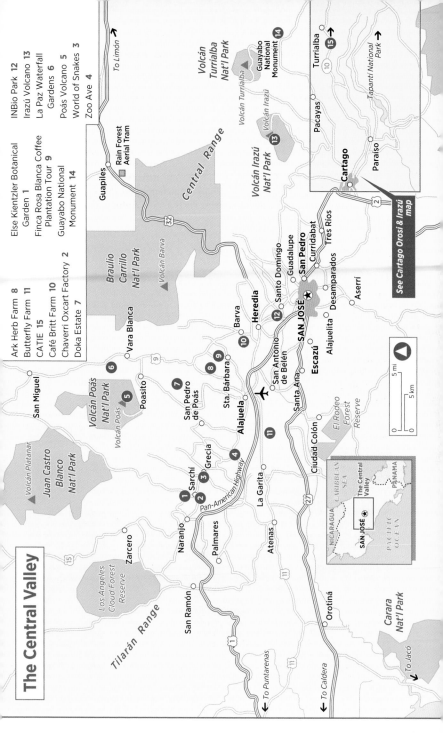

The Central Valley

Ark Herb Farm **8**
Butterfly Farm **11**
CATIE **15**
Café Britt Farm **10**
Chaverri Oxcart Factory **2**
Doka Estate **7**

Else Kientzler Botanical Garden **1**
Finca Rosa Blanca Coffee Plantation Tour **9**
Guayabo National Monument **14**

INBio Park **12**
Irazú Volcano **13**
La Paz Waterfall Gardens **6**
Poás Volcano **5**
World of Snakes **3**
Zoo Ave **4**

See Cartago Orosi & Irazú map

153

Ox Cart Derby

This area's agricultural heritage shines each year on **El Día del Boyero** (Oxcart Drivers' Day), which is celebrated on the second Sunday of March. The small town of San Antonio de Escazú is the center of the celebrations, with a street fair and a large collection of colorfully painted ox-drawn carts parading through the streets.

HORSEBACK RIDING Options are nearly endless in the mountains and along the coasts, but it's more difficult to find a place to saddle up in the Central Valley. **La Caraña Riding Academy** (© 2282-6754; www.lacarana.com) and **Centro Ecuestre Valle Yos Oy** (© 8301-4401) are both in Santa Ana, and offer riding classes as well as some guided trail rides.

Shopping

One of the country's best and largest megamalls, **Multiplaza Escazú,** is located along the Próspero Fernández Highway (CR27), just west of downtown Escazú.

Biesanz Woodworks ★★   Biesanz makes a wide range of high-quality items, including bowls, jewelry boxes, humidors, and some wonderful sets of wooden chopsticks. Biesanz Woodworks is actively involved in local reforestation, too. Bello Horizonte, Escazú. © **2289-4337.** www.biesanz.com. Call for directions and off-hour appointments.

Galería 11–12 ★★★   This outstanding gallery deals mainly in high-end Costa Rican art, from neoclassical painters such as Teodorico Quirós to modern masters such as Francisco Amighetti and Paco Zuñiga, to current stars such as Rafa Fernández, Rodolfo Stanley, Fernando Carballo, and Fabio Herrera. Plaza Itzkatzu, off the Próspero Fernández Hwy., Escazú. © **2288-1975.** www.galeria11–12.com.

Woodwork by Barry Biesanz.

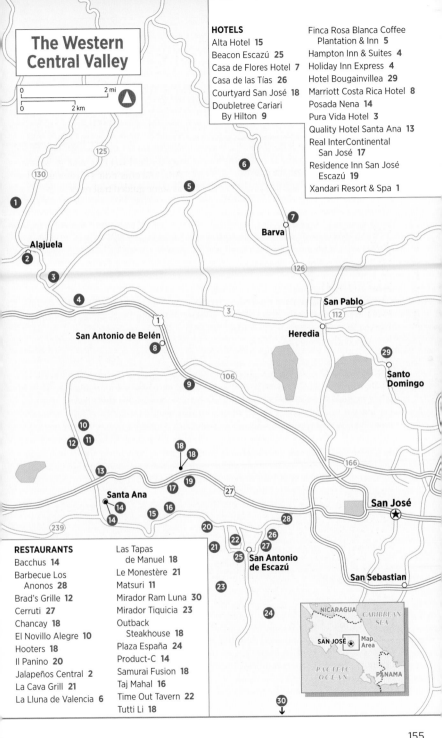

The Western Central Valley

0 — 2 mi
0 — 2 km

HOTELS
Alta Hotel **15**
Beacon Escazú **25**
Casa de Flores Hotel **7**
Casa de las Tías **26**
Courtyard San José **18**
Doubletree Cariari
By Hilton **9**
Finca Rosa Blanca Coffee
Plantation & Inn **5**
Hampton Inn & Suites **4**
Holiday Inn Express **4**
Hotel Bougainvillea **29**
Marriott Costa Rica Hotel **8**
Posada Nena **14**
Pura Vida Hotel **3**
Quality Hotel Santa Ana **13**
Real InterContinental
San José **17**
Residence Inn San José
Escazú **19**
Xandari Resort & Spa **1**

RESTAURANTS
Bacchus **14**
Barbecue Los
Anonos **28**
Brad's Grille **12**
Cerruti **27**
Chancay **18**
El Novillo Alegre **10**
Hooters **18**
Il Panino **20**
Jalapeños Central **2**
La Cava Grill **21**
La Lluna de Valencia **6**
Las Tapas
de Manuel **18**
Le Monestère **21**
Matsuri **11**
Mirador Ram Luna **30**
Mirador Tiquicia **23**
Outback
Steakhouse **18**
Plaza España **24**
Product-C **14**
Samurai Fusion **18**
Taj Mahal **16**
Time Out Tavern **22**
Tutti Li **18**

Alajuela

Barva

San Pablo

Heredia

San Antonio de Belén

Santo
Domingo

Santa Ana

San José

San Antonio
de Escazú

San Sebastian

NICARAGUA
CARIBBEAN
SEA
SAN JOSÉ
Map
Area
PACIFIC
OCEAN
PANAMA

Where to Stay

VERY EXPENSIVE

Real InterContinental San José ★★   This is a contemporary and luxurious large-scale business-class hotel, with three five-story wings. The large, open lobby has a beautiful flagstone-and-mosaic floor. The rooms are all well-appointed, with either a king-size or two double beds, a working desk, a sitting chair and ottoman, and a large armoire. The hotel is just across from a large, modern shopping-mall complex, which is nice if you want access to shopping, restaurants, and a six-plex movie theater. Overall, the InterContinental offers many of the same features and amenities as the Marriott (p. 165), although the latter gets my nod in terms of service, restaurants, and ambience.

Autopista Próspero Fernández, across from the Multiplaza mall, Escazú. www.intercontinental costarica.com. ℂ **2208-2100.** Fax 2208-2101. 372 units. $250–$350 double; $750 and up suite. AE, MC, V. Free parking. **Amenities:** 3 restaurants; 2 bars; lounge; concierge; good-size health club and spa; Jacuzzi; large free-form outdoor pool; room service; smoke-free rooms; outdoor tennis court. *In room:* A/C, TV, hair dryer, minibar, Wi-Fi.

EXPENSIVE

The **Beacon Escazú ★** (www.mybeaconescazu.com; ℂ **866/978-6168** in the U.S. and Canada, or 2228-3110) is a luxurious boutique hotel in downtown Escazú, just a block from the town's central park. The restaurant and wine bar here are both excellent.

Alta Hotel ★★   This boutique hotel is infused with old-world charm. Curves and high arches abound. My favorite touch is the winding interior alleyway that snakes down from the reception through the hotel. Most of the rooms here have great views of the Central Valley from private balconies; the others have pleasant garden patios. The rooms are all up to modern resort standards, although some have slightly cramped bathrooms. The suites are considerably larger, each with a separate sitting room with its own television, as well as large Jacuzzi-style tubs in spacious bathrooms. If you opt to rent the entire upper floor, the penthouse becomes a three-bedroom extravaganza, with a massive living room and open-air rooftop patio. The hotel's La Luz restaurant is one of the more elegant and creative dining spots in the Central Valley.

Alto de las Palomas, old road to Santa Ana. www.thealtahotel.com. ℂ **888/388-2582** in the U.S. and Canada, or 2282-4160. Fax 2282-4162. 23 units. $155 double; $179 junior suite; $230 master suite; $600 penthouse. Rates include continental breakfast. AE, DC, MC, V. Free parking. **Amenities:** Restaurant; bar; concierge; small exercise room; Jacuzzi; midsize outdoor pool; room service; sauna; smoke-free rooms. *In room:* A/C, TV, hair dryer, minibar, Wi-Fi.

MODERATE

In addition to the hotels listed below, the **Courtyard San José** (www.marriott. com; ℂ **888/236-2427** in the U.S. and Canada, or 2208-3000), **Residence Inn San José Escazú** (www.marriott.com; ℂ **888/236-2427** in the U.S. and Canada, or 2588-4300), and **Quality Hotel Santa Ana** (www.choicehotels. com; ℂ **877/424-6423** in the U.S. and Canada, or 2204-6700) are all modern business-class hotels a few miles from each other, right on the Próspero Fernández Highway.

Casa de las Tías 🎁 This old Victorian-style home is comfortable and brimming with local character. The rooms are homey and simply decorated in a sort of Costa Rican country motif. The hotel has a wonderful covered veranda for sitting and admiring the well-tended gardens, as well as a TV room and common areas inside the house. The owners live on-site and are extremely helpful and friendly—you really get the sense of staying in someone's home here. Though it's on a quiet side street, Casa de las Tías is nonetheless just a block away from a busy section of Escazú, where you'll find scores of restaurants and shops, and easy access to public transportation. The hotel is 100m (1 block) south and 150m (1½ blocks) east of El Cruce de San Rafael de Escazú.

San Rafael de Escazú. www.hotels.co.cr/casatias.html. © **2289-5517.** Fax 2289-7353. 5 units. $90 double. Rates include full breakfast. AE, MC, V. *In room:* Wi-Fi.

INEXPENSIVE

Posada Nena Housed in a converted home on a residential side street just a couple of blocks from Santa Ana's central square and church, this hotel offers spacious, comfortable rooms. The decor leans heavily on Southwest American artwork and design touches, combined with Guatemalan textiles and locally made heavy wooden furniture. My favorite rooms are the upstairs units. Rooms nos. 3 and 4 even have skylights in their bathrooms. A midsize outdoor pool, which is good for lap swimming, takes up much of the backyard, but there's also a shady lounge area out back as well. Also known as Casa Alegre, this place is under new ownership, but still a well-run ship.

Santa Ana. www.posadanena.com. © **2203-7467.** Fax 2282-0590. 8 units. $50 double. AE, DC, MC, V. **Amenities:** Outdoor pool. *In room:* TV, Wi-Fi.

Where to Eat

These two suburbs have the most vibrant restaurant scenes in San José. In addition to the places listed below, **Plaza España** ★ (© **2228-1850**) is a romantic little Spanish restaurant in an ancient adobe home in the hills of San Antonio de Escazú, while **Cerruti** ★★ (© **2228-4511**) is a top-notch, high-end Italian restaurant located near El Cruce, in San Rafael de Escazú. I also like **Il Panino** ★ (© **2228-3126;** www.ilpanino.net), an upscale sandwich shop and cafe, located in the Centro Comercial El Paco. **Time Out Tavern** ★ (© **2588-2622**) is a well-done sports bar, with good food, a friendly vibe, and a dozen or so hi-def televisions showing sporting events. You'll find this place on the "Country Club" road, just north of downtown Escazú. Come prepared; they don't accept credit cards. For good Indian fare, try **Taj Mahal** (© **2228-0980;** www. thetajmahalrestaurant.com).

A good one-stop option to consider is the Plaza Itskatzú shopping center, just off the highway and sharing a parking lot with the Courtyard San José. The wide variety of moderately priced restaurant options includes **Tutti Li** (© **2588-2405**), a good Italian restaurant and pizzeria; **Chancay** (© **2588-2327;** www. chancay.info), which serves Peruvian and Peruvian/Chinese cuisine; **Samurai Fusion** (© **2588-2240**), a fine sushi and teppanyaki joint; **Las Tapas de Manuel** ★ (© **2288-5700;** www.lastapasdemanuel.com), a Spanish-style tapas restaurant; and franchise outlets of both **Hooters** (© **2588-2241;** www. hooters.co.cr) and **Outback Steakhouse** (© **2288-0511**).

Over in Santa Ana, the stretch of road heading from the CR27 highway ramp north toward San Antonio de Belén features a steady line of strip malls with tons of excellent restaurants. Some of the top choices here include the sushi spot **Matsuri ★★** (✆ **2203-6868**); the Argentine steakhouse **El Novillo Alegre ★** (Centro Comercial Via Lindora; ✆ **2282-3242**); and the U.S.-style sports bar **Brad's Grille** (Centro Comercial Momentum; ✆ **2582-0724**).

EXPENSIVE

Bacchus ★★  ITALIAN   My favorite Italian restaurant in the San José metropolitan area is housed in a century-old historic home. This place somehow seamlessly blends the old with the new in an elegant atmosphere. The best tables are on the covered back patio, where you can watch the open kitchen and wood-burning pizza oven in action. The regularly changing menu features a range of antipasti, pastas, pizzas, and main dishes. Everything is perfectly prepared and beautifully presented. The desserts are also excellent, and the wine list is extensive and fairly priced.

Downtown Santa Ana. ✆ **2282-5441**. www.bacchus.cr. Reservations required. Main courses C4,000–C14,000. AE, MC, V. Mon–Thurs 5–11pm; Fri–Sat 11am–3pm and 5–11pm; Sun 11am–11pm.

La Cava Grill ★ COSTA RICAN/STEAK   This place is a cozy and warm spot underneath the popular yet overrated Le Monestère restaurant. While the decor is much less ornate, the service much less formal, and the menu much less French, the view is just as spectacular. Grab a window seat on a clear night and enjoy the sparkle of the lights below. The menu features a range of simply prepared meat, poultry, and fish. More adventurous diners can try the *tepezquintle* (a large rodent, also called a *paca*), which is actually quite tasty. The attached bar has live music and a festive party most weekend nights. My big complaint here is that the wine list is borrowed from the upstairs restaurant, and is pretentious and overpriced.

A *mirador* outside San José.

DINING UNDER THE stars

One of my favorite unique Costa Rica experiences is dining on the side of a volcano with the lights of San José shimmering below. These hanging restaurants, called *miradores,* are a resourceful response to the city's topography. Because San José is set in a broad valley surrounded on all sides by volcanic mountains, people who live in these mountainous areas have no place to go but up—so they do, building roadside cafes vertically up the sides of the volcanoes.

The food at most of these establishments is not spectacular, but the views often are, particularly at night, when the wide valley sparkles in a wash of lights. The town of **Aserri,** 10km (6¼ miles) south of downtown San José, is the king of *miradores,* and **Mirador Ram Luna** (*©* **2230-3060**) is the king of Aserri. Grab a window seat and, if you've got the fortitude, order a plate of *chicharrones* (fried pork rinds). There's often live music. You can hire a cab for around $12 or take the Aserri bus at Avenida 6 between calles Central and 2. Just ask the driver where to get off.

Miradores are also in the hills above Escazú and in San Ramón de Tres Ríos and Heredia. The most popular is

Le Monestère (*©* **2228-8515;** www. monastere-restaurant.com; closed Sun), an elegant converted church serving somewhat overrated French and Belgian cuisine in a spectacular setting above the hills of Escazú. I recommend coming here just for the less formal **La Cava Grill ★** (p. 158), which often features live music, mostly folk-pop but sometimes jazz. I also like **Mirador Tiquicia ★** (*©* **2289-5839;** www.miradortiquicia.com), which occupies several rooms in a sprawling old Costa Rican home and has live folkloric dance shows on Thursday. This latter place offers a free shuttle Tuesday through Friday, which you can reserve, at least 1 day in advance, at *©* **8381-3141** or tiquicia.shuttle.service@gmail.com.

1.5km (1 mile) south of Centro Comercial Paco; follow the signs to Le Monestère. *©* **2228-8515.** Reservations recommended. Main courses C7,000–C40,000. AE, MC, V. Mon–Sat 6:30pm–1:30am.

MODERATE

Barbecue Los Anonos COSTA RICAN/STEAK   Good steaks and well-prepared Costa Rican cuisine have made this homey restaurant something of an institution. Most of the seating is at rustic wooden tables covered with red-and-white checkered tablecloths, and long booths set under the shelter of low interior red-tile roofs. Aged Angus beef is served, and this is *the* place to come if you're craving a 16-ounce T-bone on the west side of town. There are also a host of chicken, pork, and fish options; I recommend the mixed-grill plate for two, which comes with a little bit of everything.

600m (6 blocks) west of the Los Anonos bridge in San Rafael de Escazú, next to the Sarretto Market. *©* **2228-0180.** Reservations recommended. Main courses C6,900–C19,000. AE, MC, V. Tues–Sat noon–3pm; Tues–Thurs 6–10pm; Fri–Sat 6–11pm; Sun 11:30am–9pm.

Product-C ★★★ SEAFOOD   Founded by the former head chef at Nectar (p. 278), this place has morphed from a simple fish and seafood outlet, into a fabulous little restaurant. A daily white-board menu features a half-dozen or so creative preparations of the freshest daily catch. These folks have also set up their own oyster farms and serve the only fresh, local oysters I've found in Costa Rica. They even have outposts in Malpaís, and over in the Avenida Escazú complex along the Próspero Fernández Highway.

Santa Ana, just north of the Red Cross (Cruz Roja). ℂ **2282-7767.** www.product-c. com. Reservations recommended. Main courses C4,500–C14,000. AE, MC, V. Tues–Sat 10:30am–10pm; Sun 10:30am–4pm.

Escazú & Santa Ana After Dark

Escazú has a host of popular bars and clubs. These are especially popular with the Central Valley's well-heeled urban youth. In addition to the place listed below, **Henry's Beach Club ★** (ℂ **2289-6250;** on the Guachipelin road in Escazú) has an upbeat casual vibe; **Mi Sala**

Musicians at Jazz Café Escazú.

(Centro Comercial Paco; ℂ **2289-4389;** www.mi-sala.com) is a chic lounge frequented by the city's hoity-toit; and the **Jazz Café Escazú ★★** (Próspero Fernández Hwy.; ℂ **2288-4740**) is a top spot for live music.

Gaira ★★ This massive club is chic and contemporary, with a large open dance space, two floors of seating, impressive lighting and design effects, and a creative drink and food menu. Next to the Ferreteria EPA, Escazú. ℂ **2288-1530.** Wed–Sat 6pm–2am. www.clubgaira.com.

ALAJUELA, POÁS ★★ & THE AIRPORT AREA

Airport: 15km (9.3 miles) NW of San José; Alajuela: 18.5km (11.5 miles) NW of San José; Poás Volcano: 37km (23 miles) northwest of San José

Most folks visiting Costa Rica land at the Juan Santamaría International Airport in Alajuela. The downtown area of Costa Rica's second largest city is just a mile or so north of the airport. The city itself is of little interest to most tourists, although it is the gateway to the Poás Volcano, and several other of the Central Valley's top attractions.

Essentials

GETTING THERE & DEPARTING   By Car: Head northwest out of San José on the Interamerican Highway (CR1).

By Bus: There are two separate lines: **Tuasa** (*𝒞* **2442-6900**) buses are red; **Station Wagon** (*𝒞* **8388-9263**) buses are beige/yellow) making the run between San José and Alajuela. Buses leave roughly every 10 minutes between 5am and 11pm, and less frequently in off hours. The fare is C450.

By Train: A commuter train runs between downtown San José and Heredia. This train runs roughly every 15 minutes between 5:30 and 8:30am, and again between 4:30 and 7:30pm, with much less frequent service during non-commuter hours. Fares range from C200 to C400, depending on the length of your ride.

ORIENTATION   Downtown Alajuela is a tight jumble of one-way streets, often choked to a standstill with gridlock traffic. Most folks will be heading up into the hills from downtown. The best way to find the route out of town is usually to follow signs for the Poás Volcano, or some other well-known attraction.

FAST FACTS   You'll find banks, ATMs, and Internet cafes all over Alajuela, especially in the central downtown area, and nearby malls and shopping centers. The **Hospital San Rafael de Alajuela** (*𝒞* **2436-1001**) is large, modern, and well-equipped. If you need a taxi, call **COOTAXA** (*𝒞* **2443-3030**) or **Taxi Radio Liga** (*𝒞* **2441-1212**).

What to See & Do

Alajuela's main church, the **Catedral de Alajuela** (Alajuela Cathedral; *𝒞* **2441-4665**) is a large, relatively ornate Catholic church, with a striking white-washed exterior, beautiful ceiling frescos, and a gold-leaf painted interior dome. The cathedral, which fronts the city's central park, received a major renovation in 2010. Mass is held Monday to Friday at 9am and 5pm; Saturday at 9am and 7pm, and Sunday at 9 and 11am, and 5 and 7pm.

Catedral de Alajuela.

The **Museo Historico Cultural Juan Santamaría,** Avenida 3 between calles Central and 2 (② **2441-4775;** www.museojuansantamaria.go.cr), isn't worth a trip of its own, but you may want to stop here before or after a trip to another nearby attraction. The museum commemorates Costa Rica's national hero, Juan Santamaría, who gave his life defending the country against a small army led by William Walker, a U.S. citizen who invaded Costa Rica in 1856, attempting to set up a slave state. The museum is open Tuesday through Saturday from 10am to 6pm; admission is free.

NEARBY ATTRACTIONS

Butterfly Farm ★ At any given time, you might see around 30 of the 80 species of butterflies raised at this butterfly farm south of Alajuela. The butterflies live in a large enclosed garden similar to an aviary and flutter about the heads of visitors during tours of the gardens. You should be certain to spot glittering blue morphos and a large butterfly that mimics the eyes of an owl. Admission includes a 2-hour guided tour. In the demonstration room, you'll see butterfly eggs, caterpillars, and pupae. There are cocoons trimmed in a shimmering gold color and cocoons that mimic a snake's head to frighten away predators. The last guided tour of the day begins at 3pm.

If you reserve in advance, the Butterfly Farm has three daily bus tours that run from many major San José hotels. The cost, including round-trip transportation and admission to the garden, is $40 for adults, $35 for students, and $25 for children 5 to 12. Buses pick up passengers at more than 20 different hotels in the San José area.

In front of Los Reyes Country Club, La Guácima de Alajuela. ② **2438-0400.** www.butterflyfarm.co.cr. Admission $19 adults, $15 students, $13 children 4–12, free for children 3 and under. Daily 8:45am–5pm.

Doka Estate This large and long-standing coffee estate in Alajuela offers up a tour that takes you from "seed to cup." Along the way, you'll get a full rundown of the processes involved in the growing, harvesting, curing, packing, and brewing of their award-winning coffee. Allow about 2½ hours.

Sabanilla de Alajuela. ② **2449-5152.** www.dokaestate.com. Admission $18 adults, $12 students with valid ID, $10 children 6–11; children 5 and under free. Packages including transportation and breakfast or lunch available. Daily 9, 10, and 11am; 1:30 and 2:30pm. Reservations required.

La Paz Waterfall Gardens ★★ ☺
The original attraction here consists of a series of trails through primary

La Paz Waterfall Gardens.

Poás Volcano.

and secondary forests alongside La Paz River, with lookouts over a series of powerful falls, including the namesake La Paz Fall. In addition to an orchid garden and a hummingbird garden, you must visit their huge butterfly garden, which is easily the largest in Costa Rica. A small serpentarium, featuring a mix of venomous and nonvenomous native snakes, several terrariums containing various frogs and lizards, and a section of wild cats and local monkey species in large enclosures are added attractions. While the admission fee is a little steep, everything is wonderfully done and the trails and waterfalls are beautiful. A buffet lunch at the large cafeteria-style restaurant costs an extra $12 for adults, or $6 for kids. This is a good stop after a morning visit to the Poás Volcano. Plan to spend 2 to 4 hours here. The hotel rooms (Peace Lodge; p. 164) are some of the nicest in the country.

6km (3¾ miles) north of Varablanca on the road to San Miguel. © **2482-2100.** www.waterfall gardens.com. Admission $35 adults, $22 children ages 3–12; children 2 and under free admission. Daily 8am–5pm. There is no bus service here, so you will need to come in a rental car or taxi, or arrange transport with the gardens.

Poás Volcano ★★ From San José, narrow roads wind through a landscape of fertile farms and dark forests to this active volcano. A paved road leads right to the top, although you'll have to hike in about 1km (½ mile) to reach the crater. The volcano stands 2,640m (8,659 ft.) tall and is located within a national park, which preserves not only the volcano but also dense stands of virgin forest. Poás's crater, said to be the second largest in the world, is more than a mile across. Geysers in the crater sometimes spew steam and muddy water 180m (590 ft.) into the air, making this the largest geyser in the world.

 DIY: Poás Volcano

If you don't have a rental car and don't want to sign on for an organized tour, a daily bus (© **2442-6900** or 2222-5325) from Avenida 2 between calles 12 and 14 leaves for the volcano at 8:30am and returns at 2pm. The fare is around C3,000 round-trip. The bus is often crowded, so arrive early. If you're driving, head for Alajuela and continue on the main road through town and follow signs for Fraijanes. Just beyond Fraijanes you will connect with the road between San Pedro de Poás and Poasito; turn right toward Poasito and continue to the rim of the volcano.

The information center shows a slideshow about the volcano, and well-groomed and marked hiking trails through the cloud forest ring the crater. About 15 minutes from the parking area, along a forest trail, is an overlook onto beautiful Botos Lake, which has formed in one of the volcano's extinct craters.

Be prepared when you come to Poás: This volcano is often enveloped in dense clouds. If you want to see the crater, it's best to come early and during the dry season. Moreover, it can get cool up here, especially when the sun isn't shining, so dress appropriately.

Poás de Alajuela. 37km (23 miles) from San José. ℂ **2482-2165.** Admission $10. Daily 8:30am–3:30pm.

Zoo Ave. ★   Dozens of scarlet macaws, reclusive owls, majestic raptors, several different species of toucans, and a host of brilliantly colored birds from Costa Rica and around the world make this one exciting place to visit. In total, over 115 species of birds are on display, including some 80 native species. Bird-watching enthusiasts will be able to get a closer look at birds they might have seen in the wild. Other species on view include iguana, deer, tapir, ocelot, puma, and monkeys—and look out for the 3.6m (12-ft.) crocodile. Zoo Ave. houses only injured, donated, or confiscated animals. It takes about 2 hours to walk the paths and visit all the exhibits.

La Garita, Alajuela. ℂ **2433-8989.** Admission $15, $13 students with valid ID. Daily 9am–5pm. Catch a bus to Alajuela on Av. 2 btw. calles 12 and 14. In Alajuela, transfer to a bus to Atenas and get off at Zoo Ave. before you get to La Garita. Fare is 60¢.

Where to Stay in & around Alajuela

Of the following hotels, the Doubletree Cariari By Hilton, Hampton Inn & Suites, Holiday Inn Express, Marriott Costa Rica Hotel, and Pura Vida Hotel are the closest to the airport.

VERY EXPENSIVE

Peace Lodge ★★ 🎁   Part of the popular La Paz Waterfall Gardens, the rooms here some of the most impressive in the country. All are quite large and feature sparkling wood floors, handcrafted four-poster beds, stone fireplaces, intricately sculpted steel light fixtures, and a host of other creative details—along with a private balcony fitted with a mosaic-tiled Jacuzzi. The deluxe bathrooms come with a second oversize Jacuzzi set under a skylight in the middle of an immense room that features a full interior wall planted with ferns, orchids, and bromeliads and fed by a functioning waterfall system. Guests here have full access to all the tours and attractions of La Paz Waterfall Gardens (p. 162) during normal operating hours and beyond.

6km (3¾ miles) north of Varablanca on the road to San Miguel. www.waterfallgardens.com. ℂ **954/727-3997** in the U.S., or 2482-2720 or 2482-2100 in Costa Rica. 17 units. $295–$465 double; $415 villa. Rates include entrance to La Paz Waterfall Gardens. AE, MC, V. **Amenities:** Restaurant; bar; Jacuzzi; 2 outdoor pools. *In room:* TV, minibar, Wi-Fi.

Xandari Resort & Spa ★★   Set on a hilltop just above the city of Alajuela, Xandari commands wonderful views of the surrounding coffee farms and the Central Valley below. The owners are artists, and their original works and innovative design touches abound. The villas are huge private affairs with high-curved ceilings, stained-glass windows, living rooms with rattan sofas and chairs, as well as small kitchenettes. All come with both an outdoor patio with a view and a private covered palapa, as well as a smaller interior terrace with chaise lounges. The adjacent "spa village" features a series of private thatch-roofed treatment rooms; a wide range of fitness classes is offered, too. The hotel grounds contain several miles of trails that pass by jungle waterfalls, lush gardens, and fruit orchards. Some of the land has been set aside as a permanent nature reserve, and they are reforesting other areas that were formerly dedicated to agriculture.

Alajuela. www.xandari.com. © **866/363-3212** in the U.S., or 2443-2020. Fax 2442-4847. 23 villas. $255–$510 villa for 2. Rates include continental breakfast. $25 for extra person; children 3 and under stay free in parent's room. AE, MC, V. **Amenities:** Restaurant; bar; lounge; several Jacuzzis; 2 lap pools; full-service spa. *In room:* Minibar.

EXPENSIVE

Doubletree Cariari By Hilton ★★ ☺   With its stone walls, open-air lobby, and lush garden plantings, the Cariari has a warm tropical feel. The rooms, which are done in subdued tones, have either one king-size bed or two double beds, although I find most of the bathrooms a bit small. The suites are similarly appointed, but are more spacious and have larger bathrooms. Families can take advantage of the dependable babysitting, children's menus, and easy access to the modern mall nearby.

Autopista General Cañas, Ciudad Cariari, San José. www.cariarisanjose.doubletree.com. © **800/ 222-8733** in the U.S. and Canada, or 2239-0022. Fax 2239-0285. 222 units. $119–$199 double; $169–$279 suite; $300–$500 presidential suite. AE, DC, MC, V. Free parking. **Amenities:** 2 restaurants; 2 bars; lounge; casino; babysitting; concierge; small exercise room; large outdoor pool w/ swim-up bar; room service; smoke-free rooms. *In room:* A/C, TV, hair dryer, minibar, Wi-Fi.

Hampton Inn & Suites   If familiarity, comfort, and proximity to the airport are important to you, then the Hampton Inn is a good bet. The rooms are what you'd expect from a well-known chain. The hotel has both standard rooms and suites. Breakfast is served, but no other dining options are on-site; a Denny's and a separate Costa Rican fast-food chicken joint are just across the parking lot, as is a large swank casino, with a popular bar. This is a good choice if your plane arrives very late or leaves very early and you don't plan to spend any time in San José. Free local calls, high-speed Internet access in all rooms, and Wi-Fi in public areas are perks that will appeal to business travelers and vacationers alike.

Autopista General Cañas, by the airport, San José. www.hamptoninncostarica.com. © **800/426- 7866** in the U.S., or 2436-0000. Fax 2442-2781. 100 units. $147–$189 double; $172–$202 suite. Rates include buffet breakfast and airport shuttle. AE, DC, MC, V. Free parking. **Amenities:** Free airport transfers; babysitting; small exercise room; small outdoor pool; smoke-free rooms. *In room:* A/C, TV, minifridge (in suites), hair dryer, Wi-Fi.

Marriott Costa Rica Hotel ★★★   For my money, the Marriott remains the best large luxury resort hotel in the San José metropolitan area. The hotel is designed in a mixed colonial style, with hand-painted Mexican tiles, antique red-clay roof tiles, and heavy wooden doors, lintels, and trim. The centerpiece is a large interior patio that somewhat replicates Old Havana's Plaza de Armas. All rooms are plush and well-appointed, with either a king-size or two double beds,

Marriott Costa Rica Hotel.

a working desk, plenty of closet space, and a small "Juliet" balcony. The bathrooms are up to par but seem slightly small for this price. The casual Antigua restaurant serves well-prepared Costa Rican and international dishes, and there's a more upscale Spanish restaurant and tapas bar. The large lobby-level bar features daily piano music and weekend jazz nights, with both indoor and patio seating.

San Antonio de Belén. www.marriott.com. ℂ **888/236-2427** in the U.S. and Canada, or 2298-0844 in Costa Rica. Fax 2298-0011. 290 units. $189–$221 double; $244–$267 executive level; $450 master suite; $750 presidential suite. AE, DC, MC, V. Valet parking. **Amenities:** 3 restaurants; bar; lounge; airport transfers; babysitting; concierge; golf driving range; small but well-appointed health club; Jacuzzi; 2 outdoor pools; room service; sauna; 2 tennis courts; smoke-free rooms. *In room:* A/C, TV, hair dryer, minibar, Wi-Fi.

Vista del Valle Plantation Inn ★★ 🎁 Individual and duplex villas are spread around the grounds here, which command an impressive view over the Río Grande and its steep-walled canyon. The architecture has a strong Japanese influence, from the open and airy villas to the comfortable wraparound decks. My favorite rooms are the Mona Lisa and Ilan-Ilan suites, set on the edge of the bluff with great views and private outdoor showers. The grounds are wonderfully landscaped, with several inviting seating areas among a wealth of flowering tropical plants. The restaurant has stunning views and features a regularly changing menu of fine international cuisine prepared with local ingredients. The hotel is 20 minutes north of the Juan Santamaría International Airport, and staying here can cut as much as an hour off your travel time if you're heading to the Pacific coast beaches, Arenal Volcano, and the Monteverde Cloud Forest.

Rosario de Naranjo, Alajuela. www.vistadelvalle.com. ☎ **2450-0800.** ☎/fax 2451-1165. 10 units. $160–$175 double. Rates include full breakfast. AE, MC, V. **Amenities:** Restaurant; Jacuzzi; mid-size outdoor tile pool w/interesting fountain/waterfall; room service; Wi-Fi. *In room:* Kitchenette (in some), minibar.

MODERATE

Pura Vida Hotel (www.puravidahotel.com; ☎ **2441-1157**) is a popular Alajuela inn that's also convenient to the airport. Finally, the **Holiday Inn Express** (www.hiexpress.com; ☎ **2443-0043**) is another good U.S.-chain hotel located right beside the Hampton Inn, just across from the airport.

Where to Eat

In addition to the restaurant reviewed below, the restaurants at **Xandari Resort & Spa, Marriott Costa Rica Hotel,** and **Vista del Valle Plantation Inn** are all excellent.

Jalapeños Central ★ MEXICAN/TEX MEX   This cozy and homey downtown spot serves well-prepared burritos, enchiladas, chalupas, nachos, and other typical Mexican and Tex-Mex specialties. You can also get burgers, fries, and onion rings. Daily lunch specials are an excellent bargain. Vegetarians will also find a few good choices on the menu here.

½ block south of the Post Office, downtown Alajuela. ☎ **2430-4027.** MC, V. Main courses C3,000–C10,000. Mon–Sat 11:30am–9pm.

HEREDIA

8.8km (5.5 miles) north of San José

Set on the flanks of the impressive Barva Volcano, this city was founded in 1706. Heredia is affectionately known as "The City of Flowers." Of all the cities in the Central Valley, Heredia has the most colonial feel to it—you'll still see adobe buildings with Spanish tile roofs along narrow streets. Heredia is also the site of the **National University,** and you'll find some nice coffee shops and bookstores near the school.

Surrounding Heredia is an intricate maze of picturesque villages and towns, including Santa Bárbara, Santo Domingo, Barva, and San Joaquín de Flores. The hills and fields surrounding these towns contain some of the best and most fertile coffee plantations in Costa Rica.

Essentials

GETTING THERE & DEPARTING   **By Car:** The road to Heredia turns north off the Interamerican Highway (CR1) between San José and the airport.

By Bus: Buses (☎ **2233-8392**) leave for Heredia every 5 minutes between 5am and 11pm from Calle 1 between avenidas 7 and 9, or from Avenida 2 between calles 12 and 14. Bus fare is C310.

ORIENTATION   Coming from San José, the most common route passes first through Santo Domingo de Heredia, although another popular route leads into downtown Heredia from San Joaquín de los Flores. The **Universidad Nacional Autonoma** (National Autonomous University) sits on the eastern edge of the city.

What to See & Do

The colonial **Catedral de la Inmaculada Concepción** ★ (Church of the Immaculate Conception; ✆ **2237-0779**), inaugurated in 1763, stands guard over Heredia's central park—the stone facade leaves no questions as to the age of the church. The altar inside is decorated with neon stars and a crescent moon surrounding a statue of the Virgin Mary.

In the middle of the palm-shaded central park is a large gazebo, known as **El Templo de la Musica** (The Music Temple). Live music is frequently performed here. Across the street, beside several red tile-roofed municipal buildings, is **El Fortin,** the tower of an old Spanish fort.

Anyone with an interest in medicinal herbs should plan a visit to the **Ark Herb Farm** ★ (✆ **8922-7599** or 2269-4847; www.arkherbfarm.com). These folks offer guided tours of their gardens, which feature more than 300 types of medicinal plants. The tour costs $12 per person, and includes a light snack and refreshments. Reservations are required. While on the road to Barva, you'll find the small **Museo de Cultura Popular** (✆ **2260-1619;** www.museo.una. ac.cr), which is open Monday through Friday from 8am to 4pm and Sunday from 10am to 5pm; admission is C1,000.

TOP ATTRACTIONS

Café Britt Farm ★ Although bananas are the main export of Costa Rica, most people are far more interested in the country's second-most-important export crop: coffee. Café Britt is one of the leading brands here, and the company has put together an interesting tour and stage production at its farm, which is 20 minutes outside of San José. Here, you'll see how coffee is grown. You'll also visit the roasting and processing plant to learn how a coffee "cherry" is turned into a delicious roasted bean. Tasting sessions are offered for visitors to experience the different qualities of coffee. There are also a restaurant and a store where you can buy coffee and coffee-related gift items. The entire tour, including transportation, takes about 3 to 4 hours. Allow some extra time and an additional $10 for a visit to their nearby working plantation and mill. You can even strap on a basket and go out coffee picking during harvest time.

A coffee tree at Café Britt.

INBio Park.

North of Heredia on the road to Barva. (②) **2277-1600.** www.coffeetour.com. Admission $20 adults, $16 children 6–11; $37 adults and $33 children, including transportation from downtown San José and a coffee drink. Add $15 for a full buffet lunch. Tour daily at 11am (an additional tour at 3pm during high season). Store and restaurant daily 8am–5pm year-round.

Finca Rosa Blanca Coffee Plantation Tour ★★   This gorgeous boutique hotel (p. 170) in Heredia also has its own organic coffee plantation, with some 16 hectares (40 acres) of shade-grown Arabica under cultivation. The hotel offers up daily coffee tours led by a very knowledgeable guide. I recommend combining the coffee tour with lunch at the open-air restaurant here; sitting under the shady gazebos, you'll enjoy a wonderful view of the Central Valley along with some fine healthy dining. The good in-house spa offers several treatments featuring home-made, coffee-based products.

Santa Bárbara de Heredia. (②) **2269-9392.** www.fincarosablanca.com. Admission $25 adults; children 11 and under free. Reservations required.

INBio Park ★★ ☺   Run by the National Biodiversity Institute (Instituto Nacional de Biodiversidad, or INBio), this place is part museum, part educational center, and part nature park. In addition to watching a 15-minute informational video, visitors can tour two large pavilions explaining Costa Rica's biodiversity and natural wonders, and hike on trails that re-create the ecosystems of a tropical rainforest, dry forest, and premontane forest. A 2-hour guided hike is included in the entrance fee, and self-guided-tour booklets are also available. There's a good-size butterfly garden, as well as a Plexiglas viewing window into the small lagoon. One of my favorite attractions is the series of wonderful animal sculptures donated by one of Costa Rica's premiere artists, José Sancho. A simple cafeteria-style restaurant is here for lunch, as well as a coffee shop and gift shop. You can easily spend 2 to 3 hours here.

Finca Rosa Blanca Coffee Plantation & Inn.

400m (4 blocks) north and 250m (2½ blocks) west of the Shell station in Santo Domingo de Heredia. ✆ **2507-8107.** www.inbio.ac.cr. Admission $23 adults, $13 children 12 and under. Tues-Fri 8:30am–5pm (admission closes at 3pm), Sat–Sun 9am–5pm. INBio Park offers packages that include transportation, entrance, and lunch for $44.

Where to Stay

While I don't recommend any hotels right in the city center, the small towns and agricultural villages surrounding Heredia are home to one of the country's finest boutique inns. In addition to the places listed below, you might want to check out the lovely little B&B the **Casa de Flores Hotel and Villa** (www.casadeflores hotel.com; ✆ **2560-4982**), high in the hills above Heredia, near the Barva Volcano.

VERY EXPENSIVE

Finca Rosa Blanca Coffee Plantation & Inn ★★★ 🎁 Finca Rosa Blanca is an eclectic architectural gem set amid the lush, green hillsides of a coffee plantation. A turret tops the main building, and walls of glass, arched windows, and curves instead of corners are at almost every turn. Throughout, the glow of polished hardwood blends with white stucco walls and brightly painted murals. If breathtaking bathrooms are your idea of luxury, consider splurging on the Rosa Blanca suite, which has a stone waterfall that cascades into a tub in front of a huge picture window, and a spiral staircase that leads to the top of the turret. All of the suites and villas have the same sense of eclectic luxury, with beautiful tile work, fabulous views, and creative design touches. The restaurant and spa here are top-notch, and the owners have a real and noticeable dedication to sustainable practices. The hotel has 14 hectares (35 acres) of organic coffee under cultivation, and their in-house coffee tour is not to be missed.

Santa Bárbara de Heredia. www.fincarosablanca.com. © **2269-9392.** Fax 2269-9555. 13 units. $295–$520 double. Rates include breakfast. AE, MC, V. Free parking. **Amenities:** Restaurant; bar; lounge; babysitting; concierge; small free-form pool set in the hillside; room service; full-service spa; all rooms smoke-free. *In room:* Minibar, Wi-Fi.

EXPENSIVE

Hotel Bougainvillea ★   The Hotel Bougainvillea is an excellent choice—a great value if you're looking for a hotel in a quiet residential neighborhood not far from downtown. It offers most of the amenities of the more expensive resort hotels around the Central Valley, but it charges considerably less. Rooms are carpeted and have small triangular balconies oriented to the wonderful views across the valley. The hillside property's gardens are beautifully designed and well tended, with pretty-good bird-watching. The hotel has an extensive recycling program and is working hard to implement sustainable tourism practices.

In Santo Tomás de Santo Domingo de Heredia, 100m (1 block) west of the Escuela de Santo Tomás, San José. www.hb.co.cr. © **2244-1414.** Fax 2244-1313. 82 units. $133 double; $147–$166 suite. AE, DC, MC, V. Free parking. **Amenities:** Restaurant; bar; babysitting; gym; midsize pool in attractive garden; room service; sauna; smoke-free rooms; 2 lighted tennis courts. *In room:* TV, hair dryer, Wi-Fi.

Where to Eat

The restaurant at Finca Rosa Blanca (see above) is superb. It's also worth making the winding drive to San Pedro de Barva de Heredia, to stop in at **La Lluna de Valencia** ★★ (© **2269-6665;** www.lallunadevalencia.com), a delightful rustic Spanish restaurant with amazing paella, delicious sangria, and a very colorful and amiable host.

Heredia After Dark

Home to the National Autonomous University, the center of Heredia is chock-full of bars and clubs frequented by college kids. Of these, **Bulevar** (© **2237-1832**), **Fresas** (© **2262-5555**), and **La Choza** (© **2237-1553**), all right near each other on Avenida Central, are the best. Down along the Interamerican Highway, in San Joaquín de los Flores, **Club 212** (© **2265-1079**) is a massive dance club with regular contemporary DJs, heavy beats, and occasional live acts.

GRECIA, SARCHÍ & ZARCERO

All of these towns are northwest of San José and can be combined into a long day trip (if you have a car), perhaps in conjunction with a visit to Poás Volcano and/or the Waterfall Gardens. The scenery here is rich and verdant, and the small towns and scattered farming communities are truly representative of Costa Rica's agricultural heartland and *campesino* tradition. This is a great area to explore on your own in a rental car, if you don't mind getting lost a bit (roads are narrow, winding, and poorly marked). If you're relying on buses, you'll be able to visit any of the towns listed below, but probably just one or two per day.

If you're heading out to this area and want some adventure mixed in, you might consider taking a leap with the folks at **Tropical Bungee** (p. 89), which is just off the Interamerican Highway, a little bit beyond the Grecia exit.

Grecia

9km (12 miles) NW of Alajuela; 37 km (23 miles) NW of San José

The picturesque little town of Grecia is noteworthy for its unusual **metal church,** which is painted a deep red with white gingerbread trim, and is just off the town's central park. About 1km (½ mile) outside of Grecia, on the old road to Alajuela, you will find the **World of Snakes** (✆ **2494-3700;** www.theworldof snakes.com). Open daily from 8am to 4pm, this serpentarium has more than 150 snakes representing more than 45 species. Admission, which includes a guided tour, is $11 for adults, and $6 for children 7 to 14.

GETTING THERE: By Car: Grecia is located just off the Interamerican Highway (CR1), on the way from San José to Puntarenas.

By Bus: Tuan (✆ **2258-2004**) buses leave San José every half-hour for Grecia from Calle 18 between avenidas 3 and 5 (on the east side of the Abonos Agros building). The fare is C610.

Sarchí ★

7km (4 miles) NW of Grecia; 44km (27 miles) NW of San José

Sarchí is Costa Rica's main artisan town. The colorfully painted miniature **oxcarts** that you see all over the country are made here. Oxcarts such as these were once used to haul coffee beans to market. Today, although you might occasionally see oxcarts in use, most are purely decorative. However, they remain a well-known symbol of Costa Rica. In addition to miniature oxcarts, many carved

Grecia's church.

An oxcart factory in Sarchí.

wooden souvenirs are made here with rare hardwoods from the nation's forests. The town has dozens of shops, and all have similar prices. Perhaps your best one-stop shop in Sarchí is the large and long-standing **Chaverri Oxcart Factory ★** (© **2454-4411;** www.sarchicostarica.net), which is right in the center of things, but it never hurts to shop around and visit several of the stores.

Built between 1950 and 1958, the town's main **church ★** is painted pink with aquamarine trim and looks strangely like a child's birthday cake. It's definitely worth a quick visit.

While Sarchí itself has no noteworthy accommodations, the plush **El Silencio Lodge & Spa** (p. 316) is about a 35-minute drive away in a beautiful mountain setting.

Close-up of an oxcart.

GETTING THERE   By Car: If you're going to Sarchí from San José, take the Interamerican Highway (CR1) north, and take the exit for Grecia. From Grecia, the road to Sarchí heads off to the left as you face the main church, but due to all the one-way streets, you'll have to drive around the church. Rural roads connect Sarchí to Naranjo, San Ramón and Zarcero.

By Bus: Tuan (☏ **2258-2004**) buses leave San José about three times throughout the day for Sarchí from Calle 18 between avenidas 3 and 5. The fare is C895. Alternatively, you can take any Grecia bus from this same station. In Grecia, they connect with the Alajuela-Sarchí buses, leaving every 30 minutes from Calle 8 between avenidas Central and 1 in Alajuela.

Else Kientzler Botanical Garden
★★ ☺ Located on the grounds of an ornamental flower farm, on the outskirts of the tourist town Sarchí, these are extensive, impressive, and lovingly laid out botanical gardens. Over 2.5km (1.5 miles) of trails run through a collection of more than 2,000 species of flora. All of the plants are labeled with their Latin names, with some further explanations around the grounds in both English and Spanish. There's a topiary labyrinth, as well as a variety of lookouts, gazebos, and shady benches on the grounds. A children's play area features some water games, jungle gym setups, and a child-friendly little zip-line canopy tour. Over 40% of the gardens are wheelchair accessible.

Else Kientzler Botanical Garden.

Sarchí, Alajuela. ☏ **2454-2070.** www.elsegarden.com. Admission C6,300 adults, C2,900 students with valid ID and children 5–12. A guided tour costs an extra C14,500 per guide per hour, for a group of up to 15 persons. Advance reservations are necessary for guided tours. Daily 8am–4pm. About 6 blocks north of the central football (soccer) stadium in the town of Sarchí.

Zarcero

60km (38 miles) NW of San José

Beyond Sarchí, on picturesque roads lined with cedar trees, is the town of Zarcero. In a small park in the middle of town is a **menagerie of sculpted shrubs** that includes a monkey on a motorcycle, people and animals dancing, an ox pulling a cart, a man wearing a top hat, and a large elephant. Behind all the topiary is a wonderful rural **church.** It's not really worth the drive just to see this park, but it's a good idea to take a break in Zarcero to walk the gardens, on the way to La Fortuna and Arenal Volcano.

GETTING THERE   By Car: Zarcero is located along the popular route from San José to La Fortuna. Take the Interamerican Highway (CR1) north to Naranjo, and follow signs to Ciudad Quesada and Zarcero.

  By Bus: Daily buses (© **2255-0567**) for Zarcero leave from San José hourly from the Atlántico del Norte bus station at Avenida 9 and Calle 12. This is actually the Ciudad Quesada–San Carlos bus. Just tell the driver that you want to get off in Zarcero, and keep an eye out for the topiary. The ride takes around 1½ hours, and the fare is around ₡875.

CARTAGO ★

24km (15 miles) SE of San José

Cartago is the original capital of Costa Rica. Founded in 1563, it was Costa Rica's first city—and was, in fact, the *only* city for almost 150 years. Irazú Volcano rises up from the edge of town, and although it's quiet these days, it has not always been so peaceful. Earthquakes have damaged Cartago repeatedly over the years, so today few of the old colonial buildings are left standing. In the center of the city, a public park winds through the ruins of a large church that was destroyed in 1910 before it could be finished.

Essentials

GETTING THERE & DEPARTING   By Car: Head east out of San José on Avenida 2, toward the suburbs of Los Yoses and San Pedro, continuing on through Curridabat. As you exit Curridabat, you will see signs to Cartago,

The topiary gardens in Zarcero.

Las Ruinas (see p. 178).

(see p. 178).

putting you on the Interamerican Highway (CR2) to Cartago. This section of the highway is also known locally as the Florencio del Castillo Highway.

By Bus: Lumaca buses (© **2537-0347**) for Cartago leave San José every 3 to 5 minutes between 4:30am and 9pm, with slightly less frequent service until midnight, from Calle 3 and Avenida 2. You can also pick up one en route at any of the little covered bus stops along Avenida Central in Los Yoses and San Pedro. The length of the trip is 45 minutes; the fare is about 70¢.

La Negrita

Legend has it that Juana Pereira stumbled upon the statue of La Negrita sitting atop a rock, while gathering wood. Juana took it home, but the next morning it was gone. She went back to the rock, and there it was again. This was repeated three times, until Juana took her find to a local priest. The priest took the statue to his church for safekeeping, but the next morning it was gone, only to be found sitting upon the same rock later that day. The priest eventually decided that the strange occurrences were a sign that the Virgin wanted a temple or shrine built to her upon the

spot. And so work was begun on what would eventually become today's impressive basilica.

Miraculous healing powers have been attributed to La Negrita, and, over the years, a parade of pilgrims has come to the shrine seeking cures for their illnesses and difficulties. August 2 is her patron saint's day. Each year, on this date, tens of thousands of Costa Ricans and foreign pilgrims walk to Cartago from San José and elsewhere in the country in devotion to this powerful statue.

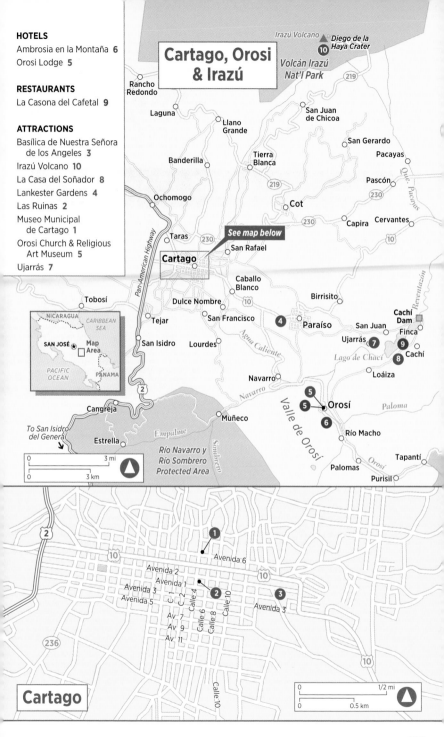

HOTELS
Ambrosia en la Montaña **6**
Orosi Lodge **5**

RESTAURANTS
La Casona del Cafetal **9**

ATTRACTIONS
Basílica de Nuestra Señora
de los Angeles **3**
Irazú Volcano **10**
La Casa del Soñador **8**
Lankester Gardens **4**
Las Ruinas **2**
Museo Municipal
de Cartago **1**
Orosi Church & Religious
Art Museum **5**
Ujarrás **7**

Cartago, Orosi & Irazú

Irazú Volcano ▲ Diego de la
Haya Crater
Volcán Irazú
Nat'l Park
219

Rancho
Redondo
San Juan
de Chicoa
Laguna
Llano
Grande
San Gerardo
Pacayas
Banderilla
Tierra
Blanca
Pascón
230
219
Ochomogo
Cot
Cervantes
Taras
230
Capira
10
Cartago
See map below
San Rafael
Caballo
Blanco
Birrisito
Cachí
Dam
Dulce Nombre
Paraíso
San Juan
Finca
10
4
Ujarrás **7**
9
Tejar
San Francisco
8 Cachí
San Isidro
Lourdes
Lago de Chací
Loáiza
Tobosí
NICARAGUA
CARIBBEAN
SEA
Navarro
SAN JOSÉ ✱
Map
Area
5
Orosí
Paloma
PACIFIC
OCEAN
PANAMA
5
6
Río Macho
Cangreja
Muñeco
Valle de Orosí
2
Empalme
Tapantí
To San Isidro
del General
Estrella
Río Navarro y
Río Sombrero
Protected Area
Palomas
Purisil
0   3 mi
0   3 km

2
10
Avenida 6
1
10
Avenida 2
Avenida 1
2
Calle 4
Calle 10
3
Avenida 3
Avenida 3
Avenida 5
Calle 6
Calle 8
Av 9
Av 11
236
10
Calle 10

Cartago
0   1/2 mi
0   0.5 km

ORIENTATION The main route into town from the highway, Avenida 2, enters downtown Cartago from the west and leads right to the center of town, and the central park and ruins. The Basilica is 6 blocks farther east, near where you pick up the road out to Paraiso and the Orosi Valley.

What to See & Do

Cartago is a quiet city, with little going on or of interest to tourists, aside from the Basilica (see below). If you spend time in the city, head to the **Parque Central** (central park), also known as **Las Ruinas** (The Ruins) ★. This is the site of the city's ill-fated original cathedral. Begun in 1575, the church was devastated by a series of earthquakes. Despite several attempts, construction was abandoned after the massive 1910 quake, and today the stone and mortar ruins sit at the heart of a neatly manicured park, with quiet paths and plenty of benches. The ruins themselves are closed off, but the park itself is lovely.

Cartago Basilica.

You might also want to stop in at the **Museo Municipal de Cartago** (Cartago Municipal Museum; ☏ **2591-1050**), on Avenida 6 between calles 2 and 4. Housed in a former, and wonderfully restored military barracks, the museum houses a series of local historical displays, as well as a range of changing exhibits, including those featuring local artists. The museum is open Tuesday to Saturday, 9am to 4pm and Sunday till 3pm. Admission is free.

With no real reason to stay in Cartago, and no hotels right in the city that I recommend highly, if you're looking to stay in the area, I recommend picking a hotel in the Orosi Valley or Turrialba region. Cartago (and the Orosi Valley) also makes a good stop along the way to visit one of the quetzal-viewing lodges in the Dota and Cerro de la Muerte region (p. 83).

Basílica de Nuestra Señora de los Angeles ★★★ Dedicated to the patron saint of Costa Rica, the impressive Basilica of Our Lady of the Angels anchors the east side of the city. Within the walls of this Byzantine-style church is a shrine containing the tiny carved figure of **La Negrita,** the Black Virgin, which is nearly lost amid its ornate altar. The walls of the shrine are covered with a fascinating array of tiny silver images left in thanks for cures affected by La Negrita. Amid the plethora of diminutive silver arms and legs, are also hands, feet, hearts, lungs, kidneys, eyes, torsos, breasts, and—peculiarly—guns, trucks,

DIY: Irazú Volcano

If you don't have a rental car and don't want to sign on for an organized tour, buses leave San José for Irazú Volcano daily at 8am from Avenida 2 between calles 1 and 3 (across the street from the entrance to the Gran Hotel Costa Rica). The fare is C3,820 round-trip, with the bus leaving the volcano at 12:30pm. This company is particularly fickle; to make sure that the buses are running, call ℰ **2530-1064,** although that might not help much, since they often don't answer their phone, and speak only Spanish.

beds, and planes. Outside the church, vendors sell a wide selection of these trinkets, as well as little candle replicas of La Negrita.

Calle 16, btw. avs. 2 and 4. ℰ **2551-0465.** Free admission. Daily 6:30am–5pm.

Attractions around Cartago

Irazú Volcano ★★   The 3,378m (11,080-ft.) **Irazú Volcano** is historically one of Costa Rica's more active volcanoes, although it's relatively quiet these days. It last erupted on March 19, 1963, the day that President John F. Kennedy arrived in Costa Rica. The landscape here is often compared to that of the moon. A good paved road leads right to the rim of the crater, where a desolate expanse of gray sand nurtures few plants and the air smells of sulfur. The drive up from Cartago has magnificent views of the fertile Meseta Central and Orosi Valley, and

Irazú Volcano.

if you're very lucky, you might be able to see both the Pacific Ocean and the Caribbean Sea. Clouds usually descend by noon, so get here as early in the day as possible. Dress in layers; this might be the Tropics, but it can be cold up at the top if the sun's not out.

A short trail leads to the rim of the volcano's two craters, their walls a maze of eroded gullies feeding onto the flat floor far below. A 2km (1.25-mile) trail loops around the rim of the Playa Hermosa Crater. The visitor center up here has information on the volcano and natural history. The park restaurant, at an elevation of 3,022m (9,912 ft.), with walls of windows looking out over the valley far below, claims to be the highest restaurant in Central America.

An orchid in bloom at Lankester Gardens.

Irazú de Cartago, 52km (32 miles) east of San José. ℂ **2200-5615.** Admission $10. Daily 8am–4pm.

Lankester Gardens ★★   Costa Rica has more than 1,400 varieties of orchids, and almost 800 species are cultivated and on display at this botanical garden in Cartago province. Created in the 1940s by English naturalist Charles Lankester, the gardens are now administered by the University of Costa Rica. The primary

A panorama of Orosi Valley.

goal is to preserve the local flora, with an emphasis on orchids and bromeliads. Paved, well-marked trails meander from open, sunny gardens into shady forests. In each environment different species of orchids are in bloom. There's an information center and a gift shop. Plan to spend between 1 and 3 hours here if you're interested in flowers and gardening; you could run through it more quickly if you're not. You can easily combine a visit here with a tour at Cartago and/or the Orosi Valley and Irazú Volcano (see above).

1km (½ mile) east of Cartago, on the road to Paraíso de Cartago. ✆ **2511-7939.** www.jbl.ucr.ac.cr. Admission $7.50 adults, $5 children 6–16. Daily 8:30am–4:30pm. Take the Cartago bus from San José, and then the Paraíso bus from a stop 1 block south and ¾ block west of the Catholic church ruins in Cartago (ride takes 30–40 min.).

THE OROSI VALLEY ★★

The Orosi Valley, southeast of Cartago, is generally considered one of the most beautiful valleys in Costa Rica. The Reventazón River meanders through this steep-sided valley until it collects in the lake formed by the Cachí Dam. A well-paved road winds a near-perfect loop around the lake, allowing for easy access to all of the attractions listed below. Scenic overlooks are near the town of Orosi, at the head of the valley, and in Ujarrás, on the banks of the lake.

GETTING THERE & DEPARTING If you're driving, take the road to Paraíso from Cartago, head toward Ujarrás, continue around the lake, and then pass through Cachí and on to Orosi. From Orosi, the road leads back to Paraíso. It is difficult to explore this whole area by public bus because this is not a densely populated region and connections are often infrequent or unreliable. However, regular buses run from Cartago to the town of Orosi. These buses run roughly every half-hour and leave the main bus terminal in Cartago. The trip takes 30 minutes, and the fare is 60¢.

Ujarrás ruins.

What to See & Do

Near **Ujarrás** are the ruins of Costa Rica's oldest church, which was built in 1693. Little remains beyond the worn brick and adobe facade of the church, but the gardens are a great place to sit and gaze at the surrounding mountains. Along the main road around the valley, especially near the town of Orosi, are several **scenic overlooks;** take the time to pull over and admire the views and snap a photo or two. In the town of **Orosi** itself is yet another **colonial church** (see below) and convent worth visiting.

From the Orosi Valley, it's a quick shot to the entrance to the **Tapantí National Park ★** (*C* **2206-5615**), where you'll find some gentle and beautiful hiking trails, as well as riverside picnic areas. The park is open daily from 8am to 4pm; admission is $10.

If you want to do any adventure activities or take an organized tour of the area, contact **Aventuras Orosi** (*C* **2533-4000;** www.aventurasorosi. com).

Orosi church.

TOP ATTRACTIONS

Orosi Church & Religious Art Museum ★   Built in 1743 by Franciscan monks, this is, in fact, the oldest functioning church in the country. The exterior is a blindingly white adobe, and inside are three painted wooden alters. The small **Museo de Arte Religioso** (Religious Art Museum) is located on the south side of the church and features a modest collection of religious arts and relics. On display are 18th-century paintings, bibles, and religious icons, as well as period pieces of clothing and furniture.

West side of the soccer field, Orosi. *C* **2533-3051.** Admission C500. Tues–Sun 8:30am–5pm.

La Casa del Soñador 🏠   The "House of the Dreamer" is the home and gallery of the late sculptor Macedonio Quesada. Quesada earned fame with his primitive sculptures of La Negrita (see "La Negrita," above) and other religious and secular characters carved on coffee tree roots and trunks. You can see some of Macedonio's original work here, including his version of *The Last Supper* carved onto one of the walls of the main building. Today, his sons carry on the family tradition. You can shop among their collection of small sculptures, carved religious icons, and ornate walking sticks.

1 km (½ mile) south of Cachí. *C* **2577-1186.** Daily 8am–4pm.

Where to Stay & Eat

If you're interested in staying out here, check out the charming little **Orosi Lodge** (www.orosilodge.com; ✆ **2533-3578**), on the south side of the tiny town of Orosi, right next to some simple hot-spring pools. A little farther out of town is **Ambrosia en la Montaña** ★ (www.ambrosiaenlamontana.com; ✆ **2533-2336**), a pretty little inn, with two individual wooden cabins, great views, and an excellent restaurant.

La Casona del Cafetal COSTA RICAN   Although clearly geared toward tourists, this popular restaurant is still an excellent option for a meal. The food is typical Tico fare. In addition to the long menu is a massive buffet and several daily options. The handmade tortillas are cooked to order. When the weather's nice, grab a patio table with a view of Lake Cachí.

Cachí. ✆ **2577-1414.** www.lacasonadelcafetal.com. Main courses C4,500–C18,000. Daily 11am–6pm.

TURRIALBA & THE GUAYABO NATIONAL MONUMENT ★

53km (33 miles) E of San José

This attractive little town is best known as the starting point and home base for many popular white-water rafting trips. Turrialba is a hot spot for active and adventure travelers. However, it's also worth a visit if you have an interest in pre-Columbian history or tropical botany.

Turrialba is situated in the heart of a rich agricultural region. Coffee and sugar cane are the principal crops. The area is lower in elevation than San José and much of the rest of the Central Valley, and for visitors (and the happy crops) this translates into generally higher temperatures. See map, "The Central Valley," p. 153.

Essentials

GETTING THERE & DEPARTING   **By Car:** If you're driving, follow the directions above to Cartago (p. 175), and then take the road from Cartago to Paraíso, through Juan Viñas, and on to Turrialba. It's pretty well marked. (Alternatively you can head toward the small town of Cot, on the road to Irazú Volcano, and then through the town of Pacayas on to Turrialba, another well-marked route.)

  By Bus: Transtusa buses (✆ **2222-4464** or 2557-5050) leave San José hourly for Turrialba between 5:45am and 10pm from Calle 13 between avenidas 6 and 8. The fare is around $2.

  Around three buses also head to Guayabo daily from the main bus terminal in Turrialba.

ORIENTATION   Turrialba itself is a bit of a jumble, and you will probably have to ask directions to get to locations in, around, and outside of town. Guayabo is about 20km (12 miles) beyond Turrialba on a road that is paved the entire way except for the last 3km (1¼ miles).

La Casa del Soñador sculptures.

What to See & Do

Most of the white-water rafting companies in Costa Rica have an operational base in Turrialba, and the put-in points for several of the more popular river trips are nearby. See chapter 4, "The Active Vacation Planner," for more information on rafting trips and operators.

In addition to rafting and kayaking, **Explornatura ★** (✆ **2556-2070;** www.explornatura.com) is an excellent local adventure tour operator that offers up a range of trips and activities, including canopy tours, horseback riding, hiking, and mountain biking.

Guayabo National Monument ★ (✆ **2559-1220**) is one of Costa Rica's only pre-Columbian sites open to the public. It's 19km (12 miles) northeast of Turrialba and preserves a town site that dates from between 1000 B.C. and A.D. 1400. Archaeologists believe that Guayabo might have supported a population of as many as 10,000 people, but no clues yet explain why the city was eventually abandoned only shortly before the Spanish arrived in the New World. Excavated ruins at Guayabo consist of paved roads, aqueducts, stone bridges, and house and temple foundations. The site also has gravesites and petroglyphs. The monument is open daily from 8am to 4pm. This is a national park, and admission is $10 at the gate. For information about other parks in this area, see also "Costa Rica's Top National Parks & Bioreserves," in chapter 4.

Botanists and gardeners will want to pay a visit to the **Center for Agronomy Research and Development (CATIE; ✆ 2556-2700;** www.catie. ac.cr), which is located 5km (3 miles) southeast of Turrialba on the road to Siquirres. This center is one of the world's foremost facilities for research into tropical agriculture. Among the plants on CATIE's 810 hectares (2,000 acres) are hundreds of varieties of cacao and thousands of varieties of coffee. The plants here have been collected from all over the world. In addition to trees used for food and other purposes, other plants grown here are strictly for ornamental purposes. CATIE is open Monday through Friday from 7am to 4pm. Guided tours are available with advance notice for $15 per person.

Hovering over the town, the **Turrialba Volcano National Park** boasts nearly 1,600 hectares (3,950 acres) of lush rainforest, as well as its namesake 3,340m (10,955-ft.) volcano. The volcano is in an extremely active phase, and the park is currently closed to the public. When open, it is possible to hike to the volcano's summit.

Where to Stay & Eat

If you're looking for luxury in this area, check out **Casa Turire** ★★ (www.hotel casaturire.com; ✆ **2531-1111**), where well-appointed rooms and suites in an elegant country mansion run between $130 and $350. The hotel is set on the banks of the lake formed by the Angostura dam project, and you can take a kayak or paddleboat out on the lake here. This place was granted "5 Leaves" by the CST Sustainable Tourism program, and the excellent restaurant here serves all organic ingredients.

Another excellent upscale option is the new **Hacienda Tayutic** ★★ (www.tayutic.com; ✆ **2538-1717**). This historic—and still functioning—family farm has been totally converted, and features plush rooms, lush gardens, spa services, and an onsite 19th-century chapel. Rates here run $295 to $325 for a double, including a buffet breakfast.

A view of the Turrialba valley.

Finally, another great bet is **Turrialtico ★** (www.turrialtico.com; ℂ **2538-1111**), a rustic yet beautiful open-air restaurant and small hotel high on a hill overlooking the Turrialba Valley. The view here is one of the finest in the area, with lush greenery far below and volcanoes in the distance. The Costa Rican food is good and reasonably priced, and a double room will cost you $52 to $75, including breakfast and taxes. This place is popular with rafting companies that bring groups here for meals and for overnights before, during, and after multiday rafting trips.

Since Turrialba is a main base for several rafting trips and operators, the town has a healthy population of rafting guides living here, and as a result, it actually has a pretty active nightlife.

GUANACASTE:
THE GOLD COAST

Guanacaste is Costa Rica's "Gold Coast"—and not because this is where the Spanish Conquistadors found vast quantities of the brilliant metal ore. Instead, it's because more and more visitors to Costa Rica are choosing Guanacaste as their first—and often only—stop. Beautiful beaches abound along this coastline. Several are packed with a mix of hotels and resorts, some are still pristine and deserted, and others are backed by small fishing villages. Choices range from long, broad sections of sand stretching on for miles, to tiny pocket coves bordered by rocky headlands.

This is Costa Rica's most coveted vacation destination and the site of its greatest tourism development. The international airport in Liberia receives daily direct flights from several major U.S. and Canadian hub cities, allowing tourists to visit some of Costa Rica's prime destinations without having to go through San José.

This is also Costa Rica's driest region. The rainy season starts later and ends earlier, and overall it's more dependably sunny here than in other parts of the country. Combine this climate with a coastline that stretches south for hundreds of miles, from the Nicaraguan border, all the way to the Nicoya Peninsula, and you have an equation that yields beach bliss.

One caveat: During the dry season (mid-Nov to Apr), when sunshine is most reliable, the hillsides in Guanacaste turn browner than the chaparral of Southern California. Dust from dirt roads blankets the trees in many areas, and the vistas are far from tropical. Driving these dirt roads without air-conditioning and the windows rolled up tight can be extremely unpleasant.

On the other hand, if you happen to visit this area in the rainy season (particularly from May–Aug), the hillsides are a beautiful, rich green, and the sun usually shines all morning, giving way to an afternoon shower—just in time for a nice siesta.

Inland from the beaches, Guanacaste remains Costa Rica's "Wild West," a land of dry plains populated with cattle ranches and cowboys, who are known here as *sabaneros,* a name that derives from the Spanish word for "savanna" or "grassland." If it weren't for those rainforest-clad volcanoes in the distance, you might swear you were in Texas.

 Guanacaste's Top Sustainable Hotels

Four Seasons Resort (p. 211)
Hacienda Guachipelin (p. 199)
Hotel Las Tortugas (p. 234)
Hotel Playa Hermosa Bosque del Mar (p. 213)

PREVIOUS PAGE: **Witch's Rock.**

Guanacaste is home to several active volcanoes and some beautiful national parks, including **Santa Rosa National Park ★**, the home to massive sea turtle nestings and the site of a major battle to maintain independence; **Rincón de la Vieja National Park ★★**, which features hot springs and bubbling mud pots, pristine waterfalls, and an active volcanic crater; and **Palo Verde National Park ★**, a beautiful expanse of mangroves, wetlands, and savannah.

LIBERIA

217km (135 miles) NW of San José; 132km (82 miles) NW of Puntarenas

Founded in 1769, Liberia is the capital of Guanacaste province, and although it can hardly be considered a bustling metropolis, it is growing rapidly, in large part as a business center to feed the growing coastal boom. Hardware stores, warehouses, malls, and shipping companies are setting up shop in Liberia, and the city serves as a housing hub for the many workers needed to man the construction and tourism boom along the coast here.

That said, Liberia offers up more colonial atmosphere than almost any other city in the country. Its narrow streets are lined with charming old adobe homes, many of which have ornate stone accents on their facades, carved wooden doors, and aged red-tile roofs. Many have beautiful large, shuttered windows (some don't even have iron bars for protection) opening onto the narrow streets. The central plaza, which occupies 2 square blocks in front of the church, remains the city's social hub and principal gathering spot.

Liberia works well as a base for exploring this region or as an overnight stop in a longer itinerary. You'll find several moderately priced hotels in the city and its

Liberia's central park.

outskirts. Still, all things considered, it's usually preferable to base yourself either at the beach or at a mountain lodge, and to visit the city on a day trip.

Essentials

GETTING THERE & DEPARTING   By Plane: The **Daniel Oduber International Airport** (✆ **2668-1010;** airport code LIR) in Liberia receives a steady stream of scheduled commercial and charter flights throughout the year. **Delta** (✆ **800/241-4141;** www.delta.com) has daily direct flights between its Atlanta hub and Liberia; **American Airlines** (✆ **800/433-7300;** www.aa.com) offers daily direct flights between Miami and Liberia, and twice-weekly flights between Dallas–Ft. Worth and Liberia; **Continental** (✆ **800/231-0856;** www.continental.com) has daily direct flights between Houston and Liberia, and three weekly direct flights between Newark and Liberia; and **US Airways** (✆ **800/622-1015;** www.usairways.com) has one weekly direct flight between Charlotte and Liberia. In addition, numerous commercial charter flights from various North American cities fly in throughout the high season. Check with your travel agent.

Sansa (✆ **877/767-2672** in the U.S. and Canada, or 2290-4100 in Costa Rica; www.flysansa.com) has two daily flights to Liberia at 8:45am and 3pm from San José's Juan Santamaría International Airport (p. 508). Return flights depart for San José at 9:45am and 4pm. The fare for the 50-minute flight is $130 each way.

Nature Air (✆ **800/235-9272** in the U.S. and Canada, or 2299-6000; www.natureair.com) has four flights daily to Liberia at 6:20 and 11:45am, and 3:20pm from Tobías Bolaños International Airport in Pavas (p. 510). Return flights leave Liberia at 7:10am and 12:35 and 4:45pm. Fares run between $85 and $133 each way.

The following car rental companies all have local agencies: **Adobe** (✆ 2667-0608), **Alamo** (✆ 2668-1111), **Avis** (✆ 2668-1138), **Budget**

⊙ An Interesting Stop on Your Way to Liberia

If you're driving to or from Guanacaste, be sure to take a brief break to check out the **Iglesia de Cañas (Cañas Church)** ★★ in Cañas. Well-known painter, installation artist, and local prodigal son Otto Apuy has designed and directed the envelopment of the entire church in colorful mosaic. The work uses whole and broken tiles in glossy, vibrant colors to depict both religious and abstract themes. The church's nearly 30m-tall (100-ft.) central tower is entirely covered in mosaic. It is estimated that more than a million pieces of ceramic were used in the work. The church is located in the center of town, just a few blocks off the highway.

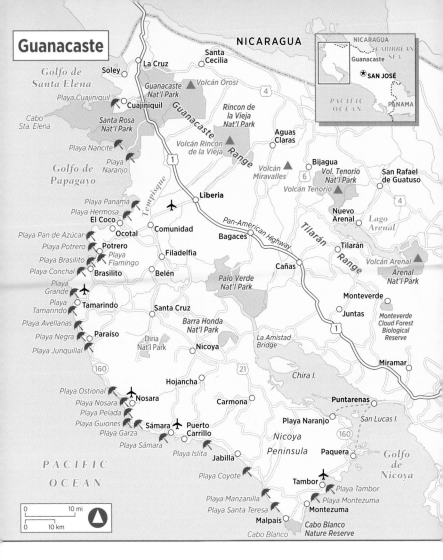

(℃ 2668-1118), **Dollar** (℃ 2668-1061), **Economy** (℃ 2666-2816), **Hertz** (℃ 2668-1048), **Thrifty** (℃ 2665-0787), and **Toyota** (℃ 2668-1212). You can also reserve with these and most major international car-rental companies via their San José and international offices (see "Getting Around," in chapter 5).

The airport is 13km (8 miles) from downtown Liberia. Taxis await all incoming flights; a taxi into town should cost around $10. The ride takes around 10 minutes.

Note: Work to expand and renovate the cramped, inefficient, and over-crowded Daniel Oduber International Airport has been plagued by delays, contractual disputes, and funding problems. As of press time, work was underway and is slated to be complete in November, 2011.

By Car: From San José, you can either take the Interamerican Highway (CR1) north all the way to Liberia from downtown San José, or first head west out of the city on the San José–Caldera Highway (CR27). When you reach Caldera, follow the signs to Puntarenas, Liberia, and the Interamerican Highway (CR1). This will lead you to the unmarked entrance to CR1. You'll want to pass under the bridge and follow the on-ramp which will put you on the highway heading north. This latter route is a faster and flatter drive. Depending upon which route you take and traffic conditions, it's a 3- to 4-hour drive.

By Bus: Pulmitan express buses (© **2222-1650** in San José, or 2666-0458 in Liberia;

A colonial-era building in Liberia.

www.pulmitandeliberia.com;) leave San José roughly every hour between 6am and 8pm from Calle 24 between avenidas 5 and 7. The ride to Liberia takes around 4 hours. A one-way fare costs C2,915.

Gray Line (© **2220-2126;** www.graylinecostarica.com) has a daily bus that leaves San José for Liberia at 3pm. The fare is $40. **Interbus** (© **2283-5573;** www.interbusonline.com) has a daily bus that leaves San José for Liberia at 7:45am; the fare is $40 to Liberia. The morning bus (for either company) makes connections to Rincón de la Vieja and Santa Rosa national parks. Both companies will pick you up at most San José–area hotels, and provide connections to and from most other destinations in Costa Rica.

Buses depart for San José and most of the area beaches and national parks from the Liberia bus station on the edge of town, 200m (2 blocks) north and 100m (1 block) east of the main intersection on the Interamerican Highway. Express buses for San José leave roughly every hour between 3am and 8pm.

FAST FACTS   Several state and private bank offices are clustered around downtown Liberia, as well as a branch of the **Banco de Costa Rica** inside the airport. The local **police** number is © **2690-0129** and the **Liberia Hospital** number is © **2690-2300.** If you need a taxi, dial © **2666-3330.** A host of Internet cafes are on the blocks surrounding and just off the central plaza.

On the southern outskirts of the city is a modern shopping mall, the place to come for a food court fix or to catch a semi-late-run movie at the local multiplex. Smaller, contemporary shopping centers can be found near

Shady Business

This province gets its name from the abundant Guanacaste *(Enterolobium cyclocarpum)*, Costa Rica's national tree. This distinctive tree is known for its broad, full crown, which provides welcome shade on the Guanacaste's hot plains and savannas. The Guanacaste is also known as the elephant-ear tree, due to the distinctive shape of its large seedpods. Its fragrant white flowers bloom between February and April.

the airport, and right at the major intersection between the Interamerican highway and the road to the beaches.

Exploring the Town

The central plaza in Liberia is a great place to people-watch, especially in the early evenings and on weekends. Grab a seat on one of the many concrete benches, or join the families and young lovers as they leisurely stroll around. On the northern edge of the Plaza Central, the **Iglesia de la Inmaculada Concepción** is Liberia's main house of worship. The church was built in 1972 and features a tall A-frame–style central nave and a separate clock tower that rises up sharply—a contemporary concrete obelisk. The main church is generally open from 6am to 6pm, though it's sometimes open later for masses.

If you venture for a few blocks down **Calle Real** ★, you'll see fine examples of the classic Spanish colonial adobe buildings with ornate wooden doors, heavy beams, central courtyards, and faded, sagging, red-tile roofs.

While the Catholic church that anchors the central plaza is unspectacular, if you head several blocks east of the plaza, you will come to **Iglesia La Ermita de la Agonía** ★. Built in 1865, this whitewashed stone church is in surprisingly good shape. Inside it is plain and bare, but it is the only remaining colonial-era church to be found in Guanacaste. The visiting hours are seriously limited (daily from 2:30–3:30pm), but not to worry: Local tour agencies can sometimes arrange visits during off hours. Even if you can't enter, you'll still get a good feel for the place by checking out its whitewashed stucco exterior.

Outdoor Adventures near Liberia

In addition to the activities listed below, Liberia is a major jumping-off point for Rincón de la Vieja National Park (p. 197).

LLANO DE CORTES WATERFALL ★

Located about 25km (16 miles) south of Liberia, the Llano de Cortes Waterfall is a beautiful and wide jungle waterfall with an excellent pool at the base for cooling off and swimming. At roughly 12m (40 ft.) wide, the falls are actually slightly wider than they are tall. This is a great spot for a picnic. The turnoff for the dirt road to the falls is well marked and about 3km (1¾ miles) north of the crossroads for Bagaces. From the turnoff, you must drive a rough dirt road to the parking area and then hike down a short steep trail to the falls. Admission is free.

BACK TO AFRICA

Since the landscape is postcard-perfect, especially in the dry season, you shouldn't be too surprised to see antelope, zebra, giraffe, and elands roaming the grassy plains of Guanacaste. **Africa Mia** (My Africa; ℂ **2666-1111;** www.africamia.net) offers safari-style open-jeep tours through its 100-hectare (247-acre) private reserve populated with a wide range of nonnative (predominantly African) species. All of the animals are herbivores, so don't expect to see any lions, hyenas, or cheetahs. The trip does provide some sense of being on the Serengeti or some other African plain and the animals have plenty of room to roam. Admission, which is C9,000 for adults, and C6,000 for children 11 and under, includes a 90-minute guided tour. Other more extensive tours include a chance to get closer to the animals, and the opportunity to feed a giraffe. Africa Mia is located just off the Interamerican Highway, 8km (5 miles) south of Liberia. The park is open daily from 9am to 5pm.

BIRDING

The **Río Tempisque Basin ★**, southwest of town, is one of the best places in the country to spot marsh and stream birds by the hundreds. This area is an important breeding ground for gallinules, jacanas, and limpkins, as well as numerous heron and kingfisher species and the roseate spoonbill. Several tour operators offer excursions and a wide range of tours in the region. **Swiss Travel Services** (ℂ **2282-4898;** www.swisstravelcr.com) is the largest and most reliable of the major operators here.

One of the most popular tours is a boat tour down the Bebedero River to **Palo Verde National Park ★**, which is south of Cañas and is best known for its migratory bird populations. Some of the best bird-watching requires no more than a little walking around the Biological Station in the park.

RAFTING TRIPS

Leisurely raft trips (with little white water) are offered by **Ríos Tropicales** (ℂ/fax **2233-6455;** www.riostropicales.com), about 40km (25 miles) south of Liberia. Its 2-hour ($55) float trips are great for families and bird-watchers. Along the way you may see many of the area's more exotic animal residents: howler

FROM LEFT: Africa Mia; A boat-billed heron.

monkeys, iguanas, caimans, coatimundis, otters, toucans, parrots, motmots, trogons, and many other species of birds. Aside from your binoculars and camera, a bathing suit and sunscreen are the only things you'll need. Rios Tropicales is based out of the Restaurant Rincón Corobicí, which is located right on the Interamerican Highway (CR1).

For a much wetter and wilder ride, the folks at **Hacienda Guachipelín** (see below) offer white-water inner-tube trips on the narrow Río Negro.

Shopping

On the road to the beaches, just west of the airport, are several large souvenir shops. These are popular stopping points on organized tours throughout this region. The best of the bunch for a one-stop shop is **Kaltak Arts & Craft Market** (✆ 2667-0696). However, you might find better selection and prices, especially for Guaitíl pottery, at some of the smaller makeshift roadside kiosks that line the road between Liberia and the Guanacaste beaches. For something different, check out the **Hidden Garden Art Gallery** (✆ 8386-6872; http://hidden garden.thevanstonegroup.com), a well-stocked contemporary art gallery, with a large stable of prominent Costa Rican and expatriate artists. This place is located 5km (3 miles) west of the Liberia airport, on the road the beaches.

Where to Stay

EXPENSIVE

Hilton Garden Inn Liberia Airport ★   Long overdue, Liberia now has a modern, business-class airport hotel. That said, with most of Guanacaste's beaches under an hour drive away (some much closer), unless your flight arrives very late, or leaves very early, there's little need to stay near the airport. Rooms and suites are up-to-date, with MP3 docking stations and complimentary Wi-Fi. The hotel is directly across the street from the airport, and a small shopping mall is next door.

Across from the airport, Liberia, Guanacaste. www.hgi.com. ✆ **877/STAY-HGI** in the U.S. and Canada, or 2690-8888 in Costa Rica. 169 units. $169 double; $210 suite. Rates include breakfast buffet. AE, DC, DISC, MC, V. **Amenities:** Restaurant; bar; exercise room; Jacuzzi; outdoor pool; room service; all rooms smoke-free. *In room:* A/C, TV, minifridge, hair dryer, Wi-Fi.

MODERATE

El Punto Bed & Breakfast ★★ ☺ 🎁   This place is a cozy, homey, intimate oasis in the middle of the hustle and bustle of Liberia. Bright primary colors and artsy touches abound. Rooms all feature a sleeping loft, making it a good option for families, and most have a private veranda with a hammock. The gardens are lush and the common areas are inviting. The restaurant serves excellent and healthy contemporary cuisine.

1½ blocks south of the intersection of CR1 and CR21, Liberia, Guanacaste. www.elpuntohotel.com. ✆ **2665-2986** or 8877-3949. 6 units. $66–$104 double. Rates include full breakfast and taxes. AE, MC, V. **Amenities:** Restaurant; bar; Wi-Fi. *In room:* A/C, minifridge.

INEXPENSIVE

Hotel Guanacaste   This basic, economical choice is primarily a hostel catering to young travelers on a tight budget. In addition to the small and simply furnished rooms—almost all of which have bunk beds with thin foam mattresses—there's a basic *soda* (diner) serving inexpensive meals. The folks here can help arrange trips to nearby national parks and tell you about other budget accommodations around the country. The best rooms here have double beds, private bathrooms, and air-conditioning and cost slightly more. Camping is also allowed, for $5 per person.

A.P. 251-5000 (1 block north and 2 blocks east of the intersection of the Interamerican Hwy. and the beach hwy.), Liberia, Guanacaste. www.higuanacaste.com. ✆ **2666-0085.** Fax 2666-2287. 27 units. $40 double. Discounts for students and those holding a valid hostel ID. MC, V. **Amenities:** Restaurant. *In room:* No phone, Wi-Fi.

Where to Eat

Liberia has plenty of standard Tico dining choices. In town, the most popular alternative is **Pizzería Pronto** (✆ **2666-2098**), which serves a wide range of wood-oven pizzas and assorted pasta dishes, in a restored old colonial home. Another favorite of mine is **El Café Liberia** ★ (✆ **2665-1660;** www.cafeliberia. com), a little French-style coffee shop and bistro that morphs into a sort of European-style hip lounge and bar at night. For some local flavor, choose one of the *sodas* around the central park. The best of these is **Restaurante Paseo Real** ★ (✆ **2666-3455**). Another option for Costa Rican cuisine is **La Choza de Laurel** (✆ **2668-1018;** www.lachozadelaurel.com), located along the main highway, about 800m (2,624 ft.) east of the Liberia airport entrance.

For seafood and a good bar scene, try **LIB** (✆ **2665-0741**), which sometimes features live music and dancing at night, and is in the Centro Comercial Santa Rosa, at the main highway crossroads.

If you want fast food, both **Burger King** and **Papa John's** are in a small shopping complex on the northwest corner of the main intersection of the Interamerican Highway and the road to the beaches, as well as an even bigger food court with more fast-food at the mall on the southern outskirts of town.

RINCÓN DE LA VIEJA NATIONAL PARK

242km (151 miles) NW of San José; 25km (16 miles) NW of Liberia

This sprawling national park begins on the flanks of the Rincón de la Vieja Volcano and includes this volcano's namesake active crater. Down lower is an area of geothermal activity similar to that of Yellowstone National Park in the United States. Fumaroles, geysers, and hot pools cover this small area, creating a bizarre, otherworldly landscape. In addition to hot springs and mud pots, you can explore waterfalls, a lake, and volcanic craters. The bird-watching here is excellent, and the views across the pasturelands to the Pacific Ocean are stunning.

What's in a Name?

Rincón de la Vieja translates literally as "the old lady's corner." In this case, "la vieja" has the connotation of a witch or hag, while "rincón" is better interpreted as a "lair" or "hangout." The smoking, belching volcanic crater and mud pots gave rise to this name.

Essentials

GETTING THERE By Car: Follow the directions above to Liberia. When you reach Liberia, head

Rincón de la Vieja National Park mud pots.

straight through the major intersection, following signs to Peñas Blancas and the Nicaraguan border.

To reach the **Las Pailas (Las Espuelas) entrance,** drive about 5km (3 miles) north of Liberia and turn right on the dirt road to the park. The turnoff is well marked. In about 12km (7½ miles), you'll pass through the small village of Curubandé. Continue on this road for another 6km (3¾ miles) until you reach the Hacienda Guachipelin. The lodge is private property, and the owners charge vehicles a C700 toll to pass through their gate and continue on to the park. I'm not sure if this is legal or mandatory, but it's not worth the hassle to protest. Pay the toll, pass through the gate, and continue for another 4km (2½ miles) until you reach the park entrance.

Two routes lead to the **Santa María entrance.** The principal route heads out of the northeastern end of Liberia toward the small village of San Jorge. This route is about 25km (16 miles) long and takes about 45 minutes. A four-wheel-drive vehicle is required. Alternatively, you can reach the entrance on a turnoff from the Interamerican Highway at Bagaces. From here, head north through Guayabo, Aguas Claras, and Colonia Blanca. Though the road is paved up to Colonia Blanca, a four-wheel-drive vehicle is required for the final, very rough 10km (6¼ miles) of gravel road.

Exploring Rincón de la Vieja National Park ★★

The Rincón de la Vieja National Park has several excellent trails. The easiest hiking is the gentle **Las Pailas loop ★**. This 3km (1.75-mile) trail is just off the Las Espuelas park entrance and passes by several bubbling mud pots and steaming fumaroles. Don't get too close, or you could get scalded. Happily, the strong sulfur smell given off by these formations works well as a natural deterrent. This gentle trail crosses a river, so you'll have to either take off your shoes or get them

La Cangrejo Waterfall.

wet. The whole loop is 3.2km (2 miles) and takes around 2 hours at a leisurely pace.

More energetic hikers can tackle the **summit** ★ and explore the several craters and beautiful lakes up here. On a clear day you'll be rewarded with a fabulous view of the plains of Guanacaste and the Pacific Ocean below. The trail is 16.6km (10.3 miles) round-trip and should take about 7 hours (the trail head begins at the ranger station). It heads pretty much straight up the volcano and is pretty steep in places. Along the way, you'll pass through several different ecosystems, including sections of tropical moist and tropical cloud forests, while climbing some 1,000m (3,280 ft.) in altitude. After about 6km (3.7 miles), the trail splits. Take the right-hand fork to the Crater Activo (Active Crater). Filled with rainwater, this crater is some 700m (2,300 ft.) in diameter and still active. Off to the side is the massive Laguna Jigueros. Because this crater emits large amounts of sulfur and acid gases, it's not recommended that you linger here long. If you have the energy, a side trail leads to the Von Seebach Crater.

My favorite hike here is to the **Blue Lake** and **La Cangrejo Waterfall** ★★. Along this well-marked 9.6km (6-mile) round-trip trail you will pass through several different ecosystems, including tropical dry forest, transitional moist forest, and open savanna. You are likely to spot a variety of birds and mammals and have a good chance of coming across a group of coatimundi—a raccoonlike local mammal. While not requiring any great climbs or descents, the hike is nonetheless arduous. Pack a lunch; at the end of your 2-hour hike in, you can picnic at the aptly named Blue Lake, where a 30m (98-ft.) waterfall empties into a small pond whose crystal-blue hues are amazing.

The park entrance fee is $10 per person per day, and the park is open daily from 7am to 3pm.

Camping will cost you an extra $2 per person per day. There are actually two entrances and camping areas here: **Santa María** and **Las Pailas** (also called Las Espuelas; *©* **2666-5051**) ranger stations. Las Pailas is by far the more popular and accessible, and it's closer to the action. These small camping areas are near each other. I recommend the one closer to the river, although the restroom and shower facilities are about 90m (295 ft.) away, at the other site. For those seeking a less rugged tour of the park, several lodges are around the park perimeter and offer guided hikes and horseback rides into the park.

Other Adventures around Rincón de la Vieja

ONE-STOP ADVENTURE SHOP

Hacienda Guachipelin (see below) offers up a range of adventure tour options, including horseback riding, hiking, white-water river inner-tubing, a waterfall canyoning and rappel tour, and a more traditional zip-line canopy tour. The most popular is the hacienda's **1-Day Adventure pass ★★**, which allows you to choose as many of the hotel's different tour options as you want and fit them into 1 adventure-packed day. The price for this is $80, including a buffet lunch and transportation. Almost all of the beach hotels and resorts of Guanacaste offer day trips here, or you can book directly with the lodge. **Be forewarned:** During the high season, the whole operation has a bit of a cattle-car feel, with busloads of day-trippers coming in from the beach. Also, I have found the inner-tube adventure to be fairly dangerous when the river is high, particularly during or just after the rainy season.

HOT SPRINGS & MUD BATHS

The active Rincón de la Vieja volcano has blessed this area with several fine hot springs and mud baths. Even if you're not staying at the **Hacienda Guachipelin** (see below) or the **Hotel Borinquen Mountain Resort** (see below), you can take advantage of their hot-spring pools and hot mud baths. Both have on-site spas offering massages, facials, and other treatments.

Just up the road from their lodge, Hacienda Guachipelin has opened the **Simbiosis Spa** (*©* **2666-8075;** www.simbiosis-spa.com). A $20 entrance fee gets you a stint in a sauna, self-application of the hot volcanic mud, and free run of the pools. **Be forewarned:** The pools are better described as warm, not hot, mud pools, and mud is the operative word here. A wide range of massages, mud wraps, facials, and other treatments are available at reasonable prices.

Horseback riding at Hacienda Guachipelin.

At the **Hotel Borinquen Mountain Resort,** a $25 entrance fee allows you access to their range of hot spring–fed pools ★, which vary from tepid to very hot, as well as their fresh volcanic mud bath area, and large fresh-water pool.

Finally, **Tizate Wellness Gardens ★★** (✆ **2666-7759;** www.buenavista lodgecr.com) is an excellent spa and adventure center run by the folks at Buena Vista Lodge, with a lovely man-made pool fed by natural hot springs. Unlike the other pools mentioned above, this one has no sulphuric smell. Entrance to the pool runs $35, but various packages, with a canopy tour, horseback ride, or other adventure activity, are available. Meals and spa treatments are also on offer.

Where to Stay & Eat

In addition to the hotels listed below, a couple of other good choices are by the park. On the Cañas Dulces road, **Buena Vista Lodge ★** (www.buenavistalodgecr. com; ✆ **2665-7759**) is set on the edge of the national park and offers a wide range of activities and attractions, including its own water slide and canopy tour.

Another good choice for adventure tourists is the new **Canyon Lodge** (www.thecanyonlodge.com; ✆ **2665-5912**), located just 3km (2 miles) inland from the main highway (CR1) on the outskirts of Liberia.

Over in the area around Aguas Claras, **Finca La Anita ★★** (laanitarainforest ranch.com; ✆ **8388-1775** or 2466-0228) is a remote and rustic, yet very cozy lodge, with a series of wooden cabins set on a working farm, on the edge of lush rain and cloud forests. The area around the lodge is home to several hot springs, and this area also provides easy access to the seldom used Santa Maria sector of Rincón de la Vieja National Park.

Hacienda Guachipelin ★ ☺
Set on the edge of Rincón de la Vieja National Park, this lodge is built around a still-operational 19th-century cattle-and-horse ranch. The superior rooms, worth the slight splurge, have a shared veranda fronting a large lawn and garden area. The older rooms are cozy and atmospheric, but generally smaller, and more rustic. These folks have implemented a variety of sustainable practices ranging from the use of solar energy for hot water and electricity to reforestation to on-site generation of bio-gas. A refreshing pool, as well as nearby rivers, creeks, and hot springs, all offer plenty of opportunities to get wet, while their extensive tour operation offers even more ways to get wild. Kids will love the working cattle and horse operations, and the range of tour activities appropriate for children of all ages. This place does a brisk business as a day-tour destination for hotels and resorts around Guanacaste, and there can be a cattle-car feel to that operation at times. See "One-Stop Adventure Shop," above, for a description of their many tour offerings.

Rincón de la Vieja (23km/14 miles northeast of Liberia). www.guachipelin.com. ✆ **2665-3303** for reservations, or 2666-8075 at the lodge. Fax 2665-2178. 59 units. $96 double; $102 superior double. Rates include breakfast and taxes. Rates higher during peak periods. AE, MC, V. Follow the directions/signs to Curubandé and Rincón de la Vieja National Park. **Amenities:** Restaurant; outdoor pool; small spa; Wi-Fi. *In room:* No phone.

Hotel Borinquen Mountain Resort ★★
This is the fanciest resort in the Rincón de la Vieja area. Individual and duplex bungalows are set on a hillside above the main lodge, restaurants, and hot springs. Rooms feature high ceilings, heavy wooden furniture, and a plush decor. All include an ample wooden deck with a view over the valley and surrounding forests. In the foot of the valley are

several natural hot-spring pools of varying temperatures, a natural sauna, and an area for full-body mud baths given with hot volcanic mud. The hotel also features a pretty, free-form outdoor pool and full-service spa, set beside a rushing creek in the middle of dense forest. The resort has good hiking and horseback riding trails and some nice waterfalls nearby. Golf carts are available to shuttle you around.

Cañas Dulces, Guanacaste. www.borinquenresort.com. © **2690-1900.** Fax 2690-1903. 39 units. $185 double villa; $206–$286 double bungalow; $323 junior suite. Rates include breakfast and unlimited use of the hot springs, sauna, and mud baths. AE, MC, V. Drive 12km (7½ miles) north of Liberia along the Interamerican Hwy., take the turnoff toward Cañas Dulces, and follow the signs. The hotel is approximately 21km (13 miles) from the highway, along a mostly rugged dirt road. **Amenities:** Restaurant; bar; large outdoor pool; small spa; all rooms smoke-free; Wi-Fi. *In room:* A/C, TV, minibar.

Río Celeste & the Tenorio Volcano

A crystalline turquoise pool at the foot of a forest waterfall, with nearby hot springs and volcanic mud make the **Río Celeste ★★** a must-see. Offering similar attractions and activities to Rincón de la Vieja, this is a much less visited, and more remote-feeling area. Río Celeste, which means "blue river," is inside the **Parque Nacional Volcán Tenorio** (Tenorio Volcano National Park; © **2206-5369**). The hike takes about 2 hours each way, and is steep in places. Above the main pool and waterfall, a loop trail will take you along the river to a few spots where underground hot springs bubble up into the blue waters. Locals have made some well-worn pools at the spots best for soaking. Along the river banks here, you can find volcanic mud deposits perfect for a free, midhike facial treatment. The park is open daily from 8am until 4pm. Entrance is $10.

If you want easy access to the Tenorio volcano and Río Celeste, I recommend the humble, yet delightful **La Carolina Lodge ★** (www.lacarolinalodge.com; © **8380-1656** or 2466-6393), which is on a working farm, next to a clear flowing river. Another good option is the **Celeste Mountain Lodge ★** (www.celeste mountainlodge.com; © **2278-6628**), a beautiful, sustainable lodge, with great views of the surrounding volcanoes. Finally, the most luxurious option in these parts is the new **Rio Celeste Hideaway ★★** (www.riocelestehideaway.com; © **2206-4000**), which is actually located on the "back side" of the Tenorio National Park, and reached via the road connecting Upala to the small town of Guatuso.

Getting There: Tenorio National Park is located near the small town of Bijagua. The road to Bijagua (CR6) heads north off of the Interamerican Highway about 5km (3 miles) northwest of Cañas. From here, it's another 30km (18½ miles) to Bijagua, and another 12km (7½ miles) to the park entrance. The last part of this is on rough dirt roads.

LA CRUZ & BAHÍA SALINAS

277km (172 miles) NW of San José; 59km (37 miles) NW of Liberia; 20km (12 miles) S of Peñas Blancas

Near the Nicaraguan border, La Cruz is a tiny hilltop town that has little to offer beyond a fabulous view of Bahía Salinas (Salinas Bay), but it does serve as a gateway to the nearly deserted beaches down below, a few mountain lodges bordering the nearby Santa Rosa and Guanacaste national parks, and the Nicaraguan border crossing at Peñas Blancas.

There's little reason to stay in La Cruz, but if you must, check out **Hotel La Mirada Inn** (www.hotel lamirada.com; ℂ **2679-9084**), a simple, well-kept local hotel. However, instead of staying in town, stay on the shores of the beaches listed below.

Essentials

GETTING THERE & DEPARTING   By Plane: The nearest airport with regular service is in Liberia (see "Liberia," earlier in this chapter).

By Car: Follow the directions above for driving to Liberia. When you reach Liberia, head straight through the major intersection, following signs to Peñas Blancas and the Nicaraguan border. Allow approximately 5 hours to get from San José to La Cruz.

Mealy parrots.

By Bus: Transportes Deldú buses (ℂ **2256-9072** in San José, or 2679-9323 in La Cruz; www.transportesdeldu.com) leave San José roughly every 2 hours (more frequently during the middle of the day) between 4am and 7pm for **Peñas Blancas** from Calle 20 and Avenida 1. These buses stop in La Cruz and will also let you off at the entrance to Santa Rosa National Park if you ask. The ride to La Cruz takes 5½ hours; a one-way fare costs between C3,300 and C4,580. Additional buses are often added on weekends and holidays.

Local buses (ℂ **2666-0517**) leave Liberia for Peñas Blancas periodically throughout the day. The ride to La Cruz takes about 1 hour and costs C1,405. Buses depart for San José from Peñas Blancas daily between 5am and 6:30pm, passing through La Cruz about 20 minutes later. Daily buses leave Liberia for San José roughly every hour between 3am and 8pm.

ORIENTATION   The highway passes slightly to the east of town. You'll pass the turnoffs to Santa Rosa National Park and Playa Caujiniquil before you reach town. For the Bahía Salinas beaches, head into La Cruz and take the road that runs along the north side of the small central park and then follow the signs down to the water.

Exploring Santa Rosa National Park

Known for its remote, pristine beaches (reached by several kilometers of hiking trails or a 4WD vehicle), **Santa Rosa National Park ★** (ℂ **2666-5051**) is a great place to camp on the beach, surf, birdwatch, or (if you're lucky) watch sea turtles nest. Located 30km (19 miles) north of Liberia and 21km (13 miles) south of La Cruz on the Interamerican Highway, Costa Rica's first national park

On to Nicaragua

Guanacaste is a popular jumping-off point for trips into Nicaragua. The main border point is at Peñas Blancas, Costa Rica. Several tour agencies and hotel desks arrange day trips to Nicaragua from resorts and hotels around Guanacaste.

Costa Rica charges no fees for entering or leaving, while Nicaragua charges $13 to enter and $3 to leave. Though it's by no means necessary, it's somewhat common to hire a helper or *gavilan* (literally, seagull), to expedite the process. These locals can occasionally cut lines, alleviate confusion, and speed up the process slightly. On the Costa Rican side, expect to spend about $5 for a bilingual *gavilan,* whereas on the Nicaraguan side, the cost should be around $3.

If you're planning on spending any time touring around Nicaragua, be sure to pick up a copy of *Frommer's Nicaragua and El Salvador.*

---

blankets the Santa Elena Peninsula. Unlike other national parks, it was founded not to preserve the land but to save a building, known as **La Casona,** which played an important role in Costa Rican independence. It was here, in 1856, that Costa Rican forces fought the decisive Battle of Santa Rosa, forcing the U.S.-backed soldier of fortune William Walker and his men to flee into Nicaragua. La

Casona was completely destroyed by arson in 2001, but it has been rebuilt, very accurately mimicking the original building, and now houses a small museum, detailing the political history of the ranch house and housing rotating temporary art exhibits. The museum descriptions, however, are in Spanish only.

La Casona has few nearby hiking trails. The best for most visitors is the **Indio Desnudo (Naked Indian) trail.** This 2.6km (1.5-mile) loop trail should take you about 45 minutes. It leads through a small patch of tropical dry forest and into overgrown former pastureland. If you're lucky, you might spot a white-tailed deer, coatimundi, black guan, or mantled howler monkey along the way.

It costs $10 per person to enter the park; day visitors can access the park daily from 8am to 4pm. Camping is allowed at several sites within the park. A campsite costs $2 per person per day. Camping is near the entrance, the principal ranger station, La Casona, and down by playas Naranjo and Nancite.

La Casona at Santa Rosa National Park.

THE BEACHES ★★   Eight kilometers (5 miles) west of La Casona, down a rugged road that's impassable during the rainy season (it's rough on 4WD vehicles even in the dry season), is **Playa Naranjo.** Four kilometers (2½ miles) north of Playa Naranjo, along a hiking trail that follows the beach, you'll find **Playa Nancite. Playa Blanca** is 21km (13 miles) down a dirt road from Caujiniquil, which itself is 20km (12 miles) north of the park entrance. None of these three beaches has shower or restroom facilities. (Playa Nancite does have some facilities, but they're in a reservation-only camping area.) Bring along your own water, food, and anything else you'll need, and expect to find things relatively quiet and deserted.

Playa Nancite is known for its *arribadas* ("arrivals," grouped egg-layings) of olive ridley sea turtles, which come ashore to nest by the tens of thousands each year in October. Playa Naranjo is legendary for its perfect surfing waves. In fact, this spot is quite popular with day-trippers who come in by boat from the Playa del Coco area to ride the waves that break around **Witch's Rock,** which lies just offshore.

On the northern side of the peninsula is **Playa Blanca,** a beautiful, remote white-sand beach with calm waters. This beach is reached by way of the small village of Caujiniquil and is accessible only during the dry season.

If you reach Caujiniquil and then head north for a few kilometers, you'll come to a small annex to the national park system at **Playa Junquillal** (*©* **2666-5051**), not to be confused with the more-developed beach of the same name farther south in Guanacaste. This is a lovely little beach that is also often good for swimming. You'll have to pay the park entrance fee ($10) to use the beach, and $2 more to camp here. There are basic restroom and shower facilities.

Fun on & over the Waves

The waters of Bahía Salinas are buffeted by serious winds from mid-November through mid-May, and this area is a prime spot for windsurfing and kiteboarding. The folks at **Ecoplaya Beach Resort** (see below) have the best windsurfing

Witch's Rock.

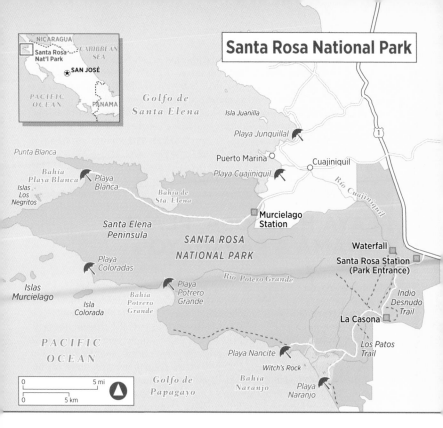

Santa Rosa National Park

operation and rental equipment in the area. If you want to try your hand at the sport of kiteboarding, check in with the folks at the **Kitesurfing Center,** who operate out of the **Blue Dream Hotel** (www.bluedreamhotel.com; ☎ **8826-5221** or 2676-1042) in Playa Copal.

Beach lovers should head to the far western tip of the Bahía Salinas, where you will find **Playa Rajada ★★**, a beautiful little white-sand beach, with gentle surf and plenty of shade trees.

Note: If you're coming to this area and aren't interested in windsurfing or kitesurfing, the winds can make your beach time rather unpleasant during the peak wind months. If you're just looking for a beach-resort vacation, I recommend heading to one of the beaches farther south in Guanacaste.

Where to Stay near La Cruz

In addition to the place listed below, **Recreo ★★** (www.recreocostarica.com; ☎ **877/268-2911** in the U.S. and Canada, or 8378-6364 in Costa Rica) is a luxurious and intimate boutique resort, offering private villas and suites, with a personal chef and hyper-personalized services.

Ecoplaya Beach Resort   This is the area's best beach hotel. The rooms are studios or junior, master, or luxury suites. Opt for one of the suites because the studios are somewhat cramped. Inside they all have high ceilings, tile floors, and plenty of varnished wood accents. The dark sand beach here is calm, although the winter winds really howl. To take advantage of this, the hotel features a fully equipped windsurf center, offering rentals and classes. This is a decent option if you're looking for isolation, or to combine some beach time with excursions to Santa Rosa National Park and/or neighboring Nicaragua, although most folks will be much happier at the more popular Guanacaste beaches described below.

La Coyotera Beach, Salinas Bay. www.ecoplaya.com. 🕿 **877/211-5512** in the U.S. and Canada, or 2228-7146 in Costa Rica. Fax 2289-4536. 43 units. $79–$98 double; $150–$245 suite. Rates include taxes. AE, MC, V. From La Cruz, take the dirt road that heads toward Bahía Salinas and Playa Soley, and then follow signs to the hotel. **Amenities:** Restaurant; bar; 2 Jacuzzis; midsize outdoor pool; extensive watersports equipment rental. *In room:* A/C, TV, kitchenette (in some).

PLAYA HERMOSA, PLAYA PANAMÁ & PAPAGAYO ★

258km (160 miles) NW of San José; 40km (25 miles) SW of Liberia

While most of Costa Rica's coast is highly coveted by surfers, the beaches here are mostly protected and calm, making them good destinations for families with kids. **Playa Hermosa ★** means "beautiful beach," which is an apt moniker for this pretty crescent of sand. Surrounded by steep forested hills, this curving gray-sand beach is long and wide and the surf is usually quite gentle. Fringing the beach is a swath of trees that stays surprisingly green even during the dry season. The shade provided by these trees, along with the calm protected waters, is a big part of the beach's appeal. Rocky headlands jut out into the surf at both ends of the beach, and at the base of these rocks are fun tide pools to explore.

Beyond Playa Hermosa you'll find **Playa Panamá ★** and, farther on, the calm waters of **Bahía Culebra ★**, a large protected bay dotted with small, private patches of beach and ringed with mostly intact dry forest. Around the north end of Bahía Culebra is the **Papagayo Peninsula ★**, home to two large all-inclusive resorts and one championship golf course. This peninsula has a half-dozen or so small to midsize beaches, the nicest of which might just be **Playa Nacascolo ★★★**, which is inside the domain of the Four Seasons Resort here—but all beaches in Costa Rica are public, so you can still visit, albeit after passing through security and parking at the public parking lot.

Essentials

GETTING THERE & DEPARTING   By Plane: The nearest airport with regularly scheduled service is in Liberia (p. 190). From there you can arrange a taxi to bring you the rest of the way. The ride takes about 25 minutes and should cost $40 to $60.

By Car: Follow the directions for getting to Liberia (p. 192). When you reach the main intersection in Liberia, take a left onto CR21, which heads towards Santa Cruz and the beaches of Guanacaste. The turnoff for the Papagayo Peninsula is prominently marked 8km (5 miles) south of the Liberia airport. At the corner here you'll see a massive Do It Center hardware store and lumber yard.

If you are going to a hotel along the Papagayo Peninsula, turn at the Do It Center and follow the paved road out and around the peninsula. If you are

Playa Hermosa.

going to Playa Panamá or Playa Hermosa, you should also turn here and take the access road shortcut that leads from a turnoff on the Papagayo Peninsula road, just beyond the Do It Center, directly to Playa Panamá. When you reach Playa Panamá, turn left for Playa Hermosa, and turn right for the Hilton Papagayo resort (p. 213).

To get to Playa Hermosa, you can also continue on a little farther west on CR21, and, just past the village of Comunidad, turn right. In about 11km (6¾ miles) you'll come to a fork in the road; take the right fork.

These roads are all relatively well marked, and a host of prominent hotel billboards should make it easy enough to find the beach or resort you are looking for. The drive takes about 4 to 4½ hours from San José.

By Bus: A **Tralapa** express bus (© 2221-7202) leaves San José daily at 3:30pm from Calle 20 and Avenida 3, stopping at Playa Hermosa and Playa Panamá, 3km (1¾ miles) farther north. One-way fare for the 5-hour trip is around C4,565.

Daily **Gray Line** (© 2220-2126; www.graylinecostarica.com) leave San José at 8am and 3:30pm for all beaches in this area. **Interbus** (© 2283-5573; www.interbusonline.com) has a daily bus that leaves San José at 7:45am for all beaches in this area. Both companies charge $40 and will pick you up at most San José–area hotels, and offer connections to most other major tourist destinations in Costa Rica.

You can take a bus from San José to Liberia (see "Essentials," earlier in this chapter) and then take a bus from Liberia to Playa Hermosa and Playa Panamá. Local buses (© 2665-7530) leave Liberia for Playa Hermosa and Playa Panamá at least a half-dozen times daily between 4:40am and 5:30pm. The trip lasts 40 minutes because the bus stops frequently to drop off and pick up passengers. The one-way fare costs C565. These bus schedules

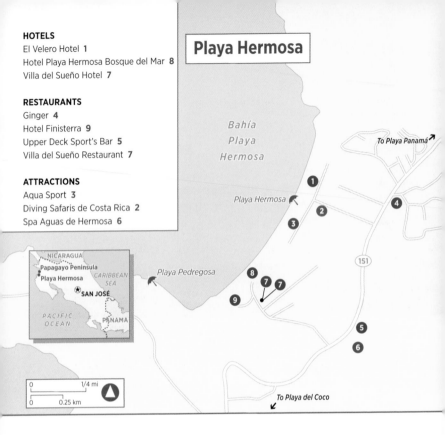

HOTELS
El Velero Hotel **1**
Hotel Playa Hermosa Bosque del Mar **8**
Villa del Sueño Hotel **7**

RESTAURANTS
Ginger **4**
Hotel Finisterra **9**
Upper Deck Sport's Bar **5**
Villa del Sueño Restaurant **7**

ATTRACTIONS
Aqua Sport **3**
Diving Safaris de Costa Rica **2**
Spa Aguas de Hermosa **6**

Playa Hermosa

Bahía Playa Hermosa

To Playa Panamá

Playa Hermosa

Playa Pedregosa

151

NICARAGUA
Papagayo Peninsula
Playa Hermosa   CARIBBEAN SEA
★ SAN JOSÉ
PACIFIC OCEAN   PANAMA

0   1/4 mi
0   0.25 km

To Playa del Coco

change from time to time, so it's always best to check in advance. During the high season and on weekends, extra buses from Liberia are sometimes added. You can also take a bus to Playa del Coco, from which playas Hermosa and Panamá are a relatively quick taxi ride away. Taxi fare should run C7,000.

One direct bus departs for San José daily at 5am from Playa Panamá, with a stop in Playa Hermosa along the way. Buses to Liberia leave Playa Panamá regularly between 6am and 7pm, stopping in Playa Hermosa a few minutes later. Ask at your hotel about current schedules, and where to catch the bus.

ORIENTATION   From the well-marked turnoff for the Papagayo Peninsula (near the prominent Do It Center hardware store), a paved road leads around to the Allegro Papagayo and Four Seasons resorts. If you are heading to the beaches a little farther south, continue on to the well-marked turnoff for Playa del Coco and Playa Hermosa. This road forks before reaching Playa del Coco. You'll come to the turnoff for Playa Hermosa first. Playa Panamá is a few kilometers farther along the same road. The road ends at the Hilton Papagayo Resort. A road connects the Papagayo Peninsula road and Playa Panamá. This 11km (6¾-mile) shortcut is definitely your quickest route to Playa Panamá.

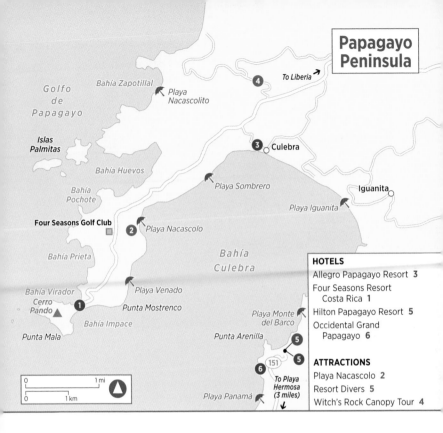

Papagayo Peninsula

Golfo de Papagayo

Bahía Zapotillal — Playa Nacascolito

4 To Liberia →

Islas Palmitas

Bahía Huevos

3 Culebra

Playa Sombrero

Iguanita

Playa Iguanita

Bahía Pochote

Four Seasons Golf Club

2 Playa Nacascolo

Bahía Prieta

Bahía Culebra

Bahía Virador
Cerro Pando **1**

Playa Venado

Punta Mostrenco

Bahía Impace

Punta Mala

Playa Monte del Barco

Punta Arenilla

5

5

151

6

To Playa Hermosa (3 miles) ↓

Playa Panamá

HOTELS

Allegro Papagayo Resort **3**
Four Seasons Resort Costa Rica **1**
Hilton Papagayo Resort **5**
Occidental Grand Papagayo **6**

ATTRACTIONS

Playa Nacascolo **2**
Resort Divers **5**
Witch's Rock Canopy Tour **4**

0 — 1 mi
0 — 1 km

Playa Hermosa is about a 450m (1,476-ft.) stretch of beach, with all the hotels laid out along this stretch. From the main road, which continues on to Playa Panamá, three access roads head off toward the beach. All the hotels are well marked, with signs pointing guests down the right access road. Playa Panamá is the least developed of the beaches out here. Somewhat longer than Playa Hermosa, it also has several access roads heading in toward the beach from the main road, which is slightly inland.

Fun on & Under the Water

Most of the beaches up here are usually quite calm and good for swimming.

If you want to do some diving, check in with **Diving Safaris de Costa Rica** ★ (☎ 2672-1259; www.costaricadiving.net), on the principal access road into Playa Hermosa, about 137m (450 ft.) before you hit the beach. This is a long-established and respected dive operation. It has a large shop and offers a wide range of trips to numerous dive spots, and it also offers night dives, multiday packages, certification classes, and Nitrox dives. These folks also offer multiday live-aboard and dive trips on their 14m (48-ft.) yacht.

Alternatively, you can check out **Resort Divers** (☎ 2672-0106; www. resortdivers-cr.com), which has set up shop at the Hilton Papagayo Resort.

Playa Panamá.

Both of the above-mentioned companies will accept divers from any of the hotels in the area, and can arrange transport. A two-tank dive should run between $70 and $140 per person, depending primarily on the distance traveled to the dive sites.

In the middle of Playa Hermosa, **Aqua Sport** (© **2672-0050**) is where to go for watersports equipment rental. Kayaks, sailboards, canoes, bicycles, beach umbrellas, snorkel gear, and parasails are available at fairly reasonable rates. You'll also find here a small supermarket, public phones, and a restaurant.

Because the beaches in this area are relatively protected and generally flat, surfers should look into boat trips to nearby **Witch's Rock ★★** (p. 219) and **Ollie's Point ★** (p. 219). **Costa Rica Surf Charters** (© **8935-2538**; www.crsurfcharters.com), **Hotel Finisterra** (© **2672-0227**), and **Aqua Sport** (© **2672-0050**) all offer trips for up to six surfers for around $60 to $120 per hour.

Most of these companies mentioned above also offer fishing trips for between $250 to $600 for groups of two to four anglers. Or you can check in with **North Pacific Tours ★** (© **2670-1564**; www.northpacifictours.com).

If you're interested in wind power, check in with the folks at the **El Velero Hotel** (see below), or any of the sailboat charter options listed in the Playa del Coco section below. All offer a range of full- and half-day tours, with snorkel stops, as well as sunset cruises.

Other Options

Both **Charlie's Adventures ★** (© **2672-0317**; www.charliesadventure.com) and **Swiss Travel Service** (© **2668-1020**; www.swisstravelcr.com) offer a wide range of activities and tours, including trips to Santa Rosa or Rincón de la Vieja national parks, and rafting on the Corobicí River. Both of these operations have desks at several of the hotels around here and will pick you up at any hotel in the area.

The best zip-line canopy tour in this area is the **Witch's Rock Canopy Tour ★★** (𝒞 **2696-7171;** www.witchsrockcanopytour.com), just before the Allegro Papagayo Resort. The 1½-hour tour covers 3km (1¾ miles) of cables touching down on 24 platforms and crossing 3 suspension bridges. The tour costs $75.

Finally, the Arnold Palmer–designed championship course at the Four Seasons Resort (see below) is hands-down the most beautiful and challenging **golf course** in the country. However, it is open only to Four Seasons' guests.

If you're looking for some pampering, whether it be a massage, facial, or body scrub, check out **Spa Aguas de Hermosa** (𝒞 **2672-1386**), which is located in the Hermosa Heights Resort Community, and offers up a wide range of treatment options.

Where to Stay

VERY EXPENSIVE

Four Seasons Resort Costa Rica ★★★ ☺   Set on a narrow spit of land between two stunning white-sand beaches, this is the most luxurious and impressive resort in Costa Rica. The architecture is unique, with most buildings featuring flowing roof designs and other touches imitating the forms of turtles, armadillos, and butterflies. Rooms are very spacious, with decorations from around the world and marble bathrooms. Each has a large private balcony with a sofa, a table, and a couple of chairs. Rooms on the third and fourth floors have the best views and are priced accordingly. Suites and villas have even more space and either a private pool, Jacuzzi, or an open-air gazebo for soaking in the views.

Four Seasons Resort Costa Rica.

The resort features the Four Seasons' renowned service (including family-friendly amenities such as kid-size bathrobes and childproof rooms), one of the best-equipped spas in the country, and a spectacular golf course that offers ocean views from 15 of its 18 holes. Despite being such a large resort, these folks have been granted "4 Leaves" by the CST Sustainable Tourism program.

Papagayo Peninsula, Guanacaste. www.fourseasons.com/costarica. ✆ **800/332-3442** in the U.S., or 2696-0000. Fax 2696-0510. 153 units. $695–$1,240 double; $1,350 and up suites and villas. Children stay free in parent's room. AE, DC, MC, V. **Amenities:** 4 restaurants; 2 bars; lounge; babysitting; children's programs; concierge; championship 18-hole golf course; 3 free-form outdoor pools; room service; smoke-free rooms; full-service spa; 2 tennis courts; watersports equipment. *In room:* A/C, TV/DVD, hair dryer, MP3 docking station, Wi-Fi.

Occidental Grand Papagayo ★★   This is the highest-end all-inclusive resort of the Occidental Hotel chain in Costa Rica. The rooms are spread over a contoured hillside overlooking the ocean, but not all rooms come with an ocean view. The resort is geared toward couples, and the vast majority of the rooms come with just one king-size bed, although some have two queen-size beds. I like the Grand Concierge rooms, which are close to the pool and restaurants, and feature marble floors. However, the Royal Club rooms and suites are the best rooms, and they come with beefed up concierge services. The protected and calm beach almost entirely disappears at peak high tide. Scheduled activities and entertainment options are offered, and a wide range of additional tours and activities can be added on.

Papagayo Peninsula, Guanacaste. www.occidentalhotels.com. ✆ **800/858-2258** in the U.S. and Canada, 2672-0191 for reservations inside Costa Rica. Fax 2672-0057. 169 units. $300 per person double occupancy; $735 Royal Club room double. Rates include food, drinks, a range of activities, and taxes. AE, MC, V. **Amenities:** 4 restaurants; 2 bars; lounge; babysitting; large health club and spa; 2 large free-form outdoor pools; smoke-free rooms; 1 lighted tennis court; watersports equipment. *In room:* A/C, TV, hair dryer, minibar, Wi-Fi.

EXPENSIVE

Over on Playa Panamá, **Casa Conde del Mar ★** (www.grupocasaconde.com; ✆ **2227-4232**) is a pretty, boutique resort, with plush rooms and lush grounds.

Allegro Papagayo Resort ★ ☺   If you're looking for an affordable all-inclusive vacation at a large modern resort with a wide range of facilities and activities, this is a good bet. The rooms are all identical in size—comfortable enough, but by no means extravagant—and housed in three-story buildings spread over a steep hillside overlooking the sea. Logically, the rooms on the upper floors in the buildings higher up the hill have the best views. The beach is an isolated patch of hard-packed salt-and-pepper sand that almost disappears at high tide. The waters here are very protected, and the drop-off is very gradual. However, most folks will want to spend their beach time at the hotel's "Fun Club" on a beautiful nearby white-sand beach. A regular boat shuttle brings folks to and fro, and the site has a snack bar/grill, watersports equipment, and activities.

Playa Manzanillo, Guanacaste (A.P. 434-1150, La Uruca). www.occidentalhotels.com. ✆ **2248-2323** reservations in San José, or 2690-9900 at the resort. Fax 2690-9910. 300 units. $113 per person double occupancy. Rates include food, drinks, a range of activities, and taxes. AE, DC, MC, V. **Amenities:** 3 restaurants; 3 bars; babysitting; children's programs; small fitness center; 2 Jacuzzis; large free-form outdoor pool; watersports equipment. *In room:* A/C, TV, hair dryer, minibar.

Hilton Papagayo Resort ★ ☺   This sprawling resort is spread across several hillsides that rise up over a small, calm section of beach. Most of the duplex villas can be separated into two rooms or shared by a family or two couples. All rooms have marble floors, large bathrooms, and small private patios or balconies. Some of the junior suites come with private plunge pools. The resort is quite spread out, so if you don't want to do a lot of walking or wait for the minivan shuttles, request a room near the main pool and restaurants. If you want a good view, ask for one on a hill overlooking the bay. The hotel has a large, modern, and plush spa facility. It also has its own small crescent-shape swath of beach, which is very calm and protected for swimming. Among the amenities offered is an excellent children's program, with a range of daily activities.

Playa Panamá, Guanacaste. www.hiltonpapagayoresort.com.✆ **800/445-8667** in the U.S. and Canada, or 2672-0000 in Costa Rica. Fax 2672-0133. 202 units. $229–$329 double; $579–$1,320 suite. Rates include food, drinks, a range of activities, and taxes. AE, DC, DISC, MC, V. **Amenities:** 3 restaurants; 2 bars; babysitting; children's programs; well-equipped health center and spa; Jacuzzi; 3-tiered main outdoor pool, small lap pool and resistance lap pool; tennis court; water-sports equipment. *In room:* A/C, TV, hair dryer, minibar, MP3 docking station, Wi-Fi.

Hotel Playa Hermosa Bosque del Mar ★★★   Following a major rebuild, this has emerged as the premier beachfront boutique hotel in the area. The oceanfront suites here are plush, and feature outdoor Jacuzzis. The garden-view suites are very similar but an indoor sauna replaces the Jacuzzi. In both cases, second floor units have better views and higher ceilings. The junior suites are all cozy and well-equipped. The whole complex was built around and among the lush existing gardens and trees, and employs sustainable practices wherever possible. Trees come up and through the main lobby and restaurant, and through some of the decks off the rooms. Three of the suites are handicapped accessible. The second-floor bar and lounge has great views through the trees to the sea.

Playa Hermosa, Guanacaste. www.hotelplayahermosa.com. ✆ **2672-0046.** Fax 2672-0019. 32 units. $175 junior suite; $275 suite. AE, MC, V. **Amenities:** Restaurant; bar; Jacuzzi; pretty outdoor pool w/sculpted waterfall; Wi-Fi. *In room:* A/C, TV, minifridge, hair dryer.

MODERATE

El Velero Hotel ★   This place is a great choice right on the beach in Playa Hermosa, especially at this price. White walls and polished tile floors give El Velero a Mediterranean flavor. The rooms are large, and those on the second floor have high ceilings. The furnishings are simple, though, and some of the bathrooms are a bit small. The hotel has its own popular little restaurant, which offers a good selection of meat, fish, and shrimp dishes, as well as weekly barbecue fests. Various tours, horseback riding, and fishing trips are arranged through the hotel; the most popular excursions are the full-day and sunset cruises on the hotel's namesake sailboat.

Playa Hermosa, Guanacaste. www.costaricahotel.net. ✆ **2672-1017.** Fax 2672-0016. 22 units. $79 double. Rates higher during peak periods, slightly lower during the off season. AE, MC, V. **Amenities:** Restaurant; bar; small outdoor pool. *In room:* A/C, TV, hair dryer, Wi-Fi.

Villa del Sueño Hotel ★   Villa del Sueño offers cozy rooms at a good price, and one of the better restaurants in Playa Hermosa. All the rooms have cool tile floors, high hardwood ceilings, ceiling fans, and well-placed windows for cross ventilation. The second-floor superior rooms have more space and larger windows. Some suites have full kitchens and multiple bedrooms. Although this hotel isn't right on the beach (it's about 1 block inland), its well-groomed lawns and gardens feel like an oasis in the dust and heat of a Guanacaste dry season. A small pool and open-air bar are in the center courtyard. In addition to fine meals, the restaurant features live music by local acts during high season.

Playa Hermosa, Guanacaste. www.villadelsueno.com. ☎ **800/378-8599** in the U.S. and Canada, or 2672-0026 in Costa Rica. Fax 2672-0021. 46 units. $75–$105 double; $130–$255 suite. Children 11 and under free. AE, MC, V. **Amenities:** Restaurant (below); bar; two outdoor pools. *In room:* A/C, Wi-Fi.

Eating & After-Dark Diversions

For nightlife, find out whether the **Villa del Sueño Restaurant** (see below) has live music. Two Saturdays a month, Villa del Sueño hosts larger concerts, featuring prominent Costa Rican acts, in its spiffy open-air amphitheater. For U.S.-style bar food and entertainment, try the **Upper Deck Sports Bar** (☎ **2672-1276**), just off the main road. For a more sedate night out, the **Embassy Cine** (☎ **2672-0173**) offers nightly, late-run movies in a small theater, with bar service.

In addition to the places listed below, you'll find good restaurants at both the **El Velero Hotel** (see "Where to Stay," above) and the **Hotel Finisterra** (see "Fun on & Under the Water," above).

Ginger ★★ 🏠 INTERNATIONAL/TAPAS   In this most creative restaurant in the area, the architecture and decor are stylish and modern, with sharp angles and loads of chrome and glass. The food is an eclectic mix of modern takes on wide-ranging international fare, all served as tapas, meant to be shared while sampling the many cocktails and wines. Still, it's easy to make a full meal. Start things off with the signature Ginger Rolls, rice paper rolls filled with poached salmon, avocado, and mango, or the spicy Firecracker shrimp, jumbo shrimp cooked over the grill, with a chili, Hoisin, honey, and lime marinade. More traditional Mediterranean and Spanish-style tapas are also on the menu, as well as delicious desserts.

On the main road, Playa Hermosa. ☎ **2672-0041.** www.gingercostarica.com. Tapas $5–$10. MC, V. Tues–Sun 5–10pm.

Villa del Sueño Restaurant ★ INTERNATIONAL   A mellow yet refined atmosphere presides under slow-turning ceiling fans at this simple open-air restaurant. In addition to lots of fresh fish are well-prepared pasta dishes and meat and poultry options. A small selection of specials is offered nightly. Live music is available many nights during high season.

At the Villa del Sueño Hotel. ☎ **2672-0026.** Main courses $12–$24. AE, MC, V. Daily 7am–9:30pm.

PLAYA DEL COCO & PLAYA OCOTAL

253km (157 miles) NW of San José; 35km (22 miles) W of Liberia

Playa del Coco is one of Costa Rica's busiest and most developed beach destinations. With a large modern mall and shopping center anchoring the eastern

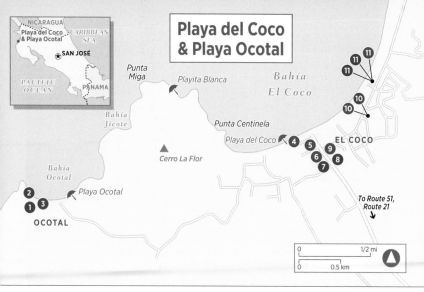

Playa del Coco & Playa Ocotal

HOTELS
Coco Beach Hotel & Casino **8**
El Ocotal Beach Resort **2**
Hotel Villa Casa Blanca **1**
The Suites at Café de Playa **11**

RESTAURANTS
Café de Playa **11**
Father Rooster **3**
La Dolce Vita **10**
Papagayo Seafood **7**
Papagayo Steak House **7**
Papagayo Sushi Boat **7**

NIGHTLIFE
Café de Playa **11**
Coconutz **6**
Kashbar **10**
La Vida Loca **4**
Lizard Lounge **9**
Zi Lounge **5**

edge of town, you'll pass through a tight jumble of restaurants, hotels, and souvenir shops for several blocks before you hit the sand and sea; homes, condos, and hotels have sprouted up along the beach in either direction. This has long been, and remains, a popular destination with middle-class Ticos and weekend revelers from San José. It's also a prime jumping-off point for some of Costa Rica's best scuba diving. The beach, which has grayish-brown sand and gentle surf, is quite wide at low tide and almost nonexistent at high tide. The crowds that come here like their music loud and constant, so if you're in search of a quiet retreat, stay away from the center of town. Still, if you're looking for a beach with a wide range of inexpensive hotels, lively nightlife, and plenty of cheap food and beer close at hand, you'll enjoy Playa del Coco.

More interesting still, in my opinion, is **Playa Ocotal ★**, which is a couple of kilometers to the south. This tiny pocket cove features a small salt-and-pepper beach bordered by high bluffs and is quite beautiful. When it's calm there's good snorkeling around some rocky islands close to shore here.

Essentials

GETTING THERE & DEPARTING   By Plane: The nearest airport with regularly scheduled flights is in Liberia (p. 190). From there you can arrange for a taxi to take you to Playa del Coco or Playa Ocotal, which is about a 25-minute drive, for $35 to $50.

Playa Ocotal.

By Car: From Liberia, head west on CR21 toward Santa Cruz. Just past the village of Comunidad, turn right. In about 11km (6¾ miles) you'll come to a fork in the road. Take the left fork. The right fork goes to Playa Hermosa. The drive takes about 4 hours from San José.

By Bus: Pulmitan express buses (© **2222-1650**) leave San José for Playa del Coco at 8am and 2 and 4pm daily from Calle 24 between avenidas 5 and 7. Allow 5 hours for the trip. A one-way ticket is C3,475. From Liberia, buses (© **2666-0458**) to Playa del Coco leave regularly throughout the day between 5am and 7pm. A one-way ticket for the 40-minute trip costs around C500. These bus schedules change frequently, so it's always best to check in advance. During the high season and on weekends, extra buses from Liberia are sometimes added. The direct bus for San José leaves Playa del Coco daily at 4am and 8:45am and 2:45pm. Local buses for Liberia leave daily between 5am and 7pm.

Gray Line (© **2220-2126**; www.graylinecostarica.com) has a daily bus that leaves San José at 8am for Playa del Coco. The fare is $40. **Interbus** (© **2283-5573**; www.interbusonline.com) has a daily bus that leaves San José at 7:45am. The fare is $40. Both companies will pick you up at most San José–area hotels, and have connections to most other tourist destinations around Costa Rica.

Depending on demand, the Playa del Coco buses sometimes go as far as Playa Ocotal; it's worth checking beforehand. Otherwise, a taxi should cost around $5.

ORIENTATION   Playa del Coco is a compact and busy beach town. Most of its hotels and restaurants are either on the water, on the road leading into town, or on the road that heads north, about 100m (328 ft.) inland from and parallel to the beach.

Playa Ocotal, which is south of Playa del Coco on a paved road that leaves the main road about 183m (600 ft.) before the beach, is a small collection of vacation homes, condos, and a couple of hotels. It has one bar and one restaurant on the beach.

GETTING AROUND   You can rent cars from any number of rental companies. Most are based in Liberia, or at the airport. See "Essentials," under "Liberia," for details and contact information.

If you can't flag down a taxi on the street, call ✆ 2670-0408.

FAST FACTS   The nearest major hospital is in Liberia (✆ **2690-2300**). For the local **health clinic,** call ✆ **2670-1717;** and for the local **pharmacy,** call ✆ **2670-2050.** For the local **police,** dial ✆ **2670-0258.** You'll find several banks and ATMs around town.

Fun on & off the Beach

Plenty of boats are anchored at Playa del Coco, and that means plenty of opportunities to go fishing, diving, or sailing. Still, the most popular activities, especially among the hordes of Ticos who come here, are lounging on the beach, hanging out in the *sodas*, and cruising the bars and discos at night. If you're interested, you might be able to join a soccer match. (The soccer field is in the middle of town.) You can also arrange horseback rides; ask at your hotel.

BEACH CLUB   If you're staying at a hotel without a pool, or just want a sense of exclusivity on the beach, you might check out **Café de Playa Beach & Dining Club** (✆ **2670-1621;** www.cafedeplaya.com). In addition to having an excellent restaurant (see below), this place offers day passes for $15

Playa del Coco.

that allow access to their pool and private grassy lawn fronting the beach, and spread with comfortable teak chaise lounges. They also have a host of watersports equipment rental and tour options, and a small spa.

CANOPY TOUR The **Congo Trail Canopy Tour** (© 2666-4422 or 2697-1801) is on the outskirts of Playa del Coco, along a dirt road that leads to Playa Pan de Azúcar. This place is set in a stand of thick, tropical dry forest. In addition to the zip-line canopy tour, these folks have a small butterfly farm, and a few zoo-enclosures, with some monkeys, and reptiles. The tour runs every day from 8am to 5pm, and costs $35 for the canopy tour, and an extra $5 to see the animals.

FOUR-WHEELING ATV tours along a deserted beach and through the surrounding forests are offered by **Fourtrax Adventures** (© 2653-4040; www.fourtraxadventure.com), which charges $75 for its 2-hour outing. You can also combine their ATV tour with a canopy tour, for $110 per person.

GOLF Located about 10km (6¼ miles) outside Playa del Coco, the **Papagayo Golf & Country Club** ★ (© 2697-0169; www.papagayo-golf.com) is a full 18-hole course, with a pro shop, driving range, and rental equipment. It costs $95 in greens fees, including a cart, and access to the pool area before or after your round. Tee time reservations are necessary on weekends. Closed Mondays during the off season.

GYM If you want to work out while in town, head to the **Coco Gym** (© 2670-2129; www.cocogym.com), which is on the road between Playa del Coco and Ocotal. Weights, cardio machines, and a range of classes are all offered. A day pass here costs just $5.

SAILING Several cruising sailboats and longtime local salts offer daily sailing excursions. The 47-foot ketch-rigged *Kuna Vela* (© 8301-3030; www.kunavela.com) and the *Seabird* (© 8880-6393; www.seabirdsailingexcursions.com), a 45-foot ketch, are two boats plying the waters off Playa

A moray eel.

Ollie's Point is named after Oliver North, the famous and felonious former lieutenant colonel at the center of the Iran-Contra scandal. The beaches and ports of northern Guanacaste were a staging ground for supplying the Nicaraguan Contra rebels. Legend has it that during a news broadcast of an interview with North, some surfers noticed a fabulous point break going off in the background. Hence, the discovery and naming of Ollie's Point.

del Coco. Both offer half- and full-day and sunset sailing options, with snorkel stops and an open bar.

SCUBA DIVING   Scuba diving is the most popular watersport in the area, and dive shops abound. **Ocotal Diving** (✆ 2670-0321; www.ocotaldiving. com), **Summer Salt** (✆ 2670-0308; www.summer-salt.com), and **Rich Coast Diving** (✆ 2670-0176; www.richcoastdiving.com) are the most established and offer equipment rentals and dive trips. A two-tank dive, with equipment, should cost between $75 and $150 per person, depending on the distance to the dive site. The more distant dive sites visited include the Catalina Islands and Bat Island. All of these operators also offer PADI certification courses.

SPORTFISHING   Full- and half-day sportfishing excursions can be arranged through any of the hotel tour desks, or with **Tranquilamar** (✆ 2670-0833; www.tranquilamar.com). A half-day of fishing, with boat, captain, food, and tackle, should cost $500 for two to four passengers; a full day should run $700.

SURFING   Playa del Coco has no surf whatsoever, but it is a popular jumping-off point for daily boat trips to Witch's Rock or Roca Bruja, and Ollie's Point up in Santa Rosa National Park (p. 202). Most of the above-mentioned sportfishing and dive operations also ferry surfers up to these two isolated surf breaks. Alternatively, you can contact **Roca Bruja Surf Operations** (✆ 2670-1020). A boat that carries five surfers for a full day, including lunch and beer, should run around $285 to $350. *Note:* Both Witch's Rock and Ollie's Point are technically within Santa Rosa National Park. Permits are sometimes required, and boats without permits are sometimes turned away. If you decide to go, be sure your boat captain is licensed and has cleared access to the park. You may also have to pay the park's $10 entrance fee.

Where to Stay

EXPENSIVE

El Ocotal Beach Resort ★   This place has been plagued with management and service issues and could use a major overhaul. That said, it's the most complete and best located resort in the Playas del Coco/Ocotal area. The guest rooms vary considerably in size and styling. Those at the top of the hill overlook a dramatic stretch of rocky coastline and have fabulous views, although if you want quick access to the beach, choose one of the lower units. Each of the six duplex bungalows shares a small oceanview plunge pool. The third-floor suite, no. 520, is the best room in the house, with a large wraparound balcony and private Jacuzzi. El Ocotal's hilltop restaurant is a great place to watch the sunset and have a drink. *Note:* It's a steep, vigorous hike from bottom to top at this resort.

Playa del Coco, Guanacaste. www.ocotalresort.com. ✆ **2670-0321.** Fax 2670-0083. 42 units, 12 bungalows, 5 suites. $125 double; $170 bungalow and suite. Rates include full breakfast. Children 11 and under free. AE, DC, MC, V. **Amenities:** 2 restaurants; exercise room; Jacuzzi; 3 outdoor pools and 3 plunge pools; lighted tennis court. *In room:* A/C, TV, minifridge, hair dryer, Wi-Fi.

MODERATE

Coco Beach Hotel & Casino   This two-story hotel is the biggest thing in Playa del Coco and is an acceptable choice if you're looking for a contemporary and well-equipped room, close to the beach, restaurants, and action. The rooms are identical in size, and come with two queen-size beds. All share a common veranda, which gets blasted by the hot afternoon sun. The casino here is the best in Playa del Coco. You can't miss this large building on your right, on the main road into Playa del Coco—about 2 blocks before you hit the beach.

Playa del Coco, Guanacaste. www.cocobeachhotelandcasino.com. ✆ **2670-0494.** Fax 2670-0555. 32 units. $102 double. Rates substantially lower in the off season. MC, V. **Amenities:** Restaurant; bar; casino; small outdoor pool; small spa. *In room:* A/C, TV, Wi-Fi.

Hotel Villa Casa Blanca ★   With friendly staff, beautiful gardens, and attractive rooms, this bed-and-breakfast inn is one of my favorite options in the area. Located about 500m (1,640 ft.) inland from the beach at Playa Ocotal, it's built in the style of a Spanish villa. All the guest rooms feature fine furnishings and are well kept. Some are a tad small, but others are quite roomy. The suites are higher up and have ocean views. My favorite has a secluded patio with lush flowering plants all around. A little rancho serves as an open-air bar and breakfast area, and beside this is a pretty little lap pool with a bridge over it. Another separate rancho serves as a sort of lounge/recreation area and they have a little in-house day spa.

Playa Ocotal, Guanacaste. www.hotelvillacasablanca.com. ✆ **2670-0518.** Fax 2670-0448. 11 units. $105 double; $125 double suite. Rates include breakfast buffet and taxes. AE, MC, V. **Amenities:** Outdoor lounge and bar; Jacuzzi; small outdoor pool; small day spa. *In room:* A/C, Wi-Fi.

The Suites at Café de Playa ★   While simple and understated, the five suites are the plushest beachfront rooms you'll find right in Playa del Coco. The design and decor are minimalist, with contemporary fixtures, furnishings, and art. Rooms are arranged around a central pool area and come with either one or two queen-size beds. The best thing about these rooms is the fact that they are just a few steps from the sand, and allow you access to the facilities and services available at Café de Playa.

Playa del Coco, Guanacaste. www.cafedeplaya.com. ✆ **2670-1621.** 4 units. $100–$140 double. Rates include full breakfast. AE, DC, MC, V. **Amenities:** Restaurant; outdoor pool; small spa. *In room:* A/C, TV, Wi-Fi.

Where to Eat

A clutch of basic open-air *sodas* is at the traffic circle in the center of El Coco village. These restaurants serve Tico standards, with an emphasis on fried fish. Prices are quite low—and so is the quality, for the most part.

You can get excellent Italian food at **La Dolce Vita** (✆ **2670-2142;** www. ladolcevitacostarica.com), in the little El Pueblito strip mall on the road running north and parallel to the beach.

Right on the main strip, you'll also find the neighboring Papagayo and Louisiana operations. Growing out of the success of their seafood restaurant, **Papagayo Seafood** (✆ **2670-0298**) has opened both the **Papagayo Steak House** (✆ **2670-0605**) and **Papagayo Sushi Boat** (✆ **2670-0298**), in an attempt to cover all possible bases.

Café de Playa ★★ 🎁 INTERNATIONAL/FUSION   This hip restaurant is the most elegant and enjoyable spot in Playa del Coco. The creative menu covers a lot of ground, with influences from Italy and across Asia most prevalent. Appetizers range from an octopus carpaccio to a cold Thai beef salad. There are several pasta choices, and a very tasty oriental rice salad with smoked tuna, caviar, and avocado. Lobster is served several ways, as are tenderloin filets. Heavy teak tables and chairs are spread around the ample open-air dining room, or out under the open sky (either sun or stars, depending upon the hour). These folks also have an excellent wine list, with plenty of Italian and French choices, in addition to the more common Chilean and Argentine fare.

On the beach, Playa del Coco. ✆ **2670-1621.** www.cafedeplaya.com. Reservations recommended. Main courses C5,500–C13,000. AE, MC, V. Daily 8am–10pm.

Father Rooster 📷 SEAFOOD/BAR   Set on the sand, just steps from Playa Ocotal, this beachfront bar and restaurant is supposed to look like a simple wooden shack. They serve up hearty and fresh lunch and dinner fare, and cool tasty cocktails. I recommend the fish tacos or beer battered shrimp. Heavy wooden tables and chairs are set under shade trees in the sand, and more ring the wraparound veranda. Inside, you'll find a pool table. Live bands occasionally set up here on weekend nights.

On the beach, Playa Ocotal. ✆ **2670-1246.** Main courses C6,200–C13,500. MC, V. Daily 11am–10pm.

Playa del Coco After Dark

Playa del Coco is one of Costa Rica's liveliest beach towns after dark. Most of the action is centered along a 2-block section of the main road into town, just before you hit the beach. Here you'll find the **Lizard Lounge** ★ (✆ **2670-0307**), which has a big party vibe. Just across the street is the large, open-air **Zi Lounge** ★★ (✆ **2670-1978**). Those looking for a gringo-influenced sports-bar hangout can try **Coconutz** ★ (✆ **2670-1982;** www.coconutz-costa rica.com).

If you head north on the dirt road running parallel to the beach you'll find **Café de Playa** (see above), which often has live music and concerts, with major acts from San José, as well as local talent filling the bills. For a Middle Eastern–inspired mellow lounge scene, you can head to **Kashbar** (✆ **2670-2141;** www. kashbar.com), in the Pueblito shopping center, located on this same road.

On the south end of the beach, reached via a rickety footbridge over the estuary, you'll find **La Vida Loca** ★ (✆ **2670-0181**), a lively beachfront bar with a pool table, Ping-Pong table, foosball table, and live bands.

En Route: Between Playas del Coco & Playa Flamingo

Hotel Sugar Beach ★★ Playa Pan de Azúcar, or Sugar Beach, is a pretty, salt-and-pepper sand beach on a small cove surrounded by rocky hills. This is the only hotel in the area, and that's what gives it most of its charm, in my opinion—lots of seclusion and privacy. Nature lovers will be thrilled to find that howler monkeys and iguanas abound on the grounds. Snorkelers should be happy here too; this cove has some good snorkeling on calm days. I like the oceanfront standard rooms, which have great views and easy access to the beach. However, the deluxe rooms and suites, which are set back on a hillside, are larger and more luxurious, and some have excellent ocean views from their private balconies. If you don't land one of the rooms with a sea view, the main lodge and restaurant have commanding views from a hillside perch.

Playa Pan de Azúcar, Guanacaste. www.sugar-beach.com. ✆ **2654-4242.** Fax 2654-4239. 30 units. $123 double; $235 suite; $700 villa. Rates include breakfast. AE, MC, V. **Amenities:** Restaurant; bar; small kidney-shape pool set on the hillside; watersports equipment rental. *In room:* A/C, TV, minifridge.

RIU Guanacaste ★ ☺ This is the largest all-inclusive resort in Costa Rica, and it offers up everything you might want or expect in this genre. Rooms are spacious and well-equipped, and most have at least some view of the ocean from a private balcony. The large, multilevel pool is the center of the action here, although plenty of tour and activity options are available, including a tennis court and a massive spa, as well as a secluded and seldom visited beach out front. The beach itself is a bit rocky and steep, with dark brown sand, but the waters are generally calm and well-protected, and a fair number of shade trees line the shore. You'll definitely get a better deal than the published rack rate if you book online.

Playa Matapalo, Guanacaste. www.riu.com. ✆ **800/748-4990** in the U.S. and Canada, or 2681-2300 at the hotel. Fax 2681-2305. 701 units. $304 double; $389 suite; $414 Jacuzzi suite. Rates include all meals, drinks, taxes, a wide range of activities, and use of nonmotorized land and watersports equipment. Spa services extra. AE, MC, V. **Amenities:** 4 restaurants; 5 bars; 2 lounges; casino; discotheque; babysitting; free bike usage; children's programs; concierge; extensive exercise facilities and spa; large free-form outdoor pool w/several Jacuzzis, smoke-free rooms; lighted tennis court; watersports equipment rental; Wi-Fi. *In room:* A/C, TV, hair dryer, minibar.

PLAYAS CONCHAL & BRASILITO

280km (174 miles) NW of San José; 67km (42 miles) SW of Liberia

Playa Conchal ★★ is the first in a string of beaches stretching north along this coast. This beach is almost entirely backed by the massive Westin Playa Conchal resort and Reserva Conchal condominium complex. The unique beach here was once made up primarily of soft crushed shells—a shell-collectors' heaven. Unfortunately, as Conchal has developed and its popularity spread, unscrupulous builders have brought in dump trucks to haul away the namesake seashells for landscaping and construction, and the impact is noticeable.

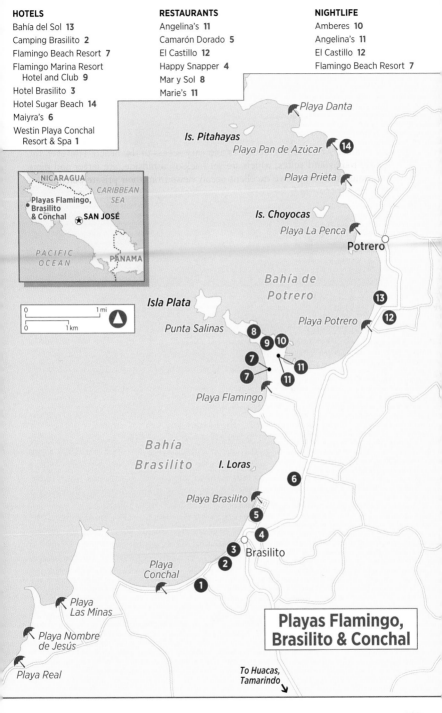

HOTELS
Bahía del Sol **13**
Camping Brasilito **2**
Flamingo Beach Resort **7**
Flamingo Marina Resort
   Hotel and Club **9**
Hotel Brasilito **3**
Hotel Sugar Beach **14**
Maiyra's **6**
Westin Playa Conchal
   Resort & Spa **1**

RESTAURANTS
Angelina's **11**
Camarón Dorado **5**
El Castillo **12**
Happy Snapper **4**
Mar y Sol **8**
Marie's **11**

NIGHTLIFE
Amberes **10**
Angelina's **11**
El Castillo **12**
Flamingo Beach Resort **7**

NICARAGUA

CARIBBEAN
SEA

Playas Flamingo,
Brasilito
& Conchal
★ SAN JOSÉ

PACIFIC
OCEAN
PANAMA

0   1 mi
0   1 km

Playa Danta

Is. Pitahayas
Playa Pan de Azúcar   **14**

Playa Prieta

Is. Choyocas
Playa La Penca
Potrero

**Bahía de
Potrero**

Isla Plata   **13**

Playa Potrero   **12**

Punta Salinas
8
9 10
7   **11**
7   **11**

Playa Flamingo

**Bahía
Brasilito**   **I. Loras**
6

Playa Brasilito
5
4
3 **Brasilito**
2
Playa
Conchal   **1**

Playa
Las Minas

Playa Nombre
de Jesús

Playa Real

**Playas Flamingo,
Brasilito & Conchal**

To Huacas,
Tamarindo

Dining on the beach at Playa Brasilito.

Just beyond Playa Conchal to the north, you'll come to **Playa Brasilito,** a tiny beach town and one of the few real villages in the area. The soccer field is the center of the village, and around its edges are a couple of little *pulperías* (general stores). The long stretch of gray sand beach has a quiet, undiscovered feel to it.

Essentials

GETTING THERE & DEPARTING   By Plane: The nearest airport with regularly scheduled flights is in Tamarindo (see "Tamarindo: Getting There; By Plane" below), although it is also possible to fly into Liberia (p. 190). From either of these places, you can arrange for a taxi to drive you to any of these beaches. Playas Brasilito and Conchal are about 25 minutes from Tamarindo and 40 minutes from Liberia. A taxi from Tamarindo should cost around $30 to $45, and between $50 and $70 from Liberia.

  By Car: Two major routes go to the beaches. The most direct is by way of the La Amistad Bridge over the Tempisque River. Take the Interamerican Highway west from San José. Forty-seven kilometers (29 miles) past the turnoff for Puntarenas, you'll see signs for the turnoff to the bridge. After crossing the Tempisque River, follow the signs for Nicoya, continuing north to Santa Cruz. About 16km (10 miles) north of Santa Cruz, just before the village of Belén, take the turnoff for playas Conchal, Brasilito, Flamingo, and Potrero. After another 20km (12 miles), at the town of Huacas, take the right fork to reach these beaches. The drive takes about 4½ hours.

  Alternatively, you can drive here via Liberia. When you reach Liberia, turn west and follow the signs for Santa Cruz and the various beaches. Just beyond the town of Belén, take the turnoff for playas Flamingo, Brasilito, and Potrero, and continue following the directions given above. This route takes around 5 hours.

By Bus: Tralapa express buses (© **2221-7202** in San José, or 2654-4203 in Flamingo) leave San José daily at 8 and 10:30am and 3pm from Calle 20 between avenidas 3 and 5, stopping at playas Brasilito, Flamingo, and Potrero, in that order. The ride takes around 5 hours. A one-way ticket costs C5,265.

Alternatively, the same company's buses to Santa Cruz (© **2680-0392**) connect with one of the several buses from Santa Cruz to Playa Potrero. Buses depart San José for Santa Cruz roughly every 2 hours daily between 7am and 6pm from Calle 20 between avenidas 3 and 5. Trip duration is around 4 hours; the fare is C4,600. From Santa Cruz, the ride is about 90 minutes; the fare is C1,100.

Gray Line (© **2220-2126;** www.graylinecostarica.com) has two daily buses that leave San José for Playa Flamingo at 8am and 3:30pm. The fare is $40. **Interbus** (© **2283-5573;** www.interbusonline.com) has two daily buses that leave San José for Playa Flamingo at 7:30am and 2:30pm. The fare is $40. Both companies will pick you up at most San José–area hotels, and offer connections to most other tourist destinations in the country.

Express buses depart **Playa Potrero** for San José at 3 and 9am and 2pm, stopping a few minutes later in playas Flamingo and Brasilito. Ask at your hotel where to catch the bus. Buses to **Santa Cruz** leave Potrero at regular intervals throughout the day and take about 90 minutes. If you're heading north toward Liberia, get off the bus at Belén and wait for a bus going north. Buses leave Santa Cruz for San José roughly every other hour between 6am and 6pm.

ORIENTATION   The pavement ends just beyond Playa Conchal as you leave the small village of Brasilito.

Fun on & off the Beach

Playa Conchal ★★, which is legendary for its crushed seashells, is also stunningly beautiful, but the drop-off is quite steep, making it notorious for its strong riptides. However, the water at **Playa Brasilito** is often fairly calm, which makes it a good swimming choice. This is also a great jumping-off point for visiting other nearby, and less popular beaches, like **Playa La Penca** ★★ and **Playa Pan de Azúcar** ★★, both of which are north of here.

All of the hotels here have tour desks offering a range of tour and activity options, including those available in the Flamingo and Potrero area (see below).

Tip: All beaches in Costa Rica are public property. But the land behind the beaches is not, and the Westin hotel owns almost all of it in Playa Conchal, so the only public access is along the soft-sand road that follows the beach south from Brasilito. Before the road reaches Conchal, you'll have to ford a small river and then climb a steep, rocky hill, so four-wheel-drive is recommended.

GOLF   The **Westin Playa Conchal Resort & Spa** ★★ (© **2654-4123**) is home to the excellent **Reserva Conchal Golf Course.** This Robert Trent Jones–designed resort course features broad open fairways, fast greens, and a few wonderful views of the ocean. It is open to the walk-in public from

The village of Playa Brasilito.

neighboring hotels and resorts. It costs $150 in greens fees for 18 holes and $95 for nine holes. If you tee off after 1pm, the price drops to $95 for all the rounds you can squeeze in.

Where to Stay

VERY EXPENSIVE

Westin Playa Conchal Resort & Spa ★★   From the massive open-air reception building down to the sprawling free-form swimming pool, everything at this resort is done on a grand scale. All rooms are suites and come with either one king-size bed or two double beds in a raised bedroom nook. Each unit has a garden patio or a small balcony. Very few rooms here have ocean views. The golf course, with its ponds and wetlands, allows for healthy populations of parrots, roseate spoonbills, and wood storks. Because the hotel owns so much land behind Playa Conchal, guests have almost exclusive access to this crushed-sea-shell beach. For years a Melia property, this place was taken over by the Westin hotel group in May 2011.

Playa Conchal, Guanacaste. www.starwoodhotels.com. © **888/336-3542** in the U.S., or 2654-3300. Fax 2654-3449. 406 units. $300–$420 double; $560 and up deluxe double. Rates include all meals, drinks, taxes, a wide range of activities, and use of nonmotorized land and watersports equipment. Golf and spa services extra. AE, MC, V. **Amenities:** 6 restaurants; 5 bars; 2 lounges; casino; babysitting; bike rental; children's programs; concierge; Robert Trent Jones II–designed 18-hole golf course and pro shop; modest exercise facilities and spa; massive free-form outdoor pool w/several Jacuzzis, another large outdoor pool for Royal Level suites; room service; all rooms smoke-free; 4 lighted tennis courts; watersports equipment rental. *In room:* A/C, TV, hair dryer, minibar, Wi-Fi.

INEXPENSIVE

A string of inexpensive cabinas line the main road leading into Brasilito, just before you hit the beach. It's also possible to camp on playas Potrero and Brasilito. At the former, contact **Maiyra's** (✆ **2654-4213**); at the latter, try **Camping Brasilito** (✆ **2654-4452**). Both of these places offer some budget rooms as well. Each charges around C2,000 per person to make camp and use the basic restroom facilities or around C5,000 to C10,000 per person to stay in a rustic room.

Hotel Brasilito ✦ This hotel, just across a sand road from the beach, offers pretty basic and small rooms that are nonetheless quite clean and well maintained. The bar and a big open-air restaurant are excellent. Even with Playa Brasilito's glut of budget options, this is one of the best values and is the closest to the water. The best rooms have balconies with ocean views, and air-conditioning. The hotel rents snorkeling equipment, kayaks, body boards, and horses and can arrange a variety of tours.

Playa Brasilito, Guanacaste. www.hotelbrasilito.com. ✆ **2654-4237.** 15 units. $40–$49 double. AE, MC, V. **Amenities:** Restaurant; watersports equipment rental. *In room:* No phone, Wi-Fi.

Where to Eat

You'll find good fresh seafood and international fare at the **Happy Snapper** (✆ **2654-4413**) in Brasilito.

Camarón Dorado 🍴 SEAFOOD With a series of tables and kerosene torches set right in the sand just steps from the crashing surf, this is one of the most perfectly placed beach restaurants in the country. More tables are in a simple, open-air dining room, for those who don't want sand in their shoes. The service is sketchy, and at times can be anything from lax to rude. The seafood is fresh and well-prepared. When I asked to see the wine list, two waiters came over carrying about 12 different bottles between them, held precariously between the straining fingers of each hand.

Playa Brasilito. ✆ **2654-4028.** Reservations recommended in high season. Main courses C5,000–C10,000. AE, MC, V. Daily 11am–10pm.

Playas Conchal & Brasilito After Dark

Pretty much all of the nightlife in Playa Conchal happens at the large Westin resort (see above), which has a range of bars, nightly entertainment, and a casino. Over in Brasilito, you might see if there's any live music or sporting events on the televisions at the **Happy Snapper** (see above).

PLAYAS FLAMINGO ★★ & POTRERO

285km (176 miles) NW of San José; 71km (44 miles) SW of Liberia

Playa Flamingo is one of the prettiest beaches in the region. A long, broad stretch of pinkish white sand, it is on a long spit of land that forms part of Potrero Bay. At the northern end of the beach is a high rock outcropping upon which most of Playa Flamingo's hotels and vacation homes are built. This rocky hill has great views.

Playa Flamingo.

If you continue along the road from Brasilito without taking the turn for Playa Flamingo, you'll come to **Playa Potrero,** which sits in a broadly curving bay, protected by the Flamingo headlands. The sand here is a brownish gray, but the beach is long, clean, deserted, and very calm for swimming. You can see the hotels of Playa Flamingo across the bay. Drive a little farther north and you'll find the still-underdeveloped beaches of **Playa Prieta ★, Playa La Penca ★** and, finally, **Playa Pan de Azúcar ★★,** or Sugar Beach.

Essentials

GETTING THERE & DEPARTING   By Plane: The nearest airport with regularly scheduled flights is in Tamarindo (see "Tamarindo: Getting There; By Plane" below), although it is also possible to fly into Liberia (p. 190). From either, you can arrange for a taxi to drive you to any of these beaches. Playas Flamingo and Potrero are about 30 minutes from Tamarindo and 45 minutes from Liberia. A taxi from Tamarindo should cost around $35 to $50, and between $50 and $70 from Liberia.

By Car: See the information for driving to Playas Conchal and Brasilito above. Playa Flamingo is the first beach you'll come to beyond Playa Brasilito. Two prominent turnoffs on your left will take you to the beach, whereas if you continue straight, and follow signs bearing right, you'll soon come to Playa Potrero.

GETTING AROUND   Economy Rent A Car (*C* **2654-4543**) has an office in Playa Flamingo.

ORIENTATION   A small collection of shops is in a couple of minimalls at the crossroads in the center of Playa Flamingo. Here you'll find a branch of **Banco de Costa Rica,** as well as the **Santa Fe Pharmacy and Medical Center** (*C* **2665-4960** or 2665-1425).

Fun on & off the Beach

Playa Flamingo ★★ is a long and beautiful stretch of soft white sand, although the surf can sometimes get a bit rough here. The beach doesn't have much shade, so be sure to use plenty of sunscreen and bring an umbrella if you can. If you're not staying here, parking spots are all along the beach road where you can park your car for the day—although do not leave anything of value inside.

Playa Potrero has much gentler surf and, therefore, is the better swimming beach. However, the beach is made up of hard-packed dark sand that is much less appealing than Playa Flamingo.

Playa Pan de Azúcar.

HORSEBACK RIDING You can arrange a horseback ride with the **Flamingo Equestrian Center** (☎ 8846-7878; www.equestriancostarica.com) or **Casagua Horses** (☎ 2653-8041; www.paintedponyguestranch.com). Depending on the size of your group, it should cost between $25 and $40 per person per hour.

LEARN THE LANGUAGE The **Centro Panamericano de Idiomas** (☎ 2654-5002; www.cpi-edu.com), which has schools in San José and Monteverde, has a branch in Flamingo, across from the Flamingo Marina, facing Potrero Bay. A 1-week course with 4 hours of classes per day costs $350. Longer course options, and homestays with local families are available.

SCUBA DIVING Scuba diving is quite popular here. **Costa Rica Diving** (☎/fax 2654-4148; www.costarica-diving.com) has a shop in Flamingo and offers trips to the Catalina Island for around $85. Alternatively, you can check in at the **Flamingo Marina Resort Hotel and Club** (p. 231).

 Flamingo Marina

In 2004, the Flamingo marina was closed down by the municipal and county authorities for operating without proper permits (it had been built and set up a decade or so earlier). Currently, it remains tied up in a slow and convoluted process of public bidding, and there's been no word on when or if it will re-open. The harbor just outside the marina break wall is big, deep, and well protected; all boats are just working from there, and are kept at anchor, instead of at dock.

A sailboat cruise near Tamarindo.

SPORTFISHING & SAILBOAT CHARTERS Although the Flamingo Marina remains in a state of legal limbo and turmoil (see box above), you still have plenty of sportfishing and sailboat charter options here. Jim McKee, the former force behind the Flamingo Marina, manages a fleet of boats. Contact him via his company, **Oso Viejo** (ⓒ **8827-5533** or 2653-8437; www. flamingobeachcr.com). A full-day fishing excursion costs between $700 and $2,200, depending on the size and quality of the boat, and distance traveled to the fishing grounds. Half-day trips cost between $500 and $700.

If you're looking for a full- or half-day sail or sunset cruise, check in with **Oso Viejo** (see above) to see what boats are available, or ask about the 52-foot cutter **Shannon.** Prices range from around $50 to $120 per person, depending on the length of the cruise. Multiday trips are also available.

Alternatively, you can ask at the **Flamingo Marina Resort Hotel and Club** (p. 231).

Where to Stay

If you plan to be here for a while or are coming down with friends or a large family, you might want to consider renting a condo or house. For information and reservations, contact the folks at **Emerald Shores Realty** (ⓒ **2654-4554;** www.emeraldshoresrealty.net) or **Century 21 Marina Trading Post** (ⓒ **2654-4004;** www.century21costarica.net).

EXPENSIVE

Bahía del Sol ★ This small resort hotel sits right on the water's edge at the heart of Playa Potrero. The rooms are all fairly large and feature contemporary tropical decor with bright primary colors at every turn, although the furnishings are rather sparse. All have either a private balcony or shared veranda, and most of these are strung with hammocks. They also have fully equipped studio and two-bedroom apartments that are a good bet for longer stays. The midsize pool features a Jacuzzi, whose water cascades down a faux-waterfall into it. The large open-air restaurant serves fresh seafood and international fare, and offers wonderful views of Potrero Bay.

Playa Potrero, Guanacaste. www.bahiadelsolhotel.com. ℂ **866/223-2463** in the U.S. and Canada, or 2654-4671 in Costa Rica. Fax 2654-5182. 28 units. $186 double; $250 suite. Rates include full breakfast. AE, MC, V. **Amenities:** Restaurant; bar; Jacuzzi; large outdoor pool; room service; small spa; Wi-Fi. *In room:* A/C, TV, hair dryer.

Flamingo Beach Resort   Located right across the road from the best section of beach at Playa Flamingo, this large resort boasts an enviable location fronting a gorgeous section of beach. The hotel is constructed in a horseshoe shape around a large pool and opens out onto the ocean. Half of the rooms have clear views of the ocean across a narrow dirt road. I definitely prefer the pool and oceanview rooms. The "mountain view" rooms aren't quite as desirable. All the rooms are clean and cool, with tile floors and comfortable bathrooms. The suites are larger and better equipped, with full-size refrigerators and kitchenettes.

Playa Flamingo, Guanacaste. www.resortflamingobeach.com. ℂ **2654-4444.** Fax 2654-4060. 120 units. $162 double; $511 suite. AE, MC, V. **Amenities:** Restaurant; 2 bars; casino; exercise room; large outdoor pool; room service; small spa; outdoor lighted tennis court; watersport equipment rental. *In room:* A/C, TV, minifridge, hair dryer, kitchenette (in suites).

MODERATE
Flamingo Marina Resort Hotel and Club ★   Uphill from the beach, the Flamingo Marina Hotel is a midsize resort with a good mix of facilities and amenities. The entire complex has received steady upkeep and makeovers over the years, although it was built in distinct stages, and lacks a sense of cohesion. Most rooms have white tile floors, bright bedspreads, and lots of light. The suites have leather couches and a wet bar in the seating area, as well as private whirlpool tubs. Condo units have full kitchenettes. All the rooms have patios or balconies, and most have pretty good bay views. While not directly on the beach (like Flamingo Beach Resort or Sugar Beach, see above), the hotel is close to Flamingo's principal beach, as well as all of the town's restaurants and nightlife options.

Playa Flamingo, Guanacaste. www.flamingomarina.com. ℂ **2654-4141.** Fax 2654-4035. 30 units, 60 apts. $119 double; $149–$189 suite; $209–$280 apt. Standard rooms include continental breakfast. AE, DC, MC, V. **Amenities:** 2 restaurants; bar; Jacuzzi; 5 small outdoor pools; tennis court; watersports equipment rental; Wi-Fi. *In room:* A/C, TV, kitchenette (in condos).

Where to Eat
You also can't go wrong with the California-style and Asian fusion cuisine at **Angelina's ★** (ℂ **2654-4839**), on the second floor of La Plaza shopping center. In Playa Potrero, **El Castillo** (ℂ **2654-4271**) is the most happening spot, with a wide-ranging menu of bar food and main courses.

Marie's ★ COSTA RICAN/SEAFOOD   This long-standing local restaurant is a large open-air affair, with a soaring thatch roof and tall, thick columns all around. The menu has grown steadily over the years, although the best option here is always some simply prepared fresh fish, chicken, or meat. Check the blackboard for the daily specials, which usually highlight the freshest catch, such as mahimahi (*dorado*), marlin, and red snapper. You'll also find such Tico favorites as *casados* (rice-and-bean dish), rotisserie chicken, and *ceviche,* as well as burritos and quesadillas.

Playa Flamingo. ✆ **2654-4136.** www.mariesrestaurantincostarica.com. Reservations recommended for dinner during the high season. Main courses C4,600–C12,000. AE, MC, V. Daily 6:30am–9:30pm.

Mar y Sol ★★ 🍴 INTERNATIONAL/SEAFOOD   French chef Alain Taulere has prepared food for regular folk and royalty. For visitors to his hilltop restaurant in Flamingo Beach, he offers a small, well-executed, and pricey selection of fresh seafood and meats. The ambience is casually formal, with the open-air main dining room dimly lit by old-fashioned lamp posts and covered by a thatch roof. Along with a surf-and-turf combo featuring filet mignon and either lobster tails or jumbo shrimp, menu highlights include a Peking-style duck served with maple-hoisin sauce. For starters, try the escargot in puff pastry, or the refreshing Gazpacho, which is a family recipe that's been passed down for generations. Call in advance for free transportation from and back to your hotel.

Playa Flamingo. ✆ **2654-4151.** www.marysolflamingo.com. Reservations recommended for dinner in high season. Main courses $14–$28. AE, DC, MC, V. Daily 5–10pm. Closed Sept–Oct.

Playa Flamingo After Dark

With both a disco and casino, **Amberes** (✆ **2654-4001**), just slightly up the hill at the north end of town, is the undisputed hot spot in this area; however, **Flamingo Beach Resort** (see above) also has a casino. You'll find a mellower bar and lounge scene at the bar of **Angelina's** ★ (see above).

In Playa Potrero, locals and tourists alike gather at **El Castillo** (see above), which sometimes has live bands.

PLAYA GRANDE ★★

295km (183 miles) NW of San José; 70km (43 miles) SW of Liberia

Playa Grande is one of the principal nesting sites for the giant leatherback turtle, the largest turtle in the world. This beach is often too rough for swimming, but the well-formed and consistent beach break here is very popular with surfers. The beach here is a long, straight stretch of soft, golden sand, with very little development at the moment. I almost hate to mention places to stay in Playa Grande because the steady influx of tourists and development is severely threatening it as a turtle-nesting site. See map "Around Tamarindo," p. 237.

Essentials

GETTING THERE & DEPARTING   By Plane: The nearest airport with regularly scheduled flights is in Tamarindo (see "Tamarindo: Getting There; By Plane" below), although it is also possible to fly into Liberia (p. 190). From either of these places, you can arrange for a taxi to drive you to Playa Grande. Playa Grande is about 15 minutes from Tamarindo and 45 minutes from Liberia. A taxi from Tamarindo should cost around $25 to $40, and between $50 and $70 from Liberia.

By Car: See the information for driving to Tamarindo below. The dirt and gravel entrance roads to Playa Grande are located along CR155 between Tamarindo and Huacas.

A nesting leatherback turtle on Playa Grande.

WATCHING NESTING SEA TURTLES Leatherback sea turtles nest on Playa Grande between early October and mid-February. The turtles come ashore to lay their eggs only at night. During the nesting season, you'll be inundated with opportunities to sign up for nightly tours, which usually cost $35 to $50 per person. No flash photography or flashlights are allowed because any sort of light can confuse the turtles and prevent them from laying their eggs; guides must use red-tinted flashlights.

Note: Turtle nesting is a natural, unpredictable, and increasingly rare event. Moreover, things have gotten worse here over the years. All indications are that excessive building and lighting close to the beach are the culprits. Even during heavy nesting years you sometimes have to wait your turn for hours, hike quite a way, and even accept the possibility that no nesting mothers will be spotted that evening.

If your hotel can't set a tour up for you, you'll see signs all over town offering tours. Make sure you go with someone licensed and reputable. Do-it-yourselfers can drive over to Playa Grande and book a $25 tour directly with the **National Parks Service** (✆ **2653-0470**). The Parks Service operates out of a small shack just before the beach, across from the Hotel Las Tortugas (see below). It opens each evening at around 6pm to begin taking reservations. They sometimes answer their phone during the day, and it's best to make a reservation in advance because only a limited number of people are allowed on the beach at one time. Spots fill up fast, and if you don't have a reservation, you may have to wait until really late, or you may not be able to go out onto the beach.

Where to Stay

In addition to the places listed below, **Hotel Bula Bula** ★ (www.hotelbulabula. com; ✆ **877/658-2880** in the U.S. and Canada, or 2653-0975 in Costa Rica) is another excellent inland option, while the **Playa Grande Surf Camp** (www.playagrandesurfcamp.com; ✆ **2653-1074**) is geared toward surfers and budget travelers.

Hotel Las Tortugas ★ 🎁 The owner of this place has led the local fight to protect the leatherback turtles that nest here, and have the surrounding area declared Las Baulas National Park. Several of the rooms are quite large, and most have interesting stone floors and shower stalls. The upper suite has a curving staircase that leads to its second room. As part of the hotel's turtle-friendly design, a natural wall of shrubs and trees shields the beach from the restaurant's light and noise, and the swimming pool is shaped like a turtle. These folks also have fully equipped apartments a few blocks inland available for weekly or monthly rental.

Playa Grande, Guanacaste. www.lastortugashotel.com. ✆ **2653-0423** or ✆/fax 2653-0458. 10 units. $90–$100 double; $135 suite. AE, MC, V. **Amenities:** Restaurant; bar; Jacuzzi; small outdoor pool. *In room:* A/C, TV (in some), no phone.

Ripjack Inn ★ This hotel is about 100m (328 ft.) inland from the beach, which is reached via a short path. The rooms are all clean and cool, with tile floors, air-conditioning, and private bathrooms. The rooms come in several sizes and a mix of bed arrangements. They feature various Indonesian-inspired and imported design touches. The hotel's restaurant and bar, on the second floor of the octagonal main building, is one of the best restaurants in Playa Grande. The hotel has a large yoga studio, with regular classes for guests and the local community.

Playa Grande, Guanacaste. www.ripjackinn.com. ✆ **800/808-4605** in the U.S. and Canada, or 2653-0480 in Costa Rica. Fax 2652-9272. 8 units. $80–$125 double. MC, V. **Amenities:** Restaurant; bar; Wi-Fi. *In room:* A/C, no phone.

Where to Eat

Dining options are pretty limited in Playa Grande. I like **Upstairs ★**, the restaurant at the Ripjack Inn (see above), or **The Great Waltini's ★**, at the Hotel Bula Bula (see above). Both are excellent restaurants serving fresh seafood and prime meats, cooked with care and creativity.

PLAYA TAMARINDO ★ & PLAYA LANGOSTA ★★

295km (183 miles) NW of San José; 73km (45 miles) SW of Liberia

Tamarindo is the biggest boomtown in Guanacaste—and in some ways, I think the boom went a bit too far, a bit too fast. The main road into Tamarindo is a helter-skelter jumble of strip malls, surf shops, hotels, and restaurants. Ongoing development is spreading up the hills inland from the beach and south to Playa Langosta. None of it seems regulated or particularly well planned out.

Still, the wide range of accommodations, abundant restaurants, and active nightlife, along with very dependable surf, have established Tamarindo as one of the most popular beaches on this coast. The beautiful beach here is a long, wide swath of white sand that curves gently from one rocky headland to another.

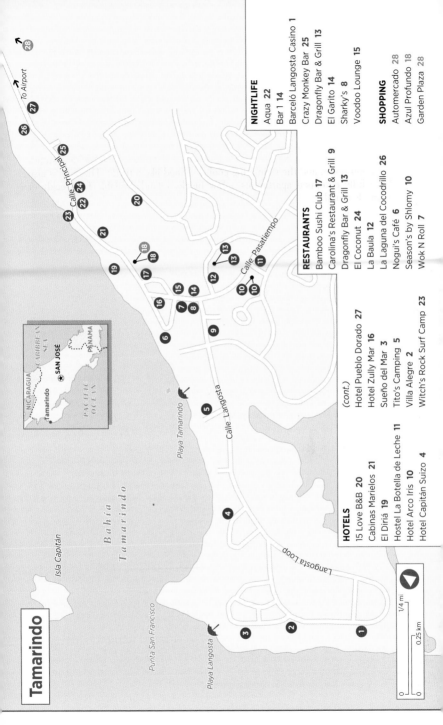

Tamarindo

NICARAGUA
CARIBBEAN SEA
★ **SAN JOSÉ**
Tamarindo
PACIFIC OCEAN
PANAMA

Isla Capitán

Bahía Tamarindo

Punta San Francisco

Playa Tamarindo

Playa Langosta

Calle Principal
To Airport

Calle Pasatiempo

Calle Langosta

Langosta Loop

0   1/4 mi
0   0.25 km

HOTELS
15 Love B&B **20**
Cabinas Marielos **21**
El Diriá **19**
Hostel La Botella de Leche **11**
Hotel Arco Iris **10**
Hotel Capitán Suizo **4**

(cont.)
Hotel Pueblo Dorado **27**
Hotel Zully Mar **16**
Sueño del Mar **3**
Tito's Camping **5**
Villa Alegre **2**
Witch's Rock Surf Camp **23**

RESTAURANTS
Bamboo Sushi Club **17**
Carolina's Restaurant & Grill **9**
Dragonfly Bar & Grill **13**
El Coconut **24**
La Baula **12**
La Laguna del Cocodrillo **26**
Nogui's Café **6**
Season's by Shlomy **10**
Wok N Roll **7**

NIGHTLIFE
Aqua **22**
Bar 1 **14**
Barceló Langosta Casino **1**
Crazy Monkey Bar **25**
Dragonfly Bar & Grill **13**
El Garito **14**
Sharky's **8**
Voodoo Lounge **15**

SHOPPING
Automercado **28**
Azul Profundo **18**
Garden Plaza **28**

Surfing in Tamarindo.

Fishing boats bob at their moorings and brown pelicans fish just beyond the breakers. A sandy islet off the southern end of the beach makes a great destination if you're a strong swimmer; if you're not, it makes a great foreground for sunsets. Tamarindo is very popular with surfers, who ply the break right here or use the town as a jumping-off place for beach and point breaks at playas Grande, Langosta, Avellanas, and Negra.

Essentials

GETTING THERE & DEPARTING **By Plane: Sansa** (© 877/767-2672 in the U.S. and Canada, or 2290-4100 in Costa Rica; www.flysansa.com) has three daily flights to Tamarindo from San José's Juan Santamaría International Airport, at 9:10 and 11:46am, and 3:10pm. Return flights leave Tamarindo at 10:17am, and 2:53 and 4:17pm for San José. The flight takes 55 minutes. The fare is $131 each way. During the high season, additional flights are sometimes added.

Nature Air (© 800/235-9272 in the U.S. and Canada, or 2299-6000; www.natureair.com) flies to Tamarindo daily at 6:20 and 11:45am, and 3:15pm from Tobías Bolaños International Airport in Pavas. Fares run $135 each way. The flight takes 55 minutes. Nature Air flights leave for San José at 7:35am and 1 and 4:20pm. Nature Air also connects Tamarindo and Arenal, Liberia, and Quepos.

Whether you arrive on Sansa or Nature Air, a couple of cabs or minivans are always waiting for arriving flights. It costs $6 to $10 for the ride into town.

If you're flying into Liberia, a taxi should cost around $75. Alternately, you can use **Tamarindo Shuttle** (© 2653-4444; www.tamarindoshuttle.com), which charges $18 per person one-way. These folks also offer a variety of tours and transfer services.

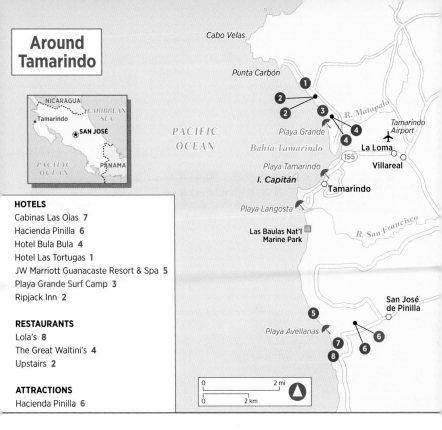

Around Tamarindo

Cabo Velas

Punta Carbón

PACIFIC OCEAN

Playa Grande
Bahía Tamarindo

Playa Tamarindo
I. Capitán

Playa Langosta

R. Matapalo

Tamarindo Airport

La Loma

Villareal

Tamarindo

Las Baulas Nat'l Marine Park

R. San Francisco

San José de Pinilla

Playa Avellanas

HOTELS

Cabinas Las Olas **7**
Hacienda Pinilla **6**
Hotel Bula Bula **4**
Hotel Las Tortugas **1**
JW Marriott Guanacaste Resort & Spa **5**
Playa Grande Surf Camp **3**
Ripjack Inn **2**

RESTAURANTS

Lola's **8**
The Great Waltini's **4**
Upstairs **2**

ATTRACTIONS

Hacienda Pinilla **6**

0 — 2 mi
0 — 2 km

By Car: The most direct route is by way of the La Amistad bridge. From San José, you can either take the Interamerican Highway (CR1) north from downtown San José, or first head west out of the city on the San José-Caldera Highway (CR27). This latter route is a faster and flatter drive. When you reach Caldera on this route, follow the signs to Puntarenas, Liberia, and the Interamerican Highway (CR1). This will lead you to the unmarked entrance to CR1. You'll want to pass under the bridge and follow the on-ramp which will put you on the highway heading north. Forty-seven kilometers (29 miles) north of the Puntarenas exit on the Interamerican Highway, you'll see signs for the turnoff to the bridge. After crossing the river, follow the signs for Nicoya and Santa Cruz. Continue north out of Santa Cruz, until just before the village of Belén, where you will find the turnoff for Tamarindo. In another 20km (12 miles), take the left fork for Playa Tamarindo at Huacas and continue on until the village of Villareal, where you make your final turn into Tamarindo. The trip should take around 4 hours.

You can save a little time, especially in the dry season, by taking a more direct but rougher route: You turn left just after passing the main intersection for Santa Cruz at the turnoff for playas Junquillal and Ostional. The road is paved until the tiny village of Veintesiete de Abril. From here, it's about 20km (12 miles) on a rough dirt road until the village of Villareal, where you make your final turn into Tamarindo.

Alternatively, you can drive here via Liberia. When you reach Liberia, turn west and follow the signs for Santa Cruz and the various beaches. Just beyond the town of Belén, take the turnoff for playas Flamingo, Brasilito, and Tamarindo, and then follow the directions for the second option above. This route takes around 5 hours.

By Bus: Alfaro express buses (© **2222-2666** in San José, or 2653-0268 in Tamarindo; www.empresaalfaro.com) leave San José daily for Tamarindo at 11:30am and 3:30pm, departing from Calle 14 between avenidas 3 and 5. **Tralapa** (© **2221-7202**) also has two daily direct buses to Tamarindo leaving at 7:15am and 4pm from their main terminal at Calle 20 between avenidas 3 and 5. The trip takes around 5 hours, and the one-way fare is around C4,785.

Alternatively, you can catch a bus to Santa Cruz from either of the above bus companies. Buses leave both stations for Santa Cruz roughly every 2 hours between 6am and 6pm. The 4-hour, one-way trip is around C4,600. Buses leave Santa Cruz for Tamarindo roughly every 1½ hours between 5:45am and 10pm; the one-way fare is C950.

Daily **Gray Line** (© **2220-2126**; www.graylinecostarica.com) buses leave San José for Tamarindo at 8am and 3:30pm. The fare is $35. **Interbus** (© **2283-5573**; www.interbusonline.com) has two daily buses from San José for Tamarindo at 7:30am and 2:30pm for $40. Both companies will pick you up at most San José–area hotels.

Direct buses leave Tamarindo for San José daily at 3:30 and 5:30am (except on Sun) and 2 and 4pm. Buses to Santa Cruz leave roughly every 2 hours between 4:30am and 8:30pm. In Santa Cruz you can transfer to one of the frequent San José buses.

ORIENTATION   The road leading into town runs parallel to the beach and ends in a small cul-de-sac just past Zully Mar. A major side road off this main road leads farther on, to Playa Langosta, from just before Zully Mar. A variety of side roads branch off this road. To reach playas Avellanas, Negra, and Junquillal, you have to first head out of town and take the road toward Santa Cruz.

FAST FACTS   The local **police** can be reached at © 2653-0283.

A **Banco Nacional** branch is at the little mall across from El Diria, and a branch of the **Banco de Costa Rica** in the Plaza Conchal mall. Several Internet cafes and a couple of pharmacies are also in town. You'll find the **Back Wash Laundry** (© 2653-0870) just past the turnoff for Playa Langosta.

GETTING AROUND   **Adobe** (© 2667-0608), **Alamo** (© 2653-0727), **Budget** (© **2436-2000**), **Economy** (© 2653-0752), **Hertz** (© 2653-1358), and **Thrifty** (© 2653-0829) have rental car offices in Tamarindo.

The town itself is very compact and you should be able to walk most places. Heck, it's not even that far a walk from Playa Langosta. Still, a large fleet of taxis are usually cruising around town, or hanging out at principal intersections and meeting points. If you need to, you can call a **taxi** at © **8816-9864** or 8834-4075.

Fun on & off the Beach

Tamarindo is a long, white-sand beach. Still, you have to be careful when and where you swim. The calmest water and best swimming are always down at the far southern end of the beach, toward Punta Langosta. Much of the sea just off the busiest part of the town is best for surfing. When the swell is up, you'll find scores of surfers in the water here. Be careful: Rocks are just offshore in several places, some of which are exposed only at low tide. An encounter with one of these rocks could be nasty, especially if you're bodysurfing. I also advise that you avoid swimming near the estuary mouth, where the currents can carry you out away from the beach.

Yo Quiero Hablar Español

If you want to try an intensive immersion program or just brush up on your rusty high school Spanish, check in with the folks at **Wayra Instituto de Español** (℡/fax 2653-0359; www.spanish-wayra.co.cr). This place is located up a side street from the dirt road that connects Tamarindo to Playa Langosta.

All of the hotel desks and tour operators here offer **turtle nesting tours** to Playa Grande (p. 233), in season, or you can contact **ACOTAM** (℡ 2653-1687), a specialized local operator.

BIKING   Bikes are available for rent at several locations in Tamarindo. Check around; you'll probably find the best bikes at the **Blue Trailz Bike Shop ★** (℡ 2653-1705; www.bluetrailz.com), which rents high-end Trek and Specialized mountain bikes for around $20 per day. These folks also offer guided mountain-bike tours and excursions.

FOUR-WHEELING   **Arenas Adventure Tours** (℡ 2653-0108; www.arenasadventures.com) offers a variety of guided ATV tours from 1 to 3 hours from $39 to $100 per person. This company also rents dirt bikes, snorkel equipment, surf and boogie boards, and jet skis and offers a full menu of other guided tours around the region. Similar ATV tours are offered by **Fourtrax Adventures** (℡ 2653-4040; www.fourtraxadventure.com), which charges $75 for its 2½-hour outing. You can also combine their ATV tour with a nearby canopy tour or horseback ride, for $110 per person.

GOLF   **Hacienda Pinilla ★★** (℡ 2680-7000; www.haciendapinilla.com) is a beautiful 18-hole links-style course located south of Tamarindo. The course is currently accepting golfers staying at all of the hotels around the area, with advance reservation. Greens fees run around $185 for 18 holes, including a cart, with discounts for guests staying at Hacienda Pinilla or the JW Marriott resort. Many folks staying in Tamarindo also play at the **Westin Playa Conchal Resort & Spa ★★**, an excellent resort course (p. 226).

HORSEBACK RIDING   Although some will be disappointed, I think it's a very good thing that horses are no longer allowed on the beach. Fortunately, you'll find plenty of opportunities to ride in the hills and forests around Tamarindo. You can go riding with **Casagua Horses ★** (℡ 2653-8041), **Arenas Adventure Tours** (℡ 2653-0108; www.arenasadventures.com), **Iguana Surf** (℡ 2653-0148; www.iguanasurf.net), or **Papagayo Excursions** (℡ 2653-0254; www.papagayoexcursions.com). Rates for horse rental, with a guide, are around $30 to $65 per hour.

The Hacienda Pinilla golf course.

SAILBOAT CHARTERS   Several boats offer cruises offshore from Tamarindo; the 40-foot catamaran *Blue Dolphin* ★ (© **8842-3204;** www.sailbluedolphin.com) and 66-foot catamaran *Marlin del Rey* (© **2653-1212;** www.marlindelrey.com) are both good choices. A half-day snorkel or shorter sunset cruise should cost $60 to $75 per person, and a full day should run between $80 and $130 per person. This usually includes an open bar and snacks on the half-day and sunset cruises, and all of that plus lunch on the full-day trip.

SCUBA DIVING   For scuba diving or snorkeling, check in with **Agua Rica Diving Center** ★ (© **2653-0094;** www.aguarica.net). These folks are the best and longest running operators in Tamarindo, and have a full-service dive shop. They offer day trips, multiday dive cruises, and standard resort and full-certification courses.

SPORTFISHING   A host of captains offer anglers a chance to go after the "big ones" that abound in the offshore waters. From the Tamarindo estuary, it takes only 20 minutes to reach the edge of the continental shelf, where the waters are filled with mostly marlin and sailfish. Although fishing is good all year, the peak season for billfish is between mid-April and August. Contact **Tamarindo Sportfishing** (© **2653-0090;** www.tamarindosportfishing.com), **Capullo Sportfishing** ★ (© **2653-0048;** www.capullo.com), or **Osprey Sportfishing** (© **2653-0162;** www.osprey-sportfishing.com).

TENNIS   You can rent court time and equipment at the **Tamarindo Tennis Club** (© **2653-0898**), which features two lighted outdoor courts on the back road on the way to the Hotel El Jardín del Edén. It is open daily from 7:30am to 8pm, and court time runs $10 per day. You can also play at **Hacienda Pinilla** (see "Golf" above) for $5 per hour during the day, and $10 per hour at night.

TOURS GALORE **Arenas Adventure Tours, Papagayo Excursions,** and **Iguana Surf** (see above for all) all offer a host of tour and activity options. Papagayo Excursions probably offers the widest selection of full- and multi-day trips, including outboard or kayak tours through the nearby estuary and mangroves, excursions to Santa Cruz and Guaitíl, raft floats on the Corobicí River, and tours to Palo Verde and Rincón de la Vieja national parks. Rates run between $30 and $140, depending on the length of the tour and group size.

There's no canopy tour available right in Tamarindo, but the **Monkey Jungle Canopy Tour** (© **2653-6982** or 8919-4242; www.canopymonkey jungle.com) and **Cartagena Canopy Tour ★** (© **2675-0801;** www.canopy tourcartagena.com) are nearby. Both charge $35 to $40 per person and include transportation from Tamarindo. Of these two, the Monkey Jungle operation is much closer, but I prefer the Cartagena tour, which has a much more lush forest setting. Still, I think your best bet is to take a day trip to Hacienda Guachipelin (p. 199) and do the "Canyon Tour" there.

WATERSPORTS If you want to try snorkeling, surfing, or sea kayaking in Tamarindo, **Agua Rica Diving Center, Iguana Surf** and **Arenas Adventure Tours** (see above) both rent all the necessary equipment. They have half-day and hourly rates for many of these items.

Tamarindo has a host of surf shops and surf schools, if you want to learn to catch a wave while in town. You can shop around town, or check in with the **Tamarindo Surf School** (© **2653-0923;** www.tamarindo surfschool.com), **Banana Surf Club** (© **2653-2463;** www.bananasurf school.com), or **Witch's Rock Surf Camp ★** (© **2653-1262;** www. witchsrocksurfcamp.com).

WELLNESS CENTERS Most of the higher-end hotels have their own spas, and most hotels can call you a massage therapist. But if you're looking for a local day spa experience, try **Cocó Day Spa** (© **2653-2562;** www.cocobeauty spa.com), which has a wide range of treatments and packages, from facials and pedicures to hot stone massages.

Alternately, you can head about 15- to 20-minutes inland to **Los Altos de Eros ★** (© **8850-4222;** www.losaltosdeeros.com) for one of their signature, full-day spa experiences.

 Pretty Pots

The lack of any long-standing local arts and crafts tradition across Costa Rica is often lamented. One of the outstanding exceptions to this rule is the small village of Guaitíl, located on the outskirts of the provincial capital of Santa Cruz. The small central plaza—actually a soccer field—of this village is ringed with craft shops and artisan stands selling a wide range of ceramic wares. Most are low-fired relatively soft clay pieces, with traditional Chorotega indigenous design motifs. All of the local tour agencies offer day trips to Guaitíl, or you can drive there yourself, by heading first to Santa Cruz, and then taking the well-marked turnoff for Guaitíl, just south of the city, on the road to Nicoya.

Shopping

Tamarindo's main boulevard is awash in souvenir stands, art galleries, jewelry stores, and clothing boutiques. For original beachwear and jewelry, try **Azul Profundo** ★ (✆ **2653-0395**), in the Plaza Tamarindo shopping center. The modern **Garden Plaza** shopping center, near the entrance to town, has several high-end shops, as well as a massive **Automercado** (supermarket).

Where to Stay

In addition to the hotels listed below, Tamarindo, Playa Langosta, and Playa Grande have a wide range of beach houses and condos for rent by the night, the week, or the month. For more information on this option, check out **Remax Tamarindo** (✆ **2653-0074;** www.remax-oceansurf-cr.com) or **Century 21** (✆ **866/978-6585** in the U.S. and Canada, or 2653-0300 in Costa Rica; www.costarica1realestate.com).

VERY EXPENSIVE

Hotel Capitán Suizo ★★ ☺ This well-appointed beachfront hotel sits on the quiet southern end of Tamarindo. The rooms are housed in a series of two-story buildings. The lower rooms have air-conditioning and private patios; the upper units have plenty of cross ventilation, ceiling fans, and cozy balconies. All have large bathrooms and sitting rooms with fold-down futon couches. The spacious bungalows are spread around the shady grounds; these all come with a tub in the bathroom and an inviting outdoor shower among the trees. The hotel's free-form pool is a delight, with tall shade trees all around. The shallow end slopes in gradually, imitating a beach, and there's also a separate children's pool. The lovely little spa is on the beachfront. Perhaps the greatest attribute here is that it's just steps from one of the calmer and more isolated sections of Playa Tamarindo.

Playa Tamarindo, Guanacaste. www.hotelcapitansuizo.com. ✆ **2653-0075** or 2653-0353. Fax 2653-0292. 28 units, 7 bungalows. $200–$225 double; $265–$305 bungalow; $370–$535 suite. Rates include breakfast buffet. AE, MC, V. **Amenities:** Restaurant; bar; babysitting; small exercise room; midsize outdoor pool and children's pool; spa; Wi-Fi. *In room:* A/C (in some), minifridge, hair dryer.

Sueño del Mar ★ 🏠 On Playa Langosta, Sueño del Mar has charming little touches and innovative design: four-poster beds made from driftwood; African dolls on the windowsills; Kokopeli candleholders; and open-air showers with sculpted angelfish, hand-painted tiles, and lush tropical plants. Fabrics are from Bali and Guatemala. Somehow all of this works well together, and the requisite chairs, hammocks, and lounges nestled under shade trees right on the beach add the crowning touch. This intimate hotel, particularly its honeymoon suite, is also consistently a top choice for weddings, honeymoons, and romantic getaways. The two casitas have their own kitchens, veranda, and sleeping loft. The honeymoon suite is a spacious second-floor room, with wraparound windows, a delightful open-air shower, and commanding ocean views. The beach right out front is rocky and a bit rough, but it does reveal some nice, quiet tidal pools at low tide; it's one of the better sunset-viewing spots in Costa Rica.

Playa Langosta, Guanacaste. www.sueno-del-mar.com. ✆/fax **2653-0284.** 4 units, 2 casitas. $195 double; $220–$295 suite or casita. Rates include full breakfast. No children 11 and under.

MC, V. **Amenities:** Small outdoor pool; free use of snorkel equipment and boogie boards; Wi-Fi. *In room:* A/C, hair dryer, kitchens (in casitas).

EXPENSIVE

El Diriá ★   This is Tamarindo's largest beachfront resort. Wedged into a narrow piece of land planted with tropical gardens and palm trees, the Diriá has an enviable spot, smack-dab in the middle of Tamarindo's long beach. I especially recommend the second- and third-floor "sunset deluxe" rooms, which feature oceanview private balconies. However, some rooms are across the street from the beach, so be sure you know what type of room you are booking when you reserve. The hotel has several swimming pools, as well as a lighted outdoor tennis court. They also have a large, open-air amphitheater that they use for weddings, private parties, and the occasional public concert, as well as a golf driving range on the outskirts of town.

Playa Tamarindo, Guanacaste. www.tamarindodiria.com. ✆ **866/603-4742** in the U.S. and Canada, or 2653-0031 in Costa Rica. Fax 2653-0208. 182 units. $230 double. Rates include breakfast buffet. AE, MC, V. **Amenities:** 2 restaurants; 2 bars; 3 outdoor pools. *In room:* A/C, TV, hair dryer, minibar (in some), Wi-Fi.

Villa Alegre ★   This small bed-and-breakfast on Playa Langosta is a well-located and homey option. You'll immediately feel part of the family here, as guests and owners share breakfast, hang around the pool, or gather for a sunset cocktail. The owners' years of globetrotting have inspired them to decorate each room in the theme of a different country. In the main house, Guatemala, Mexico, and the United States are all represented. Of these, Mexico is the most spacious, with a large open-air bathroom and shower. The smallest are Guatemala and the California casita. The latter room is quite small, in fact. Every room has its own private patio, courtyard, or balcony. The villas are spacious and luxurious, with kitchenettes. My favorite is the Japanese unit, with its subtle design touches and great woodwork. The Russian villa and the United States rooms are truly wheelchair accessible and equipped, with ramps and modified bathrooms with handrails. The beach is just a short stroll away through the trees. Breakfasts are delicious and abundant.

Playa Langosta, Guanacaste. www.villaalegrecostarica.com. ✆ **2653-0270.** Fax 2653-0287. 5 units, 2 villas. $170–$185 double; $230 villa. Rates include full breakfast. AE, MC, V. **Amenities:** Midsize outdoor pool. *In room:* A/C, kitchenettes (in villas), no phone, Wi-Fi.

MODERATE

In addition to the places listed here, **Hotel Pueblo Dorado** (www.pueblo dorado.com; ✆ **2653-0008**) is a well-located option just across from the beach, while tennis lovers (and anyone else) might want to check out the **15 Love Bed & Breakfast** (www.15lovebedandbreakfast.com; ✆ **2653-0898**), attached to the Tamarindo Tennis Club (see above).

Hotel Arco Iris ★   This stylish place is a great option in this price category. Rooms feature a slightly minimalist contemporary Asian decor. The deluxe rooms are more spacious than the bungalows, and I especially like the second-floor deluxe units. The hotel is a few blocks inland from the beach, but at times there's not much impetus to leave, thanks to the small rectangular pool and the Season's by Shlomy restaurant (see below)—one of the best in town.

Playa Tamarindo, Guanacaste. www.hotelarcoiris.com. ℂ/fax **2653-0330.** 9 units. $109 double. Rates include continental breakfast. AE, MC, V. **Amenities:** Restaurant; bar; small outdoor pool. *In room:* A/C, TV, minibar, Wi-Fi.

Hotel Zully Mar The Zully Mar had long been a favorite of budget travelers, though, the hotel has upgraded their rooms and upped their prices over the years. The best rooms here are in a two-story white-stucco building with a wide, curving staircase on the outside. They have air-conditioning, tile floors, long verandas or balconies, overhead or standing fans, large bathrooms, and doors that are hand-carved with pre-Columbian motifs. The less expensive rooms are smaller and darker and just have ceiling fans. The small free-form pool is refreshing if you don't want to walk across the street to the beach. This place is set on the busiest intersection in Tamarindo, smack-dab in the center of things, and noise can be a problem at times.

Playa Tamarindo, Guanacaste. www.zullymar.com. ℂ **2653-0140.** Fax 2653-0028. 22 units. $69 double. AE, MC, V. **Amenities:** Restaurant; small outdoor pool. *In room:* A/C, minifridge, no phone.

INEXPENSIVE

In addition to the places listed below, **Hostal La Botella de Leche** (www.la botelladeleche.com; ℂ **2653-2061**) is a popular backpacker option, while the beachfront **Witch's Rock Surf Camp** (www.witchsrocksurfcamp.com; ℂ **888/318-7873** in the U.S. and Canada, or 2653-1262) caters to young, budget surfers. Out along the road to Playa Langosta, **Tito's Camping** (no phone) charges $5 to $8 per person for camping, in a large open area just off the beach.

Cabinas Marielos ★ This place is located up a palm-shaded driveway across the road from the beach just before the center of town. Rooms are clean and well maintained, although most are small and simply furnished with air-conditioning. Some of the bathrooms are quite small, but they're clean. Guests can use a communal kitchen, and the lush gardens are beautiful and provide some welcome shade. Common verandas and balconies are cool places to sit and read a book. The staff and owners are incredibly helpful and will make you feel like part of the family—in fact, many of them are already family to each other.

Playa Tamarindo, Guanacaste. www.cabinasmarieloscr.com. ℂ/fax **2653-0141.** 24 units. $45–$60 double. Rates include taxes. MC, V. **Amenities:** Surfboard rentals. *In room:* A/C (in some), TV (in some), no phone.

Where to Eat

Tamarindo has a glut of excellent restaurants. **El Coconut** (ℂ **2653-0086;** www.elcoconut-tamarindo.com), right on the main road into town, is a long-standing option, with a wide ranging menu, specializing in fresh seafood, with a European-influenced flair.

Nogui's Café ★ (ℂ **2653-0029;** www.noguis.com) is one of the more popular places in town—and rightly so. This simple open-air cafe just off the beach on the small traffic circle serves hearty breakfasts and well-prepared salads, sandwiches, burgers, and casual meals.

Wok N Roll ★ (ℂ **2653-0156**), a half-block inland from Zully Mar along the road that leads to Playa Langosta, is a lively, open-air affair, with a big menu of healthy, fresh Asian cuisine. For pizzas, I recommend **La Baula** ★

(© 2653-1450), a delightful open-air place, on the road to Dragonfly (see below). If you want sushi, head to the **Bamboo Sushi Club ★** (© 2653-4519), on the main road, near the turnoff for Langosta. Finally, for a light bite, breakfast, or coffee break, try **Café Café ★** (© 2653-1864), on the outskirts of town, near the turnoff for Santa Rosa and Hacienda Pinilla.

Carolina's Restaurant & Grill ★★ INTERNATIONAL/FUSION   This elegant restaurant is housed in a large, enclosed space that feels like an old colonial-era home, with a red clay tile ceiling exposed through heavy wood beams, and tables decked out in white cloths and glass candleholders. Start things off with the hot ginger and papaya soup, and follow it up with some sesame seared tuna. The pastas here are also excellent. Or you can opt for one of the nightly four- or five-course tasting menus. Presentations are artful, service is impeccable, and they boast an excellent wine list.

On the road to Playa Langosta. © **2653-1946** or 8379-6834. Reservations recommended. Main courses $18–$25. AE, MC, V. Daily 6–10pm.

Dragonfly Bar & Grill ★★★ 🏠 INTERNATIONAL/FUSION   Tucked away on a back street, this place has earned ample praise and a loyal following with its excellent food, generous portions and laid-back vibe. The menu mixes and matches several cuisines, with the southwestern United States and Pacific Rim fusion being the strongest influences. The daily seafood specials might range from seared tuna to wood-fired red snapper. If you're in the mood for meat, try the thick-cut pork chop with chipotle apple chutney. The restaurant is a simple open-air affair, with a concrete floor and rough wood tree trunks as support columns. An open wood-fired oven is on one side, and a popular bar is toward the back. The restaurant has free Wi-Fi.

Down a dirt road behind the old Hotel Pasatiempo. © **2653-1506.** www.dragonflybarandgrill. com. Reservations recommended. Main courses $10–$16. AE, MC, V. Mon–Sat 6–10pm.

La Laguna del Cocodrilo ★ INTERNATIONAL/FUSION   In a crowded field, this is yet another option for fine dining and fusion cuisine in Tamarindo. When weather permits, tables are set up under the trees in their beachfront garden area. Beautiful presentations and creative use of ingredients are the norm. The menu changes regularly, but the chefs always focus on using the freshest and best ingredients available. The restaurant also has a good wine list, and a regular bar/lounge crowd.

On the main road, toward the north end of Tamarindo. © **2653-3897.** www.lalagunatamarindo. com. Reservations recommended. Main courses $14–$32. AE, MC, V. Mon–Sat 3–10pm.

Season's by Shlomy ★★ INTERNATIONAL   This is another of Tamarindo's standout restaurants. Chef and owner Shlomy Koren has earned a fond and faithful following for both his consistency and creativity. The contemporary cuisine carries a heavy Mediterranean influence: The seared tuna in a honey chili marinade is always a favorite, as is the pan fried red snapper with caramelized onions, portobello mushrooms, and a balsamic reduction. Desserts often feature homemade ice creams and sorbets. Tables are spread around an open-air dining room and poolside deck at the Hotel Arco Iris (see above).

Inside the Hotel Arco Iris. © **8368-6983.** www.seasonstamarindo.com. Reservations recommended. Main courses $12–$15. No credit cards. Mon–Sat 6–10pm.

Tamarindo After Dark

As a popular surfer destination, Tamarindo has a sometimes raging nightlife. The most happening bars in town are **Bar 1 ★★** (☎ 2653-2686) and **El Garito ★★** (☎ 2653-2017), both about a block inland, on the road leading toward Playa Langosta, and **Aqua ★** (☎ 2653-2782; www.aquadiscoteque. com), on the main road through town. Other popular spots throughout the week include the **Crazy Monkey Bar** at the Best Western Tamarindo Vista Villas (☎ 2653-0114), and the bar at the **Dragonfly Bar & Grill** (p. 245). For a chill-out dance scene, try the **Voodoo Lounge** (☎ 2653-0100), while those looking for a rocking sports bar can head to **Sharky's** (☎ 8918-4968). These latter two places are just across from each other, a little up the road that heads to Playa Langosta.

The one casino in town is at the **Barceló Playa Langosta** (☎ 2653-0363) resort down in Playa Langosta.

En Route South: Playa Avellanas & Playa Negra

Heading south from Tamarindo are several as-yet-undeveloped beaches, most of which are quite popular with surfers. Beyond Tamarindo and Playa Langosta are **Playa Avellanas** and **Playa Negra,** both with a few basic surfer cabinas, and little else. See map "Around Tamarindo," p. 237.

WHERE TO STAY

The **Mono Congo Lodge** (www.monocongolodge.com; ☎ 2652-9261), just outside of Playa Negra, is a rustically plush option in a lush, forested setting a few hundred yards from the water.

About a 15- to 20-minute drive inland is **Los Altos de Eros ★** (www.losaltosdeeros.com; ☎ 8850-4222), a small, adults-only, luxury hotel and spa.

In addition to the JW Marriott (see below), the large golf, residential, and vacation resort complex of **Hacienda Pinilla** (www.haciendapinilla.com; ☎ 2680-3000) features a couple of small hotels and condo rental units.

Very Expensive

JW Marriott Guanacaste Resort & Spa ★★★   This large-scale resort is one of Costa Rica's finest. The rooms, facilities, restaurants, amenities, and service here are all top-of-the-line. All rooms have large flatscreen televisions, a separate tub and shower, and a spacious balcony or patio, with a cooling retractable shade screen. Of the limited number of beachfront rooms, the Marimba suite (#339), a corner-view unit, is probably the best in the house. The spa here is large, modern, and luxurious. The Mansita beach just out front is a bit rocky, but beautiful stretches of Playa Avellanas and Playa Langosta lie just a short walk or shuttle ride away, and the hotel also has the largest pool in Central America—edging out the Westin Playa Conchal for the honor.

Hacienda Pinilla, Guanacaste. www.marriott.com. ☎ **888/236-2427** in the U.S. and Canada, or 2681-2000. Fax 2681-2001. 310 units. $369–$560 double; $469 suite; $1,299 presidential suite. AE, DC, DISC, MC, V. **Amenities:** 4 restaurants; 3 bars; lounge; babysitting; children's programs; concierge; championship 18-hole golf course nearby; large, modern health club and spa; massive free-form outdoor pool; room service; smoke-free rooms; tennis courts nearby; watersports equipment. *In room:* A/C, TV/DVD, hair dryer, minibar, MP3 docking station, Wi-Fi.

Moderate

Cabinas Las Olas   This collection of duplex cabins is a popular surf lodge set in the shade of some tall trees, a couple hundred meters inland from the beach and bordering a mangrove reserve. The clean and simple rooms are a good value, and close to the surf. Each comes with a little private veranda and a hammock. The beach is a long stretch of almost always uncrowded white sand. Good beach breaks for surfers are up and down the shoreline, especially toward the northern end and the Langosta estuary. Mountain bikes and sea kayaks are available for rent.

Playa Avellanas, Guanacaste. www.cabinaslasolas.co.cr. ✆ **2652-9315.** Fax 2658-9331. 10 units. $80–$90 double. AE, MC, V. **Amenities:** Restaurant; bar; bike rentals; limited watersports equipment rentals. *In room:* No phone.

Hotel Playa Negra   These thatch-roofed bungalows are set right in front of the famous Playa Negra point break. Even if you're not a surfer, you'll appreciate the beautiful beach and coastline with its coral and rock outcroppings and calm tide pools. The round bungalows each have one queen-size and two single beds, two desks, a ceiling fan, and a private bathroom. The bungalow suites are more spacious and plush, with coffeemakers and minifridges, outdoor showers, and private verandas. A few of these even come with air-conditioning. The restaurant is close to the ocean in a large open-air rancho and serves as a social hub for guests and surfers staying at more basic cabinas inland from the beach.

Playa Negra, Guanacaste. www.playanegra.com. ✆ **2652-9134.** Fax 2652-9035. 17 units. $88 bungalow; $120 bungalow suite. Rates higher during peak periods. AE, MC, V. **Amenities:** Restaurant; bar; midsize outdoor pool; Wi-Fi. *In room:* No phone.

WHERE TO EAT

In addition to the place listed below, the restaurants inside the **JW Marriott** resort (see above) are excellent, and open to the general public.

Lola's ★★★ 🍴 INTERNATIONAL/SEAFOOD   Long loved by locals, the secret is out on Lola's. Named after the owner's departed massive pet pig, this place serves up top-notch fresh fare in a beautiful open-air beachfront setting. Most of the heavy, homemade wooden tables and chairs are set in the sand, under the intermittent shade of palm trees and large canvas umbrellas. The fresh seared tuna, big healthy salads, and Belgian french fries are the favorites here, alongside the fresh fruit smoothies and delicious sandwiches on just-baked bread. You'll have to come early on weekends to get a seat.

On the beach, Playa Avellanas. ✆ **2652-9097.** Reservations not accepted. Main courses C3,900–C6,000. No credit cards. Tues–Sun 8am–sunset.

PLAYA JUNQUILLAL ★

30km (19 miles) W of Santa Cruz; 20km (12 miles) S of Tamarindo

A long, windswept beach that, for most of its length, is backed by grasslands, Playa Junquillal remains a mostly undiscovered gem on an increasingly crowded coast. With no village to speak of here and a rough road, this is a good place to get away from it all and enjoy some unfettered time on a nearly deserted beach. The long stretch of white sand is great for strolling, and the sunsets are superb. When the waves are big, this beach is great for surfing, but can be a little dangerous for swimming. When it's calm, jump right in.

Essentials

GETTING THERE & DEPARTING **By Plane:** The nearest airport with regularly scheduled flights is in Tamarindo (see earlier in this chapter). You can arrange a taxi from the airport to Playa Junquillal. The ride should take around 40 minutes and cost about $40 to $60.

By Car: From San José, you can either take the Interamerican Highway (CR1) north from downtown San José, or first head west out of the city on the San José-Caldera Highway (CR27). This latter route is a faster and flatter drive. When you reach Caldera on this route, follow the signs to Puntarenas, Liberia, and the Interamerican Highway (CR1). This will lead you to the unmarked entrance to CR1. You'll want to pass under the bridge and follow the on-ramp, which will put you on the highway heading north. Forty-seven kilometers (29 miles) past the Puntarenas on-ramp, you'll see signs and the turnoff for the La Amistad Bridge. After crossing the river, follow the signs for Nicoya and Santa Cruz. Just after leaving the main intersection for Santa Cruz, you'll see a marked turnoff for Playa Junquillal, Ostional, and Tamarindo. The road is paved for 14km (8½ miles), until the tiny village of Veintesiete de Abril. From here, it's another rough 18km (11 miles) to Playa Junquillal.

From Liberia, head south to Santa Cruz on the main road to all the beach towns, passing through Filadelfia and Belén. Then follow the directions above from Santa Cruz.

By Bus: To get here by bus, you must first head to Santa Cruz and, from there, take another bus to Playa Junquillal. Buses depart San José for Santa Cruz roughly every 2 hours between 6am and 6pm from the **Tralapa** bus station (© **2221-7202**) at Calle 20 between avenidas 3 and 5, and from the **Alfaro** bus station (© **2222-2666**) at Calle 14 between avenidas 3 and 5. The 4-hour trip is C4,600.

Buses leave Santa Cruz for Junquillal at 4:45, 6:45 and 10:15am, and 12:15, 2:15, and 5:50pm from the town's central plaza. The ride takes about 1 hour, and the one-way fare is C600. Buses depart Playa Junquillal for Santa Cruz daily at 5:30 and 8:45am, noon, and 4pm.

Playa Junquillal.

Always check with your hotel in advance as the schedule of buses between Junquillal and Santa Cruz is notoriously fickle. If you miss the connection, or there's no bus running, you can hire a taxi for the trip to Junquillal for $60. From Tamarindo, a taxi should cost $40 to $60.

What to See & Do

Other than walking on the beach, surfing, swimming when the surf isn't too strong, and exploring tide pools, there isn't much to do here—which is just fine with me. This beach is ideal for anyone who wants to relax without any distractions. Bring a few good books. You can rent bikes at the Iguanazul Hotel (see below), which is a good way to get up and down to the beach; horseback-riding tours are also popular. If you have a car, you can explore the coastline just north and south of here, as well.

For surfers, the Junquillal beach break is often pretty good. I've also heard that if you look hard enough, a few hidden reef and point breaks are around.

Several sportfishing boats operate out of Playa Junquillal. Inquire at your hotel or ask at the Iguanazul Hotel. To rent a mountain bike, you can also check in at the Iguanazul. If you want to ride a horse on the beach, call **Paradise Riding** (🕐 **2658-8162;** www.paradiseriding.com). The cost is $55 per person for a 2-hour ride and $65 per person for a 3-hour ride.

Where to Stay & Eat

You can get good pizza, homemade pasta, and fresh seafood at **Pizzería Tatanka** (🕐 **2658-8426;** www.hoteltatanka.com), which also offers simple rooms at very reasonable rates. It's near the Iguanazul Hotel on your left as you come into Junquillal, and also has good ocean and sunset views. For a more elegant dining experience, also featuring Italian cuisine, try **La Puesta del Sol** (🕐 **2658-8442**), on a hillside overlooking the sea. This is a great place to watch sunsets.

MODERATE

Iguanazul Hotel   Set on a windswept, grassy bluff above a rocky beach, Iguanazul is the biggest, best-equipped, and most happening hotel in Junquillal. The large pool features a tiny island with a palm tree growing on it, and there's also a volleyball court. If you're feeling mellow, head down to one of the quiet coves or grab a hammock in a palapa on the hillside. Guest rooms are spacious and nicely decorated with basket lampshades, wicker furniture, red-tile floors, high ceilings, and blue-and-white-tile bathrooms. Even if you're not staying here, it's a good place to dine, and the sunset views are phenomenal. These folks can also rent out fully equipped houses and condos for longer stays at their neighboring residential project.

Playa Junquillal, Guanacaste. www.iguanazul.com. 🕐 **2658-8123** or 🕐/fax 2658-8124. 24 units. $79–$124 double. Rates include full breakfast and taxes. AE, MC, V. **Amenities:** Restaurant; bar; outdoor pool; small spa. *In room:* A/C (in some), Wi-Fi.

INEXPENSIVE

In addition to the hotel listed below, **Camping Los Malinches** (🕐 **2658-8429**) has wonderful campsites on fluffy grass amid manicured gardens set on a bluff above the beach. Camping costs C2,500 per person, and includes restroom and shower privileges. You'll see a sign on the right as you drive toward Playa Junquillal, a little bit beyond the Iguanazul Hotel. The campground is about 1km (½ mile) down this dirt road. These folks also have some simple, rustic rooms.

Hotel Hibiscus 🦺 Although the accommodations are simple, the friendly German owner makes sure that everything is always in top shape. The grounds are pleasantly shady with flowering tropical flora and the beach is across the road. The rooms have cool Mexican-tile floors and firm beds. The service and ambience are excellent for the price range. The restaurant serves well-prepared international cuisine at reasonable prices.

Playa Junquillal, Guanacaste. www.hibiscus-info.com. ©/fax **2658-8437.** 4 units. $50 double. Rates include full breakfast and taxes. No credit cards. **Amenities:** Restaurant. *In room:* No phone.

PUNTARENAS
& THE
NICOYA
PENINSULA

The beaches of the Nicoya Peninsula don't get nearly as much attention or traffic as those to the north in Guanacaste. However, they are just as stunning, varied, and rewarding. Montezuma, with its jungle waterfalls and gentle surf, is the original beach destination out this way. However, it's eclipsed by the up-and-coming hot spots of Malpaís and Santa Teresa.

Farther up the peninsula lie the beaches of **Playa Sámara** and **Playa Nosara.** With easy access via paved roads and the time-saving La Amistad Bridge, Playa Sámara is one of the coastline's more popular destinations, especially with Ticos looking for a quick and easy weekend getaway. Just north of Sámara, Nosara and its neighboring beaches remain remote and sparsely visited, thanks in large part to the horrendous dirt road that separates these distinctly different destinations. However, Nosara is widely known and coveted as one of the country's top **surf spots,** with a host of different beach and point breaks from which to choose.

Top Sustainable Hotels

Cristal Azul (p. 279)
Florblanca Resort (p. 275)
The Harmony Hotel & Spa (p. 290)
Hotel Punta Islita (p. 285)
Lagarta Lodge (p. 291)
Pranamar Villas & Yoga Retreat (p. 276)
Ylang Ylang Beach Resort (p. 267)

Nearby **Puntarenas** was once Costa Rica's principal Pacific port. The town bustled and hummed with commerce, fishermen, coffee brokers, and a weekend rush of urban dwellers enjoying some sun and fun at one of the closest beaches to San José. Today, Puntarenas is a run-down shell of its former self. Still, it remains a major fishing port, and the main gateway to the isolated and coveted beaches of the Nicoya Peninsula.

PUNTARENAS

115km (71 miles) W of San José; 191km (118 miles) S of Liberia; 75km (47 miles) N of Playa de Jacó

They say you can't put lipstick on a pig, and this has proven true for Puntarenas. Despite serious investment and the steady influx of cruise ship passengers, Puntarenas can't seem to shed its image as a rough-and-tumble, perennially run-down port town. While the seafront **Paseo de los Turistas (Tourist Walk)** has a string of restaurants and souvenir stands, this town has little to interest visitors, and the beach here pales in comparison to almost any other beach destination in the country.

A 16km (10-mile) spit of land jutting into the Gulf of Nicoya, Puntarenas was once Costa Rica's busiest port, but that changed drastically when the government inaugurated nearby Puerto Caldera, a modern container port facility. After losing its shipping business, the city has survived primarily on commercial fishing.

PREVIOUS PAGE: **Curú Wildlife Refuge.**

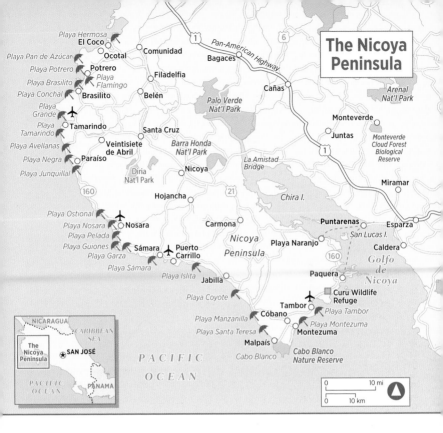

An excellent highway from San José leads to the nearby port of Caldera, so you can reach Puntarenas (on a good day, with little traffic) in little more than an hour by car, which makes it one of the closest beaches to San José. A long, straight stretch of sand with gentle surf, the beach is backed for most of its length by the Paseo de los Turistas. Across a wide boulevard from the Paseo de los Turistas are hotels, restaurants, bars, discos, and shops. The sunsets and the views across the Gulf of Nicoya are quite beautiful, and a cooling breeze usually blows in off the water. All around town you'll find unusual old buildings, reminders of the important role that Puntarenas once played in Costa Rican history. It was from here that much of the Central Valley's coffee crop was once shipped, and while the coffee barons in the highlands were getting rich, so were the merchants of Puntarenas.

Puntarenas is primarily popular as a weekend holiday spot for Ticos from San José and is at its liveliest on weekends. Puntarenas is also where you must pick up the ferries to the southern Nicoya Peninsula, and some folks like to arrive the night before and get an early start.

A Colorful Festival

If you're in Puntarenas on the Saturday closest to July 16, you can witness the **Fiesta of the Virgin of the Sea.** During this festival a regatta of colorfully decorated boats carries a statue of Puntarenas's patron saint. Boats run all along the waterfront, but the Paseo de los Turistas makes for a good place to catch the action.

Essentials

GETTING THERE & DEPARTING **By Car:** Head west out of San José on the San José–Caldera Highway (CR27). When you reach Caldera, follow the signs to Puntarenas. The drive takes a little over 1 hour. To reach Puntarenas from Liberia, just take the Interamerican Highway south, to the well-marked exit for Puntarenas.

By Bus: Empresarios Unidos express buses (© **2222-0064**) leave San José daily every hour between 6am and 7pm from Calle 16 and Avenida 12. Trip duration is 2 hours; the fare is C2,150. Buses to **San José** leave the main station daily every hour between 6am and 9pm. Buses to **Quepos** and **Manuel Antonio** (© **2777-0743;** www.transportesquepospuntarenas. com) leave the main station daily at 5, 8, and 11am and 12:30, 2:30, and 4:30pm. The trip's duration is 1 hour; the fare is C980.

The bus to **Santa Elena** leaves daily at 2:15pm from a stop across the railroad tracks from the main bus station.

The main Puntarenas bus station is cater-cornered to the main pier on the Paseo de los Turistas.

By Ferry: See "Playa Tambor" or "Playa Montezuma," below, for information on crossing to and returning from Puntarenas from Paquera or Naranjo on the Nicoya Peninsula.

ORIENTATION Puntarenas is built on a long, narrow sand spit that stretches 16km (10 miles) out into the Gulf of Nicoya and is marked by only five streets at its widest. The ferry docks for the Nicoya Peninsula are near the far end of town, as are the bus station and market. The north side of town faces an estuary, and the south side faces the mouth of the gulf. The Paseo de los Turistas is on the south side of town, beginning at the pier and extending out to the point.

FAST FACTS Several banks, Internet cafes, and general markets are all located within a 2-block radius of the town's small church and central park. The town's main post office can be found here as well.

The **Hospital Monseñor Sanabria** (© **2663-0033**), located on the outskirts of downtown, is the largest and best equipped hospital in this region.

If you need a taxi, call **Coopetico** (© **2663-2020**).

What to See & Do

Take a walk along the **Paseo de los Turistas,** which feels rather like a Florida beach town out of the 1950s. The hotels here range in style from converted old wooden homes with bright gingerbread trim to modern concrete monstrosities to tasteful Art Deco relics that need a new coat of paint.

If you venture into the center of the city, be sure to check out the **central plaza around the Catholic church.** The large, stone church itself is interesting because it has portholes for windows, reflecting the city's maritime tradition. In addition, it's one of the few churches in the country with a front entry facing east, as most face west. Here you'll also find the city's cultural center, **La Casa de la Cultura** (© **2661-1394;** www.casadelaculturapuntarenas.com). In addition to rotating exhibits and the occasional theater performance or poetry reading,

Puntarenas's Catholic church.

this place houses the **Museo Histórico** (© 2661-1394), a small museum on the city's history, especially its maritime history, with exhibits in both English and Spanish. Admission is free, and it's open Monday to Saturday from 8am to 4pm. If you're looking for a shady spot to take a break, some inviting benches are in a little park off the north side of the church.

The largest attraction in town is the **Parque Marino del Pacífico** (**Pacific Marine Park;** © 2661-5272; www.parquemarino.org), a collection of saltwater aquariums highlighting the sea life of Costa Rica. Of the 23 separate tanks, the largest re-creates the undersea environment of Isla del Coco. Despite only being a few years old, this park has a neglected and run-down feel to it. This place is 2 blocks east of the main cruise ship terminal and is open Tuesday through Sunday from 9am to 4:30pm. Admission is $10 for adults, and $5 for children 11 and under.

If you want to go swimming, the ocean waters are now said to be perfectly safe (pollution was a problem for many years), although the beach is still not very attractive. Your best bet is to head back down the spit; just a few kilometers out of town, you'll find **Playa Doña Aña,** a popular beach with picnic tables, restrooms and changing rooms, and a couple of *sodas* (diners). If you head a little farther south, you will come to **Playa Tivives,** which is virtually unvisited by tourists but quite popular with Ticos, many of whom have beach houses up and down this long, brown-sand beach. Surfers can check out the beach break here or head to the mouth of the Barranca River, which boasts an amazingly long left break. Still, surfers and swimmers should be careful; crocodiles live in both the Barranca and Tivives river mouths, and I'd be wary of pollution in the waters emptying out of the rivers here.

DIVING TRIPS TO isla del coco
(COCOS ISLAND)

This little speck of land located some 480km (300 miles) off the Pacific coast was a prime pirate hide-out and refueling station. Robert Louis Stevenson most likely modeled *Treasure Island* on Cocos. Sir Francis Drake, Captain Edward Davis, William Dampier, and Mary Welch are just some of the famous corsairs who dropped anchor in the calm harbors of this Pacific pearl. They allegedly left troves of buried loot, although scores of treasure hunters over several centuries have failed to unearth more than a smattering of the purported bounty. The Costa Rican flag was first raised here on September 15, 1869. Throughout its history, Isla del Coco has provided anchorage and fresh water to hundreds of ships and has entertained divers and dignitaries. (Franklin Delano Roosevelt visited it three times.) In 1978 it was declared a national park and protected area.

The clear, warm waters around Cocos are widely regarded as one of the most rewarding **dive destinations** ★★★ on this planet. This is a prime place to see schooling herds of scalloped hammerhead sharks. On my shallow-water checkout dive—normally, a perfunctory and uninspiring affair—I spotted my first hammerhead lurking just 4.5m (15 ft.) below me within 15 seconds of flipping into the water. Soon there were more, and soon they came much, much closer.

Other denizens of the waters around Isla del Coco include white- and silver-tipped reef sharks; marbled, manta, eagle, and mobula rays; moray and spotted eels; octopi; spiny and slipper lobsters; hawksbill turtles; squirrel fish, trigger fish, and angelfish; surgeon fish, trumpet fish, grouper, grunts, snapper, jack, and tangs; and more. Two of the more spectacular underwater residents here include the red-lipped batfish and the frogfish.

Most diving at Cocos is relatively deep (26–35m/85–115 ft.), and there are often strong currents and choppy swells to deal with—not to mention all those sharks. This is not a trip for novice divers.

The perimeter of Isla del Coco is ringed by steep, forested cliffs punctuated by dozens of majestic waterfalls cascading down in stages or steady streams for hundreds of feet. The island itself has a series of trails that climb its

Puntarenas isn't known as one of Costa Rica's prime sportfishing ports, but a few charter boats are usually available. Check at your hotel or head to the docks and ask around. Rates (for up to six people) are usually between $400 and $600 for a half-day and between $800 and $1,600 for a full day.

You can also take a yacht cruise through the tiny, uninhabited islands of the Guayabo, Negritos, and Pájaros Islands Biological Reserve. These cruises include a lunch buffet and a relaxing stop on beautiful and undeveloped **Tortuga Island ★**, where you can swim, snorkel, and sunbathe. The water is clear blue, and the sand is bright white. However, this trip has surged in popularity, and many of the tours here have a cattle-car feel. Several San José–based companies offer these excursions, with round-trip transportation from San José, but if you're already in Puntarenas, you might receive a slight discount by boarding here.

steep hills and wind through its rainforested interior. Several endemic bird, reptile, and plant species here include the ubiquitous Cocos finch, which I spotted soon after landing onshore, and the wild Isla del Coco pig.

With just a small ranger station housing a handful of national park guards, Isla del Coco is essentially uninhabited. Visitors these days come on private or charter yachts, fishing boats, or one of the few live-aboard dive vessels that make regular voyages out here. It's a long trip: Most dive vessels take 30 to 36 hours to reach Cocos. Sailboats are even slower.

Both **Aggressor Fleet Limited** (© **800/348-2628;** www.aggressor. com) and **Undersea Hunter** (© **800/ 203-2120** in the U.S., or 2228-6613 in Costa Rica; www.underseahunter.com) regularly run dive trips to Isla del Coco from Puntarenas.

Calypso Tours ★ (© **2256-2727;** www.calypsotours.com) is the most reputable company that cruises out of Puntarenas. In addition to **Tortuga Island** trips, Calypso Tours takes folks to its own private nature reserve at **Punta Coral** and even on a sunset cruise that includes dinner and some guided stargazing. Either cruise will run you $119 per person. These prices are the same whether you join them in San José or Puntarenas. If you ask around at the docks, you might find some other boats that ply the waters of the Nicoya Gulf. Some of these companies also offer sunset cruises with live music, snacks, and a bar.

Where to Stay

In addition to the places mentioned below, the **Double Tree Resort by Hilton Puntarenas** (www.puntarenas.doubletree.com; © **800/446-6677** in the U.S.

and Canada, or 2663-0808 in Costa Rica) is an all-inclusive resort set on a decidedly unspectacular patch of sand, just south of the Puntarenas peninsula. While the accommodations and service are certainly acceptable, it's still not a top beach resort pick in my book.

MODERATE

Hotel Alamar ★   This hotel is the most contemporary and best equipped option in town. Located toward the end of the Paseo de los Turistas, more than half of its units are one- or two-bedroom apartments, with fully equipped kitchens. All the rooms are spacious, clean, and modern. Walls are painted in bright primary colors and pastels. The furniture and decor are contemporary. In the center of the hotel complex are a refreshing pool and Jacuzzi. Ample breakfast buffets are served poolside. The best rooms here feature water-facing balconies and Jacuzzi tubs.

Paseo de los Turistas, Puntarenas. www.alamarcr.com. ✆ **2661-4343.** Fax 2661-2726. 34 units. $90–$110 double. Rates include buffet breakfast. AE, DC, MC, V. **Amenities:** Restaurant; bar; Jacuzzi; small outdoor pool. *In room:* A/C, TV, minifridge, hair dryer, Wi-Fi.

Hotel Las Brisas   Out near the end of the Paseo de los Turistas, you'll find this older, yet well-kept hotel with large air-conditioned rooms, a small pool out front, and the beach right across the street. All the rooms have tile floors, double or twin beds, and small televisions and tables. Large picture windows keep the rooms sunny and bright during the day. There's complimentary coffee and a secure parking lot. The hotel's small open-air restaurant serves Greek specialties, fresh seafood, and other international fare. I find the rooms here are not as nice as those at Hotel Alamar.

Paseo de los Turistas, Puntarenas. www.lasbrisashotelcr.com. ✆ **2661-4040.** Fax 2661-2120. 25 units. $95 double; $199 suite. AE, DC, MC, V. **Amenities:** Restaurant; bar; small gym; Jacuzzi; small outdoor pool. *In room:* A/C, TV, Wi-Fi.

INEXPENSIVE

Hotel La Punta ★   Most budget lodgings in Puntarenas are real port-town dives. And for decades this place was just one of many. However, a top-to-bottom remodel has transformed this into a cozy little hotel at a good price. The rooms are spread around the two-story building here, and all feature small televisions, A/C units, and a minifridge. Try for a second-floor room with a balcony. A small kidney-shaped pool is in a shady garden for cooling off during the day. The hotel has safe parking and easy access to the ferry terminal and docks.

Puntarenas (½ block south of the ferry terminal). www.hotellapunta.com. ✆ **2661-0696.** 8 units. $60 double. MC, V. **Amenities:** Restaurant; bar; small outdoor pool. *In room:* A/C, TV, no phone.

Where to Eat

You're in a seaport, so try some of the local catch. Corvina (sea bass) is the most popular offering, and it's served in various forms and preparations. My favorite dish on a hot afternoon is *ceviche,* and you'll find that just about every restaurant in town serves this savory marinated seafood concoction.

The most economical option is to pull up a table at one of the many open-air *sodas* along the Paseo de los Turistas, serving everything from sandwiches, drinks, and ice cream to fish. Sandwiches are priced at around $2, and a fish filet with rice and beans should cost around $4. If you want some seafood in a slightly more formal atmosphere, try the **Jardin Cervecero** or **Casa de los Mariscos,** or the open-air **Restaurant Aloha,** all located on the Paseo de los Turistas.

La Yunta Steakhouse ★ STEAK/SEAFOOD   This airy place bills itself as a steakhouse, but it has an ample menu of seafood dishes as well. Most of the tables are located on a two-tiered covered veranda at the front of the restaurant, overlooking the street and the ocean just beyond. Overall, this restaurant has the nicest ambience in town. The portions are immense, and the meat is tender and well prepared.

Paseo de los Turistas. ✆ **2661-3216.** Reservations recommended in high season and on Fri-Sat. Main courses C3,500–C15,000. AE, MC, V. Daily 10am–midnight.

PLAYA TAMBOR

150–168km (93–104 miles) W of San José (not including ferry ride); 20km (12 miles) S of Paquera; 38km (24 miles) S of Naranjo

Playa Tambor was the site of Costa Rica's first large-scale all-inclusive resort, the Barceló Playa Tambor Beach Resort. Despite big plans, the resort and surrounding area have never really taken off. Tambor has a forgotten, isolated feel to it.

Playa Tambor.

Part of the blame lies with the beach itself. Playa Tambor is a long, gently curving stretch of beach protected on either end by rocky headlands. These headlands give the waters ample protection from Pacific swells, making this a good beach for swimming. However, the sand is a rather unattractive, dull gray-brown color, which often receives a large amount of flotsam and jetsam brought in by the sea. Playa Tambor pales in comparison to the beaches located farther south along the Nicoya Peninsula.

However, Tambor is the site of the only major commuter airport on the southern Nicoya Peninsula, and you'll be arriving and departing here if you choose to visit Montezuma, Malpaís, or Santa Teresa by air.

Essentials

GETTING THERE & DEPARTING   By Plane: Sansa (✆ **877/767-2672** in the U.S. and Canada, or 2290-4100 in Costa Rica; www.flysansa. com) flies five times daily to **Tambor**

airport (TMU; no phone) from San José's Juan Santamaría International Airport, with the first flight at 7:40am and the last flight at 4pm. Flights begin departing for San José at 8:25am, with the last flight out at 4:45pm. Flight duration is 30 minutes; the fare is $102 each way.

Nature Air (☏ 866/735-9278 in the U.S. and Canada, or 2299-6000; www.natureair.com) flies to Tambor daily at 8am and 2pm from Tobías Bolaños International Airport in Pavas. Flight duration is 25 minutes; fares run $83 to $125 each way. Return flights for San José leave at 8:30am and 2:30pm. Nature Air also has either direct flights or connecting flights between Tambor and Liberia, Tamarindo, Quepos, Palmar Sur, and Puerto Jiménez.

The airport in Tambor is about 16km (10 miles) from Montezuma. The ride takes around 15 to 20 minutes. **Taxis** are generally waiting to meet most regularly scheduled planes, but if they aren't, you can call Gilberto (☏ 2642-0241 or 8826-9055).

By Car: The traditional route here is to drive to Puntarenas and catch the ferry to either Naranjo or Paquera. Tambor is about 30 minutes south of Paquera and about an hour and 20 minutes south of Naranjo. The road from Paquera to Tambor is paved and usually in pretty good shape, and taking the Paquera ferry will save you time and some rough, dusty driving. The road from Naranjo to Paquera is all dirt and gravel and often in very bad shape. For directions on driving to Puntarenas, see p. 254.

Naviera Tambor (☏ 2661-2084; www.navieratambor.com) car ferries to Paquera leave Puntarenas roughly every 2 hours daily between 9am and 9pm, with one early trip at 5am. The trip takes 1½ hours. The fare is C7,780 per car, including the driver; C810 for each additional adult, and C485 for children. I recommend arriving early during the peak season and on weekends because lines can be long; if you miss the ferry, you'll have to wait around 2 hours or more for the next one. Moreover, the ferry schedule changes frequently, with fewer ferries during the low season, and the occasional extra ferry added during the high season to meet demand. It's always best to check in advance.

The car ferry from Paquera to Puntarenas leaves roughly every 2 hours between 9am and 7pm, with one early trip at 6am. **Note:** If you have to wait for the ferry, do not leave your car unattended, since break-ins are common.

The **Naranjo ferry** (☏ 2661-1069; www.coonatramar.com) leaves daily at 6:30 and 10am and 2:30 and 7:30pm. The trip takes 1½ hours. Return ferries leave Naranjo for Puntarenas daily at 8am and 12:30, 5:30, and 9pm. The fare is C7,500 per car, including the driver; C860 for each additional adult; and C515 for children.

Another option is to drive via the La Amistad Bridge over the Tempisque River. I only recommend this route when the ferries are on the fritz, or when the wait for the next ferry that your car will fit on is over 2 hours. (When the lines are long, you may not find room on the next departing ferry.) Although heading farther north and crossing the bridge is more circuitous, you will be driving the whole time, which beats waiting around in the midday heat of Puntarenas. To go this route, take the Interamerican Highway west from San José. Forty-seven kilometers (29 miles) past the turnoff for Puntarenas, turn left for the La Amistad Bridge. After you cross the Tempisque River, head to Quebrada Honda and then south to Route 21, following signs for San Pablo, Jicaral, Lepanto, Playa Naranjo, and Paquera.

To drive to Tambor from Liberia, head out of town on the main road to the Guanacaste beaches, passing through Filadelfia, Santa Cruz, and Nicoya on your way toward the turnoff for the La Amistad Bridge. Continue straight at this turnoff, and follow the directions for this route as listed above.

By Bus & Ferry: Transportes Cobano (𝒞 **2221-7479;** www.transportescobanocr.com) runs two daily direct buses between San José and Cóbano, dropping passengers off in Tambor en route. The buses leave from the Coca-Cola bus terminal at Calle 12 and Avenida 5 at 6am and 2pm. The fare is C6,515, including the ferry ride, and the trip takes a little over 4 hours.

Alternately, it takes two buses and a ferry ride to get to Tambor. **Empresarios Unidos** express buses (𝒞 **2222-0064**) leave San José daily every hour between 6am and 7pm from Calle 16 and Avenida 12. The trip is 2½ hours and costs C2,150. From Puntarenas, take the car ferry to Paquera mentioned above. A bus south to Montezuma (this will drop you off in Tambor) will be waiting to meet the ferry when it arrives in Paquera. The bus ride takes about 35 minutes; the fare is around C1,000. Be careful not to take the Naranjo ferry because it does not meet with regular onward bus transportation to Tambor.

When you're ready to head back, buses originating in Montezuma, Cóbano, or Malpaís pass through Tambor roughly every 2 hours between 6am and 4:30pm. Theoretically, these should connect with a waiting ferry in Paquera. Total trip duration is 3½ hours. Buses to San José leave Puntarenas daily every hour between 5am and 8pm.

ORIENTATION   Although there's a tiny village of Tambor, through which the main road passes, the hotels themselves are scattered along several kilometers, with Tango Mar (see below), definitively outside Tambor proper. You'll see signs for all these hotels as the road passes through and beyond Playa Tambor.

If you need a bank, pharmacy, or post office, you'll have to head to nearby Cóbano.

Fun on & off the Beach

Curú Wildlife Refuge ★★ (𝒞 **2641-0100;** www.curuwildliferefuge.com), 16km (10 miles) north of Tambor, is a private reserve that has several pretty, secluded beaches, as well as forests and mangrove swamps. This area is extremely rich in wildlife. Mantled howler and white-faced monkeys are often spotted here, and quite a few species of birds. You will usually see scarlet macaws, as the refuge is actively involved in a macaw protection and repopulation effort. Horses are available to rent in the refuge for $10 per hour. Typically, the horse rentals work like this: You'll ride, with a guide, for about an hour to a lovely beach, hang out on the sand for about an hour, and then ride back. Happily, you only get charged for the time you're actually on horseback, so trips run about $20. If you'd like to take a longer ride, simply ask if they'll accommodate you. Admission for the day is $10 per person. Some rustic cabins are available with advance notice for $15 per person per day (includes entrance fee). Meals are $8. If you don't have a car, you should arrange pickup with the folks who manage this refuge. Or you can contact **Turismo Curú** (© **2641-0004;** www.curutourism.com), which specializes in guided tours to the refuge, as well as kayaking trips and other area adventures.

Both the hotels listed below offer horseback riding and various tours around this part of the peninsula and can arrange fishing and dive trips.

A woodpecker at Curú Wildlife Refuge.

Where to Stay & Eat

Aside from the hotels listed here, a few inexpensive cabinas are available near the town of Tambor, at the southern end of the beach. Most are very rustic and basic, and charge around $10 per person. Another option is **Costa Coral ★** (www.hotelcostacoral.com; © **2683-0105**), a very attractive place with a good restaurant. This place would be my top choice in Tambor, except it's unfortunately set right off the busy main road here, several hundred meters from the beach.

The **Barceló Playa Tambor Beach Resort** (www.barcelotamborbeach.com; © **2683-0303**) was Costa Rica's first all-inclusive resort, but its beach is mediocre at best, and the Barceló company has been accused of violating Costa Rica's environmental laws, ignoring zoning regulations, and mistreating workers. In late 2010, hundreds of guests were stricken by a powerful stomach virus over a period of a week or so, before the resort was closed for another week or so. Although this resort is a major presence here, I don't recommend it; much better all-inclusive options are available farther north in Guanacaste.

Tambor Tropical ★   Most of the rooms are located in five two-story octagonal buildings and a few garden suites are set back in the thick forest. The whole place is an orgy of varnished hardwoods, with purple heart and cocobolo offsetting each other at every turn. Rooms are enormous and come with large, full kitchens and a spacious sitting area. The walls are, in effect, nothing but shuttered picture windows, which give you the choice of gazing out at the ocean or shutting in for a bit of privacy. The upstairs rooms have large wraparound verandas, and the lower rooms have garden-level decks. The beach is only steps away. Plenty of coconut palms and flowering plants provide a very tropical feel.

Tambor, Puntarenas. www.tambortropical.com. © **866/890-2537** in the U.S., or 2683-0011 in Costa Rica. Fax 2683-0013. 14 units. $160–$220 double. Rates include continental breakfast. AE, MC, V. No children 15 and under. **Amenities:** Restaurant; bar; small free-form tile outdoor pool and Jacuzzi; small spa. *In room:* Kitchenette, no phone, Wi-Fi.

Tango Mar Resort ★★ Tango Mar is a great place to get away from it all. With just 18 rooms and scattered suites and villas, the resort never feels crowded. A beautiful white-sand beach is right in front, and if you choose to go exploring, you'll find seaside cliffs and a beautiful nearby waterfall. The rooms have large balconies and glass walls to soak in the views, and some have private Jacuzzis. The suites are set among shade trees and flowering vegetation. Most come with four-poster canopy beds and indoor Jacuzzis. The villas are all different, spacious, and secluded. Some suites and villas are a bit far from the beach and main hotel, so you'll need either your own car or one of the hotel's golf carts. In addition to a 9-hole par-3 golf course and two tennis courts, the hotel has a small spa and yoga space to keep you fit and busy.

Playa Tambor, Puntarenas. www.tangomar.com. ☏ **800/297-4420** in the U.S., or 2683-0001 in Costa Rica. Fax 2683-0003. 18 units. 12 tropical suites, 5 bungalows, and 4 villas. $199 double; $270 suites and bungalows; $450–$999 villa. Rates include breakfast. Rates slightly lower during the off season, higher during peak weeks. AE, DC, MC, V. **Amenities:** Restaurant; bar; bike rental; 9-hole par-3 golf course ($35 full-day greens fee) w/wonderful sea views; 4 small outdoor pools; room service; small spa; 2 lighted tennis courts; limited watersports equipment rental. *In room:* A/C, TV, minibar.

PLAYA MONTEZUMA ★★

166–184km (103–114 miles) W of San José (not including the ferry ride); 36km (22 miles) SE of Paquera; 54km (33 miles) S of Naranjo

For decades, this remote village and its surrounding beaches, forests, and waterfalls have enjoyed near-legendary status among backpackers, UFO seekers, hippie expatriates, and European budget travelers. Although it maintains its alternative vibe, Montezuma is a great destination for all manner of travelers looking for a beach retreat surrounded by some stunning scenery. Active pursuits abound, from hiking in the Cabo Blanco Absolute Nature Reserve to horseback riding to visiting a beachside waterfall. The natural beauty, miles of almost abandoned beaches, rich wildlife, and jungle waterfalls here are what first made Montezuma famous, and they continue to make this one of my favorite beach towns in Costa Rica.

A swimming hole at Playa Montezuma.

Essentials

GETTING THERE & DEPARTING By Plane: The nearest airport is in Tambor, 17km (11 miles) away (see "Playa Tambor," above, for details). Some of the hotels listed below might pick you up in Tambor for a reasonable fee. If not, you'll have to hire a taxi, which could cost anywhere between $20 and $30. **Taxis** are generally waiting to meet most regularly scheduled planes, but if they aren't, you can call **Gilberto** (✆ **2642-0241** or 8826-9055).

By Car: The traditional route here is to first drive to Puntarenas and catch the ferry to either Naranjo or Paquera. Montezuma is about 30 minutes south of Tambor, 1 hour south of Paquera, and about 2 hours south of Naranjo. The road from Paquera to Tambor is paved and usually in pretty good shape, and taking the Paquera ferry will save you time and some rough, dusty driving. The road from Naranjo to Paquera is all dirt and gravel and often in very bad shape.

For info on car ferries, see p. 260. For driving directions to Puntarenas, see p. 254.

To drive to Montezuma from Liberia, head out of town on the main road to the Guanacaste beaches, passing through Filadelfia, Santa Cruz, and Nicoya on your way toward the turnoff for the La Amistad Bridge. Continue straight at this turnoff, and follow the directions for this route as listed above.

By Bus & Ferry: Transportes Cobano (✆ **2221-7479;** www.transportescobanocr.com) runs two daily direct buses between San José and Montezuma, dropping passengers off in en route. The buses leave from the Coca-Cola bus terminal at Calle 12 and Avenida 5 at 6am and 2pm. The fare is C6,515, including the ferry ride, and the trip takes a little over 5 hours.

Alternately, it takes two buses and a ferry ride to get to Montezuma. **Empresarios Unidos** express buses (✆ **2222-0064**) to Puntarenas leave San José daily every hour between 6am and 7pm from Calle 16 and Avenida 12. The trip takes 2½ hours; the fare is C2,150. From Puntarenas, you can take the ferry to Paquera, mentioned on p. 260. A bus south to Montezuma will be waiting to meet the ferry when it arrives in Paquera. The bus ride takes about 55 minutes; the fare is C1,650. Be careful not to take the Naranjo ferry because it does not meet with regular onward bus transportation to Montezuma.

Buses are met by hordes of locals trying to corral you to one of the many budget hotels. Remember, they are getting a commission for everybody they bring in, so their information is biased. Not only that, they are often flat-out lying when they tell you the hotel you wanted to stay in is full.

When you're ready to head back, direct buses leave Montezuma daily at 5:30am and 2:30pm. Regular local buses to Paquera leave Cóbano roughly every 2 hours throughout the day starting around 4:45am. Buses to San José leave Puntarenas daily every hour between 6am and 7pm.

ORIENTATION   As the winding mountain road that descends into Montezuma bottoms out, you turn left onto a small dirt road that defines the village proper. On this 1-block road, you will find El Sano Banano Village Cafe and, across from it, a small shady park with plenty of tall trees, as well as a basketball court and children's playground. The bus stops at the end of this road. From here, hotels are scattered up and down the beach and around the village's few sand streets.

Around the center of town are several tour agencies and Internet cafes among the restaurants and souvenir stores.

Fun on & off the Beach

The ocean here is a gorgeous royal blue, and beautiful beaches stretch out along the coast on either side of town. Be careful, though: The waves can occasionally be too rough for casual swimming, and you need to be aware of stray rocks at your feet. Be sure you know where the rocks and tide are before doing any bodysurfing. The best places to swim are a couple of hundred meters north of town in front of **El Rincón de los Monos,** or several kilometers farther north at Playa Grande.

If you're interested in more than simple beach time, head for the **Montezuma waterfall ★★** just south of town—it's one of those tropical fantasies where water comes pouring down into a deep pool. It's a popular spot, and it's a bit of a hike up the stream. Along this stream are a couple of waterfalls, but the upper falls are by far the more spectacular. You'll find the trail to the falls just over the bridge south of the village (on your right just past Las Cascadas restaurant). At the first major outcropping of rocks, the trail disappears and you have to scramble up the rocks and river for a bit. A trail occasionally reappears for short stretches. Just stick close to the stream and you'll eventually hit the falls.

Buy the Book . . . or Just Borrow It

If you came unprepared or ran out of reading material, check in at **Librería Topsy** (*C* 2642-0576), which, in addition to selling books, runs a lending library and serves as the local post office. These folks also have a branch up in Cabuya.

Note: Be very careful when climbing close to the rushing water, and also if you plan on taking any dives into the pools below. The rocks are quite slippery, and several people each year get very scraped up, break bones, and otherwise hurt themselves here.

Another popular local waterfall is **El Chorro ★**, located 8km (5 miles) north of Montezuma. This waterfall cascades down into a tide pool at the edge of the ocean. The pool here is a delightful mix of fresh- and seawater, and you can bathe while gazing out over the sea and rocky coastline. When the water is clear and calm, this is one of my favorite swimming holes in all of Costa Rica. However, a massive landslide in 2004 filled in much of this pool and also somewhat lessened the drama and beauty of the falls. Moreover, the pool here is dependent upon the tides—it disappears entirely at very high tide. It's about a 2-hour hike along the beach to reach El Chorro. Alternatively, you can take a horseback tour here with any of the tour operators or horseback riding companies in town.

ON THE WING For an intimate look at the life cycle and acrobatic flights-of-fancy of butterflies, head to the **Mariposario Montezuma Gardens** (*C* 2642-1317 or 8888-4200; www.montezumagardens.com). This is perhaps the most wild and natural feeling of all the butterfly gardens in Costa Rica. Wooden walkways wind through thick vegetation under black screen meshing. Most of the butterflies in the enclosure are self-reproducing. You can also see butterflies and other wildlife on trails through open forested areas outside the enclosure. Along the dirt road heading up the hill just beyond the entrance to the waterfall trail, this place is open daily from 8am to 4pm. Admission is $8, and includes a guided tour. These folks also have a few pretty rooms they rent out, or give to volunteers in exchange for work around the gardens.

HORSEBACK RIDING　　Several people around the village will rent you horses for around $10 to $20 an hour, although most people choose to do a guided 4-hour horseback tour for $30 to $50. Any of the hotels or tour agencies in town can arrange it for you, or you can look for "Roger, the horse guy"—any local can direct you to him. However, you'll find the best-cared-for and best-kept horses at **Finca Los Caballos ★** (☎ 2642-0124; www.naturelodge. net; p. 268), which is up the hill on the road leading into Montezuma.

OTHER ACTIVITIES　　Some shops in the center of the village rent bicycles by the day or hour, as well as boogie boards and snorkeling equipment (although the water must be very calm for snorkeling).

A range of guided tour and adventure options is available in Monte-zuma. **CocoZuma Traveller** (☎ 2642-0911; www.cocozuma.com) and **Sun Trails** (☎ 2642-0808; www.montezumatraveladventures.com) can both arrange horseback riding, boat excursions, scuba-dive and snorkel tours, ATV outings, and rafting trips; car and motorcycle rentals; airport transfers; international phone, fax, and Internet service; and currency exchange.

One popular tour option here is the **Waterfall Canopy Tour ★** (☎ 2642-0808; www.montezumatraveladventures.com), which is built right alongside Montezuma's famous falls. The tour, which features eight cables connecting 10 platforms, includes a swim at the foot of the falls and costs $45 per person. Tours are offered daily at 9am and 1 and 3pm.

You'll encounter plenty of simple souvenir stores, as well as itinerant artisans selling their wares on the street, but it's worth stopping in at **Piedra Colorado ★** (☎ 2642-0612 or 8841-5855) to check out their impressive silver, stone, and polished-shell creations. This place is located in the tiny strip mall in the center of Montezuma.

An Excursion to Cabo Blanco Absolute Nature Reserve

As beautiful as the beaches around Montezuma are, the beaches at **Cabo Blanco Absolute Nature Reserve ★★** (☎ 2642-0093), 11km (6¾ miles) south of the village, are even more stunning. At the southernmost tip of the Nicoya Peninsula, Cabo Blanco is a national park that preserves a nesting site for brown pelicans, magnificent frigate birds, and brown boobies. The beaches are backed by a lush tropical forest that is home to howler monkeys. The main trail here, Sendero Sueco (Swiss Trail), is a rugged and sometimes steep hike through thick rainforest. The trail leads to the beautiful Playa Balsita and Playa Cabo Blanco, two white-sand stretches that straddle either side of the namesake Cabo Blanco point. The beaches are connected by a short trail. It's 4km (2.5 miles) to Playa Balsita. Alternately, you can take a shorter 2km (1.25-mile) loop trail through the primary forest here. This is Costa Rica's oldest official bioreserve and was set up thanks to the pioneering efforts of conservationists Karen Mogensen

Cabo Blanco Absolute Nature Reserve.

and Nicholas Wessberg. Admission is $10; the reserve is open Wednesday through Sunday from 8am to 4pm.

On your way out to Cabo Blanco, you'll pass through the tiny village of **Cabuya.** There are a couple of private patches of beach to discover in this area, off some of the deserted dirt roads, and a small offshore island serves as the town's picturesque cemetery. Snorkel and kayak trips to this island are offered out of Montezuma.

Shuttle buses head from Montezuma to Cabo Blanco roughly every 2 hours beginning at 8am, and then turn around and bring folks from Cabo Blanco to Montezuma; the last one leaves Cabo Blanco around 5pm. The fare is $2 each way. These shuttles often don't run during the off season. Alternatively, you can share a taxi: The fare is around $15 to $20 per taxi, which can hold four or five passengers. Taxis tend to hang around Montezuma center. One dependable *taxista* is **Gilberto Rodríguez** (✆ **2642-0241** or 8826-9055).

Where to Stay

EXPENSIVE

In addition to the places mentioned below, the **Anamaya Resort** ★ (www. anamayaresort.com; ✆ **2642-1289**) is a lovely and luxe new option on a high hillside above Montezuma. Anamaya specializes in yoga and wellness retreats.

Ylang Ylang Beach Resort ★★ 🎁 Set in a lush patch of forest just steps away from the sand, this hotel offers accommodations in a variety of shapes and sizes. Coco Joe's Bungalow is the largest and features a luscious wraparound balcony and a small sleeping loft. But I also like the smaller ferroconcrete geodesic domes, which look like igloos and have outdoor garden showers. Suites with private balconies and sleeping lofts are in a separate building, with standard rooms on the ground floor below them, as well as "jungalows"—large tents set on wooden platforms, with an indoor sink, small fridge, ceiling fan, and a private deck. These units share nearby bathrooms and showers. A beautiful swimming pool with a sculpted waterfall is on-site, and the whole operation is set amid lush gardens. You cannot drive in and out of the hotel, so arrival and check-in are handled at the downtown El Sano Banano Village Hotel (see below). The owners are committed environmentalists and are actively involved in local and regional conservation efforts; the restaurant serves both vegan and raw food dishes and as much locally grown organic produce as possible.

Montezuma, Cóbano de Puntarenas. www.ylangylangresort.com. (© **2642-0636.** Fax 2642-0068. 21 units. $140–$365 double. Rates include breakfast and dinner. AE, MC, V. **Amenities:** Restaurant; bar; midsize outdoor pool. *In room:* A/C (except jungalows), fridge, hair dryer, no phone, Wi-Fi.

MODERATE

The **El Sano Banano** folks also run an in-town B&B (www.elbanano.com; (© **2642-0636**), just off the popular restaurant (see below). The rooms here feature air-conditioning and satellite televisions; because of the design, you are basically forced to use the air-conditioning. Rooms are $75 per double.

El Jardin Set on a steep hill, right on the crossroads leading into "downtown," this is a good choice if you're looking for a comfortable and well-equipped room close to the action. The rooms are located in a series of different buildings spread across the hillside. Number 9 is my favorite, with pretty stone work in the bathroom, a greater sense of privacy than some of the others, and a good view from its private terrace. A fully equipped two-bedroom villa has a working kitchen for families and longer stays. A two-level pool and Jacuzzi are in a relaxing little garden area, and a small, full-service spa is on-site. Although the hotel doesn't have a restaurant, the town and its many dining options are just steps away.

Montezuma, Cóbano de Puntarenas. www.hoteleljardin.com. (©/fax **2642-0074** or (© 2642-0548. 17 units. $85–$95 double; $115 villa. AE, MC, V. **Amenities:** Jacuzzi; small outdoor pool; spa. *In room:* A/C, minifridge, no phone, Wi-Fi.

Nature Lodge Finca Los Caballos ★ This lodge is on a high ridge about 3km (1¾ miles) above Montezuma. The rooms are simple, with red tile roofs, hardwood trim, stone floors, and some pretty paintings and decorative accents. Every room has a private patio or balcony with a garden, jungle, or ocean view. The Superior Pacific rooms are the best bet, with beautiful ocean views out across the forested hills below. The hotel has a small pool, plenty of hammocks strung around for relaxing, and an in-house spa. Finca Los Caballos translates to "horse ranch," and riding is taken seriously by the hotel. The owners have 16 hectares (40 acres) of land and access to many neighboring ranches and trail systems. *Be forewarned:* If you stay here, it's a quick car ride, but very hefty hike, especially on the way back, to the beach.

Montezuma, Cóbano de Puntarenas. www.naturelodge.net. (© **2642-0124.** (©/fax 2642-0664. 12 units. $86–$146 double. Rates include breakfast. MC, V. **Amenities:** Restaurant; small outdoor pool; Wi-Fi. *In room:* Minifridge, no phone.

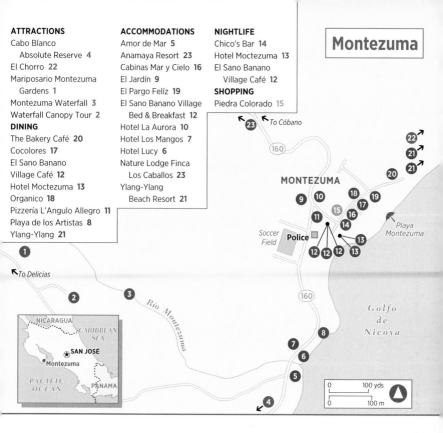

ATTRACTIONS
Cabo Blanco
  Absolute Reserve **4**
El Chorro **22**
Mariposario Montezuma
  Gardens **1**
Montezuma Waterfall **3**
Waterfall Canopy Tour **2**
DINING
The Bakery Café **20**
Cocolores **17**
El Sano Banano
Village Café **12**
Hotel Moctezuma **13**
Organico **18**
Pizzería L'Angulo Allegro **11**
Playa de los Artistas **8**
Ylang-Ylang **21**

ACCOMMODATIONS
Amor de Mar **5**
Anamaya Resort **23**
Cabinas Mar y Cielo **16**
El Jardín **9**
El Pargo Felíz **19**
El Sano Banano Village
  Bed & Breakfast **12**
Hotel La Aurora **10**
Hotel Los Mangos **7**
Hotel Lucy **6**
Nature Lodge Finca
  Los Caballos **23**
Ylang-Ylang
  Beach Resort **21**

NIGHTLIFE
Chico's Bar **14**
Hotel Moctezuma **13**
El Sano Banano
  Village Café **12**
SHOPPING
Piedra Colorado **15**

Montezuma

To Cóbano

MONTEZUMA

Playa
Montezuma

Soccer
Field   **Police**

To Delicias

Río Montezuma

NICARAGUA
CARIBBEAN
SEA
SAN JOSÉ
Montezuma
PACIFIC
OCEAN   PANAMA

Golfo
de
Nicoya

0   100 yds
0   100 m

INEXPENSIVE

In addition to the places mentioned below, **El Pargo Feliz** (www.montezuma-hotel.com; ✆ **2642-0065**) and **Cabinas Mar y Cielo** (✆ **2642-0261**) are two good budget options right in the center of town. **Hotel Los Mangos** (www.hotellosmangos.com; ✆ **2642-0384**), a bit before the waterfall on the road toward Cabo Blanco, has shared-bathroom budget rooms that are very basic, but they are a decent value and you do get access to a pool.

Amor de Mar ★ 🐚   This hotel has an idyllic setting, with a wide expanse of neatly trimmed grass sloping down to the sea, tide pools (one of which is as big as a small swimming pool), and hammocks slung from the mango trees. The rooms are housed in a two-story building, which abounds in varnished hardwoods. Although simply appointed, most rooms have plenty of space and receive lots of sunlight. However, a couple of the less expensive rooms are a bit small and dark. My favorite room is no. 5, which has exclusive access to a long second-floor balcony with a superb ocean view. Breakfast and lunch only are served on a beautiful open-air patio overlooking the sea. These folks also rent out a large fully equipped two-story, four-bedroom house next to the hotel.

Montezuma, Cóbano de Puntarenas. www.amordemar.com. ✆/fax **2642-0262.** 11 units, 9 with private bathroom. $50–$60 double with shared bathroom; $70–$110 double with private bathroom; $200 house. V, MC. **Amenities:** Restaurant. *In room:* A/C (in some), no phone.

Hotel La Aurora Just to the left as you enter the village of Montezuma, you'll find this long-standing budget hotel. The rooms are spread out over three floors in two neighboring buildings fronting the village's small park and playground. All rooms are clean and well-kept. A two-room apartment on the third floor has a private balcony and a bit of an ocean view through the treetops. The hotel also features a couple of common sitting areas, a small lending library, some hammocks and comfortable chairs for chilling out in, a communal kitchen, and flowering vines growing up the walls. In fact, the plants and vines all over La Aurora keep things cool and give the place a fitting tropical feel. Fresh coffee, tea, and hearty breakfasts are served each morning.

Montezuma, Cóbano de Puntarenas. www.hotelaurora-montezuma.com. ℰ/fax **2642-0051.** 19 units. $45–$70 double. Rates include taxes. MC, V. **Amenities:** Lounge; Wi-Fi. *In room:* A/C, TV, minifridge, no phone.

Hotel Lucy 🔑 Situated on a pretty section of beach a bit south of town, in front of Los Mangos, this converted two-story wooden home has the best location of any budget lodging in Montezuma. If you can snag a second-floor room with an ocean view, like room no. 19, you'll be in budget heaven. While very rustic and basic, the rooms are kept clean. The beach here is a bit rough and rocky for swimming, but the sunbathing and sunsets are beautiful.

Montezuma, Cóbano de Puntarenas. ℰ **2642-0273.** 17 units, 6 with bathroom. $20–$24 double with shared bathroom; $26–$30 double with private bathroom. No credit cards. **Amenities:** Smoke-free rooms. *In room:* No phone.

Where to Eat

In addition to the places listed below, you'll find several basic *sodas* and casual restaurants right in the village. My favorite of these is the **Pizzería L'Angulo Allegro** (ℰ **2642-1430**), which is at the crossroads into town and serves good thin-crust pizzas, calzones, and pastas. You might also want to check out the Spanish cuisine and fabulous setting at the downtown **Hotel Moctezuma** (ℰ **2642-0657**), or the varied international fare at **Cocolores** (ℰ **2642-0348**). For breakfast, coffee, and light meals, **Organico** ★ (ℰ **2642-1322**; bakingfairy@gmail.com) is a good option, with a range of healthy sandwiches, daily specials, and freshly baked goods. **The Bakery Café** (ℰ **2642-0458**) is another good choice, serving everything from gourmet coffee drinks to full meals from their massive menu.

El Sano Banano Village Cafe ★★ INTERNATIONAL/VEGETARIAN Delicious vegetarian meals, including nightly specials, sandwiches, and salads, are the specialty of this perennially popular Montezuma restaurant, although there's also a variety of fish and chicken dishes. Lunches feature hefty sandwiches on whole-wheat bread and filling fish and vegetarian *casados*. The natural yogurt fruit shakes are fabulous, but I like to get a little more decadent and have one of the mocha chill shakes. El Sano Banano also doubles as the local movie house. Nightly DVD releases are projected on a large screen; the selection ranges from first-run to quite artsy from a constantly growing library of more than 1,000 movies. The movies begin at 7:30pm and require a minimum purchase of $6.

On the main road into the village. ℰ **2642-0944.** Main courses $6–$14. AE, MC, V. Daily 6am–10pm.

Playa de los Artistas ★★★ 🏠 ITALIAN/MEDITERRANEAN   This open-air restaurant is housed in the back garden of an old house fronting the beach, and only has a few tables, so arrive early. If you don't get a seat and you feel hearty, try the low wooden table surrounded by tatami mats on the sand. Meals are served in large creative plates, in broad wooden bowls set on ceramic-ringed coasters, or on large wooden planks lined with banana leaves. The menu changes nightly but always features several fish dishes. The fresh grouper in a black-pepper sauce is phenomenal, as is the *moscardini* polenta, a tasty appetizer of polenta topped with grilled calamari tentacles and pecorino cheese. The outdoor brick oven and grill turns out consistently spectacular grilled seafood. All meals come with plenty of fresh bread for soaking up the delicious sauces.

Across from Hotel Los Mangos. 📞 **2642-0920.** Reservations recommended. Main courses $6.50–$20. No credit cards. Mon–Sat 10:30am–9:30pm.

Ylang Ylang ★★ INTERNATIONAL/VEGETARIAN   Located at the Ylang Ylang Beach Resort, this attractive, open-air affair features a covered dining area, as well as outdoor tables under broad canvas umbrellas, and a sculpted bar with indigenous and wildlife motifs. The menu is ample, with a prominent Asian influence, ranging from sushi to vegetarian teriyaki stir-fry. Several crepe and pasta options and plenty of fresh seafood dishes are also available. For lunch you can have a bruschetta or some cool gazpacho and be just a few steps from the sand when you're done. Vegans and even raw food fans are well taken care of here.

At the Ylang Ylang Beach Resort. 📞 **2642-0402.** Reservations recommended. Main courses $12–$25. AE, MC, V. Daily 7am–9pm.

Montezuma After Dark

Montezuma has had a tough time coming to terms with its nightlife. For years, local businesses banded together to force most of the loud, late-night activity out of town. This has eased somewhat, allowing for quite an active nightlife in Montezuma proper. The local action seems to base itself either at **Chico's Bar** ★ (📞 **2642-0526**) or at the bar at the **Hotel Moctezuma** (www.hotelmoctezuma. com; 📞 **2642-0058**). Both are located on the main strip in town facing the water. If your evening tastes are mellower, **El Sano Banano Village Cafe** (p. 270) doubles as the local movie house, with nightly late-run features projected on a large screen.

MALPAÍS & SANTA TERESA ★★

150km (93 miles) W of San José; 12km (7½ miles) S of Cóbano

Malpaís (or Mal País) translates as "badlands," and, while this may have been an apt moniker several years ago, it no longer accurately describes this booming beach area. Malpaís is a bucket term often used to refer to a string of neighboring beaches running from south to north, and including Malpaís, Playa Carmen, Santa Teresa, Playa Hermosa, and Playa Manzanillo. To a fault, these beaches are long, wide expanses of light sand dotted with rocky outcroppings. This is one of Costa Rica's hottest spots, and development continues at a dizzying pace, especially in Santa Teresa. Still, it will take some time before this place is anything like more developed destinations Tamarindo or Manuel Antonio. In

Malpaís and Santa Teresa today, you'll find a mix of beach hotels and resorts, restaurants, shops, and private houses, as well as miles of often deserted beach, and easy access to some nice jungle and the nearby **Cabo Blanco Nature Reserve** (p. 266).

Essentials

GETTING THERE & DEPARTING   By Plane: The nearest airport is in Tambor (see "Playa Tambor," p. 259, for flight details). The airport is about 22km (14 miles) away from Malpaís; the ride takes around 20 to 25 minutes. Some of the hotels listed below might be willing to pick you up in Tambor for a reasonable fee. If not, you'll have to hire a taxi, which could cost anywhere between $40 and $50. **Taxis** are generally waiting to meet most regularly scheduled planes, but if they aren't, you can call **Miguel** (🕿 **8367-4638** or 2640-0261) or **Richard** (🕿 **8317-7614** or 2640-0003) for a cab.

By Car: Follow the directions above to Montezuma (see "Playa Montezuma," earlier in this chapter). At Cóbano, follow the signs to Malpaís and Playa Santa Teresa. It's another 12km (7½ miles) down a rough dirt road that requires four-wheel-drive much of the year, especially during the rainy season.

To drive to Malpaís from Liberia, head out of town on the main road to the Guanacaste beaches, passing through Filadelfia, Santa Cruz, and Nicoya on your way toward the turnoff for the La Amistad Bridge. Continue straight at this turnoff, and follow the directions for this route as listed above.

By Bus & Ferry: Transportes Cobano (🕿 **2221-7479;** www.transportescobanocr.com) has two daily buses from San José's Coca-Cola bus station to Malpaís and Santa Teresa. The buses leave at 6am and 2pm, and the fare is C6,515, including the ferry passage. The ride takes a little over 6 hours. The return buses leave Santa Teresa at 5:15am and 2pm.

Alternately, you can follow the directions above for getting to Montezuma, but get off in Cóbano. From Cóbano are daily buses for Malpaís and Santa Teresa at 10:30am and 2:30pm. The fare is C800. Buses return daily to Cóbano at 7 and 11:30am and 3:30pm. *Be forewarned:* These bus schedules are subject to change according to demand, road conditions, and the whim of the bus company.

A surfer in Santa Teresa.

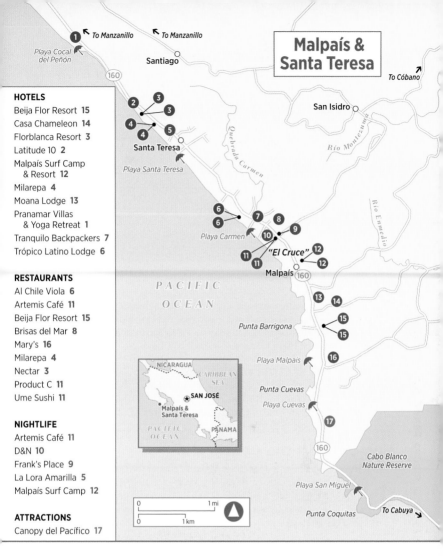

HOTELS

Beija Flor Resort **15**

Casa Chameleon **14**

Florblanca Resort **3**

Latitude 10 **2**

Malpaís Surf Camp
   & Resort **12**

Milarepa **4**

Moana Lodge **13**

Pranamar Villas
   & Yoga Retreat **1**

Tranquilo Backpackers **7**

Trópico Latino Lodge **6**

RESTAURANTS

Al Chile Viola **6**

Artemis Café **11**

Beija Flor Resort **15**

Brisas del Mar **8**

Mary's **16**

Milarepa **4**

Nectar **3**

Product C **11**

Ume Sushi **11**

NIGHTLIFE

Artemis Café **11**

D&N **10**

Frank's Place **9**

La Lora Amarilla **5**

Malpaís Surf Camp **12**

ATTRACTIONS

Canopy del Pacífico **17**

If you miss the bus connection in Cóbano, you can hire a cab to Malpaís for around $20.

ORIENTATION   Malpaís and Santa Teresa are two tiny beach villages. As you reach the ocean, the road forks; Playa Carmen is straight ahead, Malpaís is to your left, and Santa Teresa is to your right. If you continue beyond Santa Teresa, you'll come to the even-more-deserted beaches of playas Hermosa and Manzanillo (not to be confused with beaches of the same names to be found elsewhere in the country). To get to playas Hermosa and Manzanillo, you have to ford a couple of rivers, which can be tricky during parts of the rainy season.

Santa Teresa.

FAST FACTS   Currently, neither Malpaís nor Santa Teresa has a bank, but an ATM is near the crossroads at the entrance to town, along with several general stores, public phones, and Internet cafes. **Farmacia Amiga** (✆ **2640-0539**) is in the Playa Carmen Commercial Center.

If you need a taxi, call **Miguel** (✆ **8367-4638** or 2640-0261) or **Richard** (✆ **8317-7614** or 2640-0003). If you want to do the driving yourself, you can contact the local offices of **Alamo** (✆ **2640-0526;** www.alamocostarica.com) or **Budget Rent A Car** (✆ **2640-0500;** www.budget.co.cr). Or you can head to **Quads Rental Center** (✆ **2640-0178**), which has a large stock of ATVs.

Fun on & off the Beach

If you decide to do anything here besides sunbathe on the beach and play in the waves, your options include nature hikes, horseback riding, ATV tours, scuba diving, and snorkeling, which most hotels can help arrange. Surfing is a major draw, with miles of beach breaks to choose from and a few points to boot. If you want to rent a board or take a lesson, you can find a host of surf shops in Malpaís, Playa Carmen, and Santa Teresa, all of which rent boards and offer lessons. I recommend **Malpaís Surf Shop** (✆ **2640-0173**), located right on the beach in Playa Carmen.

If you've gotten beat up by the waves, or are sore from paddling out, you'll find several excellent spas in town. The best and most extensive (and most expensive) of these is at the **Florblanca Resort** (see below). But you might also check in to **Yoga & Spa Natural** (✆ **2640-0402;** www.yogaspanatural.com), which has a pretty beachfront location, at the **Trópico Latino Lodge** (see below), or the **Pranamar Villas & Yoga Retreat** (see below), also located on the beach, at the northern end of Santa Teresa.

For canopy adventures, head to **Canopy del Pacífico** (✆ **2640-0360;** www.canopydelpacifico.com), which is toward the southern end of Malpaís and just slightly inland. A 2-hour tour over the nearly 2km (1 mile) of cables touches down on 11 platforms, features two rappels, and offers good views of both the forest and the ocean below. The cost is $35. Round-trip transportation from an area hotel is just another $5 per person.

Finally, any hotel in the area can arrange a horseback-riding or ATV trip into the hills and along the beaches of this region, a guided hike through **Cabo Blanco Nature Reserve,** a sportfishing excursion out onto the high seas, or a trip over to Montezuma.

Where to Stay

VERY EXPENSIVE

In addition to the places listed below, **Casa Chameleon ★★** (www.hotelcasa chameleon.com; ℭ **888/705-0274** in the U.S. and Canada, or 2288-2879 in Costa Rica) is a collection of four plush, individual villas, each with a private pool, set on a steep hillside overlooking Malpaís.

Florblanca Resort ★★★   This lush hotel is the most luxurious option in this neck of the woods and one of the top boutique hotels in the country. The individual villas are huge, with a vast living area opening onto a spacious veranda. The furnishings, decorations, and architecture boast a mix of Latin American and Asian influences. Most overlook flowing gardens, and about half have views through to the sea. Every unit features a large open-air bathroom with a garden shower and teardrop-shape tub set amid flowering tropical foliage. Despite the luxury on display here, the owners and management are committed to sustainable tourism ideals. The modern, full-service spa with massive treatment rooms is over an amazing water feature, and complimentary classes like yoga and Pilates are regularly offered in the full-size dojo. The beautiful free-form pool is on two

Florblanca Resort.

levels, with a sculpted waterfall connecting them and a shady Indonesian-style gazebo off to one side.

Playa Santa Teresa, Cóbano, Puntarenas. www.florblanca.com. ✆ **2640-0232.** Fax 2640-0226. 11 units. $475–$600 double; $650–$750 2-bedroom villa for 4; $850 honeymoon house. Transfer to and from Tambor airstrip is included. AE, DC, MC, V. No children 13 and under. **Amenities:** Restaurant; bar; bike rental; small open-air gym; outdoor pool; room service; spa; watersports equipment rental. *In room:* A/C, kitchenette, Wi-Fi.

Latitude 10 ★★ 🎁 The individual bungalows here are architectural treats, with a heavy dose of Balinese and Indonesian art, furnishings, and overall design influences. Wraparound French doors can be opened up for access to the wraparound veranda, which in itself opens out on to lush gardens and forest. In fact, the open design of these bungalows does not include any windows, screens, or mesh. (While biting insects are not a problem, insectaphobes beware, moths and beetles will fly around as you read at night). The two master suites are the prize digs here, with massive outdoor garden bathrooms and more space than the similar, but somewhat more compact, junior suites. Thanks to the intimate vibe, it's not uncommon for a family or group of friends to rent out the whole resort.

Playa Santa Teresa, Cóbano de Puntarenas. www.latitude10resort.com. ✆ **2640-0396.** Fax 2640-0557. 6 units. $270–$320 junior suite; $440 master suite. Rates include breakfast. Rates lower in the off season. AE, MC, V. **Amenities:** Restaurant, bar; outdoor pool; all rooms smoke-free. *In room:* Minibar, no phone, Wi-Fi.

Pranamar Villas & Yoga Retreat ★★★ 🎁 Located at the far northern end of Playa Santa Teresa, this new, intimate resort features large, beautifully designed villas and bungalows, as well as daily yoga classes and delicious healthy spa cuisine. A mix of Balinese, Thai, and Central American materials and design motifs blend together seamlessly. The central salt-water pool is chemical free. A large yoga studio is in many ways the heart and soul of this place, featuring a range of daily classes, and often used by visiting groups for retreats. The owners here are dedicated to healthy living, community development, and sustainable tourism practices.

Playa Santa Teresa, Cóbano de Puntarenas. www.pranamarvillas.com. ✆ **2640-0852.** 10 units. $220–$350 double. Rates include breakfast. Rates lower in the off season; higher during peak periods. AE, MC, V. **Amenities:** Restaurant, bar; outdoor, salt-water pool; all rooms smoke-free; spa treatments; Wi-Fi. *In room:* A/C, minifridge, no phone.

EXPENSIVE

Milarepa ★ Named after a Buddhist sage, this small collection of bungalows is spread around shady grounds fronting the beach, just next door to Florblanca. The bungalows are simple, roomy, and understated. All have wooden floors, a mix of teak and bamboo furniture, beds with mosquito netting, and a private porch. An overhead fan keeps things cool, and plenty of windows make for good cross ventilation. The more expensive units are closest to the beach and have ocean views. When the surf is too rough, you can take dip in the midsize pool. The restaurant here is excellent.

Playa Santa Teresa, Cóbano, Puntarenas. www.milarepahotel.com. ✆ **2640-0023** or 2640-0663. 4 bungalows. $155–$199 double. Rates include taxes. AE, MC, V. **Amenities:** Restaurant; bar; outdoor pool. *In room:* No phone, Wi-Fi.

MODERATE

In addition to the hotels listed below, **Beija Flor Resort** (www.beijaflorresort.com; ℂ **2640-1007**) is a cozy little resort with an excellent restaurant in Malpaís.

Moana Lodge ★   Set on a steep hillside, the rooms here are all decorated in African themes. The master and junior suites have excellent views, and a few of the higher-situated standard units have a bit of an ocean view, as well. In addition to being larger, the suites come with plasma televisions and stocked minibars. The pretty free-form pool has a shady gazebo beside it, as well as some mattresses hung like swings under another shade structure. The hotel's Papaya Lounge and Restaurant are set on the highest part of the property, with stunning panoramic views.

Malpaís, Cóbano de Puntarenas. www.moanalodge.com. ℂ **2640-0230.** Fax 2640-0623. 10 units. $100–$150 double; $210–$295 suite. Rates include breakfast and taxes. MC, V. **Amenities:** Restaurant, bar; Jacuzzi; outdoor pool; all rooms are smoke-free. *In room:* A/C, hair dryer, no phone, Wi-Fi.

Trópico Latino Lodge ★   One of the first hotels in the area, this well-located beachfront spread is still a good choice. The best accommodations are the individual beachfront bungalows, and the six-room beach house, all with direct access to and views of the ocean. The older rooms are in four duplex units and are huge—the king-size bamboo bed barely makes a dent in the floor space. There's also a separate sofa bed, as well as a small desk, and closet space galore. Although none of the older rooms has any ocean view to speak of, they all have private patios with a hammock. The shady grounds are home to many native pochote trees, known for their spiky trunks. The restaurant serves up excellent fresh fish and pasta dishes, and a pretty spa and yoga studio are on-site as well.

Playa Santa Teresa, Cóbano, Puntarenas. www.hoteltropicolatino.com. ℂ **2640-0062.** Fax 2640-0117. 18 units. $105–$125 double; $135–$195 bungalow; $250–$350 suite. **Amenities:** Restaurant; bar; Jacuzzi; small free-form outdoor pool; small spa. *In room:* A/C, no phone.

INEXPENSIVE

Budget travelers can check out **Tranquilo Backpackers** (www.tranquilo backpackers.com; ℂ **2640-0589**), which is an outgrowth of a popular San José hostel. This place is located a bit inland off the road running toward Santa Teresa and has a mix of dorm-style and private rooms.

You can also pitch a tent at several spots and makeshift campsites here. Look for camping signs; you should get restroom and shower access for a few bucks.

Malpaís Surf Camp & Resort   The wide range of prices here reflects the equally wide range of accommodations. The most basic rooms are open-air ranchos with gravel floors, lathe-and-bamboo walls, bead curtain-doors, and shared bathrooms. They'll also let you set up a tent for around $10 per tent, with restroom and shower access included. From here, your options get progressively more comfortable, ranging from shared-bathroom bunk-bed rooms to deluxe poolside villas. A refreshing free-form tile pool is in the center of the complex, and the large, open main lodge area serves as a combination restaurant, bar, lounge, and surfboard-storage area. As the name implies, this place is run by and caters to surfers, and the overall vibe here is loose and funky. The restaurant serves filling, fresh, and, at times, quite creative cuisine, depending on how accomplished the itinerant surf-chef-of-the-month is. Surf rentals, lessons, and video sessions are all available.

Malpaís, Cóbano de Puntarenas. www.malpaissurfcamp.com. ℰ **2640-0031.** ℰ/fax 2640-0061. 16 units, 8 with shared bathroom. $12–$18 per person with shared bathroom; $95–$150 double with private bathroom. AE, MC, V. **Amenities:** Restaurant; bar; small exercise room; midsize outdoor pool; watersports equipment rental. *In room:* No phone, Wi-Fi.

Where to Eat

In addition to the places listed below, you might try **Mary's** (ℰ 2640-0153), a very popular open-air joint that features wood-oven baked pizzas and fresh seafood, and is toward the northern end of Malpaís. The fresh creative cooking at the **Beija Flor Resort** (www.beijaflorresort.com; ℰ 2640-1006) is another good option in Malpaís.

Right at the Playa Carmen Commercial Center, at the crossroads at the entrance to town, you'll find a small food court with a wide range of options, including the bistro-style **Artemis Café** (ℰ 2640-0579; www.artemiscafe.com) and the somewhat pricey sushi joint **Ume Sushi** (ℰ 2640-0968). My favorite, however, is **Product C ★★** (ℰ 2640-1026; www.product-c.com), a seafood retail outlet that also cooks up the daily catch, makes fresh *ceviche,* and serves fresh, farm-grown, local oysters.

Down in Santa Teresa, the fine Asian fusion cuisine served up from a chalkboard menu at **Milarepa** (see above) is worth a taste, and their Wednesday and Saturday sushi nights are a real hit. For fresh, homemade pastas and down-home Italian cuisine, head to **Al Chile Viola,** at the **Trópico Latino Lodge** (see above).

VERY EXPENSIVE

Nectar ★★★ 🎁 FUSION   The dimly lit open-air setting of this poolside and beachfront restaurant is elegant yet casual. New American and Nuevo Latino cuisines are well-represented on the menu, which changes nightly. However, you can always start with some sushi or sashimi made with the daily catch. In addition to fresh seafood and at least one vegetarian entree, you will always find a hearty meat entree, prepared with imported aged beef. Between 4 and 6pm they specialize in sushi and *bocas,* the local term for tapas. The creativity, service, and presentation are some of the best you'll find in Costa Rica. In addition, their wine and Cuban cigar cellars are the best, by far, in the area.

At Flor Blanca Resort in Santa Teresa. ℰ **2640-0232.** Reservations recommended. Main courses $16–$32. AE, MC, V. Daily 7am–9pm.

EXPENSIVE

Brisas del Mar ★★ 🎁 FUSION   With a large, open-air deck jutting out over a steep hillside, this happening spot offers up top-notch fusion fare from a chalkboard menu that changes weekly. The freshest catch and best available local ingredients are always featured, and the influence of various world cuisines is evident in the creative concoctions. Thai and Asian dishes are common, although the British-born chef and owner is also likely to throw some beer-battered fish and chips on the menu. Desserts are excellent, and they have a fine and fairly priced wine list. This is a great place to come for a sunset cocktail, and then linger on for dinner and dessert. I recommend taking a taxi here, as the walk up is daunting. Heck, even the drive up is daunting—it's a very steep hill.

On a hillside, just north of main crossroads in Malpaís. ✆ **2640-0941.** Reservations recommended. Main courses $8–$16. No credit cards. Tues–Sun 7:30–11:30am and 4–10pm.

Malpaís & Santa Teresa After Dark

The most popular bar in Malpaís is **D&N ★** (✆ 2640-0353; www.dayand nightbeachclub.com), which stands for Day & Night, and is about 1 block north of the crossroads into town, off the main road. You might try **Artemis Café** (see above) for a mellower scene. Surfers and other travelers tend to gather in the evenings at **Frank's Place,** at the crossroads of Malpaís and Playa Carmen (✆ 2640-0096) and the **Malpaís Surf Camp** (see above for both). In Santa Teresa, **La Lora Amarilla** (✆ 2640-0132) is the most happening spot. This is definitely the place to come on Saturday night, to dance some salsa and merengue with the locals.

A Truly Remote Beach: Undiscovered, For Now

The Nicoya Peninsula coastline between Santa Teresa and Playa Sámara is perhaps the last, long undeveloped stretch of Costa Rican coastline. The following hotel is located roughly midway between Santa Teresa and Playa Sámara. It can be reached year round by rough, mostly unmarked dirt roads, so it is best to carefully coordinate you transportation with the hotel.

Cristal Azul ★ Set on a hillside overlooking the long, desolate Playa San Miguel, this boutique hotel is a great getaway. The four individual villas here all have simple, tasteful decor, plenty of room, and a private balcony for enjoying the fabulous views. They also feature delightful, open-air showers. Apart from enjoying the solitude and isolation, guests here can opt for a wide range of activities and adventures, including deep sea fishing, horseback riding, and wildlife viewing. In addition to being gracious and involved hosts, the owners here are actively involved in helping improve the local community, and have earned "4 Leaves" from the CST Sustainable Tourism program.

Playa San Miguel, Guanacaste. www.cristalazul.com. ✆ **888/822-7369** in the U.S. and Canada, or 2655-8049 in Costa Rica. 4 units. $140–$190 double. Rates include full breakfast. AE, MC, V. **Amenities:** Restaurant; bar; midsize outdoor pool; Wi-Fi. *In room:* A/C, no phone.

PLAYA SÁMARA ★

35km (22 miles) S of Nicoya; 245km (152 miles) W of San José

Playa Sámara is a long, broad beach on a gently curved horseshoe-shape bay. Unlike most of the other beaches along this stretch of the Pacific coast, the water here is usually calm and perfect for swimming because an offshore island and rocky headlands break up most of the surf. Playa Sámara is popular both with Tico families seeking a quick and inexpensive getaway and with young Ticos looking to do some serious beach partying. On weekends, in particular, Sámara can get crowded and rowdy. Still, the calm waters and steep cliffs on the far side of the bay make this a very attractive spot, and the beach is so long that the crowds are usually well dispersed. Moreover, if you drive along the rugged coastal road in either direction, you'll discover some truly spectacular and isolated beaches.

Essentials

GETTING THERE & DEPARTING   **By Car:** Head west out of San José on the San José–Caldera Highway (CR27). When you reach Caldera, follow the signs to Puntarenas and the Interamerican Highway (CR1). You will actually follow signs for Liberia and San José, which are, in fact, leading you to the unmarked entrance to CR1. This road (CR23) ends when it hits the Interamerican Highway. You'll want to pass under the bridge and follow the on-ramp which will put you on the highway heading north. Forty-seven kilometers (29 miles) after you get on the Interamerican Highway heading north, you'll see signs and the turnoff for La Amistad Bridge (CR18). After crossing the bridge, continue on CR18 until it hits CR21. Take this road north to Nicoya. Turn in to the town of Nicoya, and head more or less straight through town until you see signs for Playa Sámara. From here, it's a well-marked and paved road (CR150) all the way to the beach.

To drive to Sámara from Liberia, head out of town on the main road to the Guanacaste beaches, passing through Filadelfia, Santa Cruz, and Nicoya. Once you reach Nicoya, follow the directions outlined above.

By Bus: Alfaro express buses (✆ **2222-2666;** www.empresaalfaro.com) leave San José daily at noon and 6:30pm from Avenida 5 between calles 14 and 16. The trip lasts 5 hours; the one-way fare is C3,790. Extra buses are sometimes added on weekends and during peak periods, so it's always wise to check.

Alternatively, you can take a bus from this same station to Nicoya and then catch a second bus from Nicoya to Sámara. **Alfaro** buses leave San José nearly every hour between 6am and 5pm. The fare is C3,315. The trip can take between 4 and 5½ hours, depending if the bus goes via Liberia or La Amistad Bridge. The latter route is much faster and much more frequent. **Empresa Rojas** (✆ **2685-5352**) buses leave Nicoya for Sámara and Carrillo regularly throughout the day, between 5am and 9pm. The trip's duration is 1½ hours. The fare to Sámara is C800; the fare to Carrillo is C850.

Playa Sámara.

Playa Carrillo.

Express buses to San José leave daily at 4:30 and 8am. Buses for Nicoya leave throughout the day between 5am and 6pm. Buses leave Nicoya for San José nearly every hour between 3am and 5pm.

Interbus (© **2283-5573;** www.interbusonline.com) has a daily bus that leaves San José for Playa Sámara at 8am. The fare is $40, and they will pick you up at most San José–area hotels.

ORIENTATION   Sámara is a busy little town at the bottom of a steep hill. The main road heads straight into town, passing the soccer field before coming to an end at the beach. Just before the beach is a road to the left that leads to most of the hotels listed below. This road also leads to Playa Carrillo (see below) and the Hotel Punta Islita (p. 285). If you turn right 3 blocks before hitting the beach, you'll hit the coastal road that goes to playas Buena Vista, Barrigona, and eventually Nosara.

FAST FACTS   In case of an emergency, dial © **911.** To reach the local police, dial © **2656-0436.** Sámara has a small **medical clinic** (© **2656-0166**). A branch of **Banco Nacional** (© **2656-0089**) is on the road to Playa Buena Vista, just as you head out of town. For full service laundry, head to **Green Life Laundry** (© **2656-1051**), about 3 blocks west of the Banco Nacional.

If you need a ride around Sámara, or to one of the nearby beaches, you can hire a taxi by calling **Jorge** (© **8830-3002**). Rides in town should cost $2 to $4; rides to nearby beaches might run $8 to $20, depending upon the distance.

Fun on & off the Beach

Aside from sitting on the sand and soaking up the sun, the main activities in Playa Sámara seem to be hanging out in the bars and *sodas* and dancing into the early morning hours. But if you're looking for something more, there's horseback riding either on the beach or through the bordering pastureland and forests. Other options include sea kayaking in the calm waters off Playa Sámara, sportfishing, snorkeling and scuba diving, boat tours, mountain biking, and tours to Playa Ostional to see the mass nesting of olive ridley sea turtles. You can inquire about and book any of these tours at your hotel.

You'll find that the beach is nicer and cleaner down at the south end. Better yet, head about 8km (5 miles) south to **Playa Carrillo ★★**, a long crescent of soft, white sand. With almost no development here, the beach is nearly always deserted. Loads of palm trees provide shade. If you've got a good four-wheel-drive vehicle, ask for directions at your hotel and set off in search of the hidden gems of **Playa Buena Vista** and **Playa Barrigona ★★**, which are north of Sámara, less than a half-hour drive away.

A taxi to Playa Carrillo should cost about $6 to $10 each way. Because it's a bit farther and the roads are a little rougher, expect to pay a little more to reach Playa Buena Vista, and even more for Playa Barrigona.

The folks at **Wingnuts Canopy Tours** (© 2656-0153) offer zip-line and harness "canopy tours." The 2-hour outing costs $55 per person; $35 for those under 18. You'll find their office by the giant strangler fig tree, or *matapalo,* toward the southern end of the beach.

Almost every hotel in the area can arrange sportfishing trips, or you could contact **Sámara Sport Fishing** (© 2656-0589) or **Kingfisher ★** (© 2656-0091** or 8358-9661; www.costaricabillfishing.com). Rates run from $300 to $800 for a half-day and $700 to $1,200 for a full day outing.

To learn how to surf or to rent a board, check in with **C & C Surf Shop and School** (© 2656-0590; http://cncsurfsamara.webs.com). Surfboard rentals run around $12 per day. Private lessons cost $30 per hour, including a free hour of board rental after your lesson. If you want to head out and try some scuba diving or a snorkel excursion, call **Pura Vida Diving** (© 2656-0643; www.puravidadive.com). A two-tank dive, with equipment, will run you $95.

For a bird's-eye view of the area, head over to the **Flying Crocodile** (© 2656-8048 or 8827-8858; www.flying-crocodile.com) in Playa Buena Vista. The folks here also offer flights on a two-seat (one for you, one for the pilot) Gyrocopter, the ultralight equivalent of a helicopter. Although it might feel like little more than a modified tricycle with a nylon wing and lawnmower motor, these winged wonders are very safe. A 20-minute flight will run you $75, while an hour-long tour costs $120.

All of the hotels here can help you arrange any number of tour options, including horseback rides, boat trips, sea kayaking, scuba diving, and snorkeling outings. You might also contact **Carillo Adventures** (© 2656-0380), a good all-around local tour company.

A Flying Crocodile plane.

Learn the Language

If you want to acquire or polish some language skills while here, check in with the **Sámara Language School** (© 866/978-6813 in the U.S. and Canada, or 2656-0127 in Sámara; www.samaralanguageschool.com). These folks offer a range of programs and private lessons and can arrange for a homestay with a local family. The facility even features classes with ocean views, although that might be a detriment to your language learning.

Going Down Under

Spelunkers will want to head 62km (38 miles) northeast of Playa Sámara on the road to La Amistad Bridge. If you don't have a car, your best bet is to get to Nicoya, which is about a half-hour away by bus, and then take a taxi to the park, which should cost about $15. Here, at **Barra Honda National Park ★** (© 2659-1551 or 2685-5267), is an extensive system of caves, some of which reach more than 200m (656 ft.) in depth. Human remains and indigenous relics

Terciopelo Cave at Barra Honda National Park.

have been found in other caves, but those are not open to the public. Because this is a national park, you'll have to pay the $10 entrance fee.

If you plan to descend the one publicly accessible cave, you'll need to hire a local guide at the park entrance station. These guides are always available, and will provide harnesses, helmets, and flashlights. Depending upon your group size and bargaining abilities, expect to pay between $20 to $36 per person for a visit to the **Terciopelo Cave,** including the guide, harness, helmet, and flashlight. Furthermore, the cave is open only during the dry season (mid-Nov to Apr). You begin the roughly 3-hour tour with a descent of 19m (62 ft.) straight down a wooden ladder with a safety rope attached. Inside you'll see plenty of impressive stalactites and stalagmites while visiting several chambers of varying sizes. Even if you don't descend, the trails around Barra Honda and its prominent limestone plateau are great for hiking and bird-watching. Be sure to make a stop at **La Cascada,** a gentle waterfall that fills and passes through a series of calcium and limestone pools, some of them large enough to bathe in. The entire thing is slightly reminiscent of Ocho Rios in Jamaica.

Where to Stay

MODERATE

In addition to the places listed below, **Tico Adventure Lodge** (www.ticoadventurelodge.com; © 2656-0628) is another good option, about 2 blocks from the beach, in the heart of town.

Fenix Hotel ★ Set right on the beach, the rooms here are all really studio apartments, with fully equipped kitchenettes. The rooms are simple, but they are kept clean. For cooling off, the hotel has a postage stamp–size pool and some coconut trees for shade. Hammocks are hung in the shade and the ocean is just steps away. The owners are personable and accommodating, and the full kitchens are a boon for families and those looking for longer stays.

Playa Sámara, Nicoya, Guanacaste. www.fenixhotel.com. ✆ **2656-0158.** Fax 2656-0162. 6 units. $105–$135 double. Children 17 and under stay free in parent's room. No credit cards. **Amenities:** Small outdoor pool. *In room:* Kitchenette, Wi-Fi.

Hotel Guanamar ★★ Set on a high bluff overlooking Playa Carillo, this place offers great views, large well-equipped rooms, and easy access to one of the best beaches in the region. Once a dedicated fishing resort, it's now geared toward a broad spectrum of travelers, including sportfishers. The pool has the best vantage point on the property, with large, broad wooden decks all around, and the open-air restaurant and bar share the view from under soaring thatch roofs. I recommend grabbing one of the rooms built into the hillside, in two long rows of buildings. These newer units each feature a private balcony facing the sea. However, some good options, including the suites, are higher up behind the pool and restaurants. Of these, I recommend no. 116, which has a great private balcony.

Puerto Carillo. www.guanamar.net. ✆ **2656-0054.** Fax 2232-6678. 41 units. $100–$120 double; $190 suite. Rates include full breakfast. AE, DC, MC, V. **Amenities:** Restaurant; bar; large outdoor pool; room service; Wi-Fi (in main building and around pool). *In room:* A/C, TV.

Sámara Tree House Inn ★★ Set right on the beach in the heart of town, this hotel is my top choice in Sámara. The individual units are really small studio apartments. The four namesake rooms are built on raised stilts, made from varnished tree trunks. Inside, they are awash in varnished wood. The small sitting area has large picture windows and a great view up above. And the open-air area underneath each unit is outfitted with a couple of hammocks, a table and chairs, some chaise lounges, and a barbecue. The ground-floor unit is handicap accessible and quite beautiful in its own right. Fans are in every bedroom to make up for a lack of air-conditioning.

Playa Sámara, Guanacaste. www.samaratreehouse.com. ✆ **2656-0733.** 6 units. $70–$165 double. Rates include breakfast. AE, MC, V. **Amenities:** Jacuzzi; small outdoor pool. *In room:* TV, Wi-Fi.

INEXPENSIVE

In addition to the hotels listed below, a slew of very inexpensive places to stay are along the road into town and around the soccer field. Many of the rooms at these places are less accommodating than your average jail cell.

Casa del Mar ✦ On the inland side of the beach-access road, 1 block south of the downtown, Casa del Mar is just 50m (164 ft.) from the beach. The rooms here are kept immaculate, and most of them are quite spacious. The place feels like a cool oasis from the harsh Guanacaste sun, with its open-air restaurant, shady central courtyard, and small pool/Jacuzzi. Although the units with shared bathrooms are the best bargains here, I'd opt for a second-floor room with a private bathroom. The owners and staff members are extremely friendly and helpful.

Playa Sámara, Nicoya, Guanacaste. www.casadelmarsamara.com. © **2656-0264.** Fax 2656-0129. 17 units, 11 with private bathroom. $40–$50 double with shared bathroom; $60–$85 double with private bathroom and A/C. Rates include taxes. Breakfast included for private bath rooms. AE, MC, V. **Amenities:** Bar; unheated outdoor pool/Jacuzzi. *In room:* No phone, Wi-Fi.

Hotel Belvedere ★ ✒ This long-standing German-run option is a few blocks inland and uphill from the beach. Rooms are housed in the older main building, and a newer annex, another block or so inland. Those in the annex feature modern split A/C units, one queen and one twin bed, a coffeemaker, and little fridge. The rooms in the older section are somewhat more basic, although everything is well-maintained and immaculate. Some have a small kitchenette, and so are geared toward longer stays and families. Each of the building sites has a pool. Only breakfast is served, although they run a snack bar throughout most of the day, and there's an honor bar system for beverages.

Playa Sámara. www.belvederesamara.net. ©/fax **2656-0213.** 21 units. $50–$85 double. Rates include breakfast and taxes. MC, V. **Amenities:** Lounge; Jacuzzi; 2 outdoor pools. *In room:* A/C, TV (in some), fridge.

A NEARBY LUXURY HOTEL

Hotel Punta Islita ★★★ 🎁 Set on a high bluff between two mountain ridges that meet the sea, this is one of the most exclusive and romantic luxury resorts in Costa Rica. The rooms are done in a Santa Fe style, with red terra-cotta floor tiles, and adobe-colored walls. Suites come with a separate sitting room and a private two-person plunge pool or Jacuzzi; the villas have two or three bedrooms, their own private swimming pools, and full kitchens. The beach below the hotel is a small crescent of gray-white sand with a calm, protected section at the northern end. It's about a 10-minute hike, but the hotel will shuttle you up and back

Hotel Punta Islita.

if you don't feel like walking. There's a rancho bar and grill down there for when you get hungry or thirsty, and a lap pool for when the waves are too rough.

Punta Islita is very involved with the local community, and has sponsored a wide-ranging art program that brings in prominent Costa Rican artists to teach the local residents art and craft skills, while often creating large public works in the process.

Playa Islita. www.hotelpuntaislita.com. ℗ **866/446-4053** in the U.S. and Canada, or 2656-3036 in Costa Rica. Fax 2656-2202. 58 units, 10 villas. $339 double; $542 suite; $706–$825 villa. Rates include continental breakfast. AE, MC, V. **Amenities:** 2 restaurants; 2 bars; 9-hole golf course and driving range; small exercise room and spa; Jacuzzi; small tile outdoor pool and lap pool; room service; smoke-free rooms; 2 lit tennis courts; watersports equipment rental. *In room:* A/C, TV, minibar, Wi-Fi.

Where to Eat

Sámara has numerous inexpensive *sodas,* and most of the hotels have their own restaurants. If you want to eat overlooking the water, check out **El Ancla** (℗ **2656-0254**) or **Shake Joe's** (℗ **2656-0252**). Both of these are located right on the beach a bit south of downtown.

El Lagarto ★★ 🍴 STEAK/GRILL   The first thing you notice as you enter this rustic, open-air restaurant—unless you come via the beach—is the two massive grill stations gravity-fed with fresh glowing wood coals via metal troughs from a huge overhead fire. The almost-as-massive menu features every form of meat, poultry, or fish you could imagine cooked to order over these fresh coals. The rustic open-air dining room has heavy wooden tables and chairs, some under a roof, others in the sand under shade trees and coconut palms. At night, atmospheric lighting gives this place a very romantic vibe.

On the beach, north end of Playa Sámara. ℗ **2656-0750.** www.ellagartobbq.com. Reservations recommended. Main courses $6–$28. AE, DISC, MC, V. Daily 11am–11pm.

Las Brasas SPANISH/SEAFOOD   This two-story, open-air affair serves authentic Spanish cuisine and well-prepared fresh seafood. The whole fish *a la catalana* is excellent, as is the paella. For something lighter, try the gazpacho Andaluz, a refreshing lunch choice on a hot afternoon. If you have a big party, and order a day or so in advance, they'll roast a whole pig for you. Las Brasas has a good selection of Spanish wines, a rarity in Costa Rica. Service is attentive yet informal.

On the main road into Sámara, about 90m (295 ft.) before the beach. ℗ **2656-0546.** Reservations recommended in the high season. Main courses C3,400–C17,000. MC, V. Tues–Sun noon–10pm.

Playa Sámara After Dark

After dark the most happening place in town is **Bar Arriba ★** (℗ **2656-0487**), a second-floor affair with a contemporary vibe a couple of blocks inland from the beach on the main road into town. You might also try the lounge scene at **Shake Joe's ★** (see above), **La Vela Latina** (℗ **2656-2286**), or **Tabanuco** (℗ **2656-1056**), all on the beach or fronting the water, right near the center of the action, on the main road running parallel to the beach off the center of town.

PLAYA NOSARA ★★

55km (34 miles) SW of Nicoya; 266km (165 miles) W of San José

As is the case in Malpaís, **Playa Nosara** is a bucket term used to refer to several neighboring beaches, spread along an isolated stretch of coast. In addition to the namesake beach, **Playa Guiones, Playa Pelada, Playa Garza,** and (sometimes) **Playa Ostional** are also lumped into this area. In fact, the village of Nosara itself is several kilometers inland from the beach. Playa Nosara marks the northern limit of the Nicoya Peninsula.

Playa Guiones is one of Costa Rica's most dependable beach breaks, and surfers come here in good numbers throughout the year. However, the waves are still much less crowded than you would find in and around Tamarindo.

The best way to get to Nosara is to fly, but, with everything so spread out, that makes getting around difficult after you've arrived. The roads to, in, and around Nosara are almost always in very rough shape, and there's little sign that this will improve anytime soon.

Essentials

GETTING THERE & DEPARTING   By Plane: Sansa (𝄐 **877/767-2672** in the U.S. and Canada, or 2290-4100 in Costa Rica; www.flysansa.com) has one flight to **Nosara airport** (NOB; no phone) Tuesday through Saturday, departing from San José's Juan Santamaría International Airport (p. 103) at 11:55am. The one-way fare for the 1-hour flight is $111.

Playa Guiones.

Nature Air (𝄐 **800/235-9272** in the U.S. and Canada, or 2299-6000; www.natureair.com) has two flights daily leaving at 9:30am and 2pm from Tobías Bolaños International Airport in Pavas (p. 104). The fare is $111 to $139 each way.

The return Sansa flight to San José departs Nosara at 1:20pm, and the Nature Air flights leave at 10:45am and 2:55pm.

It's usually about a 5- to 10-minute drive from the airport to most hotels. Taxis wait for every arrival; fares range between $5 and $10 to most hotels in Nosara.

By Car: Follow the directions for getting to Playa Sámara (see "Playa Sámara," earlier in this chapter), but watch for a well-marked fork in the road a few kilometers before you reach that beach. The right-hand fork leads to Nosara over another 22km (14 miles) of rough dirt road.

By Bus: Alfaro express buses (𝄐 **2222-2666** in San José, or 2282-0371 in Nosara; www.empresaalfaro.com) leave San José daily at 5:30am and noon from Avenida 5 between calles 14 and 16. The trip's duration is 5½ hours; the one-way fare is C4,250.

You can also take an Alfaro bus from San José to Nicoya and then catch a second bus from Nicoya to Nosara. **Alfaro** buses leave San José nearly every hour between 6am and 5pm. The fare is C3,315. The trip can take between 4 and 5½ hours, depending if the bus goes via Liberia or La Amistad Bridge. The latter route is much faster and much more frequent. **Empresa Rojas** buses (© 2685-5352) leave Nicoya for Nosara daily at 4:45 and 10am, noon, and 3 and 5:30pm. Trip duration is 2 hours; the one-way fare is C925.

The direct Alfaro buses to San José leave daily at 5:30am and noon. Buses to Nicoya leave Nosara daily at 4:45 and 10am, noon, and 3 and 5:30pm. Buses leave Nicoya for San José nearly every hour between 3am and 5pm.

ORIENTATION   The village of Nosara is about 5km (3 miles) inland from the beach. The small airstrip runs pretty much through the center of town; however, most hotels listed here are on or near the beach itself. You'll find the **post office** and **police station** (© 2682-1130) right at the end of the airstrip. An **EBAIS** medical clinic (© 2682-0266) and a couple of pharmacies are in the village as well. Both **Banco Popular** and **Banco Nacional** have offices in Nosara, with ATMs. There's even a tiny strip mall at the crossroads to Playa Guiones.

If you want to rent a car, both **Economy** (© 2299-2000; www. economyrentacar.com) and **National** (© 2682-0052; www.natcar.com) have offices here. Because demand often outstrips supply, I recommend you reserve a car in advance. Alternatively, you can rent an ATV from several operators around town, including **Iguana Expeditions** (see below) and **Boca Nosara Tours** (see below). If you need a taxi, call **Vino** (© 2682-0879).

FAST FACTS   An **Internet cafe** is in the village and others are at **Café de Paris** (p. 292), **Frog Pad** (© 2682-4039), and **Harbor Reef Lodge** (p. 291).

This area was originally conceived and zoned as a primarily residential community. The maze of dirt roads and lack of any single defining thoroughfare can be confusing for first-time visitors. Luckily, a host of hotel and restaurant signs spread around the area help point lost travelers in the direction of their final destination.

Fun on & off the Beach

Among the several beaches at Nosara are the long, curving **Playa Guiones** ★★, **Playa Nosara** ★, and the diminutive **Playa Pelada** ★. Because the village of Nosara is several miles inland, these beaches tend to be clean, secluded, and quiet. Surfing and bodysurfing are good here, particularly at Playa Guiones, which is garnering quite a reputation as a consistent and rideable beach break. Pelada is a short white-sand beach with three deep scallops, backed by sea grasses and mangroves. There isn't too much sand at high tide, so you'll want to hit the beach when the tide's out. At either end of the beach, rocky outcroppings reveal tide pools at low tide.

With miles of excellent beach breaks and relatively few crowds, this is a great place to learn how to surf. If you want to try to stand up for your first time, check in with the folks at **Safari Surf School** (© 866/433-3355 in the U.S.

and Canada, or 2682-0113; www.safarisurfschool.com), **Coconut Harry's Surf Shop** (℡ **2682-0574;** www.coconutharrys.com), or **Corky Carroll's Surf School** (℡ **888/454-7873** in the U.S. and Canada, or 2682-0385; www.surf school.net). All of the above offer hourly solo or group lessons, multiday packages with accommodations and meals included, and board rental.

When the seas are calm, some decent snorkeling is around the rocks and reefs just offshore. You can rent masks, snorkels, and fins at Café de Paris (p. 292) or Coconut Harry's. Bird-watchers should explore the mangrove swamps around the estuary mouth of the Río Nosara. Just walk north from Playa Pelada and follow the riverbank; explore the paths into the mangroves. In addition to numerous water, shore, and sea bird species, you're apt to spot a range of hawks and other raptors, as well as toucans and several parrot species.

SEA TURTLE WATCHING　If you time your trip right, you can do a night tour to nearby **Playa Ostional** to watch nesting olive ridley sea turtles. These turtles come ashore by the thousands in a mass egg-laying phenomenon known as an *arribada*. The *arribadas* are so difficult to predict that no one runs regularly scheduled turtle-viewing trips, but when the *arribada* is in full swing, several local guides and agencies offer tours. These *arribadas* take place 4 to 10 times between July and December; each occurrence lasts between 3 and 10 days. Consider yourself very lucky if you happen to be around during one of these fascinating natural phenomena. Your best bet is to ask the staff at your hotel or check in with Joe at **Iguana Expeditions** (℡ **2682-4089;** www.iguanaexpeditions.com). Tours are generally run at night, but because the turtles come ashore in such numbers, you can sometimes catch them in the early morning light as well. Even if it's not turtle-nesting season, you might want to look into visiting Playa Ostional just to have a long, wide expanse of beach to yourself. However, be careful swimming here because the surf and riptides can be formidable. During the dry season (mid-Nov to Apr), you can usually get here in a regular car, but during the rainy season you'll need four-wheel-drive. This beach is part of **Ostional National Wildlife Refuge** (℡ **2682-0428**). At the northwest end of the refuge is **India Point,** which is known for its tide pools and rocky outcrops.

HIKING & WILDLIFE VIEWING　Located on land surrounding the Nosara river mouth, the **Nosara Biological Reserve** (℡ **2682-0035;** www.lagarta. com) features a network of trails and raised walkways through tropical transitional forests and mangrove swamps. More than 270 species of birds have been spotted here. This private reserve is owned and managed by the folks at the **Lagarta Lodge** (see below), and the trails start right at the hotel. Admission is $6. Guided tours and guided boat tours are also available.

FISHING CHARTERS & OTHER OUTDOOR ACTIVITIES　All the hotels in the area can arrange fishing charters for $200 to $500 for a half-day, or $400 to $1,200 for a full day. These rates are for one to four people and vary according to boat size and accouterments.

HORSEBACK RIDING　The folks at **Boca Nosara Tours** (℡ **2682-0280;** www. bocanosaratours.com) have a large stable of well-cared-for horses and a range of beach, jungle, and waterfall rides to choose from. Rates run between $50 and $90 per person, depending on the size of your group and the length of the tour.

KAYAK TOURS Based out of the Gilded Iguana hotel and restaurant, **Iguana Expeditions ★** (𝄐 **2682-4089;** www.iguana expeditions.com) offers a range of full- and half-day tours around the area. Explore the inland coastal mangroves by kayak or hike to a stunning waterfall. These folks can also arrange inexpensive fishing outings in a *panga* (small craft) with a local fisherman. The kayaking expedition costs $50, and the waterfall hike costs $25.

An instructor at Nosara Yoga Institute.

YOGA & MORE If you want to spend some time getting your mind and body together, check in with the **Nosara Yoga Institute** (𝄐 866/ 439-4704 in the U.S. and Canada, or 2682-0071 in Costa Rica; www. nosarayoga.com), which offers intensive and daily yoga classes, teacher trainings, and a host of custom-designed "retreat" options. This is an internationally recognized retreat and teacher training center. Their daily, open, 90-minute classes cost just $10, and they even provide a mat.

You might also check in to see if anything is being offered up at the Harmony Hotel & Spa (see below).

Where to Stay

In addition to the places listed below, the **Nosara Beach House ★** (www.the nosarabeachhouse.com; 𝄐 **2682-0019**), on Playa Guiones, has clean and comfortable rooms and a swimming pool—and it's right on the beach to boot. **Giardino Tropicale** (www.giardinotropicale.com; 𝄐 **2682-4000**) is a similar choice, although a bit farther from the beach. For a more intimate option that's also a very good deal, check out the **Nosara B&B** (www.nosarabandb.net; 𝄐 **2682-0209**).

One final hotel that needs mentioning is the **Nosara Beach Hotel** (www. nosarabeachhotel.com; 𝄐 **2682-0121**). The tallest and most striking structure in town, you can't miss the giant Russian-style dome topping this hillside hotel. The location and view here are top notch. However, the place has been in a constant state of construction for over a decade, rooms are pretty run-down, and service is spotty at best.

VERY EXPENSIVE

The Harmony Hotel & Spa ★★ This hotel sits right in front of the beach break on Playa Guiones. All the rooms have patios or wooden decks. In fact, even the most basic rooms here, their "Coco" rooms, feature large private wooden decks out back, with an outdoor shower. The hotel is geared toward couples, and all rooms have just one king-size bed, although roll-in beds are available. The bungalows are two-bedroom affairs, with a king-size bed and fold-out sofa in each room and large shared deck area. The lush grounds have been planted to be adapted to the dry Guanacaste conditions, and the hotel has a gray water irrigation system and organic gardens. All of this has earned the hotel "5 Leaves" from the CST Sustainable Tourism program. The hotel also has a well-run spa, with various treatment options and regular yoga classes.

Playa Nosara. www.harmonynosara.com. © **2682-4114.** Fax 2682-4113. 24 units, 14 bungalows. $250 double; $300 bungalow; $460 2-bedroom bungalow. Rates include breakfast and one yoga class. AE, MC, V. **Amenities:** Restaurant; bar; complimentary bicycles; midsize outdoor pool; spa; lighted tennis court; watersports equipment rental. *In room:* A/C, TV, minifridge, Wi-Fi.

L'Acqua Viva ★   This resort hotel has the most architecturally stunning and well-equipped facilities in the Nosara area. The name translates roughly as "Living Water," and you'll find pools and water elements all around. Rooms are large, beautifully appointed, and feature LCD televisions. The restaurant, reception, lobby, and other public areas are also attractively done, with soaring thatch roofs and Balinese-inspired furnishings and decor. The biggest drawbacks here are the fact that the beach is a 10-minute drive away, and the whole complex is built close to the area's main dirt road and during the dry season dust and traffic noise can be a problem.

Playa Guiones. www.lacquaviva.com. © **2682-1087.** Fax 2682-0420. 35 units. $205 double; $310–$341 suite; $525–$735 villa. Rates include continental breakfast. AE, MC, V. **Amenities:** Restaurant; bar; Jacuzzi; 2 large outdoor pools; room service; full-service spa; Wi-Fi. *In room:* A/C, TV, hair dryer, minibar.

MODERATE

Harbor Reef Lodge ★   This hotel caters to surfers, fishermen, and all-around vacationers, with clean, spacious rooms close to the beach (about 182m/597 ft. inland from Playa Guiones). The suites come with separate sitting rooms, and a couple even have kitchenettes. The lush grounds have a cool, oasis-like feel. The best rooms are the Surf City rooms and suites, which are set around the hotel's second and larger pool, which is reserved for hotel guests—the other pool, which is just off the restaurant, is open to diners and walk-ins. The hotel offers surf lessons and sportfishing outings and even has a small general store and Internet cafe on the grounds. They also rent out a variety of private homes and villas.

Playa Nosara. www.harborreef.com. © **2682-0059.** Fax 2682-0060. 21 units. $99–$155 double; $135–$250 suite. Rates include continental breakfast. AE, MC, V. **Amenities:** Restaurant; bar; bike rental; 2 small outdoor pools; watersports equipment rental. *In room:* A/C, TV, fridge, Wi-Fi.

Lagarta Lodge   Located on a hillside high over the Nosara River, this small lodge is an excellent choice for bird-watchers and other travelers who are more interested in flora and fauna than the beach. The rooms are spartan but acceptable. The lodge borders its own private reserve, which has trails along the riverbank and through the mangrove and tropical humid forests here. The restaurant and most rooms have spectacular views over the river and surrounding forest, with the beaches of Nosara and Ostional in the distance. The six new superior rooms are larger than the standard rooms and come with air-conditioning. You'll want to have your own vehicle if you stay here: The beach is a good 10- to 15-minute hike away, and it's uphill on the way back. The hotel overseas its own biological reserve and has been granted "3 Leaves" by the CST Sustainable Tourism program.

Playa Nosara. www.lagarta.com. ☏ **2682-0035.** Fax 2682-0135. 12 units. $72–$95 double. AE, MC, V. **Amenities:** Restaurant; bar; midsize outdoor pool. *In room:* No phone, Wi-Fi.

INEXPENSIVE

The Gilded Iguana ★   This long-standing hotel and restaurant began with a few very basic budget rooms. However, it now has a swimming pool, with a high waterfall emptying into it, and six more upscale rooms. The best rooms here have high ceilings, lots of space, air-conditioning, and minifridges. They are set back from the pool in a row, and sit among some shade trees. The budget rooms are much more rustic, and located close to the road, just off the hotel's popular restaurant. These lack air-conditioning. The restaurant here is deservedly popular (see below), and in addition to feeding its guests, draws a lot of the local expatriate community to watch sporting events and listen to the occasional live band.

Playa Guiones. www.thegildediguana. com. ☏ **2682-0259.** 12 units. $50–$60 double; $75–$95 suite. AE, MC, V. **Amenities:** Restaurant; bar; midsize outdoor pool. *In room:* A/C (in some), minifridge, no phone, Wi-Fi.

> ### Yo Quiero Hablar Español
>
> You can brush up on or start up your Spanish at the **Rey de Nosara Language School** (☏/fax **2682-0215**; www.reydenosara.itgo. com). It offers group and private lessons according to demand, and can coordinate week or multiweek packages.

Where to Eat

In addition to the places mentioned below, **Marlin Bill's** (☏ 2682-0458) is a popular and massive open-air haunt on the hillside on the main road, just across from Café de Paris (see below). You can expect to get good, fresh seafood and American classics here. For Mexican food, try **Pancho's** (☏ 2682-0591). For Italian, **La Dolce Vita ★** (☏ 2682-0107), on the outskirts of town on the road to Playa Sámara, serves up good Italian fare nightly, while closer to town, **Giardino Tropicale** (☏ 2682-0258) also has good Italian fare and brick-oven pizzas. If you're looking to beat the heat, head to **Robin's Ice Cream ★** (☏ 2682-0617), on the road to the beach in Guiones, for some homemade ice cream. For local flavor, **Doña Olga's** (no phone) is a simple Costa Rican *soda* right on the beach in Playa Pelada. Finally, I've been getting good reports about the food at the new **The Rising Sun Café** (☏ 2682-0080; http://the-rising-sun.com), with hearty breakfasts, lunches, and dinners at the **Kaya Sol Surf Hotel** in Playa Guiones.

Café de Paris ★ BAKERY/BISTRO   This popular place has wonderful fresh-baked goods and a wide assortment of light bites and full-on meals. You can get pizza or nachos or filling sandwiches on fresh baguettes. Hearty salads, as well as fish, meat, and chicken dishes are also offered. I enjoy stopping in for a cup of espresso and a fresh almond croissant, and breakfasts are excellent here. Sporting events or movie videos are shown nightly, and there's even a pool table and Internet cafe.

On the main road into Nosara. ☏ **2682-0087.** www.cafedeparis.net. Main courses C2,500–C9,000. AE, MC, V. Daily 7am–11pm.

The Gilded Iguana ★ SEAFOOD/GRILL   This simple restaurant serves fish so fresh that it's still wiggling: The owner's husband, Chiqui, is a local fisherman. Other options include great burgers, Tex-Mex fare, Costa Rican *casados,* and a list of nightly specials. If you're in town fishing, they'll cook your catch. Sporting events are shown on a not-quite-big-enough television. You can also dine at a separate bar area, on the other side of their pool. Overall, the vibe is sociable and lively. Most of the tables and chairs here are low-lying affairs; plus-size travelers might find the chairs a bit challenging to get in and out of.

About 90m (295 ft.) inland from the beach at Playa Guiones. ☎ **2682-0259.** www.thegilded iguana.com. Main courses C2,500–C7,500. V. Daily 7:30am–9:30pm.

La Luna ★ INTERNATIONAL   With an enviable location overlooking the water at Playa Pelada and a casually elegant ambience, this little restaurant is an excellent choice. I especially like grabbing one of the outdoor tables closest to the waves for lunch. However, it's also quite beautiful at night, with candles generously spread around. The chalkboard menu changes regularly, but will usually include some Thai or Indian curry, as well as pasta dishes and hearty steaks. And a wood-fired pizza oven turns out excellent thin-crust pies. Prices are on the high side, and service and hospitality can be spotty at times, but this is still probably the best beachside dining to be had in Nosara.

Playa Pelada. ☎ **2682-0122.** Main courses $7–$35. No credit cards. Daily 11am–11pm.

Nosara After Dark

When evening rolls around, don't expect a major party scene. Visitors tend to gather at **Marlin Bill's** (see above) and **Casa Tucán** (☎ **2682-0113**), both near the main intersection leading to Playa Guiones. **Kaya Sol** (☎ **2682-1459**) has a lounge-style scene popular with surfers. Casa Tucán and Gilded Iguana often have live music. In "downtown" Nosara, you'll probably want to check out either the **Tropicana** (☎ **2682-0140**), the town's long-standing local disco, or the **Legends Bar** (☎ **2682-0184**), a U.S.-style bar with big-screen televisions, and pool and foosball tables.

North of Nosara

Just north of Nosara lies Playa Ostional, famous for its massive nestings of olive ridley sea turtles (see above). At the northern edge of Playa Ostional where it meets Playa San Juanillo, are a few hotels. The best of these is **Hotel Luna Azul** ★ (www.hotellunaazul.com; ☎ **2682-1400**), which features beautiful individual bungalows and a great view of the ocean—although the beach is a good distance away.

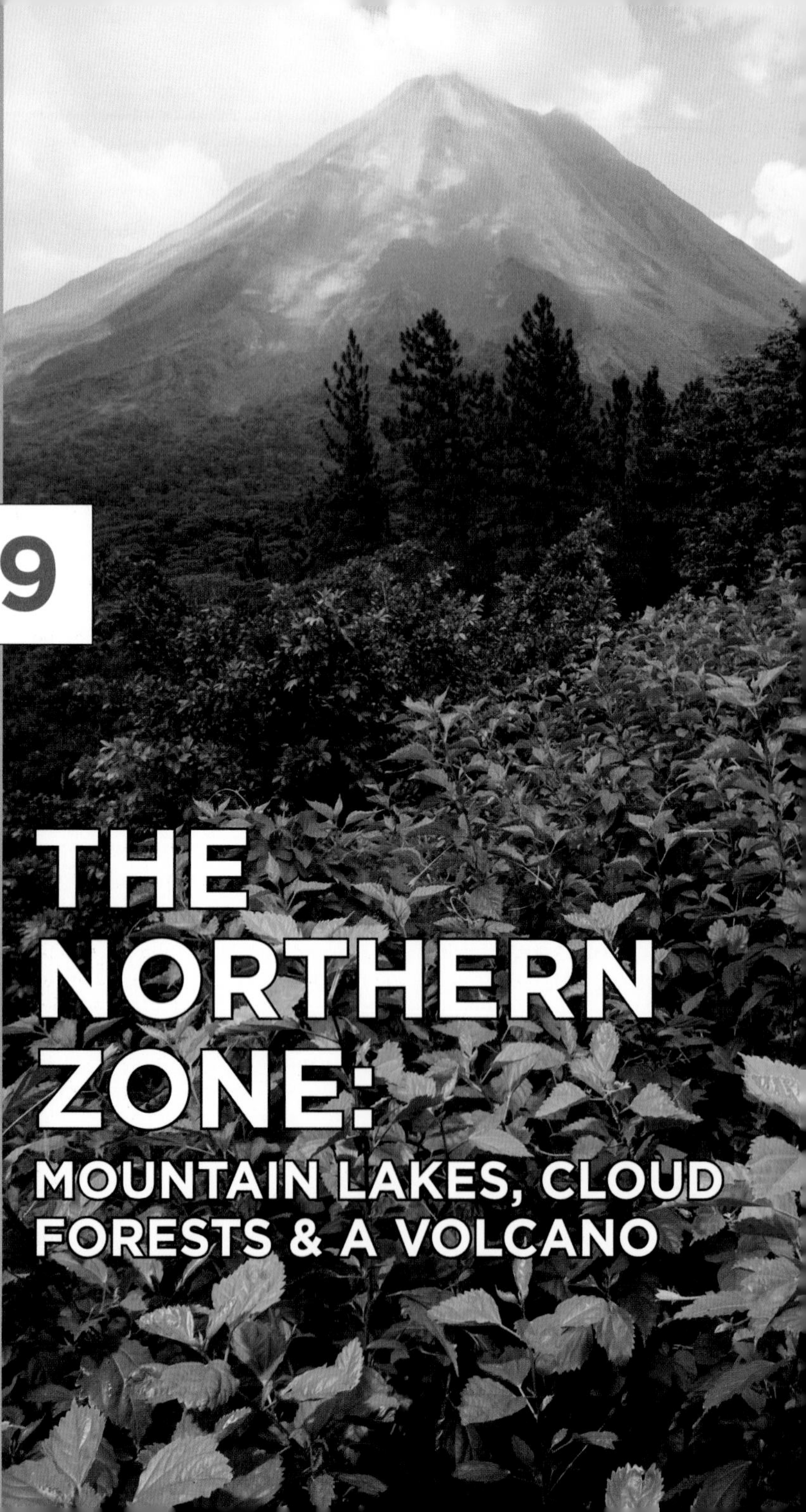

THE NORTHERN ZONE:

MOUNTAIN LAKES, CLOUD FORESTS & A VOLCANO

Costa Rica's northern zone is home to several prime ecotourist destinations, including the astoundingly active **Arenal Volcano** ★★ and the misty and mysterious **Monteverde Cloud Forest Biological Reserve** ★★★. The region has rainforests and cloud forests, jungle rivers, mountain lakes, lowland marshes, and an unbelievable wealth of birds and other wildlife. Changes in elevation create unique microclimates and ecosystems throughout the region. In addition to these natural wonders, this region also provides an intimate glimpse into the rural heart and soul of Costa Rica. Small, isolated lodges flourish, and towns and villages remain predominantly small agricultural communities.

This area is also a must for adventure travelers. The northern zone has one of the best windsurfing spots in the world, on **Lake Arenal** ★, as well as excellent opportunities for mountain biking, hiking, canyoning, and river rafting. Zip-line canopy tours and suspended forest bridges abound. And if you partake in any number of adventure activities, you'll also find several soothing natural hot springs in the area to soak your tired muscles.

ARENAL VOLCANO & LA FORTUNA ★★

140km (87 miles) NW of San José; 61km (38 miles) E of Tilarán

I've visited scores of times, and I never tire of watching red lava rocks tumble down the flanks of **Arenal Volcano,** and listening in awe to its deep rumbling. If you've never experienced them firsthand, the sights and sounds of an active volcano are awe-inspiring. At 1,607m (5,271 ft.), Arenal is one of the world's most regularly active volcanoes. In July 1968, the volcano, which had lain dormant for hundreds of years, surprised everybody by erupting with sudden violence. The nearby village of Tabacón was destroyed, and nearly 80 of its inhabitants were killed. Frequent powerful explosions send cascades of red-hot lava rocks down the volcano's steep slopes. During the day, these lava flows smoke and rumble. However, at night the volcano puts on its most mesmerizing show. If you are lucky enough to be here on a clear and active night—not necessarily a guaranteed occurrence—you'll see the night sky turned red by lava spewing from Arenal's crater.

Lying at the eastern foot of this natural spectacle is the town of **La Fortuna.** Once a humble little farming village, La Fortuna has become a magnet for volcano watchers, adventure tourists, and assorted travelers from around the

PREVIOUS PAGE: **Arenal Volcano.**

Arenal Kioro (p. 310)
Arenal Observatory Lodge (p. 313)
Caño Negro Natural Lodge (p. 317)
El Silencio Lodge & Spa (p. 316)
Hotel Poco A Poco (p. 341)
La Laguna del Lagarto Lodge (p. 318)
La Selva Biological Station (p. 348)
Monteverde Lodge & Gardens (p. 341)
Rara Avis (p. 350)
Selva Verde Lodge (p. 349)
**Tabacón Grand Spa Thermal
Resort** (p. 311)
Villa Blanca Cloud Forest & Spa (p. 317)

world. A host of budget and moderately priced hotels are in and near La Fortuna, and from here you can arrange night tours to the best volcano-viewing spots, which are 17km (11 miles) away on the western slope, on the road to and beyond the Tabacón Grand Spa Thermal Resort.

Essentials

GETTING THERE & DEPARTING
By Plane: Nature Air (✆ 800/ 235-9272 in the U.S. and Canada, or 2299-6000; www.natureair. com) flies to Arenal/La Fortuna daily at noon from Tobías Bolaños International Airport in Pavas. The flight is 30 minutes. Return flights depart for San José at 12:40pm. One-way fares are $100. Nature Air also has connecting flights between Arenal and other major destinations in the country.

Taxis are sometimes waiting for all arriving flights. If not, you can call one at ✆ 2479-9605 or 2479-8522. The fare to La Fortuna runs around C4,500. Alternately, Nature Air can arrange to have a van waiting for you, for $32 for up to four people.

By Car: Several routes connect La Fortuna and San José. The most popular is to head west on the Interamerican Highway (CR1) from San José and then turn north at Naranjo, continuing north through Zarcero to

Arenal Volcano at night.

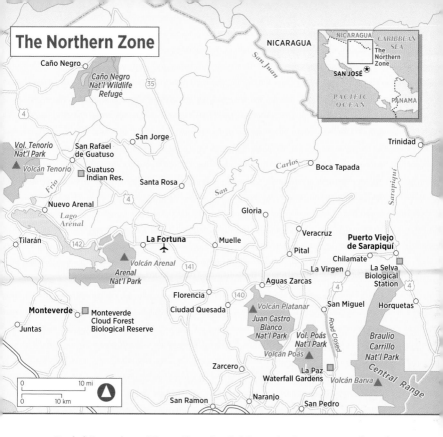

The Northern Zone

NICARAGUA

Caño Negro

Caño Negro Nat'l Wildlife Refuge

Vol. Tenorio Nat'l Park

Volcán Tenorio

San Rafael de Guatuso

Guatuso Indian Res.

San Jorge

Santa Rosa

Nuevo Arenal

Lago Arenal

Tilarán

La Fortuna ✈

Muelle

Volcán Arenal

Arenal Nat'l Park

Florencia

Ciudad Quesada

Monteverde

Monteverde Cloud Forest Biological Reserve

Juntas

Zarcero

San Ramon

Naranjo

San Pedro

Trinidad

Carlos

Boca Tapada

San

Gloria

Veracruz

Pital

Aguas Zarcas

Puerto Viejo de Sarapiquí

Chilamate

La Virgen

La Selva Biological Station

San Miguel

Horquetas

Volcán Platanar

Juan Castro Blanco Nat'l Park

Volcán Poás Nat'l Park

Volcán Poás

La Paz Waterfall Gardens

Volcán Barva

Braulio Carrillo Nat'l Park

Central Range

Road Closed

NICARAGUA

CARIBBEAN SEA

The Northern Zone

SAN JOSÉ

PACIFIC OCEAN

PANAMA

Frio

0   10 mi
0   10 km

Ciudad Quesada on CR141. From Ciudad Quesada, CR141 passes through Florencia, Jabillos, and Tanque on its way to La Fortuna. This route offers wonderful views of the San Carlos valley as you come down from Ciudad Quesada; Zarcero, with its topiary gardens and quaint church, makes a good place to stop, stretch your legs, and snap a few photos (see chapter 6, "The Central Valley," for more information).

You can also stay on the Interamerican Highway (CR1) until San Ramón (west of Naranjo) and then head north through La Tigra on CR142. This route is also very scenic and passes the Villa Blanca Cloud Forest & Spa (p. 317). The travel time on any of the above routes is roughly 3 to 3½ hours.

By Bus: Buses (☏ **2255-0567**) leave San José for La Fortuna at 6:15, 8:40, and 11:30am from the **Atlántico del Norte** bus station at Avenida 9 and Calle 12. The trip lasts 4 hours; the fare is C2,070. The bus you take might be labeled TILARÁN. Make sure it passes through Ciudad Quesada. If so, it passes through La Fortuna; if not, you'll end up in Tilarán via the Interamerican Highway, passing through the Guanacaste town of Cañas, a long way from La Fortuna.

Alternatively, you can take a bus from the same station to Ciudad Quesada and transfer there to another bus to La Fortuna. These buses depart roughly every 30 minutes between 5am and 7:30pm. The fare for the 2½-hour trip is C1,445. Local buses between Ciudad Quesada and La Fortuna run regularly through the day, although the schedule changes frequently, depending on demand. The trip lasts an hour; the fare is C750.

Buses depart **Monteverde/Santa Elena** for Tilarán every day at 7am. This is a journey of only 35km (22 miles), but the trip lasts 2½ hours because the road is in such horrendous condition. People with bad backs should think twice about making the trip, especially by bus. The return bus from Tilarán to Santa Elena leaves at 12:30pm. The fare is $2.30. Buses from Tilarán to La Fortuna depart daily at 8am and 4:30pm, and make the return trip at 7am and 12:30pm. The trip is 3 to 4 hours; the fare is C1,375.

Buses depart La Fortuna for San José roughly every 2 hours between 5am and 6:15pm; in some instances, you might have to transfer in Ciudad Quesada. From there, you can catch one of the frequent buses to San José.

Gray Line (⌀ 2220-2126; www.graylinecostarica.com) has a bus that leaves from San José to La Fortuna daily at 8am. **Interbus** (⌀ 2283-5573; www.interbusonline.com) also has two buses daily leaving San José for La Fortuna at 7:30am and 2:30pm. Both companies charge $40, and will pick you up at most San José–area hotels. And both companies also run routes from La Fortuna with connections to most other major destinations in Costa Rica.

 boats, **HORSES & TAXIS**

You can travel between La Fortuna and Monteverde by boat and taxi, or on a combination of boat, horseback, and taxi. A 10- to 20-minute boat ride across Lake Arenal cuts out hours of driving around its shores. From La Fortuna to the put-in point is about a 25-minute taxi ride. It's about a 1½-hour four-wheel-drive taxi ride between the Río Chiquito dock on the other side of Lake Arenal and Santa Elena. These trips can be arranged in either direction for between $25 and $50 per person, all-inclusive.

You can also add on a horseback ride on the Santa Elena/Monteverde side of the lake. Several routes and rides are on offer. The steepest heads up the mountains and through the forest to the town of San Gerardo, only a 30-minute car ride from Santa Elena. Other routes throw in shorter sections of horseback riding along the lakeside lowlands. With the horseback ride, this trip runs around $85 per person.

Warning: The riding is often rainy, muddy, and steep. Many find it much more arduous than awe-inspiring. Moreover, I've received numerous complaints about the condition of the trails and the treatment of the horses, so be very careful and demanding before signing on for this trip. Find out what route you will be taking, as well as the condition of the horses, if possible. **Desafío Expeditions** (⌀ 2479-9464; www.desafiocostarica.com) is one of the more reputable operators. They will even drive your car around for you while you take the scenic (and sore) route.

If you're looking to make the ride just by taxi and boat, check in with **Jeep Boat Jeep** (⌀ 2479-9955), which has a daily fixed departure in each direction at 7:30am for $28 per person.

HOTELS

Arenal Backpackers Resort **25**
Arenal Kioro **5**
Arenal Observatory Lodge **20**
Cabinas Los Guayabos **6**
Hotel La Fortuna **35**
Hotel Las Colinas **34**
Hotel Magic Mountain **24**
Hotel Royal Corin **11**
Luigi's Hotel **28**
Montaña de Fuego Inn **7**
Nayara Hotel, Spa
   & Gardens **9**
Tabacón Grand Spa Thermal
   Resort **3**
The Springs Resort & Spa **8**
Volcano Lodge **10**

RESTAURANTS

Anch'io **26**
Don Rufino **37**
El Jardin Restaurant **36**
El Novillo de Arenal **4**
El Vagabundo **22**
La Brasitas **27**
Lava Lounge **29**
Lava Rocks **30**
Los Tucanes **3**
Rancho La Cascada **33**
Restaurante Nene's **38**

ATTRACTIONS

Arenal Canopy Tour **12**
Arenal Hanging Bridges **1**
Arenal National Park **18**
Baldi Hot Springs **14**
Eco Termales **15**
Ecoglide **17**
La Fortuna Catholic Church **31**
Río Fortuna Waterfall **21**
Sky Tram **19**
Tabacón Hot Springs **2**
Tikokú **13**

SHOPPING

Original Grand Gallery **23**
Art Shop Onirica **32**

NIGHTLIFE

Volcano Look Disco **16**
Luigi's Casino **28**

ORIENTATION & FAST FACTS   As you enter La Fortuna, you'll see the massive volcano directly in front of you. La Fortuna is only a few streets wide, with almost all the hotels, restaurants, and shops clustered along the main road that leads out of town toward Tabacón and the volcano. Several information and tour-booking offices and Internet cafes, as well as a couple of pharmacies, general stores, and laundromats are on the streets that surround the small central park fronting the Catholic church. A Banco de Costa Rica, as you enter La Fortuna, is just over the Río Burío bridge, and a Banco Nacional is in the center of town, across the park from the church. Both have ATMs.

GETTING AROUND If you don't have a car, you'll need to either take a cab or go on an organized tour if you want to visit the hot springs or view the volcano eruption. La Fortuna has tons of taxis (you can flag one down practically anywhere), and a line of them is always ready and waiting along the main road beside the central park. A taxi between La Fortuna and Tabacón should cost around C7,500. Another alternative is to rent a car when you get here. **Alamo** (✆ **2479-9090;** www.alamocostarica.com) has an office in downtown La Fortuna.

Several places to rent scooters and ATVs are around town. I like **Moto Rental** (✆ **2479-7376**), which rents scooters and off-road motorcycles. Provided it's not raining too heavily, this is a good way to get around. Rates run around $45 to $60 per day for a scooter, and $50 to $90 for a dirt bike. They also offer up a 2½-hour ATV tour. The cost is $70 per person.

What to See & Do

While in the town of La Fortuna, be sure to spend some time simply people-watching from a bench or grassy spot on the central plaza. It's also worth a quick visit to tour the town's **Catholic church.** This modern church was designed by famous Costa Rican artist Teodorico Quirós, and features an interesting soaring front steeple and clock tower of concrete.

EXPERIENCING THE VOLCANO ★★★

The first thing you should know is that Arenal Volcano borders a region of cloud forests and rainforests, and the volcano's cone is often socked in by clouds and fog. Many people come to Arenal and never see the exposed cone. Moreover, the volcano does go through periods of relative quiet.

The second thing you should know is that you can't climb Arenal Volcano—it's not safe due to the constant activity. Several foolish people who have ignored this warning have lost their lives, and others have been severely injured. The most recent fatalities occurred in August 2000.

Arenal National Park

Arenal National Park ★★ (✆ **2461-8499**) constitutes an area of more than 2,880 hectares (7,114 acres), which includes the viewing and parking areas closest to the volcano. The park is open daily from 8am to 3:30pm and charges $10 admission per person. The trails through forest and over old lava flows inside the park are gorgeous and fun. (Be careful climbing on those volcanic boulders.)

The principal trail inside the park, **Sendero Coladas (Lava Flow Trail)** ★★, is just under 2km (1.25 miles) and passes through

La Fortuna and Arenal Volcano.

Arenal Volcano and the La Fortuna church.

secondary forest and open savannah. At the end of the trail, a short natural stairway takes you to a broad, open lava field left in the wake of a massive 1992 eruption. Scrambling over the cooled lava is a real treat, but be careful, as the rocks can be sharp in places. Many spots throughout the park offer great views of the volcano, but the closest view can be found at **El Mirador (The Lookout) ★**, where you can not only see the volcano better, but really hear it rumble and roar. From the parking lot near the trail head for the Lava Flow Trail, you have the option of hiking or driving the 1km (.62 mile) to El Mirador.

Arenal Volcano After Dark

Waiting for and watching Arenal's regular eruptions is the main activity in La Fortuna and is best done at night when the orange lava glows against the starry sky. Although it's sometimes possible simply to look up from the middle of town and see Arenal erupting, the view is usually best from the north and west sides of the volcano along the road to Tabacón and toward the national park entrance. In fact, the best angle for volcano viewing often changes, as the activity shifts around the cone, and side vents. If you have a car, you can ask at your hotel and around town for the best current spot to view the action and drive there. If you've arrived by bus, you will need to take a taxi or tour.

Every hotel in the area and several tour offices in La Fortuna offer night tours to the volcano. (They don't actually enter the park; they usually stop on the road that runs btw. the park entrance and the Arenal Observatory Lodge.) These tours generally cost between $10 and $30 per person. Often these volcano-viewing tours include a stop at one of the local hot springs, and the price goes up accordingly (see "Taking a Soothing Soak in Hot Springs," below, for a description of the different options and fees).

Note: Although it's counterintuitive, the rainy season is often a better time to see the exposed cone of Arenal Volcano, especially at night. I don't know why

Arenal Volcano's cooled-off lava flows.

this is, but I've had excellent volcano-viewing sessions at various points during the rainy season; during the dry season, the volcano can often be socked in solid for days at a time. The bottom line is that catching a glimpse of the volcano's cone is never a sure thing.

NATURE UP-CLOSE & PERSONAL

Located a couple of miles outside of La Fortuna, the **Ecocentro Danaus** ★ (© 2479-7019; www.ecocentrodanaus.com) is a private biological reserve and sustainable tourism project, which offers educational and engaging tours. Among the attractions here are a butterfly garden and reproduction center, botanical and medicinal plant gardens, and a small museum honoring the local Maleku indigenous culture. Open daily from 8am to 4pm, admission is $6, including a 90-minute guided tour. Night tours ($30) are offered by reservation.

OTHER ADVENTUROUS PURSUITS IN THE AREA

Aside from the impressive volcanic activity, the area around Arenal Volcano is packed with other natural wonders.

ATV The folks at **Fourtrax Adventure** (© 2479-8444; www.fourtraxadventure.com) offers a 3-hour adventure through the forests and farmlands around La Fortuna. The tour includes a stop at a jungle swimming hole, where you can cool off. You get good views of the volcano, as well as La Fortuna Waterfall. The cost is $85 per ATV. A second rider on the same ATV costs $14.

CANOPY TOURS & CANYONING There are numerous ways to get up into the forest canopy here. Perhaps the simplest way is to hike the trails and bridges of **Arenal Hanging Bridges** ★ (© 2290-0469; www.hangingbridges.com). Located just over the Lake Arenal dam, this attraction is a complex of gentle trails and suspension bridges through a beautiful tract of primary

forest. It's open daily from 7:30am to 4pm; admission is $22.

Another option is the **Sky Tram** ★★ (© **2479-9944;** www.skyadventures.travel), an open gondola-style ride that begins near the shores of Lake Arenal and rises up, providing excellent views of the lake and volcano. From here, you can hike their series of trails and suspended bridges. In the end, you can hike down, take the gondola, or strap on a harness and ride their zip-line canopy tour down to the bottom. The zip-line tour here features several very long and very fast sections, with some impressive views of the lake and volcano. The cost is $66 for the com-

TOP: A Sky Tram canopy tour. RIGHT: A canyoning tour.

bined tram ride up and zip-line down tour. It's $55 to ride the tram round-trip. The tram runs daily from 7:30am to 5pm. These folks also have a butterfly garden exhibit on-site.

Several other zip-line canopy tours in the area include the **Arenal Canopy Tour** (© 2479-9769; www.canopy.co.cr) and **Ecoglide** ★ (© **2479-7120;** www.arenalecoglide.com). The hotel **Montaña de Fuego** (p. 312) even has its own zip-line tour set up.

If you'd like a bigger rush than the canopy tours offer, you could go "canyoning" with **Pure Trek Canyoning** ★★ (© 866/569-5723 in the U.S. and Canada, or 2479-1313; www.puretrekcostarica.com) and **Desafío Expeditions** ★★ (© 866/210-0052 in the U.S. and Canada, or **2479-9464;** www.desafiocostarica.com). This adventure sport is a mix of hiking through and alongside a jungle river, punctuated with periodic rappels through and alongside the faces of rushing waterfalls. Pure Trek's trip is probably better for first-timers and families with kids, while Desafío's tour is just a bit more rugged and adventurous. The former charges $98. The latter charges $90. Both of these companies offer various combination full-day excursions, mixing canyoning with other adventure tours, and tend to have two to three daily departures, including one in the morning and one in the afternoon.

FISHING   With Lake Arenal just around the corner, fishing is a popular activity here. The big fish here is *guapote,* a Central American species of rainbow bass. However, you can also book fishing trips to Caño Negro, where snook, tarpon, and other game fish can be stalked. Most hotels and adventure-tour companies can arrange fishing excursions. Costs run around $150 to $250 per boat, and a full day goes for around $250 to $500.

HIKING & HORSEBACK RIDING   Horseback riding is a popular activity in this area, and there are scores of good rides on dirt back roads and through open fields and dense rainforest. Volcano and lake views come with the terrain on most rides. Horseback trips to the Río Fortuna waterfall are perhaps the most popular tours sold, but remember, the horse will get you only to the entrance; from there, you'll have to hike a bit. A horseback ride to the falls should cost between $20 and $40, including the entrance fee. Alternately, you can check in with the folks at **Cabalgata Don Tobias**

Horseback Riding to Cerro Chato.

(☎ 2479-1212; www.cabalgatadontobias.com), which runs a 2½-hour tour on their private land, which is a mix of farmland and forest, with some great views of the volcano. Two tours leave daily at 8:30am and 1:30pm, and the cost is $65 per person.

One popular and strenuous hike is to **Cerro Chato,** a dormant volcanic cone on the flank of Arenal with a pretty little lake. **Desafío Expeditions** ★ (☎ 2479-9464; www.desafiocostarica.com) leads a 5- to 6-hour hike for $75, including a snack.

Aventuras Arenal (☎ 2479-9133; www.arenaladventures.com), **Desafío Expeditions** ★★ (☎ 2479-9464; www.desafiocostarica.com), **Jacamar Tours** (☎ 2479-9767; www.arenaltours.com), and **Sunset Tours** (☎ 866/417-7352 in the U.S. and Canada, or 2479-9800 in Costa Rica; www.sunsettourcr.com) are the main tour operators. In addition to the above tours, each of these companies offers most of the tours listed in this section, as well as fishing and sightseeing excursions on the lake, and transfers to other destinations around Costa Rica.

LA FORTUNA FALLS Leading the list of side attractions in the area is the impressive **Río Fortuna Waterfall** ★★ (☎ 2479-8338; www.arenal adifort.com), located about 5.5km (3½ miles) outside of town in a lush jungle setting. A sign in town points the way to the road out to the falls. You can drive or hike to just within viewing distance. When you get to the entrance to the lookout, you'll have to pay a $9 entrance fee to actually check out the falls. It's another 15- to 20-minute hike down a steep and often muddy path to the pool formed by the waterfall. The hike back up will take slightly longer. You can swim, but stay away from the turbulent water at the base of the falls—several people have drowned here. Instead, check out and enjoy the calm pool just around the bend, or join the locals at the popular swimming hole under the bridge on the paved road, just after the turnoff for the road up to the falls. The trail to the falls is open daily from 8am to 5pm.

MOUNTAIN BIKING This region is very well suited for mountain biking. Rides range in difficulty from moderate to extremely challenging. You can combine a day on a mountain bike with a visit to one or more of the popular attractions here. **Bike Arenal** ★ (☎ 866/465-4114 in the U.S. and Canada, or 2479-7150; www.bikearenal.com) offers up an excellent collection of top-notch bikes and equipment and a wide range of tour possibilities.

Hard core bikers will want to come in March for the **Vuelta al Lago** ★ (☎ 2695-5297; www.vueltaallago.net), an annual 2-day race around the lake.

WHITE-WATER RAFTING, CANOEING & KAYAKING For adventurous tours of the area, check out **Desafío Expeditions** ★★ (☎ 2479-9464; www.desafio costarica.com) or **Wave Expeditions** ★★ (☎ 2479-7262; www.wave expeditions.com). Both companies offer daily raft rides of Class I to II, III, and IV to V on different sections of the Toro, Peñas Blancas, and Sarapiquí rivers. A half-day float trip on a nearby river costs between $50 and $65 per person; a full day of rafting on some rougher water costs $85 per person, depending on what section of what river you ride. Both companies also offer mountain biking and most of the standard local guided trips. If you want a wet and personal ride, try Desafío's tour in inflatable kayaks, or "duckies."

What'SUP
Stand Up Paddling (SUP) is a booming sport and fitness craze, and you can practice it on the lovely Lake Arenal, in the shadow of the lake's namesake volcano, with the folks at Desafío Expeditions (see above).

A more laid-back alternative is to take a canoe tour with **Canoa Aventura** (© **2479-8200;** www.canoa-aventura.com), which offers half-, full-, and multiday excursions on a variety of rivers in the region, which range from $50 to $150 per person.

A similar option, although in a kayak, is offered up by **Ríos Tropicales** ★★ (© **2479-0075;** www.riostropicales.com), which offers a 4-hour paddle on the lake, with drinks and a snack, for $60.

SIDE TRIPS FROM LA FORTUNA

La Fortuna is a great place from which to make a day trip to the **Caño Negro National Wildlife Refuge** ★. This vast network of marshes and rivers (particularly the Río Frío) is 100km (62 miles) north of La Fortuna near the town of Los Chiles. This refuge is best known for its amazing abundance of bird life, including roseate spoonbills, jabiru storks, herons, and egrets, but you can also see caimans and crocodiles. Bird-watchers should not miss this refuge, although keep in mind that the main lake dries up in the dry season (mid-Apr to Nov), which reduces the number of wading birds. Full-day tours to Caño Negro average between $55 and $65 per person. However, most of the tours run out of La Fortuna that are billed as Caño Negro never really enter the refuge but instead ply sections of the nearby Río Frío, which features similar wildlife and

White-water rafting the Río Toro.

Jabiru storks.

ecosystems. If you're interested in staying in this area and really visiting the refuge, check out the **Caño Negro Natural Lodge** (p. 317).

You can also visit the **Venado Caverns,** a 45-minute drive away. In addition to plenty of stalactites, stalagmites, and other limestone formations, you'll see bats and cave fish. Tours cost around $65. All of the tour agencies and hotel tour desks can arrange or directly offer trips to Caño Negro and Venado Caverns.

Shopping

La Fortuna is chock-full of souvenir shops selling standard tourist fare. However, you'll find one of my favorite craft shops here. As you leave the town of La Fortuna toward Tabacón, keep your eye on the right-hand side of the road. When you see a massive collection of wood sculptures and a building reading **Original Grand Gallery** (no phone), slow down and pull over. This local artisan and his family produce works in a variety of styles and sizes. They specialize in faces, many of them larger than a typical home's front door. You can also find a host of animal figures, ranging in style from purely representational to rather abstract. Another good shop, which features original oil paintings and acrylics, as well as other one-off jewelry and jade pieces, is **Art Shop Onirica** (𝄐 **2479-7589;** www.galeriaoniricacr.com), located next to La Fortuna's post office.

Where to Stay in La Fortuna
EXPENSIVE
Hotel Magic Mountain ★★   Located just on the outskirts of town—as you head toward Tabacón—this three-story hotel has large and luxurious rooms, with plenty of perks. All come with a private balcony facing the volcano. The junior

TAKING A SOOTHING SOAK IN hot springs

Arenal Volcano has bestowed a terrific fringe benefit on the area around it: several naturally heated thermal springs.

Located at the site of the former village that was destroyed by the 1968 eruption, **Tabacón Grand Spa Thermal Resort ★ ★ ★** (① **2519-1900;** www. tabacon.com) is the most luxurious, extensive, and expensive spot to soak your tired bones. A series of variously sized pools, fed by natural springs, are spread out among lush gardens. At the center is a large, warm, spring-fed swimming pool with a slide, a swim-up bar, and a perfect view of the volcano. One of the stronger streams flows over a sculpted waterfall, with a rock ledge underneath that provides a perfect place to sit and receive a free hydraulic shoulder massage. The extensive grounds are worth exploring. The pools and springs closest to the volcano are some of the hottest—makes sense, doesn't it? The resort also has an excellent spa on the grounds offering professional massages, mud masks, and other treatments, as well as yoga classes (appointments required). Most of the treatments are conducted in lovely open-air gazebos surrounded by the

rich tropical flora. The spa here even has several permanent sweat lodges, based on a Native American traditional design. A full-service restaurant, garden grill, and a couple of bars are available for those seeking sustenance.

Entrance fees are $85 for adults and $40 for children 11 and under. This rate includes either a buffet lunch or dinner, and allows admission for a full day. After 6pm, you can enter for $45, not including any meals. The hot springs are open

suites are even bigger, with a separate sitting area, large shower with rainwater shower head, and private volcano-view in-room Jacuzzi. I like no. 506, which is an end unit with spectacular views. The hotel has a spa and large free-form pool, with two separate outdoor Jacuzzis and separate children's pool, as well as the town's only sports bar.

La Fortuna, San Carlos. www.hotelmagicmountain.com. ① **2479-7246.** Fax 2479-7248. 42 units. $142 double; $198 suite. Rates include buffet breakfast and taxes. AE, MC, V. **Amenities:** Restaurant; bar; 2 Jacuzzis; outdoor pool; spa, Wi-Fi. *In room:* A/C, TV, hair dryer, minibar.

MODERATE

Hotel La Fortuna ★ Centrally located just 1 block south of the gas station, the Hotel La Fortuna features large, spiffy rooms with a host of modern amenities. The best of these have volcano-view private balconies—ask for a room on

daily from 10am to 10pm. The pools are busiest between 2 and 6pm. Management enforces a policy of limiting visitors, so reservations (which can be made online or by phone) are recommended. Spa treatments must be purchased separately, and reservations are required.

Baldi Hot Springs (✆ **2479-2190;** www.baldihotsprings.cr), next to the Volcano Look Disco, are the first hot springs you'll come to as you drive from La Fortuna toward Tabacón. This place has grown substantially over the years, with many different pools, slides, and bars and restaurants spread around the expansive grounds. However, I find this place far less attractive than the other options mentioned here. Baldi has much more of a party vibe, with loud music often blaring at some of the swim-up bars. Admission is $28.

Just across the street from Baldi Hot Springs is the unmarked entrance of my current favorite local hot spring, **Eco Termales** ★★ (✆ **2479-8484**). Smaller and more intimate than Tabacón, this series of pools set amid lush forest and gardens is almost as picturesque and luxurious, although it has far fewer pools, lacks a view of the volcano, and the spa services are much less extensive. Reservations are absolutely necessary here, and total admissions are limited so that it is never crowded. Admission is $32. These folks have added a restaurant serving basic local fare, but I recommend just coming for the springs.

Finally, **Tikokú** ★ (✆ **2479-7156**) is right beside Baldi and run by the folks at Arenal Kioro (p. 310). This spot features a row of eight descending sculpted pools. Admission is $24.

the fourth or fifth floor with a volcano view. This hotel has 12 rooms designed for wheelchair accessibility.

La Fortuna, San Carlos. www.fortunainn.com. ✆ **2479-9197.** Fax 2479-8563. 44 units. $70–$85 double. Rates include buffet breakfast and taxes. AE, MC, V. **Amenities:** Restaurant, bar. *In room:* A/C, TV, hair dryer, no phone, Wi-Fi.

INEXPENSIVE

La Fortuna is a tourist boomtown; basic hotels have been popping up here at a phenomenal rate for several years running. Right in La Fortuna you'll find a score of budget options. If you have time, it's worth walking around and checking out a couple. One of the better options is **Arenal Backpackers Resort** (www.arenal backpackersresort.com; ✆ **2479-7000**), which bills itself as a five-star hostel. It has both shared-bathroom dorm rooms, and more upscale private rooms, but even backpackers get to enjoy the large pool, Wi-Fi, and volcano views.

A couple of places both in town and right on the outskirts of La Fortuna allow camping, with access to basic bathroom facilities, for around $5 to $10 per person per night. If you have a car, drive a bit out of town toward Tabacón and you'll find several more basic cabins and camping sites, some that even offer views of the volcano.

Hotel Las Colinas ★ 🍃　Like the Hotel La Fortuna (see above), this long-standing downtown hotel was torn down and rebuilt. Today, Las Colinas is the centerpiece of a minimall, which features some shops and a small spa. The rooms range from simple budget accommodations to spiffy junior suites with a private volcano-view balcony and Jacuzzi. The budget rooms come with televisions, but lack the other amenities found in the rest of the rooms. The hotel's best feature is its rooftop terrace, where breakfasts are sometimes served. Eco-friendly touches include solar-heated water.

La Fortuna, San Carlos. www.lascolinasarenal.com. ☎ **2479-9305.** Fax 2479-9160. 20 units. $49 budget room double; $75 double; $90 junior suite. Rates include breakfast and taxes. AE, MC. **Amenities:** Restaurant. *In room:* A/C, TV, minifridge, Wi-Fi.

Where to Stay near the Volcano

While La Fortuna is the major gateway town to Arenal Volcano, for my money, the best places to stay are located on the road between La Fortuna and the National Park.

One other very unique alternative is to stay aboard the **Rain Goddess** (www.bluwing.com; ☎ **866/593-3168** in the U.S., or 2231-4299). This luxurious houseboat has four staterooms, ample lounge and dining areas, and cruises around Lake Arenal.

VERY EXPENSIVE

In addition to the places listed below, **Nayara Hotel, Spa & Gardens ★★** (www.arenalnayara.com; ☎ **866/311-1197** in the U.S. and Canada, or 2479-1600 in Costa Rica) is a gorgeous collection of rooms, suites, and villas, located on a lush piece of land, with great volcano views.

Arenal Kioro ★★　Set on 11 hectares (27 acres) of hilly land with two rivers and a small patch of forest, this place is extremely close to Arenal Volcano. The views from the rooms, grounds, pool, and restaurant of this hotel are truly astounding. The rooms themselves are massive, with soaring high ceilings, large picture windows and glass doors, and a private balcony or patio facing the action. Each has its own four-person modern Jacuzzi tub, with sculpted seats and numerous jets, set below a large picture window with a volcano view. The beds are also set to take in the view. Trails weave through the grounds and a host of tours and activities are on offer. The restaurant serves excellent international cuisine in a beautiful setting, with a giant wall of windows facing the volcano. The Kioro was granted "4 Leaves" by the CST Sustainable Tourism program.

On the main road btw. La Fortuna and Lake Arenal, 10km (6 miles) from La Fortuna. www.hotel arenalkioro.com. ☎ **2479-1700.** Fax 2479-1710. 53 units. $385 double. Rates include buffet breakfast. AE, DC, MC, V. **Amenities:** Restaurant; bar; exercise room; Jacuzzi; large outdoor pool; small spa. *In room:* A/C, TV, hair dryer, minibar.

Hotel Royal Corin ★★ All of the rooms at this plush resort have excellent volcano views, although those on the north wing of the large, horseshoe-shaped building have the best views. The best feature here is the large and beautiful complex of pools and Jacuzzis fed by volcanically heated natural spring water. All rooms come with volcano-facing balconies, and chic, minimalist contemporary decor. The junior and master suites are larger and have Jacuzzis and double-sized balconies. The small spa here is top-notch, and the fifth-floor Lava bar is a great place to sip a cool drink while watching the volcano.

On the main road btw. La Fortuna and Lake Arenal, 4km (2½ miles) from La Fortuna. www.royal corin.com. ℂ **877/642-6746** in the U.S. and Canada, or 2479-2201 in Costa Rica. Fax 2479-7395. 54 units. $265 double; $334–$360 suite. Rates include buffet breakfast and taxes. AE, DC, DISC, MC, V. **Amenities:** Restaurant; bar; babysitting; exercise room; 6 Jacuzzis; large outdoor complex of pools and hot springs; room service; small spa; sauna. *In room:* A/C, TV, hair dryer, minibar, Wi-Fi.

The Springs Resort & Spa ★★★ Located on a large piece of land with a great view of the volcano, this sprawling resort features plush, luxurious rooms, and some fabulous facilities. The five-story main lodge building is massive, with several restaurants, a large, full-service spa, modern exercise room; and much-needed elevator. At its base sit a series of sculpted hot and cold pools of various sizes, and below these you'll find the suites and villas. All of the rooms here are opulently appointed, and all have volcano views. The bathrooms are large, marble affairs with a huge Jacuzzi tub and separate shower. Food and service are excellent, as you would expect. ***Note:*** Do not confuse this place with the Arenal Springs Resort.

Off the main road btw. La Fortuna and Lake Arenal, 10km (6 miles) from La Fortuna. www.the springscostarica.com. ℂ **954/727-8333** in the U.S. and Canada, or 2401-3313 in Costa Rica. Fax 2401-3319. 44 units. $395–$730 suite; $1,100 and up villa for 4. AE, DC, MC, V. **Amenities:** 4 restaurants; 3 bars; large, modern exercise room; several Jacuzzis; series of outdoor pools; room service; smoke-free rooms; full-service spa. *In room:* A/C, TV/DVD, movie library, CD player, hair dryer, minibar, MP3 docking station, Wi-Fi.

Tabacón Grand Spa Thermal Resort ★★★ This is the most popular resort in the Arenal area—and for good reason. Many rooms have excellent, direct views of the volcano. Rooms on the upper floors of the 300-block building have the best vistas. Still, some have obstructed, or no, views. Be sure to specify in advance if you want a view room. Nine of the rooms are truly accessible to travelers with disabilities. Guests enjoy privileges at the spectacular hot-springs complex and spa across the street (see "Taking a Soothing Soak in Hot Springs," on p. 308), including slightly extended hours. When you consider the included entrance fee to the hot springs, the rates here are actually rather reasonable. This hotel has shown a committed and innovative approach to sustainable tourism. Guests are encouraged to make their stay carbon neutral, and the hotel is actively involved in a range of local development and conservation programs.

On the main road btw. La Fortuna and Lake Arenal, Tabacón. www.tabacon.com. ℂ **877/277-8291** in the U.S. and Canada, or 2519-1999 reservations in San José, or 2479-2020 at the resort. Fax 2519-1940. 114 units. $245–$495 suite. Rates higher during peak periods. AE, DC, MC, V.

Tabacón Grand Spa Thermal Resort.

Amenities: 2 restaurants; 2 bars; exercise room; Jacuzzi; large pool w/swim-up bar; all rooms smoke-free; extensive hot springs and spa facilities across the street. *In room:* A/C, TV, hair dryer, Wi-Fi.

EXPENSIVE

Montaña de Fuego Inn ★   This resort is a collection of individual and duplex cabins spread over hilly grounds. Most have marvelous volcano views from their spacious glass-enclosed porches. Some rooms even have back balconies overlooking a forested ravine, in addition to the volcano-facing front porch. The suites and junior suites all have a Jacuzzi tub. I actually prefer the juniors over the full suites, since the Jacuzzis in the juniors are set in front of a volcano-view picture window. Behind the hotel are some rolling hills that lead down to a small river surrounded by patches of gallery forest, where they conduct an adventurous horseback, hiking, and a zip-line canopy tour.

La Palma de la Fortuna, San Carlos. www.montanafuegohotel.com. ℂ **2479-1220.** Fax 2479-1455. 69 units. $110–$132 double; $154–$168 suite. Rates include buffet breakfast. AE, MC, V. **Amenities:** Restaurant; 2 bars; 2 Jacuzzis; outdoor pool; room service; full-service spa. *In room:* A/C, TV, hair dryer, minibar.

Volcano Lodge ☺   This large and spread-out resort has a wide range of services and amenities. All of the rooms are tastefully decorated with heavy wooden furnishings. All come with a small terrace with a couple of wooden rocking chairs, and most of these have great views of the volcano. Several rooms are wheelchair accessible. The lodge has two restaurants, as well as two outdoor pools, each with a separate heated Jacuzzi and volcano views. One also features a children's pool and playground. A wide range of tours and activities are offered.

La Fortuna de San Carlos. www.volcanolodge.com. ☎ **800/649-5913** in the U.S. and Canada, or 2479-1717. Fax 2479-1716. 64 units. $138 double. Rates include taxes and breakfast buffet. AE, MC, V. **Amenities:** 2 restaurants; 2 bars; Jacuzzis; 2 outdoor pools; small spa. *In room:* A/C, TV, hair dryer, Wi-Fi.

MODERATE

Arenal Observatory Lodge ★★ This place is built on a high ridge very close to the volcano, with a spectacular view of the cone. The best rooms here are the junior suites below the restaurant and main lodge, as well as the four rooms in the Observatory Block, and the White Hawk villa. The "Smithsonian" rooms feature massive picture windows with a direct view of the volcano. The lodge offers a number of guided and unguided hiking options, including a free morning guided hike through their trails and gardens, as well as a wide range of other tours. Five rooms are truly equipped for wheelchair access, and a paved path extends almost 1km (.5 mile) into the rainforest. When you're not hiking or touring the region, you can hang by the volcano-view swimming pool and Jacuzzi. The hotel maintains much of its land as part of a private nature reserve and is committed to sustainable and green tourism practices.

On the flanks of Arenal Volcano. To get here, head to the national park entrance, stay on the dirt road past the entrance, and follow the signs to the Observatory Lodge. A four-wheel-drive vehicle is not essential, although you'll always be better off with the clearance afforded by a four-wheel-drive vehicle. www.arenalobservatorylodge.com. ☎ **2290-7011** reservations number in San José, or 2479-1070 at the lodge. Fax 2290-8427. 51 units. $91 La Casona double; $123 standard double; $159 Smithsonian; $183 junior suite. Rates include breakfast buffet and taxes and are lower in off season. AE, MC, V. **Amenities:** Restaurant; bar; Jacuzzi; midsize outdoor pool; smoke-free rooms. *In room:* No phone.

INEXPENSIVE

While the hotels along the road between La Fortuna and the National Park tend to be geared toward higher-end travelers, more budget-conscious travelers do have a few choices. In addition to the inexpensive options in La Fortuna, if you have a car, **Cabinas Los Guayabos** (www.hotellosguayabos.com; ☎/fax **2479-1444**) is a good value, with views and a location that rival the more expensive lodgings listed above.

Luigi's Hotel This small in-town hotel has a lively, hostel-like atmosphere. The rooms are all comfortable and clean; those on the second floor have the best views of the volcano, although those on the first floor have higher ceilings. All open onto a long shared veranda or porch. Despite the name and the fact that the restaurant here is a pizza-and-pasta joint, the owners are actually Costa Rican, not Italian.

La Fortuna, San Carlos. www.luigishotel.com. ☎/fax **2479-9898**. 22 units. $48 double. Rates include breakfast. MC, V. **Amenities:** Restaurant; bar; gym; Jacuzzi; small outdoor pool. *In room:* A/C, TV, hair dryer, no phone.

Where to Eat in & Around La Fortuna

Dining in La Fortuna is nowhere near as spectacular as volcano viewing, although, given the area's popularity, options abound. The favorite meeting places in town are **El Jardín Restaurant** (☎ **2479-9360**) and **Lava Rocks** (☎ **2479-8039**); both are on the main road, right in the center of La Fortuna. Other choices include **Rancho La Cascada** (© 2479-9145) and **Restaurante Nene's** (© 2479-9192) for Tico fare, and **Las Brasitas** (© 2479-9819; www.las brasitas.com) for Mexican. For good pizza and Italian cuisine, try either **Anch'io** (© 2479-7560), near the heart of town, or **El Vagabundo** ★ (© 2479-9565), just on the outskirts.

Finally, for some fine and fancy dining, you can try **Los Tucanes** ★★ (© 2479-2020) restaurant at the Tabacón Grand Spa resort (p. 311).

Don Rufino ★ COSTA RICAN/INTERNATIONAL   Set on a busy corner in the heart of town, this restaurant is easily the best—and the busiest—option right in town. The front wall and bar area open onto the street and are often filled both with local tour guides and tourists. Try the *pollo al estilo de la abuela* (Grandma's chicken), which is baked and served wrapped in banana leaves, or one of the excellent cuts of meat. The chateaubriand and imported top sirloin steaks are huge and are meant to be shared by two. The bar stays open most nights until midnight or beyond.

Downtown La Fortuna. © **2479-9997.** www.donrufino.com. Main courses $8–$35. Reservations recommended during the high season. AE, MC, V. Daily 11am–11pm.

El Novillo del Arenal 📷 STEAK/COSTA RICAN   This place is the definition of "nothing fancy." In fact, it's just some lawn furniture (tables and chairs) set on a concrete slab underneath a high, open zinc roof. Still, it is perennially popular. The steaks are large and well prepared. The chicken and fish portions are also large and nicely done. Meals come with garlic bread, fries, and some slaw. For a real local treat, order some fried yuca as a side. If the night is clear, you can get a good view of any volcanic activity from the parking lot here.

On the road to Tabacón, 10km (6¼ miles) outside of La Fortuna. © **2479-1910.** Reservations recommended. Main courses C3,500–C9,000. MC, V. Mon–Fri noon to 10pm; Sat–Sun 10am–10pm.

Lava Lounge ★ INTERNATIONAL   This humble downtown La Fortuna open-air restaurant combines a very simple setting with a sleek and somewhat eclectic menu. Healthy and hearty sandwiches, wraps, and salads are the main offerings here. You can get a traditional burger or one made with fresh grilled tuna. More substantial fare includes traditional Costa Rican *arroz con pollo,* and a *casado,* built around a thick pork chop. You can also get several different pastas, and nightly dinner specials may include some coconut-battered shrimp with a mango salsa, or a prime sirloin steak in a green pepper or red-wine sauce. The decor consists of a series of rustic wooden tables with mostly bench seats.

Downtown La Fortuna, on the main road. © **2479-7365.** www.lavaloungecostarica.com. Main courses C4,500–C8,500. AE, MC, V. Daily 11am–11pm.

La Fortuna After Dark

La Fortuna's biggest after-dark attraction is the volcano, but the **Volcano Look Disco** (© 2479-9690) on the road to Tabacón is trying to compete. If you get bored of the eruptions and seismic rumbling, head here for heavy dance beats and mirrored disco balls. In town, the folks at Luigi's Hotel have a midsize **casino** (© 2479-9898) next door to their hotel and restaurant, while the open-to-the-street bar at **Don Rufino** (see above) is a popular spot for a drink. Finally, a cozy sports bar with a pool table and flatscreen televisions is on the second floor at the **Hotel Magic Mountain** (see above).

Where to Stay & Eat Farther Afield

All of the hotels listed in the following four sections are at least a half-hour drive from La Fortuna and the volcano. Most, if not all, offer both night and day tours to Arenal and Tabacón, but they also hope to attract you with their own natural charms.

EAST OF LA FORTUNA

The broad, flat San Carlos valley spreads out to the east of La Fortuna. This is agricultural heartland, with large plantations of yuca, papaya, and other cash crops. The popular Ciudad Quesada route to, or from, La Fortuna will take you through this area.

In addition to the places listed below, **Leaves & Lizards** (www.leavesandlizards.com; ✆ 888/828-9245 in the U.S. and Canada, or 2478-0023 in Costa Rica), near El Muelle, wins high praise as an intimate, isolated getaway.

Termales del Bosque 🎁 The best thing about this hotel is its wonderful **natural hot springs ★★**. The series of sculpted pools is set in the midst of rich rainforest, on the banks of a small river. Down by the pools are a natural

steam room (scented each day with fresh eucalyptus), a massage room, and a snack-and-juice bar. The trail down here winds through the thick forest, and, if you want to keep on walking, you can take guided or self-guided tours on a network of well-marked trails. Rooms are pretty simple and plain. Still, they are clean and spacious, and most feature a private or shared veranda with views over gardens and rolling hills. A three-bedroom bungalow has a shared bathroom and kitchenette. You can rent horses at the lodge, and a variety of tours are offered. If you aren't staying here, you can use the pools and hike the trails for C6,000.

On the road from San Carlos to Aguas Zarcas, just before El Tucano; Ciudad Quesada, San Carlos. www.termalesdelbosque.com. ✆ 2460-4740. 49 units. $75 double; $100 bungalow. Rates include full breakfast, unlimited use of the hot springs, and taxes. AE, DC, MC, V. **Amenities:** Restaurant; several hot-spring pools set beside a forest river; massage. *In room:* A/C, TV, no phone.

Termales del Bosque.

Tilajari Resort Hotel ★ ☺   This sprawling resort on the banks of the San Carlos River makes a good base for exploring the area and offers terrific bird-watching. Most rooms have views of the river; others open onto rich flowering gardens. All have a private balcony or terrace. Large iguanas are frequently sighted on the grounds, and crocodiles live in the river. There's also an orchid garden, a tropical fruit-and-vegetable garden, a medicinal herb garden, and a well-maintained butterfly garden. Tilajari is quite popular with Tico families, especially on weekends. This is a great place for your kids to have a chance to interact and play with their Costa Rican counterparts. The lodge arranges a wide range of tours of the region, and frequently hosts local tennis tournaments, too. Tilajari lies between and is connected to La Fortuna, Aguas Zarcas, and Ciudad Quesada.

Muelle (A.P. 81–4400), San Carlos. www.tilajari.com. ℂ **2462-1212.** Fax 2462-1414. 76 units. $99 double; $120 suite. Rates include full breakfast. AE, MC, V. **Amenities:** Restaurant; bar; exercise room; Jacuzzi; large outdoor pool; sauna; 6 lighted tennis courts (2 indoors); Wi-Fi. *In room:* A/C, TV, hair dryer.

SOUTH OF LA FORTUNA

In addition to the places listed below, **Finca Luna Nueva Lodge** ★(http://finca lunanuevalodge.com; ℂ **2468-4006**) is a fascinating sustainable farm and tourism project, and proud local advocate for the international "Slow Foods" movement.

Chachagua Rainforest Hotel & Hacienda ★   Sitting on 100 hectares (247 acres) of lush land, about half of which is primary rainforest, this long-standing jungle lodge has recently gotten a major makeover. Rooms now are quite cozy, with lots of space, dark-stained hardwoods, and tasteful decor. You'll pay a bit more for air-conditioning and televisions, but even the fan-equipped "rainforest bungalows" are quite comfortable. Mountain biking, horseback riding and rain-forest hiking are all offered on-site, and a host of other tours and activities are available nearby.

The tiny village of Chachagua is located 10km (6 miles) south of La For-tuna, on the main road to San Ramon. The hotel is located another 2km (1¼ miles) up a well-marked dirt road from the town.

Chachagua, Alajuela. www.chachaguarainforesthotel.com. ℂ **2468-1010.** Fax 2468-1020. 30 units. $110–$185 double. Rates include continental breakfast. AE, DC, MC, V. **Amenities:** Restaurant; bar; large outdoor pool; small spa; Wi-Fi. *In room:* No phone.

El Silencio Lodge & Spa ★★   Built and run by the folks behind Punta Islita (p. 285), this luxurious lodge is a small collection of plush individual cabins, on a hillside in an isolated mountain setting. Each room features a king-size bed with luscious bedding, a modern marble bathroom, and private outdoor Jacuzzi. The spa offers a range of excellent treatments, and the restaurant specializes in healthy spa cooking—no red meat is served. Hiking around the grounds will take you through their organic gardens, and a relatively easy loop trail passes by three nearby waterfalls. Day tours to Sarchí, Puerto Viejo de Sarapiquí, and Arenal/La Fortuna are all offered. The rooms do not have televisions, but the main lodge has a lounge area with a large plasma-screen set and modest DVD library. This place was granted "5 Leaves" by the CST Sustainable Tourism program.

To reach El Silencio, you must first get to the town of Sarchí. From the Pali supermarket in the center of town, head north and follow the signs. El Silencio is approximately 22km (13 miles) outside of Sarchí.

Bajos del Toro, Alajuela. www.elsilenciolodge.com. ☎ **2761-0301.** Fax 2232-0302. 16 units. $480 double. Rates include all meals, nonalcoholic drinks, taxes, and 1 daily hike. AE, DC, MC, V. **Amenities:** Restaurant; bar; small spa; Wi-Fi. *In room:* Hair dryer, minibar.

Villa Blanca Cloud Forest & Spa ★★   This plush mountain-retreat hotel consists of a series of Tico-style casitas surrounded by 800 hectares (1,976 acres) of farm and forest. Each casita is built of adobe and has tile floors, open beamed ceilings, and whitewashed walls. Inside you'll find a fireplace in one corner, comfortable hardwood chairs, and either one queen-size or two twin beds covered with colorful bedspreads. The deluxe units and suites have a separate sitting area with a fold-out couch and bathrooms with a whirlpool bathtub and a separate shower. In many rooms, the bathroom tubs look out through a wall of windows onto lush gardens. Some have private patios. Just outside are 11km (6.75 miles) of trails through the **Los Angeles Cloud Forest Reserve.** You can also rent horses or take an adventurous swing through the canopy on a canopy tour here. The hotel is a member of the "Green Hotels of Costa Rica" and was granted "5 Leaves" by the CST Sustainable Tourism program.

If you're driving, head west out of San José to San Ramón and then head north, following the signs to Villa Blanca. Or you can take a public bus from San José to San Ramón and then take a taxi for around $20.

San Ramón, Alajuela. www.villablanca-costarica.com. ☎ **2461-0300.** Fax 2461-0302. 34 units. $170 double; $192 deluxe; $215 suite. Rates include buffet breakfast. AE, DC, MC, V. **Amenities:** Restaurant; bar; small spa; Wi-Fi. *In room:* Stocked minifridge.

NORTH OF LA FORTUNA

Caño Negro Natural Lodge ★   This small nature lodge is the best option in the tiny village of Caño Negro, and it's near the canals and lagoons. If you really want to visit the Caño Negro Wildlife Refuge, either for bird-watching and wildlife viewing or for fishing, this is a good choice. The hotel has spacious grounds full of flowering plants, tropical palms, and fruit trees. The rooms, housed in a series of duplex buildings, are all simple but roomy, clean, and comfortable, with much needed air-conditioning and tasteful decor. The hotel is proud of its small carbon footprint and contributions to local conservation and community development efforts. To get here, drive toward Los Chiles; several kilometers before Los Chiles, you'll see signs for this hotel and the wildlife refuge. From here, it's 18km (11 miles) on a flat dirt road to the village, refuge, and hotel.

Caño Negro. www.canonegrolodge.com. ☎ **2265-3302** for reservations in San José, or 2471-1426 direct to the lodge. Fax 2265-4310. 42 units. $105 double. Rates include continental breakfast. AE, MC, V. **Amenities:** Restaurant; bar; midsize outdoor pool. *In room:* A/C.

A REALLY REMOTE NATURE LODGE

This is a very remote region, right along the San Carlos river, near the Nicaraguan border. The roads up here are rough and poorly maintained. In addition to the place listed below, **Manquenque Ecolodge ★** (www.maquenqueecolodge. com; ☎ **2479-7785**) is a great new option for getting to see the green macaw in the wild and getting to know this area.

Tip: To get here, you head first to Pital and then continue on dirt roads to the town of Boca Tapada. It's also possible, albeit difficult, to get here on public transportation (ask your lodge directions), or you can arrange for the lodge to handle your transportation from San José or La Fortuna (for a cost). Since anyone with four-wheel-drive can make the trip here independently, though, you're best off driving on your own.

La Laguna del Lagarto Lodge   This lodge is named after the two man-made lagoons that sit below the main resort buildings. Canoes are available for paddling around these and several other nearby jungle waterways. The lodge has more than 10km (6.25 miles) of well-maintained hiking trails, and offers trips on the San Carlos River, as well as horseback-riding tours. More than 380 species of birds have been spotted here, and the hotel is involved in efforts to preserve the rare green macaw, which is frequently sighted in the area. The accommodations are rustic yet comfortable. Most rooms open onto a balcony or veranda with sitting chairs and hammocks. In addition to the surrounding rainforest, the lodge sits on a small pepper plantation and has lands planted with heart of palm, pineapple, and other tropical fruits and vegetables.

6km (3¾ miles) north of Boca Tapada. www.lagarto-lodge-costa-rica.com. © **2289-8163.** Fax 2289-5295. 20 units. $68 double. AE, MC, V. **Amenities:** Restaurant; bar. *In room:* No phone.

ALONG THE SHORES OF LAKE ARENAL ★

200km (124 miles) NW of San José; 20km (12 miles) NW of Monteverde; 70km (43 miles) SE of Liberia

Despite its many charms, this remains one of the least-developed tourism regions in Costa Rica. Lake Arenal, the largest lake in Costa Rica, is the centerpiece here. A long beautiful lake, it is surrounded by rolling hills that are partly pastured and partly forested. Loads of activities and adventures are available both on the lake and in the hills and forests around it. While the towns of Tilarán and Nuevo Arenal remain quiet rural communities, several excellent hotels spread out along the shores of the lake.

Locals here used to curse the winds, which often come blasting across this end of the lake at 60 knots or greater. However, since the first sailboarders caught wind of Lake Arenal's combination of warm, fresh water, steady blows, and spectacular scenery, things have been changing quickly. Even if you aren't a fanatical sailboarder, you might enjoy hanging out by the lake, hiking in the nearby forests, riding a mountain bike on dirt farm roads and one-track trails, and catching glimpses of Arenal Volcano.

The lake's other claim to fame is its rainbow-bass fishing. These fighting fish are known in Central America as *guapote* and are large members of the cichlid family. Their sharp teeth and fighting nature make them a real challenge.

Essentials

GETTING THERE & DEPARTING   By Car: From San José, you can either take the Interamerican Highway (CR1) north all the way from San José to Cañas, or

HOTELS

Ceiba Tree Lodge **14**
Chalet Nicholas **9**
Hotel Tilawa **3**
La Mansion Inn Arenal **15**
Lucky Bug B&B **11**
Mystica **5**
Rock River Lodge **7**
Villa Decary **13**

RETAURANTS

Cabinas Mary **1**
Gingerbread **12**
Hotel La Carreta **1**
Longhorn Bar & Grill **2**
Mystica **5**
Restaurante Lajas **10**
Tom's Pan German Bakery **10**
Willy's Caballo Negro **11**

ATTRACTIONS

Tico Wind **6**
Tilawa Windsurfing Center **4**

SHOPPING

Casa Delagua **8**
Lucky Bug Gallery **11**

first head west out of San José on the San José–Caldera Highway (CR27). When you reach Caldera, follow the signs to Puntarenas and the Interamerican Highway (CR1). You will actually follow signs for Liberia and San José, which are, in fact, leading you to the unmarked entrance to CR1. This road (CR23) ends when it hits the Interamerican Highway. You'll want to pass under the bridge and follow the on-ramp which will put you on the highway heading north. This latter route is a faster and flatter drive, with no windy mountain switchbacks to contend with. In Cañas, turn east on CR142 toward Tilarán. The drive takes 3 to 4 hours. If you're continuing on to Nuevo Arenal, follow the signs in town, which will put you on the road that skirts the shore of the lake. Nuevo Arenal is about a half-hour drive from Tilarán. You can also drive here from La Fortuna, along a scenic road that winds around the lake. From La Fortuna, it's approximately 1 hour to Nuevo Arenal and 1½ hours to Tilarán.

By Bus: Transportes Tilarán buses (© **2258-5792** in San José, 2695-5611 in Tilarán) leave San José for Tilarán daily at 7:30 and 9:30am and 12:45, 3:45, and 6:30pm from Calle 20 and Avenida 3. The trip lasts from 4 to 5½ hours, depending on road conditions; the fare is C3,320.

Lake Arenal and Arenal Volcano.

Morning and afternoon buses connect **Puntarenas** to Tilarán. The ride takes about 3 hours; the fare is $3. (For details on getting to Puntarenas, see "Puntarenas," in chapter 8.) The daily bus from **Monteverde** (Santa Elena) leaves at 7am. The fare for the 2-hour trip is $2.30. Buses from **La Fortuna** leave for Tilarán daily at 8am and 4:30pm, returning at 7am and 12:30pm. The trip takes around 2 to 3 hours; the fare is C1,375.

Direct buses to San José leave from Tilarán daily at 5, 7, and 9:30am and 2 and 5pm. Buses to Puntarenas leave at 6am and 1pm daily. The bus to Santa Elena (Monteverde) leaves daily at 12:30pm. Buses also leave regularly for Cañas, and can be caught heading north or south along the Interamerican Highway.

ORIENTATION & FAST FACTS Tilarán is about 5km (3 miles) from Lake Arenal. All roads into town lead to the central park, which is Tilarán's main point of reference for addresses. If you need to exchange money, check at one of the hotels listed here, or go to the Banco Nacional. If you need a taxi to get to a lodge on Lake Arenal, call **Taxis Unidos Tilarán** (© **2695-5324**). For a taxi in Nuevo Arenal, call **Taxis Nuevo Arenal** (© **2694-4415**).

What to See & Do

ARTS, CRAFTS & DOWN-HOME COOKING About halfway between Nuevo Arenal and Tilarán is **Casa Delagua** ★ (© **2692-2101**), the studio, gallery, and coffee shop of Costa Rican artist Juan Carlos Ruiz. These folks also have a good used book and DVD collection on sale.

The **Lucky Bug Gallery** ★★ is an excellent roadside arts-and-crafts and souvenir shop, attached to the Lucky Bug Bed & Breakfast (p. 323). This place features a host of functional and decorative pieces produced locally.

FISHING   Ask at your hotel if you want to try your hand at fishing for *guapote*. A half-day fishing trip should cost around $150 to $250 per boat, and a full day goes for around $250 to $500. The boats used will usually accommodate up to three people fishing. If you're interested in fishing, I recommend you check in with **Captain Ron** at **Arenal Fishing Tours** (✆ **2694-4678;** www.arenalfishing.com).

HORSEBACK RIDING   Any of the hotels in the area can hook you up with a horseback-riding tour for around $10 to $20 per hour.

SWIMMING & HIKING   Up above Lake Arenal on the far side of the lake from Tilarán, you'll find the beautiful little heart-shape **Lake Coter.** This lake is surrounded by forest and has good swimming. (UFO watchers also claim that this is a popular pit stop for extraterrestrials.) A taxi to Lake Coter costs around C15,000.

If you feel like strapping on your boots, some hiking trails are on the far side of Lake Arenal, near the smaller Lake Coter.

WINDSURFING & KITEBOARDING   If you want to try windsurfing, **Tilawa Windsurfing Center** (✆ **2695-5050;** www.windsurfcostarica.com) rents equipment at its facilities on one of the lake's few accessible beaches, about 8km (5 miles) from Tilarán on the road along the west end of the lake. Boards rent for around $50 per day, and lessons are available. These folks also offer classes and rentals for the high-octane sport of kiteboarding. Another option that is especially popular with serious sail- and kiteboarders is **Tico Wind** (✆ **2692-2002;** www.ticowind.com), which sets up shop on

A fisherman with a guapote at Lake Arenal.

Windsurfing on Lake Arenal.

the shores of the lake each year from December 1 to the end of April, when the winds blow. Rates run around $85 per day, including lunch, with multiday packages available. If you can't reach them via the phone or website, the folks at **Mystica** (see "Where to Stay," below) can hook you up.

WAKEBOARDING Lake Arenal is a big lake with plenty of calm quiet corners to practice wakeboarding. If you're interested in lessons, or just a reliable pull on a wakeboard or water skis, contact **Fly Zone** (✆ **8339-5876;** www.flyzone-cr.com). Simple pulls behind their specialized boat run around $95 per hour, including boards, skis, and any other necessary gear.

Where to Stay

In addition to the places listed below, the **Ceiba Tree Lodge** (www.ceibatree-lodge.com; ✆ 2692-8050) is a small, simple lodge with a beautiful view and lovely gardens on a hill above the lake. **La Mansion Inn Arenal** (www.lamansionarenal.com; ✆ 2692-8018) is an upscale option with a great setting and cozy cabins.

MODERATE

Chalet Nicholas 🐾 This friendly American-owned bed-and-breakfast is 2.5km (1½ miles) west of Nuevo Arenal and sits on a hill above the road. This converted home is set on 6 hectares (15 acres) and has pretty flower gardens, an organic vegetable garden, and an orchid garden. Behind the property are acres of forest through which you can hike in search of birds, orchids, butterflies, and other tropical beauties. The upstairs loft room is the largest unit, with its own private deck. All three rooms are nonsmoking and have a view of Arenal Volcano in the distance. Owners John and Catherine Nicholas go out of their way to make their guests feel at home, although their three Great Danes might intimidate you when you first drive up. All around, it's a really good deal. Three-hour horseback riding tours are offered for just $25 per person.

Tilarán. www.chaletnicholas.com. ✆ **2694-4041.** 3 units. $68 double. Rates include full breakfast. No credit cards. *In room:* No phone.

Hotel Tilawa ☺ Built to resemble the Palace of Knossos on the island of Crete, the Hotel Tilawa sits high on the slopes above the lake and has a sweeping

9

THE NORTHERN ZONE | Along the Shores of Lake Arenal

vista down to the water. It's primarily a windsurfers' and kiteboarders' hangout, and often has an untended or sloppy feel, particularly in terms of service and upkeep. Unusual colors and antique paint effects give the hotel a weathered look; inside are murals and other artistic paint treatments. Rooms have dyed cement floors, Guatemalan bedspreads, and big windows. Some have kitchenettes. Tilawa can arrange windsurfing, kiteboarding, mountain-biking, horseback-riding, and fishing trips. The hotel even has a small skate park for radical skateboarders and BMX freestyle bikers, which makes this a good place to bring teenagers.

On the road btw. Tilarán and Nuevo Arenal. www.tilawa.com. ☎ **2695-5050.** 22 units. $70–$80 double; $110 apt. No credit cards. **Amenities:** Restaurant; bar; Jacuzzi; outdoor pool; small spa; unlit outdoor tennis court; skateboard park; sailboard and kiteboard rental. *In room:* No phone, Wi-Fi.

Lucky Bug Bed & Breakfast ★　An outgrowth of this family's successful restaurant, gallery, and gift shop, this hotel's rooms are artistic and cheery. Each features an animal motif, from the handmade wood and metal beds, to the hand-painted bathroom tiles, to the individual artworks and wall hangings. The Butterfly and Frog rooms are the best, and each comes with a small balcony. Most have one king-size bed. The largest room is the one ground-floor unit, although I prefer those on the second floor. The rooms are located just above the small lake that's behind the restaurant and gift shop. This lake is stocked with *guapote*, which you can fish for, and, if you're lucky, have cooked up for you at the restaurant.

Nuevo Arenal. www.luckybugcr.net. ☎ **2694-4515.** 5 units. $89–$129 double. Rates include full breakfast. MC, V. **Amenities:** Restaurant; Wi-Fi. *In room:* No phone.

Mystica ★ ✦　Set on a high hill above Lake Arenal (about midway btw. Nuevo Arenal and Tilarán), this establishment has simple but spacious and cozy rooms. The painted cement floors are kept immaculate, and the rooms get good ventilation from their large windows. All rooms open onto a long and broad shared veranda with a great view of the lake. The one private villa has a kitchenette, fireplace, and beautiful open deck area. The owners can help you book a wide range of adventures and tours. The hotel has a large open-air yoga platform and sometimes hosts retreats. Perhaps the star attraction here is the hotel's excellent little Italian restaurant and pizzeria by the same name (p. 324).

On the road btw. Tilarán and Nuevo Arenal. www.mysticaretreat.com. ☎ **2692-1001.** Fax 2692-2097. 7 units. $100 double; $145 villa. Rates include continental breakfast. MC, V. **Amenities:** Restaurant; bar. *In room:* No phone.

Villa Decary ★ ♟　Named after a French explorer (and a rare palm species that he discovered and named), this small bed-and-breakfast is nestled on a hill above Lake Arenal, midway between the town of Nuevo Arenal and the Arenal Botanical Gardens. Each room comes with one queen-size and one twin bed, large picture windows, and a spacious balcony with a lake view. The rooms get plenty of light, and the bright Guatemalan bedspreads and white-tile floors create a vibrant look. The separate casitas have full kitchens and even better views of the lake from their slightly higher perches. Breakfasts are extravagant, with a steady stream of fresh fruits and juice; strong coffee; homemade pancakes, waffles, or muffins; and usually an excellent omelet or soufflé. The hotel grounds are great for bird-watching and howler monkeys are common guests here as well.

Nuevo Arenal. www.villadecary.com. ✆ **800/556-0505** in the U.S. and Canada, or 2694-4330 in Costa Rica. 5 units, 3 casitas. $99 double; $129–$149 casita for 2. Rates include full breakfast. Extra person $15. MC, V. **Amenities:** Wi-Fi. *In room:* No phone.

INEXPENSIVE

Rock River Lodge ★ ✦   Set high on a grassy hill above the lake, this place has fabulous lake and sunset views. Recently re-opened after a 3-year hiatus, the hotel is under new management. Midsize rooms are housed in a long, low wooden building set on stilts. The bungalows, which are farther up the hill, offer more privacy and space and have small sculpted bathtubs in larger bathrooms. It's a long walk down to the lake (not to mention the walk back up), so a car is recommended.

On the road btw. Tilarán and Nuevo Arenal. www.rockriverlodgecr.com. ✆ **2692-1180.** 6 units, 8 bungalows. $30–$35 double; $60–$65 bungalow. Rates include full breakfast. AE, MC, V. **Amenities:** Restaurant; bar; Wi-Fi. *In room:* No phone.

Where to Eat

Numerous inexpensive places to eat are in the town of Tilarán, including the restaurant at **Hotel La Carreta** (✆ 2695-6593; www.lacarretacr.com) and **Cabinas Mary** (✆ 2695-5479). Just outside of town, on the road to Nuevo Arenal, the **Longhorn Bar & Grill ★** (✆ 2695-5663; http://site. longhornbarandgrill.com) is a very popular spot, that's part steakhouse, part sports bar.

In Nuevo Arenal, try the pizzas and pastas at **Restaurante Lajas** (✆ 2694-4780). For breakfast, snacks, lunch, and fresh-baked goods, check out **Tom's Pan German Bakery** (✆ 2694-4547; www.tomspan.com). The lakeside **Gingerbread ★** (✆ 2694-0039; www.gingerbreadarenal.com) has an Israeli chef-owner who is turning out top-notch fusion fare in a lively, welcoming environment, on the outskirts of Nuevo Arenal.

Mystica ★ ITALIAN/PIZZA   The restaurant in this Italian-run hotel has a wonderful setting high on a hill overlooking the lake. The most striking features, aside from the view, are the large open fireplace on one end and, on the other, the large brick oven, in the shape of a small cottage, which turns out pizzas. The pastas and delicious main dishes are authentically northern Italian. Whenever possible, Mystica uses fresh ingredients from its own garden.

On the road btw. Tilarán and Nuevo Arenal. ✆ **2692-1001.** www.mysticacostarica.com. Main courses C4,900–C6,000. MC, V. Daily noon–9pm.

Willy's Caballo Negro ★ INTERNATIONAL/VEGETARIAN   The German owners of this attractive little roadside cafe serve up two different types of schnitzel, bratwurst, veal *cordon bleu,* and a host of other old-world dishes. However, vegetarians are well served here, and will find several tasty and filling options on the menu, including stuffed potatoes, garden burgers, and eggplant Parmesan. Wooden tables are set around the edges of the round dining room, with a high peaked roof. Candles and creative lighting give the place a cozy and warm feel. There's a small, picturesque lake behind the restaurant, a small B&B

(Lucky Bug Bed & Breakfast; p. 323), and the very interesting Lucky Bug Gallery (p. 321), run by the owner's triplet daughters.

Nuevo Arenal (about 3km/1¾ miles out of town on the road to Tilarán). ✆ **2694-4515.** Main courses $8–$15. MC, V. Dinner by reservation only. Daily 7am–5pm.

MONTEVERDE ★★

167km (104 miles) NW of San José; 82km (51 miles) NW of Puntarenas

Monteverde, which translates as "Green Mountain," is one of world's first and finest ecotourism destinations. The mist enshrouded and marvelous Monteverde Cloud Forest Biological Reserve and extensive network of neighboring private reserves are rich and rewarding. Bird-watchers flock here for a chance to spot the myth-inspiring Resplendent Quetzal, scientists study its bountiful biodiversity, and a bevy of attractions and adventures await everyone else.

Active Pursuits   **Hike** the area's cloud forest reserves on foot, but also try riding the trails and dirt roads on **horseback** or an **ATV.** For real adrenaline junkies, there are several **zip-line canopy tours** and an even wetter and wilder **canyoning** adventure. The cloud forest's sounds are more palpable and its animal residents much more active when experienced on a fascinating **night tour.**

Flora & Fauna   Cloud forests are formed as moist air swept in off the ocean is forced upward by mountain slopes, and, cooling as it rises, forms clouds. Branches of huge trees are draped thick with epiphytic **orchids, ferns,** and **bromeliads,** which in turn host an incredibly diverse population of wildlife. Beyond the **Resplendent Quetzal,** the Monteverde area boasts more than 2,500 species of plants, 450 types of **orchids,** 400 species of **birds,** and 100 species of **mammals.**

Monteverde Cloud Forest Biological Reserve.

Tours   The high mountain terrain here produces some of Costa Rica's best coffee, and you can tour a local **coffee plantation,** or see how sugar cane is harvested and processed on the **El Trapiche tour.** In the town of Santa Elena, you'll want to visit the **Orchid Garden, Frog Pond,** and **World of Insects,** while on the road to the reserve, the **Bat Jungle** and **Butterfly Garden** are well worth the price of admission.

Essentials

GETTING THERE & DEPARTING   By Car: The principal access road to Monteverde and Santa Elena is located along the Interamerican Highway (CR1); about 20km (12 miles) north of the exit for Puntarenas is a marked turnoff for Sardinal, Santa Elena, and Monteverde. From this turnoff, the road is paved for 15km (9½ miles), to just beyond the tiny town of Guacimal. From here, it's another 20km (12 miles) to Santa Elena.

Today's Forecast . . . Misty & Cool

The climatic conditions that make Monteverde such a biological hot spot can leave many tourists feeling chilled to the bone. More than a few visitors are unprepared for a cool, windy, and wet stay in the middle of their tropical vacation, and can find Monteverde a bit inhospitable, especially from August through November.

From San José, you can either take the Interamerican Highway (CR1) north all the way to the turnoff, or first head west out of San José on the San José–Caldera Highway (CR27). When you reach Caldera, follow the signs to Puntarenas and the Interamerican Highway (CR1). You will actually follow signs for Liberia and San José, which are, in fact, leading you to the unmarked entrance to CR1. This road

An ATV on the road between Monteverde and Santa Elena.

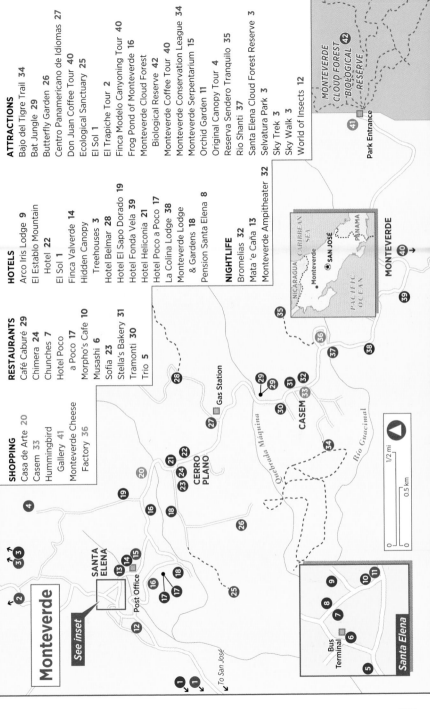

Monteverde

See inset

To San José

ATTRACTIONS
Bajo del Tigre Trail **34**
Bat Jungle **29**
Butterfly Garden **26**
Centro Panamericano de Idiomas **27**
Don Juan Coffee Tour **40**
Ecological Sanctuary **25**
El Sol **1**
El Trapiche Tour **2**
Finca Modelo Canyoning Tour **40**
Frog Pond of Monteverde **16**
Monteverde Cloud Forest Biological Reserve **42**
Monteverde Coffee Tour **40**
Monteverde Conservation League **34**
Monteverde Serpentarium **15**
Orchid Garden **11**
Original Canopy Tour **4**
Reserva Sendero Tranquilo **35**
Rio Shanti **37**
Santa Elena Cloud Forest Reserve **3**
Selvatura Park **3**
Sky Trek **3**
Sky Walk **3**
World of Insects **12**

HOTELS
Arco Iris Lodge **9**
El Establo Mountain Hotel **22**
El Sol **1**
Finca Valverde **14**
Hidden Canopy Treehouses **3**
Hotel Belmar **28**
Hotel El Sapo Dorado **19**
Hotel Fonda Vela **39**
Hotel Heliconia **21**
Hotel Poco a Poco **17**
La Colina Lodge **38**
Monteverde Lodge & Gardens **18**
Pension Santa Elena **8**

NIGHTLIFE
Bromelias **32**
Mata 'e Caña **13**
Monteverde Ampitheater **32**

SHOPPING
Casa de Arte **20**
Casem **33**
Hummingbird Gallery **41**
Monteverde Cheese Factory **36**

RESTAURANTS
Café Caburé **29**
Chimera **24**
Chunches **7**
Hotel Poco a Poco **17**
Morpho's Cafe **10**
Musashi **6**
Sofia **23**
Stella's Bakery **31**
Tramonti **30**
Trio **5**

MONTEVERDE CLOUD FOREST BIOLOGICAL RESERVE

Park Entrance

SANTA ELENA
Post Office

CERRO PLANO

Gas Station

Quebrada Máquina

CASEM

Rio Guacimal

Santa Elena

Bus Terminal

NICARAGUA
CARIBBEAN SEA
PANAMA
Monteverde
★ SAN JOSÉ
PACIFIC OCEAN
MONTEVERDE

N

0   0.5 km
0   1/2 mi

(CR23) ends when it hits the Interamerican Highway. You'll want to pass under the bridge and follow the on-ramp which will put you on the highway heading north. This latter route is a faster and flatter drive.

Another access road to Santa Elena is found just south of the Río Lagarto Bridge. This turnoff is the first you will come to if driving from Liberia. From the Río Lagarto turnoff, it's 38km (24 miles) to Santa Elena, and the road is unpaved the entire way.

Once you arrive, the roads in and around Santa Elena are paved, including all the way to Cerro Plano, and about halfway to the Cloud Forest Preserve.

To drive from Monteverde to La Fortuna, head out of Santa Elena toward Sky Trek and the Santa Elena Cloud Forest Reserve. Follow signs for Tilarán, which are posted at most of the critical intersections. If there's no sign, stick to the most well-worn road. This is a rough dirt road, all the way to Tilarán. From Tilarán, you have mostly well-marked and okay paved roads around the lake, passing first through Nuevo Arenal, and then over the dam and through Tabacón, before reaching La Fortuna.

By Bus: Transmonteverde express buses (☏ **2222-3854** in San José, or 2645-5159 in Santa Elena) leave San José daily at 6:30am and 2:30pm from Calle 12 between avenidas 7 and 9. The trip takes around 4 hours; the fare is C2,350. Buses arrive at and depart from Santa Elena. If you're staying at one of the hotels or lodges toward the reserve, arrange pickup if possible, or take a taxi or local bus.

Three daily Transmonteverde buses depart Puntarenas for Santa Elena at 7:50am, and 1:50 and 2:15pm. The bus stop in Puntarenas is across the street from the main bus station. The fare for the 2½-hour trip is C1,300. A daily bus from Tilarán (Lake Arenal) leaves at 12:30pm. Trip duration, believe it or not, is 2 hours (for a 40km/25-mile trip); the fare is C1,150. The express bus departs for San José daily at 6:30am and 2:30pm. The buses from Santa Elena to Puntarenas leave daily at 4:30 and 6am and 3pm.

Gray Line (☏ **2220-2126**; www.graylinecostarica.com) has a daily bus that leaves San José for Monteverde at 8am. **Interbus** (☏ **2283-5573**; www.interbusonline.com) has two daily buses that leave San José for Monteverde at 7:30am and 2:30pm. Both of the above companies charge $40, and will pick you up and drop you off at most San José and Monteverde area hotels.

 Alternative Transport

You can travel between Monteverde and La Fortuna by boat and taxi, or on a combination boat, horseback, and taxi trip. See "Boats, Horses & Taxis," on p. 298, for details. Any of the trips described there can be done in the reverse direction departing from Monteverde. Most hotels and **Desafío Expeditions** (☏ **2645-5874**; www.monteverdetours. com) can arrange this trip for you. Desafío also offers multiday hikes from Monteverde to Arenal; you spend the night in rustic research facilities inside the Bosque Eterno de los Niños.

Peace, Love & Ecotourism

Monteverde was settled in 1951 by Quakers from the United States who wanted to leave behind the fear of war, as well as their obligation to support continued militarism through paying U.S. taxes. They chose Costa Rica, a country that had abolished its army a few years earlier, in 1948. Although Monteverde's founders came here to farm the land, they wisely recognized the need to preserve the rare cloud forest that covered the mountain slopes above their fields, and to that end, they dedicated the largest adjacent tract of cloud forest as the Monteverde Cloud Forest Biological Reserve.

If you want an in-depth look into the lives and history of the local Quaker community, try to pick up a copy of the *Monteverde Jubilee Family Album.* Published in 2001 by the Monteverde Association of Friends, this collection of oral histories and photographs is 260 pages of local lore and memoirs. It's very simply bound and printed but well worth the $20 price.

If you're heading to Manuel Antonio, take the Santa Elena/Puntarenas bus and transfer in Puntarenas. To reach Liberia, take any bus down the mountain and get off as soon as you hit the Interamerican Highway. You can then flag down a bus bound for Liberia (almost any bus heading north). The Santa Elena/Tilarán bus leaves daily at 7am. Both **Gray Line** and **Interbus** offer routes with connections to most major destinations in Costa Rica.

GETTING AROUND Some six buses daily connect the town of Santa Elena and the Monteverde Cloud Forest Biological Reserve. The first bus leaves Santa Elena for the reserve at 6:15am and the last bus from the reserve leaves there at 4pm. The fare is around C600. Periodic van transportation also runs between the town of Santa Elena and the Santa Elena Cloud Forest Reserve. Ask around town and you should be able to find the current schedule and book a ride for around $2 per person. A **taxi** (✆ **2645-6969** or 2645-6666) between Santa Elena and either the Monteverde Reserve or the Santa Elena Cloud Forest Reserve costs around C3,500 for up to four people. Count on paying between C3,000 and C3,500 for the ride from Santa Elena to your lodge in Monteverde. Finally, several places around town rent **ATVs,** or all-terrain vehicles, for around $50 to $75 per day. Hourly rates and guided tours are also available. If this is up your alley, try **Aventura** (✆ **2645-6959;** www.cienporcientoaventura.com).

ORIENTATION The tiny town of **Santa Elena** is the gateway to Monteverde and the Monteverde Cloud Forest Biological Reserve, which is located 6km (3¾ miles) outside of town along a windy road that dead-ends at the reserve entrance. As you approach Santa Elena, take the right fork in the road if you're heading directly to Monteverde. If you continue straight, you'll come into the little town center of tiny **Santa Elena,** which has a bus stop, a health clinic, a bank, a supermarket and a few general stores, and a collection of simple restaurants, budget hotels, souvenir shops, and tour offices. Heading just out of town, toward Monteverde, is a small strip mall with a large and prominent Megasuper supermarket. **Monteverde,** on the other hand, is not a village in the traditional sense of the word. There's no center of town—only dirt lanes leading off from the main road to various farms. This main road has signs for all the hotels and restaurants mentioned here, and it dead-ends at the reserve entrance.

For a map of the Cloud Forest Reserve, see the inside front cover of this book.

FAST FACTS   The telephone number for the **local clinic** is ✆ **2645-5076;** for the **Red Cross,** ✆ **2645-6128;** and for the **local police,** ✆ **911** or 2645-6248. The **Farmacia Monteverde** (✆ **2449-5495**) is right downtown. A **Banco Nacional** (✆ **2645-5610**) is in downtown Santa Elena, and a **Coopemex** (✆ **2645-6948**) is on the road out to Santa Elena, near Finca Valverde; both have 24-hour ATMs.

Tip: Fill up on gas before heading up to Monteverde, as the local gas station has been closed for some years. A large service station is right at the main turnoff for Monteverde from the Interamerican Highway (CR1).

Exploring the Monteverde Cloud Forest Biological Reserve ★★★

The **Monteverde Cloud Forest Biological Reserve** (✆ **2645-5122;** www. cct.or.cr) is one of the most developed and well-maintained natural attractions in Costa Rica. The trails are clearly marked, regularly traveled, and generally gentle in terms of ascents and descents. The cloud forest here is lush and largely untouched. Still, keep in mind that most of the birds and mammals are rare, elusive, and nocturnal. Moreover, to all but the most trained of eyes, those thousands of exotic ferns, orchids, and bromeliads tend to blend into one large mass of indistinguishable green. However, with a guide hired through your hotel, or on one of the reserve's official guided 2- to 3-hour hikes, you can see and learn far

A hanging bridge in a Monteverde-area cloud forest.

A SELF-GUIDED hike THROUGH THE RESERVE

I know I strongly recommend going on a guided tour, but if you're intent on exploring the reserve on your own, or heading back for more, I suggest starting off on the **Sendero El Río (River Trail)** ★★. This trail, which heads north from the reserve office, puts you immediately in the midst of dense primary cloud forest, where heavy layers of mosses, bromeliads, and epiphytes cover every branch and trunk. This very first section of trail is a prime location for spotting a Resplendent Quetzal.

After 15 or 20 minutes, you'll come to a little marked spur leading down to a *catarata*, or waterfall. This diminutive fall fills a small, pristine pond and is quite picturesque, but if you fail in your attempts to capture its beauty, look for its image emblazoned on postcards at souvenir stores all around the area. The entire trek to the waterfall should take you an hour or so.

From the waterfall, turn around and retrace your steps along the River Trail until you come to a fork and the **Sendero Tosi (Tosi Trail).** Follow this shortcut, which leads through varied terrain, back to the reserve entrance.

Once you've got the River Trail and waterfall under your belt, I recommend a slightly more strenuous hike to a lookout atop the Continental Divide. The **Sendero Bosque Nuboso (Cloud Forest Trail)** ★ heads east from the reserve entrance. As its name implies, the trail leads through thick, virgin cloud forest. Keep your eyes open for any number of bird and mammal species, including toucans, trogans, honeycreepers, and howler monkeys. Some great specimens of massive strangler fig trees are on the trail. These trees start as parasitic vines and eventually engulf their host tree. After 1.9km (1.2 miles), you will reach the Continental Divide. Despite the sound of this, there's only a modest elevation gain of some 65m (213 ft.).

A couple of lookout points on the Divide are through clearings in the forest, but the best is **La Ventana (The Window)** ★, just beyond the end of this trail and reached via a short spur trail. Here you'll find a broad, elevated wooden deck with panoramic views. Be forewarned: It's often misty and quite windy up here.

On the way back, take the 2km (1.2-mile) **Sendero Camino (Road Trail).** As its name implies, much of this trail was once used as a rough all-terrain road. Since it is wide and open in many places, this trail is particularly good for birdwatching. About halfway along, you'll want to take a brief detour to a **suspended bridge** ★. Some 100m (330-ft.) long, this midforest bridge gives you a bird's-eye view of the forest canopy. The entire loop should take around 3 hours.

more than you could on your own. At $17 per person, the reserve's tours might seem like a splurge, especially after you pay the entrance fee, but I strongly recommend that you go with a guide.

Perhaps the most famous resident of the cloud forests of Costa Rica is the quetzal, a robin-size bird with iridescent green wings and a ruby-red breast, which has become extremely rare due to habitat destruction. The male quetzal also has two long tail feathers that can reach nearly .6m (2 ft.) in length, making

Seeing the Forest for the Trees, Bromeliads, Monkeys, Hummingbirds . . .

Because the entrance fee to Monteverde is valid for a full day, I recommend taking an early-morning walk with a guide and then heading off on your own either directly after that hike or after lunch. A guide will certainly point out and explain a lot, but there's also much to be said for walking quietly through the forest on your own or in very small groups. This will also allow you to stray from the well-traveled paths in the park.

it one of the most spectacular birds on earth. The best time to see quetzals is early morning to midmorning, and the best months are February through April (mating season).

Other animals that have been seen in Monteverde, although sightings are extremely rare, include jaguars, ocelots, and tapirs. After the quetzal, Monteverde's most famous resident used to be the golden toad *(sapo dorado)*, a rare native species. However, the golden toad has disappeared from the forest and is feared extinct. Competing theories of the toad's demise include adverse effects of a natural drought cycle, the disappearing ozone layer, pesticides, and acid rain.

ADMISSION, HOURS & TOURS The reserve is open daily from 7am to 4pm, and the entrance fee is $17 for adults and $9 for students and children. Because only 220 people are allowed into the reserve at any one time, you might be forced to wait. Most hotels can reserve a guided walk and entrance to the reserve for the following day for you, or you can get tickets in advance directly at the reserve entrance.

Some of the trails can be very muddy, depending on the season, so ask about current conditions. Before venturing into the forest, have a look around the information center. Several guidebooks are available, as well as posters and postcards of some of the reserve's more famous animal inhabitants.

Night tours of the reserve leave every evening at 6:15pm. The cost is $17, including admission to the reserve, a 2-hour hike, and, most important, a guide with a high-powered searchlight. For an extra $3, they'll throw in round-trip transportation to and from your area hotel.

Santa Elena Cloud Forest Reserve.

What to See & Do outside the Reserve

BIRD-WATCHING & HIKING

You can also find ample bird-watching and hiking opportunities outside the reserve boundaries. Avoid the crowds at Monteverde by heading 5km (3 miles) north from the village of Santa Elena to the **Santa Elena Cloud Forest Reserve** ★★ (𝄐 **2645-5390;** www.reservasantaelena.org). This 310-hectare (765-acre) reserve has a maximum elevation of 1,680m (5,510 ft.), making it the highest cloud forest in the Monteverde area. There are 13km (8 miles) of hiking trails, as well as an information center. Because it borders the Monteverde Reserve, a similar richness of flora and fauna is found here, although quetzals are not nearly as common. The $14 entry fee at this reserve goes directly to support local schools. The reserve is open daily from 7am to 5pm. Three-hour guided tours are available for $15 per person, not including the entrance fee. (Call the number above to make a reservation for the tour.)

    Sky Walk ★★ (𝄐 **2645-5238;** www.skyadventures.travel) is a network of forest paths and suspension bridges that provides visitors with a view previously reserved for birds, monkeys, and the much more adventurous traveler. The bridges reach 39m (128 ft.) above the ground at their highest point, so acrophobia could be an issue. The Sky Walk and its sister attraction, **Sky Trek** (see "Canopy & Canyoning Tours," below), are about 3.5km (2¼ miles) outside the town of Santa Elena, on the road to the Santa Elena Cloud Forest Reserve. The Sky Walk is open daily from 7am to 4pm; admission is $30, which includes a knowledgeable guide. For $75 per person, you can do the Sky Trek canopy tour and then walk the trails and bridges of the Sky Walk. Reservations are recommended for the Sky Trek; round-trip transportation from Santa Elena is just $5 per person.

    To learn even more about Monteverde, stop in at the **Monteverde Conservation League** (𝄐 **2645-5003;** www.acmcr.org), which administers the 22,000-hectare (54,000-acre) private reserve **Bosque Eterno de Los Niños (Children's Eternal Forest),** as well as the Bajo del Tigre Trail. The Conservation League has an information center and small gift shop at the trail head/entrance to the Bajo del Tigre Trail. In addition to being a good source for information, it also sells books, T-shirts, and cards, and all proceeds go to purchase more land for the Bosque Eterno de Los Niños. The **Bajo del Tigre Trail** ★ is a 3.5km (2.3-mile) trail that's home to several different bird species not usually found within the reserve. You can take several different loops, lasting anywhere

---

 If Not Here, Where?

For many, the primary goal in visiting Monteverde is to glimpse the rare and elusive **quetzal,** a bird once revered by the pre-Columbian peoples of the Americas. However, if you just care about seeing a quetzal, you should also consider visiting other cloud forest areas. In particular, San Gerardo de Dota and Cerro de la Muerte areas are home to several specialty lodges (see "Cerro de la Muerte & San Gerardo de Dota: Where to See Quetzals in the Wild," in chapter 10), where you'll find far fewer crowds and often better chances of seeing the famed quetzal.

from 1 hour to several hours. The trail starts a little past the CASEM artisans' shop (see "Shopping," below) and is open daily from 8am to 4pm. Admission is $10 for adults and $7 for students. These folks also do a 2-hour night hike that departs at 5:30pm, and costs $20 per adult, and $17 per student. Children under 12 are free.

You can also go on guided 3-hour hikes at the **Reserva Sendero Tranquilo ★** (© **2645-5010;** www.sapodorado.com), run by the folks at the Sapo Dorado (p. 340) and which has 80 hectares (198 acres) of land, two-thirds of which is in virgin forest. This reserve is up the hill from the cheese factory (p. 339). Both day and night hikes are offered here, and the group size is always small. Prices run $25 for the 3- to 4-hour day tour, and $20 for the 2½-hour night tour.

Finally, you can walk the trails and grounds of the **Ecological Sanctuary ★** (© **2645-5869;** www.santuarioecologico.com), a family-run wildlife refuge and private reserve located down the Cerro Plano road. This place has four main trails through a variety of ecosystems, and wildlife viewing is often quite good. A couple of pretty waterfalls are off the trails. It's open daily from 7am to 5:30pm; admission is $10 for self-guided hiking on the trails; $25 during the day for a 2-hour guided tour; and $20 for the 2-hour guided night tour at 5:30pm.

CANOPY & CANYONING TOURS

Selvatura Park ★★ (© **2645-5929;** www.selvatura.com), located close to the Santa Elena Cloud Forest Reserve, is the best one-stop shop for various adventures and attractions in the area. In addition to an extensive canopy tour, with 13 cables connecting 15 platforms, they also have a network of trails and suspended bridges, a huge butterfly garden, a hummingbird garden, a snake exhibit, and a wonderful insect display and museum. Prices vary depending upon how much you want to see and do. Individually, the canopy tour costs $45; the walkways and bridges, $25; the snake and reptile exhibit, $12; and the butterfly garden and the insect museum, $12 each. Packages to combine the various exhibits are available, although it's definitely confusing, and somewhat annoying, to pick the perfect package. For $120, you get the run of the entire joint, including the tours, lunch, and round-trip transportation from your Monteverde hotel. It's open daily from 7am to 4:30pm.

Another popular option is offered by the folks at **Sky Trek ★★** (© **2645-5238;** www.skyadventures. travel), which is part of a large complex of aerial adventures and hiking trails. This is one of the more extensive canopy tours in the country, and begins with a cable car ride (or **Sky Tram**) up into the cloud forest, where their zipline canopy tour commences. This tour features 10 zip-line cables. The longest of these is some 770m (2,525 ft.) long, high above the forest floor. There are

A green iguana.

no rappel descents here, and you brake using the pulley system for friction. This tour costs $60.

One of the oldest canopy tours in the country is run by the **Original Canopy Tour ★** (© 2645-5243; www.canopytour.com). This is one of the more interesting canopy tours in Costa Rica because the initial ascent is made by climbing up the hollowed-out interior of a giant strangler fig. The tour has 13 platforms and one rappel. The 2- to 2½-hour tours run four times daily and cost $45 for adults, $35 for students, and $25 for children 11 and under.

Finally, if you want to add a bit more excitement, and definitely more water, to your adventure, you can try the **Finca Modelo Canyoning Tour** (© 2645-5581; www.familiabrenestours.com). This tour involves a mix of hiking and then rappelling down the face of a series of forest waterfalls. The tallest of these waterfalls is around 39m (130 ft.). You will get wet on this tour. The cost is $50.

The Monteverde area has a glut of canopy tours, and I can only recommend those mentioned above. Anybody in average physical condition can do any of the adventure tours in Monteverde, but they're not for the fainthearted or acrophobic. Try to book directly with the companies listed above or through your hotel. Beware of touts on the streets of Monteverde, who make a small commission and frequently try to steer tourists to the operator paying the highest percentage.

HORSEBACK RIDING

Monteverde has excellent terrain for horseback riding. **La Estrella Stables** (© 2645-5075) and **Sabine's Smiling Horses** (© 2645-6894; www.smiling horses.com) are the most established operators, offering guided rides for around $15 to $20 per hour. Horseback/boat trips link Monteverde/Santa Elena with La Fortuna (p. 298).

Another option is to set up a day tour and sauna at **El Sol ★** (© 2645-5838; www.elsolnuestro.com). Located about a 10-minute car ride down the mountain from Santa Elena, these folks take you on a roughly 3-hour ride either to San Luis or to an isolated little waterfall with an excellent swimming hole. After the ride back, you'll find the wood-burning traditional Swedish sauna all fired up, with a refreshing and beautiful little pool beside it. The half-day tour costs $60 per person, including lunch. El Sol also has two rustically luxurious private cabins ($95–$125 double), with excellent views.

OTHER ATTRACTIONS IN MONTEVERDE

It seems as if Monteverde has an exhibit or attraction dedicated to almost every type of tropical fauna. It's a pet peeve of mine, but I really wish these folks would band together and offer some sort of general pass. However, as it stands, you'll have to shell out for each individual attraction.

Butterflies abound here, and the **Butterfly Garden ★** (© 2645-5512; www.monteverdebutterflygarden.com), located near the Pensión Monteverde Inn, displays many of Costa Rica's most beautiful species. Besides the hundreds of preserved and mounted butterflies, there is a garden and a greenhouse where you can watch live butterflies. With over 20 years in business, the garden is open daily from 8:30am to 4pm, and admission is $12 for adults and $9 for students and $4 for children, including a guided tour. The best time to visit is between 9:30am and 1pm, when the butterflies are most active.

If your taste runs toward the slithery, you can check out the informative displays at the **Monteverde Serpentarium** ★ (© 2645-5238; www.snaketour.com), on the road to the reserve. It's open daily from 8am to 8pm and charges $11 for admission. The **Frog Pond of Monteverde** ★ (© 2645-6320; www.frogpondmonteverde.com), a couple of hundred meters north of the Monteverde Lodge, is probably a better bet. The $12 entrance gets you a 45-minute guided tour, and your ticket is good for 2 days. A variety of

An orchid at the Orchid Garden.

amphibians populates a series of glass terrariums. In addition, these folks have a butterfly garden. It's open daily from 9am to 8:30pm. I especially recommend that you stop by at least once after dark, when the tree frogs are active.

Fans of invertebrates will want to head to **World of Insects** (© 2645-6859), which features more than 30 terrariums filled with some of the area's more interesting creepy-crawlies. My favorites are the giant horned beetles. This place is 300m (984 ft.) west of the supermarket in Santa Elena. It's open daily from 9am to 7pm; admission is $10.

The **Bat Jungle** ★★ (© 2645-6566 or 2645-7701; www.batjungle.com) provides an in-depth look into the life and habits of these odd flying mammals. A visit here includes several different types of exhibits, from skeletal remains to a large enclosure where you get to see various live species in action—the enclosure and room are kept dark, and the bats have had their biological clocks tricked into thinking that it's night. It's quite an interesting experience. The Bat Jungle is open daily from 9am to 7:30pm, but keep in mind the last tour starts at 6:45pm. Admission is $11 for adults and $9 for students. In addition, there's a good gift shop and separate coffee shop, where they make homemade chocolate.

If you've had your fill of birds, snakes, bugs, butterflies, and bats, you might want to stop at the **Orchid Garden** ★★ (© 2645-5308; www.monteverde orchidgarden.com), in Santa Elena across from the Pension El Tucano. This botanical garden boasts more than 450 species of orchids. The tour is fascinating, especially the fact that you need (and are given) a magnifying glass to see some of the flowers in bloom. Admission is $10 for adults and $7 for students. It's open daily from 8am to 5pm.

Several options are available for those looking for a glimpse into the practices and processes of daily life in this region. My favorite is **El Trapiche Tour** ★ (© 2645-7780 or 2645-7650; www.eltrapichetour.com), which gives you a peek at the traditional means of harvesting and processing coffee and sugar cane. The 2-hour tour also includes a ride in an ox-drawn cart, and a visit to their coffee farms. Depending upon the season, you may even get to pick a bushel of raw coffee beans. Back at the farmhouse you get to see how the raw materials are turned into cane liquor, raw sugar, and roasted coffee. The tour costs $30 for adults, and $13 for children 6 through 12.

If your primary interest is java, you can take a tour of several different local coffee farms. The **Monteverde Coffee Tour** (© 2645-5901; www.monteverde-coffee.com) is run by the folks at the Cooperativa Santa Elena, a local Fair Trade coffee producer, with a shop right next to CASEM. They offer a 3-hour tour to a working coffee farm and mill for $30. **Don Juan Coffee Tour** ★ (© 2645-7100; www.donjuancoffeetour.com) is a local, family farm operation, which offers a similar 2-hour tour for $25.

Because the vegetation in the cloud forest is so dense, most of the forest's animal residents are rather difficult to spot. If you were dissatisfied with your sightings, you might want to consider attending a slide show of photographs taken in the reserve. Various daily slide shows are offered around Monteverde. The longest running of these takes place at the **Monteverde Lodge, Hotel El Sapo Dorado, Hotel Belmar** (see "Where to Stay," below), and **Humming-bird Gallery** (see below). Dates, showtimes, and admissions vary, so inquire at your hotel or one of the places mentioned above.

Almost all of the area hotels can arrange a wide variety of other tours and activities, including guided night tours of the cloud forest and night trips to the Arenal Volcano (a tedious 4-hr. ride, each way).

Learn the Language

The **Centro Panamericano de Idiomas** ★ (© 2645-5441; www.cpi-edu.com) offers immersion language classes in a wonderful setting. A 1-week program with 4 hours of class per day and a homestay with a Costa Rican family costs $480. They offer language seminars on topics such as social work,

Sampling sugar cane on El Trapiche Tour.

medicine, and security. Be sure to check their website for the dates the seminars are taking place.

Loose & Limber

If you're interested in a massage treatment or yoga class, head to **Río Shanti** (✆ **2645-6121;** www.rioshanti.com). This delightful spot offers regular, open yoga classes, private lessons, and various massage treatments. Their little boutique and shop sells handmade jewelry, clothing, and a range of oils, scents, and lotions, most made with organic local ingredients.

Shopping

The best-stocked gift shop in Monteverde is the **Hummingbird Gallery** ★ (✆ **2645-5030**), just outside the reserve entrance. Several hummingbird feeders here attract more than seven species of these tiny birds. At any given moment, several dozen hummingbirds might be buzzing and chattering around the building and your head. Inside you will find many beautiful color prints of hummingbirds and other local flora and fauna, as well as a wide range of craft items, T-shirts, and other gifts. The Hummingbird Gallery is open daily from 8am to 5pm.

Another good option is **CASEM** ★ (✆ **2645-5190**), on the right side of the main road, just across from Stella's Bakery. This crafts cooperative sells embroidered clothing, T-shirts, posters, and postcards with photos of the local flora and fauna, Boruca weavings, locally grown and roasted coffee, and many other items to remind you of your visit to Monteverde. CASEM is open Monday through Saturday from 7am to 5pm and Sunday from 10am to 4pm (closed Sun May–Oct). A well-stocked **gift shop** is at the entrance to the Monteverde Cloud Forest Biological Reserve. You'll find plenty of T-shirts, postcards, and assorted crafts here, as well as a selection of science and natural-history books.

Birds at the Hummingbird Gallery.

Shopping in Monteverde.

Over the years, Monteverde has developed a nice little community of artists. Around town you'll see paintings by local artists such as Paul Smith and Meg Wallace, whose works are displayed at the Fonda Vela Hotel and Stella's Bakery, respectively. You should also check out **Casa de Arte ★★** (✆ 2645-5275), which has a mix of arts and crafts in many media.

Finally, it's also worth stopping by the **Monteverde Cheese Factory** (✆ 2645-5150; www. monteverde.net) to pick up some of the best cheese in Costa Rica. (You can even watch it being processed and get homemade ice cream.) The cheese factory is right on the main road about midway between Santa Elena and the reserve. They offer 1-hour tours at 9am and 2pm, at a cost of $10.

Where to Stay

When choosing a place to stay in Monteverde, be sure to check whether the rates include a meal plan. In the past almost all the lodges included three meals a day in their prices, but this practice is waning. Check before you assume anything.

VERY EXPENSIVE

El Establo Mountain Hotel   From a working stable (*El Establo* translates as "the stable") owned by a local Quaker family, with just a handful of budget rooms, this place has morphed into the largest hotel in Monteverde. However, the design and scale are somewhat out of place with the vibe and aesthetic of Monteverde, and the service and food consistently fall short. The rooms are all very large and have balconies or patios taking in spectacular views. The honeymoon suites have fabulous views and a private Jacuzzi, but the 400-block of rooms are my favorites. There's one midsize outdoor swimming pool and another slightly smaller pool built under a high open-air roof. El Establo owns 48 hectares (119 acres) of land backing the hotel, and half of that is primary forest. They also have an on-site canopy tour and spa.

Monteverde. www.hotelelestablo.com. ✆ **2645-5110.** Fax 2645-5041. 155 units. $210 double; $295 suite. Rates include breakfast and taxes. AE, MC, V. **Amenities:** 2 restaurants; bar; babysitting; 2 outdoor pools; all rooms smoke-free; small spa. *In room:* TV, hair dryer, minifridge.

EXPENSIVE

Hidden Canopy Treehouses ★★ 🎁   The individual villas here are the most unique accommodations in the area. All are built at treetop level on stilts, making them feel at one with the surrounding forest. All also feature tons of varnished hardwood, custom furniture, and a sculpted waterfall shower. Most have a four-poster handmade bed, and some sort of canopy-level balcony or outdoor deck area. My favorite is "Eden," a two-level unit, with a sitting area and large deck upstairs, and bedroom, fireplace, and glassed-in 2-person Jacuzzi surrounded by forest below. Breakfast and sunset tea are served in the main lodge, which has spectacular views—especially at sunset—of the Nicoya gulf. This is also where you'll find two more economical room options.

On the road to the Santa Elena Cloud Forest Reserve. www.hiddencanopy.com. ☎ **2645-5447.** Fax 2645-9952. 6 units. $165 double; $245–$295 double treehouse. Rates include breakfast, afternoon tea, and taxes. Extra person $25. No children 9 or under. MC, V. **Amenities:** Lounge; Wi-Fi. *In room:* Hair dryer, minibar.

Hotel El Sapo Dorado   On a steep hill between Santa Elena and the reserve, El Sapo Dorado (named for Monteverde's famous golden toad) offers individual and duplex cabins. The cabins, which are relatively spartan, still feel romantic and intimate. They are built of hardwoods both inside and out and are surrounded by a grassy lawn and gardens, and backed by forest. Big windows let in lots of light, and high ceilings keep the rooms cool during the day. Some of the cabins have fireplaces, a welcome feature on chilly nights and during the rainy season. My favorite rooms are the sunset suites, which have private terraces with views to the Gulf of Nicoya and wonderful sunsets. Not only does El Sapo Dorado own and manage the Reserva Sendero Tranquilo, but it also has a network of well-maintained trails into primary forest on-site.

Just outside of Santa Elena, on the road to the Monteverde Cloud Forest Reserve. www.sapo dorado.com. ☎ **800/407-3903** in the U.S. and Canada, or 2645-5010 in Costa Rica. Fax 2645-5181. 30 units. $138 double. Rates include continental breakfast and taxes. Lower rates in the off season. AE, MC, V. **Amenities:** 2 restaurants; bar; Wi-Fi.

Hotel Fonda Vela ★★   Although it's one of the older hotels here, Fonda Vela remains one of my top choices in Monteverde. Moreover, this is one of the closer lodges to the Cloud Forest Reserve, a relatively easy 15-minute walk away. Guest rooms are in a series of separate buildings scattered among the forests and pastures of this former farm, and most have views of the Nicoya Gulf. The junior suites all come with cable television. The newer block of junior suites, some of which have excellent views, are the best rooms in the house, and I prefer them to the older and larger junior suites. The dining room has great sunset views, and sometimes features live music. Throughout the hotel, you'll see paintings by co-owner Paul Smith, who also handcrafts violins and cellos and is a musician himself.

On the road to the Monteverde Cloud Forest Reserve. www.fondavela.com. ☎ **2645-5125.** Fax 2645-5119. 40 units. $124 double; $146 junior suite. Extra person $10. AE, MC, V. **Amenities:** 2 restaurants; 2 bars; Jacuzzi; outdoor pool. *In room:* TV, hair dryer, minibar.

Hotel Heliconia   The Heliconia's main lodge building is a three-story affair, located high on a hill behind the rest of the hotel's several buildings. Here you'll find most of the suites and junior suites, which are immense rooms featuring varnished wood walls, carpeted floors, two king-size beds, and huge private balconies. All of the rooms on the second and third floors get great sunset views. Rooms in the older buildings down by the road are done in floor-to-ceiling hardwoods that give them the rustic feel of a classic mountain resort. Some of these have large picture windows facing dense forest. All around are paths that lead through attractive gardens and to a hot tub in a bamboo grove; additional trails lead from the hotel up to and through a 240-hectare (593-acre) private reserve of virgin forest with scenic views of the Nicoya Gulf.

Monteverde (A.P. 10921–1000, San José). www.hotelheliconia.com. ✆ **2645-5109.** Fax 2645-5570. 50 units. $129 double; $147 suite. MC, V. **Amenities:** Restaurant; bar; Jacuzzi.

MODERATE

In addition to the hotels listed below, **El Sol ★** (www.elsolnuestro.com; ✆ **2645-5838**), about 10 minutes south of Santa Elena, is on the road to the Interamerican Highway. Also check out **Hotel Belmar** (www.hotelbelmar.net; ✆ **2645-5201**), a Swiss chalet–style hotel with moderate rates.

Arco Iris Lodge ★★ 🍃   This is my favorite hotel in the town of Santa Elena and an excellent value to boot. The rooms are spread out in a variety of separate buildings, including several individual cabins. All have wood or tile floors and plenty of wood accents. My favorite is the "honeymoon cabin," which has a Jacuzzi tub and its own private balcony with a forest view and good bird-watching, although nos. 16 and 17 are also good choices, with their own small private balconies. The management here is helpful, speaks five languages, and can arrange a wide variety of tours. Although they don't serve lunch or dinner, breakfast is offered in a spacious and airy dining and lounge building, where refreshments are available throughout the day and evening.

Santa Elena. www.arcoirislodge.com. ✆ **2645-5067.** Fax 2645-5022. 21 units. $85–$110 double; $195 honeymoon cabin. AE, MC, V. **Amenities:** Lounge. *In room:* No phone, Wi-Fi.

Finca Valverde ★   This place is right on the outskirts of Santa Elena, yet once you head uphill to the rooms, you'll feel far from the hustle and bustle of the tiny burg. The standard rooms are set behind the main lodge and restaurant and are reached via a small suspension bridge over a small forest creek. Most have one queen-size and two twin beds. All share a broad common veranda. The superior rooms are larger, more private, and feature televisions, small refrigerators, and coffeemakers. The grounds are lush and well-tended.

Santa Elena. www.monteverde.co.cr. ✆ **2645-5157.** Fax 2645-5216. 40 units. $90–$136 double. Rates include taxes. AE, MC, V. **Amenities:** Restaurant; bar; Wi-Fi.

Hotel Poco a Poco ★ ☺   Located just outside of Santa Elena, this hotel provides many of the perks and comforts of a luxury hotel, at good prices. Some rooms are on the small side, but the beds are firm, and everything is kept neat and contemporary. The best rooms are higher up, away from the road, and have a small private balcony. All rooms come with DVD players, and the hotel maintains a movie-lending library of over 4,000 titles. A heated pool and Jacuzzi are on-site, and the restaurant is excellent. The children's pool and easy access to several nearby attractions make this a good choice for families. This hotel was granted "4 Leaves" by the CST Sustainable Tourism program.

Santa Elena. www.hotelpocoapoco.com. ✆ **2645-6000.** Fax 2645-6264. 32 units. $113 double. Rates include breakfast and taxes. AE, MC, V. **Amenities:** Restaurant; bar; small outdoor pool; spa. *In room:* TV/DVD, movie library, hair dryer, Wi-Fi.

Monteverde Lodge & Gardens ★★ ☺   This was one of the first ecolodges in Monteverde, and it remains one of the best. Rooms are large and cozy. Most feature angled walls of glass with chairs and a table placed so that avid bird-watchers can do a bit of birding without leaving their rooms. The gardens and secondary forest surrounding the lodge have some gentle groomed trails and are home to quite a few species of birds. Perhaps the lodge's most popular attraction is the large hot tub in a big atrium garden. The dining room offers great views, excellent food, and attentive service. The adjacent bar is a popular gathering spot, and there are regular evening slide shows focusing on the cloud forest. Scheduled bus service to and from San José is available, as is a shuttle to the reserve, horseback riding, and a variety of optional tours.

Santa Elena. www.monteverdelodge.com. ☎ **2257-0766** reservations office in San José, or 2645-5057 at the lodge. Fax 2257-1665. 28 units. $98–$197 double. Rates slightly lower in off season; higher during peak periods. AE, MC, V. **Amenities:** Restaurant; bar; Jacuzzi; Wi-Fi.

INEXPENSIVE

In addition to the hotels listed below, quite a few pensions and backpacker specials are in Santa Elena and spread along the road to the reserve. The best is the **Pensión Santa Elena** (www.pensionsantaelena.com; ☎ 2645-5051).

Finally, it's possible to stay in a room right at the **Monteverde Cloud Forest Biological Reserve** (www.cct.or.cr; ☎ **2645-5122**). A bunk bed, shared bathroom, and three meals per day here run $53 per person. For an extra $11 you can get a room with a private bathroom. Admission to the reserve is included in the price.

La Colina Lodge One of the older lodges in Monteverde, the former Flor Mar Pension remains a steady and solid budget choice. The rooms are housed in two separate buildings. Most rooms have one double and one single bed, although a couple still have bunk beds. The restaurant area is warm and cozy, with a big fireplace, and a separate common lounge area has satellite television. Service is friendly and attentive, and they even allow camping here, with access to the shared bathrooms. The lodge is pretty close to the reserve, which is a plus for budget travelers without a car.

A.P. 60–5655, Santa Elena, Puntarenas, Monteverde. www.lacolinalodge.com. ☎ **2645-5009.** Fax 2645-5580. 11 units, 7 with private bathroom. $15 per person with shared bathroom; $35 double with private bathroom; $5 per person camping. MC, V. **Amenities:** Restaurant; bakery; lounge. *In room:* No phone, Wi-Fi.

Where to Eat

Most lodges in Monteverde have their own dining rooms, and these are the most convenient places to eat, especially if you don't have a car. Because most visitors want to get an early start, they usually grab a quick breakfast at their hotel. It's also common for people to have their lodge pack them a bag lunch to take with them to the reserve, although a decent little *soda* is now at the reserve entrance, and another coffee shop next to the **Hummingbird Gallery** (see above), just before the reserve entrance.

In addition to the places listed below, you can get good pizzas and pastas at **Tramonti** (☎ 2645-6120; www.tramonticr.com), along the road to the reserve, and passable sushi and Japanese fare at **Musashi** (☎ 2645-7160) in downtown Santa Elena. Also, the restaurant at the **Hotel Poco a Poco** (☎ 2645-6000) gets good marks for its wide range of international dishes.

A popular choice for lunch is **Stella's Bakery** (☎ 2645-5560), across from the CASEM gift shop. The restaurant is bright and inviting, with lots of varnished woodwork, as well as a few outdoor tables. The selection changes regularly but might include vegetarian quiche, eggplant parmigiana, and different salads. Stella's also features a daily supply of decadent baked goods.

EXPENSIVE

Sofia ★★★ COSTA RICAN/FUSION   This restaurant serves top-notch eclectic cuisine in a beautiful setting. Start everything off with a mango-ginger mojito and then try one of their colorful and abundant salads. Main courses range from seafood *chimichangas* to chicken breast served in a guava reduction. The tenderloin comes with a chipotle butter sauce, or in a roasted red-pepper and cashew sauce, either way served over a bed of mashed sweet potatoes. Everything is very well prepared and reasonably priced. Of the two good-size dining rooms here, the best seats are close to the large arched picture windows overlooking the forest and gardens.

Cerro Plano, just past the turnoff to the Butterfly Farm, on your left. (C) **2645-7017.** Reservations recommended during high season. Main courses $14–$17. AE, DC, DISC, MC, V. Daily 11:30am–9:30pm.

MODERATE

Café Caburé ★★ DESSERT/ARGENTINE   Specializing in homemade artisanal truffles and other organic chocolate creations, this cozy spot is a good call for breakfast, lunch, dinner, or a sinfully sweet coffee break. Although they advertise themselves as an Argentine restaurant, I find that description lacking. The menu includes excellent curries and chicken mole, as well as an Argentine–style breaded steak, and fresh baked empanadas. A large, simple space, this place is located on the second floor of the Bat Jungle (p. 336). Be sure to save room for some chocolates for dessert, or their chocolate-walnut soufflé.

On the road btw. Santa Elena and the reserve, at the Bat Jungle. (C) **2645-5020.** www.cabure. net. Reservations recommended during high season. Main courses C6,000–C7,500. AE, MC, V. Mon–Sat 9am–8pm.

Chimera ★★ FUSION/TAPAS   The small menu at this creative, yet casual tapas restaurant has a broad scope, with influences ranging from Asia to Latin America to the Old World. Standout dishes include slow-cooked pork with white beans and caramelized onions and coconut shrimp "lollipops" with a mango-ginger dipping sauce. And for dessert, don't pass up the chocolate mousse with sangria syrup. A variety of creative and contemporary cocktails, as well as good wines, are also offered.

Cerro Plano, on the road btw. Santa Elena and the reserve, on your right. (C) **2645-6081.** Reservations recommended during high season. Tapas $2.50–$12. AE, DC, DISC, MC, V. Daily 11:30am–9:30pm.

Trio ★★ FUSION   Karen Nielsen, the force behind Sofia and Chimera (see above), has brought her restaurant magic to downtown Santa Elena. A great spot for lunch or dinner, this place serves up a healthy and varied menu. I recommend the hamburger, which has sundried tomatoes mixed into the meat, and is served with figs, arugula, and caramelized onions on a home-baked bun. The fish tacos feature local sea bass with a green plantain coating and chipotle sauce. For a more substantial option, try the beef tenderloin with a Manchego cheese and Dijon mustard sauce.

Downtown Santa Elena, below the supermarket. ✆ **2645-7254.** Reservations recommended during high season. Main courses $9.25–$17; sandwiches $6.75–$8.75. AE, DC, DISC, MC, V. Daily 11:30am–9:30pm.

INEXPENSIVE

Morpho's Café COSTA RICAN/INTERNATIONAL   Probably the best and definitely the most popular restaurant in the town of Santa Elena, this simple second-floor affair serves up hearty and economical meals. Soups, sandwiches, and *casados* (plates of the day) are available for lunch and dinner, and delicious fresh-fruit juices, ice-cream shakes, and home-baked desserts are ready throughout the day. The tables and chairs are made from rough-hewn lumber and whole branches and trunks, and the place brims with a light convivial atmosphere. Morpho's is a very popular hangout for backpackers.

In downtown Santa Elena, next to the Orchid Garden. ✆ **2645-5607.** Main courses C2,400–C10,000. AE, MC, V. Daily 11am–9pm.

Monteverde After Dark

The most popular after-dark activities in Monteverde are night hikes in one of the reserves and a natural-history slide show (see "Other Attractions in Monteverde," earlier in this chapter). However, if you want a taste of the local party scene, head to **Mata 'e Caña ★★** (✆ **2645-5883**), just outside of downtown Santa Elena next to the entrance to Finca Valverde. With a contemporary club vibe, this place attracts a mix of locals and tourists, cranks its music loud, often gets people dancing, and occasionally has live bands. Alternatively, **Bromelias ★** (✆ **2645-6272**), located up a steep driveway from Stella's Bakery, sometimes features live music, theater, or open-mic jam sessions. These folks also run the neighboring **Monteverde Amphitheater,** a beautiful open-air performance space, which is the site of regular performances by acts visiting from San José and beyond.

> **Take a Break**
>
> If all the activities in Monteverde have worn you out, stop in at **Chunches** (✆ **2645-5147**), a bookstore with a small coffee shop and espresso bar that also doubles as a laundromat.

PUERTO VIEJO DE SARAPIQUÍ ★

82km (51 miles) N of San José; 102km (63 miles) E of La Fortuna

The Sarapiquí region, named for the principal river that runs through this area, lies at the foot of the Cordillera Central mountain range. To the west is the rainforest of **Braulio Carrillo National Park,** and to the east are **Tortuguero National Park ★★** and **Barra del Colorado National Wildlife Refuge ★**. In between these protected areas lay thousands of acres of banana, pineapple, and palm plantations. Here you see the great contradiction of Costa Rica: On the one hand, the country is known for its national parks, which preserve some of the largest tracts of rainforest left in Central America; on the other hand, nearly every acre of land outside of these parks, save a few private reserves, has been clear-cut and converted into plantations—and the cutting continues.

Within the remaining rainforest are several lodges that attract naturalists (both amateur and professional). Two of these lodges, **La Selva** and **Rara Avis,** are famous for the research that's conducted on their surrounding reserves. Birdwatching and rainforest hikes are the primary attractions, but more adventure-oriented travelers will find plenty of activities available here, including canopy tours and boating and rafting trips along the Sarapiquí River.

Essentials

GETTING THERE & DEPARTING   By Car: The Guápiles Highway (CR32), which leads to the Caribbean coast, heads north out of downtown San José on Calle 3. Turn

A pineapple plantation.

north before reaching Guápiles on the road to Río Frío (CR4), and continue north through Las Horquetas, passing the turnoffs for Rara Avis, La Selva, and El Gavilán lodges before reaching Puerto Viejo.

A more scenic route goes through Heredia, Barva, Varablanca, and San Miguel before reaching Puerto Viejo. This route passes very close to the Poás Volcano and directly in front of La Paz waterfall. If you want to take this route, head west out of San José, then turn north to Heredia and follow the signs for Varablanca and La Paz Waterfall Gardens. *Note:* A major March 2009 earthquake shut down this route, which is expected to reopen in late 2011.

Tip: If you plan to stop on the way to see **La Paz Waterfall Gardens** (p. 162) or ride the **Rain Forest Aerial Tram** (p. 146), budget at least 2 hours to visit either attraction.

By Bus: Empresarios Guapileños buses (*©* **2222-0610** in San José, or 2710-7780 in Puerto Viejo) leave San José roughly every hour between 6:30am and 6pm from the **Gran Terminal del Caribe,** on Calle Central, 1 block north of Avenida 11. The trip takes around 2 hours; the fare is C1,710. Buses for San José leave Puerto Viejo roughly every hour between 5:30am and 5:30pm.

 Getting Loopy

If you connect the two routes mentioned above, you get what is sometimes referred to as "The Sarapiquí Loop." This loop is a pretty drive, punctuated with attractions and tour opportunities, and it also connects quite nicely with an alternative route to La Fortuna and the Arenal volcano area (p. 296).

ORIENTATION   Puerto Viejo is a very small town, with a soccer field at its center. If you continue past the soccer field on the main road and stay on the paved road, and then turn right at the Banco Nacional, you'll come to the Río Sarapiquí and the dock, where you can look into arranging a boat trip.

What to See & Do

BOAT TRIPS   For the adventurous, Puerto Viejo is a jumping-off point for trips down the Río Sarapiquí to Barra del Colorado National Wildlife Refuge and Tortuguero National Park on the Caribbean coast. A boat for up to 10 people will cost you around $400 to $500 to Barra del Colorado or $500 to $600 to Tortuguero. If you're interested in this trip, it's worth checking at your hotel or with **Oasis Nature Tours** (*C* **2766-6108;** www.oasisnature tours.com). Alternatively, you can head down to the town dock on the bank of the Sarapiquí and see if you can arrange a less expensive boat trip on your own by tagging along with another group or, better yet, with a bunch of locals.

In addition to the longer trips, you can take shorter trips on the river for between $10 and $20 per person per hour. A trip down the Sarapiquí, even if it's for only an hour or two, provides opportunities to spot crocodiles, caimans, monkeys, sloths, and dozens of bird species.

CANOPY TOUR & MORE   Hacienda Pozo Azul ★ (*C* **877/ 810-6903** in the U.S. and Canada, or 2761-1360 in Costa Rica; www.pozoazul.com) is a working cattle farm and one-stop shop for a wide range of adventure activities. These folks have an extensive zip-line canopy tour operation, with 12 platforms connected by 9 different cable runs, in addition to offering white-water rafting, horseback riding, and guided hikes. They even run a tent-camp and separate rustic lodge in deep rainforest sites here. Several differently priced combo packages are offered, and the property is open daily from 8am to 6pm.

A red-eyed tree frog.

HIKING & GUIDED TOURS   Anyone can take advantage of the 56km (35 miles) of well-maintained **trails at La Selva ★★** (p. 348). If you're not staying there, however, you'll have to take a guided hike, led by experienced and well-informed naturalists. Half- and full-day hikes ($30 and $38, respectively) are offered daily, but you must reserve in advance (*C* **2524-0607;** www.threepaths.co.cr). The half-day tours leave at 8am and 1:30pm daily.

My favorite hike starts off with the Cantarrana ("singing frog") trail, which includes a section of low bridges over a rainforest swamp. From here, you can join up with either the near or far circular loop trails—**CCC** and **CCL.** Another good hiking option is the trails and suspended bridges at the **Centro Neotrópico SarapiquíS** (p. 350).

For a more orderly introduction to the local flora, head to a botanical garden, like the **Chester Field Biological Gardens** (see below), or the nearby **Heliconia Island** (⊘ 2764-5220; www.heliconiaisland.com), an interesting garden with over 70 varieties of heliconia, on a small island. This place is open daily from 8am to 5pm. Admission is $10 for a self-guided walk, or $15 for a guided tour.

A NATURAL-HISTORY THEME PARK The **SarapiquíS Rainforest Lodge** (p. 350) is a multifaceted natural-history project and tourist attraction. The **Alma Ata Archaeological Park** is basically an ongoing dig of a modest pre-Columbian gravesite; so far, 12 graves, some petroglyphs, and numerous pieces of ceramic and jewelry have been unearthed. Plans for the park include the reconstruction of a small indigenous village. The hotel also has a small museum that displays examples of the ceramics, tools, clothing, and carvings found here, as well as other natural-history exhibits. Just across the hotel's driveway, you'll find the Chester Field Biological Gardens, which feature well-tended displays of local medicinal and ornamental plants and herbs, as well as food crops. Admission to the archaeological park, museum, and gardens costs $30. If you just want to visit the museum, the cost is $15; it's open daily from 6am to 5pm. A self-guided walk through the botanical gardens is free.

Across the river from the SarapiquíS Rainforest Lodge is the 300-hectare (741-acre) private **Tirimbina Rainforest Center** ★ (⊘ 2761-1579; www.tirimbina.org), with a small network of trails and several impressive suspension bridges, both over the river and through the forest canopy. A self-guided walk of the bridges and trails of the reserve costs $15 per person, and a 2-hour guided tour costs $22 per person—definitely worth the extra few bucks. The center is open daily from 7am to 5pm, and from 7:30 to 9:30pm for night tours; specialized bird-watching tours are also available.

RAFTING & KAYAKING If you want a fast, wild ride on the river, check in with **Aguas Bravas** (⊘ 2292-2072; www.aguas-bravas.co.cr) or **Aventuras del Sarapiquí** ★ (⊘ 2766-6768; www.sarapiqui.com). Both companies run trips on a variety of sections of the Sarapiquí and Puerto Viejo rivers, ranging from Class I to Class IV. Trips cost between $50 and $80 per person. Aventuras del Sarapiquí also runs mountain-biking and horseback-riding tours in the area. They rent kayaks, give kayaking classes, and offer kayak trips for more experienced and/or daring river rats, and offer innertube floats for those with lesser skill sets still looking to get wet.

SNAKES UNDER GLASS Just a few blocks west of the Centro Neotrópico SarapiquíS, you'll find **Jardin de Serpientes** (**Snake Garden;** ⊘ 2761-1059), a collection of over 50 snakes, both venomous and nonvenomous, and other reptiles and amphibians. One of the prize attractions here,

A Rain Forest Aerial Tram hike.

An eyelash viper.

although not native, is a massive, yellow Burmese python. All are kept in clean, well-lit displays. Admission is $8 adults, $6 children and it's open daily from 9am to 5pm.

ONE MAJOR ATTRACTION EN ROUTE If you're driving to Puerto Viejo de Sarapiquí via the Guápiles Highway, you might want to stop at the **Rain Forest Aerial Tram ★**. You'll see the entrance on your right shortly after passing through the Zurquí tunnel. For more information, see "Side Trips from San José," in chapter 5.

Where to Stay & Eat

All the lodges listed below arrange excursions throughout the region, including boat trips on the Sarapiquí, guided hikes in the rainforest, and horseback or mountain-bike rides. Also note that rates for the lodges in the "Expensive" category include all meals, taxes, and usually a tour or two, greatly reducing their real cost. In addition to the hotels listed below, **Peace Lodge** (p. 164), located at La Paz Waterfall Gardens, is almost close enough to be considered lodging in this region.

EXPENSIVE

La Selva Biological Station ★ This place caters primarily to students and researchers but also accepts visitors seeking a rustic rainforest adventure. The atmosphere is definitely that of a scientific research center. La Selva, operated by the Organization for Tropical Studies (OTS), covers 1,614 hectares (3,656 acres). The contiguous Braulio Carrillo National Park, has miles of well-maintained hiking trails to explore. Rooms are basic but large, and the high ceilings help keep them cool. Most have bunk beds and shared bathrooms, although eight have private bathrooms and twin beds, and the two-room family units have a mix of twin and queen-size beds. There's no price difference, so be specific when reserving a room. Rates are pretty high for what you get, but you can take some solace in the fact that you're helping to support valuable and valiant research and conservation efforts.

Puerto Viejo. www.threepaths.co.cr. ☏ **2524-0607** reservations office in San José, or 2766-6565 at the lodge. Fax 2524-0608. 24 units, 16 with shared bathroom. $84 per person double occupancy. Rates include all meals, half-day tour, and taxes. Rates lower for researchers and student groups. AE, MC, V. **Amenities:** Restaurant. *In room:* No phone.

Selva Verde Lodge ★ ☺ This is one of the pioneering ecotourist ventures in Costa Rica. The main lodge is a series of buildings connected by covered walkways that keep you dry even though this area receives more than 381cm (150 in.) of rain each year. The bungalows are across the road and 500m (1,640 ft.) into the forest; they're not as close to the main compound as the lodge rooms, but they offer more privacy, as well as air-conditioning and a private screened veranda. Meals are served buffet-style in a beautiful large dining room that overlooks the river. Across the river is a large rainforest preserve. The grounds have trails, a wonderful suspension bridge with a separate zip-line adventure across the river to more trails, and modest butterfly and botanical gardens. Swimming options include a pretty free-form pool and separate children's pool, as well as a natural swimming hole right on the river.

Chilamate, Sarapiquí. www.selvaverde.com. ☏ **800/451-7111** in the U.S. and Canada, or 2766-6800. Fax 2766-6011. 53 units, 5 bungalows. $185–$211 double. Rates include 3 meals daily and taxes. AE, DC, DISC, MC, V. **Amenities:** 2 restaurants; bar; outdoor pool; smoke-free rooms. *In room:* Hair dryer.

Sueño Azul Resort ★★ ☺ This lodge and wellness retreat offers the best accommodations in the area. Set at the juncture of two rivers and backed by forested mountains, the setting's pretty sweet, as well. All rooms are spacious, with high ceilings, large bathrooms, and a private porch overlooking either one of the rivers or a small lake. Junior suites come with a private outdoor Jacuzzi. Meals are served in an open-air dining room set to take in the view, and a pool, Jacuzzi, and bar are down by the river's edge. The best place to cool off is in the massive outdoor pool, fed and filled by river water, although there's a traditional freshwater pool, and you can simply swim in the river at various spots. A wide range of spa treatments, tours, and activities is offered, including rainforest hikes, horseback riding, mountain biking, and fly-fishing.

Las Horquetas de Sarapiquí. www.suenoazulresort.com. ☏ **2253-2020** reservation number in San José, 2764-1000 at the lodge. Fax 2764-1048. 64 units. $122 double; $174 suite. Rates include taxes. Add $20 for A/C. AE, MC, V. **Amenities:** Restaurant; Jacuzzi; 2 outdoor pools; room service. *In room:* A/C, TV (in some), hair dryer, minibar.

MODERATE

Although I highly recommend you choose one of the more atmospheric nature lodges listed in this section, if you absolutely must (or for some reason prefer to) stay in Puerto Viejo de Sarapiquí proper, **Hotel El Bambú** (www.elbambu.com; ℂ **2766-6005**) is a clean, comfortable, and almost modern option.

In addition to the places outside town that are reviewed below, the **Tirimbina Rainforest Center** ★ (www.tirimbina.org; ℂ **2761-1579**) also has rooms.

La Quinta de Sarapiquí Country Inn   This small, family-run lodge makes a good base for exploring the Sarapiquí region. On the banks of the Sardinal River about 15 minutes west of Puerto Viejo, La Quinta caters primarily to nature lovers and bird-watchers. The rooms are in a half-dozen buildings dispersed among richly flowering gardens and connected by covered walkways. They're simple but clean, with good lighting and comfortable bathrooms. Each room has a small patio with a sitting chair or two for gazing out into the garden. The superior rooms have air-conditioning. A small gift shop, a butterfly garden, a frog garden, an extensive insect display, and a vegetable garden and reforestation project are also on hand. Meals are either buffet- or family-style in the main lodge.

Chilamate, Sarapiquí. www.laquintasarapiqui.com. ℂ 2761-1300. Fax 2761-1395. 35 units. $110 double; $125 suite. Children 11 and under stay free in parent's room. AE, MC, V. **Amenities:** Restaurant; bar; small outdoor pool.

Rara Avis 👣   Rara Avis is one of the first, most responsible, biologically rich, and isolated ecolodge operations in Costa Rica. Of the several options here, the Waterfall Lodge is by far the most popular. It has rustic but comfortable rooms in a two-story building near the main lodge, dining room, and namesake waterfall. Each unit here is a corner room with a wraparound porch. For those who want a closer communion with nature, Rara Avis has a two-room cabin set deep in the forest beside a river, about a 10-minute hike from the main lodge, as well as three more rustic two-bedroom cabins with shared bathrooms in a small clearing about a 5-minute walk from the lodge. Meals are basic Tico-style dishes with lots of beans and rice. *Bird-watchers, take note:* More than 367 species of birds have been sighted here, and the lodge consistently has excellent guides and naturalists.

When making reservations, get directions for how to get to Las Horquetas and information on coordinating your ride on the lodge's tractor. The tractor leaves just once daily for the very bumpy and plodding 3-hour ride to the lodge.

15km (9⅓ miles) from Las Horquetas. www.rara-avis.com. ℂ 2764-1111 for reservations or 2710-8032 at the lodge. Fax 2764-1114. 16 units, 10 with private bathroom. $55 per person with shared bathroom; $75–$90 double with private bathroom. Rates include transportation from Las Horquetas, guided hikes, all meals, and taxes. AE, MC, V. **Amenities:** Restaurant. *In room:* No phone.

SarapiquíS Rainforest Lodge ★   On a high bluff fronting the Sarapiquí River, this complex is the most unique project in the Sarapiquí region. Rooms are housed in three large, round buildings, or *palenques,* based on the traditional pre-Columbian constructions of the area. Each *palenque* has a towering thatch roof. All rooms are of good size, although a little dark. Each has a door leading out to the shared veranda that encircles the building. The hotel has several interesting attractions, including a small natural-history museum, an on-site excavation of a pre-Columbian graveyard, and a well-marked botanical garden. Just across the river lies the 300-hectare (741-acre) Tirimbina Rainforest Center, with a small network of trails and several impressive suspension bridges, both over the river and through the forest canopy.

La Virgen de Sarapiquí. www.sarapiquis.org. ✆ **2761-1004.** Fax 2761-1415. 40 units. $104 double. AE, MC, V. **Amenities:** 2 restaurants; bar; babysitting; room service; smoke-free rooms.

INEXPENSIVE

The **Posada Andrea Cristina** (www.andreacristina.com; ✆ **2766-6265**), just on the outskirts of Puerto Viejo, is run by Alex Martínez, an excellent local guide and pioneering conservationist in the region. You may also consider staying at the jungle tent camp or isolated Magsasay Lodge at **Hacienda Pozo Azul ★** (www.pozoazul.com; ✆ **877/810-6903** in the U.S. and Canada, or 2438-2616).

Gavilán Sarapiquí River Lodge On the banks of the Río Sarapiquí just south of Puerto Viejo, Gavilán is surrounded by 100 hectares (247 acres) of forest reserve (secondary forest) and 14 hectares (35 acres) of gardens planted with lots of flowering ginger, heliconia, orchids, and bromeliads. Guest rooms are basic and simply furnished. All have fans, hot water, and fresh-cut flowers. The four "superior" rooms have much more contemporary appointments and amenities. An unheated Jacuzzi is in the garden and several open-air ranchos have hammocks strung up for afternoon siestas. Tico and Continental meals are served buffet-style with plenty of fresh fruits and juices. Guided hikes through the forest, horseback rides, and river trips are all offered for around $35 per person.

Puerto Viejo de Sarapiquí. www.gavilanlodge.com. ✆ **2234-9507** reservation office in San José, 2766-7131 or 8343-9480 at the lodge. Fax 2253-6556. 20 units. $50 double; $70 superior double. AE, MC, V. **Amenities:** Restaurant; bar; Jacuzzi. *In room:* No phone, Wi-Fi.

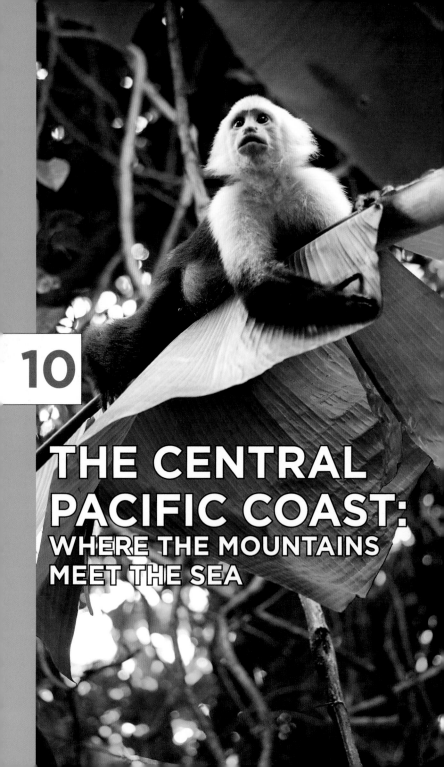

10

THE CENTRAL PACIFIC COAST:
WHERE THE MOUNTAINS
MEET THE SEA

A fter Guanacaste, the beaches of Costa Rica's central Pacific coast are the country's most popular. Options here range from the surfer and snowbird hangout of Jacó, to the ecotourist mecca of Manuel Antonio, to remote and diminutive Dominical, with its jungle-clad hillsides and rainforest waterfalls. With the 2010 opening of a modern highway connecting San José to the coast, and improvements along the Costanera Sur highway heading south, this region has gotten much easier to visit.

Jacó is the closest major beach destination to San José. It has historically been a top choice for young surfers and city-dwelling Costa Ricans. Just north of Jacó and Playa Herradura sits **Carara National Park ★★**, one of the few places in Costa Rica where you can see the disappearing dry forest join the damp, humid forests that extend south down the coast. It's also a great place to see scarlet macaws in the wild.

For its part, Manuel Antonio remains one of the country's foremost ecotourist destinations, with a host of hotel and lodging options and an easily accessible national park that combines the exuberant lushness of a lowland tropical rainforest with several gorgeous beaches. **Manuel Antonio National Park ★★** is home to all four of Costa Rica's monkey species, as well as a wealth of other easily viewed flora and fauna.

If you're looking to get away from it all, **Dominical** and the **beaches south of Dominical ★** should be your top choice on this coast. Still a small village, the beach town of Dominical is flanked by even more remote and undeveloped beaches, including those found inside **Ballena Marine National Park ★★**.

Finally, if you can tear yourself away from the beaches and coastline here, and head slightly inland, you'll find **Chirripó National Park ★★**, a misty cloud forest that becomes a barren páramo (a region above 3,000m/ 9,840 ft.) at the peak of its namesake, Mount Chirripó—the tallest peak in Costa Rica.

The climate here is considerably more humid than that farther north in Guanacaste, but it's not nearly as steamy as along the southern Pacific or Caribbean coasts.

 The Central Pacific Coast's Top Sustainable Hotels

Arenas Del Mar (p. 386)
Cuna del Angel (p. 404)
El Parador (p. 388)
Gaia Hotel & Reserve (p. 386)
Hacienda Baru (p. 398)
Hotel Sí Como No (p. 388)
La Cusinga Lodge (p. 404)
Monte Azul (p. 411)
Savegre Mountain Hotel (p. 412)

PREVIOUS PAGE: **A capuchin monkey.**

If you're coming for an extended stay with your family or a large group, **Mead Brown ★** (www.meadbrown.com; 𝄐 866/567-1516 in the U.S. and Canada, or 2637-8561 in Costa Rica) rents a broad selection of luxurious private villas and condos in the Los Sueños resort complex and around Jacó.

PLAYA HERRADURA

108 km (67 miles) W of San José; 9km (6 miles) NW of Playa de Jacó.

Playa Herradura is the first major beach you'll hit as you head south along the Southern Coastal Highway. **Playa Herradura** is a long stretch of brown sand that is home to the massive **Los Sueños Marriott Ocean & Golf Resort** and its attached marina. North of Herradura, you'll find a few other small beaches and resorts, including the elegant boutique hotel **Villa Caletas ★★★** (p. 360).

Essentials

GETTING THERE & DEPARTING **By Car:** Head west out of San José on the San José–Caldera Highway (CR27). Just past the toll booth at Pavón, this road connects with the Costanera Sur (CR34), or Southern Coastal Highway. The exit is marked for Jacó and CR34. From here it's a straight and flat shot down the coast to Playa Herradura. The trip should take about an hour.

By Bus No direct buses run all the way into Playa Herradura. All buses to Jacó will drop off passengers at the entrance to Playa Herradura, which is about 1km (½ mile) or so from the beach and Los Sueños resort complex. See "Jacó: Getting There," below, for bus info.

Gray Line (𝄐 **2220-2126;** www.graylinecostarica.com) has one bus that leaves San José for Jacó daily at 8am. **Interbus** (𝄐 **2283-5573;** www.interbusonline.com) has two buses that leave San José for Jacó daily at 8am and 2pm. Both companies charge $30 and will drop you off at any hotel in or around Playa Herradura. Both companies will also pick you up at most San José–area hotels. Both also offer connections to most major tourist destinations in the country.

Buses from San José to **Quepos** and Manuel Antonio also pass by Playa Herradura. (They let passengers off on the hwy. about 1km/½ mile from town.) However, during the busy months, some of these buses will refuse passengers getting off in Playa Herradura or will accept them only if they pay the full fare to Quepos or Manuel Antonio. For information and departure times of these buses, see p. 377.

ORIENTATION Playa Herradura is a short distance off the Southern Coastal Highway. Just before you hit the beach, you'll see the entrance to the Los Sueños resort complex and marina on your right. One dirt road runs parallel to the beach, with a few restaurants and a makeshift line of parking spaces all along its length.

FAST FACTS Playa Herradura has no real town. At the main intersection with the Southern Coastal Highway, you'll find a modern strip mall, with a large Automercado supermarket, and some restaurants, shops, and a couple of bank ATMs.

The Central
Pacific Coast

The Costanera Highway passes over the Tárcoles River just outside the entrance to **Carara National Park,** about 23km (14 miles) south of Orotina. This is a popular spot to pull over and spot some gargantuan crocodiles. Some can reach 3.7 to 4.6m (12–15 ft.) in length. Usually anywhere from 10 to 20 are easily visible, either swimming in the water or sunning on the banks. But be careful. First, you'll be walking on a narrow sidewalk along the side of the bridge with cars and trucks speeding by. And second, car break-ins are common here, including in the seemingly safe restaurant parking lots at the north end of the bridge.

Although a police post has somewhat reduced the risk, I recommend that you don't leave your car or valuables unguarded for long, or better yet, leave someone at the car and take turns watching the crocs.

Fun on & off the Beach

Playa Herradura is a calm and protected beach, although the dark sand is rocky in places and not very attractive. The calmest section of beach is toward the north end, where you'll find the **Los Sueños Marriott Ocean & Golf Resort.** Aside from sunbathing and swimming, there's not too much to do here. When the swell is big, the center section of beach here can be a good place to body surf, boogie board, or try some beginning surf moves.

Punta Leona, just a few kilometers north of Playa Herradura, is a cross between a hotel, a resort, and a private country club, and it has some of the nicer beaches in the area. Although they effectively have restricted access to their beaches for years, this is technically illegal in Costa Rica, and you have the right to enjoy both playas **Manta ★** and **Blanca ★**, two very nice white-sand beaches inside the Punta Leona complex. The public access beach road is south of the main Punta Leona entrance and is not very well marked.

In contrast to the dryness of Guanacaste, these are the first beaches on the Pacific coast to have a tropical feel. The humidity is palpable, and the lushness of the tropical forest is visible on the hillsides surrounding town. In hotel gardens, flowers bloom profusely throughout the year.

Because they're so close, many folks staying in Playa Herradura take advantage of the tours and activities offered out of Jacó and even those offered out of Quepos and Manuel Antonio. See the respective sections below for more details.

Finally, just beyond Carara National Park on the Costanera Sur in the direction of Jacó is a turnoff for the **Pura Vida Botanical Gardens ★**(✆ **2645-1001;** www.puravidagarden.com) and some beautiful waterfalls around the town of **Bijagual.** Admission for the gardens is $20, and it's open daily from 8am to 5pm. The fee includes free run of the gardens and trails, which lead to a couple of smaller local waterfalls.

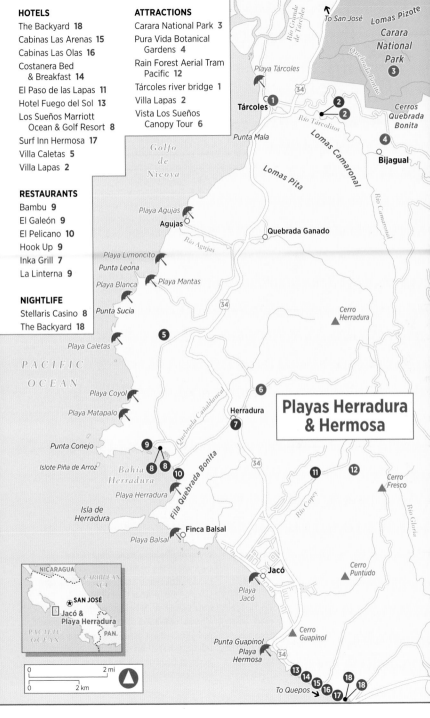

HOTELS

The Backyard **18**
Cabinas Las Arenas **15**
Cabinas Las Olas **16**
Costanera Bed & Breakfast **14**
El Paso de las Lapas **11**
Hotel Fuego del Sol **13**
Los Sueños Marriott Ocean & Golf Resort **8**
Surf Inn Hermosa **17**
Villa Caletas **5**
Villa Lapas **2**

RESTAURANTS

Bambu **9**
El Galeón **9**
El Pelicano **10**
Hook Up **9**
Inka Grill **7**
La Linterna **9**

NIGHTLIFE

Stellaris Casino **8**
The Backyard **18**

ATTRACTIONS

Carara National Park **3**
Pura Vida Botanical Gardens **4**
Rain Forest Aerial Tram Pacific **12**
Tárcoles river bridge **1**
Villa Lapas **2**
Vista Los Sueños Canopy Tour **6**

Map labels

To San José
Lomas Pizote
Carara National Park **3**
Río Grande de Tárcoles
Quebrada Bonita
Playa Tárcoles
1
Tárcoles
2
2
Cerros Quebrada Bonita
Río Tárcolitos
Punta Mala
Lomas Camaronal
4
Bijagual
Golfo de Nicoya
Lomas Pita
Río Camaronal
Playa Agujas
Agujas
Río Agujas
Quebrada Ganado
Playa Limoncito
Punta Leona
Playa Mantas
Playa Blanca
Punta Sucia
5
Cerro Herradura
Playa Caletas
PACIFIC OCEAN
Playa Coyol
6
Quebrada Cañablanca
Herradura
Playas Herradura & Hermosa
Playa Matapalo
7
Punta Conejo
9
Islote Piña de Arroz
Bahía Herradura
8 **8**
10
11
12
Cerro Fresco
Playa Herradura
Fila Quebrada Bonita
Río Copey
Isla de Herradura
Finca Balsal
Playa Balsal
Río Gloria
Jacó
Cerro Puntudo
NICARAGUA
CARIBBEAN SEA
SAN JOSÉ
Jacó & Playa Herradura
PACIFIC OCEAN
PAN.
Playa Jacó
Cerro Guapinol
Punta Guapinol
Playa Hermosa
13
14
15
16
17
18 **18**
To Quepos
0 | 2 mi
0 | 2 km

However, the largest waterfall here is a 180m (590-ft.) multitiered affair reached by a rather vigorous 45-minute hike. The entrance fee for the hike in is $20 per person, and is collected at a makeshift kiosk (no phone) at the entrance to the trail head, which is on private land.

To get here, turn off at the signs for Hotel Villa Lapas. From there, it's a rough 8km (5 miles) up to the gardens and waterfalls.

CANOPY TOURS   **Vista Los Sueños Canopy Tour ★** (© 8342-3683; www. canopyvistalossuenos.com) is set in the hills above Playa Herradura. This place also has 13 zip-lines and some excellent views, and boasts the longest cable in the area, at almost a half-mile in length. Both of the above operations charge $60 per person, and can also arrange transportation.

Nearby, **Villa Lapas** (p. 361) has two different tours through the treetops outside of Jacó. The better and cheaper option is a guided hike on its network of trails and five suspended bridges ($20 per person). The operator also has a relatively low-adrenaline zip-line canopy tour ($30 per person), with seven platforms connected by six cables.

GOLF   The excellent **La Iguana,** an 18-hole golf course at the **Los Sueños Marriott Ocean & Golf Resort** (© 2630-9028; www.golflaiguana. com), is open to nonguests. See p. 360 for details. Greens fees are $160 for a full round. The price drops to $130 if you tee off after noon. Club and shoe rentals are available. Marriott guests pay slightly less to play here.

SPORTFISHING, SCUBA DIVING & SEABORNE FUN   Since the Los Sueños Marriott Resort (p. 360) and its adjacent 250-slip marina opened, most local maritime activity has shifted over here. If you're interested in doing some sportfishing, scuba diving, or any other waterborne activity, I recommend that you check with your hotel or at the marina. Dependable operators that have set up here include **Maverick Sportfishing Yachts** (© 866/888-6426 in the U.S., or 2637-8824 in Costa Rica; www.maverickyachtscosta rica.com), **Costa Rica Dreams** (© 732/901-8625 ext. 246 in the U.S. and Canada, or 2637-8942 in Costa Rica; www.costaricadreams.com), and **Central Pacific Sport Fishing** (© 707/962-4470 in the U.S. and Canada; www.costarica-fishingcharters.com). A half-day fishing trip for four people costs around $700 to $1,200, and a full day costs between $1,000 and $1,700.

Carara National Park ★★

A little more than 17.5km (11 miles) north of Playa Herradura is **Carara National Park** (© 2637-1054 for visitor center), a world-renowned nesting ground for **scarlet macaws.** It has a few kilometers of trails open to visitors. The **Sendero Accesso Universal (Universal Access Trail),** which heads out from the national park office, is broad, flat, and

 En Route to Jacó: An Isolated Boutique Beauty

If you're planning on heading to the beaches of the central Pacific coast via Ciudad Colón and Puriscal, you might consider a stop at **Ama Tierra Retreat & Wellness Center ★** (www.amatierra.com; © 866/659-3805 in the U.S. and Canada, or 2419-0110 in Costa Rica), a lovely little boutique hotel and retreat center about 1½ hours outside of San José along this route, and approximately 1 hour from Jacó.

A scarlet macaw.

wheelchair-accessible (hence the trail name). The first half of this 1km (.7-mile) stretch leads into the forest and features various informative plaques, in both English and Spanish, pointing out prominent flora. About 10 or 15 minutes into your hike, you'll see that the trail splits, forming a loop (you can go in either direction). The entire loop trail should take you about an hour. The macaws migrate daily, spending their days in the park and their nights among the coastal mangroves. It's best to view them in the early morning when they arrive, or around sunset when they head back to the coast for the evening, but a good guide can usually find them for you during the day. Whether or not you see them, you should hear their loud squawks. Among the other wildlife that you might see here are caimans, coatimundis, armadillos, pacas, peccaries, and, of course, hundreds of species of birds.

Be sure to bring along insect repellent or, better yet, wear light cotton long sleeves and pants. (I was once foolish enough to attempt a quick hike while returning from Manuel Antonio, still in beach clothes and flip-flops.) The reserve is open daily from 7am to 4pm. Admission is $10 per person at the gate.

Most hotel desks can arrange for a guided hike to Carara National Park, or you can contact **Jaguar Riders** (© **2643-0180;** www.jaguariders.com) in Jacó to set one up. Although you can certainly hike the gentle and well-marked trails of Carara independently, my advice is to take a guided tour; you'll learn a lot more about your surroundings.

If you're staying in any of the nearby beach towns, you might consider taking a boat tour of the river and mangroves here. Several companies offer such a tour, and every hotel and tour agency in the area can arrange it for you. Nearly all the operators bring along plenty of freshly killed chickens to attract the crocs and pump up the adrenaline—a practice I cannot endorse. That's why I suggest going with **Jungle Crocodile Safari ★** (© **2637-0338;** www.junglecrocodilesafari. com). The cost of the 2-hour tour is $35 for adults and $25 for children ages 4 to 12 (children 3 and under free). Transportation from Jacó, Playa Herradura,

Manuel Antonio, or San José is available. Jungle Crocodile Safari's trips depart daily at 8:30 and 10:30am, and 1:30 and 3:30pm.

Where to Stay

VERY EXPENSIVE

In addition to its hotel rooms, the Los Sueños resort has scores of condominium units for rent. All come with kitchens, access to swimming pools, and rights to use the golf course here. These are excellent options for families who want to do some cooking, and for longer stays. If you want to rent a condo here, contact **Costa Rica Luxury Rentals** (www.crluxury.com; ☎ **866/525-2188** in the U.S. and Canada, or 2637-7105 in Costa Rica). Rates are upwards of $451 nightly for one- and two-bedroom units, to over $1,320 for some of the more luxurious three-bedroom units.

Los Sueños Marriott Ocean & Golf Resort ★★ ☺ This large resort is done in a Spanish colonial style, with stucco walls, heavy wooden doors, and red-clay roof tiles. Every room has a balcony, but all are not created equal. Most have only small Juliet-style balconies. Those facing the ocean are clearly superior, and a few of the ocean-facing rooms even have large balconies with chaise lounges and garden furniture. The pool is a vast, intricate maze built to imitate the canals of Venice, with private nooks and grottoes; kids love exploring it. Parents will appreciate the excellent children's program. The beach here is calm and good for swimming, although it's one of the least attractive beaches on this coast, with a mix of rocks and hard-packed, dark-brown sand. The excellent, if not particularly challenging, golf course winds through some of the neighboring forest. The Stellaris Casino is the largest and plushest I've found at a beach resort in Costa Rica.

Playa Herradura (A.P. 502–4005), San Antonio de Belén. www.marriott.com. ☎ **888/236-2427** in the U.S. and Canada, 2298-0844 or 2630-9000 in Costa Rica. Fax 2630-9090. 200 units. $325–$399 double; $650 suite; $1,500 presidential suite. AE, MC, V. **Amenities:** 4 restaurants; coffee shop; 2 bars; lounge; children's program; concierge; golf course and pro shop; 9-hole miniature golf course; extensive health club and spa; large outdoor pool; room service; smoke-free rooms; 4 outdoor lit tennis courts; Wi-Fi (for a fee) in most public areas. *In room:* A/C, TV, hair dryer, Internet (for a fee), minibar.

Villa Caletas ★★★ Perched above the sea, Villa Caletas enjoys commanding views of the Pacific over forested hillsides. The rooms are all elegantly appointed, but you'll want to stay in a villa or suite. All feature ornate neoclassical decor and a private terrace for soaking up the views. The larger junior suites come with their own outdoor Jacuzzis. The suites and master suites are larger still—and come with their own swimming pools. Of the two master suites, one is a vigorous hike downhill from the main hotel building and restaurants. The same is true of some of the villas and juniors. The Zephyr Palace is a seven-suite addition, located a bit apart from the main hotel and villas. The rooms here are immense and thematically designed—you can choose from an African suite, an Arabian suite, an Oriental suite, and more. All have beautiful ocean views, home theater systems, Jacuzzis, private balconies, and personal concierge service.

A.P. 12358–1000, San José. www.hotelvillacaletas.com. ☎ **2630-0505.** Fax 2637-0404. 52 units. $180 double; $250 villa; $380 suite; $550–$1,500 Zephyr Palace suites. Rates slightly lower in off season; higher during peak periods. Extra person $35. AE, MC, V. **Amenities:** 2 restaurants; bar; concierge; 2 midsize outdoor pools w/spectacular view; spa. *In room:* A/C, TV, minibar.

EXPENSIVE

In addition to the place listed below, **El Paso de las Lapas** (www.elpasodelas lapas.com; ☏ **2643-5678**) is a boutique hotel and spa, located on a hillside a bit inland, between Playa Herradura and Jacó.

Villa Lapas   Located on a lush piece of property along the Río Tarcolitos bordering Carara National Park, Villa Lapas is a good choice if you're looking to combine a bit of ecoadventure and bird-watching with some beach time. The hotel's best feature is its massive, open-air restaurant and deck, which overlooks the river and where meals are served. Villa Lapas has 217 hectares (536 acres) of land with excellent trails, a series of suspended bridges crossing the river, and its own canopy tour. The hotel also features a small re-creation of a typical Costa Rican rural village of times gone by. This riverside attraction has three massive gift shops, an atmospheric old-style Costa Rican bar, and a small chapel, too. The hotel is about 15 to 25 minutes from the beaches of Jacó, Hermosa, and Herradura.

Tárcoles (A.P. 419–4005, San Antonio de Belén). www.villalapas.com. ☏ **2637-0232.** Fax 2637-0232, ext. 249. 56 units. $220 double. Rates include 3 meals daily and taxes. AE, MC, V. **Amenities:** 2 restaurants; 2 bars; small outdoor pool. *In room:* A/C, Wi-Fi.

Where to Eat

Several restaurants, including some fast-food outlets and the Peruvian chain **Inka Grill** (☏ **2637-8510**), are in the strip mall on the highway near the entrance to the beach. At the Los Sueños marina you'll find several other options, including **Bambu,** a sushi bar and Pan-Asian restaurant; **La Linterna,** a fancy Italian restaurant; and **Hook Up,** an excellent American-style grill and restaurant, serving great lunch and light fare, with a second-floor perch and good views. You can make reservations at any of the marina restaurants by calling ☏ **2630-4444.**

VERY EXPENSIVE

El Galeón ★★ FUSION   This is the top restaurant in a complex of restaurants found at the Los Sueños resort and marina. The setting is elegant, service refined, and the menu wide-ranging, creative, and eclectic. Appetizers range from an inventive plate of scallop sliders, to crisp Asian-spiced soft-shell crabs and sea bass *ceviche* served with avocado and a local salsa. For a main course, I recommend the pumpkin, ricotta, and basil–filled ravioli served with grilled Creole jumbo shrimp.

At the marina of the Los Sueños Marriott Resort (p. 360). ☏ **2630-4555.** Reservations recommended. Main courses $18–$40. AE, MC, V. Wed–Sun 6–10pm.

MODERATE

El Pelicano SEAFOOD/COSTA RICAN   This simple beachfront restaurant is a lot like El Hicaco was before success went to its head. Heavy wooden tables and chairs are spread around a large, open-air dining room facing the beach and boats bobbing at anchor off Playa Herradura. The menu features a range of *ceviche,* salads, and main courses, with a heavy—and logical—emphasis on fresh seafood. The *corvina al ajillo* (sea bass in garlic sauce) is excellent, as is the *arroz con mariscos* (rice with seafood). To get here, drive the Playa Herradura road until you hit the beach, and then turn left on the narrow sandy access road.

On the beach in Playa Herradura. (☎ **2637-8910.** Reservations recommended during high season. Main courses C6,500–C39,000. AE, MC, V. Daily noon to 10pm.

Playa Herradura After Dark

Playa Herradura doesn't have much in the way of nightlife. However, if you're into gaming, you'll want to head to the **Stellaris Casino ★★** (☎ **2630-9143**) at the Los Sueños Marriott Resort (p. 360). This is the most elegant and elaborate casino in country.

PLAYA DE JACÓ

Jacó: 117km (73 miles) W of San José; 75km (47 miles) S of Puntarenas

Playa de Jacó is a long stretch of beach strung with a dense hodgepodge of hotels in all price categories, souvenir shops, seafood restaurants, pizza joints, and rowdy bars. The main strip here, which runs parallel to the shoreline, is an overcrowded and congested collection of restaurants, shops, and small strip malls, where pedestrians, bicycles, scooters, cars, and ATVs vie for right of way both day and night.

The number-one attraction here is the surf, and this is definitely a surfer-dominated beach town. Surfers love the consistent beach break; however, the beach itself is not particularly appealing. It consists of dark-gray sand with lots of little rocks, and it's often pretty rough for swimming. Still, given its proximity to San José, Jacó is almost always packed with a mix of foreign and Tico vacationers. Beyond the surf, Jacó is also known for its nightlife. A range of raging bars here offer everything from live music venues to chill lounge environments to beachfront sports bars with pool and foosball tables.

Essentials

GETTING THERE & DEPARTING   By Car: Head west out of San José on the San José–Caldera Highway (CR27). Just past the toll booth at Pavón, this road connects with the Costanera Sur (CR34), or Southern Coastal Highway. The exit is marked for Jacó and CR34. From here, it's a straight and flat shot down the coast to Jacó. The trip should take a little over an hour.

By Bus   Transportes Jacó express buses (☎ **2223-1109** or 2643-3472) leave San José daily every 2 hours between 7am and 7pm from the Coca-Cola bus terminal at Calle 16 between avenidas 1 and 3. The trip takes between 2½ and 3 hours; the fare is C1,945. On weekends and holidays, extra buses are sometimes added, so it's worth calling to check.

Gray Line (☎ **2220-2126;** www.graylinecostarica.com) has one bus that leaves San José for Jacó daily at 8am. The fare is $30. **Interbus** (☎ **2283-5573;** www.interbusonline.com) has two buses that leave San José for Jacó daily at 8am and 2pm, and the fare is $30. Both companies will pick you up at most San José–area hotels. Both also offer connections to most major tourist destinations in the country.

Buses from San José to **Quepos** and Manuel Antonio also pass by Jacó. (They let passengers off on the hwy. about 1km/½ mile from town.) However, during the busy months, some of these buses will refuse passengers getting off in Jacó or will accept them only if they pay the full fare to

A Jacó surf shop.

Quepos or Manuel Antonio. For information and departure times of these buses, see p. 254.

From **Puntarenas,** you can catch daily **Transportes Quepos Puntarenas** (✆ **2777-0743;** www.transportesquepospuntarenas.com) Quepos-bound buses at 5, 8, and 11am and 12:30, 2:30, and 4:30pm. The buses drop you off on the highway outside of town. The trip's duration is 1 hour; the fare is C980.

The Jacó bus station is at the north end of town, at a small mall across from the Jacó Fiesta Hotel. Buses for San José leave daily every 2 hours between 5am and 5pm. Buses returning to San José from Quepos pass periodically and pick up passengers on the highway. Because schedules can change, it's best to ask at your hotel about current departure times.

ORIENTATION Playa de Jacó is a short distance off the southern highway. One main road runs parallel to the beach, with a host of arteries heading toward the water; you'll find most of the town's hotels and restaurants off these roads.

GETTING AROUND Almost everything is within walking distance in Jacó, but you can call **Asotaxi** (✆ **2643-2020** or 2643-1919) for a cab.

You can also rent a bicycle or scooter from a variety of different shops and streetside stands along the main street. A bike rental should run you around $9 to $15 per day, and a scooter should cost between $30 and $60 per day.

For longer excursions, you can rent a car from **Budget** (✆ **2643-2665**), **Economy** (✆ **2643-1098**), **National/Alamo** (✆ **2643-1752**), **Payless** (✆ **2643-3224**), or **Zuma** (✆ **2643-3207**). Expect to pay approximately $45 to $90 for a 1-day rental. You might also consider talking to a local taxi driver, who'd probably take you wherever you want to go for about the same price, saving you some hassle and headache.

FAST FACTS The **Banco Nacional** (© 2643-3072) and the **Banco de Costa Rica** (© 2643-3695) have branches in town on the main road. Also on the main road, you can find the **Farmacia Jacó** (© 2643-3205), which is right in the center of town. A gas station is on the main highway, between Playa Herradura and Jacó, and a 24-hour gas station, **El Arroyo,** is on the highway on the southern edge of Jacó. The **health center** (© 2643-3667) and **post office** (© 2643-2175) are at the Municipal Center at the south end of town. However, the best-equipped medical center is the **Pro-Salud** (© 2643-5059), located 4 blocks inland from the Pop's ice-cream shop.

A **public phone office,** where you can make international calls, is in the ICE building on the main road. This office is open Monday through Saturday from 8am to noon and 1 to 5pm. Half a dozen or more **Internet cafes** are in town, as well as several inexpensive full-service laundromats; a **Western Union office** in a small strip mall across from La Hacienda restaurant; a large **Más × Menos** supermarket on the main drag in the center of town; and an even larger and more modern **Automercado** supermarket in the strip mall on the main highway near the entrance to Playa Herradura.

Fun on & off the Beach

Jacó beach has a reputation for dangerous riptides (as does most of Costa Rica's Pacific coast). Even strong swimmers have been known to drown in the power rips. In general, the far southern end of the beach is the calmest and safest place to swim.

As an alternative to Playa de Jacó, you may want to visit other nearby beaches, like **Playa Manta, Playa Blanca, Playa Hermosa, Esterillos,** and **Playa Bejuco.** These beaches are easily reached by car, moped, or even bicycle—if you've got a lot of energy. All are signposted, so you'll have no trouble finding them. These are just south of Jacó. See the sections above and below for more information on these beaches.

Activities & Tours

ATV TOURS Several operations take folks out on ATV tours through the surrounding countryside. Tours range in length from 2 to 6 hours and cost between $65 and $140 per person. Contact **Fourtrax Adventure** (© 2643-2373; www.fourtraxadventure.com), or **Jaguar Riders** (© 2643-0180; www.jaguariders.com).

BIKING You can rent a bike for around $9 to $15 per day or $2 to $3 per hour. Bikes are available from a slew of shops along the main road. Shop around, and make sure you get a bike that is in good condition and that is comfortable.

BUNGEE JUMPING Thrill-seekers can get some serious adrenaline pumping with a trip to **Pacific Bungee** (© 2643-6682; www.pacificbungee.com). In addition to a traditional bungee jump from a 40m tall (120-ft.) steel tower, these folks offer the opportunity for a water immersion at the end of your jump and night-time jumps, as well as other thrilling rides, including their "rocket launch" and "giant swing." The views are fabulous from the top of their tower. Rates run $45 for a single jump, launch, or swing; $70 for two activities; and $100 for three. This place is located 1 block south of the Red Cross (Cruz Roja) toward the southern end of Jacó.

CANOPY TOURS   The easiest way to get up into the canopy here is on the **Rain Forest Aerial Tram Pacific** (*C* **2257-5961;** www.rfat.com; see map "Playas Herradura & Hermosa"). A sister project to the original Rain Forest Aerial Tram (p. 146), this attraction features modified ski-lift type gondolas that take you through and above the transitional forests bordering Carara National Park. The $55 entrance fee includes the guided 40-minute tram ride, and a guided 45-minute hike on a network of trails. You can also hike the company's trails for as long as you like. These folks have a zip-line canopy tour on the same grounds, and offer guided tours, including transportation from both San José and any hotel in the area. The Aerial Tram is a few kilometers inland from an exit just north of the first entrance into Jacó.

Quite a few zip-line and harness-style canopy tours are in this area. **Chiclets Tree Tour** (*C* **2643-1880**) offers up a canopy adventure in nearby Playa Hermosa. This is an adventurous tour, with 16 platforms set in transitional forest, with some sweeping views of the Pacific.

GOLF   The excellent **La Iguana,** an 18-hole golf course at the **Los Sueños Marriott Ocean & Golf Resort** (*C* **2630-9028;** www.golflaiguana. com), is open to nonguests. See p. 360 for details.

HORSEBACK RIDING   Horseback-riding tours give you a chance to get away from all the development in Jacó and see a bit of nature. The best operator in the area, with the best horses, is **Discovery Horseback** (*C* **8838-7550** or 2643-7151; www.horseridecostarica.com) down in Playa Hermosa. It's $65 per person for a 2½-hour tour.

KAYAKING   **Kayak Jacó** (*C* **2643-1233;** www.kayakjaco.com) runs a couple of different trips. Tours are offered in single and tandem sea kayaks, as well as 8-person outrigger canoes. Along the way you'll be able to admire the beautiful coastline, and—when conditions permit—take a snorkel break. Kayak fishing tours and sailing trips aboard a 7.5m (25 ft.) Trimaran are also available. Most options run around 4 hours and include transportation to and from the put-in, as well as fresh fruit and soft drinks during the trip. The tours cost between $55 and $75 per person, depending on the particular trip and group size.

ORGANIZED TOURS FARTHER AFIELD   If you'll be spending your entire Costa Rican visit in Jacó but would like to see some other parts of the country, you can arrange tours through the local offices of **Gray Line Tours** (*C* **2643-3231**), which operates out of the Best Western Jacó Beach Resort (p. 367). Gray Line offers day tours to Arenal and Poás volcanoes; white-water rafting trips; and cruises to Tortuga Island, among its many options. Rates range from $86 to $132 for day trips. Overnight trips are also available. Thanks to improvements to the road, you can reach **Manuel Antonio** in about 1 hour from Jacó. In addition to the above-mentioned companies, many local operators offer a variety of tour options in Manuel Antonio, including trips to the national park, the Rainmaker Nature Refuge, and the Damas Island estuary. See the "Manuel Antonio National Park" section (later in this chapter) for more details on the types of tours and activities available there.

Fishing vessels at the Los Sueños Marina.

SPA   The **Serenity Spa ★** (© 2643-1624; www.serenityspacr.net) offers massages, as well as mud packs, face and body treatments, and manicures and pedicures. The spa's Jacó branch is on the first floor, among a tiny little cul-de-sac of shops next to Zuma Rent-A-Car. These folks also have operations at Villa Caletas.

SPORTFISHING, SCUBA DIVING & SEABORNE FUN   Since the Los Sueños Marriott Resort (p. 360) and its adjacent 250-slip marina opened, most local maritime activity has shifted over there. See p. 358 for information on these activities in this area.

SURFING   The same waves that often make Playa de Jacó dangerous for swimmers make it one of the most popular beaches in the country with surfers. Nearby **Playa Hermosa, Playa Tulin,** and **Playa Escondida** are also excellent surfing beaches. Those who want to challenge the waves can rent surfboards for around $3 an hour or $10 to $15 per day, and boogie boards for $2 an hour, from any one of the numerous surf shops along the main road. If you want to learn how to surf, try the **Jacó Surf School** (© 8829-4697 or 2643-1905; www.jacosurfschool.com), or contact Johnny at **Jaguar Riders** (© 2643-0180; www.jaguariders.com) or ask for him at Club del Mar (see below).

Shopping

If you try to do any shopping in Jacó, you'll be overrun with shops selling T-shirts, cut-rate souvenirs, and handmade jewelry and trinkets. Most of the offerings are of pretty poor quality. A notable exception is **Guacamole ★** (© 2643-1120), a small clothing store that produces its own line of batik beachwear. Guacamole is on the main street through town, close to the center of town.

Where to Stay

Because Playa Herradura, Playa Hermosa de Jacó (not to be confused with either Playa Hermosa in Guanacaste, or Playa Hermosa on the Nicoya Peninsula), Playa Esterillos, and Playa Bejuco are close, many people choose accommodations in these beach towns as well. Selected listings for these towns can be found above and below.

Playa de Jacó

0 — 1/4 mi
0 — 0.25 km

To Playa Herradura and San José

PACIFIC OCEAN

Parque Lapa Verde

To Playa Hermosa & Quepos/Manuel Antonio

ACCOMMODATIONS

Apartotel Girasol **28**
Arenal Pacífico **30**
Best Western Jacó Beach **5**
Club del Mar Condominiums & Resort **32**
El Hicaco Camping **24**
Hotel Catalina **29**
Hotel Nine **31**
Hotel Mar de Luz **18**
Hotel Poseidon **12**
Pochote Grande **1**

SHOPPING

Guacamole **15**

NIGHTLIFE

Beatle Bar **6**
Clarita's Beach Bar & Grill **2**
Congas **3**
Ganesha **20**
Hotel Copacabana **10**
Hotel Poseidon **12**
Jacó Taco **9**
Jazz Casino **33**
Jungle Bar **11**
Le Loft **23**
Los Amigos **16**
Tabacón **13**

RESTAURANTS

Café del M@r **8**
Caliche's Wishbone **19**
El Barco de Mariscos **22**
El Hicaco **25**
El Recreo **4**
Lemon Zest **27**
Los Amigos **16**
Pili Pili **26**
Rioasis **21**
Taco Bar **17**
Tsunami Sushi **14**
Wahoo Restaurant **7**

EXPENSIVE

Best Western Jacó Beach Resort   Situated right on the beach, this five-story hotel offers all the amenities and services you could want at a pretty good price. Still, this is a cut-rate resort, with little charm, romance, or true ambience here. The hotel is often packed throughout the high season, and a party atmosphere pervades the place. The open-air lobby is surrounded by lush gardens, and covered walkways connect the hotel's buildings. Rooms are adequate and have tile floors and walls of glass facing balconies; however, not all of the rooms have good views (some face another building), and many of them show the wear and tear of age and heavy occupancy. Ask for a room on a higher floor and with an ocean view. A large percentage of guests opt for the all-inclusive package; even so, I think you'd do better to sample some of the many restaurants and dining options around Jacó.

Playa de Jacó, Puntarenas. www.bestwerncostarica.com. (C) **800/528-1234** in the U.S. and Canada, or 2643-1000 in Costa Rica. Fax 2643-3833. 125 units. $160 double. Rates include breakfast buffet. AE, DC, MC, V. **Amenities:** Restaurant; bar; bikes; well-equipped gym; 2 circular outdoor pools; room service; tennis court; volleyball; free calls to the U.S. and Canada. *In room:* A/C, TV, Wi-Fi.

Club del Mar Condominiums & Resort ★★ ☺   This has perennially been my top choice in Playa de Jacó. It has a fabulous location, friendly management, and attractively designed rooms. Club del Mar is at the far southern end of the beach, where the rocky hills meet the sand, and where the swimming is probably the safest in town. Most of the rooms are actually one- or two-bedroom condo units, with full kitchens. All are spacious and feature private balconies or porches. Eight rooms are also on the second floor of the large main building, as well as two huge and luxurious penthouse suites up on the third floor. All units come with an ocean view, although some are more open and expansive than others. The grounds are lush and chock-full of flowering heliconia and ginger. The resort has a midsize multipurpose pool, an excellent open-air restaurant, and some modest spa facilities. Thanks to its welcoming, family-friendly vibe, this is a great choice for those traveling with children.

Playa de Jacó, Puntarenas. www.clubdelmarcostarica.com. ✆ **866/978-5669** in the U.S. and Canada, or 2643-3194 in Costa Rica. Fax 2643-3550. 32 units. $151 double; $228–$332 condo; $409 penthouse. AE, DC, MC, V. **Amenities:** Restaurant; bar; babysitting; concierge; midsize free-form outdoor pool; room service; small spa; Wi-Fi (in main building and around pool). *In room:* A/C, TV, fridge.

MODERATE

In addition to the places listed below, the oceanfront **Apartotel Girasol** ★ (www.girasol.com; ✆ **800/923-2779** or 2643-1591), with 16 fully equipped one-bedroom apartments, is a good option, especially for longer stays. **Hotel Poseidon** (www.hotel-poseidon.com; ✆ **888/643-1242** in the U.S. and Canada, or 2643-1642) is a pretty boutique hotel in the heart of downtown, while **Hotel Catalina** (www.hotelcatalinacr.com; ✆ **2643-1237**) is another good beachfront choice.

Arenal Pacífico ★   This is a good midrange option, and it's right on the beach to boot. The rooms are nothing special—and almost none offer an ocean view—but they are clean and cool, and most are pretty spacious. The grounds are lush by Jacó standards—you have to cross a shady bridge over a little stream to get from the parking lot and reception to the rooms and restaurant. I like the second-floor rooms, which have private balconies. The superior rooms are larger, and come with coffeemakers and minifridges. There are two outdoor pools—one with a little waterfall filling it, another with a round children's pool. The open-air restaurant serves standard Tico and international fare.

Playa de Jacó (A.P. 962–1000, San José), Puntarenas. www.arenalpacifico.com. ✆ **2643-3419.** Fax 2643-3770. 40 units. $99 double; $129–$137 superior double; $240 junior suite. Rates include continental breakfast. AE, MC, V. **Amenities:** Restaurant; bar; bicycle rental; 2 outdoor pools; surf- and boogie-board rental. *In room:* A/C, TV, Wi-Fi.

Hotel Mar de Luz ★   About 1 block inland from the main drag, all the rooms at this small hotel are immaculate and comfortable. Some feature stone walls, small sitting areas, and one or two double beds placed on a raised sleeping nook. My only complaint is that in most rooms, the windows are too small and mostly sealed, forcing you to use air-conditioning. In the gardens just off the pools are a couple of grills for guest use. A comfortable common sitting area has magazines and books, and there's a game room for the kids. The Dutch owner, Victor Keulen, seems driven to offer as much comfort, quality, and service as he can for the price.

Playa de Jacó, Puntarenas. www.mardeluz.com. ✆/fax **2643-3259.** 29 units. $109 double. Rates include breakfast and taxes. AE, MC, V. **Amenities:** Babysitting; Jacuzzi; 2 outdoor small-to-mid-size adult pools and children's pool; smoke-free rooms. *In room:* A/C, TV, minifridge, Wi-Fi.

Hotel Nine ★   This hotel features contemporary architectural design touches that would be right at home on Miami's South Beach. This is appropriate, as the L-shaped, three-story building fronts the sand toward the southern end of Jacó beach. Inside, the rooms have tropical-style wood and rattan furnishings and bold colors. The premium suites have a small kitchenette with microwave oven. Laundry service and surfboards are both complimentary. The excellent restaurant here bills itself primarily as a steakhouse, but fresh seafood options are also available.

Playa de Jacó, Puntarenas. www.hotelnine.com. ✆ **2643-5335.** 12 units. $90–$150 double; $180 suite. Rates include continental breakfast. AE, DC, MC, V. **Amenities:** Restaurant; bar; Jacuzzi; midsize outdoor pool; room service; all rooms smoke-free; surfboards. *In room:* A/C, TV, minibar, Wi-Fi.

Pochote Grande   This well-kept hotel is located just off the beach toward the far north end of Jacó. All of the rooms are quite large, although sparsely furnished, and have white-tile floors, one queen-size and one single bed, a small fridge, and a balcony or patio. I prefer the second-floor rooms, which are blessed with high ceilings. The modest restaurant and snack bar serve a mixture of Tico, German, and American meals. (The owners are German by way of Africa.) The grounds and surrounding properties here were once shady and lush, but encroaching construction all around has left this place feeling a bit exposed.

Playa de Jacó, Puntarenas. www.hotelpochotegrande.net. ✆ **2643-3236.** Fax 2289-3204. 24 units. $85 double. Add $5 for a room with TV. AE, MC, V. **Amenities:** Restaurant; bar; outdoor pool. *In room:* A/C, fridge, no phone, Wi-Fi.

INEXPENSIVE

Quite a few budget hotels are around town. Most cater to itinerant surfers, backpackers, and Ticos. If you're looking to stay on the cheap, your best bet is to simply walk the strip and see who's got the best room at the best price.

You can try camping at **El Hicaco** (✆ **2643-3004**), which is very centrally located and close to the beach, but it's also nearby the Disco La Central, so don't expect to get much sleep if you stay here. In addition, you'll need to be very careful with your belongings; I've heard several complaints of robberies at the campsites here. Camping runs around C3,500 per person per night.

Where to Eat

Playa de Jacó has a wide range of restaurants. Many cater to surfers and budget travelers. In addition to the places listed below, if you're looking for simply prepared fresh seafood, **El Barco de Mariscos** (✆ **2643-2831**) and **El Recreo** (✆ **2643-3012**) are both good bets that serve standard Tico beach fare—fresh seafood, sandwiches, chicken, and steak. For a coffee break and newly baked pastries and breads, head to **Café del M@r** (✆ **2643-1250**). **Wahoo Restaurant** (✆ **2643-1876**) offers good fresh seafood. **Pili Pili** ★ (✆ **2643-5535** or 8995-4946) serves up fusion fare, with dominant African and French flavors. And sushi lovers should head to **Tsunami Sushi** (✆ **2643-3678;** www.tsunami sushicr.com), inside the El Galeone strip mall.

EXPENSIVE

El Hicaco ♨ COSTA RICAN/SEAFOOD   This beachside restaurant is too popular for its own good. The whole operation has a cattle-car feel to it, and the food is overpriced and quality has declined. But the setting is still wonderful: right on the edge of the beach, with the majority of the tables outdoors. At night you sit under the stars, surrounded by tall palm trees, with some interesting lighting overhead. If you do come here, stick with the freshly caught grilled seafood or lobster, although the menu has plenty of meat and chicken selections as well.

On the beach in downtown Jacó. ℂ **2643-3226.** www.elhicaco.net. Reservations recommended during high season. Main courses C8,300–C33,500. AE, MC, V. Daily 11am–11pm.

Lemon Zest ★★★ SEAFOOD/FUSION   Former Le Cordon Bleu instructor, chef Richard Lemon runs what is easily the best restaurant in Jacó. Set on the second-floor of a small strip-mall, right on Jacó's main strip, the decor is elegant, with subdued lighting and white cloth-covered tables. I recommend starting things off with the lobster and manchego quesadilla, or the Korean BBQ satay skewers served with homemade banana ketchup. Seafood main courses include macadamia-crusted mahimahi and fresh seared tuna. For a splurge, try the sesame-and-panko-crusted lobster with a pineapple risotto and sweet chile sauce. You can also choose from daily specials and some outrageous desserts. The wine list here is well-priced, with several good selections offered by the glass.

Downtown Jacó. ℂ **2643-2591.** www.lemonzestjaco.com. Reservations recommended during high season. Main courses $4–$32. AE, MC, V. Mon–Sat 5:30–10pm, Sun 5–9pm.

INEXPENSIVE

Caliche's Wishbone ★ SEAFOOD/MEXICAN   This casual spot is popular with surfers and offers Tex-Mex standards and homemade pizzas. However, you can also get excellent seafood dishes, as well as a variety of sandwiches served in homemade pita bread. The portions are huge. It almost always has fresh tuna lightly seared and served with a soy-wasabi dressing. The nicest tables are streetside on a covered veranda. Inside are more tables, as well as a bar with television sets showing surf videos.

On the main road in Jacó. ℂ **2643-3406.** Reservations not accepted. Main courses $6–$25. AE, MC, V. Thurs–Tues 12–10pm.

Los Amigos INTERNATIONAL/SEAFOOD   Set on a large corner of a busy intersection in the heart of Jacó, this restaurant serves fresh seafood and adventurous international fare at very reasonable prices. Sturdy wooden tables are spread around the small dining room and open-air patio here. I prefer the patio seating, which looks out over flowering heliconia to the bustle of Jacó's main drag. Fresh tuna can be had Cajun-style or with a spicy mango salsa. Several traditional Thai dishes are also on the menu, as well as some wraps and hearty salads. At night, they play electronic music and have a lively bar scene.

On the main road in Jacó. ℂ **2643-2961.** www.losamigosjaco.com. Main courses $7–$20. AE, MC, V. Sun–Thurs 11am–11pm, Fri–Sat 11am–1am.

Rioasis ☺ PIZZA/MEXICAN   Rioasis serves hearty burritos, simple pasta dishes, and a wide array of freshly baked wood-oven pizzas. My favorite item is the Greek pizza, with olives, feta cheese, and anchovies, but the barbecue chicken pizza is also delicious. Choose from both indoor and terrace seating, or the bar area, complete with a pool table, dartboards, and a couple of TVs for sports events and surf videos.

On the main road in Jacó. ℂ **2643-3354.** Reservations not accepted. Main courses C3,000–C9,500. MC, V. Daily noon to 10pm.

Taco Bar ★ MEXICAN/INTERNATIONAL   This casual little open-air joint serves up excellent food at great prices. The best option here is to order a one-, two-, or three-taco plate with the accompanying salad bar. Choose from fresh fish, chicken, shrimp, calamari, or any combination of them. My favorites are the coconut shrimp and spicy fish fillings. The well-stocked salad bar features a wide range of stand-alone salads, as well as numerous toppings to finish off your tacos. You won't leave here hungry. A few wooden tables are set outdoors under large umbrellas, but most of the seating is around a large U-shaped bar. The seats are either high stools or wood planks hung from ropes, like swings. They also serve breakfast, pizzas, and a small selection of full entrees, and offer free Wi-Fi for diners.

A half-block inland from Pop's, central Jacó. (✆ **2643-0222** or 8836-2049. www.tacobar.info. Reservations not accepted. Main courses C3,300–C6,700. MC, V. Tues–Sun 7:30am–10pm, Mon noon–10pm.

Playa de Jacó After Dark

Playa de Jacó is the central Pacific's party town, with tons of bars and several discos. My favorite bar in town is the beachfront **Ganesha Lounge ★★**, which has a laid-back Ibiza-like club vibe, while **Le Loft ★**, on the main street and near the center of town, seeks to attract a more sophisticated and chic clubbing crowd.

For a more casual atmosphere, head to either **Los Amigos** or **Tabacón ★** on the main street through Jacó, near the center of town. Tabacón has popular pool and foosball tables, and often has live music.

Other popular bars in town are the **Beatle Bar** (www.thebeatlebar.com), **Jungle Bar,** and **Jacó Taco.** All of the aforementioned bars are along the main strip through town. *Note:* Jacó has a good amount of prostitution. It's not uncommon to find working women at any of the above-mentioned places, particularly the Beatle Bar, as well as cruising other bars around town.

For a dance scene, try **Congas ★**, which often has live salsa bands, and is toward the south end of town. Congas usually charges a nominal cover charge.

Sports freaks can catch the latest games at **Clarita's Beach Bar & Grill, Hotel Copacabana** (both are right on the beach toward the north end of town), or **Hotel Poseidon** (on a side street near the center of town). The first two serve up good reasonably priced burritos, burgers, and bar food, while the latter offers much the same, as well as some items from their much better restaurant downstairs.

If you're into gaming, head to the **Stellaris Casino ★★** (✆ **2630-9143**) at the Los Sueños Marriott Resort (p. 360), or the **Jazz Casino** (✆ **2643-2316**) at the Hotel Amapola. The latter is a modest casino situated toward the southern end of the main road through Jacó (Av. Pastor Díaz), about a block beyond where it takes a sharp turn inland toward the Costanera Sur.

En Route South: Playas Hermosa, Esterillos & Bejuco

South of Jacó, Costa Rica's coastline is a long, almost entirely straight stretch of largely undeveloped beach backed by thick forests and low lying rice and African palm plantations.

Playa Esterillos.

Playa Hermosa ★, 10km (6¼ miles) southeast of Jacó, is the first beach you'll hit as you head down the Southern Coastal Highway. This is primarily a surfers' beach, but it is still a lovely spot to spend some beach time. In fact, even though the surf conditions here can be rather rough and unprotected, and the beach is made of dark volcanic sand, I find Playa Hermosa and the beaches south of it much more attractive than Jacó. Be careful on Playa Hermosa, as the fine dark sand can get extremely hot in the tropical sun, so be sure to have adequate footwear and a large towel or mat to lay out on the sand. Aside from a small grouping of hotels and restaurants, most of Playa Hermosa is protected, as **olive ridley sea turtles** lay eggs here from July to December. During turtle nesting season, all of the hotel tour desks and local tour agencies can help you arrange a nighttime turtle nesting tour, for around $40 to $50 per person.

Playa Hermosa is the only beach in this section located right along the Southern Coastal Highway; all of the rest are a kilometer or so set in from the road and reached by a series of dirt access roads. If you exit the highway in Playa Hermosa, you can follow a dirt-and-sand access road that runs parallel to the shore along several miles of deserted, protected beach, as Playa Hermosa eventually becomes **Playa Tulin,** near the Tulin river mouth. This is another popular surf spot. Still be careful, crocodiles live in the Tulin river.

As you continue down the coastal highway from Playa Hermosa you will hit Esterillos. **Playa Esterillos,** 22km (14 miles) south of Jacó, is long and wide and almost always nearly deserted. Playa Esterillos is so long, in fact, that it has three separate entrances and sections, Esterillos Oeste, Centro, and Este—West, Center, and East, in order as you head away from Jacó.

If you keep heading south (really southeast), you next come to **Playa Bejuco,** another long, wide, nearly deserted stretch of sand. Playa Bejuco, which features a very narrow strip of land fronting the beach, with mangroves and swampland behind, has very little development.

Note: While beautiful, isolated, and expansive, the beaches of Hermosa, Esterillos, and Bejuco can be quite rough at times and dangerous for swimming. Caution is highly advised here.

WHERE TO STAY IN PLAYA HERMOSA
Moderate
In addition to the places listed below, you might want to check out **Surf Inn Hermosa** (www.surfinnhermosa.com; ✆ **2643-7184**), which offers 1-bedroom

studios with a kitchenette, and 2-bedroom fully equipped condo units, right on the beach.

The Backyard This perennially popular bar and restaurant also has some of the most comfortable accommodations in Playa Hermosa, although they're definitely overpriced for what you get. The two-story building features large rooms with dark red terra-cotta tile floors and simple furnishings. The second-floor rooms are better than those on the ground floor. The oceanfront end units are classified as suites. They are a bit bigger and do have excellent ocean views. The small pool features a little sculpted-rock waterfall and is quite refreshing on hot days. Despite the more elaborate facilities and amenities, this place is still quintessentially a surfer joint, and the main reason to stay here is that this hotel sits directly in front of the principal peaks on Playa Hermosa. At night, most folks find their way to the raucous surfer bar here, with a pool table, darts, and hearty food.

Playa Hermosa de Jacó, Puntarenas. www.backyardhotel.com. ✆/fax **2643-7011.** 8 units. $110–$175 double. AE, MC, V. **Amenities:** Restaurant; bar; small outdoor pool. *In room:* A/C, TV.

Hotel Fuego del Sol ★ This place is right on the beach and offers clean, cool, and comfortable rooms, and easy access to the waves. Most of the rooms are housed in a long, two-story block set perpendicular to the beach. Each comes with a queen-size and twin bed and a private balcony overlooking the free-form pool. Those closest to the water will also give you a glimpse of the sea. The suites come with king-size beds, a separate sitting room, and a fully stocked kitchenette. Everything is well maintained, and the restaurant has a good view of the beach action. This place is a bit better value, and definitely a mellower option, than the Backyard (see above).

Playa Hermosa de Jacó, Puntarenas. www.fuegodelsolhotel.com. ✆ **2643-7171.** Fax 2288-0123. 24 units. $98 double; $155 suite. Rates include breakfast. Lower rates in off season. MC, V. **Amenities:** Restaurant; bar; pool. *In room:* A/C, TV.

Inexpensive

Playa Hermosa has a host of simple hotels and cabinas catering to surfers. Prices, conditions, and upkeep can vary greatly. If you've got the time, your best bet is to visit a few until you find the best deal on the cleanest room. **Costanera Bed & Breakfast** (www.costaneraplayahermosa.com; ✆ **2643-7044**), **Cabinas Las Arenas** (www.cabinaslasarenas.com; ✆ **2643-7013**), and **Cabinas Las Olas** (www.lasolashotel.com; ✆ **2643-7021**) are three good options.

WHERE TO STAY IN PLAYA ESTERILLOS

If you're looking for something even more remote and undeveloped than the hotel listed below, head to Playa Esterillos Este and the **Pelican Hotel** (www.pelicanbeachfronthotel.com; ✆ **2778-8105**), a simple, cozy beachfront bed-and-breakfast.

Very Expensive

Alma del Pacifico Hotel ★★ 📖 Formerly known as Xandari By The Pacific, this beachfront boutique resort features large, private villas, with high, curved ceilings and loads of artistic touches. I especially like the open, mosaic tile showers that let out onto lush gardens. The Maxima villas are the top option and come with their own private plunge pool. Most of the villas are beachfront, but those that aren't have large gardens and a wonderful sense of seclusion and romance.

The open-air seafront restaurant serves excellent international fare, with an equal emphasis on healthy fresh ingredients and creative cooking combinations. **Note:** This place was bought by Rock Resorts in late 2010. Major remodeling and updating is slated to take place in late 2011, just in time for the 2012 season.

Playa Esterillos Centro, Puntarenas. www.legendarylodging.com. ℰ **866/495-7625** in the U.S. and Canada, or 2778-7070 in Costa Rica. Fax 2778-7878. 20 units. $354–$678 double. Rates include full breakfast. AE, MC, V. **Amenities:** Restaurant; bar; concierge; Jacuzzi; 2 outdoor lap pools; room service; all rooms smoke-free; full-service spa; Wi-Fi. *In room:* A/C, kitchenette, minibar.

WHERE TO STAY IN PLAYA BEJUCO
Moderate
Hotel Playa Bejuco ★ ☺ A half-block off the beach at Playa Bejuco, this is a younger sister to the popular Mar de Luz hotel in Jacó (p. 368). The two-story hotel is an L-shape around a central swimming pool and gardens and faces the ocean. The construction features various walls and details made from heavy, smooth river stones. Rooms are spacious and cool, with tile floors and simple wooden furnishings. The second-floor rooms are the biggest, and most feature high ceilings with sleeping lofts, making them good options for families with children.

Playa Bejuco, Puntarenas. www.hotelplayabejuco.com. ℰ/fax **2778-8181.** 20 units. $121 double. Rates include breakfast and taxes. Lower rates in off season. AE, MC, V. **Amenities:** Restaurant; bar; outdoor pool. *In room:* A/C, TV, minifridge, Wi-Fi.

MANUEL ANTONIO NATIONAL PARK ★★

140km (87 miles) SW of San José; 69km (43 miles) S of Playa de Jacó

Manuel Antonio was Costa Rica's first major ecotourist destination and remains one of its most popular. The views from the hills overlooking Manuel Antonio are spectacular, the beaches (especially those inside the national park) are idyllic, and its rainforests are crawling with howler, white-faced, and squirrel monkeys, among other forms of exotic wildlife. The downside is that you'll have to pay more to see it, and you'll have to share it with more fellow travelers than you would at other rainforest destinations around the country. Moreover, development has begun to destroy what makes this place so special. What was once a smattering of small hotels tucked into the forested hillside has become a long string of lodgings along the 7km (4⅓ miles) of road between Quepos and the national park entrance. Hotel roofs now regularly break the tree line, and there seems to be no control over zoning and unchecked ongoing construction. A jumble of snack shacks, souvenir stands, and makeshift parking lots choke the beach road just outside the park, making the entrance road look more like a shanty than a national park.

Still, this remains a beautiful destination, with a wide range of attractions and activities. Gazing down on the blue Pacific from high on the hillsides of Manuel Antonio, it's almost impossible to hold back a gasp of delight. Offshore, rocky islands dot the vast expanse of blue, and in the foreground, the rich, deep green of the rainforest sweeps down to the water. Even cheap disposable cameras

A squirrel monkey.

A palm plantation nearby Quepos.

regularly produce postcard-perfect snapshots. It's this superb view that keeps people transfixed on decks, patios, and balconies throughout the area.

One of the most popular national parks in the country, Manuel Antonio is also one of the smallest, covering fewer than 680 hectares (1,680 acres). Its several nearly perfect small beaches are connected by trails that meander through the rainforest. The mountains surrounding the beaches quickly rise as you head inland from the water; however, the park was created to preserve not its beautiful beaches but its forests, home to endangered squirrel monkeys, three-toed sloths, purple-and-orange crabs, and hundreds of other species of birds, mammals, and plants. Once, this entire stretch of coast was a rainforest teeming with wildlife, but now only this small rocky outcrop of forest remains.

Those views that are so bewitching also have their own set of drawbacks. If you want a great view, you aren't going to be staying on the beach—in fact, you probably won't be able to walk to the beach. This means that you'll be driving back and forth, taking taxis, or riding the public bus. Also keep in mind that it's hot and humid here, and it rains a lot. However, the rain is what keeps Manuel Antonio lush and green, and this wouldn't be the Tropics if things were otherwise.

If you're traveling on a rock-bottom budget or are mainly interested in sport-fishing, you might end up staying in the nearby town of **Quepos,** which was once a quiet banana port and now features a wide variety of restaurants, souvenir and crafts shops, and lively bars; the land to the north was used by Chiquita to grow its bananas. Disease wiped out most of the banana plantations, and now the land is planted primarily with African oil-palm trees. To reach Quepos by road, you pass through miles of these **oil-palm plantations;** see the box "Profitable Palms," below, for info.

Despite the above caveats, Manuel Antonio is still a fabulous destination with a wealth of activities and attractions for all types and all ages. If you plan carefully, you can avoid many of the problems that detract from its appeal. If you steer clear of the peak months (Dec–Mar), you'll miss most of the crowds. If you must come during the peak months, try to avoid weekends, when the beach is packed with families and young Ticos from San José. If you visit the park early in the morning, you can leave when the crowds begin to show up at midday. In the afternoon, you can lounge by your pool or on your patio.

Essentials

GETTING THERE & DEPARTING   **By Plane: Sansa** (© 877/767-2672 in the U.S. and Canada, or 2290-4100 in Costa Rica; www.flysansa.com) has seven daily flights to the **Quepos airport** (no phone; airport code: XQP) beginning at 6am, with the final flight departing at 3:30pm from San José's Juan Santamaría International Airport. The flight's duration is 30 minutes; the fare is $82 each way.

   Nature Air (© 800/235-9272 in the U.S. and Canada, or 2299-6000 in Costa Rica; www.natureair.com) flies to Quepos daily at 9am and 2pm from Tobías Bolaños International Airport in Pavas (p. 104). The flight duration is 30 minutes; the fare is $83 each way.

   Both Sansa and Nature Air provide minivan airport-transfer service coordinated with their arriving flights. The service costs around $8 per person each way, depending on where your hotel is located. Speak to your airline's agent when you arrive to confirm your return flight and coordinate a pickup at your hotel for that day if necessary. Taxis meet incoming flights as well. Expect to be charged between $10 and $15 per car for up to four people, depending on the distance to your hotel.

   When you're ready to depart, **Sansa** (© 2777-1912 in Quepos) flights begin departing at 8:40am, with the final flight leaving at 3:30pm. **Nature Air** (© 2777-2548 in Quepos) flights leave for San José daily at 7:50 and 10:45am and 1:25 and 5pm.

   By Car: From San José, take the San José–Caldera Highway (CR27) west to Orotina. Just past the toll booth at Pavón, this road connects with the Costanera Sur (CR34), or Southern Coastal Highway. The exit is marked for Jacó and CR34. From here, it's a straight and flat shot down the coast to Quepos and Manuel Antonio.

   If you're coming from Guanacaste or any point north, take the Interamerican Highway to the Puntarenas turnoff and follow signs to the San José–Caldera Highway (CR27). Take this east toward Orotina, where it connects with the Costanera Sur (CR34). It's about a 4½-hour drive from Liberia to Quepos and Manuel Antonio.

   By Bus: Express buses (© 2223-5567) to Manuel Antonio leave San José daily at 6 and 9am, noon, and 2:30, 6, and 7:30pm from the Coca-Cola bus terminal at Calle 16 between avenidas 1 and 3. Trip duration is 3½ hours; the fare is C3,785. These buses go all the way to the park entrance and will drop you off at any of the hotels along the way.

10

THE CENTRAL PACIFIC COAST | Manuel Antonio National Park

Regular buses (☎ 2223-5567) to Quepos leave San José daily at 6, 7, 9, and 10am, and 12, 2, 2:20, 3, 4, 5, 6, and 7:30pm. Trip duration is 4 hours; the fare is C3,530. These buses stop in Quepos. From here, if you're staying at one of the hotels on the road to Manuel Antonio, you must take a local bus or taxi to your hotel.

Gray Line (☎ 2220-2126; www.graylinecostarica.com) has one daily bus that leaves San José for Quepos and Manuel Antonio at 8am. The return bus leaves at 3pm for San José. Interbus (☎ 2283-5573; www.interbusonline.com) has two daily buses that leave San José for Quepos and Manuel Antonio at 7:30am and 2:30pm. Return buses leave at 8am and 1pm. Both companies charge $40 one-way and will pick you up at most San José—and Manuel Antonio—area hotels and also offer connections to various other popular destinations around Costa Rica.

Buses leave **Puntarenas** for Quepos daily at 5, 8, and 11am and 12:30, 2:30, and 4:30pm. The ride takes 2 hours; the fare is C1,635.

Many of the buses for Quepos stop to unload and pick up passengers in **Playa de Jacó.** If you're in Jacó heading toward Manuel Antonio, you can try your luck at one of the covered bus stops out on the Interamerican Highway (see "Playa de Jacó, Playa Hermosa & Playa Herradura," earlier in this chapter).

When you're ready to depart, the **Quepos bus station** (☎ 2777-0263) is next to the market, which is 3 blocks east of the water and 2 blocks north of the road to Manuel Antonio. Express buses to San José leave daily at 4, 6, and 9:30am, noon, and 2:30 and 5pm. Local buses to San José (duration is 4 hr.) leave at 5, 6, and 10am, noon, and 2 and 4:45pm.

In the busy winter months, tickets sell out well in advance, especially on weekends; if you can, purchase your ticket several days in advance. However, you must buy your Quepos-bound tickets in San José and your San José return tickets in Quepos. If you're staying in Manuel Antonio, you can buy your return ticket for a direct bus in advance in Quepos, and then wait along the road to be picked up. There is no particular bus stop; just make sure you are out to flag down the bus and give it time to stop—you don't

Profitable Palms

On any drive to or from Quepos and Manuel Antonio, you will pass through miles and miles of African palm plantations. Native to West Africa, *Elaeis guineensis* was planted along this stretch in the 1940s by United Fruit, in response to a blight that was attacking their banana crops. The palms took hold and soon proved quite profitable, being blessed with copious bunches of plum-size nuts that are rich in oil. This oil is extracted and processed in plantations that dot the road between Jacó and Quepos. The smoke and distinct smell of this processing is often easily noticed. The processed oil is eventually shipped overseas and used in a wide range of products, including soaps, cosmetics, lubricants, and food products.

These plantations are a major source of employment in the area—note the small, orderly "company towns" built for workers—but their presence is controversial. The palm trees aren't native, and the farming practices are thought by some to threaten Costa Rica's biodiversity.

want to be standing in a blind spot when the bus comes flying around a tight corner.

Buses for **Puntarenas** leave daily at 4:30, 7:30, and 10:30am and 12:30, 3, and 5:30pm. Any bus headed for San José or Puntarenas will let you off in Playa de Jacó.

ORIENTATION Quepos is a small port city at the mouth of the Boca Vieja Estuary. If you're heading to Manuel Antonio National Park, or any hotel on the way to the park, after crossing the bridge into town, take the lower road (to the left of the high road). In 4 blocks, turn left, and you'll be on the road to Manuel Antonio. This road winds through town a bit before starting over the hill to all the hotels and the national park.

GETTING AROUND A taxi between Quepos and Manuel Antonio (or any hotel along the road toward the park) costs between C3,500 and C4,000, depending upon the distance. At night or if the taxi must leave the main road (for hotels such as La Mariposa, Parador, Makanda, and Arenas del Mar), the charge is a little higher. If you need to call a taxi, dial ✆ **2777-3080** or 2777-0425. Taxis are supposed to use meters, although this isn't always the case. If your taxi doesn't have a meter, or the driver won't use it, try to negotiate in advance. Ask your hotel desk what a specific ride should cost, and use that as your guide.

The bus between Quepos and Manuel Antonio (✆ **2777-0318**) takes 15 minutes each way and runs roughly every half-hour from 5:30am to 9:30pm daily. The buses, which leave from the main bus terminal in Quepos, near the market, go all the way to the national park entrance before turning around and returning. You can flag down these buses from any point on the side of the road. The fare is C210.

You can also rent a car from **Adobe** (✆ **2777-4242**), **Alamo/National** (✆ **2777-3344**), **Economy** (✆ **2777-5260**), or **Hertz** (✆ **2777-3365**) for around $45 to $90 a day. All have offices in downtown Quepos or Manuel Antonio, but with advance notice, someone will meet you at the airport with your car for no extra charge.

If you rent a car, never leave anything of value in it unless you intend to stay within sight of the car at all times. Car break-ins are common here. A couple of parking lots just outside the park entrance cost around $3 for the entire day. You should definitely keep your car in one of these while exploring the park or soaking up sun on the beach. And although these lots do offer a modicum of protection and safety, you still should not leave anything of value exposed in the car. The trunk is probably safe, though.

FAST FACTS The telephone number of the **Quepos Hospital** is ✆ 2777-0922. In the event of an emergency, you can also call the **Cruz Roja** (Red Cross; ✆ **2777-0116**). For the **local police,** call ✆ **2777-1511.**

The **post office** (✆ **2777-1471**) is in downtown Quepos. Several pharmacies are in Quepos, as well as a pharmacy at the hospital, and another close to the park entrance. A half-dozen or so laundromats and laundry services are in town.

Several major Costa Rican banks have branches and ATMs in downtown Quepos, and a couple of ATMs have sprung up along the road to the national park. An ample array of **Internet cafes** can be found around Quepos and along the road to Manuel Antonio, and many hotels have them as well.

THE CENTRAL PACIFIC COAST | Manuel Antonio National Park

Exploring the National Park

Manuel Antonio is a small park with three major trails. Most visitors come primarily to lie on a beach and check out the white-faced monkeys, which sometimes seem as common as tourists. A guide is not essential here, but unless you're experienced in rainforest hiking, you'll see and learn a lot more with one. A 2- or 3-hour guided hike should cost between $25 and $50 per person. Almost any of the hotels in town can help you set up a tour of the park. Bird-watchers might want to book a tour with **Ave Natura** (© **2777-0973**), a local tour agency that special-

A Manuel Antonio National Park trail.

izes in birding. If you decide to explore the park on your own, see the trail map on the inside front cover of this book.

ENTRY POINT, FEES & REGULATIONS The park (© **2777-5185**) is closed on Monday but is open Tuesday through Sunday from 7am to 4pm year-round. The entrance fee is $10 per person. The principal park entrance is at **Playa Espadilla,** the beach at the end of the road from Quepos. To reach the park station, you must cross a small, sometimes polluted stream that's little more than ankle-deep at low tide but that can be knee- or even waist-deep at high tide. It's even reputed to be home to a crocodile or two. For years there has been talk of building a bridge over this stream; in the meantime you'll have to either wade it or pay a boatman a small voluntary tip for the very quick crossing. Just over the stream and over a small rise is a small ranger station. Another ranger station is inland at the end of the side road that leads off perpendicular to Playa Espadilla just beyond Marlin Restaurant.

MINAE, the national ministry that oversees the park, has been frus-tratingly inconsistent about which entrance visitors must use. As of this writing, tickets are being sold only at the inland entrance. The trail from here begins with about 20 to 30 minutes of hiking along an often muddy access road before you get to the beach and principal park trails. If this is still the situation when you visit, I recommend buying your ticket here, then heading back to the principal beach entrance to begin your exploration of the park. **Note:** The Parks Service allows only 600 visitors to enter each day, which could mean that you won't get in if you arrive in midafternoon during the high season. Camping is not allowed.

THE BEACHES **Playa Espadilla Sur** (as opposed to Playa Espadilla, which is just outside the park; see "Hitting the Water," below) is the first beach within the actual park boundaries. It's usually the least crowded and one of the best places to find a quiet shade tree to plant yourself under. However, if there's any surf, this is also the roughest beach in the park. If you want to explore further, you can walk along this soft-sand beach or follow a trail through the rainforest parallel to the beach. **Playa Manuel Antonio,** which is the most popular beach inside the park, is a short, deep crescent of

Playa Espadilla Sur.

white sand backed by lush rainforest. The water here is sometimes clear enough to offer good snorkeling along the rocks at either end, and it's usually fairly calm. At low tide, Playa Manuel Antonio shows a very interesting relic: a circular stone turtle trap left by its pre-Columbian residents. From Playa Manuel Antonio, another slightly longer trail leads to **Puerto Escondido,** where a blowhole sends up plumes of spray at high tide.

THE HIKING TRAILS From either Playa Espadilla Sur or Playa Manuel Antonio, you can take a circular loop trail (1.4km/0.9-mile) around a high promontory bluff. The highest point on this hike, which takes about 25 to 30 minutes round-trip, is **Punta Catedral ★★**, where the view is spectacular. The trail is a little steep in places, but anybody in average shape can do it. I have done it in sturdy sandals, but you might want to wear good hiking shoes. This is a good place to spot monkeys, although you're more likely to see a white-faced monkey than a rare squirrel monkey. Another good place to see monkeys is the **trail inland** from Playa Manuel Antonio. This is a linear trail and mostly uphill, but it's not too taxing. It's great to spend hours exploring the steamy jungle and then take a refreshing dip in the ocean.

 Helping Out

If you want to help efforts in protecting the local environment and the severely endangered squirrel monkey *(mono titi),* make a donation to the **Mono Titi Alliance** (☎ 2777-2306; www.monotiti.org), an organization supported by local businesses and individual donors, or to **Kids Saving The Rainforest** (☎ 2777-2592; www.kidssavingthe rainforest.org), which was started in 1999 by a couple of local children.

Finally, a trail connects Puerto Escondido (see above) and **Punta Surrucho,** which has some sea caves. Be careful when hiking beyond Puerto Escondido: What seems like easy beach hiking at low tide becomes treacherous to impassable at high tide. Don't get trapped.

Hitting the Water

BEACHES OUTSIDE THE PARK   **Playa Espadilla,** the gray-sand beach just outside the park boundary, is often perfect for board surfing and bodysurfing. At times it's a bit rough for casual swimming, but with no entrance fee, it's the most popular beach with locals and visiting Ticos. Some shops by the water rent boogie boards and beach chairs and umbrellas. A full-day rental of a beach umbrella and two chaise lounges costs around $10. (These are not available inside the park.) This beach is actually a great spot to learn how to surf, because several open-air shops renting surfboards and boogie boards are along the beachfront road. Rates run $5 to $10 per hour, and around $20 to $30 per day. If you want a lesson, I recommend the **Manuel Antonio Surf School** (✆ **2777-4842;** www.masurfschool.com), which has a kiosk on the road to Manuel Antonio.

BOATING, KAYAKING, RAFTING & SPORTFISHING TOURS   **Iguana Tours** (✆ **2777-2052;** www.iguanatours.com) is the most established and dependable tour operator in the area, offering river rafting, sea kayaking, mangrove tours, and guided hikes.

The above company, as well as **Rios Tropicales** (✆ **2777-4092;** www.aventurash2o.com), offer full-day rafting trips for around $85 to $110. Large multiperson rafts are used during the rainy season, and single-person "duckies" are broken out when the water levels drop. Both of the above companies also offer half-day rafting adventures and sea-kayaking trips for around $65. Depending on rainfall and demand, they will run either the Naranjo or Savegre rivers. I very much prefer the **Savegre River ★★** for its stunning scenery.

Another of my favorite tours in the area is a mangrove tour of the **Damas Island estuary.** These trips generally include lunch, a stop on Damas Island, and roughly 3 to 4 hours of cruising the waterways. You'll see loads of wildlife. The cost is usually around $60 to $80.

White-water rafting the Savegre River.

A Damas Island boat tour.

Among the other boating options around Quepos/Manuel Antonio are excursions in search of dolphins and sunset cruises. **Iguana Tours** (see above) and **Planet Dolphin ★** (𝒞/fax **2777-1647;** www.planetdolphin. com) offer these tours for $75 per person, depending upon the size of the group and the length of the cruise. Most tours include a snorkel break and, if lucky, dolphin sightings. **Jungle Coast Jets** (𝒞 **2777-1706;** www.jungle coastjets.com) offers 2-hour jet-ski tours for $95 per person. This tour plies the same waters and includes some snorkeling and the possibility of a dolphin encounter.

Quepos is one of Costa Rica's billfish centers, and sailfish, marlin, and tuna are all common in these waters. In the past year or so, fresh and brackish water fishing in the mangroves and estuaries has also become popular. If you're into sportfishing, try hooking up with **Blue Fin Sportfishing** (𝒞 **2777-0000;** www.bluefinsportfishing.com) or **Luna Tours Sportfishing** (𝒞 **2777-0725;** www.lunatours.net). A full day of fishing should cost between $550 and $1,800, depending on the size of the boat, distance traveled, tackle provided, and amenities. With so much competition here, it pays to shop around.

SCUBA DIVING & SNORKELING   **Oceans Unlimited ★** (𝒞 **2777-3171;** www. oceansunlimitedcr.com) offers both scuba diving and snorkel outings, as well as certification and resort courses. Because of river run-off and often less-than-stellar visibility close to Quepos, the best trips involve some travel time. Tours around Manuel Antonio run $95 per person for a two-tank scuba dive, and $220 for a four-person snorkel.

However, **Isla del Caño** (p. 421) is only about a 90-minute ride each way. This is one of the best dive sites in Costa Rica, and I highly recommend it. Trips to Isla del Cano are $139 for snorkeling and $189 for two-tank scuba diving.

Other Activities in the Area

ATV   If you want to try riding a four-wheel ATV (all-terrain vehicle), check in with the folks at **Fourtrax Adventure** (𝒞 **2777-1829;** www.fourtrax adventure.com). Their principal tour is a 4-hour adventure through African palm plantations, rural towns, and secondary forest to a jungle waterfall, where you stop for a dip. You cross several rivers and a long suspension bridge. Either breakfast or lunch is served, depending on the timing. The cost is $95 per ATV. A second rider on the same ATV costs $30.

BIKING   If you want to do some mountain biking while you're here, contact **Estrella Tour** (© **2777-1286**) in downtown Quepos. These folks offer a number of different guided tours according to skill level, for between $45 and $75 per day, as well as multiday expeditions.

BUTTERFLY GARDEN   **Fincas Naturales/The Nature Farm Reserve ★★** (© **2777-0850;** www.wildliferefugecr.com) is just across from (and run by) Hotel Sí Como No (p. 388). A lovely bi-level **butterfly garden ★** is the centerpiece attraction here, but there is also a private reserve and a small network of well-groomed trails through the forest. A 1-hour guided tour of the butterfly garden costs $20 per person. This is also a good place to do a night tour ($39).

CANOPY ADVENTURES   The most adventurous local canopy tour is by **Canopy Safari ★** (© **2777-0100;** www.canopysafari.com), which features 18 treetop platforms connected by a series of cables and suspension bridges. Adventurers use a harness-and-pulley system to "zip" between platforms, using a leather-gloved hand as their only brake. The **Titi Canopy Tour** (© **2777-3130;** www.titicanopytours.com) is a

BOTTOM: A Planet Dolphin sailing tour; TOP: A butterfly at Fincas Naturales.

similar but mellower setup. A canopy tour should run you between $50 and $70 per person.

About 20 minutes outside of Quepos is **Rainmaker Nature Refuge** (℡ **2777-3565;** www.rainmakercostarica.org). The main attraction here is a system of connected suspension bridges strung through the forest canopy, crisscrossing a deep ravine. Of the six bridges, the longest is 90m (295 ft.) across. The refuge also has a small network of trails and some great swimming holes. The refuge is open daily from 7am to 5pm. The entrance fee is $15 and $10 additional for a guided tour.

HORSEBACK RIDING While you can still sometimes find locals renting horses on the beaches outside the national park, I discourage this, as there are just too many crowds, the beach is too short, and the droppings are a problem. Better yet, head back into the hills and forests. Both **Finca Valmy** (℡ **2779-1118;** www.valmytours.com) and **Brisas del Nara** (℡ **2779-1235;** www.horsebacktour.com) offer horseback excursions that pass through both primary and secondary forest and feature a swimming stop or two at a jungle waterfall. Full-day tours, including breakfast and lunch, cost between $55 and $90 per person. Finca Valmy also offers an overnight tour for serious riders, with accommodations in rustic, but cozy cabins in the Santa Maria de Dota mountains.

SOOTHE YOUR BODY & SOUL The best of the local day spas are **Raindrop Spa** (℡ **2777-2880;** www.raindropspa.com), **Spa Uno** ★ (℡ **2777-2607;** www.spauno.com), and **Serenity Spa** ★ at the Hotel Sí Como No (p. 388). A wide range of treatments, wraps, and facials are available at all of the above.

Sivana Yoga (℡ **2777-3899** or 8899-2987; www.sivanayoga.com) has open classes ($12) Monday, Wednesday, and Friday at 8am in the event center at Hotel Costa Verde. Private classes are also offered.

SPICE UP YOUR LIFE Located 16km (10 miles) outside of Quepos, **Villa Vanilla** ★★ (℡ **2779-1155** or 8839-2721; www.rainforestspices.com) offers an informative and tasty tour of their open-air botanical gardens and spice farm. Their on-site commercial vanilla operation is the centerpiece of the show, but you'll also learn about a host of other tropical spices and other assorted flora. You'll even sample some sweet and savory treats and drinks made with the on-site bounty. The half-day guided tour runs daily at 9am and 1pm, and costs $50, including round-trip transportation from any area hotel. Be sure to stock up at their small shop, which offers pure vanilla, cinnamon, and locally grown pepper.

TAKE A TOUR ON THE TICO SIDE ★ For a good taste of local Tico rural culture, mixed in with some fabulous scenery and adventure, sign up for the **Santa Juana Mountain Tour** (℡ **2777-0850**). This full-day tour takes you to a local farming village about an hour outside of Quepos. Depending upon your needs and interests, you can tour coffee and citrus farms, take part in carbon-offset tree planting, hike the trails, swim in rainforest pools, fish for tilapia, see how sugar cane is processed, and/or ride horseback. A typical Tico lunch is included.

BIRD'S EYE VIEWING If you want a really good view of Manuel Antonio's spectacular scenery, you might sign up with the folks at **Costa Rica Flying**

Manuel Antonio National Park

THE CENTRAL PACIFIC COAST

Escuela D'Amore (𝄞/fax **2777-0233**; www.academiadamore.com) runs language-immersion programs out of a former hotel with a fabulous view on the road to Manuel Antonio. A 2-week conversational Spanish course, including a homestay and two meals daily, costs $845. Or you can try the **Costa Rica Spanish Institute** (COSI; 𝄞 **2234-1001** or 2777-0021; www.cosi.co.cr), which charges $1,570 for a similar 2-week program with a homestay.

Boat (𝄞 **2777-9208** or 8368-1426), who offer ultralight flights out of Quepos. A 20-minute flight runs around $80.

Another good option for getting high and enjoying the scenery is to go parasailing. The folks at **Aguas Azules** (𝄞 **2777-9193**; www.costarica parasailing.com) set up shop every morning on Playa Espadilla and offer parasailing tows behind a speedboat. A 15-minute ride costs $75, while a 30-minute jaunt will cost just $140.

Shopping

If you're looking for souvenirs, you'll find plenty of beach towels, beachwear, and handmade jewelry in a variety of small shops in Quepos and at impromptu stalls down near the national park.

For higher-end gifts, check out Hotel Sí Como No's **Regálame** (www. regalameart.com) gift shop, which has a wide variety of craft works, clothing, and original paintings and prints. Finally, one of my favorite shops from Jacó has a branch in Manuel Antonio.

Downtown Quepos.

Where to Stay

Take care when choosing your accommodations in Quepos/Manuel Antonio. You won't have much luck finding a hotel where you can walk directly out of your room and onto the beach as Manuel Antonio has very few true beachfront hotels. In fact, most of the nicer hotels here are 1km (½ mile) or so away from the beach, high on the hill overlooking the ocean.

If you're traveling on a rock-bottom budget, you'll get more for your money by staying in Quepos and taking the bus to the beaches at Manuel Antonio. The rooms in Quepos might be small, but they're generally cleaner and more appealing than those available in the same price category closer to the park.

VERY EXPENSIVE

In addition to the places listed below, **Bella Vista Villas and Casas** (www. buenavistavillas.net; ✆ 866/569-6241 in the U.S. and Canada, or 2777-0580 in Costa Rica) is a current incarnation of the former Tulemar Resort, and, after years of ups and downs, they've finally got this superbly located property running in good shape.

If you're coming for an extended stay with your family or a large group, look into **Escape Villas** ★★ (www.escapevillas.com; ✆ 800/340-2407 in the U.S., or 2777-5258 in Costa Rica), which rents a broad selection of very large and luxurious private villas with all the amenities and some of the best views in Manuel Antonio.

Arenas del Mar ★★★ 🏨   This place has it all—direct beach access, a rainforest setting, fabulous views, and luxurious accommodations. Designed and built by the folks behind Finca Rosa Blanca (p. 170), Arenas del Mar is deeply committed to sustainability. Not all rooms have ocean views, so be sure to specify if you want one. However, all are spacious, with cool tile floors and stylish decorative accents. Most have outdoor Jacuzzi tubs on private balconies. The apartments are immense two-bedroom, three-bathroom affairs with a kitchenette, perfect for families and longer stays. The restaurant, lobby, and main pool are set on the highest point of land here, and several spots have fabulous views of Manuel Antonio's Punta Catedral. *Note:* The beautiful patch of beach right in front of Arenas has for decades been the town's de facto nude beach. Those who might find this offensive can walk farther down the beach or stick to the pools.

Manuel Antonio. www.arenasdelmar.com. ✆/fax **2777-2777.** 38 units. $320 double; $490 suite; $770 2-bedroom apt. Rates include full breakfast. AE, MC, V. **Amenities:** 2 restaurants; bar; snack bar; babysitting; concierge; 2 small outdoor pools; room service; spa. *In room:* A/C, TV, minibar, Wi-Fi.

Gaia Hotel & Reserve ★★   This hotel features chic, postmodern design and decor, with large, well-equipped rooms, tons of amenities, and personalized service. Set on a hilly private reserve, the rooms, spa, and restaurant are housed in a series of tall, blocky buildings. The large rooms all have wooden floors, contemporary furnishings, plasma-screen televisions with complete home theater systems, and elaborate bathrooms with massive Jacuzzi tubs. Each guest is assigned a personal concierge and gets 20 minutes of free spa services. The deluxe suites feature a private rooftop terrace, with a reflecting pool, and shaded lounge chairs. The spa is extensive and well-run, with a wide range of treatment options and free daily yoga classes. Despite the over-the-top luxury here, this hotel is

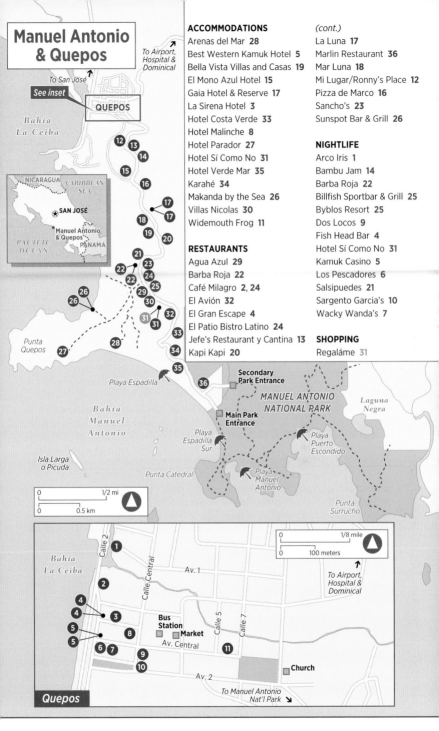

Manuel Antonio & Quepos

To Airport, Hospital & Dominical

To San José

See inset

QUEPOS

Bahía La Ceiba

NICARAGUA · CARIBBEAN SEA · SAN JOSÉ · Manuel Antonio & Quepos · PANAMA · PACIFIC OCEAN

ACCOMMODATIONS
Arenas del Mar **28**
Best Western Kamuk Hotel **5**
Bella Vista Villas and Casas **19**
El Mono Azul Hotel **15**
Gaia Hotel & Reserve **17**
La Sirena Hotel **3**
Hotel Costa Verde **33**
Hotel Malinche **8**
Hotel Parador **27**
Hotel Sí Como No **31**
Hotel Verde Mar **35**
Karahé **34**
Makanda by the Sea **26**
Villas Nicolas **30**
Widemouth Frog **11**

RESTAURANTS
Agua Azul **29**
Barba Roja **22**
Café Milagro **2, 24**
El Avión **32**
El Gran Escape **4**
El Patio Bistro Latino **24**
Jefe's Restaurant y Cantina **13**
Kapi Kapi **20**

(cont.)
La Luna **17**
Marlin Restaurant **36**
Mar Luna **18**
Mi Lugar/Ronny's Place **12**
Pizza de Marco **16**
Sancho's **23**
Sunspot Bar & Grill **26**

NIGHTLIFE
Arco Iris **1**
Bambu Jam **14**
Barba Roja **22**
Billfish Sportbar & Grill **25**
Byblos Resort **25**
Dos Locos **9**
Fish Head Bar **4**
Hotel Sí Como No **31**
Kamuk Casino **5**
Los Pescadores **6**
Salsipuedes **21**
Sargento Garcia's **10**
Wacky Wanda's **7**

SHOPPING
Regaláme **31**

Punta Quepos

Bahía Manuel Antonio

Isla Larga o Picuda

Punta Catedral

Playa Espadilla

Secondary Park Entrance

MANUEL ANTONIO NATIONAL PARK

Laguna Negra

Main Park Entrance

Playa Espadilla Sur

Playa Puerto Escondido

Playa Manuel Antonio

Punta Surrucho

0 — 1/2 mi
0 — 0.5 km

Quepos

Calle 2 · Calle Central · Av. 1 · Calle 5 · Calle 7

Bahía La Ceiba

Bus Station · Market · Av. Central

To Airport, Hospital & Dominical

0 — 1/8 mile
0 — 100 meters

Church

Av. 2

To Manuel Antonio Nat'l Park

dedicated to sustainable and green tourism practices and was granted "4 Leaves" by the CST Sustainable Tourism program.

Manuel Antonio. www.gaiahr.com. ☎ **800/226-2515** in the U.S., or 2777-9797 in Costa Rica. Fax 2777-9126. 20 units. $260–$330 double; $440–$495 suite; $840 Gaia suite. Rates include full breakfast. AE, MC, V. No children 15 and under. **Amenities:** Restaurant, bar; concierge; small gym; multilevel outdoor pool; room service; extensive spa. *In room:* A/C, TV/DVD, minibar, MP3 docking station, Wi-Fi.

Hotel Sí Como No ★★ ☺ 🎁 This local favorite is a lively, upscale, midsize resort that blends in with and respects the rainforests and natural wonders of Manuel Antonio. The hotel is equally suited to families traveling with children and to couples looking for a romantic getaway. All the wood used is farm-grown, and while the rooms have energy-efficient air-conditioning units, guests are urged to use them only when necessary. The standard rooms are quite acceptable, but it's worth the splurge for a superior or deluxe room or a suite. Most of these are on the top floors of the two- to three-story villas, with spectacular tree-top views out over the forest and onto the Pacific. The deluxe suites have lots of space and large garden bathrooms, some of which have private Jacuzzis. This hotel has earned "5 Leaves" in the CST Sustainable Tourism program, and the parent organization, Green Hotels of Costa Rica, was honored in 2009 as a corporate leader in sustainability by the Rainforest Alliance.

Manuel Antonio. www.sicomono.com. ☎ **2777-0777.** Fax 2777-1093. 52 units. $205–$290 double; $315–$375 suite. Rates include breakfast buffet. Extra person $30. Children 5 and under stay free in parent's room. AE, MC, V. **Amenities:** 2 restaurants; 2 bars; babysitting; concierge; 2 Jacuzzis; 2 midsize outdoor pools, including 1 w/small water slide; all rooms smoke-free; modest spa, Wi-Fi. *In room:* A/C, hair dryer, minibar.

Makanda by the Sea ★★ A wonderful collection of studio apartments and private villas, Makanda is a great option for anyone looking for an intimate, romantic getaway in Manuel Antonio. If you combine villa no. 1 with the three studios, you get one very large four-bedroom villa, great for a family or a small group (although children 15 and under are not allowed, unless you rent out the entire hotel). Every choice comes with a full kitchenette, cable television, MP3 docking station, and either a terrace or a balcony. The grounds are well tended, and intermixed with tropical flowers and Japanese gardens. A full breakfast is delivered to your room each morning. The hotel's pool and Jacuzzi combine intricate and colorful tile work with a view of the jungle-covered hillsides and the Pacific Ocean. The hotel is set in thick forest, and, despite the name, is a hefty hike—or short drive—from the beach.

Manuel Antonio. www.makanda.com. ☎ **888/625-2632** in the U.S., or 2777-0442 in Costa Rica. Fax 2777-1032. 11 units. $265 studio; $400 villa. Rates include full breakfast. AE, MC, V. **Amenities:** Restaurant; bar; concierge; Jacuzzi; midsize outdoor pool; room service; massage and spa services. *In room:* TV, kitchenette, minibar, MP3 docking station, Wi-Fi.

EXPENSIVE

Hotel Parador ★★ This hotel is spread out over more than 4.8 hectares (12 acres) of land on a low peninsula. The main building here is loaded with antiques, including 17th-century Dutch and Flemish oil paintings, a 300-year-old carved wooden horse, a 16th-century church and castle doors, and an amazing, museum-quality massive model ship. The spacious suites are located in a tall building on the top of a hill, giving a good view of the sea and Punta Catedral in the distance; the "Vista Suites" are the highest rooms here and have the best views. Despite being a large, resort-style hotel, this place has earned "5 Leaves" in the CST Sustainable Tourism program. The new executive chef here has also really improved the dining experience at all of the hotel's restaurants, especially its sushi bar and Nuevo Latino options.

Manuel Antonio. www.hotelparador.com. © **877/506-1414** in the U.S. and Canada, or 2777-1414 in Costa Rica. Fax 2777-1437. 129 units. $195–$235 double; $300–$325 premium; $450 suite; $975 presidential suite. Rates include breakfast buffet. Rates slightly higher during peak weeks; significantly lower in off season. AE, MC, V. **Amenities:** 3 restaurants; 2 bars; babysitting; concierge; health club and spa; Jacuzzi; 3 outdoor pools, including one large free-form pool w/swim-up bar and central fountain; room service; unlit outdoor tennis court. *In room:* A/C, TV, hair dryer, minibar, Wi-Fi.

Karahé The Karahé is one of the original beachfront hotels in Manuel Antonio. If you stay in one of the more expensive beachfront units, you'll have a plain room with tile floors, two double beds, and a small patio. The least-expensive rooms are just off the reception area and offer neither views nor easy access to the ocean. Be aware that if you opt for one of the villas, you'll have a steep uphill climb from the beach; on the other hand, a couple of these have great views. The lush gardens have flowering ginger that often attracts hummingbirds. The hotel can arrange a wide variety of tours and charters, including sportfishing. Karahé is located on both sides of the road about 450m (1,476 ft.) before you reach Playa Espadilla.

Manuel Antonio. www.karahe.com. © **2777-0170.** Fax 2777-1075. 33 units. $113–$170 double. Rates include continental breakfast and taxes. AE, MC, V. **Amenities:** Restaurant; bar; Jacuzzi; small outdoor pool. *In room:* A/C.

MODERATE

In addition to the hotels mentioned below, the **Best Western Kamuk Hotel** (www.kamuk.co.cr; © **2777-0811**) and **La Sirena Hotel** (www.lasirenahotel.com; © **2777-0572**) are two dependable options right in downtown Quepos. Both are popular with sportfishing enthusiasts.

El Mono Azul Hotel 🖋 On the road to Manuel Antonio, just outside Quepos, the "Blue Monkey" offers clean and comfortable rooms at a good price. The more expensive rooms feature air-conditioning and/or a small television with cable. The villas have red-tile floors, separate sitting rooms, and a kitchenette. One room even has a Jacuzzi tub. Though all the rooms are rather spartan, the place has a lively, hostel-like vibe. The owners are active in a children's arts program aimed at helping preserve the local rainforest and the endangered squirrel monkey. In fact, 10% of your bill goes to this program. The restaurant/pizzeria here is quite popular. Staff can arrange longer-term rentals of fully equipped apartments and villas.

Manuel Antonio. www.monoazul.com. © **800/381-3578** in the U.S., or 2777-2572 in Costa Rica. Fax 2777-1954. 31 units. $60–$85 double; $140 villa. AE, DC, MC, V. **Amenities:** Restaurant; bar; lounge; 3 small outdoor pools. *In room:* A/C, TV, no phone, Wi-Fi.

Hotel Costa Verde ★ Costa Verde has rooms in a wide range of sizes and prices. The best rooms here have ocean views, kitchenettes, private balconies, and loads of space; some of these don't have air-conditioning, but feature huge screened walls to encourage cross ventilation. The enormous penthouse suite has a commanding view of the spectacular surroundings. The most unique option here is the 727 Fusilage suite, a 2-bedroom affair inside the converted fuselage of an old jet airliner. Three small pools are set into the hillside, with views out to the ocean, and the hotel has a couple of miles of private trails through the rainforest. Some of the buildings are quite a hike from the hotel's reception and restaurants, so be sure you know exactly what type of room you'll be staying in and where it's located.

Manuel Antonio. ✆ **866/854-7958** in the U.S. and Canada, or 2777-0584 in Costa Rica. Fax 2777-0560. www.costaverde.com. 75 units. $115–$174 double; $500 727 Fusilage suite. AE, MC, V. **Amenities:** 4 restaurants; 4 bars; 3 small outdoor pools. *In room:* A/C (in some units), TV (in some units), Wi-Fi.

Hotel Verde Mar ★   This hotel is a great choice for proximity to the national park and the beach, and I recommend it much more than the similarly priced hotel Karahé. From your room, it's just a short walk to the beach (Playa Espadilla) via a raised wooden walkway. All the rooms here have plenty of space, nice wrought-iron queen-size beds, tile floors, a desk and chair, a fan, and a small porch. All but two of the rooms come with a basic kitchenette. Some of the larger rooms even have two queen-size beds. The hotel has no restaurant, but plenty are within walking distance. When the surf is too rough you can enjoy the small pool here.

Manuel Antonio. www.verdemar.com. ✆ **2777-1805.** Fax 2777-1311. 24 units. $110 double; $125 suite. MC, V. **Amenities:** Restaurant; small outdoor pool; Wi-Fi. *In room:* A/C, kitchenette (in some), no phone.

Villas Nicolás ★   These large villas offer a lot of bang for your buck. Built as terraced units up a steep hill in deep forest, they really give you the feeling that you're in the jungle. Most are quite large and well appointed, with wood floors, throw rugs, and comfortable bathrooms; some rooms even have separate living rooms and full kitchenettes, which make longer stays comfortable. My favorite features, though, are the balconies, which come with sitting chairs and a hammock. Some of these balconies are massive and have incredible views. In fact, the rooms highest up the hill have views that I'd be willing to pay a lot more for, and a few of them even have air-conditioning. During the high season, the hotel opens an informal restaurant/bar near the pool that serves breakfast and sometimes lunch and dinner, depending on demand.

Manuel Antonio. www.villasnicolas.com. ✆ **2777-0481.** Fax 2777-0451. 19 units. $115 double; $175 suite. Weekly, monthly, and off-season (May–Nov) rates available. Rates include full breakfast. AE, MC, V. **Amenities:** Small outdoor pool; Wi-Fi. *In room:* A/C (in some units), fridge.

INEXPENSIVE

In addition to the place listed below, the **Widemouth Frog** (www.widemouth frog.org; ✆ **2777-2798**) is a hostel option in downtown Quepos, which even has its own swimming pool.

Hotel Malinche   A good choice for budget travelers, the Hotel Malinche has consistently been my top choice in this category right in Quepos. The standard rooms are small but have hardwood or tile floors and clean bathrooms. Some of those on the second floor even have small private balconies that open on to a small interior courtyard. The more expensive rooms are larger and have air-conditioning, TVs, and carpets.

Half-block west of downtown bus terminal, Quepos. ✆ **2777-3723.** Fax 2777-0093. 24 units. $30–$60 double. AE, MC, V. *In room:* No phone, Wi-Fi.

Where to Eat

Scores of dining options are available around Manuel Antonio and Quepos, and almost every hotel has some sort of restaurant. For the cheapest meals around, try a simple *soda* in Quepos, or head to one of the open-air joints on the beach road before the national park entrance. The standard Tico menu prevails, with prices in the $4-to-$8 range. Of these, **Marlin Restaurant** (✆ **2777-1134**), right in front of Playa Espadilla, and **Mar Luna** (✆ **2777-5107**), on the main road just beyond Hotel La Colina, are your best bets. For simple pasta, pizzas, and Italian gelato, head to **Pizza de Marco** (✆ **2777-9400;** in the Plaza Yara shopping center). For Tex-Mex cuisine, margaritas and a sports bar scene, you can head to **Jefe's Restaurante y Cantina** at the Hotel Plinio (✆ **2777-0055;** www.hotelplinio.com), or for more traditional Mexican-style cooking, try the new **Sancho's** (✆ **2777-0340**), across from the Barba Roja. In addition to the places listed below, another good option, on the outskirts of Quepos, is **Mi Lugar,** or **"Ronny's Place"** (✆ **2777-5120**).

For a taste of the high life, head to **La Luna ★** restaurant at Gaia Hotel & Reserve (see above) for their sunset tapas menu. The views are great and the creative tapas are very reasonably priced.

Finally, one of my favorite hangouts has always been **Café Milagro ★★** (✆ **2777-1707;** www.cafemilagro.com), a homey coffeehouse and gift shop with two locations in the area. The folks here roast their own beans and also have a mail-order service to keep you in Costa Rican coffee year-round. The menu includes a daily selection of freshly baked sweets, simple sandwiches, and breakfast items, and a wide range of coffee drinks. You'll find local art for sale on the walls and a good selection of Cuban cigars and international newspapers, too. The original storefront is located just over the bridge on your left as you enter Quepos, and another branch is on the main road to Manuel Antonio, right across from the turnoff for Hotel La Mariposa.

EXPENSIVE

Agua Azul ★★ INTERNATIONAL With a fabulous perch and panoramic view, this open-air restaurant serves up fresh fish, and what can best be described as upscale bar food. Tables by the railing fill up fast, so get here well before sunset if you want to snag one. Start things off with a Tuna Margarita, an inventive version of *ceviche* with a lime-and-tequila marinade. Main dishes include coconut-crusted mahimahi and panko-crusted tuna. For lunch are giant burgers and fresh fish sandwiches. The long wooden bar is a popular hangout, and a good place to order up some appetizers and drinks.

Manuel Antonio, near Villas del Parque. ✆ **2777-5280.** www.cafeaguaazul.com. Reservations not accepted. Main courses $15–$21. V. Thurs–Tues 11am–10pm.

El Avión SEAFOOD/INTERNATIONAL Set on the edge of Manuel Antonio's hillside with a great view of the ocean and surrounding forests, this restaurant is housed under some permanent tents and the starboard wing of a retired army transport plane, hence the name El Avión, which means "the Plane." This specific plane was actually shot down by the Sandinista army, leading to a scandal that uncovered illegal CIA supply missions to the Contra rebels in Nicaragua. Today you can enjoy a wide range of seafood and steaks as you take in the unique surroundings and glow of history. However, food quality and service are inconsistent here—I've had both excellent and roundly disappointing meals—although the setting never falters. Inside the fuselage you'll also find a small bar.

Manuel Antonio. ✆ **2777-3378.** www.elavion.net. Reservations recommended. Main courses C4,700–C25,000. AE, MC, V. Daily noon to 10pm.

El Patio Bistro Latino ★★★ NUEVO LATINO/FUSION   This relaxed, yet refined restaurant is an outgrowth of the popular coffeehouse and roasting company Café Milagro. The same attention to detail and focus on quality carries over here. By day, you can get a wide range of coffee drinks and specialties, as well as full breakfasts, fresh-baked sweets, and a variety of salads, sandwiches, wraps, and light lunch dishes. By night, things get more interesting. The menu features inventive main dishes that take advantage of local ingredients and various regional culinary traditions. Fresh mahimahi comes steamed in a banana leaf with a spicy *mojo*, and the tenderloin features a tamarind glaze and is served over roasted local yuca puree. You may even find some of their home-roasted coffee used as an ingredient in a glaze, sauce, or dessert.

On the road btw. Quepos and Manuel Antonio. ✆ **2777-0794.** www.elpatiobistrolatino.com. Reservations recommended. Main courses C6,000–C8,500. AE, MC, V. Daily 6am–10pm.

Kapi Kapi ★★ FUSION/NUEVO LATINO   This place features elegant understated Asian-influenced decor and an inventive wide-ranging menu. At night, the ample, open-air dining room is candlelit and romantic. Start things off with the Asian-spice glazed baby back ribs or some seared fresh yellow-fin tuna. Or, save the seared tuna for your main course, where it comes encrusted in peppercorns and served with a green papaya salad. For a sample of local flavors, order up the grilled shrimp, which are served on sugar-cane skewers, with a glaze made from local rum, tamarind, and coconut. For dessert try their hot chocolate soufflé. These folks have an excellent and very fairly priced wine list, as well.

On the road btw. Quepos and Manuel Antonio. ✆ **2777-5049.** www.restaurantekapikapi.com. Reservations recommended. Main courses C14,000–C17,000. MC, V. Daily 4–10pm.

Sunspot Bar & Grill ★★ INTERNATIONAL   Dining by candlelight under a purple canvas tent at one of the few poolside tables here is one of the most romantic dining experiences to be had in Manuel Antonio. The menu changes regularly but features prime meats and poultry and fresh fish, excellently prepared. The rack of lamb might get a light jalapeño-mint or mango chutney, and the chicken breast might be stuffed with feta cheese, kalamata olives, and roasted red peppers and topped with a blackberry sauce. The menu also includes nightly specials and a good selection of salads, appetizers, and desserts.

At Makanda by the Sea (p. 388). ✆ **2777-0442.** Reservations recommended. Main courses C4,000–C15,000. MC, V. Daily noon–10pm.

MODERATE

Barba Roja SEAFOOD/INTERNATIONAL   Perched high on a hill with stunning views over jungle and ocean, the Barba Roja has long been one of the more popular restaurants in Manuel Antonio, although mostly for its lively ambience and stellar location, as the food and service can be inconsistent. The most current incarnation here features a creative fusion menu and sushi bar. The interior is done with local hardwoods and bamboo, which gives the open-air dining room a warm glow. You can sit for hours taking in the view or the stars on the outdoor patio. A gallery attached to the restaurant displays original art by local artists.

Manuel Antonio. ✆ **2777-0331.** www.barbarojarestaurant.com. Reservations recommended in high season. Main courses C5,900–C8,800. AE, MC, V. Tues–Sun 10am–10pm; Mon 4–10pm.

El Gran Escape ★★ SEAFOOD   This Quepos landmark is consistently one of the top restaurants in the area. The fish is fresh and expertly prepared, portions are generous, and the prices are reasonable. If that's not enough of a recommendation, the atmosphere is lively, the locals seem to keep coming back, and the service is darn good for a beach town in Costa Rica. Sturdy wooden tables and chairs take up the large indoor dining room, and sportfishing photos and an exotic collection of masks fill up the walls. If you venture away from the fish, the menu features hearty steaks and giant burgers; the wide assortment of delicious appetizers, includes fresh tuna sashimi, and an excellent breakfast menu. El Gran Escape's Fish Head Bar is usually crowded and spirited, and if there's a game going on, it will be on the television here.

On the main road into Quepos, on your left just after the bridge. ✆ **2777-0395.** www.elgran escape.com. Reservations recommended in high season. Main courses $5–$20. Wed–Mon 8am–11pm.

Manuel Antonio After Dark

The bars at the **Barba Roja** restaurant (see above), about midway along the road between Quepos and Manuel Antonio, and the **Hotel Sí Como No** (p. 388) are good places to hang out and meet people in the evenings. To shoot some pool, I head to the **Billfish Sportbar & Grill** ★ at the Byblos Resort (on the main road btw. Quepos and the park entrance). For tapas and local *bocas,* try **Salsipuedes** (roughly midway along the road btw. Quepos and the National Park entrance), which translates as "get out if you can." If you want live music, **Bambu Jam** ★ (along the road btw. Quepos and the park entrance; www.bambujam.com) and **Dos Locos** (in the heart of downtown) are your best bets. In downtown Quepos, **Los Pescadores, Sargento Garcia's, Wacky Wanda's,** and the **Fish Head Bar** at El Gran Escape (see above) are all popular hangouts.

Night owls and dancing fools have several choices here, although the bulldozing of Mar y Sombra down by the beach has really hurt the scene. The live music at **Bambu Jam** is often salsa and merengue, perfect for dancing. For real late-night action, the local favorite appears to be the **Arco Iris,** just before the bridge heading into town. Admission is usually around $3.

The **Hotel Kamuk** in Quepos and the **Byblos Resort** on the road to Manuel Antonio both have small casinos and will even foot your cab bill if you try your luck and lay down your money. If you want to see a flick, check what's playing at **Hotel Sí Como No**'s (p. 388) little theater, although you have to eat at the restaurant or spend a minimum at the bar to earn admission.

En Route to Dominical: Playa Matapalo

Playa Matapalo is a long expanse of flat beach that's about midway between Quepos and Dominical. It's an easy but bumpy 26km (16 miles) south of Quepos on the Costanera Sur. It's nowhere near as developed as either of those two beaches, but that's part of its charm. The beach here seems to stretch on forever, and it's usually deserted. The surf and strong riptides frequently make Matapalo too rough for swimming, although surfing and boogie-boarding can be good. Foremost among this beach's charms are peace and quiet.

WHERE TO STAY

Matapalo is a tiny coastal village, although the actual beach is about 1km (½ mile) away. A few very small and intimate lodges are located right on the beach. One of the more interesting is **Bahari Beach Bungalows** (www.baharibeach.com; ✆ **2787-5014**), which offers deluxe tents with private bathrooms, and more standard rooms, right on the beach, or **Dreamy Contentment** (www.dreamy contentment.com; ✆ **2787-5223**), a more traditional beachfront hotel. **El Coquito del Pacifico** hotel (www.elcoquito.com; ✆ **2787-5028**) has a restaurant popular with tourists and locals alike.

DOMINICAL ★

29km (18 miles) SW of San Isidro; 42km (26 miles) S of Quepos; 160km (99 miles) S of San José

With a stunning setting, and miles of nearly deserted beaches backed by rainforest-covered mountains, Dominical and the coastline south of it are excellent places to find uncrowded stretches of sand, spectacular views, remote jungle waterfalls, and abundant budget lodgings. The beach at Dominical itself is one of the prime surf destinations in Costa Rica, with both right and left beach breaks. When the swell is big, the wave here is a powerful and hollow tube, and the town is often packed with surfers. In fact, while the beach at Dominical gets broad, flat, and beautiful at low tide, its primary appeal is to surfers. It is often too rough for casual bathers. However, you will find excellent swimming, sunbathing, and

A campground in Dominical.

strolling beaches just a little farther south at **Dominicalito, Playa Hermosa,** and inside **Ballena Marine National Park ★★**.

Leaving Manuel Antonio, the road south to Dominical runs by mile after mile of oil-palm plantations. However, just before Dominical, the mountains again meet the sea. From Dominical south, the coastline is dotted with tide pools, tiny coves, and cliff-side vistas. Dominical is the largest village in the area and has several small lodges both in town and along the beach to the south. The village enjoys an enviable location on the banks of Río Barú, right where it widens considerably before emptying into the ocean. The banks of the river and throughout the surrounding forests offer good birding. Along the coast and rivers, you're likely to see numerous shore and sea birds, including herons, egrets, and kingfishers, while the forests are home to colorful and lively tanagers, toucans, and trogons.

Essentials

GETTING THERE & DEPARTING   By Plane: The nearest airport with regular service is in Quepos (see "Essentials" under "Manuel Antonio National Park," earlier in this chapter). From there you can hire a taxi, rent a car, or take the bus.

By Car: The traditional route from San José involves heading east out of town (toward Cartago), and then south on the Interamerican Highway (CR2) to the city of San Isidro de El General. From San Isidro, a well-marked and well-traveled route (CR243) leads to Dominical and the coast. The entire drive takes about 4 hours.

However, it's faster and easier to take the San José–Caldera Highway (CR27) west to Orotina. Just past the toll booth at Pavón, this road connects with the Costanera Sur (CR34), or Southern Coastal Highway. The exit is marked for Jacó and CR34. From here, it's a straight and flat shot down the coast. When you reach Quepos, follow the signs for Dominical. This route should take you just over 3 hours.

The Costanera Sur (CR34) heading south from Dominical to Palmar Norte, passing all the beaches mentioned below, is in excellent shape.

By Bus: To reach Dominical, you must first go to San Isidro de El General or Quepos. Buses leave San José for San Isidro roughly every hour between 4:30am and 5:30pm. See "Getting There & Departing" in "San Isidro de El General: A Base for Exploring Chirripó National Park," later in this chapter. The trip takes 3 hours; the fare is C2,705. The main bus stop in Dominical is in the heart of town, near the soccer field and San Clemente restaurant.

From Quepos, **Transportes Blanco** buses (☎ **2771-4744**) leave daily at 5:30 and 11:30am, and 3:30pm. The trip is 1½ hours and costs C1,800.

From San Isidro de El General, **Transportes Blanco** buses (☎ **2771-4744**) leave for Dominical at 7, 9, and 11:30am, and 3:30 and 4pm. The bus station in San Isidro for rides to Dominical is 1 block south of the main bus station and 2 blocks west of the church. Trip duration is 1½ hours; the fare is C1,240.

When you're ready to leave, buses depart Dominical for San Isidro at 6 and 7am and 1, 2, and 4:30pm. Buses leave San Isidro for San José roughly every hour between 5:30am and 5:30pm. Buses to Quepos leave Dominical at approximately 8:30am and 1 and 4pm.

ORIENTATION   Dominical is a small village on the banks of the Río Barú. The village is to the right after you cross the bridge (heading south) and stretches out along the main road parallel to the beach. As you first come into town, you'll see the small Pueblo Del Rio shopping center dead ahead of you, where the road hits a "T" intersection. On your left is the soccer field and the heart of the village. To the right, a rough road heads to the river and up along the riverbank. If you stay on the Costanera Highway heading south, just beyond the turnoff into town is a little strip mall, **Plaza Pacífica,** with a couple of restaurants, a pharmacy, bank, and a grocery store.

FAST FACTS   You can purchase stamps and send mail from the **San Clemente Bar & Grill** (see below). In the little mall built beside this restaurant, you'll also find an Internet cafe, and they'll change dollars. A small branch of the **Banco de Costa Rica,** with an ATM, is in the Plaza Pacifica.

Taxis tend to congregate in front of the soccer field. If you need a car, **Solid Rental Car** (© **2787-0111;** www.solidcarrental.com) will arrange drop-off and pickup at any area hotel.

Exploring the Beaches South of Dominical & Ballena Marine National Park

The open ocean waters just in front of town and toward the river mouth are often too rough for swimming. However, you can swim in the calm waters of the Río Barú, just in from the river mouth, or head down the beach a few kilometers to the little sheltered cove at **Roca Verde.**

Dominicalito.

Ballena Marine National Park.

If you have a car, you should continue driving south, exploring beaches as you go. You will first come to **Dominicalito,** a small beach and cove that shelters the local fishing fleet and can be a decent place to swim, but continue on a bit. You'll soon hit **Playa Hermosa,** a long stretch of desolate beach with fine sand. As in Dominical, this is unprotected and can be rough, but it's a nicer place to sunbathe and swim than Dominical.

At the village of Uvita, 16km (10 miles) south of Dominical, you'll reach the northern end of the **Ballena Marine National Park ★★**, which protects a coral reef that stretches from Uvita south to Playa Piñuela and includes the little Isla Ballena, just offshore. To get to **Playa Uvita** (which is inside the park), turn in at the village of Bahía and continue until you hit the ocean. The beach here is actually well protected and good for swimming. At low tide, an exposed sandbar allows you to walk about and explore another tiny island. This park is named for the whales that are sometimes sighted close to shore in the winter months. If you ever fly over this area, you'll also notice that this little island and the spit of land that's formed at low tide compose the perfect outline of a whale's tail. An office at the entrance here regulates the park's use and even runs a small turtle-hatching shelter and program. Entrance to the national park is $10 per person. Camping is allowed here for $2 per person per day, including access to a public restroom and shower.

Dominical is a major surf destination. The long and varied beach break here is justifiably popular. In general, the beach boasts powerful waves best suited for experienced surfers. Nevertheless, beginners should check in with the folks at the **Green Iguana Surf Camp** (© **2787-0157** or 8825-1381; www.greeniguana surfcamp.com), who offer lessons and comprehensive "surf camps." Rates run around $695 to $1,255 per person, based on double occupancy, for a 1-week program including accommodations, lessons, unlimited surfboard use, transportation to various surf breaks, and a T-shirt.

Other Activities in the Area

Several local farms offer horseback tours through forests and orchards, and some of these farms offer overnight accommodations. **Hacienda Barú ★ (✆ 2787-0003;** fax 2787-0057; www.haciendabaru.com) offers several different hikes and tours, including a walk through mangroves and along the riverbank (for some good bird-watching), a rainforest hike through 80 hectares (198 acres) of virgin jungle, an all-day trek from beach to mangrove to jungle that includes a visit to some Indian petroglyphs, an overnight camping trip, and a combination horse-back-and-hiking tour. The operation, which is dedicated to conservation and reforestation, even has tree-climbing tours and a small canopy platform 30m (98 ft.) above the ground, as well as one of the more common zip-line canopy tours. Tour prices range from $20 for the mangrove hike to $98 for the jungle overnight. If you're traveling with a group, you'll be charged a lower per-person rate, depending on the number of people. In addition to its eco- and adventure tourism activities, Hacienda Barú also has six comfortable cabins with two bedrooms each, full kitchens, and even a living room (prices range from $65 to $85 for a double, including breakfast). Hacienda Barú is about 1.5km (1 mile) north of Dominical on the road to Manuel Antonio.

The jungles just outside of Dominical are home to two spectacular water-falls. The most popular and impressive is the **Santo Cristo** or **Nauyaca Water-falls ★**, a two-tiered beauty with an excellent swimming hole. Most of the hotels in town can arrange for the horseback ride up here, or you can contact **Don Lulo** (✆ **2787-8013;** www.cataratasnauyaca.com) directly. A full-day tour, with both breakfast and lunch, should cost around $85 per person, including transportation to and from Dominical. The tour is a mix of hiking, horseback riding, and hanging out at the falls. It is also possible to reach these falls by horseback from an entrance near the small village of Tinamaste. (You will see signs on the road.) Similar tours (at similar prices) are offered to the **Diamante Waterfalls,** which

Nauyaca Waterfalls.

A basilisk lizard.

are a three-tiered set of falls with a 360m (1,180-ft.) drop, but not quite as spacious and inviting a pool as the one at Santo Cristo.

If you're looking for a bird's-eye view of the area, **Skyline Ultralights** (✆ 2743-8037; www.ultralighttour.com) offers a variety of airborne tours of the area. Near the beach in Uvita, these folks offer options ranging from a 20-minute introductory flight for $110 to a roughly hour-long circuit exploring the Ballena Marine National Park and neighboring mangrove forests for $235.

If you want to take a scuba-diving trip out to the rocky sites off Ballena National Park or all the way out to Isla del Caño, call **Mystic Dive Center** (✆ 2786-5217; www.mysticdivecenter.com), which has its main office in a small roadside strip mall down toward Playa Tortuga and Ojochal. These folks are only open from December 1 through April 15, and prices for Ballena National Park are $65 for snorkeling and $95 for a two-tank dive; prices for Isla del Caño are $95 for snorkeling and $145 for a two-tank dive.

For sportfishing, I recommend the folks at **Sportfishing Dominical** (✆ 2787-8012; www.sportfishingdominical.co.cr), who are based out of the hotel Cuna del Angel (p. 404).

Other adventure activities offered in Dominical include kayak tours of the mangroves, river floats in inner tubes, day tours to Caño Island and Corcovado National Park, and sportfishing. To arrange any of these activities, check in with **Dominical Adventures** (✆ 2787-0431; www.dominicalsurfadventures.com), **Southern Expeditions** (✆ 2787-0100; www.southernexpeditionscr.com), or the folks at the **Hotel Roca Verde** (✆ 2787-0036; www.rocaverde.net).

For a fun side trip for anyone interested in snakes and other little critters, head to **Parque Reptilandia** ★★ (✆ 2787-0343; www.crreptiles.com), a few miles outside Dominical on the road to San Isidro. In my opinion, this is the best snake and reptile attraction in Costa Rica. With more than 55 well-designed and spacious terrariums and enclosed areas, the collection includes a wide range of snakes, frogs, turtles, and lizards, as well as crocodiles and caimans. Some of my favorite residents here are the brilliant eyelash pit viper and sleek golden vine snake. Both native and imported species are on display, including the only Komodo dragon in Central America. For those looking to spice up their visit, Fridays are feeding days. It's open daily from 9am to 4:30pm; admission is $10.

Finally, if you're looking to learn or bone up on your Spanish, **Adventure Education Center** (℡ 800/237-2730 in the U.S. and Canada, or 2787-0023 in Costa Rica; www.adventurespanishschool.com), located right in the heart of town, offers a variety of immersion-style language programs. A standard, 1-week program including 20 hours of class, homestay, and breakfasts and dinners costs $460.

Where to Stay

In addition to the places listed below, a host of beautiful private homes on the hillsides above Dominical regularly rent out rooms. Most come with several bedrooms and full kitchens, and quite a few have private pools. If you're here for an extended stay and have a four-wheel-drive vehicle (a must for most of these), check in with **Paradise Costa Rica** (www.paradisecostarica.com; ℡ 800/708-4552 in the U.S. and Canada) or with the folks at **Cabinas San Clemente** or **Hotel Roca Verde** (see below for both of these).

EXPENSIVE

Cascadas Farallas Waterfall Villas ★★ 🎁   Although not on the beach, this boutique hotel is truly special. Set in deep, lush forest on the edge of a beautiful jungle waterfall, the villas here are plush and luxurious, and loaded with beautiful art and striking architectural details. Most are two-room affairs that can be rented whole or split up. Several rooms feature Jacuzzi tubs, and all come with a fabulous rainforest and/or waterfall view balcony. This place frequently functions as a wellness retreat center, and has daily yoga classes. Fabulous healthy meals are served, and those on vegetarian, vegan, and even raw food diets are well-cared for.

8km (5 miles) northeast of Dominical, on the road to San Isidro. www.waterfallvillas.com. ℡ **2787-8378.** 6 units. $115–$225 double. Rates include breakfast and a welcome glass of wine. MC, V. **Amenities:** Restaurant. *In room:* No phone.

MODERATE

Domilocos   This place offers basic, comfortable rooms at a reasonable price. Rooms are simply furnished and on the plain side, with bamboo furnishings, air-conditioning, and large bathrooms. All open onto a common veranda. In the small, central garden area, you'll find a large Jacuzzi. Since it's about 1 block inland from the beach, this hotel has an isolated location; still, the restaurant and bar are both popular here, so things can get lively.

Dominical. www.domilocos.com. ℡ **2787-0244.** 25 units. $75 double. Rates include breakfast. MC, V. **Amenities:** Restaurant; bar; Jacuzzi. *In room:* A/C, Wi-Fi.

Hotel Diuwak   This little complex offers the best-equipped rooms right near the surf break, although that's definitely not saying much. The rooms are spartan, but bright. About half the rooms come with air-conditioning, and a few suites and bungalows are for larger groups and families. Most have some sort of private or semiprivate veranda. A refreshing pool is at the center of the complex. About 50m (164 ft.) inland from the beach, this place is a decent option for surfers seeking a little extra comfort just steps away from the waves. However, service and upkeep can be very spotty here.

Dominical. www.diuwak.com. ☎ **2787-0087.** Fax 2787-0089. 36 units. $65–$160 double. Rates include full breakfast. AE, MC, V. **Amenities:** Restaurant; bar; midsize outdoor pool. *In room:* Wi-Fi.

Hotel Roca Verde ★   This popular hotel offers the best beachfront accommodations in Dominical. Located a bit south of town, the setting is superb—on a protected little cove with rocks and tide pools. The rooms are in a two-story building beside the swimming pool. Each room comes with one queen-size and one single bed, and a small patio or balcony. A large open-air restaurant with a popular bar really gets going on Saturday nights. The rooms are a bit close to the bar, so it can sometimes be hard to get an early night's sleep, especially during the high season if the bar is raging.

1km (½ mile) south of Barú River Bridge in Dominical, just off the coastal hwy. www.rocaverde.net. ☎ **2787-0036.** 9 units. $85 double. AE, MC, V. **Amenities:** Restaurant; bar; small outdoor pool. *In room:* A/C, no phone.

Pacific Edge ★   This place is away from the beach, but the views from the individual bungalows are so stunning that you might not mind. Spread along a lushly planted ridge on the hillside over Dominical, the hotel features four individual wooden cabins. Their best feature is the private porch with a comfortable hammock in which to laze about and enjoy the sweeping views. The restaurant serves breakfast, and dinners are served upon request. A wide range of tours and activities also can be arranged here, and there's a refreshing swimming pool. Pacific Edge is 4km (2½ miles) south of Dominical, and then another 1.2km (¾ mile) up a steep and rocky road; four-wheel-drive vehicles are recommended.

Dominical. www.pacificedge.info. ☎/fax **2787-8010.** 4 units. $70–$100 double. AE, MC, V. **Amenities:** Restaurant; midsize outdoor pool. *In room:* Minifridge, no phone.

INEXPENSIVE

As a popular surfer destination, budget lodgings abound in Dominical. I've tried to list the best below, but if you're really counting pennies, it's always a good idea to walk around and check out what's currently available. Another good budget option is **Montanas de Agua** (☎ **2787-0200**), about a block and a half inland from the beach, across from Domilocos (p. 400). There are plenty of camping options as well. I recommend **Piramys** (piramys@hotmail.com; ☎ **2787-0196**) or **Camping Antorchas** (www.campingantorchas.net; ☎ **2787-0307**), both of which offer basic rooms very close to the beach.

Cabinas San Clemente ✦   In addition to running the town's most popular restaurant (see below) and serving as the social hub for the surfers, beach bums, and expatriates passing through, this place offers a variety of accommodations to fit most budgets. Located about 1km (½ mile) from the in-town restaurant, San Clemente has rooms in three separate buildings, right on the beach. Some of the second-floor rooms have wood floors and wraparound verandas and are a good deal in this price range. The grounds are shady and have plenty of hammocks. The cheapest rooms are bunk-bed hostel-style affairs in a separate building dubbed the **Dominical Backpacker's Hostel.** Rooms here come with access to a communal kitchen.

Dominical. ☎ **2787-0026** or 2787-0055. Fax 2787-0063. 21 units, 12 with private bathroom. $10 per person with shared bathroom; $30–$40 double with private bathroom. AE, MC, V. **Amenities:** Restaurant; bar; Wi-Fi. *In room:* No phone.

Tortilla Flats This long-standing surfer hotel is another good budget option on the beach. The several styles of rooms include options with fans, rooms with air-conditioning, and larger rooms fitted out for groups of surfers. I recommend the second-floor rooms with ocean views. Because the rooms differ so much in size and comfort levels, you should definitely take a look at a few of them before choosing one.

Dominical. www.tortillaflatsdominical.com. ©/fax **2787-0033.** 18 units. $30–$45 double. AE, MC, V. **Amenities:** Restaurant; bar. *In room:* No phone, Wi-Fi.

Where to Eat

On the beach, **Tortilla Flats** (© **2787-0033**) is the best and most happening spot, and their menu features some excellent fresh-fish dishes and a touch of fusion cuisine. If you head a bit south of town, you can check out the restaurant at the **Hotel Roca Verde** (p. 401), which is usually pretty good for grilled fish, steaks, and burgers.

Soda Nanyoa (© **2787-0164**) is a basic Tico restaurant on the main road, just down a bit from the soccer field, serving local food and fresh seafood at good prices.

Coconut Spice ★★ THAI/INDIAN   Near the mouth of the river, this place continues to serve up excellent and reasonably authentic Thai, Malaysian, Indonesian, and Indian cuisine. The lemon-grass soup and pad Thai are both excellent. Chicken, pork, and shrimp are all served up in a selection of red, green, yellow, and Panang curry sauces. The open-air dining room has wood floors and paneling, heavy wooden tables and chairs, and a smattering of Asian decorations.

In the Pueblo del Rio shopping complex, Dominical. © **2787-0073** or 8829-8397. Reservations recommended during the high season. Main courses $10–$20. MC, V. Daily 1–9pm.

Maracutú ★ INTERNATIONAL/VEGETARIAN   This open-air roadside restaurant has a lively party scene. The heart of the menu is vegetarian and vegan cuisine, but they also serve up some fish and seafood dishes. Much of the food here is locally grown and organic. For starters, you can get a range of Middle Eastern standards, such as falafel and tabouli, as well as delicious homemade guacamole, and fresh yuca chips. The menu also has a range of large, filling salads and pasta dishes. I also recommend the fresh seared tuna or the coconut shrimp baked in a rich and creamy coconut milk and butter sauce. Most nights feature either live music or a DJ and dancing.

Across from the soccer field, Dominical. © **2787-0091.** Reservations not accepted. Main courses $4.50–$11. AE, MC, V. Daily 11am–11pm.

San Clemente Bar & Grill ★★ MEXICAN/AMERICAN   The large wooden tables and bench seats at this convivial place fill up fast most nights. The menu has a large selection of Mexican-American fare ranging from tacos and burritos to sandwiches. You can get any of the former with fresh fish. There are also more substantial plates, as well as nightly specials and excellent breakfasts. Just off the restaurant is a large indoor space that has a pool and foosball table, and which becomes one of the town's more popular nightspots, particularly on Fridays. An interesting (and sobering) decorative touch here is the ceiling full of broken surfboards. If you break a board out on the waves, bring it in; they'll hang it and even buy you a bucket of beer.

Dominical's coastline.

Next to the soccer field, Dominical. ✆ **2787-0055.** Reservations not accepted. Main courses $3.50–$8. AE, MC, V. Daily 11am–10pm.

Dominical After Dark

The big party scenes shift from night to night. **Maracutú** (see above) hosts an open jam session every Sunday and a ladies' night every Wednesday. The loud and late-night dancing scene usually takes place Fridays at **San Clemente** and Saturdays at **Roca Verde;** see above for info. In addition, **Thrusters** in the center of town is a popular surfer bar with pool tables and dartboards, and the bar at **Rio Lindo Resort,** which is several hundred meters inland along the Río Barú, has a mellow scene, with occasional concerts.

South of Dominical

The beaches south of Dominical are some of the nicest and most unexplored in Costa Rica. With the paving of the Costanera Sur, hotels and cabinas have begun popping up all along this route. This is a great area to roam in a rental car—it's a beautiful **drive ★★**. One good itinerary is to make a loop from San Isidro to Dominical, down the Costanera Sur, hitting several deserted beaches, and then returning along the Interamerican Highway.

Among the beaches you'll find are **Playa Ballena, Playa Uvita, Playa Piñuela, Playa Ventanas,** and **Playa Tortuga.** *Tip:* Most of these beaches are considered part of **Ballena Marine National Park** (p. 396) and are subject to the national park entrance fee of $6 per person. If you're visiting several of these beaches in 1 day, save your ticket—it's good at all of them.

WHERE TO STAY

In addition to the places listed here, you'll find a campground at Playa Ballena and a couple of basic cabinas in Bahía and Uvita. The best of these is the **Tucan**

Hotel (www.tucanhotel.com; ✆ **2743-8140**), with a mix of private rooms and dorm accommodations and a friendly hostel-like vibe.

However, if you want to be closer to the beach, check out **Canto de Ballenas** (www.hotelcantoballenas.com; ✆ **2743-8085**), an interesting local cooperative with neat rooms located about .7km (a little less than a half-mile) from the national park entrance at Playa Uvita.

Just south of Dominical, on a point over Dominicalito beach, **La Parcela** (www.laparcela.net; ✆ **2787-0016**) offers up four simple, but ideally located individual cabins that sleep up to four people, for $100, per night, while the nearby **Coconut Grove** (www.coconutgrovecr.com; ✆ **2787-0130**) offers a mix of cottages and guesthouses with direct access to Dominicalito, for between $75 and $135 per double.

Expensive

Cuna del Angel ★★   This hotel has the plushest accommodations along this stretch of coast. The name of this place translates roughly as the Angel's Cradle. All rooms are named after angels, and angel motifs are abundant, as are stained-glass windows and lampshades, carved wood details, tile mosaics, and other artistic touches. The hotel is a bit set in, away from the ocean, but many rooms and common areas have pretty good sea views, over the thick forest and gardens here. Rooms come with either an open front patio fronting the pool, or a private balcony. I prefer the second-floor rooms, with the balconies. A wide range of treatments is available at the spa, and they have several well-equipped boats for deep-sea sportfishing. These folks were awarded "4 Leaves" by the CST Sustainable Tourism program.

9km (5½ miles) south of Dominical, just off the coastal hwy. www.cunadelangel.com. ✆ **2787-8436.** Fax 2787-8015. 23 units. $151–$255 double. Rates include full breakfast. AE, MC, V. **Amenities:** Restaurant; bar; Jacuzzi; midsize outdoor pool; sauna; all rooms smoke-free; small spa. *In room:* A/C, TV, minifridge, hair dryer, Wi-Fi.

La Cusinga Lodge ★   La Cusinga is a wonderful, low-impact sustainable lodge, with a true commitment to environmental protection and education. This should be a top choice for bird-watchers and those looking for a comfortable lodge that also feels entirely in touch with the natural surroundings. The individual and duplex cabins feature lots of varnished woodwork and large screened windows on all sides for cross ventilation. The small complex is set on a hill overlooking Ballena National Park and Playa Uvita. Heavy stone paths connect the main lodge to the various individual cabins. The "honeymoon cabin" is large, with a private garden sitting area and a large bathroom with rustic stonemasonry and its own Jacuzzi tub. This place also has a beautiful, large yoga space and caters to yoga groups. They have an extensive recycling and wastewater treatment program, serve almost entirely organic and locally harvested foods, and used reforested lumber in all construction.

> ### Get the Scoop
>
> If you're venturing south of Dominical, you might want to stop in at the **Uvita Tourist Information Center** (✆ **2743-8072**; www.uvita.info), right on the Costanera Sur, at the main intersection in Uvita. These folks are a wealth of knowledge, have a tour booking agency and rental car operation, and even function as the local branch of the Costa Rican post office, DHL, and UPS.

Bahía Ballena. www.lacusingalodge.com. ℭ/fax **2770-2549.** 9 units. $150 double. Rates include breakfast. MC, V. **Amenities:** Restaurant. *In room:* No phone.

Moderate

Costa Paraiso Lodge   This hotel offers spacious and functional individual rooms on a rocky point at the north end of Dominicalito beach. All but one of the units come with either a full kitchen or kitchenette, and most have high ceilings and plenty of light and ventilation. The Toucan Nest is the best room here, set off from the rest, with a private deck and great view of the ocean. There is a small swimming pool, as well as some beautiful tide pools in front of the hotel; the beach is a short walk away.

2km (1¼ miles) south of Dominical, just off the coastal hwy., Dominicalito. www.costa-paraiso. com. ℭ **2787-0025.** Fax 2787-0340. 5 units. $110–$140 double. Rates include taxes. AE, DC, MC, V. **Amenities:** Small outdoor pool. *In room:* A/C, fridge, kitchenette (in some), no phone, Wi-Fi.

Hotel Villas Gaia ★   Located off the Costanera Sur just before the town of Ojochal, this small hotel is a collection of separate, spacious wood bungalows. Each bungalow has one single and one double bed, a private bathroom, a ceiling fan, and a small veranda with a jungle view. I prefer the bungalows farthest from the restaurant, up on the high hill by the swimming pool. The pool area has wonderful views over the forest to the sea. A large, open-air dining room down by the parking lot is too close to the highway for my liking but serves tasty, well-prepared international fare. A wide range of tours are available, including trips to Isla del Caño, Corcovado National Park, and Wilson Botanical Gardens.

Playa Tortuga. www.villasgaia.com. ℭ/fax **2244-0316** reservations in San José, or 2786-5044 at the lodge. 14 units. $80 double. AE, MC, V. **Amenities:** Restaurant; bar; small outdoor pool. *In room:* A/C ($10), no phone.

WHERE TO EAT

In addition to the places mentioned below, in Ojochal you'll also find the charming **Ylang-Ylang** (ℭ **2786-5054**), which serves up Indonesian fare.

Citrus Restaurante ★★★ BISTRO/FUSION   With an open, airy feel and sense of laid-back refinement, this is my favorite restaurant in the area. You'll find a broad mix of world cuisine on the bistro-style menu, with dishes showing influences as far flung as Asia, North Africa, and France. In addition to the fixed menu are daily blackboard specials, and rich, delicious desserts. You can start things off with wine-steamed mussels, some coconut-milk tuna *ceviche,* or a fresh salad with rich goat cheese and organic, homegrown garden herbs. This place serves up cool cocktails and fruit juices fit for the hot steamy climate here, and occasionally features live music on weekend nights.

Just inland from the turnoff for Ojochal, in front of the Police station. ℭ **2786-5175.** restocitrus@ yahoo.ca. Reservations recommended. Main courses $8–$22. MC, V. Daily 11am–10pm.

Exotica ★★ 🍴 FRENCH/INTERNATIONAL   This place is tucked away along one of the dirt roads that run through Ojochal. With polished concrete floors, bamboo screens for walls, and only a few tree-trunk slab tables and plastic lawn chairs for furniture, it is nonetheless one of the most popular restaurants in the area. The chalkboard menu changes regularly but might feature such dishes as shrimp in a coconut curry sauce or Chicken Exotica, which is stuffed with bacon, prunes, and cheese and topped with a red-pepper coulis.

The lunch menu is much more limited, with a selection of fresh salads and a few more filling mains.

1km (½ mile) inland from the turnoff for Ojochal. ✆ **2786-5050.** Reservations recommended. Lunch $4–$16; main courses $6–$26. MC, V. Mon–Sat 11am–9pm.

La Parcela SEAFOOD/INTERNATIONAL   This open-air restaurant has a lovely setting on a rocky bluff overlooking the ocean. Try to get one of the tables by the railing and you'll be able to watch the waves crashing on the rocks below. The menu features fresh seafood, meat, and poultry dishes, as well as a selection of pastas. Start things off with a tuna tartare tower, and then try either their fresh mahimahi with a mango relish, or the filet mignon in a porcini mushroom sauce. This place has a truly wonderful view, although the food and service can be inconsistent.

At Punto Dominical. ✆ **2787-0016.** www.laparcela.net. Reservations recommended. Main courses C3,000–C30,000. AE, MC, V. Daily 11am–10pm.

SAN ISIDRO DE EL GENERAL: A BASE FOR EXPLORING CHIRRIPÓ NATIONAL PARK

120km (74 miles) SE of San José; 123km (76 miles) NW of Palmar Norte; 29km (18 miles) NE of Dominical

San Isidro de El General is just off the Interamerican Highway in the foothills of the Talamanca Mountains and is the largest town in this region. Although there isn't much to do right in town, this is the jumping-off point for trips to **Chirripó National Park.**

Essentials

GETTING THERE & DEPARTING   **By Car:** The long and winding stretch of the Interamerican Highway between San José and San Isidro is one of the most difficult sections of road in the country. Not only are there the usual car-eating potholes and periodic landslides, but you must also contend with driving over the 3,300m (10,824-ft.) **Cerro de la Muerte (Mountain of Death).** This aptly named mountain pass is legendary for its dense afternoon fogs, blinding torrential downpours, steep drop-offs, severe switchbacks, and unexpectedly breathtaking views. (Well, you wanted adventure travel, so here you go!) Drive with extreme care, and bring a sweater or sweatshirt—it's cold up at the top. It'll take you about 3 hours to get to San Isidro.

   Tip: If you want a break from the road, stop for a coffee or meal at **Mirador Valle del General** (✆ **8384-4685** or 2200-5465; www.valledel general.com; at Km 119), a rustic roadside joint with a great view, gift shop, hiking trails, and orchid collection. These folks also have a few rustic cabins, as well as a zip-line canopy tour.

   By Bus: Musoc buses (✆ **2222-2422** in San José, or 2771-3829 in San Isidro) leave from their terminal at Calle Central and Avenida 22 roughly hourly between 5:30am and 5:30pm. **Tracopa** (✆ **2221-4214** or 2771-0468) also runs express buses between San José and San Isidro that

> ## Little Devils
>
> If you're visiting the San Isidro area in February, head out to the nearby **Rey Curré** village for the **Fiesta of the Diablitos,** where costumed Boruca Indians perform dances representative of the Spanish conquest of Central America. The 3-day event also includes fireworks and an Indian handicraft market—this is *the* best place in Costa Rica to buy hand-carved Boruca masks. The date varies, so it's best to call the **Costa Rica Tourist Board** (☎ **866/267-8274** in the U.S. and Canada) for more information.

leave 6 and 8:30am and 12:30, 2:30, 4, and 6:30pm from Calle 5, between avenidas 18 and 20. Whichever company you choose, the trip takes a little over 3 hours, and the fare is roughly C2,705. Return buses depart San Isidro for **San José** roughly every hour between 4:30am and 5:30pm.

Buses from **Quepos** to San Isidro leave daily at 5:30 and 11:30am and 3:30pm. Trip duration is 3 hours; the fare is C2,015. Buses to or from **Golfito** and **Puerto Jiménez** will also drop you off in San Isidro.

ORIENTATION   Downtown San Isidro is just off the Interamerican Highway. A large church fronts the central park, and you'll find several banks, and a host of restaurants, shops, and hotels within a 2-block radius of this park. The main bus station is 2 blocks west of the north end of the central park.

Exploring Chirripó National Park ★★

At 3,819m (12,526 ft.) in elevation, Mount Chirripó is the tallest mountain in Costa Rica. If you're headed up this way, come prepared for chilly weather. Actually, dress in layers and come prepared for all sorts of weather: Because of the great elevations, temperatures frequently dip below freezing, especially at night. However, during the day, temperatures can soar—remember, you're still only 9 degrees from the equator. The elevation and radical temperatures have produced an environment here that's very different from the Costa Rican norm. Above 3,000m (9,840 ft.), only stunted trees and shrubs survive in páramos. If you're driving the Interamerican Highway between San Isidro and San José, you'll pass through a páramo on the Cerro de la Muerte.

Hiking up to the top of Mount Chirripó is one of Costa Rica's best adventures. On a clear day (usually in the morning), an unforgettable **view ★★★** is your reward: You can see both the Pacific Ocean and the Caribbean Sea from the summit. You can do this trip fairly easily on your own if you've brought gear and are an experienced backpacker. Although it's possible to hike from the park entrance to the summit and back down in 2 days (in fact, some daredevils even do it in 1 day), it's best to allow 3 to 4 days for the trip in order to give yourself time to enjoy your hike fully and spend some time on top, because that's where the glacier lakes and páramos are. For much of the way, you'll be hiking through

Mount Chirripó.

cloud forests that are home to abundant tropical fauna, including the spectacular **quetzal,** Costa Rica's most beautiful bird. However, quetzal sightings on summit climbs are rare. If you really want to see one of these birds, head to one of the specialized lodges listed below.

Several routes lead to the top of Mount Chirripó. The most popular, by far, leaves from **San Gerardo de Rivas.** However, it's also possible to start your hike from the nearby towns of **Herradura** or **Canaan.** All these places are within a mile or so of each other, reached by the same major road out of San Isidro. San Gerardo is the most popular because it's the easiest route to the top and has the greatest collection of small hotels and lodges, as well as the National Parks office. Information on all of these routes is available at the parks office.

When you're at the summit lodge, you have a number of hiking options. Just in front of the lodge are Los Crestones (the Crests), an impressive rock formation, with trails leading up and around them. The most popular, however, is to the actual summit (the lodge itself is a bit below), which is about a 2-hour hike that passes through the Valle de los Conejos (Rabbit Valley) and the Valle de los Lagos (Valley of Lakes). Other hikes and trails lead off from the summit lodge, and it's easy to spend a couple of days hiking around here. A few trails will take you to the summits of several neighboring peaks. These hikes should be undertaken only after carefully studying an accurate map and talking to park rangers and other hikers.

ENTRY POINT, FEES & REGULATIONS   Although it's not that difficult to get to Chirripó National Park from nearby San Isidro, it's still rather remote. And to see it fully, you have to be prepared to hike. To get to the trail head, you have three choices: car, taxi, or bus. If you choose to drive, take the road out of San Isidro, heading north toward San Gerardo de Rivas, which is some 20km (12 miles) down the road. Otherwise, you can catch a bus in San Isidro that will take you directly to the trail head in San Gerardo de Rivas. Buses leave daily at 5am from the western side of the central park in San Isidro. It costs C425 one-way and takes 1½ hours. Another bus departs at 2pm from a bus station 200m (656 ft.) south of the park. Buses return to

San Isidro daily at 7am and 4pm. A taxi from town should cost around C7,000 to C10,000. Because the hike to the summit of Mount Chirripó can take between 6 and 12 hours, depending on your physical condition, I recommend taking a taxi or the early bus so that you can start hiking when the day is still young. Better still, you should arrive the day before and spend the night in San Gerardo de Rivas (there are inexpensive cabinas and one nice hotel there) before setting out early the following morning.

Before climbing Mount Chirripó, you must make a reservation and check in with the **National Parks office** (☎ **2742-5083**) in San Gerardo de Rivas. The office is open from 6:30am to 4:30pm daily. Even if you have a reservation, I recommend checking in the day before you plan to climb. If you plan to stay at the lodge near the summit, you must make reservations in advance because accommodations are limited (see "Staying at the Summit Lodge," below). Note that camping is not allowed in the park. It's possible to have your gear carried up to the summit by horseback during the dry season (Dec–Apr). Guides work outside the park entrance in San Gerardo de Rivas. They charge between $20 and $30 per pack, depending on size and weight. In the rainy season, the same guides work, but they take packs up by themselves, not by horseback. The guides like to take up the packs well before dawn, so arrangements are best made the day before. The entrance fee to the national park is $15 per day.

STAYING AT THE SUMMIT LODGE   Reservations for lodging on the summit of Mount Chirripó must be made with the National Parks office listed above. This is an increasingly popular destination, and you must reserve well in advance during the dry season. The lodge holds only 30 people and fills up quickly and frequently. However, a few last-minute spaces are usually released each day on a first-come, first-served basis.

Once you get to the lodge, you'll find various rooms with bunk beds, several bathrooms and showers, and a common kitchen area. It has good drinking water. However, blankets, lanterns, and cookstoves are no longer for rent up top, so you have to pack all your own gear, as well as food and water (for the hike up). *Note:* It gets cold up here at night, and the lodge

 Movin' On Up

From San Gerardo de Rivas, the 14.5km (9-mile) trail to the summit lodge is well marked and well maintained. The early parts of the trail are pretty steep and will take you through thick cloud forests and rainforests. After about 7.5km (4.7 miles), you will reach the "Water Ridge," a flat ridge that features a small shelter and water spigot. This is roughly the midway point to the lodge and a great place to take a break.

From Water Ridge, three steep uphill sections remain: Cuesta de Agua (Water Hill), Monte Sin Fe (Mountain without Hope), and La Cuesta de los Arrepentidos (The Hill of Regret). As you continue to climb, you will notice the flora changing. The entire elevation gain for this hike is 2,200m (7,215 ft.). La Cuesta de los Arrepentidos, your final ascent, brings you to a broad flat valley, where you'll find the summit lodge. This hike can take anywhere from 6 to 10 hours, depending on how long you linger along the way.

seems to have been designed to be as cold, dark, and cavernous as possible. The showers are freezing. It costs $10 per person per night to stay here.

Warning: It can be dangerous for more inexperienced or out-of-shape hikers to climb Chirripó, especially by themselves. It's not very technical climbing, but it is a long, arduous hike. If you're

Race to the Top

If simply climbing the tallest peak in Costa Rica is a bit too mundane for you, why not join the annual **Carrera Campo Traviesa Al Cerro Chirripó** (☎ 2771-8731; www.carrera chirripo.com). Held the third or fourth Saturday of February, this is a grueling 34km (21-mile) race from the base to the summit and back. The record time, to date, is 3 hours, 15 minutes, and 3 seconds.

not sure you're up for it, you can just take day hikes out of San Isidro and/or San Gerardo de Rivas, or ask at your hotel about guides.

Other Adventures in & Around San Isidro

If you want to undertake any other adventures while in San Isidro, contact **Costa Rica Trekking Adventures** (☎ 2771-4582; www.chirripo.com), which offers organized treks through Chirripó National Park, as well as white-water rafting trips and other adventure tours and activities.

Just 7km (4⅓ miles) from San Isidro is **Las Quebradas Biological Center** (☎ 2771-4131), a community-run private reserve with 2.7km (1.75 miles) of trails through primary rainforest. The rustic lodge for visitors and researchers is C20,000 per person (C11,500 per person, if part of group, including three meals), and camping is also permitted. You can hike the trails here and visit the small information center on-site for C1,500. From San Isidro, you can take a local bus to Quebradas, but you'll have to walk the last mile to the entrance. You can also take a taxi for around C5,000. If you're driving, take the road to Morazán and Quebradas.

Where to Stay & Eat in San Isidro

San Isidro doesn't have much of a dining scene. Sure, the town has its fair share of local joints, but most visitors are content at their hotel restaurant; see below for ideas. If you do venture beyond your hotel, your first stop should be the local outpost of **Citrus ★★** (☎ 2771-9393, p. 405) in the small downtown strip mall, Plaza Villa Herrera. While nowhere near as atmospheric as its jungle-clad sister down in Ojochal, this place still serves up excellent fusion cuisine. Other good options include the **Pizzería El Tenedor** (☎ 2771-0881), just off the central park, and **Taquería México Lindo** (☎ 2772-8222), in the Centro Comercial Pedro Perez Zeledon, just across from the central park. Although the food is mediocre, the second-floor, open-air balcony seating at **La Cascada** (☎ 2771-6479), right in the town center, offers some excellent opportunities for people-watching, and is a great place to mingle with locals. For a coffee break or light meal, I like **Kafe de la Casa ★** (☎ 2770-4816), which is next to the **Hotel Diamante Real** (www.hoteldiamantereal.com; ☎ 2770-6230), and offers up free Wi-Fi, along with its regular breakfast, lunch, and dinner menu.

Hotel Los Crestones This two-story hotel is a few blocks south of downtown, and away from most of the traffic noise of this busy little city, although it is still on the main route that heads out of town toward Dominical. All rooms are relatively large and come with air-conditioning. The televisions, however, are pretty small. I recommend the units on the second floor, which share a broad tiled veranda. The hotel has a midsize outdoor swimming pool and Jacuzzi.

San Isidro de El General (southwest side of the stadium). www.hotelloscrestones.com. ☎ **2770-1200.** Fax 2770-5047. 27 units. C25,500–C30,000 double. AE, MC, V. **Amenities:** Restaurant; Jacuzzi; outdoor pool. *In room:* A/C, TV, Wi-Fi.

Where to Stay Closer to the Trail Head

If you're climbing Mount Chirripó, you'll want to spend the night as close to the trail head as possible. As mentioned above, several basic cabinas right in San Gerardo de Rivas charge between $10 and $20 per person. The best of these are **El Descanso** (☎ **2742-5061**), **Casa Mariposa** (www.hotelcasamariposa.net; ☎ **2742-5037**), and **Roca Dura** (hotelrocadura@hotmail.com; ☎ **2742-5071**). If you're looking for a little more comfort, check out **El Pelicano** (www.hotelpelicano.net; ☎ **2742-5050**) or the hotels listed below.

For good general information on the tiny village and its surrounding area, check out www.sangerardocostarica.com.

Monte Azul ★★★   This boutique hotel is artsy, chic, and luxurious. Set among lush gardens, the casitas are spacious and loaded with contemporary art. All feature a queen-size bed, kitchenette, and a private garden patio. Casa Palo Alto is a large two-bedroom villa on a high point of land, with its own swimming pool, massive living room, and fully equipped kitchen. A range of spa treatments is offered in the comfort of your room or villa, and meals at the hotel's Café Blue restaurant are excellent, and focus on locally grown organic fruits, vegetables, and herbs. Various arts and crafts classes are regularly held, and the hotel has an extensive network of trails, as well as easy access to the relatively nearby Chirripó National Park.

Rivas, San Isidro. www.monteazulcr.com. ☎ **2742-5222.** 6 units. $190 casita; $1,390 Casa Palo Alto. Rates include full breakfast. AE, MC, V. **Amenities:** Restaurant; bar; concierge; all rooms smoke-free. *In room:* No phone, minifridge, Wi-Fi.

Talari Mountain Lodge ★ This small mountain getaway is nothing fancy, but it is one of the nicer options right around San Isidro, and it also makes a good base for exploring the region or climbing Mount Chirripó. The rooms are in two separate concrete-block buildings. Most come with one double and one single bed, although one room can handle a family of four in one double and two single beds. I prefer the four rooms that face the Talamanca Mountains. The grounds are planted with fruit trees and offer good bird-watching. (They've identified more than 222 bird species here.) The hotel borders the Río General and

---

Rest Your Weary Muscles Here

If you're tired and sore from so much hiking, be sure to check out the small **Aguas Termales Gevi** (☎ **2742-5016**), located off the road between San Gerardo de Rivas and Herradura. The entrance to these humble hot springs is 1km (½ mile) beyond San Gerardo de Rivas. There are two small pools here, as well as showers and changing rooms. The entrance fee is C2,800.

maintains some forest trails. Talari is 8km (5 miles) outside of San Isidro, and a staff member picks you up in town for free with advance notice. This lodge is also about 11km (6¾ miles) from San Gerardo de Rivas, so you'll probably have to arrange transportation to and from the park entrance if you plan on climbing Chirripó.

Rivas, San Isidro. www.talari.co.cr. (℃)/fax **2771-0341.** 12 units. $72 double. Rates include full breakfast. AE, MC, V. **Amenities:** Restaurant; bar; Jacuzzi; small outdoor pool and separate children's pool; indoor lit tennis court. *In room:* Fridge, no phone.

Cerro de la Muerte & San Gerardo de Dota: Where to See Quetzals in the Wild

Between San José and San Isidro de El General, the Interamerican Highway climbs to its highest point in Costa Rica and crosses over the **Cerro de la Muerte** (The Mountain of Death). About midway between San Isidro and Cartago, a deep valley descends toward the Pacific coast and the tiny town of San Gerardo de Dota. This area is one of the best places in Costa Rica to see quetzals. March, April, and May is nesting season for these birds, and this is usually the best time to see them. However, it's often possible to spot them year-round here. On my first visit here, during a 2-hour hike without a guide, my small group spotted eight of these amazing birds. I was hooked.

If you plan on spending any time in the region and want to take an organized tour, contact **Santos Tours ★** (℃ **8855-9386;** www.santostour.net), a local, community tourism project that offers a range of active adventures, including waterfall hikes, coffee plantation tours, and even a canopy tour.

In addition to the places listed below, **Dantica Cloud Forest Lodge ★** (www.dantica.com; ℃ **2740-1067**) is a small collection of private bungalows in a beautiful forested setting near the town of San Gerardo de Dota.

Albergue Mirador de Quetzales This family-run lodge is also known as Finca Eddie Serrano. The rooms in the main lodge are quite basic, with wood floors, bunk beds, and shared bathrooms. Eight separate A-frames provide a bit more comfort and a private bathroom. Meals are served family-style in the main lodge. But quetzals, not comfort, are the main draw here, and if you come between December and May, you should have no trouble spotting plenty. The cloud forest has good hiking trails and the Serrano family are genial hosts and good guides. On a clear day, you can see the peaks of five volcanoes from the hotel's lookout—but it's not clear that often.

Carretera Interamericana Sur Km 70, about 1km (½ mile) down a dirt road from the hwy. www. elmiradordequetzales.com.(℃)/fax **8381-8456** or 2200-5915. 15 units. $50 per person. Rate includes breakfast and dinner, a 2-hr. tour, and taxes. MC, V. **Amenities:** Restaurant. *In room:* No phone.

Savegre Mountain Hotel ★ This working apple-and-pear farm, which also has more than 240 hectares (593 acres) of primary forest, has a well-earned reputation for superb bird-watching—it's one of the best places in the country to see quetzals. The rooms are clean and comfortable, but spartan, but if you're serious about birding, this shouldn't matter. In addition to the quetzals, some 170 other species have been spotted here. Hearty Tico meals are served, and if you want to try your hand at trout fishing, you might luck into a fish dinner. The owners of this place are a local family dedicated to local conservation and community development efforts. You'll find the lodge 9km (5½ miles) down a dirt road off the Interamerican Highway. This road is steep and often muddy, and four-wheel-drive is recommended, although not necessary.

Carretera Interamericana Sur Km 80, San Gerardo de Dota. www.savegre.co.cr. (C) **2740-1028.** Fax 2740-1027. 41 cabins. $186–$265 double. Rates include all meals, nonalcoholic drinks, entrance to their reserve, and taxes. Rates slightly lower in the off season. AE, MC, V. **Amenities:** Restaurant; 2 bars; Wi-Fi.

Trogon Lodge ★ 👜 This is the most attractive and comfortable of the area's lodges. The rooms are still rather basic, but the grounds, setting, and overall decor are a bit nicer than at the lodges listed above. The rooms are all of good size, with wood floors and walls, a shared veranda, and one double and one twin bed. Room nos. 15 and 16 are my favorites; they are the farthest from the main lodge and have great views of the river. The family-style meals often feature fresh trout from their well-stocked trout ponds; as at Savegre Mountain Hotel, more than half the fun is catching it yourself. These folks also have their own little zip-line canopy tour.

Carretera Interamericana Sur Km 80, San Gerardo de Dota. www.grupomawamba.com. (C) **2293-8181** in San José, or 2740-1051 at the lodge. Fax 2239-7657. 23 units. $79 double; $130 junior suite with Jacuzzi. A full meal package runs $24 per person. AE, MC, V. **Amenities:** Restaurant; bar; lounge. *In room:* No phone.

THE SOUTHERN ZONE

Costa Rica's southern zone is an area of jaw-dropping beauty, with vast expanses of virgin lowland rainforest, loads of wildlife, tons of adventure opportunities and few cities, towns, or settlements. Lushly forested mountains tumble into the sea, streams still run clear and clean, scarlet macaws squawk raucously in the treetops, and dolphins frolic in the Golfo Dulce. The Osa Peninsula is the most popular attraction in this region and one of the premier ecotourism destinations in the world. It's home to Corcovado National Park ★★★, the largest single expanse of lowland tropical rainforest in Central America, and its sister, Piedras Blancas National Park ★★. Scattered around the edges of these national parks and along the shores of the Golfo Dulce are some of the country's finest nature lodges. These lodges, in general, offer comfortable to nearly luxurious accommodations, attentive service, knowledgeable guides, and a wide range of activities and tours, all close to the area's many natural wonders.

But this beauty doesn't come easy. You must have plenty of time (or plenty of money—or, preferably, both) and a desire for adventure. It's a long way from San José, and many of the most fascinating spots can be reached only by small plane or boat—although hiking and four-wheeling will get you into some memorable surroundings as well. In many ways, this is Costa Rica's final frontier, and the cities of Golfito and Puerto Jiménez are nearly as wild as the jungles that surround them. Tourism is still underdeveloped here, with no large resorts in this neck of the woods. Moreover, the heat and humidity are more than some people can stand. It's best to put some forethought into planning a vacation down here, and wise to book your rooms and transportation in advance.

 The Southern Zone's Top Sustainable Hotels

Bosque del Cabo Rainforest Lodge (p. 439)
Casa Corcovado (p. 425)
El Remanso (p. 439)
Golfo Dulce Lodge (p. 447)
Iguana Lodge (p. 438)
La Paloma Lodge (p. 425)
Lapa Ríos (p. 440)
Luna Lodge (p. 440)
Playa Nicuesa Rainforest Lodge (p. 447)
Tiskita Jungle Lodge (p. 454)

PREVIOUS PAGE: **Climbing a Strangler fig on the Psycho Tour.**

DRAKE BAY ★★

145km (90 miles) S of San José; 32km (20 miles) SW of Palmar

While Drake Bay remains one of the more isolated spots in Costa Rica, the small town located at the mouth of the **Río Agujitas** has boomed a bit in recent years. Most of that is due to the year-round operation of the small airstrip here, and the sometimes passable condition of the rough dirt road connecting Drake Bay to the coastal highway—just a decade or so ago there was no road, and the nearest regularly functioning airstrip was in Palmar Sur. That said, the village of Drake Bay is still tiny, and the lodges listed here remain quiet and remote getaways catering to naturalists, anglers, scuba divers, and assorted vacationers. Tucked away on the northern edge of the Osa Peninsula, Drake Bay is a great place to get away from it all.

The bay is named after Sir Francis Drake, who is believed to have anchored here in 1579. Emptying into a broad bay, the tiny Río Agujitas acts as a protected harbor for small boats and is a great place to do a bit of canoeing or swimming. Many of the local lodges dock their boats and many **dolphin and whale-watching tours** leave from here. Stretching south from Drake Bay are miles of deserted beaches and dense primary tropical rainforest. Adventurous explorers will find tide pools, spring-fed rivers, waterfalls, forest trails, and some of the best bird-watching in all of Costa Rica. If a paradise such as this appeals to you, Drake Bay makes a good base for exploring the peninsula.

South of Drake Bay are the wilds of the **Osa Peninsula,** including **Corcovado National Park.** This is one of Costa Rica's most beautiful regions, yet it's also one of its least accessible. Corcovado National Park covers about half of the peninsula and contains the largest single expanse of virgin lowland rainforest in Central America. For this reason, Corcovado is well known among naturalists and researchers studying rainforest ecology. If you come here, you'll learn

Spotting a common dolphin.

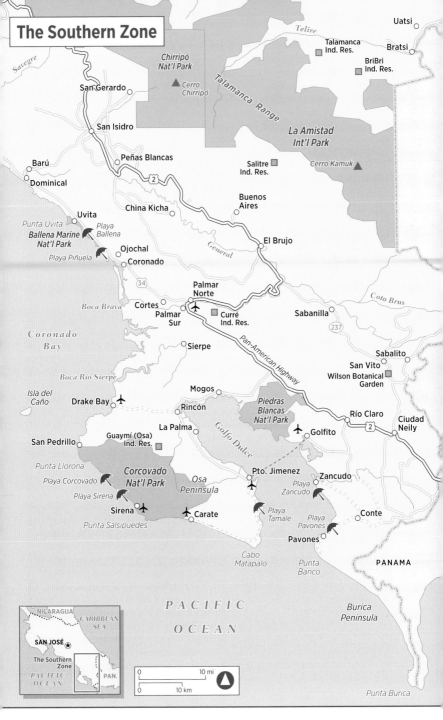

The Southern Zone

Uatsi

Telire

Talamanca
Ind. Res.

Bratsi

BriBri
Ind. Res.

Savegre

Chirripó
Nat'l Park

Cerro
Chirripó

Talamanca Range

La Amistad
Int'l Park

San Gerardo

San Isidro

Peñas Blancas

Salitre
Ind. Res.

Cerro Kamuk

Barú

Dominical

Buenos
Aires

China Kicha

El Brujo

Punta Uvita   Uvita
Ballena Marine
Nat'l Park

Playa
Ballena

General

Coto Brus

Playa Piñuela

Ojochal

Coronado

Boca Brava

Cortes

Palmar
Norte

Curré
Ind. Res.

Sabanilla

Palmar
Sur

Coronado
Bay

Sierpe

Pan-American Highway

Sabalito

San Vito
Wilson Botanical
Garden

Boca Río Sierpe

Mogos

Isla del
Caño

Drake Bay

Rincón

Piedras
Blancas
Nat'l Park

Río Claro

Ciudad
Neily

La Palma

Golfo Dulce

Golfito

San Pedrillo

Guaymí (Osa)
Ind. Res.

Punta Llorona

Playa Corcovado

Corcovado
Nat'l Park

Osa
Peninsula

Pto. Jimenez

Zancudo

Playa
Zancudo

Playa Sirena

Sirena

Carate

Playa
Tamale

Playa
Pavones

Conte

Punta Salsipuedes

Cabo
Matapalo

Punta
Banco

Pavones

PANAMA

PACIFIC

OCEAN

Burica
Peninsula

NICARAGUA

CARIBBEAN
SEA

SAN JOSÉ

The Southern
Zone

PACIFIC
OCEAN

PAN.

0   10 mi
0   10 km

Punta Burica

firsthand why they call them rainforests: Some parts of the peninsula receive more than 635cm (250 in.) of rain per year.

Puerto Jiménez (p. 426) is the best base if you want to spend a lot of time hiking in and camping inside Corcovado National Park. Drake Bay is primarily a collection of mostly high-end hotels, very isolated and mostly accessible only by boat. Travelers using these hotels can have great day hikes and guided tours into Corcovado Park, but Puerto Jiménez is the place if you want to have more time in the park or to explore independently. (It has budget hotels, the parks office, and "taxi/bus" service to Carate and Los Patos, from which visitors can hike into the various stations.) From the Drake Bay side, you're much more dependent on a boat ride/organized tour from one of the lodges to explore the park; these lodges offer many other guided outings in addition to visits to the park.

Essentials

Because Drake Bay is so remote, I recommend that you have a room reservation and transportation arrangements (usually arranged with your hotel) before you arrive. Most of the lodges listed here are scattered along several kilometers of coastline, and it is not easy to go from one to another looking for a room.

Tip: A flashlight and rain gear are always useful to have on hand in Costa Rica; they're absolutely essential in Drake Bay.

GETTING THERE   By Plane: Most people fly directly into the little airstrip at Drake Bay (no phone), although some tourists still fly to Palmar Sur (p. 416): All lodges will either arrange transportation for you, or include it in their packages. **Sansa** (✆ **877/767-2672** in the U.S. and Canada, or 2290-4100 in Costa Rica; www.flysansa.com) flies directly to Drake Bay daily at 9:50am and 3pm from San José's Juan Santamaría International Airport. The return flights leave Drake Bay at 10:53am and 4pm. The flight takes 50 minutes; the fare is $133 each way. Flights also depart San José daily at 9:20 and 9:40am for Palmar Sur; the fare is $120 each way.

Nature Air (✆ **800/235-9272** in the U.S. and Canada, or 2299-6000; www.natureair.com) has direct flights to Drake Bay departing daily from Tobías Bolaños International Airport in Pavas at 8:20 and 11:30am. The flight duration is 40 minutes; the fare is $105 to $134 each way. Return flights leave Drake Bay at 9:05am and 12:20pm. It also has a daily flight to Palmar Sur that departs at 9am and sometimes stops at Quepos en route. The flight takes a little over an hour, and the fare is $123 each way.

If your travels take you to Drake Bay via Palmar Sur, you must then take a 15-minute bus or taxi ride over dirt roads to the small town of

Helping Out

If you want to help local efforts in protecting the fragile rainforests and wild areas of the Osa Peninsula, contact the **Corcovado Foundation** (✆ **2297-3013**; www.corcovado foundation.org) or the **Friends of the Osa** (✆ **2735-5756**; www.osaconservation.org).

Moreover, if you're looking to really lend a hand, both of the aforementioned groups have volunteer programs ranging from trail maintenance to environmental and English-language education to sea-turtle-nesting protection programs.

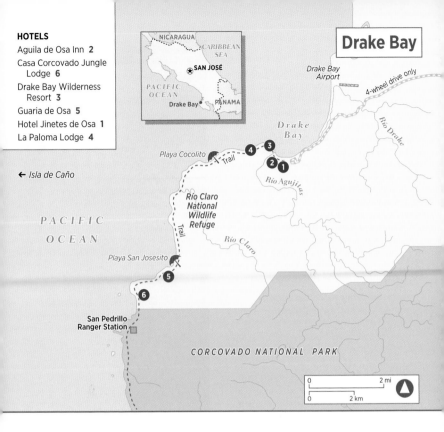

HOTELS

Aguila de Osa Inn **2**

Casa Corcovado Jungle
Lodge **6**

Drake Bay Wilderness
Resort **3**

Guaria de Osa **5**

Hotel Jinetes de Osa **1**

La Paloma Lodge **4**

← *Isla de Caño*

Drake Bay

NICARAGUA

CARIBBEAN SEA

SAN JOSÉ

PACIFIC OCEAN

PANAMA

Drake Bay

Drake Bay Airport

4-wheel drive only

Río Drake

Drake Bay

Playa Cocolito

Trail

Río Aguijitas

Río Claro National Wildlife Refuge

PACIFIC OCEAN

Trail

Río Claro

Playa San Josesito

San Pedrillo Ranger Station

CORCOVADO NATIONAL PARK

0   2 mi

0   2 km

Sierpe. This bumpy route runs through several **banana plantations** and quickly past some important archaeological sites. In Sierpe, you board a small boat for a 40km (25-mile) ride to Drake Bay; see "By Taxi & Boat from Sierpe," below. The first half of this trip snakes through a maze of mangrove canals and rivers before heading out to sea for the final leg to the bay. ***Warning:*** Entering and exiting the Sierpe River mouth is often treacherous; I've had several very white-knuckle moments here.

    By Bus: Tracopa buses (*☎* **2221-4214** or 2258-8939; www.tracopa cr.com) leave San José daily for the southern zone throughout the day, between 5am and 6:30pm from Calle 5 between avenidas 18 and 20. Almost all stop in Palmar Norte, although be sure to ask. The ride takes around 6 hours; the fare is C4,850.

    Once in Palmar Norte, ask when the next bus goes out to Sierpe. If it doesn't leave for a while (buses aren't frequent), consider taking a taxi (see below).

    By Taxi & Boat from Sierpe: When you arrive at either the Palmar Norte bus station or the Palmar Sur airstrip, you'll most likely first need to take a taxi to the village of Sierpe. The fare should be around $15. If you're booked into one of the main lodges, chances are your transportation is included. Even if you're not booked into one of the lodges, a host of taxi and minibus drivers offer the trip. When you get to Sierpe, head to the dock and try to find space on a boat. This should run you another $20 to $40. If you don't arrive early enough, you might have to hire an entire boat, which usually runs around $90 to $150 for a boat that can carry up to six passengers. Make sure that you feel confident about the boat and skipper, and, if possible, try to find a spot on a boat from one of the established lodges in Drake Bay.

By Car: I don't recommend driving to Drake Bay. But if you insist, take the San José–Caldera Highway (CR27) to the first exit past the Pozón toll booth, where you will pick up the Southern Highway or Costanera Sur (CR34). Take this south through Jacó, Quepos, and Dominical to Palmar Norte, where you'll meet up with the Interamerican Highway (CR2). Take this south to the turnoff for La Palma, Rincón, and

A flowering banana plant.

Puerto Jiménez (at the town of Chacarita; it's clearly marked). Then at Rincón, turn onto the rough road leading into Drake Bay. This road fords some 10 rivers and is often not passable during the rainy season. Moreover, it only reaches into the small heart of the village of Drake Bay, though almost all of the hotels I list below are farther out along the peninsula, where only boats reach. The only hotels that you can actually drive up to are very basic cabins in town. For the rest, you'd have to find someplace secure to leave your car and either haul your bags quite a way or get picked up in a boat.

DEPARTING If you're not flying directly out of Drake Bay, have your lodge arrange a boat trip back to Sierpe for you. Be sure that the lodge also arranges for a taxi to meet you in Sierpe for the trip to Palmar Sur or Palmar Norte. (If you're on a budget, you can ask around to see whether a late-morning public bus is still running from Sierpe to Palmar Norte.) In the two Palmars you can make onward plane and bus connections. At the Palmar Norte bus terminal, almost any bus heading north will take you to San José, and almost any bus heading south will take you to Golfito.

What to See & Do

Beaches, forests, wildlife, and solitude are the main attractions of Drake Bay. Although Corcovado National Park (see "Puerto Jiménez: Gateway to Corcovado National Park," below) is the area's star attraction, plenty of other attractions are in and around Drake Bay. The Osa Peninsula is home to an unbelievable variety of plants and animals: more than 140 species of mammals, 390 species of birds, and 130 species of amphibians and reptiles. You aren't likely to see anywhere near all of these animals, but you can expect to see quite a few, including several types of monkeys, coatimundis, scarlet macaws, parrots, and hummingbirds. Other park inhabitants include jaguars, tapirs, sloths, and crocodiles. If you're lucky, you might even see one of the region's namesake *osas*, or giant anteaters.

Around Drake Bay and within the national park are many miles of trails through rainforests and swamps, down beaches, and around rock headlands. All of the lodges listed below offer guided excursions into the park. It's also possible to begin a hike around the peninsula from Drake Bay.

One of the most popular excursions from Drake Bay is a trip out to **Isla del Caño** and the **Caño Island Biological Reserve ★★** for a bit of exploring and snorkeling or scuba diving. The island is about 19km (12 miles) offshore from Drake Bay and was once home to a pre-Columbian culture about which little is known. A trip to the island will include a visit to an ancient cemetery, and you'll also be able to see some of the stone spheres believed to have been carved by this area's ancient inhabitants (see the box below, "Those Mysterious Stone Spheres"). Few animals or birds live on the island, but the coral reefs just offshore teem with life and are the main reason most people come here. This is one of Costa Rica's prime **scuba spots ★★**. Visibility is often quite good, and the beach has easily accessible snorkeling. All of the lodges listed below offer trips to Isla del Caño.

A baird's tapir.

Snorkelers at Caño Island Biological Reserve.

All lodges in the area also offer a host of half- and full-day tours and activities, including hikes in Corcovado National Park, horseback rides, and sportfishing. In some cases, tours are included in your room rate or package; in others, they must be bought a la carte. Other options include mountain biking and sea kayaking. Most of these tours run between $60 and $120, depending on the activity, with scuba diving ($90–$125 for a two-tank dive) and sportfishing ($450–$1,500, depending on the size of the boat and other amenities) costing a bit more.

One of the most interesting tour options in Drake Bay is a 2-hour **night tour** ★★ (© **8701-7356;** www.thenighttour.com; $35 per person) offered by Tracie Stice, who is affectionately known as the "Bug Lady." Equipped with flashlights, participants get a bug's-eye view of the forest at night. You might see reflections of some larger forest dwellers, but most of the tour is a fascinating exploration of the nocturnal insect and arachnid world. Consider yourself lucky if she finds the burrow of a trap-door spider or large tarantula. Avoid this tour if you are helplessly arachnophobic. Any hotel in Drake Bay can book the tour for you. However, the travel distance makes it impossible for those staying at hotels outside of walking distance of the town.

Drake Bay is one of the best places to go **whale-watching** in Costa Rica; humpback whales are most commonly spotted in the

 Where's The Beach?

While the beach at Drake Bay itself is acceptable and calm for swimming, it's far from spectacular. The most popular swimming beach is a pretty small patch of sand, known locally as Cocalito beach, about a 7-minute hike down from La Paloma Lodge. The nicest beaches around involve taking a day trip to either Isla del Caño or San Josesito. The latter is a stunning beach farther south on the peninsula with excellent snorkeling possibilities.

THOSE MYSTERIOUS stone spheres

Although Costa Rica lacks the great cities, giant temples, and bas-relief carvings of the Maya, Aztec, and Olmec civilizations of northern Mesoamerica, its pre-Columbian residents did leave a unique legacy that continues to cause archaeologists and anthropologists to scratch their heads and wonder. Over a period of several centuries, hundreds of painstakingly carved and carefully positioned granite spheres were left by the peoples who lived throughout the Diquis Delta, which flanks the Terraba River in southern Costa Rica. The orbs, which range from grapefruit size to more than 2m (6½ ft.) in diameter, can weigh up to 15 tons, and many reach near-spherical perfection.

Archaeologists believe that the spheres were created during two defined cultural periods. The first, called the Aguas Buenas period, dates from around A.D. 100 to 500. Few spheres survive from this time. The second phase, during which spheres were created in apparently greater numbers, is called the Chiriquí period and lasted from approximately A.D. 800 to 1500. The "balls" believed to have been carved during this time frame are widely dispersed along the entire length of the lower section of the Terraba River. To date, only one known quarry for the spheres has been discovered, in the mountains above the Diquis Delta, which points to a difficult and lengthy transportation process.

Some archaeologists believe that the spheres were hand-carved in a very time-consuming process, using stone tools, perhaps aided by some sort of firing process. However, another theory holds that granite blocks were placed at the bases of powerful waterfalls, and the hydraulic beating of the water eventually turned and carved the rock into these near-perfect spheres. And more than a few proponents have credited extraterrestrial intervention for the creation of the stone balls.

Most of the stone balls have been found at the archaeological remains of defined settlements and are associated with either central plazas or known burial sites. Their size and placement have been interpreted to have both social and celestial importance, although their exact significance remains a mystery. Unfortunately, many of the stone balls have been plundered and are currently used as lawn ornaments in the fancier neighborhoods of San José. Some have even been shipped out of the country. The **Museo Nacional de Costa Rica** (p. 129) has a nice collection, including one massive sphere in its center courtyard. It's a never-fail photo op. You can also see the stone balls near the small **airports in Palmar Sur** and **Drake Bay,** and on **Isla del Caño** (which is 19km/12 miles off the Pacific coast near Drake Bay).

area between late July and November and December through March. There are currently no dedicated whale-watching operators in the area, but all the hotels listed below can arrange whale-watching, as well as dolphin-spotting, trips. Two

A humpback whale.

resident marine biologists, Shawn Larkin and Roy Sancho, are often hired by the better hotels, but depending on demand and availability, the hotels may send you out with one of their own guides and/or captains.

If you want more information on the local whale watching scene, or to contact Shawn Larkin directly, head to the website **www.costacetacea.com**. These folks also offer deep-water free diving and snorkel tours aimed at providing the chance to swim in close proximity to the large pelagic fish, mammals, and reptiles found in the area.

Finally, if you want to try a zip-line canopy adventure, **The Drake Bay Canopy Tour** (© 8314-5454; canopytourdrakebay.com) has six cable runs, several "Tarzan swings," and a hanging bridge, all set in lush forests just outside of Drake Bay. The 2-hour tour costs $39.

Where to Stay & Eat

Given the remote location and logistics of reaching Drake Bay, as well as the individual isolation of each hotel, nearly all of the hotels listed below deal almost exclusively in package trips that include transportation, meals, tours, and taxes. I list the most common packages, although all the lodges will work with you to accommodate longer or shorter stays. Nightly room rates are listed only where they're available and practical, generally at the more moderately priced hotels.

In addition to the places listed below, **Guaria de Osa ★** (www.guaria deosa.com; © **510/235-4313** or 908/998-1020 in the U.S.) is a beautiful lodge near the Río Claro that specializes in yoga, spiritual, and educational retreats.

VERY EXPENSIVE

Aguila de Osa Inn ★   This luxurious hillside lodge is a great choice for serious sportfishers and scuba divers, because it has a private fleet of sportfishing and dive vessels. On a hill overlooking Drake Bay and the Pacific Ocean, the Aguila de Osa Inn offers large, attractively decorated rooms, with hardwood or tile floors, ceiling fans, large bathrooms, and excellent views. Varnished wood and bamboo abound. A bar is built atop some rocks on the bank of the Río Agujitas, and the open-air dining room is set amid lush foliage with a partial view of the bay through the leaves, close to river level. Meals are excellent and filling, and the kitchen leaves a fresh thermos of coffee outside each room every morning. Service, upkeep, and attention are top-notch here. The biggest drawback, however, is the lack of a swimming pool, which most of the other high-end places here have.

Drake Bay. www.aguiladeosainn.com. ⓒ **866/924-8452** in the U.S. and Canada, 2296-2190 in San José, or 8840-2929 at the lodge. Fax 2232-7722. 13 units. $544–$665 for 3 days/2 nights; $818 and up for 4 days/3 nights. Rates are per person based on double occupancy and include round-trip transportation from Palmar Sur, all meals, one daily guided tour, and taxes. Lower rates in off season. AE, MC, V. **Amenities:** Restaurant; bar; watersports rentals. *In room:* No phone, minibar.

Casa Corcovado Jungle Lodge ★   This isolated jungle lodge is the closest to Corcovado National Park on this end of the Osa Peninsula. The rooms are all large private bungalows built on the grounds of an old cacao plantation on the jungle's edge. Access is strictly by small boat, and sometimes the beach landing can be a bit rough and wet. When the sea is calm, the beach is great for swimming; when it is rough, it's a great place to grab a hammock in the shade and read a book. The lodge has two pretty swimming pools, both surrounded by thick rainforest, and late afternoons are usually enjoyed from a high point overlooking the sea and sunset, with your beverage of choice in hand. The owners here are strong supporters of local community development projects and environmental protection organizations.

Osa Peninsula. www.casacorcovado.com. ⓒ **888/896-6097** in the U.S., or 2256-3181 in Costa Rica. Fax 2256-7409. 14 units. $929 per person for 3 days/2 nights with 1 tour; $1,149 for 4 days/3 nights with 2 tours. Rates are based on double occupancy and include round-trip transportation from San José, all meals, daily tours, park fees, and taxes. Rates higher during peak weeks; lower in off season. Closed Sept 15–Nov 14. AE, MC, V. **Amenities:** Restaurant; 2 bars; 2 outdoor pools. *In room:* Minibar, no phone.

La Paloma Lodge ★★★ 🏨   On a steep hill overlooking the Pacific, with Isla del Caño in the distance, the luxurious bungalows at La Paloma offer expansive ocean views that make this my top choice in Drake Bay. All of the bungalows feature private verandas, and are set among lush foliage facing the Pacific. The large two-story Sunset Ranchos are the choice rooms here, with fabulous panoramic views. The other cabins are a tad smaller, but all are plenty spacious, beautifully appointed, and feature luxurious bathrooms and pretty good ocean views as well. Standard rooms, located in one long building, are smaller and less private than the cabins, but are still attractive and have good views from their hammock-equipped balcony. The beach is about a 7-minute hike down a winding jungle path. The restaurant serves hearty and delicious family-style meals. The owners are committed environmentalists and actively work on conservation and local development issues.

Drake Bay. www.lapalomalodge.com. ✆ **2293-7502** or ✆/fax 2239-0954. 11 units. $1,195–$1,525 per person for 4 days/3 nights with 2 tours; $1,360–$1,765 per person for 5 days/4 nights with 2 tours. Rates are based on double occupancy and include round-trip transportation from San José, all meals, park fees, indicated tours, and taxes. Rates slightly lower in off season. MC, V. **Amenities:** Restaurant; bar; small tile pool w/spectacular view; Wi-Fi (main lodge). *In room:* Minibar, no phone.

MODERATE

Drake Bay Wilderness Resort ★   This is one of the best-located lodges at Drake Bay. It backs onto the Río Agujitas and fronts the Pacific. The rooms here are less fancy than those at the resort lodges listed above, but they are clean and cozy, with ceiling fans, small verandas, good mattresses on the beds, and private bathrooms. A few have air-conditioning. The best room is a pretty, deluxe honeymoon suite on a little hill toward the rear of the property, with a great view of the bay. Three budget cabins share bathroom and shower facilities. Because it's on a rocky spit, the beach doesn't have good swimming, but a saltwater pool is in front of the bay, and, depending on the tide, you can bathe in a beautiful small tide pool.

Drake Bay. www.drakebay.com. ✆ **2725-1716** or 8825-4130 in Costa Rica. 25 units. $55 per person per day with shared bathroom; $90–$130 per person per day standard and deluxe. Rates include all meals and taxes. $790 per person for 4 days/3 nights with 2 tours, including all meals and taxes. AE, MC, V. **Amenities:** Restaurant; bar; small saltwater pool; free use of canoes and kayaks. *In room:* No phone, Wi-Fi.

Hotel Jinetes de Osa 🤿   This is a good option right on the edge of the village of Drake Bay, and a popular choice for serious divers and adventure tourists. Although no longer a budget lodging, it does offer a reasonable alternative to the more upscale options in the area. The best rooms here are spacious and well-appointed, and even have a view of the bay. The hotel is pretty close to the docks on the Río Agujitas, which is a plus for those traveling independently or with heavy bags. A wide range of tours and activities are available, as are dive packages, weekly packages, and PADI certification courses. For true budget travelers, camping is allowed just behind the main lodge.

Drake Bay. www.drakebayhotel.com. ✆ **866/553-7073** in the U.S. and Canada, or ✆/fax 2231-5806 in Costa Rica. 9 units, 7 with private bathroom. $70–$92 per person. Rates include 3 meals daily. AE, MC, V. **Amenities:** Restaurant; bar. *In room:* No phone, Wi-Fi.

PUERTO JIMÉNEZ: GATEWAY TO CORCOVADO NATIONAL PARK

35km (22 miles) W of Golfito by water (90km/56 miles by road); 85km (53 miles) S of Palmar Norte

Don't let its small size and languid pace fool you. **Puerto Jiménez ★** is actually a bustling little burg, where rough jungle gold-panners mix with wealthy ecotourists, budget backpackers, serious surfers, and a smattering of celebrities seeking a small dose of anonymity and escape. Located on the southeastern tip of the Osa Peninsula, the town itself is just a couple of streets wide in any direction, with a ubiquitous soccer field, a handful of general stores, some inexpensive

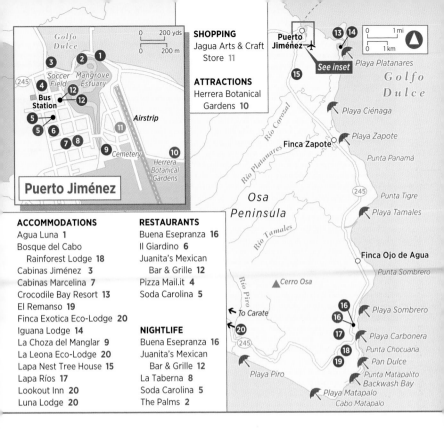

sodas (diners), and several bars. Scarlet macaws fly overhead, and mealy parrots provide wake-up calls.

Corcovado National Park has its headquarters here, and this town makes an excellent base for exploring this vast wilderness area. Signs in English on walls around town advertise a variety of tours, including a host of activities outside of the park. If the in-town accommodations are too budget-oriented, you'll find several far more luxurious places farther south on the Osa Peninsula. This is also a prime surf spot. **Cabo Matapalo** (the southern tip of the Osa Peninsula) is home to several very dependable right point breaks. When it's working, the waves at Pan Dulce and Backwash actually connect, and can provide rides almost as long and tiring as those to be had in more famous Pavones (see "Playa Pavones: A Surfer's Mecca," later in this chapter).

Essentials

GETTING THERE & DEPARTING   By Plane: Sansa (© 877/767-2672 in the U.S. and Canada, or 2290-4100 in Costa Rica; www.flysansa.com) has three daily flights to Puerto Jiménez from San José's Juan Santamaría International Airport. The cost is $133 each way. A direct flight takes around 55 minutes; add on about 10 minutes if there's a stop.

Hiking in Corcovado National Park.

Nature Air (© **800/235-9272** in the U.S. and Canada, or 2299-6000; www.natureair.com) has flights to Puerto Jiménez departing from Tobías Bolaños International Airport in Pavas at 6, 8:30, and 11am and 3:15pm daily. The flight is 50 minutes and costs $136 each way. Nature Air flights to San José depart daily at 7 and 9:30am, noon, and 4:15pm.

Note that due to the remoteness of this area and the unpredictable flux of traffic, both Sansa and Nature Air frequently improvise on scheduling. Sometimes this means an unscheduled stop in Quepos or Golfito either on the way to or from San José, which can add some time to your flight. Less frequently, it might mean a change in departure time, so it's always best to confirm. Also, lodges down here sometimes run charters, so it pays to ask them as well.

Taxis are generally waiting to meet all incoming flights. A ride into downtown Puerto Jiménez should cost around $3. If you're staying at a hotel outside of downtown, it's best to have them arrange for a taxi to meet you. Otherwise you can hire one at the airstrip. Depending upon how far out on the peninsula you are staying, it could cost up to $80 for a rugged four-wheel-drive vehicle that can carry up to four people.

By Car: Take the San José–Caldera Highway (CR27) to the first exit past the Pozón toll booth, where you will pick up the Southern Highway or Costanera Sur (CR34). Take this south through Jacó, Quepos, and Dominical to Palmar Norte, where you'll meet up with the Interamerican Highway (CR2). Take this south to the turnoff for La Palma, Rincón, and Puerto Jiménez.

By Bus: Transportes Blanco-Lobo express buses (© **2257-4121** in San José, or 2771-4744 in Puerto Jiménez) leave San José daily at 8am and noon from Calle 12 between avenidas 7 and 9. The trip takes 7 to 8 hours; the fare is C6,250. Buses depart Puerto Jiménez for San José daily at 5am and 9am.

By Boat: Several speedboats work as boat taxis between Puerto Jiménez and Golfito. The fare is $5, and the ride takes a little under 30 minutes. These boats leave five or six times throughout the day, or whenever they fill up, beginning at around 5am and finishing up at around 5pm. Ask around town, or at the docks for current schedules.

There is also a daily passenger launch. This slower boat takes 1½ hours and is $3. The ferry leaves the public dock in Golfito at 7:30 and 10am and 3pm for Puerto Jiménez. The return trip to Golfito leaves Puerto Jiménez's municipal dock at 2:30 and 4pm. It's possible to charter a water taxi in Golfito for the trip across to Puerto Jiménez as well. You'll have to pay around $100 for an entire launch, some of which can carry up to 12 people.

ORIENTATION   Puerto Jiménez is a dirt-lane town on the southern coast of the Osa Peninsula. The public dock is over a bridge past the north end of the soccer field; the bus stop is 2 blocks east of the center of town. You'll find a couple of Internet cafes in town; the best of these is **Cafe Net El Sol** (© **2735-5719;** www.soldeosa.com), which is a great place to book tours and get information, and is also a Wi-Fi hot spot.

Four-wheel-drive taxis are actually fairly plentiful in Puerto Jiménez. You can usually find them cruising or parked along the main street in town.

The Puerto Jiménez dock.

Surfers at Backwash.

Alternatively, have your hotel or restaurant call one for you. You can even rent a car down here from **Solid Car Rental** (© **2735-5777;** www.solid carrental.com).

What to See & Do

While Puerto Jiménez has typically been a staging ground for adventures much farther out toward Carate and the park, quite a few activities and tours can be undertaken closer to town.

If you're looking to spend some time on the beach, head just east of town for a long pretty stretch of sand called **Playa Plantanares.** The waves are generally fairly gentle, and quite a few hotels have begun to pop up here. If you head farther out on the peninsula, you'll come to the beaches of **Pan Dulce, Backwash,** and **Matapalo,** all major surf spots with consistently well-formed right point breaks. When the waves aren't too big, these are excellent places to learn how to surf.

Kayaking trips around the estuary and up into the mangroves and out into the gulf are very popular. The two main operators in town are **Escondido Trex ★** (© **2735-5210;** www.escondidotrex.com), which has an office in the Soda Carolina (p. 438), and **Aventuras Tropicales** (© **2735-5195;** www. aventurastropicales.com), which is set up in front of the soccer field. Trips include daily paddles through the mangroves, as well as sunset trips where you can sometimes see dolphins. Both of these operations offer guided rainforest hikes and can have you rappelling down the face of a jungle waterfall. More adventurous multiday kayak and camping trips are also available, in price and comfort ranges from budget to luxury (staying at various lodges around the Golfo Dulce and Matapalo). Escondido Trex can even take you gold-panning (although there are no guarantees that your panning will pay for the trip).

One unique option is the chocolate tour at **Finca Kobo** ★ (② 8398-7604; www.fincakobo.com), which is located near La Palma, 17km (10½ miles) northwest of Puerto Jiménez. These folks offer an informative tour through their organic cacao plantation. You'll learn about and see all the various stages involved in the process of growing cacao and transforming these precious beans into chocolate. At the end of the tour, you'll get to sample some of their handiwork, dipping some local fruit into fresh melted chocolate fondue. The tour costs $32; children 8 and under half-price.

If you're in Puerto Jiménez, be sure to check out the **Herrera Botanical Gardens** ★ (② 2735-5256). These gardens are just outside of town, and the entrance is across from Crocodile Bay. The whole project encompasses over 101 hectares (260 acres) of botanical gardens, working permaculture gardens, and secondary forest. A few platforms built high in the trees are reached by climbing a ladder. A 2½-hour guided tour of the gardens costs $20, although you can wander the gardens yourself, with a self-guiding map, for $4.

For a real adventure, check in with **Psycho Tours** ★★ (② 8353-8619; www.psychotours.com). These folks, who also call themselves Everyday Adventures, run a variety of adventure tours, but their signature combo trip features a free climb up (with a safety rope attached) the roots and trunks of a 60m-tall (200-ft.) Strangler fig. You can climb as high as your ability allows, but most try to reach a natural platform at around 18m (60 ft.), where you take a leap of faith into space and are belayed down by your guide. This is preceded by an informative hike through primary rainforest, often wading through a small river, and followed by a couple of rappels down jungle waterfalls, the highest of which is around 30m (100 ft.). You can do either one of the above adventures separately, but I recommend the 5- to 6-hour combo tour, which costs $120.

Kayaking with Escondido Trex.

If you're interested in doing some **bill-fishing** or **deep-sea fishing,** you'll probably want to stay at or fish with **Crocodile Bay Lodge** (www.crocodilebay. com; ⓒ **800/733-1115** in the U.S. and Canada, or 2735-5631 in Costa Rica). This upscale fishing lodge is close to the Puerto Jiménez airstrip. Alternatively, you can ask at your hotel, or contact the **Osa Yacht Club** (ⓒ **2735-5298;** www.costaricasportsman.com). Rates can run between $800 and $2,200 for a full day, or between $500 and $900 for a half-day, depending on the boat, tackle, number of anglers, and fishing grounds.

If you want to learn to surf, contact **Pollo's Surf School ★** (ⓒ **8366-6559;** www.pollosurfschool.com), which is near some excellent learning waves on Pan Dulce beach. A 2-hour lesson runs $55 per person.

Osa Aventura (ⓒ/fax **2735-5758** or 8372-6135; www.osaaventura.com) and **Sol de Osa** (ⓒ **2735-5702;** www.corcovadoguide.com) are local tour companies that offer a host of guided tours and wildlife watching expeditions around the Osa Peninsula and into Corcovado National Park. Rates run between $120 and $300 per person, depending upon group size and the tour.

Exploring Corcovado National Park ★★★

Exploring Corcovado National Park is not something to be undertaken lightly, but neither is it the expedition that some people make it out to be. The weather is the biggest obstacle to overnight backpacking trips through the park. Within a couple of hours of Puerto Jiménez (by 4WD vehicle) are several entrances to the park; however, the park has no roads, so once you reach any of the entrances, you'll have to start hiking. The heat and humidity are often quite extreme, and frequent rainstorms can make trails fairly muddy. If you choose the alternative—hiking on the beach—you'll have to plan your hiking around the tides when often there is no beach at all and some rivers are impassable.

Corcovado National Park is amazingly rich in biodiversity. It is one of the only places in Costa Rica that is home to all four of the country's monkey species—howler, white-faced, squirrel, and spider. Its large size makes it an ideal

A hummingbird.

Corcovado National Park

La Palma
Guaymí (Osa) Indigenous Reserve
San Pedrillo Ranger Station
Los Patos Ranger Station
Punta Llorona
Playa Llorona
CORCOVADO NATIONAL PARK
Osa Peninsula
Laguna Corcovado
Playa Corcovado
Cerro Rincón
Río Corcovado
Río Pavón
Río Rincón
Río Tigre
Río Claro
Sirena Ranger Station
Playa Sirena
La Leona Ranger Station
Carate
PACIFIC OCEAN
Punta Salsipuedes
Playa Madrigal
245

NICARAGUA
CARIBBEAN SEA
SAN JOSÉ
Corcovado Nat'l Park
PACIFIC OCEAN
PANAMA

habitat for wildcat species, including the endangered jaguar, as well as other large mammals, like Baird's Tapir. Apart from the jaguar, other cat species found here include the ocelot, margay, jaguarundi, and puma. More than 390 species of birds have been recorded inside the park. Scarlet macaws are commonly sighted here. Other common bird species include any number of antbirds, manakins, toucans, tanagers, hummingbirds, and puffbirds. Once thought extinct in Costa Rica, the harpy eagle has been spotted here as well. Most rivers in Corcovado are home to crocodiles; moreover, at high tide, they are frequented by bull sharks. For this reason, river crossings must be coordinated with low tides.

Because of its size and remoteness, Corcovado National Park is best explored over several days; however, it is possible to enter and hike a bit of it on day trips. The best way to do this is to book a tour with your lodge on the Osa Peninsula, from a tour company in Puerto Jiménez, or through a lodge in Drake Bay (see "Where to Stay & Eat," above).

GETTING THERE & ENTRY POINTS   The park has four primary entrances, which are really just ranger stations reached by rough dirt roads. When you've reached them, you'll have to strap on a backpack and hike. Perhaps the easiest one to reach from Puerto Jiménez is **La Leona ranger station,** accessible by car, bus, or taxi.

Trail Distances in Corcovado National Park

It's 14km (8.7 miles) from La Leona to Sirena. From Sirena to San Pedrillo, it's 23km (14 miles) along the beach. From San Pedrillo, it's 20km (13 miles) to Drake Bay. It's 19km (12 miles) between Sirena and Los Patos.

If you choose to drive, take the dirt road from Puerto Jiménez to Carate (Carate is at the end of the road). From Carate, it's a 3km (1.75-mile) hike to La Leona. To travel there by "public transportation," pick up one of the collective buses (actually, a 4WD pickup truck with a tarpaulin cover and slat seats in the back) that leave Puerto Jiménez for Carate daily at 6am and 1:30pm, returning at 8am and 4pm. Remember, these "buses" are very informal and change their schedules regularly to meet demand or avoid bad weather, so always ask in town. The one-way fare is around $9. A small fleet of these pickups leaves just south of the bus terminal, and will stop to pick up anyone who flags them down along the way. Your other option is to hire a taxi to suit your schedule, which will charge between $60 and $100 (depending on road conditions) to or from Carate.

En route to Carate, you will pass several campgrounds and small lodges as you approach the park. If you are unable to get a spot at one of the campsites in the park, you can stay at one of these and hike the park during the day.

You can also travel to **El Tigre,** about 14km (8¾ miles) by dirt road from Puerto Jiménez, site of another ranger station. But note that trails from El Tigre go only a short distance into the park.

The third entrance is in **Los Patos,** which is reached from the town of La Palma, northwest of Puerto Jiménez. From here, a 19km (12-mile) trail runs through the center of the park to **Sirena,** a ranger station and research facility (see "Beach Treks & Rainforest Hikes," below). Sirena has a landing strip used by charter flights.

The northern entrance to the park is **San Pedrillo,** which you can reach by hiking from Sirena or by taking a boat from

A Corcovado National Park trail.

Drake Bay or Sierpe (see "Beach Treks & Rainforest Hikes," below). It's 14km (8¾ miles) from Drake Bay.

If you're not into hiking in the heat, you can charter a plane in Puerto Jiménez to take you to Carate or Sirena. A five-passenger plane costs between $200 to $400 one-way, depending on your destination. Contact **Alfa Romeo Air Charters** (© **2735-5353** or 2735-5112; www.alfa romeoair.com) for details.

FEES & REGULATIONS   Park admission is $10 per person per day. Only the Sirena station is equipped with dormitory-style lodgings and a simple *soda,* but the others have basic campsites and toilet facilities. All must be reserved in advance by contacting the **ACOSA** (Area de Conservacion de Osa) in Puerto Jiménez (© **2735-5036** pncorcovado@gmail.com). For a good overview of the park and logistics, check out **www.corcovado.org**. Its offices are adjacent to the airstrip. Only a limited number of people are allowed to camp at each ranger station, so make your reservations well in advance.

BEACH TREKS & RAINFOREST HIKES   The park has quite a few good hiking trails. Two of the better-known ones are the beach routes, starting at either La Leona or San Pedrillo ranger stations. Between any two ranger stations, the hiking is arduous and takes all or most of a day, so it's best to rest for a day or so between hikes if possible. Remember, this is quite a wild area. Never hike alone, and take all the standard precautions for hiking in a rainforest. In addition, be especially careful about crossing or swimming in any isolated rivers or river mouths. Most rivers in Corcovado are home to crocodiles; moreover, at high tide, some are frequented by bull sharks. For this reason, river crossings must be coordinated with low tides. During the wet months (July–Nov) parts of the park may be closed. One of the longest and most popular hikes, between San Pedrillo and La Sirena, can be undertaken only during the dry season.

Sirena is a fascinating destination. As a research facility and ranger station, it's frequented primarily by scientists studying the rainforest. The network of trails here can easily keep you busy for several days. Just north of the station lies the mouth of the Río Sirena. Most days at high tide, bull sharks swarm and feed in this river mouth. Large crocodiles also inhabit

---

 Important Corcovado Tips

If you plan to hike the beach trails from La Leona or San Pedrillo, be sure to pick up a tide table at the park headquarters' office in Puerto Jiménez. The tide changes rapidly; when it's high, the trails and river crossings can be dangerous or impassable.

If you plan to spend a night or more in the park, you'll want to stock up on food, water, and other essentials in Puerto Jiménez. Carate has a minimarket with a limited selection. Although most of the stations have simple *sodas,* you need to reserve in advance if you plan to take your meals at any of these.

these waters, so swimming is seriously discouraged. Still, it's quite a spectacle. The **Claro Trail** will bring you to the mouth of the Río Claro. A bit smaller, this river also houses a healthy crocodile population, although allegedly fewer bull sharks. However, if you follow the Claro trail upstream a bit, you can find several safe and appropriate swimming spots.

WHERE TO STAY & EAT IN THE PARK: CAMPSITES, CABINS & CANTINAS   Reservations are essential at the various ranger stations if you plan to eat or sleep inside the park (see "Fees & Regulations," above). **Sirena** has a modern research facility with dormitory-style accommodations for 28 persons, as well as a campground, *soda*, and landing strip for charter flights. Camping is available at **La Leona, Los Patos,** and **San Pedrillo** ranger stations. Every ranger station has potable water, but it's advisable to pack in your own; whatever you do, don't drink stream water. Campsites in the park are $4 per person per night. A dorm bed at the Sirena station will run you $8— you must bring your own sheets, and a mosquito net is highly recommended—and meals here are $15 breakfast, $20 lunch, and $20 dinner. Everything must be reserved in advance.

Shopping

Jagua Arts & Craft Store ★★ (© 2735-5267) is near the airstrip, and is definitely worth a visit. Owner Karen Herrera has found excellent local and regional art and craft works, including some fine jewelry and blown glass. *Tip:* Many folks head to this store while waiting for their departing flight out of Puerto Jiménez. Be sure to give yourself enough time, as the store has a somewhat extensive collection.

Where to Stay in Puerto Jiménez

VERY EXPENSIVE

Crocodile Bay Resort ★   Originally, and still primarily a sportfishing resort, this place also caters to other sorts of adventure travelers. The rooms are the most comfortable you'll find right in Puerto Jiménez, with tons of space and private balconies or verandas—try for a garden-facing second-floor unit. The hotel has excellent facilities and expansive grounds. In addition to a large modern fleet of fishing boats, with top-notch crew and equipment, they have a well-staffed activities and tour desk, and a large spa. The food and service here are also excellent.

Puerto Jiménez. www.crocodilebay.com. © **800/733-1115** in the U.S. and Canada, or 2735-5631 in Costa Rica. 40 units. $550 double. Rates include breakfast, lunch, and dinner and alcoholic beverages. A wide range of fishing and adventure-tour packages are available. AE, MC, V. **Amenities:** Restaurant; bar; Jacuzzi; outdoor pool; large modern spa; watersports equipment rental. *In room:* A/C.

INEXPENSIVE

In addition to the places listed below, **Cabinas Marcelina** (www.jimenezhotels. com/cabinasmarcelina; © **2735-5007**) is a good, clean, dependable budget option right in the heart of town.

Agua Luna   Agua Luna is located right at the foot of the town's public dock and backs up to a mangrove forest. The original rooms directly face the gulf

Costa Rican Family Robinson

For a truly unique family vacation, think about renting the **Lapa's Nest Tree House** ★★ (www.treehouseincostarica. com; ℂ 508/714-0622 in the U.S., or 8372-3529 in Costa Rica), an impressive lodge built up and around a giant Guanacaste tree in the midst of thick forest. This gorgeous home, just 13km (8 miles) north of Puerto Jiménez, is chock-full of creative design touches. Spread over six levels, it features three bedrooms, two bathrooms, and a full kitchen and is available for weekly rentals. The price for all of this ranges from $1,800 to $2,500, depending on the season.

across a fenced-in gravel parking area. The best thing about these rooms is the bathroom, which features a huge picture window that looks into the mangroves. The rooms have two double beds and a tiled veranda out front, with hammocks and chairs for lounging. Annex rooms are a half-block away and are smaller and less attractive than those in the original building, although room nos. 4 and 5 in this building do overlook the mangroves.

In front of the public dock, Puerto Jiménez. ℂ/fax **2735-5393**. 13 units. $50 double. MC, V. **Amenities:** Restaurant. *In room:* A/C, TV.

Cabinas Jiménez ★★ ✦ This is my top hotel choice right in Puerto Jiménez. On the waterfront at the north end of the soccer field, this perennial budget favorite has improved with age. All of the rooms have air-conditioning, tile floors, hot-water showers, and hand-carved headboards and Guatemalan bedspreads. Some have little fridges and coffeemakers. Three units even have views of the water, with a broad shared veranda in front, and the one private bungalow is the choice room in the house. The range in prices, in fact, reflects the range in size and location of the rooms. But even the most basic room here is a good option, and a good value. These folks have their own boat, and offer excellent dolphin-watching, mangrove, and snorkel tours around the gulf. The biggest downside here is that the town's main disco is fairly close by, and the pounding bass and tunes can be a problem for some on weekend nights.

Downtown, 50m (164 ft.) north of the soccer field, Puerto Jiménez, Puntarenas. www.cabinas jimenez.com. ℂ **2735-5090**. 11 units. $50–$90 double. MC, V. **Amenities:** Small outdoor pool. *In room:* A/C, no phone, Wi-Fi.

La Choza del Manglar ✦ A short distance from the airstrip, this long-standing hotel is one of the better in-town options. The rooms are clean and comfortable, probably the most modern and tastefully decorated rooms you'll find in Puerto Jiménez proper. All rooms have air-conditioning, and about half have televisions. However, the private cabins have fans only. The hotel has several acres of mangroves and gardens, and the bird-watching and wildlife viewing are pretty good. The restaurant serves Costa Rican and international fare in a large, open-air space with colorful murals. While this is a good in-town option, you're still several hundred meters or more from the water and from downtown Puerto Jiménez.

125m (410 ft.) west of the airstrip, Puerto Jiménez. www.manglares.com. ℂ **888/467-3181** in the U.S. and Canada, or ℂ/fax 2735-5605 in Costa Rica. 11 units. $39–$99 double. Rates include breakfast and taxes. Rates higher during peak weeks; lower in off season. MC, V. **Amenities:** Restaurant; bar. *In room:* No phone, Wi-Fi.

Where to Stay in Playa Plantanares

EXPENSIVE

Iguana Lodge ★★ This place has a variety of rooms and bungalows. The two-story casitas are their top option: These are set amid lush gardens just steps from the sand. Hardwood floors, bamboo furniture, and mosquito netting over orthopedic mattresses all add up to rustic tropical elegance. The lower units have delightful semi-outdoor garden showers, and all come with either a large covered balcony or veranda. Still, I recommend trying for a second-floor room, for the views and elevation. These folks also rent out a separate, private three-bedroom villa. There's also a lovely lap pool, with an attached Jacuzzi, and a beautiful large yoga space. The lodge incorporates a wide range of sustainable and responsible tourism practices.

Playa Plantanares. www.iguanalodge.com. *©* **8829-5865** or 8848-0752. Fax 2735-5436. 19 units. $135 double club room; $330 casita double; $550 3-bedroom villa. Rates for club room include breakfast. Rates of the casita include dinner as well, while rates for the villa do not include any meals. MC, V. **Amenities:** 2 restaurants; bar; Jacuzzi; outdoor lap pool; spa; water-sports equipment rental. *In room:* No phone.

Where to Eat in Puerto Jiménez

For pizzas and homemade pastas, you should head to **Pizza Mail.it** (*©* **2735-5483**), next to the post office. You can also get pizzas, as well as other excellent Italian fare, and even find the occasional sushi night at the open-air downtown Italian joint, **Il Giardino** ★ (*©* **2735-5129**).

Juanita's Mexican Bar & Grille ★ 🍴 MEXICAN This place offers good, hearty California-style Mexican food and seafood served up in a lively, convivial atmosphere. You can get fajitas with chicken, beef, fish, or even grilled vegetables. Juanita's also has pizza by the slice or pie, and will deliver, although I'm not sure how far out on the peninsula their drivers will go. There are nightly specials and a popular happy hour.

Downtown, Puerto Jiménez. *©* **2735-5056.** www.juanitasmexican.com. Reservations not accepted. Main courses C3,000–C7,500. No credit cards. Daily 5am–11pm.

Soda Carolina 📷 COSTA RICAN Set in the center of the town's main street, and otherwise known as the "Bar, Restaurante y Cabinas Carolina," this is the town's main budget travelers' hangout and also serves as an unofficial information center. The walls are painted with colorful jungle and wildlife scenes. As for the fare, seafood is the way to go. There's good fried fish as well as a variety of *ceviche*. The black-bean soup is usually tasty, and the *casados* (plates of the day) are filling and inexpensive.

On the main street. *©* **2735-5185.** Reservations not accepted. Main courses C3,000–C5,000. AE, MC, V. Daily 6am–10pm.

Where to Stay & Eat around the Osa Peninsula

As with most of the lodges in Drake Bay, the accommodations listed in this section include three meals a day in their rates and do a large share of their bookings in package trips. Per-night rates are listed, but the price categories have been adjusted to take into account the fact that all meals are included. Ask about package rates if you plan to take several tours and stay awhile: They could save you money.

In addition to the lodges listed below, several other options range from small bed-and-breakfasts to fully equipped home rentals. Surfers, in particular, might want to inquire into one of the several rental houses located close to the beach at Matapalo. Your best bet for alternative accommodations is to contact **Jimenez Hotels** (www.jimenezhotels.com; ☏ **2735-5702**), which also handles a host of house rentals around the area.

Finally, Carate has several lodges. In addition to the lodges listed below, you can look into **Finca Exotica Eco-Lodge** ★ (www.fincaexotica.com; ☏ **2735-5230**), a delightful new beachfront lodge; **La Leona Eco-Lodge** ★ (www.laleonaecolodge.com; ☏ **2735-5705**), a tent-camp option on the outskirts of the national park; and **Lookout Inn** (www.lookout-inn.com; ☏ **757/644-5967** in the U.S., or 2735-5431 in Costa Rica), a more traditional lodge option right in Carate.

This is a very isolated area, with just one rough dirt road connecting all the lodges, nature reserves, and parks. Almost all visitors here take all their meals at their hotel or lodge. If you want to venture away for some good fresh food and simple home cooking, head to Martina's **Buena Esperanza** (no phone) on the main road, near Matapalo.

VERY EXPENSIVE

The following lodges are some of the best ecolodges Costa Rica has to offer, and most are pretty pricey. However, keep in mind that despite paying top dollar, the rooms have no TVs, no telephones, no air-conditioning, and the town has no discos, very limited shopping, and no paved roads. Consequently, there are also no crowds and very few modern distractions.

Bosque del Cabo Rainforest Lodge ★★★ 🎁   This lodge is my favorite spot in this neck of the woods. The large individual cabins are attractively furnished, have wooden decks or verandas to catch the ocean views, and are set amid beautiful gardens. The deluxe cabins come with king-size beds and more deck space. The Congo cabin is my choice for its spectacular view of the sunrise from your bed. All cabins have indoor bathrooms; while tiled showers are set outdoors amid flowering heliconia and ginger. About half of the units also have outdoor bathtubs.

One trail leads to a jungle waterfall, and several others wind through the rainforests of the lodge's 260-hectare (650-acre) private reserve. If you're too lazy to hike down to the beach, a beautiful pool is by the main lodge. Other attractions include a canopy platform 36m (118 ft.) up a Manu tree, reached along a 90m (295-ft.) zip line, as well as a bird- and wildlife-watching rancho set beside a little lake. These folks also rent out four separate, fully equipped houses that are quite popular, along with a couple of cabins set inland by their gardens. In addition to conservation and reforestation efforts, the owners here are actively involved in a host of local environmental and educational causes, and the lodge has been awarded "4 Leaves" by the CST Sustainable Tourism program.

Osa Peninsula. www.bosquedelcabo.com. ☏/fax **2735-5206** or 8389-2846. 17 units. $210–$330 per person. Rates include 3 meals daily and taxes. $30 per person, round-trip transportation from Puerto Jiménez. **Amenities:** Restaurant; bar; midsize outdoor pool; surfboard rental. *In room:* No phone.

El Remanso ★★   This collection of individual cabins and two-story units is set in a deep patch of primary forest. The best view of the ocean, over and through thick forest, can be had from the two-story deluxe La Vanilla unit, which can be rented whole or split into two separate one-bedroom affairs. The upstairs room here is the best in the house, with plenty of space, varnished wood floors, and a spacious balcony. All of the private cabins feature polished cement floors, a queen-size bed, and separate fold-down futon. If you want an individual cabin, Azul de Mar has the best view. A host of adventure activities are available, including tree climbing, waterfall rappelling, and a zip-line canopy tour. They also have a large, open-air yoga platform, and frequently host yoga groups. For chilling out, a small oval pool set is in a stone deck area with great views to the ocean. Breakfasts can be taken on a platform high atop a rainforest tree. The owners are committed to environmental protection. In fact, Joel and Belen Stewart met aboard the Greenpeace vessel *Rainbow Warrior,* which Joel captained for a number of years.

Osa Peninsula. www.elremanso.com. ⓒ **2735-5569** or 8814-5775. Fax 2735-5938. 14 units. $165–$195 per person. Rates include 3 meals daily and all taxes. MC, V. **Amenities:** Restaurant; bar; small outdoor pool. *In room:* No phone.

Lapa Ríos ★★   This is one of Costa Rica's pioneering ecolodges. Although half of a duplex, each spacious room is totally private and oriented toward the view, with open screen walls and a high-peaked thatch roof. A large deck and small tropical garden, complete with a hammock and outdoor shower, more than double the living space. There's an indoor shower as well, which features screen walls letting out on the view, so it's not all that different from being outdoors. **Note:** It's a bit of a hike back and forth from the main lodge to the farthest rooms.

The centerpiece of the lodge's large open-air dining room is a 15m (49-ft.) spiral staircase that leads to an observation deck tucked beneath the peak of the thatch roof. Just off the main lodge is a pretty little pool with great views. The beach, however, is a good 15-minute hike away. Lapa Ríos is surrounded by its own 400-hectare (988-acre) private rainforest reserve, home to scarlet macaws, toucans, parrots, hummingbirds, monkeys, and myriad other wildlife.

Osa Peninsula. www.laparios.com. ⓒ **2735-5130.** Fax 2735-5179. 16 units. $760 double. Rates include 3 meals daily, 2 guided tours per stay, round-trip transportation btw. the lodge and Puerto Jiménez, and taxes. Discounts for children 10 and under. AE, MC, V. **Amenities:** Restaurant; bar; small outdoor pool; all rooms smoke-free. *In room:* No phone.

Luna Lodge ★★   Set on a high hill, among thick rainforest, Luna Lodge is often used for yoga and wellness retreats. Accommodations range from lush private cabins with great views over the jungle, to a string of cozy rooms, and even some semipermanent large tents on sturdy platforms for more budget-conscious travelers. The biggest drawback here is that the beach is a short hike away—it's downhill on the way to the water, but a steep, vigorous hike back. Luckily, the lodge has a delightful little pool. Among the various environmental and conservation causes she supports, owner Lana Wedmore is especially involved in White Hawk and Harpy Eagle monitoring and protection programs, and the whole operation is powered by low-impact, on-site solar and hydro power.

Carate, Osa Peninsula. www.lunalodge.com. ⓒ **888/762-4069** in the U.S. and Canada, or 2206-5859 in Costa Rica. 8 units. $100–$105 per person in tent; $120–$135 per person, room; $145–$175 per person, private cabin. Rates are double occupancy, and include 3 meals daily. A range of package tours, including round-trip transportation btw. the lodge and Puerto Jiménez, tours and yoga classes, and taxes are also available. AE, MC, V. **Amenities:** Restaurant; bar; small outdoor pool; all rooms smoke-free. *In room:* No phone.

Puerto Jiménez After Dark

If you're looking for any after-tours action in Puerto Jiménez, I recommend you start off at either **Juanita's Mexican Bar & Grille** (p. 438), or **Soda Carolina** (p. 438), both of which are popular with locals, guides, and tourists. For a much more local scene, stop in for an Imperial at **La Taberna** (✆ 2735-9533). You also might take a walk down along the water to see if anything is happening at **The Palms** (✆ 2735-5012; www.thepalmscostarica.com).

If you're staying farther out on the Osa and want to hang with some locals, head to **Buena Esperanza** (see above). This place can actually get pretty lively on a Friday or Saturday night.

GOLFITO: GATEWAY TO THE GOLFO DULCE

87km (54 miles) S of Palmar Norte; 337km (209 miles) S of San José

Despite being the largest and most important city in Costa Rica's southern zone, Golfito, in and of itself, is neither a popular nor a particularly inviting tourist destination. In its prime, this was a major banana port, but following years of rising taxes, falling prices, and labor disputes, United Fruit pulled out in 1985. Things may change in the future, as rumors perennially abound about the potential construction of an international airport nearby, major marina right on the bay, or large-scale tuna farm just offshore. But for the moment, none of these megaprojects have gotten off the drawing board.

That said, Golfito is still a major sportfishing center and a popular gateway to a slew of nature lodges spread along the quiet waters, isolated bays, and lush rainforests of the Golfo Dulce, or "Sweet Gulf." In 1998, much of the rainforest bordering the Golfo Dulce was officially declared the **Piedras Blancas National Park ★★**, which includes 12,000 hectares (29,640 acres) of primary forests, as well as protected secondary forests and pasturelands.

Golfito is set on the north side of the Golfo Dulce, at the foot of lush green mountains. The setting alone gives Golfito the potential to be one of the most attractive cities in the country. However, the areas around the municipal park and public dock are somewhat seedy and the "downtown" section is quite run-down. Still, if you go a little bit farther along the bay, you come to the old United Fruit Company housing. Here you'll find well-maintained wooden houses painted bright colors and surrounded by neatly manicured gardens. Toucans are commonly sighted. It's all very lush and green and clean—an altogether different picture from that painted by most port towns in this country. When a duty-free zone was opened here, these old homes experienced a minor renaissance and several were converted into small hotels. Ticos come here in droves on weekends and throughout December to take advantage of cheap prices on name-brand goods and clothing at the duty-free zone; sometimes all these shoppers make finding a room difficult.

The Golfito shoreline.

Essentials

GETTING THERE & DEPARTING   By Plane: Sansa (📞 877/767-2672 in the U.S. and Canada, or 2290-4100 in Costa Rica; www.flysansa.com) has three daily flights to the Golfito airstrip (no phone; airport code: GLF), with the first one departing San José's Juan Santamaría International Airport at 5:45am, followed by one at 9:25am and 2:55pm. Trip duration is 1 hour; the fare is $130 each way. Sansa flights return to San José daily at 7am, with the last flight departing at 2:43pm in the low season, and at 4:08pm in the high season.

Nature Air (📞 800/235-9272 in the U.S. and Canada, or 2299-6000; www.natureair.com) has daily flights to Golfito from Tobías Bolaños International Airport in Pavas at 6am and 3:15pm. The direct morning flight is 50 minutes, and the later flight is 70 minutes and stops first in Puerto Jiménez; the fare is $133 each way.

By Car: Take the San José–Caldera Highway (CR27) to the first exit past the Pozón toll booth, where you will pick up the Southern Highway or Costanera Sur (CR34). Take this south through Jacó, Quepos, and Dominical to Palmar Norte, where you'll meet up with the Interamerican Highway (CR2). Take this south. When you get to Río Claro, you'll notice a couple of gas stations and quite a bit of activity. Turn right here and follow the signs to Golfito. If you end up at the Panama border, you've missed the turnoff by about 32km (20 miles). The complete drive takes about 6 hours.

By Bus: Express buses leave San José daily at 7am and 3:30pm from the **Tracopa** bus station (📞 2221-4214 or 2775-0365; www.tracopacr.com) on the Plaza Viquez at Calle 5 between avenidas 18 and 20. The trip takes 7 hours; the fare is C6,145. Buses depart Golfito for San José daily at 5am and 1:30pm from the bus station near the municipal dock.

By Boat: Several speedboats work as boat taxis between Golfito and Puerto Jiménez. The fare is $5, and the ride takes a little under 30 minutes. These boats leave five or six times throughout the day, or whenever they fill up, beginning at around 5am and finishing up at around 5pm. Ask at the *muellecito* (public dock) for current schedules.

There is also a daily passenger launch. This slower boat takes 1½ hours, and the fare is $3. The ferry leaves the public dock in Golfito at 7:30 and 10am and 3pm for Puerto Jiménez. The return trip to Golfito leaves Puerto Jiménez's municipal dock at 2:30pm and 4pm.

It's also possible to charter a water taxi in Golfito for the trip across to Puerto Jiménez. You'll have to pay between $40 and $80 for an entire launch, some of which can carry up to 12 people.

GETTING AROUND   Taxis are plentiful in Golfito, and are constantly cruising the main road, all the way from the entrance of town to the duty-free port. A taxi ride anywhere in town should cost around $1. Local buses also ply this loop. The fare for the bus is 20¢.

If you drive down here and head out to one of the remote lodges on the gulf, you can leave your car at Samoa del Sur (see "Where to Stay," below) for around $10 per day.

If you need to rent a car in Golfito, check in with **Solid Car Rental** (© **2775-3333;** www.solidcarrental.com).

If you can't get to your next destination by boat, bus, commuter airline, or car, **Alfa Romeo Air Charters** (© **2735-5353** or 2735-5178; www.alfaromeoair.com) runs charters to most of the nearby destinations, including Carate, Drake Bay, Sirena, and Puerto Jiménez. A five-passenger plane should cost around $290 to $450 one-way, depending on your destination.

FAST FACTS   To avoid the bureaucracy and frequently long lines at the banks, you can **exchange money** at the gas station, or La Bomba, in the middle of town. A **laundromat** on the upper street of the small downtown charges around $6 for an average-size load.

Exploring the Area

You won't find any really good swimming beaches right in Golfito. The closest spot is **Playa Cacao,** a short boat ride away, although this is not one of my favorite beaches in Costa Rica. You should be able to get a ride here for around $5 per person from one of the boat taxis down at the public docks. However, you might have to negotiate hard because these boatmen like to gouge tourists whenever possible. If you really want some beach time, I recommend staying at one of the hotels in the Golfo Dulce (see "Where to Stay," below) or heading over to **Playa Zancudo** (see "Playa Zancudo," later in this chapter).

With a trail head located just on the outskirts of town, the **Golfito National Wildlife Reserve ★** is the closest place to Golfito for a hike in one of the area's typical local lowland rainforests. This reserve is home to much of the same wildlife and flora you'll find in other, more famous national parks. A well-marked trail begins near the ranger station, just beyond the city's airstrip. You can hike it yourself or go as part of an organized tour with **Land Sea Tours** (© **2775-1614**). Admission is $10, and the refuge is open daily 8am to 4pm.

About a 20-minute drive over a rough dirt road from Golfito will bring you to the **Cataratas y Senderos Avellán** (Avellán Waterfall & Trails; no phone).

Admission to the site costs $5 and includes a 2-hour guided hike through the forests and a visit to a beautiful forest waterfall, with several refreshing pools perfect for swimming. A taxi should charge around $20 for the ride, one-way. Horseback riding is available, and they even have a zip-line canopy tour. Camping is also allowed, and meals are served by the friendly owners of the land, the local Gamba family. However, for most folks, the best way to visit this site is to go as part of an organized trip with **Land Sea Tours.**

A sportfishing vessel in Golfito.

The waters off Golfito also offer some of the best **sportfishing** in Costa Rica. Most game fish species can be caught here year-round, including blue and black marlin, sailfish, and roosterfish. November through May is the peak period for sailfish and blue marlin. If you'd like to try hooking into a possible world-record marlin or sailfish, contact **Banana Bay Marina** (✆ **2775-0838;** www.bananabaymarina.com). These folks have a full-service marina, a few waterside rooms for guests, and a fleet of sportfishing boats and captains. A full-day fishing trip costs between $950 and $1,500. You can also try **The Zancudo Lodge** (www.thezancudolodge.com; ✆ **800/854-8791** in the U.S. and Canada, or 2776-0008 in Costa Rica), which is based out of the Zancudo Beach Resort (p. 451) in nearby Playa Zancudo. The lodge can arrange pickup in Golfito, and I much prefer the Zancudo lodgings and scenery to what you'll find in Golfito.

About 30 minutes by boat out of Golfito, you'll find **Casa Orquídeas ★★** (✆ **8829-1247**), a private botanical garden lovingly built and maintained by Ron and Trudy MacAllister. Most hotels in the area offer trips here, including transportation and a 2-hour tour of the gardens. During the tour, you'll sample a load of fresh fruits picked right off the trees. If your hotel can't, you can book a trip out of Golfito with **Land Sea Tours** (✆ **2775-1614**). If you decide to do it yourself, the entrance and guided tour is only $5 per person, but it will cost you between $80 and $100 to hire a boat for the round-trip ride; the gardens are open daily from 8am to 4pm. Closed Fridays. Regularly scheduled tours are on Thursdays and Sundays at 8:30am (three-person minimum).

If you have a serious interest in botanical gardens or bird-watching, consider an excursion to **Wilson Botanical Gardens ★★★** at the Las Cruces Biological Station (✆ **2524-0607** in San José, or 2773-4004 at the gardens; www.threepaths.co.cr), just outside the town of San Vito, about 65km (40 miles) to the northeast. The gardens are owned and maintained by the Organization for Tropical Studies and include more than 7,000 species of tropical plants from around the world. Among the plants grown here are many endangered species, which make the gardens of interest to botanical researchers. Despite the scientific aspects of the gardens, with so many beautiful and unusual flowers amid the manicured grounds, even a neophyte can't help but be astounded. All this luscious flora has attracted at least 360 species of birds. A full-day guided walk, including lunch, costs $53; a half-day guided walk costs $18. If you'd like to stay the night here, 12 well-appointed rooms are available. Rates include one guided walk, three meals, and taxes, and run around $84 per person. Reservations are essential if you want to spend the night, and it's usually a good idea to make a reservation for a simple day visit and hike. The gardens are about 6km (3¾ miles) before San Vito. To get here from Golfito, drive out to the Interamerican Highway and continue south toward Panama. In Ciudad Neily, turn north. A taxi from Golfito should cost around $45 each way.

Wilson Botanical Gardens.

Where to Stay

IN GOLFITO

Moderate

Casa Roland Marina Resort ★ If you want a contemporary, well-appointed room in Golfito, this miniresort is your best bet. Located in the old banana company housing area, near the airport and duty-free zone, this place is geared equally toward business travelers, vacationers, and sportfishers. However, the hotel is several blocks from the water, so I find the use of "marina" in the title a bit misleading. Still, the rooms are large and well equipped, with interesting art works and comfortable, heavy wood furnishings.

Old American zone, near the duty-free zone, Golfito. www.casarolandgolfito.com. ✆ **2775-0180.** Fax 2775-1506. 53 units. $110–$165 double; $185–$250 suite. Rates include continental breakfast. AE, MC, V. **Amenities:** Restaurant; bar; midsize outdoor pool; room service; spa. *In room:* A/C, TV, Internet, minibar.

Hotel Sierra This resort-style hotel is set right beside the airstrip, within walking distance to the duty-free zone. The Hotel Sierra was originally built as a business-class option geared toward middle-class Ticos in town to shop, and that's still its primary market. The Sierra is constructed to be as open and breezy as possible, and covered walkways connect the hotel's various buildings. The rooms are large and have windows on two sides to let in plenty of light. The swimming pool is the largest and most appealing in town, and the restaurant serves good, affordable international fare. One of the biggest draws here is the small casino, which is popular with guests and locals alike.

Beside the airstrip (A.P. 37), Golfito. www.hotelsierra.com. ℂ **888/790-5264** in the U.S. and Canada, or 2775-0666 in Costa Rica. Fax 2775-0506. 72 units. $69–$79 double. AE, MC, V. **Amenities:** Restaurant; bar; casino; midsize outdoor pool; room service. *In room:* A/C, TV.

Las Gaviotas Hotel   Situated just at the start of Golfito proper—a short taxi or bus ride from the "downtown"—Las Gaviotas is a local institution. The waterfront location is the hotel's greatest asset. The long pier attracts the sailboat and sportfishing crowd. For landlubbers, there's a small pool built out near the gulf. Guest rooms all face the ocean, and while regular maintenance has kept them up to date, they still feel a bit spartan. Small, tiled patios are in front of all the rooms, and the cabanas have little kitchens. A large, open-air restaurant looks over the pool to the gulf; it's a great view, but the food and service can be spotty. Just around the corner is a large, open-air bar.

A.P. 12–8201, Golfito. www.lasgaviotasmarinaresort.com. ℂ **2775-0062.** Fax 2775-0544. 18 units, 3 cabanas. $83 double; $98 suite. AE, DC, MC, V. **Amenities:** Restaurant; bar; small outdoor pool; room service. *In room:* A/C, TV.

Inexpensive

Centro Turístico Samoa del Sur ☺   This is the best-located hotel on the waterfront, and it features a popular restaurant and bar. The rooms are spacious and clean. Varnished wood headboards complement two firm and comfortable queen-size beds. With red-tile floors, modern bathrooms, and carved-wood doors, the rooms all share a long, covered veranda that's set perpendicular to the gulf, so the views aren't great. If you want to watch the water, you're better off grabbing a table at the restaurant, or walking out to the docks at their small marina. The hotel also has a swimming pool, children's playground, and a volleyball court that are popular with locals using it for a daily fee, as well as a large gift shop with an extensive shell-and-coral collection that they bill as a museum.

100m (328 ft.) north of the public dock, Golfito. www.samoadelsur.com. ℂ **2775-0233.** Fax 2775-0573. 14 units. $60 double. AE, MC, V. **Amenities:** Restaurant; bar; midsize outdoor pool; room service; kayak rentals. *In room:* A/C, TV.

El Gran Ceibo ⚡   This little motel-like option at the entrance to Golfito is a decent choice. It's named after the giant ceibo tree you'll see standing over it near the entrance. The rooms are clean, bright, comfortable, and relatively spacious. All feature small verandas with some sitting chairs. About half of them come with air-conditioning and cable TV; although you pay more for these, they're still quite affordable. The others have just fans and cold-water showers. The grounds and some of the rooms have nice views over the gulf.

On the left, just as you enter Golfito. ℂ **2775-0403.** Fax 2775-2303. 27 units. C22,000–C27,000 double. AE, MC, V. **Amenities:** Restaurant; bar; small outdoor pool. *In room:* A/C (in some units), TV, no phone.

ALONG THE SHORES OF THE GOLFO DULCE

The lodges listed here are on the shores of the Golfo Dulce. This area has no roads, so you must get to the lodges by boat. I recommend that you have firm reservations when visiting this area, so your transportation should be arranged. If worse comes to worst, you can hire a boat taxi at the *muellecito* (little dock), on the water just beyond the gas station, or La Bomba, in Golfito, for between $30 and $70, depending on your lodging destination.

Both of the below hotels are extremely committed to environmental protection and education. Another excellent option, but with an emphasis on luxury, is **Villas Corcovado** ★ (www.villacorcovado.com; ✆ **8817-6969**).

Golfo Dulce Lodge ★   This small, Swiss-run lodge is just down the beach from Casa Orquídeas (p. 444), about a 30-minute boat ride from Golfito. The five separate cabins and main lodge buildings are all set back from the beach about 500m (1,640 ft.) into the forest. The cabins are spacious and airy, and feature either a twin and a double bed or three single beds. In addition, there are large bathrooms, solar hot-water showers, a small sitting area, and a porch with a hammock. The rooms are all comfortable and well appointed, and even feature private verandas, but they are not nearly as nice as the cabins. The lodge offers jungle hikes, river trips, and other guided tours. This lodge has been granted "4 Leaves" by the CST Sustainable Tourism program and is a member of the International Ecotourism Society.

Golfo Dulce (A.P. 137–8201, Golfito). www.golfodulcelodge.com. ✆ **8821-5398.** Fax 2775-0573. 8 units. $95–$115 per person double occupancy. Rates include 3 meals daily and taxes. Add $30 per person for transportation to and from Golfito. No credit cards. **Amenities:** Restaurant; bar; small outdoor pool. *In room:* No phone.

Playa Nicuesa Rainforest Lodge ★★★ 🏠   Set on its own private bay and black-sand beach, this is the most impressive lodge along the shores of the Golfo Dulce. While the four Mango Manor rooms are certainly very cozy, you'll definitely want to snag one of the individual cabins. These are all set amid dense forest and are made almost entirely of wood, with large open-air showers, private verandas, and a true sense of being in touch with nature. The main lodge building is a huge, open-air affair with an abundance of varnished wood and a relaxed inviting vibe that induces one to grab a book, board game, or chat with other guests. An excellent network of trails snakes through the lodge's 66 hectares (165 acres), and a whole host of tours and activities are offered. The dedicated environmentalist owners have actively implemented a series of sustainable practices. The family-style meals are inventive and tasty.

Golfo Dulce. www.nicuesalodge.com. ✆ **866/504-8116** in the U.S., or 2258-8250 in Costa Rica. 11 units. $190–$210 per person per day, double occupancy. Children 6–12, $105. Rates include all meals, taxes, and transfers to and from either Golfito or Puerto Jiménez. A 2-night minimum stay is required during low season, and a 4-night minimum stay is required during high season. AE, MC, V. **Amenities:** Restaurant; bar; watersports equipment. *In room:* No phone.

EN ROUTE TO WILSON BOTANICAL GARDENS

While the Wilson Botanical Gardens themselves offer up the best accommodations in or around the tiny town of San Vito, the place below is a rare exception. The French-owned and inspired restaurant here is a great place for lunch or dinner on your way to or from the gardens, although call in advance, as the hours are extremely limited.

Morphose Mountain Retreat ★★ 🏠   This isolated, boutique lodge offers up fabulous views, rich bird and wildlife, and delicious dining. Guests can either rent out the entire two-bedroom Balinese-designed guesthouse, or share. A common living area has cable television and a fully equipped kitchen. Both of the bedrooms, as well as the restaurant and common areas, offer spectacular views over green hillsides and valleys all the way to the Golfo Dulce. The owners are a friendly and accommodating French-American family, and the food served here is the best in the area.

9km (5½ miles) outside of Ciudad Neily, on the road to San Vito. www.morphosecr.com. ℂ **8843-8626.** 2 units. $75–$95 double; $250 suite. Rates include full breakfast. AE, MC, V. **Amenities:** Restaurant; bar; outdoor pool. *In room:* No phone.

Where to Eat

Bilge Bar, Restaurant & Grill ★ INTERNATIONAL/SEAFOOD   This open-air restaurant attached to the Banana Bay Marina is the best restaurant in Golfito. The seafood is fresh and excellently prepared, but you can also get hearty steaks and great burgers. I personally recommend the fresh fish burger. Breakfasts are also hearty and well-prepared. Grab a table toward the water and watch the boats bob up and down while you enjoy your meal.

At the Banana Bay Marina, on the waterfront in downtown Golfito. ℂ **2775-0838.** Main courses $5–$15. MC, V. Daily 7am–9pm.

Samoa del Sur INTERNATIONAL   This large, open-air place features an extensive menu of Continental and French dishes (the owners are French), including such specialties as onion soup, salade niçoise, filet of fish meunière, and, in a nod to their southern neighbor, paella. Pizzas and spaghetti are also offered. In addition to the food, the giant rancho houses a pool table, several high-quality dartboards, and two big-screen TVs. The bar sometimes stays open all night.

100m (328 ft.) north of the public dock. ℂ **2775-0233.** www.samoadelsur.com. Reservations not accepted. Main courses C2,000–C20,000. AE, MC, V. Daily 6am–midnight.

Golfito After Dark

Golfito is a rough-and-tumble port town, and it pays to be careful here after dark. Most folks stick pretty close to their hotel bar and restaurant. Of these, the bar/restaurants at **Las Gaviotas, Samoa del Sur,** and **Bilge Bar, Restaurant & Grill ★** are, by far, the liveliest. If you're feeling lucky, you can head to the **casino** at the **Hotel Sierra** (p. 445). Another popular, if somewhat unlikely, spot is **La Pista** (ℂ **2775-9015**) bar, near the airstrip.

PLAYA ZANCUDO ★

19km (12 miles) S of Golfito by boat; 35km (22 miles) S of Golfito by road

Playa Zancudo is one of Costa Rica's most isolated and undeveloped beach destinations. If you're looking for a remote and low-key beach getaway, it's hard to beat Zancudo. It's pretty far from just about everything, and with relatively few places to stay, it's virtually never crowded. However, the small number of hotel rooms to be had means that the better ones, such as those listed here, can fill up fast in the high season. The beach itself is long and flat, and because it's protected from the full force of Pacific waves, it's one of the calmest beaches on this coast and

Park It

If you drive down to Golfito, you can leave your car at Samoa del Sur (see "Where to Stay," above) and take one of the waterborne routes mentioned above. They charge around $10 per day, and the lot is very secure.

relatively good for swimming, especially toward the northern end. There's a splendid view across the Golfo Dulce, and the sunsets are hard to beat.

Essentials

GETTING THERE   **By Plane:** The nearest airport is in Golfito. See "Golfito: Gateway to the Golfo Dulce," earlier in this chapter, for details. To get from the airport to Playa Zancudo, your best bets are by boat or taxi.

A fishing vessel at Playa Zancundo.

By Boat: Water taxis can be hired in Golfito to make the trip out to Playa Zancudo; however, trips depend on the tides and weather conditions. When the tide is high, the boats take a route through the mangroves. This is by far the calmest and most scenic way to get to Zancudo. When the tide is low, they must stay out in the gulf, which can get choppy at times. It costs around $15 to $20 per person for a water taxi, with a minimum charge of $40. If you can round up any sort of group, be sure to negotiate. The ride takes about 30 minutes.

Also, there's a passenger launch from the *muellecito* (little dock) in Golfito, which normally leaves daily at around noon. Because the schedule sometimes changes, be sure to ask in town about current departure times. The trip lasts 40 minutes; the fare is $5. The *muellecito* is next to the town's principal gas station, La Bomba.

If you plan ahead, you can call **Zancudo Boat Tours** (© **2776-0012;** www.loscocos.com) and arrange for pickup in Golfito or Puerto Jiménez. The trip costs $20 per person each way from Golfito or Puerto Jiménez, with a $50 minimum from Golfito and $60 minimum from Puerto Jiménez. Zancudo Boat Tours also includes land transportation to your hotel in Playa Zancudo—a very nice perk because the town has so few taxis.

By Car: If you've got a four-wheel-drive vehicle, you can make it out to Zancudo even in the rainy season. To get here, follow the directions for driving to Golfito, but don't go all the way into town. The turnoff for playas Zancudo and Pavones is at El Rodeo, about 4km (2½ miles) outside of Golfito, on the road in from the Interamerican Highway. It's mostly rough, gravel and dirt roads. Follow the few signs and the flow of traffic (if there is any) or stick to the most worn route when in doubt.

An alternative route from Paso Canoas (at the border) is via the towns of La Cuesta and Laurel. This route meets the route mentioned above at the small village of Conte.

A four-wheel-drive **taxi** costs around $75 from Golfito. It takes about 1 hour when the road is in good condition, and about 2 hours when it's not. For info on getting here from San José, see p. 443.

By Bus: It's possible to get to Zancudo by bus, but I highly recommend coming by boat from Golfito, or your own car. If you insist, you can catch one of the Pavones buses in front of the gas station La Bomba in downtown Golfito and get off in the village of Conte. In theory, a Zancudo–bound bus should be waiting. However, this is not always the case, and you may have to wait, hitchhike, or spring for a cab, if any can be found. The entire trip takes about 3 hours; the fare is $3.50.

DEPARTING   The public launch to Golfito leaves daily at 7am from the dock near the school, in the center of Zancudo. You can also arrange a water taxi back to Golfito, but it's best to work with your hotel owner and make a reservation at least 1 day in advance. **Zancudo Boat Tours** will take you for $20 per person, with a $50 minimum. Zancudo will also take you to the **Osa Peninsula.** It costs the same $20 per person, but there's a minimum charge of $60. The bus to Golfito leaves Zancudo each morning at 5:30am. You can catch the bus anywhere along the main road.

ORIENTATION   Zancudo is a long, narrow peninsula (sometimes only 90m/ 295 ft. or so wide) at the mouth of the Río Colorado. On one side is the beach; on the other is a mangrove swamp. There is only one road that runs the length of the beach, and along this road, spread out over several kilometers of long, flat beach, you'll find the hotels I mention here. It's about a 20-minute walk from the public dock near the school to the popular Cabinas Sol y Mar.

What to See & Do (or How to Not Do Anything)

The main activity at Zancudo is relaxing, and people take it seriously. Every lodge has hammocks, and if you bring a few good books, you can spend quite a number of hours swinging slowly in the tropical breezes. The beach along Zancudo is great for swimming. It's generally a little calmer on the northern end and gets rougher (good for bodysurfing) as you head south. There are a couple of bars and even a disco, but visitors are most likely to spend their time just hanging out at their hotel or in restaurants meeting like-minded folks, reading a good book, or playing board games. If you want to take a horseback ride on the beach, ask at your hotel; they should be able to arrange it for you.

Susan and Andrew England, who run Cabinas Los Cocos, also operate **Zancudo Boat Tours** (© 2776-0012; www.loscocos.com), which offers snorkeling trips, kayaking tours, trips to the Casa Orquídeas Botanical Garden, hikes on the Osa Peninsula, a trip up the Río Coto to watch birds and wildlife, and more. A boat trip through

A blue-crowned motmot.

the Río Coto mangroves will turn up a remarkable number of sea and shore birds, as well as the chance to see a crocodile resting on a river bank, or a white-faced monkey leaping overhead. Tour prices are $50 to $75 per person per tour, with discounts available for larger groups.

For fishing, ask at your hotel, or contact the **Zancudo Beach Resort** (see below). A full day of fishing with lunch and beer should cost between $500 and $1,600 per boat.

Because a mangrove swamp is directly behind the beach, mosquitoes and sand flies can be a problem when the winds die down, so be sure to bring insect repellent.

Where to Stay

Quite a few fully equipped beach houses are for rent for long stays. Once again, Susan and Andrew at **Los Cocos** (www.loscocos.com; ✆ 2776-0012) are your best bet for lining up one of these houses.

VERY EXPENSIVE

Zancudo Beach Resort ★★ ☺   Located at the north end of Zancudo, this is, by far, the most luxurious option around. All of the rooms look out onto a bright green lawn of soft grass and the small swimming pool. The beach, which is almost always calm and perfect for swimming, is just a few steps beyond. Two units come with a kitchenette, which comes in handy for families, or during longer stays. Formerly a dedicated fishing lodge, boasting more than 60 world-record catches, this place still offers world-class fishing outings under the name **The Zancudo Lodge** (www.thezancudolodge.com).

Playa Zancudo. www.zancudobeachresort.com. ✆ **800/854-8791** in the U.S. or Canada, or 2776-0008 in Costa Rica. Fax 2776-0011. 15 units. $146–$160 double; $250 suite. Rates higher during peak periods. AE, DISC, DC, MC, V. **Amenities:** Restaurant; bar; outdoor pool. *In room:* A/C, TV, minibar.

MODERATE

Cabinas Los Cocos ★ 🏠   If you've ever pondered throwing it all away, downsizing, and moving to the beach, these cabins are a good choice for a trial run. Four individual cabins are set beneath palm trees just a few meters from the beach. Two of them served as banana-plantation housing in a former life, until they were salvaged and moved here. These wood houses have big verandas and bedrooms, and large eat-in kitchens. Bathrooms are down a few steps in back and have hot water. The other cabins also offer plenty of space, small kitchenettes, and a private veranda, as well as comfortable sleeping lofts. The owners, Susan and Andrew Robertson, run Zancudo Boat Tours, so if you want to do some exploring or need a ride into Golfito or Puerto Jiménez, they're the folks to see. Finally, these folks also rent out several wonderful beach houses around Zancudo.

Playa Zancudo. www.loscocos.com. ✆/fax **2776-0012.** 4 units. $65 double. Weekly discounts available. No credit cards. *In room:* Kitchenette, no phone.

INEXPENSIVE

Cabinas Sol y Mar ★ 🎣   This friendly owner-run establishment is one of the most popular lodgings in Zancudo. There are two individual bungalows and two rooms in a duplex building with a shared veranda. I prefer the individual rooms for their privacy. The bathrooms in these have unusual showers that feature a tiled platform set amid smooth river rocks. The small budget cabin is quite a good deal, as well as a fully equipped house for longer stays. You can even camp here for a few bucks per night. All of the options are just steps away from the sand. The hotel's open-air restaurant is one of the best and most popular places to eat in Zancudo.

Playa Zancudo. www.zancudo.com. ✆ **2776-0014.** 6 units. $28–$45 double. MC, V. **Amenities:** Restaurant; bar. *In room:* No phone, Wi-Fi.

Where to Eat

In addition to the place listed below, you might try the tasty Italian meals at **Restaurante Macondo** (✆ **2776-0157**) or **Alberto's Puerta Negra ★** (✆ **2776-0181**). And if you want basic Tico fare and some local company, head to **Soda Sussy** (✆ **2776-0107**) or **Soda Katherine** (✆ **2776-0124**).

Finally, for a good breakfast, lunch, or dinner, or perhaps just a midday ice-cream treat, check out the open-air restaurant at **Oceanos Cabinas ★** (✆ **2776-0921;** www.oceanocabinas.com).

Sol y Mar ★★ 🖊 INTERNATIONAL/SEAFOOD   This is the best and most popular restaurant in Playa Zancudo. The reasonably priced menu is heavy on seafood, but features some items you won't find at most places in town, including thick-cut pork chops in a teriyaki sauce. The fresh seared tuna is always excellent, as are the twice-weekly barbecues on Monday and Friday. Saturday is Taco Night, a regular horseshoe tournament takes place on Sundays throughout the high season, and free Wi-Fi is always available at the bar and restaurant. This is also my top choice for breakfast—the breakfast burrito should get you through most of the day.

At Cabinas Sol y Mar. ✆ **2776-0014.** Main courses C2,700–C7,900. MC, V. Daily 7am–9pm.

PLAYA PAVONES: A SURFER'S MECCA ★

40km (25 miles) S of Golfito

Hailed as the world's longest rideable left point break, Pavones is a legendary destination for surfing. It takes around 1.8m (6 ft.) of swell to get this wave cranking, but when the surf's up, you're in for a long, long ride—so long, in fact, that it's much easier to walk back through town to where the wave is breaking than to paddle back. The swells are most consistent during the rainy season, but you're likely to find surfers here year-round. Locals tend to be pretty possessive of their turf, so don't be surprised if you receive a cool welcome.

Other than surfing, nothing much goes on here; however, the surrounding rainforests are quite nice, and the beaches feature some rocky coves and points that give Pavones a bit more visual appeal than Zancudo. If you're feeling energetic, you can go for a horseback ride or hike into the rainforests that back up this beach town, or stroll south on the beaches that stretch toward Punta Banco and beyond, all the way to the Panamanian border. This is a forgotten and isolated destination catering almost exclusively to backpackers. So be prepared,

Surfing in Pavones.

Pavones is a tiny village with few amenities, and most of the accommodations are quite basic.

Essentials

GETTING THERE & DEPARTING **By Plane:** The nearest airport with regularly scheduled flights is in Golfito (p. 442). Tiskita Jungle Lodge (see below) has a private airstrip. Depending on space, you might be able to arrange transportation to Pavones on one of its charter flights even if you are not staying there.

By Car: If you've got a four-wheel-drive vehicle, you can make it out to Pavones even in the rainy season. To get here, follow the directions for driving to Golfito (p. 442), but don't go all the way into town. The turnoff for playas Zancudo and Pavones is at El Rodeo, about 4km (2½ miles) outside of Golfito, on the road in from the Interamerican Highway. It's mostly rough, gravel and dirt roads. Follow the few signs and the flow of traffic (if there is any) or stick to the most worn route when in doubt.

An alternative route from Paso Canoas (at the border) goes via the towns of La Cuesta and Laurel. This route meets the route mentioned above at the small village of Conte.

By Bus: Two daily buses (no phone) go to Pavones from Golfito at 10am and 3pm. Trip duration is 2½ hours; the fare is around $3. Buses to Golfito depart Pavones daily at 5:30am and 12:30pm. This is a very remote destination, and the bus schedule is subject to change, so it always pays to check in advance.

ORIENTATION You can find an Internet connection at **Esquina del Mar** in the heart of the village. If there are no waves, or you want some other form of exercise, check in with the folks at **Shooting Star Yoga** (© **2776-2107;** www.yogapavones.com). For board rentals, head to **Sea Kings Surf Shop** (© **2776-2015;** www.surfpavones.com).

A WILD ride

Surfers first discovered the amazing wave off of Pavones in the late 1970s. When conditions are right, this wave peels off in one continuous ribbon for over 2km (1.25 miles). Your skills better be up to snuff, and your legs better be in good shape, if you want to ride this wave.

Pavones got some good press in Allan Weisbecker's 2001 novel *In Search of Captain Zero: A Surfer's Road Trip Beyond The End of the Road*. The word was out and surfers began flocking to Pavones from all over. On any given day—when the wave is working—you are likely to find surfers from the United States, Brazil, Argentina, Israel, Australia, Peru, and any other number of countries.

However, the town and wave are not without their controversy. Aside from the typical territorial squabbles that erupt over most popular waves, Pavones has been the site of a series of prominent squabbles and controversies that include land disputes, drug busts, fist fights, and even murders. For a unique and in-depth account of the town, its wave, and some of these controversies, check out Weisbecker's *Can't You Get Along with Anyone?: A Writer's Memoir and a Tale of a Lost Surfer's Paradise*.

Where to Stay & Eat

In addition to the hotels listed below, **Riviera Riverside Villas** (www.pavones riviera.com; © 2776-2396) offers modern, plush individual cabins, as well as several fully equipped house rentals, a block or so inland from the water, right alongside the Río Claro (Clear River). **Cabinas La Ponderosa ★** (www.la ponderosapavones.com; © 954/771-9166 in the U.S., or 2776-2076 in Costa Rica) is a small, beachfront collection of cabins and private, rustic villas, a bit out of town, on the way to Punta Banco.

Right in Pavones, several very basic lodges cater to itinerant surfers by renting rooms for between $10 and $20 per night for a double room; most take walk-in reservations since they don't have phones. That said, for in-town budget lodgings, I recommend **Mira Olas** (www.miraolas.com; © 2776-2006), about 2 blocks uphill from the soccer field.

A couple of simple *sodas* where you can get Tico meals are in town. The most popular spot for both cheap meals and an afternoon-to-evening bar scene is **Esquina del Mar** (© 2776-2005), right on the beach's edge, in front of the fattest part of the surf break.

For better and more healthy meals, I recommend **Café de la Suerte ★** (© 2776-2388; www.cafedelasuerte.com), a lively little joint across from Esquina del Mar that serves breakfasts and lunches and specializes in vegetarian items, freshly baked goods, and fresh-fruit smoothies. These folks also serve dinner during the high season, and rent out a cozy A/C-equipped cabin.

VERY EXPENSIVE

Tiskita Jungle Lodge ★★ 🎁 This remote ecolodge is nearly on the Panamanian border. Everything is set on a tall hillside a few hundred meters from the beach and commands a superb view of the ocean. There's a dark-sand beach, tide pools, jungle waterfalls, a farm and forest to explore, and great bird-watching.

Most of the land here is primary rainforest; the rest is a mix of secondary forest, reforestation projects, orchards, and pastures. These folks actively work on projects to reintroduce scarlet macaws to the area, to protect the local turtle nesting sites, and to preserve and restore the surrounding forest lands. Accommodations are in cozy rustic cabins with screen walls and verandas. My favorite cabin is no. 6, which has a great view and ample deck space. Some cabins have two or three rooms, perfect for families but less private for couples.

6km (3¾ miles) southeast, down the road from Pavones. www.tiskita.com. © **2296-8125.** Fax 2296-8133. 17 units. $150 per person. Rates include all meals. Packages with transportation to and from Golfito or Puerto Jiménez are available. AE, MC, V. **Amenities:** Restaurant; bar; small outdoor pool; limited watersports equipment. *In room:* No phone.

MODERATE

Casa Siempre Domingo   This small hillside inn offers up the best accommodations right in Pavones. The rooms all feature high ceilings, tile floors, and two double beds (one room has two doubles and a twin). The high beds are custom-made constructions, and they're uncommonly high off the ground. The owner says the design helps capture the breeze from the picture windows, but if there's not enough, you can always crank up the air-conditioning. Meals are served on picnic tables in the large interior common space. The nicest feature is the huge deck, with its ocean view.

Pavones, several hundred meters south of downtown Pavones. www.casa-domingo.com. © **8820-4709** or 2776-2185. 3 units. $100 double. Rate includes breakfast and taxes. No credit cards. *In room:* A/C, no phone, Wi-Fi.

12

THE CARIBBEAN COAST

Costa Rica's Caribbean coast is a world apart from the rest of the country. The pace is slower, the food is spicier, the tropical heat is more palpable, and the rhythmic lilt of patois and reggae music fills the air. This remains one of Costa Rica's least discovered and explored regions. More than half of the coastline here is still inaccessible except by boat or small plane. This inaccessibility has helped preserve large tracts of virgin lowland rainforest, which are now set aside as Tortuguero National Park ★★ and Barra del Colorado National Wildlife Refuge ★. These two parks, on the coast's northern reaches, are among Costa Rica's most popular destinations for adventurers and ecotravelers. Of particular interest are the sea turtles that nest here. Farther south, Cahuita National Park ★★ is another popular national park, located just off its namesake beach village. It was set up to preserve 200 hectares (494 acres) of coral reef, but its palm tree–lined white-sand beaches and gentle trails are stunning.

So remote was the Caribbean coast from Costa Rica's population centers in the Central Valley that it developed a culture all its own. The original inhabitants of the area included people of the Bribri, Cabécar, and Kéköldi tribes, and these groups maintain their cultures on indigenous reserves in the Talamanca Mountains. In fact, until the 1870s, this area had few non-Indians. However, when Minor Keith (p. 34) built the railroad to San José and began planting bananas, he brought in black laborers from Jamaica and other Caribbean islands to lay the track and work the plantations. These workers and their descendants established fishing and farming communities up and down the coast. Today dreadlocked Rastafarians, reggae music, Creole cooking, and the English-based patois of this Afro-Caribbean culture give this region a quasi-Jamaican flavor, a striking contrast with the Spanish–derived Costa Rican culture.

The Caribbean Coast's Top Sustainable Hotels

Almonds and Corals Hotel (p. 502)
Casa Marbella (p. 471)
Casa Verde Lodge (p. 495)
Punta Mona Center for Sustainable Living & Education (p. 501)
Selva Bananito Lodge (p. 476)
Tortuga Lodge (p. 470)
Tree House Lodge (p. 503)

FACING PAGE: **Surfboards at Playa Cocles.**

To Go, or Not to Go? The Weather is Nobler

The Caribbean coast has a very unique weather pattern. Whereas you'll almost never get even a drop of rain in Guanacaste during Costa Rica's typical dry season (mid-Nov to Apr), on the Caribbean coast it can rain, at least a bit, almost any day of the year. However, the months of September and October, when torrential rains pound most of the rest of the country, most of the time, are oddly two of the drier and more dependably sunny days along the Caribbean coast.

The Caribbean coast has only one major city, **Limón,** a major commercial port and popular cruise ship port of call. However, the city itself is of little interest to most visitors, who quickly head south to the coast's spectacular beaches, or north to the jungle canals of Tortuguero.

Over the years, the Caribbean coast has garnered a reputation as being a dangerous, drug-infested zone, rife with crime and danger. This is somewhat deserved because of several high-profile crimes in the area; petty theft is a major problem. Still, overall this reputation is exaggerated. The same crime and drug problems found here exist in San José and most of the more popular beach destinations on the Pacific coast. Use common sense and take normal precautions and you should have no problems on the Caribbean coast.

BARRA DEL COLORADO ★

115km (71 miles) NE of San José

Most visitors to Barra del Colorado come for the fishing. Tarpon and snook fishing are world-class, or you can head farther offshore for some deep-sea action. Barra del Colorado is part of the same ecosystem as Tortuguero National Park (see below); as in Tortuguero, an abundance of wildlife and rainforest fauna lives in the rivers and canals.

Named for its location at the mouth of the Río Colorado up near the Costa Rica–Nicaragua border, Barra del Colorado can be reached only by boat or small plane. No roads go in or out of Barra del Colorado. The town itself is a small, ramshackle collection of raised stilt houses, and it supports a diverse population of Afro-Caribbean and Miskito Indian residents, Nicaraguan emigrants, and transient commercial fishermen.

It's hot and humid here most of the year, and it rains a lot, so although some of the lodges have at times risked offering a "tarpon guarantee," they're generally hesitant to promise anything in terms of the weather.

Essentials

GETTING THERE & DEPARTING   **By Plane:** Most folks come here on multiday fishing packages, and most of the area's lodges either include charter flights as part of their package trips or will book you a flight.

    By Boat: It is also possible to travel to Barra del Colorado by boat from **Puerto Viejo de Sarapiquí** (see chapter 9). Expect to pay $400 to $600

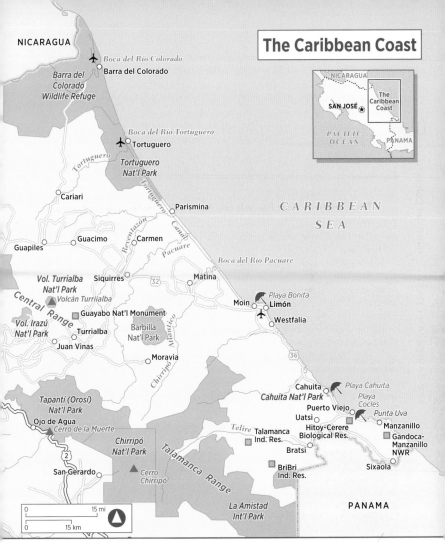

The Caribbean Coast

each way for a boat that holds up to 10 people. Check at the public dock in Puerto Viejo de Sarapiquí or call **Oasis Nature Tours** (☏ 2766-6108; www.oasisnaturetours.com).

Río Colorado Lodge (☏ 800/243-9777 in the U.S. and Canada, or 2232-4063; www.riocoloradolodge.com) runs its own launch between Barra del Colorado and Puerto Viejo de Sarapiquí (and sometimes btw. Barra and Limón), including land transportation between Puerto Viejo de Sarapiquí and San José. If you're staying at the Río Colorado Lodge, be sure to ask about this option (for at least one leg of your trip) when booking; the hotel doesn't discriminate—you can arrange transportation even if you aren't staying there. For $370 per person, you can arrange a San José pickup, a minibus to the boat, a river trip to Barra, overnight accommodations at Río Colorado Lodge, and a return trip the next day, with all meals and taxes included.

ORIENTATION   The Río Colorado neatly divides the town of Barra del Colorado. The airstrip is in the southern half of town, as are most of the lodgings. The lodges that are farther up the canals will meet you at the airstrip with a small boat.

Fishing, Fishing & More Fishing

Almost all the lodges here specialize in fishing packages. If you don't fish, you may wonder just what in the world you're doing here. Even though there are excellent opportunities for bird-watching and touring jungle waterways, most lodges still merely pay lip service to ecotourists and would rather see you with a rod and reel.

Fishing takes place year-round. You can do it in the rivers and canals, in the very active river mouth, or offshore. Most anglers come in search of the tarpon, or silver king. **Tarpon** can be caught year-round, both in the river mouth and, to a lesser extent, in the canals; however, they are much harder to land in July and August—the 2 rainiest months—probably because the river runs so high and is so full of runoff and debris. **Snook,** an aggressive river fish, peak in April, May, October, and November; fat snook, or *calba,* run heavy November through January. Depending on how far out to sea you venture, you might hook up with **barracuda, jack, mackerel** (Spanish and king), **wahoo, tuna, dorado, marlin,** or **sailfish.** In the rivers and canals, fishermen regularly bring in *mojarra, machaca,* and *guapote* (rainbow bass).

An angler pulling in a tarpon in Barra del Colorado.

Following current trends in sportfishing, more and more anglers have been using fly rods, in addition to traditional rod-and-reel setups, to land just about all the fish mentioned above. To fish here, you'll need a fishing license ($24), which covers both salt and fresh water. The lodges here either include these in your packages or can readily provide the licenses for you.

Nonfishers should see whether their lodge has a good naturalist guide or canoes or kayaks for rent or use.

Where to Stay & Eat

Almost all of the hotels here specialize in package tours, including all your meals, fishing and tackle, taxes, and usually your transportation and liquor too, so rates are high. With no dependable budget hotels, Barra remains a remote and difficult destination for independent and budget travelers.

Río Colorado Lodge This riverside outpost is one of the country's oldest and best-known fishing lodges. It was founded and built more than 35 years ago by local legend Archie Fields. The rooms are comfortable but decidedly rustic, with many showing the wear and tear of the years. Two of the rooms are wheelchair accessible. The nicest feature here is the large covered deck out by the river, where breakfast is served. Lunch is served at the large bar with satellite TV, a pool table, and a dartboard. The lodge runs a small "zoo" and participates in a macaw breeding project, as well as local education efforts. While their hearts may be in the right place, I find the zoo and cage conditions here rather desultory.

Barra del Colorado (A.P. 5094-1000, San José). www.riocoloradolodge.com. ℂ **800/243-9777** in the U.S. and Canada, or 2232-4063 in Costa Rica. Fax 2231-5987. 18 units. $2,453–$3,051 per person double occupancy for 7 days/6 nights with 4 full days of fishing, including 2 nights lodging in San José, all meals and drinks at the lodge, boat, guide, fuel, licenses, and taxes. Nonfishing guests $120–$170 per person per day. AE, MC, V. **Amenities:** Restaurant; bar; Jacuzzi. *In room:* A/C, no phone.

Silver King Lodge ★★ 🛎 This is the most upscale lodge in Barra del Colorado. They take their fishing seriously here—with a large selection of modern boats and equipment, as well as a full tackle shop—but Silver King also emphasizes comfort. The rooms are immense, with two double beds, a desk and chair, fishing racks, air-conditioning, an overhead fan, and a roomy closet. The floors and walls are all varnished hardwood, and the ceilings are finished in bamboo. The entire complex is built on raised stilts and connected by covered walkways. Excellent and abundant buffet meals are served, and free daily laundry service is provided.

Barra del Colorado (mailing address: Interlink P.O. Box 373, Gloucester, MA 01930). www.silver kinglodge.net. ℂ **800/335-0755** in the U.S., or 2794-0139 in Costa Rica. 10 units. $2,255–$3,600 per person double occupancy for 3 full days of fishing, round-trip air transportation btw. San José and the lodge, all meals at the lodge, liquor, and taxes; $375–$420 per person per extra day, including all fishing, meals, liquor, and taxes. AE, MC, V. Closed throughout the months of June, July, Aug, Nov, and Dec. **Amenities:** Restaurant; bar; Jacuzzi; small outdoor pool; sauna. *In room:* A/C, TV, no phone, Wi-Fi.

TORTUGUERO NATIONAL PARK ★★

250km (155 miles) NE of San José; 79km (49 miles) N of Limón

Sometimes dubbed "the Venice of Costa Rica," Tortuguero is connected to Limón, and the rest of mainland Costa Rica, by a series of rivers and canals. This aquatic highway is lined almost entirely with a dense tropical rainforest that is home to howler and spider monkeys, three-toed sloths, toucans, and great green macaws. A trip through the canals is nothing like touring around Venice in a gondola, but it is a lot like cruising the Amazon basin—on a much smaller scale.

"Tortuguero" comes from the Spanish name for the giant sea turtles (*tortugas*) that nest on the beaches of this region every year from early March to mid-October (prime season is July–Oct, and peak months are Aug–Sept). The chance to see this nesting attracts many people to this remote region, but just as many come to explore the intricate network of jungle canals that serve as the region's main transportation arteries.

Very important: More than 508cm (200 in.) of rain fall here annually, so you can expect a downpour at any time of the year. Most of the lodges will provide you with rain gear (including ponchos and rubber boots), but it can't hurt to carry your own.

Independent travel is not the norm here, although it's possible. Most travelers rely on their lodge for boat transportation through the canals and into town. At most of the lodges around Tortuguero, almost everything (bus rides to and from, boat trips through the canals, and even family-style meals) is done in groups.

Essentials

GETTING THERE & DEPARTING   By Plane: Nature Air (✆ **800/235-9272** in the U.S. and Canada, or 2299-6000; www.natureair.com) has one flight that departs daily at 6:15am for **Tortuguero** airstrip (no phone) from Tobías Bolaños International Airport in Pavas. The flight takes approximately 30 minutes; the fare is $95 each way. The return flight leaves Tortuguero daily at around 7am for San José.

Additional flights are often added during the high season, and departure times can vary according to weather conditions. In addition, many local lodges operate charter flights as part of their package trips.

Be sure to arrange with your hotel to pick you up at the airstrip. Otherwise you'll have to plead with one of the other hotels' boat captains to give you a lift, which they will usually do, either for free or for a few dollars.

By Car: It's not possible to drive to Tortuguero. If you have a car, your best bet is either to leave it in San José and take an organized tour, or drive it to Limón or Moín, find a secure hotel or public parking lot, and then follow the directions for arriving by boat below. La Pavona has a secure parking useful for those meeting the boats plying the Cariari and La Pavona route outlined below.

By Boat: Flying to Tortuguero is convenient if you don't have much time, but a boat trip through the canals and rivers of this region is often the highlight of any visit. However, be forewarned: Although this trip can be

stunning and exciting, it can also be long, tiring, and uncomfortable. You'll first have to ride by bus or minivan from San José to Moín, Caño Blanco, or one of the other embarkation points; then it's 2 to 3 hours on a boat, usually with hard wooden benches or plastic seats. All of the more expensive lodges listed offer their own bus and boat transportation packages, which include the boat ride through the canals. However, if you're coming here on the cheap and plan to stay at one of the less expensive lodges or at a budget cabina in Tortuguero, you will have to arrange your own transportation. In this case, you have a few options.

The most traditional option is to get yourself first to Limón and then to the public docks in **Moín,** just north of Limón, and try to find a boat on your own. You can reach Limón easily by public bus from San José (see "Getting There & Departing" under "Limón: Gateway to Tortuguero National Park & Southern Coastal Beaches," later in this chapter). If you're coming by car, make sure you drive all the way to Limón or Moín, unless you have prior arrangements out of Cariari or Caño Blanco Marina.

If you arrive in Limón by bus, you might be able to catch one of the periodic local buses to Moín (around 50¢) at the main bus terminal. Otherwise, you can take a taxi for around $6, for up to four people. At the docks, you should be able to negotiate a fare of between $50 and $80 per person

A Tortuguero National Park boat tour.

round-trip with one of the boats docked here. These boats tend to depart between 8 and 10am every morning. You can stay as many days as you like in Tortuguero, but be sure to arrange with the captain to be there to pick you up when you're ready to leave. The trip from Moín to Tortuguero takes between 3 and 4 hours.

It is possible to get to Tortuguero by bus and boat from Cariari. For backpackers and budget travelers, this is the cheapest and most reliable means of reaching Tortuguero from San José. To take this route, begin by catching the 9 or 10:30am direct bus to Cariari from the **Gran Terminal del Caribe,** on Calle Central, 1 block north of Avenida 11 (© **2222-0610**). The fare is C1,400. This bus will actually drop you off at the main bus terminal in Cariari, from which you'll have to walk 4 blocks east to a separate bus station, known locally as *"la estación vieja,"* or the old station. Look for a booth marked **COOPETRACA** or **Clic Clic** ★. At these booths you can buy your bus ticket for La Pavona. The bus fare is C1,200. Buy a ticket for the 11:30am bus (a later bus leaves at 3pm).

A boat or two will be waiting to meet the bus at the dock at the edge of the river at around 2:30pm (and again at 4pm). Check out the boats heading to Tortuguero, and pick the one that looks most comfortable and safe, then pay on board. The boat fare to Tortuguero is not regulated, and the price sometimes varies for foreigners. It can be as low as C1,600 each way, which is what locals pay. However, the boat captains often try to gouge tourists. Stand firm; you should not have to pay more than C3,500 (or $7). Return boats leave Tortuguero for La Pavona every morning at 6 and 11:30am, and 3pm, making return bus connections to Cariari.

Warning: Be careful if you decide to take this route. I've received reports of unscrupulous operators providing misinformation to tourists. Folks from a company called **Bananera** have offices at the Gran Terminal del Caribe and in Cariari, offering to sell you "packaged transportation" to Tortuguero. However, all they are doing is charging you extra to buy the individual tickets described above. Be especially careful if the folks selling you boat transportation aggressively steer you to a specific hotel option, claim that your first choice is full, or insist that you must buy a package with them that includes the transportation, lodging, and guide services. If you have doubts or want to check on the current state of this route, check out the site **www.tortugerovillage.com ★**, which has detailed directions about how to get to Tortuguero by a variety of routes.

Finally, it's also possible, albeit expensive, to travel to Tortuguero by boat from **Puerto Viejo de Sarapiquí** (see chapter 9). Expect to pay $450 to $650 each way for a boat that holds up to 10 people. Check at the public dock in Puerto Viejo de Sarapiquí if you're interested. The ride usually takes about 3 to 4 hours, and the boats tend to leave in the morning.

ORIENTATION   Tortuguero is one of the most remote locations in Costa Rica. With no roads into this area and no cars in the village, all transportation is by boat or foot. Most of the lodges are spread out over several kilometers to the north of Tortuguero Village on either side of the main canal; the small airstrip is at the north end of the beachside spit of land. At the far northern end of the main canal, you'll see the **Cerro de Tortuguero (Turtle Hill),** which, at some 119m (390 ft.), towers over the area. The hike to the top of this hill is a popular half-day tour and offers some good views of the Tortuguero canal and village, as well as the Caribbean Sea.

A Tortuguero stilt house.

Tortuguero Village is a small collection of houses connected by foot-paths. The village is spread out on a thin spit of land, bordered on one side by the Caribbean Sea and on the other by the main canal. At most points, it's less than 300m (984 ft.) wide. In the center of the village, you'll find a small children's playground, the town's health clinic, and a soccer field.

If you stay at a hotel on the ocean side of the canal, you'll be able to walk into and explore the village at your leisure; if you're across the canal, you'll be dependent on the lodge's boat transportation. However, some of the lodges across the canal have their own network of jungle trails that might appeal to naturalists.

FAST FACTS Tortuguero has no banks, ATMs, or currency-exchange houses, so be sure to bring sufficient cash in colones to cover any expenses and inci-dental charges. The local hotels and shops generally charge a commission to exchange dollars. An Internet cafe (no phone) is right across from the main dock in town, although I prefer the one found at **La Casona** (*②* **2709-8092**), a small restaurant and budget hotel in the heart of the village.

Exploring the National Park

According to existing records, sea turtles have frequented Tortuguero National Park since at least 1592, largely due to its extreme isolation. Over the years, tur-tles were captured and their eggs were harvested by local settlers; by the 1950s, this practice became so widespread that turtles faced extinction. Regulations controlling this mini-industry were passed in 1963, and in 1970 Tortuguero National Park was established.

Today four different species of sea turtles nest here: the green turtle, the hawksbill, the loggerhead, and the giant leatherback. The park's beaches are excellent places to watch sea turtles nest, especially at night. As appeal-ingly long and deserted as they are, however, the beaches are not appro-priate for swimming. The surf is usually very rough, and the river mouths attract sharks that feed on the turtle hatchlings and many fish that live here.

Green turtles are the most common turtle found in Tortuguero, so you're more likely to see one of them than any other species if you visit during the prime nesting season from **July to mid-October** (Aug–Sept are peak months). **Logger-heads** are very rare, so don't be disappointed if you don't see one. The **giant leatherback** is perhaps the most spectacular sea turtle to watch laying eggs. The largest of all turtle species, the leatherback can grow to 2m (6½ ft.) long and weigh

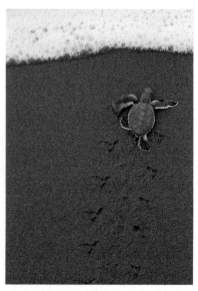

A turtle hatchling heading to sea.

Turtle Tips

- Visitors to the beach at night must be accompanied by a licensed guide. Tours generally last between 2 and 4 hours.

- Sometimes you must walk quite a bit to encounter a nesting turtle. Wear sneakers or walking shoes rather than sandals. The beach is very dark at night, and it's easy to trip or step on driftwood or other detritus.

- Wear dark clothes. White T-shirts are not permitted.

- Flashlights, flash cameras, and lighted video cameras are prohibited on turtle tours.

- Smoking is prohibited on the beach at night.

well over 1,000 pounds. It nests from late February to June, predominantly in the southern part of the park. See the "In Search of Turtles" box on p. 92 for more information.

You can explore the park's rainforest, either by foot or by boat, and look for some of the incredible varieties of wildlife that live here: jaguars, anteaters, howler monkeys, collared and white-lipped peccaries, some 350 species of birds, and countless butterflies, among others. Some of the more colorful and common bird species you might see in this area include the rufescent and tiger herons, keel billed toucan, northern jacana, red lored parrot, and ringed kingfisher. Boat tours are far and away the most popular way to visit this park, although one frequently very muddy trail starts at the park entrance and runs for about 2km (1.25 miles) through the coastal rainforest and along the beach.

Although it's a perfect habitat, West Indian manatees (*Trichechus manatus*) are rare and threatened in the canals, rivers, and lagoons of Costa Rica's Caribbean coast. Hunting and propeller injuries are the prime culprits. Your chances of seeing one of these gentle aquatic mammals is extremely remote.

ENTRY POINT, FEES & REGULATIONS   The Tortuguero National Park entrance and ranger station are at the south end of Tortuguero Village. The ranger station is inside a landlocked old patrol boat, and a small, informative open-air kiosk explains a bit about the park and its environs. Park admission is $10. However, most people visit Tortuguero as part of a package tour. Be sure to confirm whether the park entrance is included in the price. Moreover, only certain canals and trails leaving from the park station are actually within the park. Many hotels and private guides take their tours to a series of canals that border the park and are very similar in terms of flora and fauna but don't require a park entrance. When the turtles are nesting, arrange a night tour in advance with either your hotel or one of the private guides working in town. These guided tours generally run between $10 and $15. Flashlights and flash cameras are not permitted on the beach at night because the lights discourage the turtles from nesting.

ORGANIZED TOURS   Most visitors come to Tortuguero on an organized tour. All of the lodges listed below, with the exception of the most inexpensive accommodations in Tortuguero Village, offer package tours that include various hikes and river tours; this is generally the best way to visit the area.

In addition, several San José–based tour companies offer budget 2-day/1-night excursions to Tortuguero, including transportation, all meals, and limited tours around the region. Prices for these trips range between $120 and $220 per person, and—depending on price—guests are lodged either in one of the basic hotels in Tortuguero Village or one of the nicer lodges listed below. Reputable companies offering these excursions include **Exploradores Outdoors** ★★ (✆ 2222-6262; www.exploradoresoutdoors. com), **Jungle Tom Safaris** (✆ 2221-7878; www.jungletomsafaris.com), and **Iguana Verde Tours** (✆ 2231-6803; www.iguanaverdetours.com). Jungle Tom Safaris also offers 1-day trips in which tourists spend almost all their time coming and going but that do allow for a quick tour of the canals and lunch in Tortuguero. These trips are good for travelers who like to be able to say, "Been there, done that," and they generally run between $80 and $100 per person. However, these trips spend most of their time traveling to and from Tortuguero. If you really want to experience Tortuguero, I recommend staying for at least 2 nights.

Alternately, you could go with **Fran and Modesto Watson** ★ (✆ 2226-0986; www.tortuguerocanals.com), who are pioneering guides in this region and operate their own boat. The couple offers a range of overnight and multiday packages to Tortuguero, with lodging options at most of the major lodges here.

BOAT CANAL TOURS Aside from watching the turtles nest, the unique thing to do in Tortuguero is tour the canals by boat, keeping your eye out for tropical birds and native wildlife. Most lodges can arrange a canal tour for you, but you can also arrange a tour through one of the operators in Tortuguero Village. I recommend **Daryl Loth** (✆ 8833-0827; http://casamarbella.tripod. com), who runs the Casa Marbella (see below) in the center of the village. I also recommend **Ernesto Castillo,** who can be reached through Cabinas Sabina or by asking around the village. If neither of these guides is available, ask for a recommendation at the **Jungle Shop** (✆ 2709-8072) or at the **Caribbean Conservation Corporation's Museum** (✆ 2709-8091). Most guides charge between $15 to $25 per person for a tour of the canals. If you travel through the park, you'll also have to pay the park entrance fee of $10 per person.

Exploring the Village

The most popular attraction in town is the small **Caribbean Conservation Corporation's Visitors' Center and Museum** ★ (✆ 2709-8091; www. cccturtle.org). The museum has information and exhibits on a whole range of native flora and fauna, but its primary focus is on the life and natural history of the sea turtles. Most visits to the museum include a short, informative video on the turtles. All the proceeds from the small gift shop go toward conservation and turtle protection. The museum is open daily from 10am to noon and 2 to 5pm. Admission is $2, but more generous donations are encouraged.

In the village you can also rent dugout canoes, known in Costa Rica as *cayucos* or *pangas*. Be careful before renting and taking off in one of these; they tend to be heavy, slow, and hard to maneuver, and you might be getting more than you bargained for. **Miss Junie** (✆ 2709-8102) rents lighter and more modern fiberglass canoes for around $5 for 3 hours.

Tortuguero Village.

You'll find a handful of souvenir shops spread around the center of the village. The **Paraíso Tropical Gift Shop** has the largest selection of gifts and souvenirs. But I prefer the **Jungle Shop,** which has a higher-end selection of wares and donates 10% of its profits to local schools.

Where to Stay

Although the room rates below may appear high, keep in mind that they usually include round-trip transportation from San José (which amounts to approx. $100 per person), plus all meals, taxes, and usually some tours. When broken down into nightly room rates, most of the lodges are really charging only between $60 and $120 for a double room. ***Note:*** When I list package rates below, I have always listed the least expensive travel option, which is a bus and boat combination both in and out. All of the lodges also offer packages with the option of a plane flight either one or both ways.

VERY EXPENSIVE

Manatus Hotel ★★   This intimate hotel offers the most luxurious accommodations in Tortuguero. The large rooms are plush and well-equipped, with two queen-size four-poster beds, high ceilings, wood floors, tasteful local furnishings, and a host of amenities you won't find anywhere else in the area, including a stocked minibar. Meals and service are top-notch, and they have the best little spa of any local hotel, as well as an on-site art gallery. The amoeba-shaped pool is set just off the dark waters of the Tortuguero Canal, with a broad deck and plenty of inviting chaise lounges surrounding it. Only children over 10 years of age are allowed.

Tortuguero. www.manatushotel.com. ✆ **2239-4854** reservations in San José, or 2709-8197 at the hotel. Fax 2239-4857. 12 units. $391 per person for 2 days/1 night; $498 per person for 3 days/2 nights. Rates are double occupancy, and include round-trip transportation from San José, 3 meals daily, taxes, and daily tours. AE, MC, V. No children 10 and under allowed. **Amenities:** Restaurant; bar; outdoor pool; room service; small spa and exercise room. *In room:* A/C, TV, minibar, Wi-Fi.

EXPENSIVE

Laguna Lodge ★   This popular lodge is 2km (1¼ miles) north of Tortuguero Village, on the ocean side of the main canal (which allows you to walk along the beach and into town). Most of the rooms have wood walls, waxed hardwood floors, and tiled bathrooms. Each room also has a little veranda overlooking flowering gardens. The large dining area is on a deck that extends out over the Tortuguero Canal. Another covered deck, also over the water, is strung with hammocks for lazing away the afternoons. Several palapa huts, also strung with hammocks, have been built among the flowering ginger and hibiscus. There's a large landscaped pool, with a poolside bar and grill, as well as a butterfly garden and botanical garden.

Tortuguero (A.P. 173–2015, Zapote). www.lagunatortuguero.com. ✆ **2272-4943** for reservations, or 2709-8082 at the lodge. Fax 2272-4927. 100 units. $236 per person for 2 days/1 night; $265 per person for 3 days/2 nights. Rates are double occupancy and include round-trip transportation from San José, tours, taxes, and 3 meals daily. Children 5–11 pay half-price. Children 4 and under, free. AE, DC, MC, V. **Amenities:** Restaurant; 2 bars; large free-form outdoor pool. *In room:* No phone.

Mawamba Lodge ★   Located just north of Tortuguero on the ocean side of the canal, Mawamba lies within easy walking distance of the village. All rooms are painted in bright Caribbean colors. A few "superior rooms" come with king-size beds and a few extra amenities, like hair dryers and a bathtub. The gardens are lush and overgrown with flowering ginger, heliconia, and hibiscus, and include a frog garden, butterfly garden, and iguana garden. Plenty of hammocks are around for anyone who wants to kick back and a beach volleyball court for those who don't. The newest option here is a floating restaurant, where you can enjoy lunch or dinner while slowly cruising the canals. These folks also offer an extensive menu of kayaking tours and excursions, including one package in which you actually kayak part of the way into Tortuguero.

Tortuguero (A.P. 10980–1000, San José). www.grupomawamba.com. ✆ **2293-8181** or 2709-8100. Fax 2239-7657. 58 units. $200 per person for 2 days/1 night; $285 per person for 3 days/2 nights. Rates are double occupancy, and include round-trip transportation from San José, 3 meals daily, taxes, and some tours. Discounts for children 5–11. Children 4 and under, free. AE, MC, V. **Amenities:** Restaurant; bar; free-form outdoor pool. *In room:* Hair dryer (in superior rooms), no phone.

Tortuga Lodge ★★ ☺   One of the oldest lodges in Tortuguero, this is still one of the best. My favorite feature here is the long multilevel deck off the main dining room, where you can sit and dine, sip a cool drink, or just take in the view as the water laps against the docks at your feet. The lovely pool built by the water's edge is designed to look like it blends into Tortuguero's main canal. All the rooms are large and feature loads of freshly varnished hardwood. A two-bedroom, two-bathroom second-floor suite is also available. Several acres of forest behind the lodge have well-maintained trails winding their way through the trees. This is a great place to look for howler monkeys and colorful poison-arrow frogs. The hotel is run by Costa Rica Expeditions, one of the pioneers in the field of sustainable travel.

Tortuguero. www.costaricaexpeditions.com. © **800/886-2609** in the U.S. and Canada, or 2257-0766 reservations in San José or 2709-8034 at the lodge. Fax 2257-1665. 27 units. $178 double; $278 penthouse. Package rates with transportation, meals, and tours are available. AE, MC, V. **Amenities:** Restaurant; bar; small outdoor pool. *In room:* No phone.

Turtle Beach Lodge ★   This isolated ecolodge is 8km (5 miles) north of the village of Tortuguero, about 20 minutes away by boat. The grounds are set on a narrow strip of land between the Caribbean Sea and the Caño Palma canal. The accommodations are somewhat more spartan than those at the lodges listed above, but they are still clean and comfortable. The rooms are housed in a series of long buildings. Most feature exterior walls that are solid on the bottom half and pure screening above. The best rooms are the corner units, which get the most airflow and circulation. All have some form of shared or private verandas. Given its location, this is one of the more convenient lodges for viewing the turtle nestings. A small, turtle-shaped pool is in the center of the grounds, and a stable of horses is available for riding tours.

Caño Palma, Tortuguero. www.turtlebeachlodge.com. © **2248-0707** in San José, or 8837-6969 at the lodge. Fax 2257-4409. 55 units. $210 per person for 2 days/1 night; $288 per person for 3 days/2 nights. Rates double occupancy, and include round-trip transportation from San José, 3 meals daily, taxes, and tours. MC, V. **Amenities:** Restaurant; bar; lounge w/satellite TV; Internet; outdoor pool. *In room:* No phone.

INEXPENSIVE

Several basic cabinas in the village of Tortuguero offer budget lodgings for between $15 and $25 per person. **Cabinas Miss Junie** (© **2709-8102**) and **Cabinas Miss Miriam** (© **2709-8002**) are the traditional favorites, although in my opinion, the best of the batch are the **Cabinas Icaco** (www.hotelelicaco. com; © **2709-8044**), **Cabinas La Casona** (© **2709-8092**), and **Cabinas Tortuguero** (© **2709-8114**).

Casa Marbella ★ 🍃   Right in Tortuguero Village, this converted house is an excellent option for budget travelers looking for a bit more comfort and care than that offered at most of the other inexpensive in-town options. It's also a good alternative for those wishing to avoid the large groups and cattle-car–like operations of most big lodges here. The rooms all have high ceilings, tile floors, and firm mattresses. Co-owner Daryl Loth is a longtime resident and well-respected naturalist guide. He and his wife are dedicated environmentalists and actively involved in local community development and environmental conservation efforts. Breakfast is served on a little patio facing the main Tortuguero canal in back of the house. A library and lounge area complement the facilities, and a wide range of tours can be arranged. The best choices here are the two "superior" rooms, with direct views of the canal.

Tortuguero, Limón. http://casamarbella.tripod.com. ©/fax **2709-8011** or © 8833-0827. 11 units. $50 double; $60 superior. Rates include breakfast. No credit cards. *In room:* No phone, Wi-Fi.

Where to Eat

Most visitors take all their meals, as part of a package, at their hotel. The town has a couple of simple *sodas* (diners) and restaurants. The best of these are **La Casona** (☏ 2709-8092) and the **Miss Junie's** (☏ 2709-8102).

Budda Café ★ INTERNATIONAL   With a laid-back, hip vibe, this is my favorite restaurant in Tortuguero Village. Most of the seating here is on an open-air deck out over the water. The heart of the menu here is the thin-crust pizzas, crepes and pastas, but you can also get delicious salads, a just-caught tuna carpaccio, or some fresh river prawns, head-on, with a garlic butter sauce. There's a good selection of wines and cocktails, as well.

On the main canal, next to the ICE building, Tortuguero Village. ☏ **2709-8084.** www.budda cafe.com. Main courses C3,200–C12,000. No credit cards. Daily noon to 10pm.

LIMÓN: GATEWAY TO TORTUGUERO NATIONAL PARK & SOUTHERN COASTAL BEACHES

160km (99 miles) E of San José; 55km (34 miles) N of Puerto Viejo

It was just offshore from present-day Limón, in the lee of Isla Uvita, that Christopher Columbus is said to have anchored in 1502, on his fourth and final voyage to the New World. Believing that this was potentially a very rich land, he christened it Costa Rica ("Rich Coast"). While never supplying the Spanish crown with much in the way of gold or jewels, the spot where he anchored has proved over the centuries to be the best port on Costa Rica's Caribbean coast—so his judgment wasn't all bad. Today Limón is a rough-around-the-edges port city that ships millions of pounds of bananas northward every year. It also receives a fair share of the country's ocean-borne imports and a modest number of cruise ship callings. On days when a cruise ship is in port, you'll find the city bustling far beyond the norm.

Limón is not generally considered a tourist destination, and few tourists take the time to tour the city, except those stopping here on cruise ships. Very few choose to stay here, and I don't recommend it except during Carnaval—and even then you're better off in Cahuita or Puerto Viejo.

 A Fall Festival

Limón's biggest yearly event, and one of the liveliest festivals in Costa Rica, is **Carnaval**, around Columbus Day (Oct 12). For a week, languid Limón shifts into high gear for a nonstop bacchanal orchestrated to the beat of reggae, soca, and calypso music. During the revelries, residents don costumes and take to the streets in a dazzling parade of color. Festivities include marching bands, dancers, and parade floats. If you want to experience Carnaval, make your reservations early because hotels fill up fast. (This advice goes for the entire coast.)

If you want to get in some beach time while you're in Limón, hop in a taxi or a local bus and head north a few kilometers to **Playa Bonita,** a small public beach. Although the water isn't very clean and is usually too rough for swimming, the setting is much more attractive than downtown. This beach is popular with surfers.

Essentials

GETTING THERE & DEPARTING   By Car: The Guápiles Highway (CR32) heads north out of San José on Calle 3 before turning east and passing close to Barva Volcano and through the rainforests of Braulio Carrillo National Park en route to Limón. The drive takes about 2½ hours and is spectacularly beautiful, especially when it's not raining or misty. Alternately, you can take the old highway, which is also scenic but much slower. This highway heads east out of San José on Avenida Central and passes through San Pedro and then Curridabat before reaching Cartago. From Cartago on, the narrow and winding road passes through Paraíso and Turrialba before descending out of the mountains to Siquirres, where the old highway meets the new. This route takes around 4 hours, more or less, to get to Limón.

Along the Way

If you're driving to the Caribbean coast, you should consider combining the trip with a stop at the Rainforest Aerial Tram (p. 146), or the Puerto Viejo de Sarapiquí area (p. 344).

By Bus: Transportes Caribeños buses (② **2222-0610** in San José, or 2758-2575 in Limón) leave San José every hour daily between 5am and 7pm from the Caribbean bus terminal (Gran Terminal del Caribe) on Calle Central, 1 block north of Avenida 11. Friday and Sunday, the last bus leaves an hour later at 8pm. The trip duration is around 3 hours. The buses are either direct or local *(corriente),* and they don't alternate in any particularly predictable fashion. The local buses are generally older and less comfortable and stop en route to pick up passengers from the roadside. I highly recommend taking a direct bus, if possible. The fare is C2,650 one-way.

Buses leave Limón for San José every hour between 5am and 7pm, and similarly alternate between local and direct, with the last bus leaving 1 hour later on Sundays. The Limón bus terminal is on the main road into town, several blocks west of the downtown area and Parque Vargas. Buses (② **2758-1572** for the terminal) to **Cahuita** and **Puerto Viejo** leave from here roughly every hour from 5am to 7pm daily. Buses to **Punta Uva** and **Manzanillo,** both of which are south of Puerto Viejo, leave Limón daily at 5:30, 6, and 10:30am and 3 and 6pm, from the same station.

ORIENTATION   Nearly all addresses in Limón are measured from the central market, which is aptly located smack-dab in the center of town, or from Parque Vargas, which is at the east end of town fronting the sea. The cruise ship dock is just south of Parque Vargas. A pedestrian mall runs from Parque Vargas to the west for several blocks.

Cruise ships at dock in Limón.

FAST FACTS   A host of private and national banks are in the small downtown area. You can reach the **local police** at ✆ **2758-0365** and the **Red Cross** at ✆ **2758-0125**. The **Tony Facio Hospital** (✆ **2758-0580**) is just outside of downtown on the road to Playa Bonita.

What to See & Do

Limón has little for tourists to do or see. The closest true attraction, **Veragua Rainforest Park** (see below), is about a 40-minute drive.

If you end up spending any time in Limón, be sure to take a seat in **Parque Vargas** along the seawall and watch the city's citizens go about their business. Occupying 1 city block on the waterfront, this is a lush and quiet oasis in the heart of downtown. You may even spot some sloths living in the trees here. If you want to shop for souvenirs, head to the **cruise ship terminal** whenever a ship is in port, and you'll find more than your fair share of vendors. Finally, if you're interested in architecture, take a walk around town. When banana shipments built this port, local merchants erected elaborately decorated buildings, several of which have survived the city's many earthquakes, humid weather, and salty sea air. There's a certain charm in the town's fallen grace, drooping balconies, rotting woodwork, and chipped paint. One of the city's most famous buildings is known locally as the **Black Star Line** (✆ **2798-1948**), located on Avenida 5 and Calle 6. Also called Liberty Hall, this building was built in 1922, as the headquarters for Marcus Garvey's United Negro Improvement Association. Recently restored, it serves today as the city's social and cultural meeting place.

Check here for traveling art exhibits, and the occasional live music, dance, or theater performance.

Just be careful: Limón is a rough and impoverished port town. Street crime and violence are problems. Tourists should stick to the very well-worn city center, and spots mentioned here. In addition, I don't recommend walking anywhere at night. And even in the daytime, it's probably best to travel in small groups.

A ONE-STOP SHOP RAINFOREST TOURISM SPOT

Located outside of Limón in a patch of thick rainforest south of the banana town of Liverpool, **Veragua Rainforest Park** ★ (𝄢 **2296-5056;** www.veraguarainforest.com) is primarily a destination for cruise ship excursions. However, this extensive complex is a worthy stop for anyone visiting the area. Attractions include a serpentarium, butterfly garden and breeding exhibit, hummingbird garden, extensive insect exhibit, free-range rainforest frog room, zip-line canopy tour, and a short tram ride that takes you to their rainforest trail system. Along the trails, you'll find a beautiful little waterfall. A half-day tour runs $55 per adult and $45 per child, and a full-day tour runs $89 per adult and $65 per child; these tour prices don't include transportation or lunch. The park is open Tuesday through Sunday from 8am to 3pm.

Where to Stay

Hotel Playa Westfalia ★ 🛏 This is my favorite hotel in the Limón area. Located right on the beach about 10 minutes south of the city, and just a mile or so beyond the airstrip, this place offers up cool, contemporary rooms, in a quiet, laid-back environment. Rooms all feature red-tile floors, and bathrooms adorned in lively blue and yellow Mexican tiles. The second-floor master suite has a great view of the ocean. A waterfall and raised unheated Jacuzzi feed a midsized pool, and the hotel's restaurant serves good local and international cuisine. The whole thing fronts a stretch of nearly deserted beach.

Just south of Limón, just beyond the airstrip. www.hotelplayawestfalia.com. 𝄢 **2756-1300** or 2756-1661. Fax 3756-1174. 8 units. $85–$95 double; $105–$135 suite. Rates include full breakfast and taxes. AE, DC, MC, V. **Amenities:** Restaurant; Jacuzzi; outdoor pool; smoke-free rooms. *In room:* A/C, TV, minifridge, Wi-Fi.

Park Hotel ★ This is easily, and perennially, the best option in Limón proper—although there really isn't any competition. The hotel has an excellent location fronting the ocean, across the street from the fire station, and just down from Parque Vargas. Unlike much of Limón, which seems to be in a state of prolonged and steady decay, the Park Hotel receives regular and fairly competent upkeep year in and year out. Ask for a room on the ocean side of the hotel because these are brighter, quieter, and cooler than those that face the fire station, although they're also slightly more expensive. The suites have private oceanview balconies and larger bathrooms with tubs. The large, sunny dining room off the lobby serves standard Tico fare at very reasonable prices.

Av. 3, btw. calles 1 and 3 (A.P. 35–7300), Limón. 𝄢 **2798-0555.** Fax 2758-4364. 32 units. $67 double. AE, MC, V. **Amenities:** Restaurant. *In room:* A/C, TV.

Where to Eat

Dining options are pretty limited in Limón. In addition to the place listed below, the restaurant at the **Park Hotel** (see above) is a good bet. Feel free to sample some *pati*. A local staple, this fried dough concoction is stuffed with a slightly spicy ground meat filling. You'll find *pati* vendors all over downtown Limón.

Brisas del Caribe SEAFOOD/COSTA RICAN The increase in cruise ship traffic here has been a shot in the arm for this local landmark. The local cuisine served up here is dependable, if not particularly special or memorable. Still, order up a plate of fresh fish with rice and beans and some *patacones* (fried plantain chips), and you'll do fine. When the weather permits, grab a table on the sidewalk, under a big umbrella.

North side of Parque Vargas, Limón. 📞 **2758-0138.** Main courses C1,950–C6,900. AE, DC, MC, V. Daily 7:30am–9pm.

En Route South

Staying at the place listed below is a great way to combine some quiet beach time on the Caribbean coast with a more active ecolodge and bird-watching experience into one compact itinerary.

Selva Bananito Lodge ★★ 💼 The spacious raised-stilt cabins here feature an abundance of varnished woodwork, large private bathrooms, and a wraparound veranda with a hammock. Half the cabins have views of the Bananito River and a small valley; the other half have views of the Matama Mountains (part of the Talamanca mountain range). Hot water is provided by solar panels, and lighting is provided by a mix of gas lanterns and candles. The wide range of tours and activities includes rainforest hikes and horseback rides in the jungle, tree climbing, self-guided trail hikes, and even the opportunity to rappel down the face of a jungle waterfall. The owners are very involved in conservation efforts in this area, and approximately two-thirds of the 1,000 hectares (2,471 acres) here are primary forest managed as a private reserve. This place has earned "5 Leaves" in the CST Sustainable Tourism program.

Bananito (A.P. 2333-2050, San Pedro). www.selvabananito.com. 📞 **2253-8118.** Fax 2280-0820. 11 units. $260–$280 double. Rates include 3 meals daily and all taxes. No credit cards. **Amenities:** Restaurant. *In room:* No phone. You'll need a four-wheel-drive vehicle to reach the lodge itself, although most leave their rental cars in Bananito and let the lodge drive them the final bit. You can also arrange to be picked up in San José.

CAHUITA ★

200km (124 miles) E of San José; 42km (26 miles) S of Limón; 13km (8 miles) N of Puerto Viejo

Cahuita is a small beach village and the first "major" tourist destination heading south out of Limón. Nevertheless, the boom going on in Puerto Viejo and the beaches south of Puerto Viejo have in many ways passed Cahuita by. Depending on your point of view, that can be a reason to stay or to decide to head farther south. Any way you slice it, Cahuita is one of the more laid-back villages in Costa Rica. The few dirt and gravel streets here are host to a languid parade of pedestrian traffic, parted occasionally by a bicycle, car, or bus. After a short time, you'll find yourself slipping into the heat-induced torpor that affects anyone who ends up here.

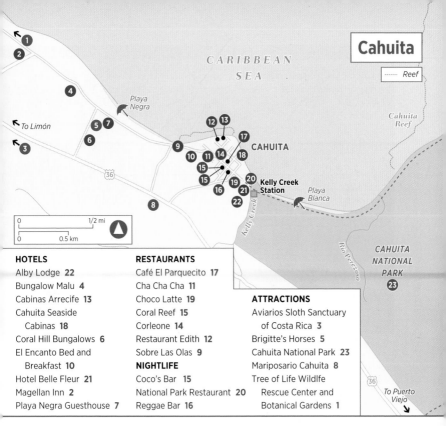

Cahuita

······ Reef

CARIBBEAN SEA

Playa Negra

To Limón

CAHUITA

Kelly Creek Station

Playa Blanca

CAHUITA NATIONAL PARK

To Puerto Viejo

0   1/2 mi
0   0.5 km

HOTELS
Alby Lodge **22**
Bungalow Malu **4**
Cabinas Arrecife **13**
Cahuita Seaside
    Cabinas **18**
Coral Hill Bungalows **6**
El Encanto Bed and
    Breakfast **10**
Hotel Belle Fleur **21**
Magellan Inn **2**
Playa Negra Guesthouse **7**

RESTAURANTS
Café El Parquecito **17**
Cha Cha Cha **11**
Choco Latte **19**
Coral Reef **15**
Corleone **14**
Restaurant Edith **12**
Sobre Las Olas **9**
NIGHTLIFE
Coco's Bar **15**
National Park Restaurant **20**
Reggae Bar **16**

ATTRACTIONS
Aviarios Sloth Sanctuary
    of Costa Rica **3**
Brigitte's Horses **5**
Cahuita National Park **23**
Mariposario Cahuita **8**
Tree of Life Wildlfe
    Rescue Center and
    Botanical Gardens **1**

The village traces its roots to Afro-Caribbean fishermen and laborers who settled in this region in the mid-1800s, and today the population is still primarily English-speaking blacks whose culture and language set them apart from other Costa Ricans.

People come to Cahuita for its miles of pristine beaches, which stretch both north and south from town. The southern beaches, the forest behind them, and the coral reef offshore (one of just a handful in Costa Rica) are all part of **Cahuita National Park ★★**. Silt and pesticides washing down from nearby banana plantations have taken a heavy toll on the coral reefs, so don't expect the snorkeling to be world-class. But on a calm day, it can be pretty good, and the beaches are idyllic every day. It can rain almost any time of year here, but the most dependably dry months are September and October.

Essentials

GETTING THERE & DEPARTING   By Car: Follow the directions above for getting to Limón. As you enter Limón, about 5 blocks before the busiest section of downtown, watch for a paved road to the right, just before the railroad tracks. Take this road (CR36) south to Cahuita, passing the airstrip and the beach on your left as you leave Limón. Alternatively, a turnoff with signs for

A Cahuita National Park trail.

Sixaola and La Bomba is several miles before Limón. This winding shortcut skirts the city and puts you on the coastal road (CR36) several miles south of Limón.

By Bus: Mepe express buses (© **2257-8129**) leave San José daily at 6 and 10am, noon, and 2 and 4pm from the Caribbean bus terminal (Gran Terminal del Caribe) on Calle Central, 1 block north of Avenida 11. The trip's duration is 4 hours; the fare is C3,910. During peak periods, extra buses are often added. However, it's wise to check because this bus line (Mepe) is one of the most fickle.

Alternatively, you can catch a bus to **Limón** (see above) and then transfer to a Cahuita- or Puerto Viejo–bound bus (© **2758-1572**) in Limón. These latter buses leave roughly every hour between 5am and 7pm from the main bus terminal in Limón. Buses from Limón to Manzanillo also stop in Cahuita and leave from the same spot at 6 and 10:30am, and 3 and 6pm. The trip takes 1 hour; the fare is C1,005.

Interbus (© **2283-5573;** www.interbusonline.com) has a daily bus that leaves San José for Cahuita at 7:50am. The fare is $40. Interbus buses leave Cahuita daily at both 7:20am and 3:15pm. Interbus will pick you up at most area hotels in both San José and Cahuita, and offers connections to various other destinations around Costa Rica.

Buses departing **Puerto Viejo** and Sixaola (on the Panama border) stop in Cahuita roughly every hour between 8am and 8pm en route to San José. However, the schedule is far from precise, so it's always best to check with your hotel. Moreover, these buses are often full, particularly on weekends and throughout the high season. To avoid standing in the aisle all the way to San José, it is sometimes better to take a bus first to Limón and then catch one of the frequent Limón–San José buses. Buses to Limón pass through Cahuita regularly throughout the day. Another tactic I've used is to take a morning bus to Puerto Viejo, spend the day down there, and board a direct bus to San José at its point of origin, thereby snagging a seat.

ORIENTATION Cahuita only has about eight dirt streets. The highway runs parallel to the coast, with three main access roads running perpendicular. The northernmost of these access roads bypasses town and brings you to the northern end of Playa Negra. It's marked with signs for the Magellan Inn and other hotels up on this end. The second road in brings you to the southern end of Playa Negra, a half-mile closer to town. The third road is the principal entrance into town. The village's main street in town, which runs parallel to the highway, dead-ends at the national park entrance (a footbridge over a small stream).

Buses drop their passengers off at a bus terminal at the back of a small strip mall on the main entrance road into town. If you come in on the bus and are staying at a lodge on Playa Negra, there will be cabs waiting. Alternately, you can head out walking north on the street that runs between Coco's Bar and the small park. This road curves to the left and continues a mile or so out to Playa Negra.

FAST FACTS The police station (℅ **2755-0217**) is located where the road from Playa Negra turns into town. The post office (℅ **2755-0096**) is next door. You'll find a well-equipped pharmacy, **Farmacia Cahuita** (℅ **2755-0505**), as well as a Banco de Costa Rica and ATM, in the small strip mall in front the bus station. Several Internet cafes are around the central downtown area of the village. If you can't find a **cab** in town, ask your hotel to call you one, or try **Alejandro** (℅ **8875-3209**) or **Dino** (℅ **2755-0012** or 8340-2354).

Exploring Cahuita National Park ★★

This little gem of a national park sits at the southern edge of Cahuita town. Although the pristine white-sand beach, with its picture-perfect line of coconut palms and lush coastal forest backing it, is the main draw here, the park was actually created to preserve the 240-hectare (787-acre) **coral reef** that lies just offshore. The reef contains 35 species of coral and provides a haven for hundreds of brightly colored tropical fish. You can walk on the beach itself or follow the trail that runs through the forest just behind the beach to check out the reef.

 You Can Bring It with You

I recommend packing a picnic lunch, plenty of water, and some snorkel gear and hiking out along the inland rainforest trail, all the way out to Punta Cahuita. Once there, you can spread out a blanket or some towels, snorkel on the reef, and swim in the tide pools, before enjoying your lunch. You can walk along the beach for most of the return trip to town, and stop for a cooling dip or two if the mood strikes.

One of the best places to swim is just before or beyond the **Río Perezoso (Lazy River),** several hundred meters inside Cahuita National Park. The trail behind the beach is great for bird-watching, and if you're lucky, you might see some monkeys or a sloth. The loud grunting sounds you'll hear off in the distance are the calls of howler monkeys, which can be heard from more than a kilometer away. Nearer at hand, you're likely to hear crabs scuttling amid the dry leaves on the forest floor—a half-dozen or so species of land crabs live in this region—my favorites are the bright orange-and-purple ones.

The trail behind the beach stretches a little more than 9km (5.6 miles) to the southern end of the park at **Puerto Vargas** (© **2755-0302**), where you'll find a beautiful white-sand beach. The best section of reef is off the point at Punta Cahuita, and you can snorkel here. If you don't dawdle, the 3.8km (2.35-mile) hike to Punta Cahuita should take a little over an hour each way—although I'd allow plenty of extra time to marvel at the flora and fauna, and take a dip or two in the sea. Bring plenty of mosquito repellent because this area can be buggy.

Although you can snorkel from the shore at Punta Cahuita, it's best to have a boat take you out to the nicest coral heads just offshore. A 3-hour **snorkel trip** costs between $15 and $30 per person, with equipment. You can arrange one with any of the local tour companies listed below. **Note:** These trips are best taken when the seas are calm—for safety's sake, visibility, and comfort.

ENTRY POINTS, FEES & REGULATIONS The **in-town park entrance** is just over a footbridge at the end of the village's main street. It has restroom facilities, changing rooms, and storage lockers. This is the best place to enter if you just want to spend the day on the beach and maybe take a little hike in the bordering forest.

Howler monkeys.

Cahuita National Park beach.

The alternate park entrance is at the southern end of the park in **Puerto Vargas.** This is where you should come if you plan to camp at the park or if you don't feel up to hiking a couple of hours to reach the good snorkeling spots. The road to Puerto Vargas is approximately 5km (3 miles) south of Cahuita on the left.

Officially, **admission** is $10 per person per day, but this is collected only at the Puerto Vargas entrance. You can enter the park from the town of Cahuita for free or with a voluntary contribution. The park is open from dawn to dusk for day visitors.

GETTING THERE **By Car:** The turnoff for the Puerto Vargas entrance is clearly marked 5km (3 miles) south of Cahuita.

By Bus: Your best bet is to get off a Puerto Viejo- or Sixaola-bound bus at the turnoff for the Puerto Vargas entrance (well marked, but tell the bus driver in advance). The guard station/entrance is only about 500m (1,640 ft.) down this road. However, the campsites are several kilometers farther, so it's a long hike with a heavy pack.

 Damaged & Endangered

While patches of living, vibrant reef survive off Costa Rica's Caribbean coast, much of it has been killed off, or is severely threatened by over-fishing, pollution, rain, and mud run-off during the rainy season. Much of the damage can be traced to the massive banana plantations that line this coastline, which have had a direct role in increasing the amount of muddy run-off and dumped tons of plastic and pesticides into the fragile, inshore reef systems.

Beaches & Activities Outside the Park

Outside the park the best place for swimming is **Playa Negra.** The stretch right in front of the Playa Negra Guesthouse (p. 485) is my favorite spot. The waves here are often good for bodysurfing, boogie boarding, or surfing. If you want to rent a board or try a surf lesson, check in with Rennie at **Willie's Tours** (see below).

Cahuita has plenty of options for organized adventure trips or tours. I recommend **Cahuita Tours** (✆ **2755-0000;** www.cahuitatours.com), on the village's main street heading out toward Playa Negra. They offer a wide range of tour and activity options, including snorkeling trips ($25–$35 per person) and jungle hikes ($25–$30).

Willie's Tours (✆ **2755-1024;** www.williestourscostarica.com), also on the main road in the center of town, and **Roberto Tours** (✆ **2755-0117**), on the main road a half-block south of the small central park, offer similar tours at similar prices. Most of the companies offer multiday trips to Tortuguero, as well as to Bocas del Toro, Panama.

Brigitte (✆ **2755-0053;** www.brigittecahuita.com) offers guided horse-back tours for $35 to $75. She also rents mountain bikes for C3,500 per day, and even has a few rooms available.

On the main highway, just north of the main entrance to Cahuita, is the **Mariposario Cahuita** (✆ **2755-0361**), a large, informative butterfly-farm attraction that charges $10 and is open Monday to Friday from 9am to 4pm, and weekends by appointment. It's best to come in the early morning on a sunny day, when the butterflies are most active.

Bird-watchers and sloth lovers should head north 9km (5½ miles) to **Aviarios Sloth Sanctuary of Costa Rica** ★★ (✆/fax **2750-0775;** www.sloth rescue.org). Their signature tour features an informative visit to their sloth reha-bilitation project and learning center, as well as a 1-hour canoe tour through the

A sloth at the Aviarios Sloth Sanctuary of Costa Rica.

Cahuita locals.

surrounding estuary and river system. More than 330 species of birds have been spotted here. You'll get an up-close look at a range of rescued wild sloths, both adults and babies, as well as several bred in captivity. After, you can hike their trail system and look for sloths in the wild. Tours begin at 8am, with the last tour of the day leaving at 2:30pm. It's best to make reservations in advance. These folks also offer up a few cozy and quaint rooms right on-site if you want to spend more time exploring the bird-watching, wildlife, and sloth rescue project here.

Toward the northern end of the dirt road leading out beyond Playa Negra is the **Tree of Life Wildlife Rescue Center and Botanical Gardens** (📞 **2755-0014;** www.treeoflifecostarica.com). Stroll through extensive, well-maintained gardens, where a series of large cages house a range of rescued and recovering local fauna, including toucans, monkeys, coatimundi, deer, wild pigs, or peccaries. This place is open daily from 8am to 3pm. Admission is $12.

If you're looking to study Spanish here, check in with **Icari The Spanish School** (📞 **2755-1096;** www.icari-spanishlearning.com). A variety of group and individual class options are available.

Shopping

For a wide selection of beachwear, local crafts, cheesy souvenirs, and batik clothing, try **Boutique Coco,** which has moved to the small strip mall near the bus terminal, or **Boutique Bambata,** which is on the main road near the entrance to the park. The latter is also a good place to have your hair wrapped in colorful threads and strung with beads. Right in the center of town, **Bodhi's Books & Gifts** is another good option for souvenirs. Heading north out of town, similar wares are offered at the **Cahuita Tours** gift shop. For something less formal, local and itinerant artisans in makeshift stands near the park entrance sell handmade jewelry and crafts.

Cahuita's Calypso Legend

Walter "Gavitt" Ferguson, who turned 92 in 2011, is a living legend. For decades, Ferguson labored and sang in obscurity. Occasionally he would record a personalized cassette tape of original tunes for an interested tourist willing to part with $5. Finally, in 2002, Ferguson was recorded by the local label Papaya Music (www.papayamusic.com). Today, he has two CDs of original songs, *Babylon* and *Dr. Bombodee.* Ask around town and you should be able to find a copy. If you're lucky, you might even bump into Gavitt himself.

If you're interested in the region, pick up a copy of Paula Palmer's *What Happen: A Folk-History of Costa Rica's Talamanca Coast.* The book is a history of Costa Rica's Caribbean coast based on interviews with many of the area's oldest residents. Much of it is in the traditional Creole language, from which the title is taken. It makes for a fun and interesting read, and you just might meet someone mentioned in the book.

Where to Stay

In addition to the places listed below, **Bungalow Malu** (✆ 2755-0114) is a pretty collection of individual bungalows located just across the dirt road from a long stretch of Black Beach, while **Coral Hill Bungalows** ★ (www.coralhill bungalows.com; ✆ 2755-0479) offers up three individual bungalows and a separate two-story house, in a lush garden setting, about a block or so inland from the beach.

MODERATE

El Encanto Bed & Breakfast ★★   The individual bungalows at this little bed-and-breakfast are set in from the road on spacious and well-kept grounds. The bungalows themselves are also spacious and have attractive touches that include wooden bed frames, arched windows, Mexican-tile floors, Guatemalan bedspreads, and framed Panamanian *molas* hanging on the walls. A separate two-story, three-bedroom, two-bathroom house has a full kitchen. Hearty breakfasts are served in the small open dining room surrounded by lush gardens. The hotel also has a small kidney-shaped pool, a wood-floored meditation and yoga hall, and an open-air massage room.

Cahuita (just outside of town on the road to Playa Negra). www.elencantocahuita.com. ✆ **2755-0113.** Fax 2755-0432. 8 units. $75 double; $190 house. Rates include full breakfast. Rates slightly lower in off season; higher during peak weeks. MC, V. **Amenities:** Small outdoor pool; Wi-Fi. *In room:* No phone.

Magellan Inn ★   With an understated sense of tropical sophistication, this small inn has thrived over the years. The tile-floor rooms have French doors, vertical blinds, compact bathrooms with hardwood counters, and two joined single beds. Each room has its own tiled veranda with a Persian rug and bamboo sitting chairs. Half of the rooms have air-conditioning, and one has satellite television. Although a ceiling fan spins over each bed, the non-air-conditioned rooms could use a bit more ventilation. The combination bar/lounge and dining room features even more Persian-style rugs and wicker furniture. Most memorable of all are the hotel's sunken pool and lush gardens, both of which are built into a crevice in the ancient coral reef that underlies this entire region.

At the far end of Playa Negra (about 2km/1¼ miles north of Cahuita), Cahuita. www.magellaninn. com. ☎/fax **2755-0035**. 6 units. $68–$74 double; $90–$96 double with A/C. Rates include continental breakfast. Rates slightly lower in off season; higher during peak weeks. AE, MC, V. **Amenities:** Bar; lounge; small outdoor pool. *In room:* A/C (in some), no phone, Wi-Fi.

Playa Negra Guesthouse ★★ ☺ Expansive gardens and grounds, a beautiful pool, attentive owners, cozy accommodations, and direct beach access make this my top choice in Cahuita. Rooms are immaculate and well-lit and most come with a wet bar, in addition to the coffeemaker and minifridge. My favorite option for couples are the two private cabins, while the two independent two-bedroom cottages are perfect for families, with plenty of space, a full kitchen, and large veranda. The hotel is just across the road from a wonderful section of Playa Negra.

On Playa Negra (about 1.5km/1 mile north of town), Cahuita. www.playanegra.cr. ☎ **2755-0127**. Fax 2755-0481. 6 units. $60–$80 double room; $75–$85 cabin; $100–$120 cottage. AE, MC, V. **Amenities:** Small outdoor pool. *In room:* Minifridge, no phone, Wi-Fi.

INEXPENSIVE

In addition to the places listed below, **Cahuita Seaside Cabinas** (www.cahuita side.net; ☎ **2755-0027**) and its somewhat funky collection of budget rooms is worth considering; its rooms are set just a few feet from the water in the heart of town. Another option is **Hotel Belle Fleur** (www.hotelbellefleur.com; ☎ **2755-0283**), which has neat and cheery rooms set near the main road, close to the national park entrance.

Alby Lodge ★ ✦ With the feel of a small village, Alby Lodge is a fascinating little place hand-built by its German owners. Although the four small cabins are close to the center of the village, they're surrounded by a large lawn and feel secluded. The cabins are quintessentially tropical, with thatch roofs, mosquito nets, hardwood floors and beams, big shuttered windows, tile bathrooms, and a hammock slung on the front porch. There's no restaurant here, but you may cook your own meals in a communal kitchen area if you wish. The turnoff for the lodge is on your right just before you reach the national park entrance; the hotel is about 136m (446 ft.) down a narrow, winding lane from here.

Cahuita. www.albylodge.com. ☎/fax **2755-0031**. 4 units. $50 double. $5 for extra person. No credit cards. *In room:* No phone, Wi-Fi.

Cabinas Arrecife Located near the water, next to Restaurant Edith (p. 486), this row of basic rooms is an excellent budget choice in Cahuita. Each room comes with a double and a single bed, a table fan, and tile floors. There's not a lot of room to move around, but things are pretty clean and well kept for this price range. A shared veranda offers a glimpse of the sea through a dense stand of coconut palms. The tiny pool fronts the ocean. If you want to be closer to the sea, grab one of the hammocks strung on the palms or sit in the small, open restaurant, which serves breakfast every day and dinners on demand.

Cahuita (about 100m/328 ft. east of the post office). www.cabinasarrecife.com. ☎/fax **2755-0081**. 12 units. $30 double. AE, MC, V. **Amenities:** Restaurant; outdoor pool. *In room:* No phone.

Where to Eat

Coconut meat and milk figure into a lot of the regional cuisine here. Most nights, local women cook up pots of various local specialties and sell them from the front porches of the two discos or from streetside stands around town; a full meal will cost you around $2 to $5.

In addition to the places listed below, **Corleone** (℡ **2755-0341;** toward the north end of the main road in town) is the place to go for pizza, pastas, and Italian specialties. **Coral Reef** (℡ **2755-0133,** at the main crossroads in town) is a good local restaurant, with a cozy open-air second-floor dining space that's great for people-watching. Another favorite is **Café El Parquecito** (℡ **2755-0279**), which serves up local and international fare throughout the day, in an open-air space next to the small park in the center of town, as well as popular breakfasts featuring fresh crepes.

Cha Cha Cha ★★ SEAFOOD/INTERNATIONAL   Fresh seafood and grilled meats, simply and expertly prepared—what more could you ask for from a casual, open-air restaurant in a funky beach town? In addition to the fresh catch of the day and filet mignon, the eclectic menu here includes everything from jerk chicken to Thai shrimp salad. The grilled squid salad with a citrus dressing is one of the house specialties and deservedly so. The restaurant occupies the ground floor of an old wooden building, with only a half-dozen or so tables that fill up fast.

On the main road in town, 3 blocks north of Coco's Bar. ℡ **8780-2593.** Reservations recommended during the high season. Main courses C5,000–C10,000. No credit cards. Tues–Sun 2–10pm.

Choco Latte ★ COFFEEHOUSE/CREOLE   Light, airy, and cheerful, this simple yellow clapboard cafe is a great choice for breakfast or lunch. I recommend grabbing a table on the small outdoor patio. The open kitchen turns out great waffles, pancakes, and eggs for breakfast. Lunch options range from juicy burgers to *casados*. Throughout the day, fresh baked goods (cinnamon rolls, carrot cake, muffins, and such) are offered up, along with cold and hot coffee concoctions.

On the main road in town, ½ block south of Coco's Bar. ℡ **2755-0010.** Main courses C1,500–C3,000. No credit cards. Tues–Fri 6:30am–2pm, Sat–Sun 6:30am–midnight.

Restaurant Edith CREOLE/SEAFOOD   This place is a local institution. Miss Edith's daughters do most of the cooking and serving these days, but you will often find the restaurant's namesake matriarch on hand. The long menu has lots of local seafood dishes and Creole combinations such as yuca in coconut milk with meat or vegetables. The sauces' spice and zest are a welcome change from the typically bland fare served up elsewhere in Costa Rica. It's often crowded, so don't be bashful about sitting down with total strangers at any of the big tables. Hours can be erratic; it sometimes closes without warning, and service can be slow and gruff at times. After you've ordered, it's usually no more than 45 minutes until your meal arrives. As an added bonus, these folks also offer cooking classes, so you can whip up some of the Caribbean classics when you get home.

By the police station, Cahuita. ℡ **2755-0248.** Reservations are accepted. Main courses $5–$23. No credit cards. Mon–Sat 7am–10pm.

Sobre Las Olas ★ SEAFOOD/ITALIAN   Set on a slight rise of rocks above a coral cove and breaking waves, this place has by far the best location in Cahuita.

The Italian owners dish up a mix of local and Italian fare. They serve excellent fresh squid or shrimp in a tangy local coconut milk sauce, as well as a host of pasta dishes. The fresh grilled snapper is always a good way to go. I especially like this place for lunch, since you can really enjoy the view of the clear blue Caribbean Sea then. If weather permits, grab one of the outdoor tables set in the shade of coconut palms. After you finish eating, slide over and into one of the hammocks strung between those palms.

Just north of town on the road to Playa Negra. ☎ **2755-0109.** Main courses C5,700–C12,500. AE, MC, V. Wed–Mon noon–10pm.

Cahuita After Dark

Coco's Bar ★, a classic Caribbean watering hole at the main crossroads in town, has traditionally been the place to spend your nights (or days, for that matter) if you like cold beer and very loud reggae and soca music. Toward the park entrance, the **National Park Restaurant** has a popular bar and disco on most nights during the high season and on weekends during the off season, while out toward Playa Negra, the **Reggae Bar** has a convivial vibe, with thumping tropical tunes blasting most nights.

PUERTO VIEJO ★★

200km (124 miles) E of San José; 55km (34 miles) S of Limón

Puerto Viejo is the Caribbean coast's hottest destination. And not just because of the sometimes stifling heat. Even though Puerto Viejo is farther down the road from Cahuita, it's much, much more popular, with a distinctly livelier vibe and

A beached barge by Puerto Viejo.

many more hotels and restaurants to choose from. Much of this is due to the scores of surfers who come to ride the town's famous and fearsome Salsa Brava wave, and only slightly mellower Playa Cocles (p. 504) beach break. Nonsurfers can enjoy other excellent swimming beaches, plenty of active adventure options, nearby rainforest trails, and the collection of great local and international restaurants.

This area gets plenty of rain, just like the rest of the coast (Feb–Mar and Sept–Oct are your best bets for sun, although it's not guaranteed).

Essentials

GETTING THERE & DEPARTING   By Car: To reach Puerto Viejo, continue south from Cahuita on CR36 for another 16km (10 miles). Watch for a prominent and well-marked fork in the highway. The right-hand fork continues on to Bribri, Sixaola, and the Panamanian border. The left-hand fork (it actually appears to be a straight shot) takes you into Puerto Viejo on 5km (3 miles) of sporadically paved road.

By Bus: Mepe express buses (© **2257-8129** in San José, or 2750-0023 in Puerto Viejo) to Puerto Viejo leave San José daily at 6 and 10am, noon, and 2 and 4pm from the Caribbean terminal (Gran Terminal del Caribe) on Calle Central, 1 block north of Avenida 11. The trip's duration is 4½ to 5 hours; the fare is C4,545. During peak periods extra buses are sometimes added. Always ask if the bus is continuing on to **Manzanillo** (especially helpful if you're staying in a hotel south of town).

Interbus (© **2283-5573;** www.interbusonline.com) has a daily bus that leaves San José for Puerto Viejo at 7:30am. The fare is $40. Interbus buses leave Puerto Viejo daily at 7am and 2pm. Interbus will pick you up at most hotels in both San José and Puerto Viejo, and offers connections to various other destinations around Costa Rica.

Alternatively, you can catch a bus to **Limón** (p. 472) and then transfer to a Puerto Viejo–bound bus in Limón. These latter buses (© **2758-1572**) leave roughly every hour between 5am and 7pm from the main terminal in Limón. Buses from Limón to Manzanillo also stop in Puerto Viejo and leave daily at 5:30, 6, and 10:30am and 3 and 6pm. The trip takes 1½ hours; the fare is C1,505.

If you arrive in Puerto Viejo by bus, be leery of hucksters and touts offering you hotel rooms. In most cases, they work on a small commission from whatever hotel or cabina is hiring, and, in some cases, they'll steer you away from one of my recommended hotels or falsely claim that it is full.

Express buses leave Puerto Viejo for San José daily at 9 and 11am and 4pm. Buses for Limón leave daily roughly every hour between 7am and 8pm. However, this schedule is subject to change, so it's always best to check with your hotel. Buses to **Punta Uva** and **Manzanillo** leave Puerto Viejo about a half-dozen times throughout the day.

ORIENTATION   The road in from the highway runs parallel to Playa Negra, or Black Sand Beach (not the beach in Cahuita), for a couple of hundred meters before entering the village of Puerto Viejo, which has all of about 10 dirt streets. The sea is on your left and forested hills on your right as you come into town. It's another 15km (9⅓ miles) south to Manzanillo. This road is paved all the way to Manzanillo, although many sections are nonetheless in fairly rough shape.

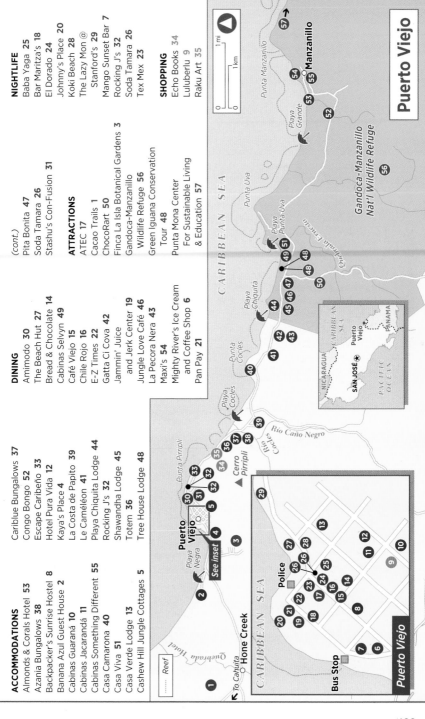

ACCOMMODATIONS

Almonds & Corals Hotel 53
Azania Bungalows 38
Backpacker's Sunrise Hostel 8
Banana Azul Guest House 2
Cabinas Guaraná 10
Cabinas Jacarandá 11
Cabinas Something Different 55
Casa Camarona 40
Casa Verde Lodge 13
Casa Viva 51
Cashew Hill Jungle Cottages 5

Cariblue Bungalows 37
Congo Bongo 52
Escape Caribeño 33
Hotel Pura Vida 12
Kaya's Place 4
La Costa de Papito 39
Le Caméléon 41
Playa Chiquita Lodge 44
Rocking J's 32
Shawandha Lodge 45
Totem 36
Tree House Lodge 48

DINING

Amimodo 30
The Beach Hut 27
Bread & Chocolate 14
Cabinas Selvyn 49
Café Viejo 15
Chile Rojo 16
E-Z Times 22
Gatta Ci Cova 42
Jammin' Juice
  and Jerk Center 19
Jungle Love Café 46
La Pecora Nera 43
Maxi's 54
Mighty River's Ice Cream
  and Coffee Shop 6
Pan Pay 21

(cont.)
Pita Bonita 47
Soda Tamara 26
Stashu's Con-Fusion 31

ATTRACTIONS

ATEC 17
Cacao Trails 1
ChocoRart 50
Finca La Isla Botanical Gardens 3
Gandoca-Manzanillo
  Wildlife Refuge 56
Green Iguana Conservation
  Tour 48
Punta Mona Center
  For Sustainable Living
  & Education 57

NIGHTLIFE

Baba Yaga 25
Bar Maritza's 18
El Dorado 24
Johnny's Place 20
Koki Beach 28
The Lazy Mon @
  Stanford's 29
Mango Sunset Bar 7
Rocking J's 32
Soda Tamara 26
Tex Mex 23

SHOPPING

Echo Books 34
Luluberlu 9
Raku Art 35

Puerto Viejo

A handful of taxi drivers are in town. You'll either find them hanging around the *parquecito* (little park), or you can try calling **Bull** (© 2750-0112 or 8836-8219) or **Taxi Kale** (© 8340-2338). You can rent scooters and bicycles from several operators in town. I like **Red Eye Scooter Rentals** (© 8860-8588), which is on the south side of town, across from Stanfords.

FAST FACTS **Public phones** are located around town and at several hotels. Those looking to change money should head to the **Banco de Costa Rica** branch on the main road in town. A **Banco Nacional** branch is in Bribri, about 10km (6 miles) away. Both of these banks have ATMs. You'll find the **post office** (© 2750-0404) in a small strip mall behind Café Viejo. A **Guardia Rural police office** (© 2750-0230) is on the beach, near Johnny's Place (see later in this chapter).

Several little Internet cafes are around town. There are also a couple of self- and full-service laundromats—the one at **Café Rico** (© 2750-0510) will give you a free cup of coffee, cappuccino, or espresso while you wait.

What to See & Do

CULTURAL & ADVENTURE TOURS The **Asociación Talamanqueña de Ecoturismo y Conservación ★★** (ATEC; Talamancan Association of Ecotourism and Conservation; © 2750-0398 or ©/fax 2750-0191; www.ateccr.org), across the street from the Soda Tamara, is a local organization concerned with preserving the environment and cultural heritage of this area and promoting ecologically sound development. (If you plan to stay in Puerto Viejo for an extended period of time and would like to contribute to the community, ask about volunteering.) In addition to functioning as the local information center, Internet cafe, and traveler's hub, ATEC runs a little shop that sells T-shirts, maps, posters, and books.

ATEC also offers quite a few tours, including **half-day walks** that focus on nature and either the local Afro-Caribbean culture or the indigenous Bribri culture. These walks pass through farms and forests, and along the way you'll learn about local history, customs, medicinal plants, and Indian mythology, and have an opportunity to see sloths, monkeys, iguanas, keel-billed toucans, and other wildlife. A range of

A bare-throated tiger heron.

Cacao fruit.

different walks lead through the nearby **Bribri Indians' Kéköldi Reserve,** as well as more strenuous hikes through the primary rainforest. **Bird walks** and **night walks** will help you spot more of the area wildlife; there are even overnight treks. The local guides have a wealth of information and make a hike through the forest a truly educational experience. ATEC can arrange snorkeling trips to the nearby coral reefs, as well as snorkeling and fishing trips in dugout canoes, and everything from surf lessons to dance classes. ATEC can also help you arrange overnight and multiday **camping trips** into the Talamanca Mountains and through neighboring indigenous reserves, as well as trips to Tortuguero and even a 7- to 10-day transcontinental trek to the Pacific coast. Half-day tours (and night walks) are $25 to $45, and full-day tours run between $50 and $75. Some tours require minimum groups of 5 or 10 people and several days' advance notice. The ATEC office is open daily from 8am to 9pm.

Local tour operators **Aventuras Bravas** ★★ (© 2750-0626; www.braveadventure.net), **Exploradores Outdoors** ★★ (© 2750-2020; www.exploradoresoutdoors.com), and **Terraventuras** ★ (© 2750-0750; www.terraventuras.com) all offer a host of half- and full-day adventure tours into the jungle or sea for between $35 and $150 per person. One popular tour is Terraventuras' zip-line canopy tour, which features 23 treetop platforms, a large harnessed swing, and a rappel.

For horseback riding, check in with **Seahorse Stables** (© 8859-6435; www.horsebackridingincostarica.com).

Scuba divers can check in with **Reef Runners Dive Shop** (© 2750-0480; www.reefrunnerdivers.com) or **Puerto Viejo Scuba Dive** ★ (© 2750-0919; http://puertoviejoscuba.com). Both operators frequent a variety of dive sites between Punta Uva and Manzanillo, and if you're lucky the seas will be calm and visibility good—although throughout most of the year it can be a bit rough and murky here. Reef Runners has an office in downtown Puerto Viejo. Rates run between $75 and $110 for a two-tank boat dive.

A LITTLE MIND & BODY REVITALIZATION   If you're looking for some day-spa pampering, check out **Indulgence Spa** ★★ (© 2750-0536). Located at La Costa de Papito (see below), these folks have a wide range of massage and treatment options at reasonable rates. They make many of their own oils, masks, wraps, and exfoliants. They also have an in-house salon.

Bliss Massage Center (© 2756-8224; www.blisscostarica.com) offers up a similar menu of treatment options in the minimall in the center of downtown.

A spa treatment at Pure Jungle Spa.

Cacao beans drying in the sun.

Better suited to a longer stay or organized retreat, **Samasati** (www. samasati.com; © **800/563-9643** in the U.S., or 2756-8015 in Costa Rica) is a lovely jungle yoga retreat and spa, with spectacular hillside views of the Caribbean Sea and surrounding forests. Rates here run between $115 and $185 per person per day, depending on occupancy and room type, and include three vegetarian meals per day and taxes. A wide range of tour, massage, and yoga packages are available. If you're staying elsewhere in Puerto Viejo or Cahuita, you can come up for yoga classes ($15), meditation ($5), or private massages ($110–$200) with advance notice. Samasati is located a couple of kilometers before Puerto Viejo (near the turnoff for Bribri) and roughly 1.6km (1 mile) up into the jungle.

NOT YOUR EVERYDAY GARDENS One of the nicest ways to spend a day in Puerto Viejo is to visit the **Finca La Isla Botanical Gardens ★★** (© **2750-0046** or 8886-8530; www.costaricacaribbean.com), a couple hundred meters inland from the Black Sand Beach on a side road just north of El Pizote lodge. Peter Kring and his late wife Lindy poured time and love into the creation of this meandering collection of native and imported tropical flora. You'll see medicinal, commercial, and just plain wild flowering plants, fruits, herbs, trees, and bushes. Visitors get to gorge on whatever is ripe at the moment. A rigorous rainforest loop trail leaves from the grounds. The gardens are generally open Friday through Monday from 10am to 4pm, but visits at other times can sometimes be arranged in advance. Entrance to the garden is $5 per person for a self-guided tour of the trails (you can buy their trail map for an extra $1), or $10 for a 2½ hour guided tour (minimum of three people).

Cacao Trails ★ (© 2756-8186; www.cacaotrails.com) is a one-stop attraction featuring botanical gardens, a small serpentarium, an open-air museum demonstrating cacao cultivation and processing, and a series of trails. There's also a large open-air restaurant, and a swimming pool. You can take canoe rides on the bordering Carbon River, and even watch leatherback sea turtles lay their eggs during the nesting season (p. 233). Admission to the attraction is $25, including a guided tour. A full-day tour, including lunch and a canoe trip, as well as the guided tour, costs $47. During turtle nesting season, they do night tours to watch sea turtles lay their eggs.

SUNNING & SURFING **Surfing** has historically been the main draw here, but increasing numbers of folks are coming for the miles of beautiful and uncrowded **beaches ★★**, acres of lush rainforests, and laid-back atmosphere. If you aren't a surfer, the same activities that prevail in any quiet beach town are the norm here—sunbathe, go for a walk on the beach, read a book, or take a nap. If you have more energy, there's a host of tours and hiking options, or you can rent a bicycle or a horse. For swimming and sunbathing, locals like to hang out on the small patches of sand in front of the Lazy Mon @ Stanford's and Johnny's Place. Small, protected tide pools are in front of each of these bars for cooling off. The Lazy Mon has several hammocks and you're likely to stumble upon a pickup beach volleyball match or soccer game here.

If you want a more open patch of sand and sea, head north out to **Playa Negra,** along the road into town, or, better yet, to the beaches south of town around Punta Uva and all the way down to Manzanillo, where the coral reefs keep the surf much more manageable (see "Manzanillo & the Manzanillo–Gandoca Wildlife Refuge," below).

Just offshore from the tiny village park is a shallow reef where powerful storm-generated waves sometimes reach 6m (20 ft.). **Salsa Brava ★★★**, as it's known, is the prime surf break on the Caribbean coast. Even when the waves are small, this spot is recommended only for very experienced surfers because of the danger of the reef. Other popular beach breaks are south of town on Playa Cocles. If you're interested in surf lessons or want to rent a board, check in with **Aventuras Bravas ★★** (© 2750-0626; www.braveadventure.net), which offers a range of group and private surf lessons, as well as weeklong all-inclusive surf camps.

Several operators and makeshift roadside stands offer bicycles, scooters, boogie boards, surfboards, and snorkel gear for rent. Shop around to compare prices and the quality of the equipment before settling on any one.

ANOTHER WAY TO GET WET & WILD **Exploradores Outdoors ★★** (© 2222-6262 in San José, or 2750-2020 in Puerto Viejo; www.exploradoresoutdoors.com) runs daily white-water rafting trips on the Pacuare and Reventazón rivers. The full-day trip, including transportation, breakfast, and lunch, is $99. If you want to combine white-water rafting with your transportation to or from the Caribbean coast, they can pick you up at your hotel in San José or La Fortuna with all your luggage, take you for a day of white-water rafting, and drop you off at day's end at your hotel anywhere on the Caribbean coast from Cahuita to Manzanillo. You can choose to use the option in the other direction, getting dropped off at the hotel of your choosing either in San

José or the La Fortuna/Arenal Volcano area. These folks also offer a combination kayaking and hiking tour to Punta Uva, as well as overnight tours to Tortuguero.

Shopping

Puerto Viejo attracts a lot of local and international bohemians, who seem to survive solely on the sale of handmade jewelry, painted ceramic trinkets (mainly pipes and cigarette-lighter holders), and imported Indonesian textiles. You'll find them at makeshift stands set up by the town's *parquecito* (little park), which comprises a few wooden benches in front of the sea between Soda Tamara and Stanford's.

In addition to the makeshift outdoor stands, a host of well-stocked gift and crafts shops are spread around town. **Luluberlu ★** (© **2750-0394**), located inland across from Cabinas Guaraná, features locally produced craftwork, including shell mobiles and mirrors with mosaic-inlaid frames, as well as imports from Thailand and India.

Tip: My favorite local purchase is locally produced chocolate, which comes wrapped in wax paper the size and shape of a roll of quarters. They come plain or flavored with coconut, peanuts, mint, ginger, or raisins, and can be found for sale at many gift shops and restaurants around town.

Where to Stay

For a longer stay, close to town, you might want to check out **Cashew Hill Jungle Cottages** (www.cashewhilllodge.co.cr; © 2750-0256). On a hill just on the outskirts of town, these are simple but immaculate individual one- and two-bedroom bungalows, with kitchenettes.

MODERATE

In addition to the hotels listed below, **Escape Caribeño** (www.escapecaribeno.com; © **2750-0103**) is another good option in this price range, located on the outskirts of town, just south of Salsa Brava.

Banana Azul Guest House ★★ 🏠 At the northern end of Playa Negra, on the north end of town, this hotel has earned fast friends and hearty praise. Rooms abound in varnished hardwoods. Inside they are quite simple, with minimal furnishings and amenities, and an overhead or floor fan. Most are on the second floor of the main lodge building, and open onto a broad veranda with ocean views. The end-unit Howler Monkey suite is my favorite room here. The garden bath suites are larger units, with a large open-air bathtub in their private gardens—hence, the name. The cute little free-form pool has an attached and elevated unheated Jacuzzi tub under a thatch-roof palapa. A virtually private section of beach sits just in front of the hotel, and stretches on for miles north, all the way to Cahuita National Park.

Playa Negra Puerto Viejo, Limón. www.bananaazul.com. © **877/284-5116** in the U.S. and Canada, or 2750-2035 in Costa Rica. 14 units. $69–$99 double; $139–$149 suite or apt. Rates include full breakfast. Discounts offered for cash payments. AE, DC, DISC, MC, V. No children 15 and under allowed. **Amenities:** Restaurant; bar; bike rental; Jacuzzi; outdoor pool; watersports equipment rental. *In room:* TV (in some), no phone, Wi-Fi.

INEXPENSIVE

True budget hounds will find an abundance of basic hotels and cabinas in downtown Puerto Viejo in addition to those listed below. Of these, **Hotel Pura Vida** (www.hotel-puravida.com; ✆/fax **2750-0002**) and **Backpackers Sunrise Hostel** (www.sunrisepuertoviejo.com; ✆ **2750-0028**) are both good bets, while **Kaya's Place** (www.kayasplace.com; ✆ **2750-0690**) is a budget traveler's favorite just on the northern outskirts of town across from Playa Negra.

Cabinas Guaraná   This is one of the better options right in town. The spacious rooms are painted in bright primary colors, with equally bright and contrasting trim. Rooms come with either two or three full-size beds, or a queen-size with one or two full beds. All come with tile floors, a ceiling fan, and mosquito netting. Guests can use the hotel's fully equipped kitchen to whip up meals, and an interesting little sitting area is on a platform high up a tree on the property.

1½ blocks inland from Café Viejo, Puerto Viejo, Limón. www.hotelguarana.com. ✆/fax **2750-0244**. 12 units. $41 double. Rates slightly lower in off season; higher during peak weeks. AE, DC, MC, V. **Amenities:** Lounge; Wi-Fi. *In room:* No phone.

Cabinas Jacarandá ✦   This small hotel has a few nice touches that set it apart from the others in the area. Guatemalan bedspreads add a dash of color and tropical flavor, as do tables made from sliced tree trunks. Most rooms and walkways feature intricate and colorful tile work; in addition, Japanese paper lanterns cover the lights, mosquito nets hang over the beds, and covered walkways connect the various buildings in this budding compound. Massage and yoga classes are offered on-site. If you're traveling in a group, you'll enjoy the space and atmosphere of the biggest room here. If the hotel is full, the owners also rent a few nearby bungalows.

1½ blocks inland from Café Viejo, Puerto Viejo, Limón. www.cabinasjacaranda.net. ✆/fax **2750-0069**. 14 units, 13 with private bathroom. $32–$45 double. AE, MC, V. *In room:* No phone.

Casa Verde Lodge ★★ ✦   This is my favorite hotel right in Puerto Viejo, regardless of the price. A quiet sense of tropical tranquillity pervades this place. Most rooms here are large, with high ceilings, tile floors, private bathrooms, and a private veranda. Those with shared bathrooms are housed in a raised building with a wide, covered breezeway between the rooms. Two fully equipped apartments are available in a neighboring duplex. The hotel also features lush gardens, a small but well-stocked gift shop, a good-size outdoor pool with a waterfall, and an outdoor massage hut. Even though it's an in-town choice, there's great bird-watching all around the grounds. The owners here are deeply involved in \improving the environmental and educational opportunities in the region.

A.P. 37-7304, Puerto Viejo, Limón. www.cabinascasaverde.com. ✆ **2750-0015**. Fax 2750-0047. 17 units, 9 with private bathroom. $50 double with shared bathroom; $70 double with private bathroom. Rates include taxes. Rates slightly lower in off season; higher during peak weeks. Discounts offered for cash payments. AE, MC, V. **Amenities:** Outdoor pool; massage hut. *In room:* TV (in some), no phone.

Rocking J's ★ ✦   This is, hands-down, the top backpacker hangout in the area. Whimsy pervades this sprawling compound of dorm rooms, covered camping spaces, and private suites. The "hammock hotel" is a large, common room strung with a dozen or two hammocks. Guests here get a private locker and use of the shared bathrooms and showers. Throughout, you'll find places to hang out, or play board games, or shoot some pool. The restaurant and bar here are always packed and lively, and they have an excellent in-house tour operation, run by Aventuras Bravas (p. 491).

Just south of downtown, Puerto Viejo, Limón. www.rockingjs.com. ⓒ **2750-0665** or 2750-0657. 35 units, 3 with private bathroom. $4–$6 per person in a tent; $5 hammock; $7 dorm room; $20–$25 double with shared bathroom; $70 double with private bathroom; $50–$60 suite. AE, MC, V. **Amenities:** Restaurant; bar; Wi-Fi. *In room:* No phone.

Where to Eat

To really sample the local cuisine, you need to look up a few local women. Ask around for **Miss Dolly, Miss Sam, Miss Isma,** and **Miss Irma,** who all serve up sit-down meals in their modest little *sodas.* In addition to locally seasoned fish and chicken served with rice and beans, these joints are usually a great place to find some *pan bon* (a local sweet, dark bread), ginger cakes, *paty* (meat-filled turnovers), and *rondon* (see below). Just ask around for these women, and someone will direct you to them.

> ### That Run-down Feeling
>
> *Rondon* soup is a spicy coconut milk–based soup or stew made with anything the cook can "run down"—it usually includes a mix of local tubers (potato, sweet potato, or yuca), other vegetables (carrots or corn), and often some seafood. Be sure to try this authentic taste of the Caribbean.

If you're looking for a light bite for breakfast, lunch, or a snack, check out **Pan Pay** (ⓒ **2750-0081**), a French-run bakery and sandwich shop next to Johnny's Place (see "Puerto Viejo After Dark," below). Also, **Jammin' Juice and Jerk Center** ★ (ⓒ **2750-2083** or 8826-4332), in the same building, specializes in jerk chicken, salads, and fresh juices. For casual fare, try **E-Z Times** (ⓒ **2750-0663**), right in front of the water near the heart of town.

Puerto Viejo has a glut of excellent Italian restaurants; in addition to the places listed below, **Amimodo** ★ (ⓒ **2750-0257**) is a fine restaurant.

Finally, if you're just looking for something to cool you off, try **Mighty River's Ice Cream & Coffee Shop** (ⓒ **2750-0850**), which has delicious home-made ice cream.

The Beach Hut ★★ 💼 INTERNATIONAL   This restaurant is a downtown gem. Tables are set on gravel in a small covered courtyard with a large tree in its center, although a few more tables are set under an adjacent open-roof closer to the water. The open-kitchen is abuzz with activity. There's a broad selection of soups, salads, and appetizers to get you going. I recommend the steamed mussels or the sautéed squid and black-eyed peas, or some of the garlicky carrot soup. You can also choose from excellent fresh fish and seafood options, as well as such tasty terrestrial fare as slow-grilled pork and tasty tenderloin in a green pepper-corn sauce. They occasionally have live music or a DJ.

On the waterfront, downtown Puerto Viejo. ⓒ **2750-0895.** Main courses C4,000–C9,000. MC, V. Tues–Sun 7am–noon, 3–11pm.

Bread & Chocolate ★ ☺ BREAKFAST/AMERICAN   A top spot for break-fast or lunch, this place is almost always bustling and full. Breakfasts feature waffles, French toast, and pancakes served with some namesake fresh chocolate sauce, or egg dishes served with home-baked biscuits, bagels, or whole wheat bread. For lunch, sandwiches, served on the aforementioned homemade bread, include BLTs and Jerk chicken. Those with kids or a child within might want to sample the PB&J or PB&Chocolate, again made with homemade ingredients. Both breakfast and lunch are served all day. Don't leave without trying or buying some of their brownies and truffles.

Half-block south of Café Viejo. © **2750-0723.** Main courses C2,400–C3,000. No credit cards. Wed–Sat 6:30am–6:30pm; Sun 6:30am–2:30pm.

Café Viejo ITALIAN   This place is set on the busiest corner of "downtown" Puerto Viejo. White gauze curtains help to slightly shield this open-air spot from the hustle and bustle just outside. Still, it's often loud and crowded inside as well, and that's part of the charm of this popular place. You can get a wide range of pastas and thin-crust wood-oven pizzas, and substantial fish, chicken, and meat entrees. On weekends, a late-night lounge scene sometimes erupts, with electronic music and dancing.

On the main road. © **2750-0817.** Main courses C4,000–C33,000. MC, V. Wed–Mon 6–11:30pm.

Chile Rojo ★ 🍴 PAN-ASIAN/MEDITERRANEAN   Housed in a large second floor space of Puerto Viejo's largest minimall, this long-standing restaurant serves up excellent Pan-Asian, Mediterranean, and vegetarian fare at very reasonable prices. Bright tablecloths, a lively bar scene, and an open kitchen make this place inviting. If you want to people-watch, grab a seat at the long line of stools that line the street-facing, open-air wall that runs along one side of the restaurant. Standout menu options are green Thai curry served with fish, chicken, or vegetables or seared fresh tuna steak with a ginger-soy dressing. There are also selections of sushi rolls and nigiri, daily specials, and occasional live concerts here.

2nd floor of shopping mall downtown. © **2750-0025.** Main courses C5,200–C6,800. AE, MC, V. Thurs–Tues 7am–11pm.

Soda Tamara 🍴 COSTA RICAN   This little restaurant has long been popular with budget-conscious travelers and has an attractive setting for such an economical place. The painted picket fence in front gives the restaurant a homey feel, and the best seats are on the front veranda facing the street, or in the large open-air dining area. The menu features standard fish, chicken, and meat entrees, served with a hefty helping of Caribbean-style rice and beans. You can also get *patacones* (fried plantain chips) and a wide selection of fresh-fruit juices. A second-floor open-air bar is open nightly from 6pm until the last straggler calls it quits.

On the main road. © **2750-0148.** Main courses C3,500–C11,000. AE, MC, V. Thurs–Tues 11:30am–10pm.

Stashu's Con-Fusion ★★ INTERNATIONAL   A friendly, hippie vibe pervades this open-air restaurant. Seating is at heavy wooden tables, and if the few smaller, more private tables are taken, you can take any empty seat at one of the larger communal tables. The short menu features several vegetarian items, as well as fresh fish and some chicken and meat dishes, prepared in curry, Thai, and Mexican sauces. Live music here ranges from reggae to jazz to Latin American folk. Historically known as El Loco Natural, longtime chef Stash, is now the restaurant's owner and namesake.

On the main road just south of downtown, about 1 block beyond Stanford's. ℭ **2750-0530**. www.loconaturalrestaurant.com. Main courses C3,200–C17,000. No credit cards. Thurs–Tues 6–10pm.

Puerto Viejo After Dark

The town has two main disco/bars. **Johnny's Place ★★** (ℭ 2750-0623) is near the Rural Guard station, about 100m (328 ft.) or so north of the ATEC office. The action spills out from the dance floor and on to the beach on most nights, where you'll find candle-lit tables set near the water's edge. Another good waterfront nightspot is the **Lazy Mon @ Stanford's** (ℭ 2750-0608; www. thelazymon.com), with a bit more of a sport's bar vibe to it and features regular live bands or DJs. Formerly known as "Stanford's" and now under new ownership, this bar will be eventually called the Lazy Mon. However, "Stanford's" is still used as a reference point in town when giving directions. Both have small dance floors with ground-shaking reggae, dub, and rap rhythms blaring.

One of the more popular places in town is the **Tex Mex** (ℭ 2750-0525) restaurant and bar, right where the main road hits the water. Another option is the **Mango Sunset Bar ★★** (ℭ 8757-8356), which is near the water, beside the bus station, and features either live music or a DJ most nights. For a more sophisticated ambience, try the downtown **Baba Yaga ★** (ℭ 8388-4359), or the oceanfront **Koki Beach ★** (ℭ 2275-0902; www.kokibeach.com).

An open-air bar on the second floor of **Soda Tamara** (p. 497) is a casual and quiet place to gather after dark. **Rocking J's** (p. 495) often features live music. Finally, for a more local scene, check out **Bar Maritza's** (ℭ 2750-0003), in the center of town, right across from the basketball court, which really seems to go off on Sunday nights.

You can also take advantage of the pool table, board games, and DirecTV (usually showing sporting events) at **El Dorado** (ℭ 2750-0604), in front of the ATEC office (p. 490), as an alternative to the loud music and dance scenes of the other joints mentioned above.

PLAYAS COCLES, CHIQUITA, MANZANILLO & SOUTH OF PUERTO VIEJO ★★★

200km (124 miles) E of San José; 55km (34 miles) S of Limón

As you continue south on the coastal road from Puerto Viejo, you'll come to several of Costa Rica's best beaches. Soft white sands are fronted by the Caribbean Sea and backed by thick rainforest. **Playa Cocles** is a popular surf spot, with a powerful and dependable beach break. South of here, the isolated **Playa Chiquita** is characterized by small pocket coves, and calm pools formed by dead coral reefs raised slightly above sea level by the 1991 earthquake. Beyond this lies **Punta Uva,** a long curving swath of beach punctuated by its namesake point (or *punta*), a rainforest-clad mound of land that looks vaguely like a bunch of grapes from the distance. If you come here, be sure to hike the short loop trail up and

Surfers at Playa Cocles.

around the point. From Punta Uva the coastline stretches to **Manzanillo.** Along the way, the white sands are fronted by a living coral reef, which breaks up the waves and keeps the swimming here generally calm and protected. When it's calm (Aug–Oct), the waters down here are some of the clearest anywhere in the country, with good snorkeling among the nearby coral reefs. The tiny village of Manzanillo is literally the end of the road. The shoreline heading south from Manzanillo, located inside the **Gandoca–Manzanillo Wildlife Reserve,** is especially beautiful, with a series of pocket coves and small beaches, featuring small islands and rocky outcroppings offshore, and backed by thick rainforest. This park stretches all the way to the Panamanian border.

Essentials

GETTING THERE & DEPARTING   By Car: A single two-lane road runs out south out of Puerto Viejo and ends in Manzanillo. A few dirt roads lead off this paved, but rutted road, both toward the beach and into the mountains.

By Bus: Follow the directions above for getting to Puerto Viejo. Local buses to Punta Uva and Manzanillo leave Puerto Viejo about a half-dozen times throughout the day.

GETTING AROUND   A taxi from Puerto Viejo should run you around $7 to Punta Uva or $12 to Manzanillo. Alternatively, it's about 1½ hours each way by bicycle, with only two relatively small hills to contend with. Although the road is ostensibly paved all the way to Manzanillo, between the near-constant potholes and washed-out sections, it's almost like riding an off-road trail. Most of the hotels in this area either offer free bicycles, or will help arrange a rental.

It's also possible to walk along the beach all the way from Puerto Viejo to Manzanillo, with just a couple of short and well-worn detours inland around rocky points. However, I recommend you catch a ride down to Manzanillo and save your walking energies for the trails and beaches inside the refuge.

ORIENTATION As you drive south, the first beach you will hit is **Playa Cocles** ★, which is 2km (1¼ miles) from Puerto Viejo. A little farther you'll find **Playa Chiquita** ★, which is 5km (3 miles) from Puerto Viejo, followed by **Punta Uva** ★★ at 8.4km (5¼ miles) away, and **Manzanillo** ★★ some 13km (8 miles) away.

FAST FACTS There are no true towns, and no major services to be found along this stretch of coast. However, you can find a few scattered internet cafes and small markets mixed in with the sporadic string of hotels, private homes, and restaurants that line the main road.

What to See & Do

For all intents and purposes, this string of beaches is an extension of Puerto Viejo, and all of the tours, activities, and attractions mentioned above can be enjoyed by those staying here. For organized scuba diving, snorkeling, sportfishing excursions, or dolphin-sighting tours around Manzanillo and the beaches south of Puerto Viejo, check in with the **Asociación de Guías Autóctonos Naturalistas de Manzanillo-Talamanca** (Association of Naturalist Guides; ℂ **2759-9064**) or a Puerto Viejo tour operator.

Manzanillo & the Gandoca–Manzanillo Wildlife Refuge ★★

13km (8 miles) south of Puerto Viejo

The **Gandoca–Manzanillo Wildlife Refuge** encompasses the small village and extends all the way to the Panamanian border. Manatees, crocodiles, and more than 350 species of birds live within the boundaries of the reserve. The

The Punta Uva shoreline.

FROM TOP: **A Manzanillo offshore rock; A green turtle.**

reserve also includes the coral reef off-shore—when the seas are calm, this is the best **snorkeling** and **diving** spot on this entire coast. Four species of **sea turtles** nest on one 8.9km (5½-mile) stretch of beach within the reserve between March and July. Three species of dolphins also inhabit and frolic in the waters just off Manzanillo. The waters here are home to Atlantic spotted, bottlenose, and the rare tucuxi. This latter species favors the brackish estuary waters, but has actually been observed in mixed species mating with local bottlenose dolphins. Many local tour guides and operators offer boat trips out to spot them.

If you want to explore the refuge, you can easily find the single, well-maintained trail by walking along the beach just south of town until you have to wade across a small river. On the other side, you'll pick up the trail head. Otherwise, you can ask around the village for local guides. For dolphin-spotting tours and information, you might want to check in with **The Talamanca Dolphin Foundation** (© 8856-1348; www.dolphinlink.org).

IGUANA MAMAS ★★ Down in Playa Chiquita, at the Tree House Lodge (see below), is the **Green Iguana Conservation Tour** (© 2750-0706; www.iguanaverde.com). This educational tour focuses on the life cycle, habits, and current situation of this endangered reptile. The tour features a walk around a massive natural enclosure, as well as a video presentation. The cost is $15. Regular tours are offered Tuesday and Thursday at 10am. Additional tours may be arranged by appointment.

SWEET STUFF ★ Another great educational tour is the 2-hour **ChocoRart** (© 2750-0075) through a working organic cacao plantation and chocolate production facility. The tour shows you the whole process of growing, harvesting, and processing cacao, and of course there's a tasting at the end. The tour is run by reservation only, and costs $22 per person or $12 for kids under 12, with a four-person minimum.

(ORGANIC) PEAS & LOVE ★ Inside the Manzanillo–Gandoca refuge is the **Punta Mona Center For Sustainable Living & Education** ★ (no phone; www.puntamona.org). With organic permaculture gardens and a distinctly alternative vibe, this place is open for day visits, overnight stays, and work-exchange and educational programs.

Shopping

If you need a book to read on the beach, head to **Echo Books** (✆ **2756-8323;** www.echobookscostarica.com) just inland from Playa Cocles. This place has a good supply of new and used books in English, Spanish, Dutch, German, and Italian, as well as a small cafe and gift shop. The owner also makes homemade truffles and other chocolate treats from local cacao.

For ceramics, head south to Playa Chiquita and check out the traditional Japanese-style works at **Raku Art** (✆ **2750-0548**).

Where to Stay between Puerto Viejo & Manzanillo

I recommend that you rent a car if you plan to stay at one of these hotels because public transportation is sporadic and taxis aren't always available. If you arrive by bus, however, a rented bicycle or scooter might be all you need to get around once you are settled.

VERY EXPENSIVE

Almonds & Corals Hotel ★   Originally a tent camp, this place has morphed into a rustic, yet plush jungle lodge. The safari-style pavilions are set on large raised platforms, under high-pitched thatch roofs; the suites and rooms feature four-poster beds with mosquito netting, large screen windows, and private balconies. The whole complex is set in dense secondary forest, with wooden walkways connecting the rooms to the main lodge and dining area. Perhaps the best part is Manzanillo Beach, just a short walk away through the jungle. Snorkel equipment, sea kayaks, and a variety of tours are also available, and a zip-line canopy tour through the forest here ends right at the beach. These folks have done much

Manzanillo beach.

The Tree House Lodge.

to conserve the forests and wildlife around the hotel, and their efforts have earned them "4 Leaves" from the CST Sustainable Tourism program.

Manzanillo, Limón. www.almondsandcorals.com. ⓒ **2272-2024** reservations in San José, or 2759-9057 at the hotel. Fax 2272-2220. 25 units. $300–$400 double. Rates include breakfast, dinner, and taxes. Children 6–9 $40–$50; children 5 and under free. AE, MC, V. **Amenities:** Restaurant; bar; bicycle rental; Jacuzzi; small spa; all rooms smoke-free; watersports equipment rental. *In room:* No phone.

Le Caméléon ★★ This hotel offers up the most luxurious and contemporary accommodations on this coast. Rooms are spacious and well-equipped. Everything, aside from a few throw pillows, the flatscreen TV, a single painting, and some flowers, is pure white—floors, walls, doors, furnishings, and linens. The throw pillows, flowers, and paintings are changed daily, adding a sense of whimsy and variety. However, while the decor is certainly chic, the all-white theme is very quick to show wear and spotting. The hotel has an inviting pool area, as well as a hip lounge scene at their bar most nights. In addition, their beach club provides beach lounge chairs, hammocks, private shaded gazebos, and waiter service all day long on a beautiful stretch of Playa Cocles, just across the road from the hotel.

Playa Cocles, Puerto Viejo, Limón. www.lecameleonhotel.com. ⓒ **2750-0501.** 23 units. $295–$354 double; $425–$509 suite. AE, MC, V. **Amenities:** Restaurant; bar; Jacuzzi; small outdoor pool. *In room:* A/C, TV, hair dryer, minibar, MP3 docking station, Wi-Fi.

Tree House Lodge ★★★ 🎁 The individual houses here are the most unique and stylish options on this coast. All are distinct and quite large, with fluid and fanciful architectural details and tons of brightly varnished woodwork. As the name implies, the Tree House is built into and around a large *sangrillo* tree. The Beach House is closest to the sea and has an ocean view from its kitchen and broad deck. However, the crowning achievement is the three-bedroom, two-bathroom Beach Suite, with its spectacular domed bathroom, sunlit by scores of colored glass skylights. All of the houses are beautiful, and you'll spend much of your time here marveling at the creative touches and one-off furniture. This property is right off Punta Uva, one of the best swimming beaches in the area. In addition to their Iguana preservation project (see above), this place has earned "4 Leaves" in the CST Sustainable Tourism program.

Punta Uva, Puerto Viejo, Limón. www.costaricatreehouse.com. ⓒ **2750-0706.** 2 units. $300 double. Rates include breakfast. No credit cards. **Amenities:** Jacuzzi. *In room:* A/C (in some), kitchen.

MODERATE

In addition to the places listed below, surfers might look into **Totem** (www. totemsite.com; ⓒ **2750-0758**), which offers comfortable rooms, set just off the road, right in front of the Playa Cocles beach break, while **Casa Viva** (www. puntauva.net; ⓒ **2750-0089**) offers beautiful, fully equipped one- and two-bedroom houses just steps from the sand on Punta Uva.

Azania Bungalows ★   This collection of individual bungalows is an excellent option for those seeking a quiet, romantic tropical getaway. The spacious bungalows are set apart from each other amid the hotel's high flowering gardens, giving each a sense of seclusion. All come with one queen-size bed and one double bed downstairs and another double bed in the small loft. The high-pitched thatch roofs, combined with large screened windows, allow for good cross ventilation. The lounge area features a television with satellite TV, a small lending library, and a collection of board games. Some of the best features here include the refreshing free-form swimming pool and the open-air thatch-roofed poolside restaurant.

Playa Cocles, Puerto Viejo, Limón. www.azania-costarica.com. ⓒ **2750-0540.** Fax 2750-0371. 10 bungalows. $90 double. Rates include full breakfast. AE, DC, MC, V. **Amenities:** Restaurant; bar; bike rental; outdoor pool; Wi-Fi. *In room:* Fridge, no phone.

Cariblue Bungalows ★★   This intimate resort is a wonderful choice. The rooms are spread around well-tended and lush grounds. My favorites are the older raised-stilt wood bungalows, with spacious bedrooms and a small veranda with a hammock. The standard rooms are in a series of concrete-block buildings with high-pitched thatch roofs. They are also spacious and comfortable, but not quite as private or charming as the bungalows. Deluxe rooms and bungalows come with televisions and air-conditioning. Another option is a two-bedroom house with a full kitchen, for families or for longer stays. A large free-form swimming pool has a swim-up bar, and the restaurant here serves up excellent Italian and local cuisine. Cariblue is about 90m (295 ft.) or so inland from the southern end of Playa Cocles.

Playa Cocles, Puerto Viejo, Limón. www.cariblue.com. ⓒ **2750-0035** or ⓒ/fax 2750-0057. 22 units, 1 house. $110–$135 double; $265 house. Rates include breakfast buffet. Rates slightly lower in off season. AE, MC, V. **Amenities:** Restaurant; bar/lounge; bike rental; Jacuzzi; outdoor pool. *In room:* A/C (in some), TV, hair dryer, no phone, Wi-Fi.

Casa Camarona   Casa Camarona has the enviable distinction of being one of the very few hotels in this area right on the beach. There's no road to cross and no long path through the jungle—just a small section of shady gardens separates you from a pretty section of Playa Cocles and the Caribbean Sea. The rooms are in two separate two-story buildings. Definitely get a room on the second floor: Up there you'll find spacious rooms painted in pleasant pastels, with plenty of cross ventilation and a wide shared veranda. The hotel keeps some chaise lounges on the beach under the shade of palm trees, and a beach bar is open during the day, so you barely have to move to quench your thirst.

Playa Cocles, Puerto Viejo, Limón. www.casacamarona.co.cr. ℰ **2283-6711** or 2750-0151. Fax 2750-0210. 18 units. $63–$98 double. Rates include continental breakfast and taxes. AE, MC, V. **Amenities:** Bar. *In room:* A/C (in some), no phone.

La Costa de Papito ★ 🗝 This small collection of individual and duplex cabins is just across from Playa Cocles, about 1.6km (1 mile) south of Puerto Viejo. The wooden bungalows come with one or two double beds, artfully tiled bathrooms, and an inviting private porch with a table and chairs and either a hammock or a swing chair. There's also a larger, two-bedroom unit, an excellent restaurant, and the Indulgence Spa (see above).

Playa Cocles, Puerto Viejo, Limón. www.lacostadepapito.com. ℰ **2750-0704** or ℰ/fax 2750-0080. 13 units. $89 double. AE, DISC, MC, V. **Amenities:** Restaurant; bar; bike rental; small spa. *In room:* No phone.

Shawandha Lodge ★ Remote and romantic, the individual bungalows here are rustically luxurious. Creative flourishes abound. The thatch-roofed, raised bungalows feature high-pitched ceilings, varnished wood floors, and either one king-size bed or a mix of queen-size and single beds. The bathrooms feature original, intricate mosaics of hand-cut tile highlighting a large, open shower. Every bungalow has its own spacious balcony, with both a hammock and a couch, where you can lie and look out on the lush, flowering gardens. The beach is accessed by a private path, and a host of activities and tours can be arranged. The restaurant is romantic and quite good. The newest addition here is a wonderful outdoor pool.

Puerto Viejo, Limón. www.shawandhalodge.com. ℰ **2750-0018.** Fax 2750-0037. 13 units. $115 double. Rates include full breakfast. AE, MC, V. **Amenities:** Restaurant; small outdoor pool. *In room:* No phone.

INEXPENSIVE

Down in Manzanillo, the simple **Cabinas Something Different** (ℰ **2759-9014**) is a good option, while **Congo Bongo** (www.congo-bongo.com; ℰ **2759-9016**) offers fully equipped houses in a lush forest setting.

Playa Chiquita Lodge ☺ Set amid the shade of large old trees a few kilometers south of Puerto Viejo toward Punta Uva (watch for the sign), this lodge has several wooden buildings set on stilts and connected by a garden walkway. Wide verandas offer built-in seating and rocking chairs. The spacious rooms are painted in bright colors. A short trail leads down to a semiprivate little swimming beach with tide pools and beautiful turquoise water. This stretch of beach is the site of a daily 4pm volleyball game.

Puerto Viejo, Limón. www.playachiquitalodge.com. ℰ **2750-0062** or ℰ/fax 2750-0408. 8 units. $60 double. Rates include breakfast. AE, MC, V. **Amenities:** Restaurant. *In room:* No phone, Wi-Fi.

Where to Eat

In addition to the restaurants listed above and below, **Cabinas Selvyn** (no phone) at Punta Uva is an excellent option for local cuisine and fresh seafood, while **Pita Bonita** (ℰ **2756-8173**) serves up wonderful Middle Eastern cuisine at an open-air spot between Playa Chiquita and Punta Uva.

Jungle Love Café ★★ INTERNATIONAL This hidden gem is intimate and romantic. Five tables are spread around a circular, open-air deck, and a few more tables are in an open-air dining area. The creative chef and owner serves up

> ### On to Panama
>
> Costa Rica's southern zone, particularly Puerto Viejo, is a popular jumping-off point for trips into Panama. The nearest and most popular destination is the island retreat of Bocas del Toro. Most tour agencies and hotel desks in the area can arrange tours to Panama. The most reliable and easiest way to get to Bocas del Toro is to take the daily **Caribe Shuttle** (© 2750-0626; www.caribeshuttle.com), which will take you via land and boat for $32 each way; check the website or call for departure times. These folks also offer a 1-day tour to Bocas, including all transport; a snorkel and dolphin-watching tour around Bocas; lunch, drinks, and snacks. The tour takes all day, and costs $95.
>
> If you're planning on spending any time touring around Panama, be sure to pick up a copy of *Frommer's Panama*.

excellent California-style cuisine, fresh pizzas, and a selection of nightly specials. I highly recommend the shrimp and pasta, with leeks and carrots in a spicy brandy cream sauce—a family heirloom recipe. You also can't go wrong with the Tokyo Tuna or Chipotle chicken.

Playa Chiquita. www.junglelovecafe.com. © **2750-0162.** Main courses $33–$65. No credit cards. Tues–Sun 5–9:30pm.

La Pecora Nera ★★★ ITALIAN   This open-air joint on the jungle's edge has a deserved reputation as the finest Italian restaurant in the region, if not the country. Owner Ilario Giannoni is a whirlwind of enthusiasm and activity, switching hats all night long from maitre d' to chef to waiter to busboy in an entertaining blur. Sure, he's got some help, including his grandmother, who makes gnocchi, but it sometimes seems like he's doing it single-handedly. The menu has a broad selection of pizzas and pastas, but your best bet is to just ask Ilario what's fresh and special for that day, and to trust his instincts and inventions. I've had fabulous fresh pasta dishes and top-notch appetizers every time I've visited. The various carpaccios are fabulous, and the gnocchi here is light and mouthwatering. These folks also run **Gatta Ci Cova,** a less formal pizzeria and trattoria on the main road, near the entrance to La Pecora Nera.

50m (164 ft.) inland from a well-marked turnoff on the main road south just beyond the soccer field in Cocles. © **2750-0490.** Reservations recommended. Main courses C6,000–C15,000. AE, MC, V. Tues–Sun 5:30–10pm.

Maxi's ★   This second floor, oceanfront restaurant is almost always packed, especially for lunch. The kitchen specializes in locally caught seafood simply prepared and served alongside the local rice 'n' beans, fried plantain chips, and cabbage salad. Portions are large and filling. The best seats are next to large open windows that overlook the beach and sea.

On the beach, Manzanillo. © **2759-9086.** Main courses C3,500–C9,500; lobster C10,500–C24,500. MC, V. Daily noon–10pm.

13

PLANNING YOUR TRIP TO COSTA RICA

C osta Rica is no longer the next new thing. Neither is it old hat. As Costa Rica has matured as a tourist destination, things have gotten easier and easier for international travelers. That said, most travelers—even experienced travelers and repeat visitors—will want to do some serious pre-trip planning. This chapter provides a variety of planning tools, including information on how to get there; tips on accommodations; and quick, on the ground resources.

GETTING THERE
By Plane

It takes between 3 and 7 hours to fly to Costa Rica from most U.S. cities, the origin of most direct and connecting flights. Most international flights still land in San José's **Juan Santamaría International Airport** (© **2437-2626** for 24-hr. airport information; www.alterra.co.cr; airport code: SJO). However, more and more direct international flights are touching down in Liberia's **Daniel Oduber International Airport** (© **2668-1010;** airport code: LIR).

Liberia is the gateway to the beaches of the Guanacaste region and the Nicoya Peninsula, and a direct flight here eliminates the need for a separate commuter flight in a small aircraft or roughly 5 hours in a car or bus. If you are planning to spend all, or most, of your vacation time in the Guanacaste region, you'll want to fly in and out of Liberia. However, San José is a much more convenient gateway if you are planning to head to Manuel Antonio, the Central Pacific coast, the Caribbean coast, or the Southern zone.

Numerous airlines fly into Costa Rica. Be warned that the smaller Latin American carriers tend to make several stops (sometimes unscheduled) en route to San José, thus increasing flying time.

From North America, **Air Canada, American Airlines, Continental, Delta, Frontier, Grupo Taca, JetBlue, Spirit Air, United,** and **US Airways** all have regular direct flights to Costa Rica.

From Europe, **Iberia** is the only airline with regular routes to San José, some direct and others with one connection. Alternately, you can fly to any major U.S. hub-city and make connections to one of the airlines mentioned above.

For info on the airlines that travel to Costa Rica, please see "Airline Websites," p. 528.

By Bus

Bus service runs regularly from Panama City, Panama, and Managua, Nicaragua. If at all possible, it's worth the splurge for a deluxe or express bus. In terms of travel time and convenience, it's always better to get a direct bus rather than one

PREVIOUS PAGE: **A Costa Rican oxcart.**

that stops along the way—and you've got a better chance of getting a working restroom in a direct/express or deluxe bus. Some even have television sets showing video movies.

Several bus lines with regular daily departures connect the major capital cities of Central America. Call **King Quality** (☎ **2258-8834**; www.king-qualityca.com), **Transnica** (☎ **2223-4242**; http://transnica.com), or **Tica Bus Company** (☎ **2221-0006**; www.ticabus.com) for further information. All of these lines service Costa Rica directly from Panama City and Managua, with connections to the other principal cities of Central America. None of them will reserve a seat by telephone, and schedules change frequently according to season and demand, so buy your ticket in advance—several days in advance, if you plan to travel on weekends or holidays. From Panama City, it's a 20-hour, 900km (558-mile) trip. The one-way fare is around $37. From Managua, it's 11 hours and 450km (279 miles) to San José, and the one-way fare is around $21.

Whenever you're traveling by bus through Central America, try to keep a watchful eye on your belongings, especially at rest and border stops, whether they're in an overhead bin or stored below decks in a luggage compartment.

By Car

It's possible to travel to Costa Rica from North America by car, but it can be difficult. After leaving Mexico, the Interamerican Highway (Carretera Interamericana, also known as the Pan-American Hwy.) passes through Guatemala, El Salvador, Honduras, and Nicaragua before reaching Costa Rica. This highway then travels the length of Costa Rica before entering Panama. All of these countries can be problematic for travelers for a variety of reasons, including internal violence, crime, corrupt border crossings, and visa formalities. If you do decide to undertake this adventure, take the **Gulf Coast route** from the border crossing at Brownsville, Texas, because it involves traveling the fewest miles through Mexico. Those planning to travel this route should purchase a copy of *You Can Drive to Costa Rica in 8 Days!* by Dawn Rae Lessler, which is available from the major online bookstores. You might also try to find a copy of *Driving the Pan-Am Highway to Mexico and Central America,* by Audrey and Raymond Pritchard, which is harder to find. A wealth of information is also online at **www.sanborns insurance.com** and **www.drivemeloco.com**.

CAR DOCUMENTS You will need a current driver's license, as well as your vehicle's registration and the original title (no photocopies), to enter the country.

CENTRAL AMERICAN AUTO INSURANCE Contact **Sanborn's Insurance Company** (☎ **800/222-0158** or 956/686-0711; www.sanbornsinsurance.com), which has agents at various border towns in the United States. These folks have been servicing this niche for more than 50 years. They can supply you with trip insurance for Mexico and Central America (you won't be able to buy insurance after you've left the U.S.), driving tips, and an itinerary.

CAR SAFETY Be sure your car is in excellent working order. It's advisable not to drive at night because of the danger of being robbed by bandits, especially in Mexico, Guatemala, El Salvador, and Honduras.

For information on car rentals and gasoline (petrol) in Costa Rica, see "Getting Around by Car," later in this section.

By Boat

More than 200 cruise ships stop each year in Costa Rica, calling at Limón on the Caribbean coast, and at Puerto Caldera and Puntarenas on the Pacific coast. Many are part of routes that cruise through the Panama Canal. Cruise lines that offer stops in Costa Rica include **Crystal Cruises** (© **888/722-0021;** www.crystalcruises.com), **Celebrity Cruises** (© **800/647-2251;** www.celebritycruises.com), **Holland America** (© **877/932-4259;** www.hollandamerica.com), **Norwegian Cruise Line** (© **866/234-7650;** www.ncl.com), **Royal Caribbean** (© **866/562-7625;** www.rccl.com), **Regent Seven Seas Cruises** (© **877/505-5370;** www.rssc.com), **Silver Sea Cruises** (© **954/759-5098;** www.silversea.com), and **Windstar Cruises** (© **800/258-7245;** www.windstarcruises.com).

It might pay off to book through a travel agency that specializes in cruises; these companies buy in bulk and stay on top of the latest specials and promotions. Try the **Cruise Company** (© **800/289-5505;** www.thecruisecompany.com) or **World Wide Cruises** (© **800/882-9000;** www.wwcruises.com).

GETTING AROUND

By Plane

Flying is one of the best ways to get around Costa Rica. Because the country is quite small, flights are short and not too expensive. The domestic airlines of Costa Rica are Sansa and Nature Air.

Sansa (© **877/767-2672** in the U.S. and Canada, or 2290-4100 in Costa Rica; www.flysansa.com) operates from a separate terminal at San José's **Juan Santamaría International Airport** (see above).

Nature Air (© **800/235-9272** in the U.S. and Canada, or 2299-6000; www.natureair.com) operates from **Tobías Bolaños International Airport** (© **2232-2820;** airport code: SYQ) in Pavas, 6.4km (4 miles) from San José. The ride from downtown to Pavas takes about 10 minutes, and a metered taxi should cost $10 to $20. Nature Air also provides a regularly scheduled shuttle between the Tobías Bolaños and Juan Santamaría airports for $8 per person.

In the high season (late Nov to late Apr), be sure to book reservations well in advance. Both companies have online booking systems via their websites.

By Car

Renting a car in Costa Rica is no idle proposition. The roads are riddled with potholes, most rural intersections are unmarked, and, for some reason, sitting behind the wheel of a car seems to turn peaceful Ticos into homicidal maniacs. But unless you want to see the country from the window of a bus or pay exorbitant amounts for private transfers, renting a car might be your best option for independent exploring. (That said, if you don't want to put up with any stress on your vacation, it might be worthwhile springing for a driver.)

Be forewarned, however: Although rental cars no longer bear special license plates, they are still readily identifiable to thieves and are frequently targeted. (Nothing is ever safe in a car in Costa Rica, although parking in guarded parking lots helps.) Transit police also seem to target tourists; never pay money directly to a police officer who stops you for any traffic violation.

Before driving off with a rental car, be sure that you inspect the exterior and point out to the rental-company representative every tiny scratch, dent, tear, or any other damage. It's a common practice with many Costa Rican car-rental companies to claim that you owe payment for minor dings and dents that the company finds when you return the car. Also, if you get into an accident, be sure that the rental company doesn't try to bill you for a higher amount than the deductible on your rental contract.

These caveats aren't meant to scare you off from driving in Costa Rica. Thousands of tourists rent cars here every year, and the large majority of them encounter no problems. Just keep your wits about you and guard against car theft (see p. 525 for info), and you'll do fine. Also, keep in mind that four-wheel-drives are particularly useful in the rainy season (May to mid-Nov) and for navigating the bumpy, poorly paved roads year-round.

Note: It's sometimes cheaper to reserve a car in your home country rather than book when you arrive in Costa Rica. If you know you'll be renting a car, it's always wise to reserve it well in advance for the high season because the rental fleet still can't match demand.

Among the major international agencies operating in Costa Rica are **Alamo, Avis, Budget, Hertz, National, Payless,** and **Thrifty.** For a complete list of car-rental agencies and their contact information, see the "Getting Around" sections of major tourist destinations in this book.

GASOLINE (PETROL) Gasoline is sold as "regular" and "super." Both are unleaded; super is just higher octane. Diesel is available at almost every gas station as well. Most rental cars run on super, but always ask your rental agent what type of gas your car takes. When going off to remote places, try to leave with a full tank of gas because gas stations can be hard to find. If you need to gas up in a small town, you can sometimes get gasoline from enterprising families who sell it by the liter from their houses. Look for hand-lettered signs that say GASOLINA. At press time, a liter of super cost C681, or roughly $2.90 per liter, and $5.16 per gallon.

ROAD CONDITIONS The awful road conditions throughout Costa Rica are legendary, and deservedly so. Despite constant promises to fix the problem and sporadic repair attempts, the hot sun, hard rain, and rampant corruption outpace any progress made toward improving the condition of roads. Even paved roads are often badly potholed, so stay alert. Road conditions get especially tricky during the rainy season, when heavy rains and runoff can destroy a stretch of pavement in the blink of an eye.

Note: Estimated driving times are listed throughout this book, but bear in mind that it might take longer than estimated to reach your destination during the rainy season or if roads have deteriorated.

Route numbers are somewhat sporadically and arbitrarily used. You'll also find frequent signs listing the number of kilometers to various towns or cities. Still, your best bets for on-road directions are billboards and advertisements for hotels. It's always a good idea to know the names of a few hotels at your destination, just in case your specific hotel hasn't put up any billboards or signs.

Most car rental agencies now offer the opportunity to rent out GPS units along with your car rental. Rates run between $10 to $15 per day. If you have your own GPS unit, several maps to Costa Rica are available.

While you still can't simply enter a street address, most commercial GPS maps of Costa Rica feature hundreds of prominent points of interest (POI), and you should be able to plug in a POI close to your destination.

RENTER'S INSURANCE Even if you hold **your own car-insurance policy** at home, coverage doesn't always extend abroad. Be sure to find out whether you'll be covered in Costa Rica, whether your policy extends to all persons who will be driving the rental car, how much liability is covered in case an outside party is injured in an accident, and whether the *type* of vehicle you are renting is included under your contract.

DRIVING RULES A current foreign driver's license is valid for the first 3 months you are in Costa Rica. Seat belts are required for the driver and front-seat passengers. Motorcyclists must wear helmets. Highway police use radar, so keep to the speed limit (usually 60–90kmph/37–56 mph) if you don't want to be pulled over. Speeding tickets can be charged to your credit card for up to a year after you leave the country if they are not paid before departure.

To reduce congestion and fuel consumption, a rotating ban on rush-hour traffic takes place in the central core of San José Monday through Friday from 7 to 8:30am and from 4 to 5:30pm. The ban affects cars with licenses ending in the digits 1 or 2 on Monday; 3 or 4 on Tuesday; 5 or 6 on Wednesday; 7 or 8 on Thursday; and 9 or 0 on Friday. If you are caught driving a car with the banned license plate during these hours on a specified day, you will be ticketed.

In 2010, Costa Rica passed a new comprehensive traffic law, which severely increased the monetary penalties for traffic offenses. It's still too early to tell if this will help reign in the general chaos and improve Ticos' driving habits, but it should.

BREAKDOWNS Be warned that emergency services, both vehicular and medical, are extremely limited outside San José, and their availability is directly related to the remoteness of your location at the time of breakdown. You'll find service stations spread over the entire length of the Interamerican Highway, and most of these have tow trucks and mechanics. The major towns of Puntarenas, Liberia, Quepos, San Isidro, Palmar, and Golfito all have hospitals, and most other moderately sized cities and tourist destinations have some sort of clinic or health-services provider.

If you're involved in an accident, contact the **National Insurance Institute (INS)** at ✆ **800/800-8000.** You should probably also call the **Transit Police** (✆ **2222-9330** or 2222-9245); if they have a unit close by, they'll send one. An official transit police report will greatly facilitate any insurance claim. If you can't get help from any of these, try to get written statements from any witnesses. Finally, you can also call ✆ **911,** and they should be able to redirect your call to the appropriate agency.

If the police do show up, you've got a 50-50 chance of finding them helpful or downright antagonistic. Many officers are unsympathetic to the problems of what they perceive to be rich tourists running around in fancy cars with lots of expensive toys and trinkets. Success and happy endings run about equal with horror stories.

If you don't speak Spanish, expect added difficulty in any emergency or stressful situation. Don't expect that rural (or urban) police officers, hospital personnel, service-station personnel, or mechanics will speak English.

If your car breaks down and you're unable to get well off the road, check your trunk for reflecting triangles. If you find some, place them as a warning for approaching traffic, arranged in a wedge that starts at the shoulder about 30m (98 ft.) back and nudges gradually toward your car. If your car has no triangles, try to create a similar warning marker using a pile of leaves or branches.

Finally, although not endemic, there have been reports of folks being robbed by seemingly friendly Ticos who stop to give assistance. To add insult to injury, there have even been reports of organized gangs who puncture tires of rental cars at rest stops or busy intersections, only to follow them, offer assistance, and make off with belongings and valuables. If you find yourself with a flat tire, try to ride it to the nearest gas station. If that's not possible, try to pull over into a well-lit public spot. Keep the doors of the car locked and an eye on your belongings while changing the tire, by yourself.

By Bus

This is by far the most economical way to get around Costa Rica. Buses are inexpensive and relatively well maintained, and they go nearly everywhere. The two types are: **Local buses,** the cheapest and slowest, stop frequently and are generally a bit dilapidated. **Express buses** run between San José and most beach towns and major cities; these tend to be newer units and more comfortable, although very few are so new or modern as to have restroom facilities, and they sometimes operate only on weekends and holidays.

Two companies run regular, fixed-schedule departures in passenger vans and small buses to most of the major tourist destinations in the country. **Gray Line** (✆ 800/719-3905 in the U.S. and Canada, or 2220-2126; www.grayline costarica.com) has about 10 departures leaving San José each morning and heading or connecting to Jacó, Manuel Antonio, Liberia, Playa Hermosa, La Fortuna, Tamarindo, and playas Conchal and Flamingo. There are return trips to San José every day from these destinations and a variety of interconnecting routes. A similar service, **Interbus** (✆ 2283-5573; www.interbusonline.com) has a slightly more extensive route map and more connections. Fares run between $30 and $55, depending upon the destination. Gray Line offers an unlimited weekly pass for all of its shuttle routes for $145.

Beware: Both of these companies offer pickup and drop-off at a wide range of hotels. This means that if you are the first picked up or last dropped off, you might have to sit through a long period of subsequent stops before finally hitting the road or reaching your destination. Moreover, I've heard some horror stories about both lines, concerning missed or severely delayed connections and rude drivers. For details on how to get to various destinations from San José, see the "Getting There" sections in the preceding chapters.

Another option is **Costa Rica Drivers** (✆ 8840-2646; www.costarica driver.net), which offers private, custom trips and transfers for groups large and small, to any destination in Costa Rica.

By Taxi

Taxis are readily available in San José and most popular tourist towns and destinations. In San José, your best bet is usually just to hail one down in the street.

However, during rush hours and rain storms, and in more remote destinations, it is probably best to call a cab. Throughout the book, I list numbers for local taxi companies in the "Getting Around" sections. If no number is listed, ask at your hotel, or, if you're out and about, at the nearest restaurant or shop; someone will be more than happy to call you a cab.

All city taxis, and even some rural cabs, have meters (*marías*), although drivers sometimes refuse to use them, particularly with foreigners. If this is the case, be sure to negotiate the price up front. Always try to get drivers to use the meter first (say *"ponga la maría, por favor"*). The official rate at press time is C530 per kilometer (½ mile) and C10 every 4 seconds of wait time. If you have a rough idea of how far it is to your destination, you can estimate how much it should cost from these figures, or you can ask at your hotel how much a specific ride should cost. After 10pm, taxis are legally allowed to add a 20% surcharge. Some of the meters are programmed to include the extra charge automatically, but be careful: Some drivers will use the evening setting during the daytime or (at night) to charge an extra 20% on top of the higher meter setting.

By Thumb

Although buses serve most towns in Costa Rica, service can be infrequent in the remote regions, so local people often hitchhike to get to their destinations sooner. If you're driving a car, people will frequently ask you for a ride. In remote rural areas, a hitchhiker carrying a machete is not necessarily a great danger, but use your judgment. Hitchhiking is not recommended on major roadways or in urban areas. In rural areas, it's usually pretty safe. (However, women should be extremely cautious about hitchhiking anywhere in Costa Rica.) If you choose to hitchhike, keep in mind that if a bus doesn't go to your destination, there probably aren't too many cars going there, either. Good luck.

STAYING HEALTHY

Staying healthy on a trip to Costa Rica is predominantly a matter of being a little cautious about what you eat and drink, and using common sense. Know your physical limits, and don't overexert yourself in the ocean, on hikes, or in athletic activities. Respect the tropical sun and protect yourself from it. As you climb above 10,000 ft (3000m), you may feel the effects of altitude sickness. Be sure to drink plenty of water and not overexert yourself. Limit your exposure to the sun, especially during the first few days of your trip and, thereafter, from 11am to 2pm. Use sunscreen with a high protection factor, and apply it liberally. Remember that children need more protection than adults. I recommend buying and drinking bottled water or soft drinks, but the water in San José and in most of the country's heavily visited spots is safe to drink.

General Availability of Health Care

In general, Costa Rica has a high level of medical care and services for a developing nation. The better private hospitals and doctors in San José are very good. In fact, given the relatively budget nature of care and treatment, a sizable number of Americans come to Costa Rica each year for elective surgery and other care.

Pharmacies are widely available, and generally well stocked. In most cases you will not need a doctor's script to fill or refill a prescription.

I list **additional emergency numbers** in the various destination chapters, as well as in "Fast Facts" below.

If You Get Sick

Your hotel front desk should be your best source of information and assistance if you get sick while in Costa Rica. In addition, your local consulate in Costa Rica can provide a list of area doctors who speak English. The local English-language newspaper, the *Tico Times,* is another good resource. I list the best hospitals in San José in "Fast Facts: San José," in chapter 5; these have the most modern facilities in the country. Most state-run hospitals and walk-in clinics around the country have emergency rooms that can treat most conditions, although I highly recommend the private hospitals in San José if your condition is not life-threatening and can wait for treatment until you reach one of them.

I list **additional emergency numbers** in the various destination chapters, as well as in the "Fast Facts," below.

Regional Health Concerns

TROPICAL ILLNESSES   Your chance of contracting any serious tropical disease in Costa Rica is slim, especially if you stick to the beaches or traditional spots for visitors. However, malaria, dengue fever, and leptospirosis all exist in Costa Rica, so it's a good idea to know what they are.

Malaria is found in the lowlands on both coasts and in the northern zone. Although it's rarely found in urban areas, it's still a problem in remote wooded regions and along the Caribbean coast. Malaria prophylaxes are available, but several have side effects, and others are of questionable effectiveness. Consult your doctor regarding what is currently considered the best preventive treatment for malaria. Be sure to ask whether a recommended drug will cause you to be hypersensitive to the sun; it would be a shame to come down here for the beaches and then have to hide under an umbrella the whole time. Because malaria-carrying mosquitoes usually come out at night, you should do as much as possible to avoid being bitten after dark. If you are in a malaria-prone area, wear long pants and long sleeves, use insect repellent, and either sleep under a mosquito net or burn mosquito coils (similar to incense, but with a pesticide).

Of greater concern is **dengue fever,** which has had periodic outbreaks in Latin America since the mid-1990s. Dengue fever is similar to malaria and is spread by an aggressive daytime mosquito. This mosquito seems to be most common in lowland urban areas, and Puntarenas, Liberia, and Limón have been the worst-hit cities in Costa Rica. Dengue is also known as "bone-break fever" because it is usually accompanied by severe body aches. The first infection with dengue fever will make you very sick but should cause no serious damage. However, a second infection with a different strain of the dengue virus can lead to internal hemorrhaging and could be life threatening.

Many people are convinced that taking B-complex vitamins daily will help prevent mosquitoes from biting you. I don't think the American Medical Association has endorsed this idea yet, but I've run across it in enough places to think that there might be something to it.

One final tropical fever that I think you should know about (because I got it myself) is **leptospirosis.** There are more than 200 strains of leptospires, which are animal-borne bacteria transmitted to humans via contact with drinking, swimming, or bathing water. This bacterial infection is easily treated with antibiotics; however, it can quickly cause very high fever and chills, and should be treated promptly.

If you develop a high fever accompanied by severe body aches, nausea, diarrhea, or vomiting during or shortly after a visit to Costa Rica, consult a physician as soon as possible.

Costa Rica has historically had very few outbreaks of cholera. This is largely due to an extensive public-awareness campaign that has promoted good hygiene and increased sanitation. Your chances of contracting cholera while you're here are very slight.

DIETARY RED FLAGS   Even though the water in San José and most popular destinations in Costa Rica is generally safe, and even if you're careful to buy bottled water, order *frescos en leche* (fruit shakes made with milk rather than water), and drink your soft drink without ice cubes, you still might encounter some intestinal difficulties. Most of this is just due to tender stomachs coming into contact with slightly more aggressive Latin American intestinal flora. In extreme cases of diarrhea or intestinal discomfort, it's worth taking a stool sample to a lab for analysis. The results will usually pinpoint the amoebic or parasitic culprit, which can then be readily treated with available over-the-counter medicines.

Except in the most established and hygienic of restaurants, it's also advisable to avoid *ceviche*, a raw seafood salad, especially if it has any shellfish in it. It could be home to any number of bacterial critters.

BUGS, BITES & OTHER WILDLIFE CONCERNS   Although Costa Rica has Africanized bees (the notorious "killer bees" of fact and fable) and several species of venomous snakes, your chances of being bitten are minimal, especially if you refrain from sticking your hands into hives or under rocks in the forest. If you know that you're allergic to bee stings, consult your doctor before traveling.

At the beaches, you'll probably be bitten by *pirujas* (sand fleas). These nearly invisible insects leave an irritating welt. Try not to scratch because this can lead to open sores and infections. *Pirujas* are most active at sunrise and sunset, so you might want to cover up or avoid the beaches at these times.

Snake sightings, much less snakebites, are very rare. Moreover, the majority of snakes in Costa Rica are nonpoisonous. If you do encounter a snake, stay calm, don't make any sudden movements, and do not try to handle it. As recommended above, avoid sticking your hands under rocks, branches, and fallen trees.

Scorpions, black widow spiders, tarantulas, bullet ants, and biting insects of many types can all be found in Costa Rica. In general, they are not nearly the danger or nuisance most visitors fear. Watch where you stick your hands; in addition, you might want to shake out your clothes and shoes before putting them on to avoid any unpleasant and painful surprises.

TROPICAL SUN   Limit your exposure to the sun, especially during the first few days of your trip and, thereafter, from 11am to 2pm. Use a sunscreen with a high protection factor, and apply it liberally. Remember that children need more protection than adults.

RIPTIDES   Many of Costa Rica's beaches have riptides: strong currents that can drag swimmers out to sea. A riptide occurs when water that has been dumped on the shore by strong waves forms a channel back out to open water. These channels have strong currents. If you get caught in a riptide, you can't escape the current by swimming toward shore; it's like trying to swim upstream in a river. To break free of the current, swim parallel to shore and use the energy of the waves to help you get back to the beach.

TIPS ON ACCOMMODATIONS

When the Costa Rican tourist boom began in the late 1980s, hotels popped up like mushrooms after a heavy rain. By the 1990s the country's first true megaresorts opened, more followed, and still more are under construction or in the planning phase. Except during the few busiest weeks of the year, there's a relative glut of rooms in Costa Rica. That said, most hotels are small to midsize, and the best ones fill up fast most of the year. You'll generally have to reserve well in advance if you want to land a room at any of the hotels on my "Best of" lists in chapter 1. Still, in broader terms, the glut of rooms is good news for travelers and bargain hunters. Less popular hotels that want to survive are being forced to reduce their rates and provide better service.

Your best bet in Costa Rica is negotiating directly with the hotels themselves, especially the smaller hotels. Almost every hotel in Costa Rica has e-mail, if not its own website, and you'll find the contact information in this book. However, be aware that response times might be slower than you'd like, and many of the smaller hotels might have some trouble communicating back and forth in English.

 Skip the Motel

You'll want to avoid motels in Costa Rica. To a fault, these are cut-rate affairs geared toward lovers consummating their affairs—usually illicit. Most rent out rooms by the hour, and most have private garages with roll-down doors outside each room, so that snoopy spouses or ex-lovers can't check for cars or license plates.

Throughout this book, I separate hotel listings into several broad categories: **Very Expensive,** $200 and up; **Expensive,** $125 to $199; **Moderate,** $60 to $124; and **Inexpensive,** under $60 for a double. *Rates given in this book do not include the 13% room taxes, unless otherwise specified.* These taxes will add considerably to the cost of your room.

Throughout Costa Rica, rates generally fluctuate somewhat according to season and demand, with a majority of hotels offering lower rates in the off season, and charging higher rates during peak periods.

Hotel Options

Costa Rica has hotels to suit every budget and travel style. In addition to the Four Seasons and JW Marriott, the host of amazing boutique hotels around the country will satisfy the high-end and luxury traveler.

Still, the country's strong suit is its **moderately priced hotels.** In the $60-to-$124 price range, you'll find comfortable and sometimes outstanding accommodations almost anywhere in the country. However, room size and quality vary quite a bit within this price range, so don't expect the kind of uniformity that you may find at home.

If you're even more budget- or bohemian-minded, you can find quite a few good deals for less than $50 a double. ***But beware:*** Budget-oriented lodgings often feature shared bathrooms and either cold-water showers or showers heated by electrical heat-coil units mounted at the shower head, affectionately known as "suicide showers." If your hotel has one, do not adjust it while the water is running. Unless specifically noted, all rooms listed in this guide have a private bathroom.

Note: Air-conditioning is not necessarily a given in many midrange hotels and even some upscale joints. In general, this is not a problem. Cooler nights and a well-placed ceiling fan are often more than enough to keep things pleasant, unless I mention otherwise in the hotel reviews.

Bed-and-breakfasts are also abundant. Although the majority are in the San José area, you'll also find B&Bs (often gringo-owned and -operated) throughout the country. Another welcome hotel trend in the San José area is the renovation and conversion of old homes into **small hotels.** Most are in the Barrio Amón district of downtown San José, which means that you'll sometimes have to put up with noise and exhaust fumes, but these establishments have more character than any other hotels in the country. You'll find similar hotels in the Paseo Colón and Los Yoses districts.

Costa Rica has many small nature-oriented **ecolodges.** These lodges offer opportunities to see wildlife (including sloths, monkeys, and hundreds of species of birds) and learn about tropical forests. They range from spartan facilities catering primarily to scientific researchers, to luxury accommodations that are among the finest in the country. Keep in mind that although the nightly room rates at these lodges are often quite moderate, prices start to climb when you throw in transportation (often on chartered planes), guided excursions, and meals. Also, just because you can book a reservation at most of these lodges doesn't mean that they're not remote. Be sure to find out how you get to and from the ecolodge, and what tours and services are included in your stay. Then think long and hard about whether you really want to put up with hot, humid weather (cool and wet in the cloud forests); biting insects; rugged transportation; and strenuous hikes to see wildlife.

A couple of uniquely Costa Rican accommodations types that you might encounter are the **apartotel** and the **cabina.** An apartotel is just what it sounds like: an apartment hotel where you'll get a full kitchen and one or two bedrooms, along with daily maid service. Cabinas are Costa Rica's version of cheap vacation lodging. They're very inexpensive and very basic—often just cinder-block buildings divided into small rooms. Occasionally, you'll find a cabina in which the units are actually cabins, but these are a rarity. Cabinas often have clothes-washing sinks (*pilas*), and some come with kitchenettes; they cater primarily to Tico families on vacation.

For tips on surfing for hotel deals online, visit Frommers.com.

[FastFACTS] COSTA RICA

Area Codes There are no area codes in Costa Rica. All phone numbers are eight-digit numbers.

Business Hours Banks are usually open Monday through Friday from 9am to 4pm, although many have begun to offer extended hours. Post offices are generally open Monday through Friday from 8am to 5:30pm, and Saturday from 7:30am to noon. (In small towns, post offices often close on Sat.) Stores are generally open Monday through Saturday from 9am to 6pm (many close for 1 hr. at lunch) but stores in modern malls generally stay open until 8 or 9pm and don't close for lunch. Most bars are open until 1 or 2am, although some go later.

Car Rental See "Getting There by Car," earlier in this chapter.

Cellphones See "Mobile Phones," later in this section.

Crime See "Safety," later in this section.

Customs Visitors to Costa Rica are permitted to bring in all manner of items for personal use, including cameras, video cameras and accessories, tape recorders, personal computers, and music players. Customs officials in Costa Rica seldom check tourists' luggage.

Disabled Travelers Although Costa Rica does have a law mandating Equality of Opportunities for People with Disabilities, and some facilities have been adapted, in general, there are relatively few buildings or public buses for travelers with disabilities in the country. In San José, sidewalks are particularly crowded and uneven, and they are nonexistent in most of the rest of the country. Few hotels offer wheelchair-accessible accommodations. In short, it can be difficult for a person with disabilities to get around San José and Costa Rica.

However, one local agency specializes in tours for travelers with disabilities and restricted ability. **Vaya Con Silla de Ruedas** (☏/fax **2454-2810,** or ☏ 8391-5045; www.gowithwheelchairs.com) has a ramp- and elevator-equipped van and knowledgeable, bilingual guides. It charges very reasonable prices and can provide anything from simple airport transfers to complete multiday tours.

Doctors Your hotel front desk will be your best source of information on what to do and where to go for treatment. Most have the number of a trusted doctor on hand. In addition, your local consulate in Costa Rica can provide a list of area doctors who speak English. Also see "Staying Healthy" earlier in this chapter.

Drinking Laws Alcoholic beverages are sold every day of the week throughout the year, with the exception of the 2 days before Easter and the 2 days before and after a presidential election. The legal drinking age is 18, although it's only sporadically enforced. Liquor—everything from beer to hard spirits—is sold in specific liquor stores, as well as at most supermarkets and even convenience stores.

Driving Rules See "Getting Around," earlier in this chapter.

Electricity The standard in Costa Rica is the same as in the United States and Canada: 110 volts AC (60 cycles). However, three-pronged outlets can be scarce, so it's helpful to bring along an adapter. Wherever you go, bring a **connection kit** of the right power, plus phone adapters, a spare phone cord, and a spare Ethernet network cable—or find out whether your hotel supplies them to guests.

Embassies & Consulates The following are located in San José: **United States Embassy,** Calle 120 and Avenida 0, Pavas (☏ **2519-2000,** or 8863-4895 after hours in case of emergency; http://sanjose.usembassy.gov); **Canadian Embassy,** Oficentro Ejecutivo La Sabana, Edificio 5 (☏ **2242-4400;** http://costarica.gc.ca); and **British Embassy,** Edificio Colón, 11th Floor, Paseo Colón between calles 38 and 40 (☏ **2258-2025;** http://ukincostarica.fco.gov.uk/en). There are no Australian, Irish, or New Zealand embassies in San José.

Emergencies In case of any emergency, dial ☏ **911** (which should have an English-speaking operator); for an ambulance, call ☏ **1028;** and to report a fire, call ☏ **1118.** If 911 doesn't work, you can contact the police at ☏ **2222-1365** or 2221-5337, and hopefully they can find someone who speaks English.

Family Travel Hotels in Costa Rica often give discounts for children, and allow children to stay for free in a parent's room. Still, discounts for children and the cutoff ages vary according to the hotel, and, in general, don't assume that your kids can stay in your room for free.

Some hotels, villas, and cabinas come equipped with kitchenettes or full kitchen facilities. These can be a real money-saver for those traveling with children, and I list many of these accommodations in the destination chapters in this book.

Hotels offering regular, dependable babysitting service are few and far between. If you will need babysitting, make sure that your hotel offers it, and be sure to ask whether the babysitters are bilingual. In many cases, they are not. This is usually not a problem with infants and toddlers, but it can cause problems with older children.

To locate accommodations, restaurants, and attractions that are particularly kid-friendly, look for the "Kids" icon throughout this guide.

Gasoline Please see "Getting There By Car," earlier in this chapter.

Insurance For information on traveler's insurance, trip cancellation insurance, and medical insurance while traveling, please visit http://www.frommers.com/planning.

Internet & Wi-Fi Cybercafes can be found all over Costa Rica, especially in the more popular tourist destinations. Moreover, an ever increasing number of hotels, restaurants, cafes, and retailers around Costa Rica are offering high-speed Wi-Fi access, either free or for a small fee. Throughout the book, I list which hotels provide free, or for a fee, Wi-Fi and high-speed Ethernet access.

Language Spanish is the official language of Costa Rica. However, in most tourist areas, you'll be surprised by how well Costa Ricans speak English. *Frommer's Spanish PhraseFinder & Dictionary* is probably the best phrase book to bring with you; also see chapter 15 for some key Spanish terms and phrases.

Legal Aid If you need legal help, your best bet is to first contact your local embassy or consulate. See "Embassies & Consulates," above, for contact details. Alternatively, you can pick up a copy of the *Tico Times,* which usually carries advertisements from local English-speaking lawyers.

LGBT Travelers Costa Rica is a Catholic, conservative, macho country where public displays of same-sex affection are rare and considered somewhat shocking. Public figures, politicians, and religious leaders periodically denounce homosexuality. However, gay and lesbian tourism to Costa Rica is quite robust, and gay and lesbian travelers are generally treated with respect and should not experience any harassment.

For a general overview of the current situation, info on LGBT friendly hotels, bars, and tour agencies, and news of any special events or meetings, the website **www.costaricagaymap.com** is your best bet, especially for gay men, and to a much lesser extent for lesbian women. If you speak Spanish, you'll want to connect with the **Comunidad Arco Iris** (CARI; ✆ **2221-1636;** www.caricr.com), which serves as a meeting place and information clearinghouse for the entire LGBT community.

The **International Gay and Lesbian Travel Association** (**IGLTA;** ✆ **954/630-1637;** www.iglta.org) is the trade association for the gay and lesbian travel industry, and offers an online directory of gay- and lesbian-friendly travel businesses and tour operators.

Mail At press time, it cost C350 to mail a letter to the United States, and C395 to Europe. You can get stamps at post offices and at some gift shops in large hotels. Given the Costa Rican postal service's track record, I recommend paying an extra C500 to have anything of any value certified. Better yet, use an international courier service or wait until you get home to post it. **DHL,** on Paseo Colón between calles 30 and 32 (✆ **2209-6000;** www.dhl.com); **EMS Courier,** with desks at most post offices nationwide (✆ **800/900-2000** in Costa Rica; www.correos.go.cr); **FedEx,** which is based in Heredia but will arrange pickup anywhere in the metropolitan area (✆ **800/463-3339;** www.fedex.com); and **United Parcel Service,** in Pavas (✆ **2290-2828;** www.ups.com), all operate in Costa Rica.

If you're sending mail *to* Costa Rica, it generally takes between 10 and 14 days to reach San José, although it can take as much as a month to get to the more remote corners of the country. Plan ahead. Also note that many hotels and ecolodges have mailing addresses in the United States. Always use these addresses when writing from North America or Europe. Never send cash, checks, or valuables through the Costa Rican mail system.

Throughout the book, I only list physical addresses for hotels. In this day of e-mails and fax communications, traditional mail between hotels and clients is extremely rare. That said, hotel addresses can easily be attained via their websites, and in fact, many hotels and ecolodges in Costa Rica maintain a mailing address in the United States.

Medical Requirements No shots or inoculations are required to enter Costa Rica. The exception to this is for those who have recently been traveling in a country or region known to have yellow fever. In this case, proof of a yellow fever vaccination is required. Also see "Staying Healthy," earlier in this chapter.

Mobile Phones Costa Rica primarily uses **GSM** (Global System for Mobile Communications) networks. If your cellphone is on a GSM system, and you have a world-capable multiband phone, you should be able to make and receive calls in Costa Rica. Just call your wireless operator and ask for "international roaming" to be activated on your account. Per-minute charges can be high, though—up to $5 in Costa Rica, depending upon your plan.

You can purchase a **pre-paid SIM card for an unlocked GSM phone** at the airport and offices of the Costa Rican Electrical Institute (ICE) around the country. A 30-day SIM card costs around $4. You'll need an 1800mHz band, unlocked phone. You can buy minutes separately via phone cards or at ICE offices.

Moreover, as this book goes to press, two new cellphone operators, Claro and Telefonica, were making final preparations to enter into the Costa Rican market. This will most certainly open the availability and range of options for tourists and visitors.

Several local firms rent cellphones. However, none of the rental companies has a booth or office at the airport, so you'll have to contact them either beforehand or from your hotel. Most will deliver the phone to your hotel. **Cell Service** (✆ **2296-5553;** www.cellservicecr.com) and **Costa Rica Cellular Connection** (✆ **866/353-6492** in the U.S. and Canada, or 8876-1776 in Costa Rica; www.costaricacellularconnection.com) both rent cellphones. Rates run around $5 to $8 per day or $30 to $50 per week for the rental, with charges of 50¢ to $1.50 per minute for local calls and $1 to $3 per minute for international calls. In addition to the above companies, most of the major car-rental agencies offer cellphone rentals, for rates similar to those listed above.

Money & Costs   The unit of currency in Costa Rica is the **colón.** Frommer's lists exact prices. In this book, prices are listed in the currency you are most likely to see them quoted. Hence, nearly all hotel prices and most tour and transportation prices are listed in dollars, since the hotels, airlines, tour agencies, and transport companies quote their prices in dollars. Many restaurants do as well. Still, a good many restaurants, as well as taxis and other local goods and services, are advertised and quoted in colones. In those cases, prices listed are in colones (C).

The colón is divided into 100 **céntimos.** Currently, two types of coins are in circulation. You'll find gold-hued 5-, 10-, 25-, 50-, 100-, and 500-colón coins, as well as lightweight silver-colored alloy coins in the 5- and 10- colón denominations.

Paper notes come in denominations of 1,000, 2,000, 5,000, 10,000 and 20,000 colones. You might also encounter a special-issue 5-colón bill that is a popular gift and souvenir. It is valid currency, although it sells for much more than its face value. You might hear people refer to a *rojo* or *tucán,* which are slang terms for the 1,000- and 5,000-colón bills, respectively. One-hundred-colón denominations are called *tejas,* so *cinco tejas* is 500 colones. I've yet to encounter a slang equivalent for the 2,000, 10,000, and 20,000 bills.

Forged bills are not entirely uncommon. When receiving change in colones, it's a good idea to check the larger-denomination bills, which should have protective bands or hidden images that appear when held up to the light.

WHAT THINGS COST IN COSTA RICA	US$
Taxi from the airport to downtown San José	22.00–32.00
Double room, moderate	90.00
Double room, inexpensive	45.00
Three-course dinner for one without wine, moderate	15.00–25.00
Bottle of beer	1.00–1.50
Cup of coffee	1.00–1.50
1 gallon/1 liter of premium gas	4.70/1.25
Admission to most museums	2.00–5.00
Admission to most national parks	10.00

You can change money at all banks in Costa Rica. The principal state banks are **Banco Nacional** and **Banco de Costa Rica.** However, be forewarned that service at state banks can be slow and tedious. You're almost always better off finding a private bank. Luckily, there are hosts of private banks around San José and in most major tourist destinations.

Since banks handle money exchanges, Costa Rica has very, very few exchange houses. One major exception to this is the **Global Exchange** (✆ **2431-0670;** www.globalexchange.co.cr) office at the airport. However, be forewarned they exchange at more than 10% below the official exchange rate. Airport taxis accept U.S. dollars, so there isn't necessarily any great need to exchange money the moment you arrive.

Hotels will often exchange money and cash traveler's checks as well; there usually isn't much of a line, but they might shave a few colones off the exchange rate.

Be very careful about exchanging money on the streets; it's extremely risky. In addition to forged bills and short counts, street money-changers frequently work in teams that can leave you holding neither colones nor dollars. Also be very careful when leaving a bank. Criminals are often looking for foreigners who have just withdrawn or exchanged cash.

The currency conversions provided below were correct at press time. However, rates fluctuate, so before departing consult a currency exchange website such as **www.oanda.com/currency/converter** to check up-to-the-minute rates.

THE VALUE OF THE COLÓN VS. OTHER POPULAR CURRENCIES

Colónes	Aus$	Can$	Euro (€)	NZ$	UK £	US$
500	A$098	C0.97	€0.71	NZ$1.32	61p	$1

MasterCard and **Visa** are the most widely accepted credit cards in Costa Rica, followed by American Express. Most hotels and restaurants accept all of these, especially in tourist destination areas. Discover and Diners Club are far less commonly accepted.

Beware of hidden credit card fees while traveling. Check with your credit or debit card issuer to see what fees, if any, will be charged for overseas transactions. Recent reform legislation in the U.S., for example, has curbed some exploitative lending practices. But many banks have responded by increasing fees in other areas, including fees for customers who use credit and debit cards while out of the country—even if those charges were made in U.S. dollars. Fees can amount to 3% or more of the purchase price. Check with your bank before departing to avoid any surprise charges on your statement.

Costa Rica has a modern and widespread network of ATMs. You should find ATMs in all but the most remote tourist destinations and isolated nature lodges. In 2009, in response to a rash of "express kidnappings" in San José, in which folks were taken at gunpoint to an ATM to clean out their bank accounts, both Banco Nacional and Banco de Costa Rica stopped ATM service between the hours of 10pm and 5am. Other networks still dispense money 24 hours a day.

It's probably a good idea to change your PIN to a four-digit PIN. While many ATMs in Costa Rica will accept five- and six-digit PINs, some will only accept four-digit PINs.

For help with currency conversions, tip calculations, and more, download Frommer's convenient Travel Tools app for your mobile device. Go to http://www.frommers.com/go/mobile and click on the Travel Tools icon.

Newspapers & Magazines   Costa Rica has a half-dozen or so Spanish-language dailies and one English-language weekly, the *Tico Times.* In addition, you can get *Time, Newsweek,* and several U.S. newspapers at some hotel gift shops and a few of the bookstores in San José. If you understand Spanish, *La Nación* is the paper you'll want. Its "Viva" and "Tiempo Libre" sections list what's going on in the world of music, theater, dance, and more.

Packing   Everyone should be sure to pack the essentials: sunscreen, insect repellent, camera, bathing suit, a wide-brimmed hat, all prescription medications, and so forth. You'll want good hiking shoes and/or beach footwear, depending upon your itinerary. I also like to have a waterproof headlamp or flashlight and refillable water bottle. Lightweight long-sleeved shirts and long pants are good protection from both the sun and insects. Surfers use "rash guards," quick-drying lycra or polyester shirts, which provide great protection from the sun while swimming.

If you're just heading to Guanacaste between December and March, you won't need anything for the rain. Otherwise, I recommend either or both an umbrella or some rain gear. Most high-end hotels provide umbrellas. If you plan to do any wildlife viewing, bringing your own binoculars is a good idea, as is a field guide (see p. 531 for recommendations).

For more helpful information on packing for your trip, download Frommer's convenient Travel Tools app for your mobile device. Go to and click on the Travel Tools icon.

Passports   Citizens of the United States, Canada, Great Britain, and most European nations may visit Costa Rica for a maximum of 90 days. No visa is necessary, but you must have a valid passport, which you should carry with you at all times while you're in Costa Rica. Citizens of Australia, Ireland, and New Zealand can enter the country without a visa and stay for 30 days, although once in the country, visitors can apply for an extension.

If you overstay your visa or original entry stamp, you will have to pay around $45 for an exit visa. If you need to get an exit visa, a travel agent in San José can usually obtain one for a small fee and save you the hassle of dealing with Immigration. If you want to stay longer than the validity of your entry stamp or visa, the easiest thing to do is cross the border into Panama or Nicaragua for 72 hours and then reenter Costa Rica on a new entry stamp or visa. However, be careful: Periodically the Costa Rican government has cracked down on "perpetual tourists"; if it notices a continued pattern of exits and entries designed simply to support an extended stay, it might deny you reentry.

It is advised to always have at least one or two consecutive blank pages in your passport to allow space for visas and stamps that need to appear together. It is also important to note when your passport expires. Many countries require your passport to have at least 6 months left before its expiration in order to allow you into the destination.

See "Embassies & Consulates," above, for whom to contact if you lose your passport while traveling. For other information, contact the following agencies:

Australia   Australian Passport Information Service (© **131-232;** www.passports.gov.au).

Canada Passport Office, Department of Foreign Affairs and International Trade, Ottawa, ON K1A 0G3 (☎ **800/567-6868;** www.ppt.gc.ca).

Ireland Passport Office, Setanta Centre, Molesworth St., Dublin 2 (☎ **01/671-1633;** www.foreignaffairs.gov.ie).

New Zealand Passports Office, Department of Internal Affairs, 47 Boulcott St., Wellington, 6011 (☎ **0800/225-050** in New Zealand or 04/474-8100; www.passports.govt.nz).

United Kingdom Visit your nearest passport office, major post office, or travel agency or contact the **Identity and Passport Service (IPS),** 89 Eccleston Square, London, SW1V 1PN (☎ **0300/222-0000;** www.ips.gov.uk).

United States To find your regional passport office, check the U.S. State Department website (travel.state.gov/passport) or call the **National Passport Information Center** (☎ **877/487-2778**) for automated information.

Petrol Please see "Getting Around by Car," earlier in this chapter.

Police In most cases, dial ☎ **911** for the police, and you should be able to get someone who speaks English on the line. Other numbers for the **Judicial Police** are ☎ **2222-1365** and 2221-5337. The numbers for the **Traffic Police (Policía de Tránsito)** are ☎ **800/8726-7486** toll-free nationwide, or 2222-9330.

Safety Although most of Costa Rica is safe, petty crime and robberies committed against tourists are endemic. San José, in particular, is known for its pickpockets, so never carry a wallet in your back pocket. A woman should keep a tight grip on her purse (keep it tucked under your arm). Thieves also target gold chains, cameras and video cameras, prominent jewelry, and nice sunglasses. Be sure not to leave valuables unsecured in your hotel room, or unattended on the beach. Given the high rate of stolen passports in Costa Rica, mostly as collateral damage in a typical pickpocketing or room robbery, it is recommended that, whenever possible, you leave your passport in a hotel safe, and travel with a photocopy of the pertinent pages. Don't park a car on the street in Costa Rica, especially in San José; plenty of public parking lots are around the city.

Rental cars generally stick out and are easily spotted by thieves. Don't leave anything of value in a car parked on the street, not even for a moment. Be wary of solicitous strangers who stop to help you change a tire or take you to a service station. Although most are truly good Samaritans, there have been reports of thieves preying on roadside breakdowns. See "Getting Around, By Car," above, for more info.

Inter-city buses are also frequent targets of stealthy thieves. Try not to check your bags into the hold of a bus, if they will fit in the rack above your seat. If this can't be avoided, keep your eye on what leaves the hold. If you put your bags in an overhead rack, be sure you can see the bags at all times. Try not to fall asleep.

Single women should use common sense and take precaution, especially after dark. I don't recommend that single women walk alone anywhere at night, especially on seemingly deserted beaches, or dark uncrowded streets.

Senior Travel Be sure to mention that you're a senior when you make your travel reservations. Although it's not common policy in Costa Rica to offer senior discounts, don't be shy about asking for one anyway. You never know. Always carry some kind of identification, such as a driver's license, that shows your date of birth, especially if you've kept your youthful glow.

Many reliable agencies and organizations target the 50-plus market. **Elderhostel** (☎ **800/454-5768** in the U.S. and Canada; www.elderhostel.org) arranges Costa Rica study programs for those ages 55 and older, as well as intergenerational trips good for families. **ElderTreks** (☎ **800/741-7956** in the U.S. and Canada; 0808-234-1714 in the U.K.; www.eldertreks.com) offers small-group tours to Costa Rica, restricted to travelers 50 and older.

Smoking Many Costa Ricans smoke, and public smoking regulations and smoke-free zones have yet to take hold. A comprehensive tobacco and smoking reform law is currently stalled in the legislature. Restaurants are required by law to have nonsmoking areas, but enforcement is often lax, air-circulation poor, and the separating almost nonexistent. Bars, as a whole, are often very smoke-filled in Costa Rica.

Most higher-end hotels have at least some nonsmoking rooms. However, many midrange hotels and most budget options are pretty laissez-faire when it comes to smoking. Whenever possible, the presence of nonsmoking rooms is noted in hotel listing description information.

Student Travel In Costa Rica, there is one travel agency that specializes in student and youth travel: **OTEC** (☎ **2523-0500;** www.otecviajes.com). These folks have three offices in San José, located in downtown, Escazú, and the university district of San Pedro, and another office across from the National University in Heredia. OTEC also has sister operations throughout Central America, and are official representatives of STA Travel, the leader in international student travel.

Although you won't find any discounts at the national parks, most museums and other attractions around Costa Rica do offer discounts for students. It always pays to ask.

Taxes The national 13% value added tax (often written as i.v.i. in Costa Rica) is added to all goods and services. This includes hotel and restaurant bills. Restaurants also add on a 10% service charge, for a total of 23% more on your bill.

The airport departure tax is $26. This tax must be purchased prior to check-in. Desks where you can pay this tax are in the main terminal of all international airports. Some local travel agencies and hotels offer to purchase the departure tax in advance, as a convenience for tourists. You must give them authorization, as well as your passport number, and pay a small service fee.

Although you can pay the airport exit tax with a credit card, it is charged as a cash advance. Most credit card companies hit this kind of transaction with a fee and begin charging interest on it immediately. It is best to pay the airport tax in cash, either dollars or colones.

Telephones Costa Rica has an excellent and widespread phone system. A phone call within the country costs around C10 per minute. Pay phones take a calling card or 5-, 10-, or 20-colón coins. Calling cards are much more practical, and coin-operated phones are getting harder and harder to find. You can purchase calling cards in a host of gift shops and pharmacies. However, there are several competing calling-card companies, and certain cards work only with certain phones. **CHIP** calling cards work with a computer chip and just slide into specific phones, although these phones aren't widely available. Better bets are the **197** and **199** calling cards, which are sold in varying denominations. These have a scratch-off PIN and can be used from any phone in the country. Generally, the 197 cards are sold in smaller denominations and are used for local calling, while the 199 cards are deemed international and are easier to find in larger denominations. Either card can be used to make any call, however, provided that the card can cover the costs. Another perk of the 199 cards is the fact that you can get the instructions in English. For local calls, it is often easiest to call from your hotel, although you will likely be charged around C150 to C300 per call.

To call Costa Rica from abroad:

1. Dial the international access code: 011 from the U.S. and Canada; 00 from the U.K., Ireland, or New Zealand; or 0011 from Australia.
2. Dial the country code 506.
3. Dial the 8-digit number.

To make international calls: To make international calls from Costa Rica, first dial 00 and then the country code (U.S. or Canada 1, U.K. 44, Ireland 353, Australia 61, New Zealand 64). Next you dial the area code and number. For example, if you wanted to call the British Embassy in Washington, D.C., you would dial 00-1-202-588-7800.

For directory assistance: Dial 1113 if you're looking for a number inside Costa Rica, and dial 1024 for numbers to all other countries.

For operator assistance: If you need operator assistance in making a call, dial 1116 if you're trying to make an international call, and 0 if you want to call a number in Costa Rica.

Toll-free numbers: Numbers beginning with 0800 or 800 within Costa Rica are toll-free, but calling a 1-800 number in the States from Costa Rica is not toll-free. In fact, it costs the same as an overseas call.

Time   Costa Rica is on Central Standard Time (same as Chicago and St. Louis), 6 hours behind Greenwich Mean Time. Costa Rica does not use daylight saving time, so the time difference is an additional hour April through October.

For help with time translations, and more, download Frommer's convenient Travel Tools app for your mobile device. Go to and click on the Travel Tools icon.

Tipping   Tipping is not necessary in restaurants, where a 10% service charge is always added to your bill (along with a 13% tax). If service was particularly good, you can leave a little at your own discretion, but it's not mandatory. Porters and bellhops get around C500 to C1,000 per bag. You don't need to tip a taxi driver unless the service has been superior; a tip is not usually expected.

For help with tip calculations, currency conversions, and more, download Frommer's convenient Travel Tools app for your mobile device. Go to http://www.frommers.com/go/mobile and click on the Travel Tools icon.

Toilets   These are known as *sanitarios, servicios sanitarios,* or *baños.* They are marked *damas* (women) and *hombres* or *caballeros* (men). Public restrooms are hard to come by. You will almost never find a public restroom in a city park or downtown area. Public restrooms are usually at most national-park entrances, and much less frequently inside the national park. In towns and cities, it gets much trickier. One must count on the generosity of some hotel or restaurant. Same goes for most beaches. However, most restaurants, and, to a lesser degree, hotels, will let you use their facilities, especially if you buy a soft drink or something. Bus and gas stations often have restrooms, but many of these are pretty grim. In some restrooms around the country, especially more remote and natural areas, it's common practice not to flush any foreign matter, aside from your business, down the toilet. This includes toilet paper, sanitary napkins, cigarette butts, and so forth. You will usually find a little sign advising you of this practice in the restroom.

VAT See "Taxes" earlier in this section.

Visitor Information In the United States or Canada, you can get basic information on Costa Rica by contacting the **Costa Rican Tourist Board** (**ICT,** or Instituto Costarricense de Turismo; ☏ **866/267-8274** in the U.S. and Canada, or 2299-5800 in Costa Rica; www.visitcostarica.com). Travelers from the United Kingdom, Australia, and New Zealand will have to rely primarily on this website, or call direct to Costa Rica, because the ICT does not have toll-free access in these countries.

In addition to this official site, you'll be able to find a wealth of Web-based information on Costa Rica with a few clicks of your mouse. In fact, you'll be better off surfing, as the ICT site is rather limited and clunky. See "The Best Websites About Costa Rica," on p. 27, for some helpful suggestions about where to begin your online search.

You can pick up a map at the ICT's information desk at the airport when you arrive, or at their downtown San José offices (although the destination maps and fold-out map that come with this book are sufficient for most purposes). Perhaps the best map to have is the waterproof country map of Costa Rica put out by **Toucan Maps** (www. mapcr.com), which can be ordered directly from their website, or any major online bookseller, like Amazon.com.

Water Although the water in San José is generally safe to drink, water quality varies outside the city. Because many travelers have tender digestive tracts, I recommend playing it safe and sticking to bottled drinks as much as possible. Also avoid ice. See p. 516 for more advice.

Wi-Fi See "Internet & Wi-Fi," earlier in this section.

Women Travelers For lack of better phrasing, Costa Rica is a typically "macho" Latin American nation. Single women can expect catcalls, hisses, whistles, and car horns, especially in San José. In most cases, while annoying, this is harmless and intended by Tico men as a compliment. Nonetheless, women should be careful walking alone at night throughout the country. Also, see "Safety," earlier in this section.

AIRLINE WEBSITES

MAJOR AIRLINES

Aeroméxico
www.aeromexico.com

Air France
www.airfrance.com

Air New Zealand
www.airnewzealand.com

Alitalia
www.alitalia.com

American Airlines
www.aa.com

British Airways
www.british-airways.com

Caribbean Airlines (formerly BWIA)
www.caribbean-airlines.com

Continental Airlines
www.continental.com

Delta Air Lines
www.delta.com

Frontier Airlines
www.frontierairlines.com

Iberia Airlines
www.iberia.com

Japan Airlines
www.jal.co.jp

JetBlue Airways
www.jetblue.com

Korean Air
www.koreanair.com

Lan Airlines
www.lan.com

Lufthansa
www.lufthansa.com

Qantas Airways
www.qantas.com

TACA
www.taca.com

United Airlines
www.united.com

US Airways
www.usairways.com

Virgin Atlantic Airways
www.virgin-atlantic.com

DOMESTIC AIRLINES

Nature Air
www.natureair.com

Sansa
www.flysansa.com

14

COSTA RICAN WILDLIFE

F or such a small country, Costa Rica is incredibly rich in biodiversity. With just .01% of the earth's landmass, the country is home to some 5% of its biodiversity. Whether you come to Costa Rica to check 100 or more species off your lifetime list, or just to check out of the rat race for a week or so, you'll be surrounded by a rich and varied collection of flora and fauna.

In many instances, the prime viewing recommendations should be understood within the reality of actual wildlife viewing. Most casual visitors and even many dedicated naturalists will never see a wild cat or kinkajou. However, anyone working with a good guide should be able to see a broad selection of Costa Rica's impressive flora and fauna. The information below is meant to be a selective introduction to some of what you might see.

Scores of good field guides are available; two of the best general guides are *The Field Guide to the Wildlife of Costa Rica,* by Carrol Henderson, and *Costa Rica: Traveller's Wildlife Guides,* by Les Beletsky. Bird-watchers will want to pick up one or both of the following two books: *A Guide to the Birds of Costa Rica,* by F. Gary Stiles and Alexander Skutch and *Birds of Costa Rica,* by Richard Garrigues and Robert Dean. Other specialized guides to mammals, reptiles, insects, flora, and more are also available. In Costa Rica, **Seventh Street Books,** on Calle 7 between avenidas 1 and Central in San José (© **2256-8251**), always has a great selection, including many of the specialized guides which they produce under their own publishing house imprint, Zona Tropical (www.zonatropical.net).

See "The Lay of the Land," in chapter 2, for more information, as well as "Tips on Health, Safety & Etiquette in the Wilderness," in chapter 4.

FAUNA
Mammals

Costa Rica has more than 230 species of mammals. Roughly half of these are bats. While it is very unlikely that you will spot a wildcat, you have good odds of catching a glimpse of a monkey, coatimundi, peccary, or sloth, or more likely any number of bats.

Jaguar

Jaguar (Panthera onca)   This cat measures from 1 to 1.8m (3½–6 ft.) plus tail and is distinguished by its tan/yellowish fur with black spots. Often called simply *tigre* (tiger) in Costa Rica. Jaguars are classified as nocturnal, although some say it would be more accurate to describe them as crepuscular, most active in the periods around dawn and dusk. **Prime Viewing:** Major tracts of primary and secondary forest in

PREVIOUS PAGE: **A Resplendent Quetzal.**

Costa Rica, as well as some open savannas; the greatest concentration is in Corcovado National Park (p. 426) on the Osa Peninsula. However, jaguars are endangered and extremely hard to see in the wild.

Ocelot

Jaguarundi

Paca

Tayra

Baird's Tapir

Ocelot (Leopardus pardalis)   Known as *manigordo,* or "fat paws," in Costa Rica, the tail of this small cat is longer than its rear leg, which makes for easy identification. Ocelots are mostly nocturnal, and they sleep in trees. **Prime Viewing:** Forests in all regions of Costa Rica, with the greatest concentration found on the Osa Peninsula.

Jaguarundi (Herpailurus yaguarondi)   This small to midsize cat has a solid black, brown, or reddish coat and an oval-shaped face often compared to that of a weasel or otter, giving it a unique look for a wild cat. The jaguarundi is a diurnal hunter; it can occasionally be spotted in a clearing or climbing a tree. **Prime Viewing:** Most frequently spotted in middle elevation moist forests.

Paca (Agouti paca)   The paca, known as *tepezquintle* in Costa Rica, is a nocturnal rodent that feeds on fallen fruit, leaves, and tubers it digs from the ground. It features dark brown to black fur on its back, usually with three to five rows of white spots. Its belly fur tends to be lighter in color. However, since this species is nocturnal, you're more likely to see its cousin, the diurnal agouti or *guatusa,* which in addition to being smaller, is of a lighter brown coloring, with no spots. **Prime Viewing:** Most often found near water throughout many habitats of Costa Rica, from river valleys to swamps to dense tropical forest.

Tayra (Eira Barbara)   Known as *tolumuco* or *gato de monte* in Costa Rica, this midsize rodent is in the weasel family. Tayras run from dark brown to black, with a brown to tan head and neck. Long and low to the ground, they have a long, bushy tail. **Prime Viewing:** Tayras are found across the country, in forests as well as plain areas, and in trees, as well as on the ground.

Baird's Tapir (Tapirus bairdii)   Known as the *danta* or *macho de monte,* Baird's tapir is the largest land mammal in Costa Rica. An endangered species, tapirs are active both day and night, foraging along riverbanks, streams, and forest clearings. **Prime Viewing:** Tapirs can be found in wet forested areas, particularly on the Caribbean and south Pacific slopes.

Coatimundi (Nasua narica) Known as *pizote* in Costa Rica, the raccoonlike coatimundi can adapt to habitat disturbances and is often spotted near hotels and nature lodges. Active both day and night, they are social animals, often found in groups of 10 to 20. Coatimundi are equally comfortable on the ground and in trees. **Prime Viewing:** Found in a variety of habitats across Costa Rica, from dry scrub to dense forests, on the mainland as well as the coastal islands.

Coatimundi

Collared Peccary (Tayassu tajacu) Called *saino* or *chancho de monte* in Costa Rica, the collared peccary is a black or brown piglike animal that travels in groups and has a strong musk odor. **Prime Viewing:** Low- and middle-elevation forests in most of Costa Rica.

Collared Peccary

Northern Tamandua (Tamandua Mexicana) Also known as the collared anteater (*oso hormiguero* in Spanish), the Northern Tamandua grows up to 77cm (30 in.) long, not counting its thick tail, which can be as long as its body. It is active diurnally and nocturnally. **Prime Viewing:** Low- and middle-elevation forests in most of Costa Rica.

Northern Tamandua

Three-Toed Sloth (Bradypus variegates) The larger and more commonly sighted of Costa Rica's two sloth species, the three-toed sloth has long, coarse, brown-to-gray fur and a distinctive eye-band. Each fore leg has three long, sharp claws. Except for brief periods to defecate, these slow-moving creatures are entirely arboreal. **Prime Viewing:** Low- and middle-elevation forests in most of Costa Rica. While sloths can be found in a wide variety of trees, they are most commonly spotted in the relatively sparsely leaved Cecropia (see later in this chapter).

Three-Toed Sloth

Mantled Howler Monkey (Alouatta palliate) Known locally as *mono congo,* the highly social mantled howler monkey grows to 56cm (22 in.) in size and often travels in groups of 10 to 30. The loud roar of the male can be heard as far as 1.6km (1 mile) away. **Prime Viewing:** Wet and dry forests across Costa Rica. Almost entirely arboreal, they tend to favor the higher reaches of the canopy.

Mantled Howler Monkey

White-Faced Monkey (Cibus capucinus) Known as both *mono cariblanca* and *mono capuchin* in Costa Rica, the white-faced or capuchin monkey is a mid-size species (46 cm/18 in.) with distinct white fur around its face, head, and forearms. It can be found in forests all around the country and often travels in large troops or family groups. **Prime Viewing:** Wet and dry forests across Costa Rica.

White-Faced Monkey

Red-Backed Squirrel Monkey

Red-Backed Squirrel Monkey (Saimiri oerstedii) The smallest and friskiest of Costa Rica's monkeys, the red-backed squirrel monkey, or *mono tití,* is also its most endangered. Active in the daytime, these monkeys travel in small to midsize groups. Squirrel monkeys do not have a prehensile (grasping) tail. **Prime Viewing:** Manuel Antonio National Park and Corcovado National Park.

Central American Spider Monkey

Central American Spider Monkey (Ateles geoffroyi) Known as both *mono araña* and *mono colorado* in Costa Rica, the spider monkey is one of the more acrobatic monkey species. A large monkey (64 cm/25 in.) with brown or silvery fur, it has long thin limbs and a long prehensile tail. It is active both day and night, and travels in small to midsize bands or family groups. **Prime Viewing:** Wet and dry forests across Costa Rica.

Nine-Banded Armadillo

Nine-Banded Armadillo (Dasypus novemcinctus) This is the most common armadillo species. Armadillo is Spanish for "little armored one," and that's an accurate description of this hard-carapace carrying mammal. The nine-banded armadillo can reach 65cm (26 in.) in length and weigh up to 4.5kg (9.9 lb.). These prehistoric-looking animals are nocturnal and terrestrial. The female gives birth to identical quadruplets from one single egg. **Prime Viewing:** Low- and middle-elevation forests, as well as farm lands, in most of Costa Rica.

Birds

Costa Rica has more than 880 identified species of resident and migrant birds. The variety of habitats and compact nature of the country make it a major bird-watching destination.

Jabiru Stork

Jabiru Stork (Jabiru mycteria) One of the largest birds in the world, this stork stands 1.5m (5 ft.) tall and has a wingspan of 2.4m (8 ft.) and a 30cm-long (1-ft.) bill. An endangered species, the jabiru is very rare, with only a dozen or so nesting pairs in Costa Rica. **Prime Viewing:** The wetlands of Palo Verde National Park and Caño Negro Wildlife Reserve are the best places to try to spot the jabiru stork. The birds arrive in Costa Rica from Mexico in November and fly north with the rains in May or June.

Keel-Billed Toucan (Ramphastos sulfuratus) The rainbow-colored canoe-shape bill and brightly colored feathers make the keel-billed toucan a favorite of bird-watching tours. The toucan can grow to about 51cm (20 in.) in length. Aside from its bill coloration, it is similar in shape and coloring to the chestnut-mandibled toucan. Costa Rica also is home to several smaller toucanet and aracari species. **Prime Viewing:** Lowland forests on the Caribbean and north Pacific slopes, up to 1,200m (4,000 ft.).

Scarlet Macaw (Ara macao) Known as *guacamaya* or *lapa* in Costa Rica, the scarlet macaw is a long-tailed member of the parrot family. It can reach 89cm (35 in.) in length, including its long pointed tail. The bird is endangered over most of its range, mainly because it is coveted as a pet. Its loud squawk and rainbow-colored feathers are quite distinctive. **Prime Viewing:** Carara National Park, Corcovado National Park, and Piedras Blancas National Park.

Resplendent Quetzal (Pharomchrus mocinno) Arguably the most spectacular bird in Central America, the Resplendent Quetzal, of the trogon family, can grow to 37cm (15 in.). The males are distinctive, with bright red chests, iridescent blue-green coats, yellow bills, and tail feathers that can reach another 76cm (30 in.) in length. The females lack the long tail feathers and have a duller beak and less pronounced red chest. **Prime Viewing:** High-elevation wet and cloud forests, particularly in the Monteverde Cloud Forest Biological Reserve and along the Cerro de la Muerte.

Magnificent Frigate Bird (Fregata magnificens) The magnificent frigate bird is a naturally agile flier, and it swoops (unlike other seabirds, it doesn't dive or swim) to pluck food from the water's surface—or more commonly, it steals catch from the mouths of other birds. **Prime Viewing:** Often seen soaring high overhead, along the shores and coastal islands of both coasts.

Montezuma's Oropendola (Psarocolius Montezuma) Montezuma's oropendola has a black head, brown body, a yellow-edged tail, a large black bill with an orange tip, and a blue patch under the eye. These birds build long, teardrop-shaped hanging nests, often found in large groups. They have several distinct loud calls, including one that they make while briefly hanging upside down. **Prime Viewing:** Low and middle elevations along the Caribbean slope, and some sections of eastern Guanacaste.

Keel-Billed Toucan

Scarlet Macaw

Resplendent Quetzal

Magnificent Frigate Bird

Montezuma's Oropendola

Roseate Spoonbill

Cattle Egret

Boat-Billed Heron

Laughing Falcon

Mealy Parrot

Roseate Spoonbill (Ajaia ajaja) The roseate spoonbill is a large water bird, pink or light red in color and with a large spoon-shaped bill. Also known as *garza rosada* (pink heron). The species almost became extinct in the United States because its pink wing feathers were used to make fans. **Prime Viewing:** Found in low-lying freshwater and saltwater wetlands nationwide, although rare along the Caribbean coast and plains. Common on the Pacific coast, north-central lowlands, and in the Golfo de Nicoya and Golfo Dulce areas.

Cattle Egret (Bubulcus ibis) The cattle egret is a snow-white bird, with a yellow bill and irises, and black legs. It changes color for the breeding season: A yellowish buff color appears on the head, chest, and back, and a reddish hue emerges on the bill and legs. **Prime Viewing:** Found near cattle, or following tractors, throughout Costa Rica.

Boat-Billed Heron (Cochlearius cochlearius) The midsize boat-billed heron (about 51cm/20 in.) has a large black head, a large broad bill, and a rusty brown color. **Prime Viewing:** Throughout the country, near marshes, swamps, rivers, and mangroves.

Laughing Falcon (Herpetotheres cachinnans) The laughing falcon is also known as the *guaco* in Costa Rica. It gets its name from its loud, piercing call. This largish (56cm/22-in.) bird of prey's wingspan reaches an impressive 94cm (37 in.). It specializes in eating both venomous and nonvenomous snakes but will also hunt lizards and small rodents. **Prime Viewing:** Throughout the country, most commonly in lowland areas, near forest edges, grasslands, and farmlands.

Mealy Parrot (Amazona farinose) Called *loro* or *loro verde* this large, vocal parrot is common in lowland tropical rainforests on both coasts. Almost entirely green, it has a touch of blue on the top of its head, and small red and blue accents on its wings. *Loro* means parrot, and *verde* means green, so you and locals alike may confuse this parrot with any number of other local species. **Prime Viewing:** Lowland rainforests on the Caribbean and Pacific coasts.

Scarlet Rumped Tanager (Ramphocelus costaricensis) With a striking scarlet red patch on its backside, this is one of the most commonly sighted tanagers in Costa Rica. It is known locally as *sargento* or *sangre de toro.* For true ornithologists, a reclassification has divided the Costa Rican scarlet rumped tanagers into two distinct species, Passerini's Tanager, which is found on the Caribbean slope and lowlands, and Cherrie's Tanager, which is found along the Pacific slope and lowlands. **Prime Viewing:** Throughout the country, in lowland and midelevation areas.

Osprey (Pandion haliatus) This large (.6m/2-ft.-tall, with a 1.8m/6-ft. wingspan) brownish bird with a white head is also known as *gavilan pescador,* or "fishing eagle." In flight, the osprey's wings "bend" backward. **Prime Viewing:** Found in lowland coastal areas and wetlands throughout Costa Rica; seen flying or perched in trees near water. A small population is resident year-round, although most are winter migrants, arriving September to October and departing April to May.

Ferruginous Pygmy Owl (Glaucidium brasilianum) Unlike most owls, this small (about 38cm/15-in.) grayish brown or reddish brown owl is most active during the day. **Prime Viewing:** In wooded areas, forest edges, and farmlands of low and middle elevations along the northern Pacific slope.

Violet Sabrewing (Campylopterus hemileucurus) The largest hummingbird found in Costa Rica, the violet sabrewing shines a deep purple when the sun strikes it right. Its beak is long, thick, and gently curving. **Prime Viewing:** Mid- and higher-elevation cloud forests and rainforests countrywide.

Clay-Colored Robin (Turdus grayi) In a country with such a rich variety of spectacularly plumaged bird species, this plain brown robin is an unlikely choice to be Costa Rica's national bird. However, it is extremely widespread and common, especially in urban areas of the Central Valley, and it has a wide range of pleasant calls and songs. Known locally as the *yiguirro,* it has uniform brown plumage, with a lighter brown belly and yellow bill. **Prime Viewing:** Low and middle elevations nationwide, especially in clearings, secondary forests, and amid human settlements.

Scarlet Rumped Tanager

Osprey

Pygmy Owl

Violet Sabrewing

Clay-Colored Robin

Amphibians

Frogs and toads are actually some of the most beguiling, beautiful, and easy-to-spot residents of tropical forests.

Marine Toad

Marine Toad (Bufo marinus) The largest toad in the Americas, the 20cm (8-in.) wart-covered marine toad is also known as the cane toad, or *sapo grande* (giant toad). Females are mottled in color, while males are uniformly brown. These voracious toads have been known to eat small mammals, other toads, lizards, and just about any insect within range. They have a very strong chemical defense mechanism. Glands spread across their back and behind their eyes secrete a powerful toxin when threatened. **Prime Viewing:** Despite the misleading name, this terrestrial toad is not found in marine environments, but can be found in forests and open areas throughout Costa Rica.

Red-Eyed Tree Frog

Red-Eyed Tree Frog (Agalychnis callidryas) The colorful 7.6-cm (3-in.) red-eyed tree frog usually has a pale or dark green back, sometimes with white or yellow spots, with blue-purple patches and vertical bars on the body, orange hands and feet, and deep red eyes. This nocturnal amphibian is also known as the gaudy leaf frog or red-eyed tree frog. **Prime Viewing:** This arboreal amphibian is most frequently found on the undersides of broad leaves, in low- and middle-elevation wet forests throughout Costa Rica. If you don't find this beautiful, distinctive-looking frog in the wild, you will certainly see its image on T-shirts and postcards.

Green and Black Poison Arrow Frog

Green and Black Poison Arrow Frog (Dendrobates auratus) Also called the harlequin poison-arrow frog, the small green and black poison arrow frog ranges between 2.5 and 4cm (1–1½ in.) in length. It has distinctive markings of iridescent green mixed with deep black. **Prime Viewing:** On the ground, around tree roots, and under fallen logs, in low- and middle-elevation wet forests on the Caribbean and southern Pacific slopes.

Reptiles

Costa Rica's reptile species range from the frightening and justly feared fer-de-lance pit viper and massive American crocodile to a wide variety of turtles and lizards. ***Note:*** Sea turtles are included in the "Sea Life" section below.

Boa Constrictor (Boa constrictor) Adult boa constrictors (*bécquer* in Costa Rica) average about 1.8 to 3m (6–10 ft.) in length and weigh over 27 kilograms (60 lb.). Their coloration camouflages them. Look for patterns of cream, brown, gray, and black ovals and diamonds. **Prime Viewing:** Low- and middle-elevation wet and dry forests, countrywide. They often live in the rafters and eaves of homes in rural areas.

Boa Constrictor

Fer-de-Lance (Bothrops atrox) Known as *terciopelo* in Costa Rica, the aggressive fer-de-lance can grow to 2.4m (8 ft.) in length. Beige, brown, or black triangles flank either side of the head, while the area under the head is a vivid yellow. These snakes begin life as arboreal but become increasingly terrestrial as they grow older and larger. **Prime Viewing:** Predominantly lower elevation forests, but has spread to almost all regions up to 1,300m (4,265 ft.), including towns and cities in agricultural areas.

Fer-de-Lance

Mussurana (Clelia clelia) This bluish black, brown, or grayish snake grows to 2.4m (8 ft.) in length. While slightly venomous, this snake has rear fangs and is of little danger to humans. In fact, it is prized and protected by locals, since its primary prey happens to be much more venomous pit vipers, like the fer-de-lance. **Prime Viewing:** Open forests, pastures, and farmlands across Costa Rica.

Mussurana

Tropical Rattlesnake (Crotalus durissus) Known as *cascabel* in Costa Rica, this pit viper has a triangular head, a pronounced ridge running along the middle of its back, and (of course) a rattling tail. It can reach 1.8m (6 ft.) in length. **Prime Viewing:** Mostly found in low elevation dry forests and open areas of Guanacaste.

Tropical Rattlesnake

Green Iguana (Iguana iguana) Despite its name, the green iguana comes in a range of coloring. Individuals can vary in color, ranging from bright green to a dull grayish green, with quite a bit of red and orange mixed in. Predominantly arboreal, it often perches on a branch overhanging a river and will plunge into the water when threatened. **Prime Viewing:** All lowland regions of the country, living near rivers and streams, along both coasts.

Green Iguana

COSTA RICAN WILDLIFE | Fauna

Basilisk

American Crocodile

Litter Skink

Slender Anole

Basilisk (Basiliscus vittatus) The basilisk can run across the water's surface for short distances on its hind legs, holding its body almost upright; thus its alternate name, "Jesus Christ lizard." **Prime Viewing:** In trees and on rocks located near water in wet forests throughout the country.

American Crocodile (Crocodylus acutus) Although an endangered species, environmental awareness and protection policies have allowed the massive American crocodile to mount an impressive comeback in recent years. While these reptiles can reach lengths of 6.4m (21 ft.), most are much smaller, usually less than 4m (13 ft.). **Prime Viewing:** Near swamps, estuaries, large rivers, and coastal lowlands, countrywide. Guaranteed viewing from the bridge over the Tarcoles River, on the coastal highway to Jacó and Manuel Antonio.

Litter Skink (Sphenomorphus cherriei) This small, brown lizard has a proportionally large head and neck, and short legs. A black stripe extends off the back of its eyes and down its sides, with a yellowish area below. **Prime Viewing:** Common on the ground and in leaf litter of low- and middle-elevation forests throughout the country.

Slender Anole (Anolis [norops] limifrons) This thin, olive-colored lizard can reach 5.1cm (2 in.) in length. There are some 25 related species of *anolis* or *norops* lizards. **Prime Viewing:** Lowland rainforests nationwide.

Sea Life

Boasting over 1,290km (780 miles) of shoreline on both the Pacific and Caribbean coasts, Costa Rica has a rich diversity of underwater flora and fauna.

Whale Shark (Rhincodon typus)   Although the whale shark grows to lengths of 14m (45 ft.) or more, its gentle nature makes swimming with them a special treat for divers and snorkelers. **Prime Viewing:** Can occasionally be spotted off Isla del Caño, and more frequently off Isla del Coco.

Whale Shark

Green Turtle (Chelonia mydas)   A large sea turtle, the green turtle has a teardrop-shaped carapace that can range in color from dull green to dark brown. Adults reach some 1.5m (4.9 ft.) and weigh an average of 200kg (440 lb.). **Prime viewing**: Carribean coast around Tortuguero National Park, from July through mid-October, with August through September their peak period.

Green turtle

Leatherback Sea Turtle (Dermochelys coriacea)   The world's largest sea turtle (reaching nearly 2.4m/8 ft. in length and weighing more than 544kg/1,200 lb.), the leatherback sea turtle is now an endangered species. Unlike most other turtle species, the leatherback's carapace is not a hard shell, but rather a thick, leathery skin. **Prime Viewing:** Playa Grande, near Tamarindo, is a prime nesting site from early October through mid-February; also nests off Tortuguero in much lesser numbers from February through June, peaking during the months of March and April.

Leatherback Sea Turtle

Olive Ridley Sea Turtle (Lepidochelys olivacea)   Also known as *tortuga lora,* the olive ridley sea turtle is the most common of Costa Rica's sea turtles, famous for its massive group nestings, or *arribadas.* **Prime Viewing:** Large *arribadas* occur from July through December, and to a lesser extent from January through June. Playa Nancite in Santa Rosa National Park and Playa Ostional, north of Nosara, are the prime nesting sites.

Olive Ridley Sea Turtle

Moray Eel (Gymnothorax mordax)   Distinguished by a swaying serpent-head and teeth-filled jaw that continually opens and closes, the moray eel is most commonly seen with only its head appearing from behind rocks. At night, however, it leaves its home along the reef to hunt for small fish, crustaceans, shrimp, and octopus. **Prime Viewing:** Rocky areas and reefs off both coasts.

Moray Eel

Humpbacked Whale

Bottle-Nosed Dolphin

Manta Ray

Brain Coral

Humpbacked Whale (Megaptera novae-angliae)   The migratory humpbacked whale spends the winters in warm southern waters and has been increasingly spotted close to the shores of Costa Rica's southern Pacific coast. These mammals have black backs and whitish throat and chest areas. Females have been known to calve here. **Prime Viewing:** Most common in the waters off Drake Bay and Isla del Caño, from December through April.

Bottle-Nosed Dolphin (Tursiops truncates)   A wide tail fin, dark gray back, and light gray sides identify bottle-nosed dolphins. Dolphins grow to lengths of 3.7m (12 ft.) and weigh up to 635 kilograms (1,400 lb.). **Prime Viewing:** Along both coasts and inside the Golfo Dulce.

Manta Ray (Manta birostris)   The manta is the largest species of ray, with a wingspan that can reach 6m (20 ft.) and a body weight known to exceed 1,360kg (3,000 lb.). Despite its daunting appearance, the manta is quite gentle. If you are snorkeling or diving, watch for one of these extraordinary and graceful creatures. **Prime Viewing:** All along the Pacific coast.

Brain Coral (Diploria strigosa)   The distinctive brain coral is named for its striking physical similarity to a human brain. **Prime Viewing:** Reefs off both coasts.

Invertebrates

Creepy-crawlies, biting bugs, spiders, and the like give most folks chills. But this group, which includes moths, butterflies, ants, beetles, bees, and even crabs, features some of the most abundant, fascinating, and easily viewed fauna in Costa Rica. In fact, Costa Rica has nearly 500,000 recorded species of invertebrates, with more than 9,000 species of butterflies and moths alone.

Blue Morpho

Leafcutter Ants

Blue Morpho (Morpho peleides) The large blue morpho butterfly, with a wingspan of up to 15cm (6 in.), has brilliantly iridescent blue wings when opened. Fast and erratic fliers, they are often glimpsed flitting across your peripheral vision in dense forest. **Prime Viewing:** Country-wide, particularly in moist environments.

Leafcutter Ants (Atta cephalotes) You can't miss the miniature rainforest highways formed by these industrious red ants carrying their freshly cut payload. The ants do not actually eat the leaves, but instead feed off a fungus that grows on the decomposing leaves in their massive underground nests. **Prime Viewing:** Can be found in most forests countrywide.

Golden Silk Spider (Nephila clavipes) The common Neotropical golden silk spider weaves meticulous webs that can be as much as .5m (2 ft.) across. The adult female of this species can reach 7.6cm (3 in.) in length, including the legs, although the males are tiny. The silk of this spider is extremely strong and is being studied for industrial purposes. **Prime Viewing:** Lowland forests on both coasts.

Mouthless Crab (Gecarcinus quadratus) The nocturnal mouthless crab is a distinctively colored land crab with bright orange legs, purple claws, and a deep black shell or carapace. **Prime Viewing:** All along the Pacific coast.

Sally Lightfoot Crab (Grapsus grapsus) Known simply as *cangrego* or "crab," this is the most common crab spotted in Costa Rica. It is a mid-size crab with a colorful carapace that can range from dark brown to deep red to bright yellow, with a wide variation in striations and spotting. **Prime Viewing:** On rocky outcroppings near the water's edge all along both coasts.

Golden Silk Spider

Mouthless Crab

Sally Lightfoot Crab

Ceiba

FLORA
Trees

Despite the cliche to the contrary, it's often a good thing to be able to identify specific trees within a forest. I include illustrations of leaves, flowers, seeds, and fruit to get you started.

Ceiba (Ceiba pentandra) Also known as the kapok tree, the ceiba tree is typically emergent (its large umbrella-shape crown emerges above the forest canopy), reaching as high as 60m (197 ft.); it is among the tallest trees of Costa Rica's tropical forest. The ceiba tree has a thick columnar trunk, often with large buttresses. Sometimes called the silk cotton tree in English, the ceiba's seed pod produces a light, airy fiber that is resilient, buoyant, and insulating. Throughout history this fiber has been used for bedding, and as stuffing for pillows, clothing, and even life jackets. Ceiba trees may flower as infrequently as once every 5 years, especially in wetter forests. **Prime Viewing:** Tropical forests throughout Costa Rica.

Guanacaste (Enterolobium cyclocarpum) The guanacaste gives its name to Costa Rica's northwestern-most province, and is the country's national tree. With a broad and pronounced crown, the guanacaste can reach heights of over 39m (130 ft.), and its trunk can measure more than 1.8m (6 ft.) in diameter. Guanacaste is prized as a shade tree, and is often planted on pasture lands to provide relief to cattle from the hot tropical sun. **Prime Viewing:** Low elevation forests and plains throughout Costa Rica. Most commonly viewed in the open plains and savannahs of Guanacaste.

Guanacaste

Strangler Fig (Ficus aurea) This parasitic tree gets its name from the fact that it envelops and eventually strangles its host tree. The *matapalo* or strangler fig begins as an epiphyte, whose seeds are deposited high in a tree's canopy by bats, birds, or monkeys. The young strangler then sends long roots down to the earth. The sap is used to relieve burns. **Prime Viewing:** Primary and secondary forests countrywide.

Strangler Fig

Cecropia (Cecropia obtusifolia) Several Cecropia (trumpet tree) species are found in Costa Rica. Most are characterized by large, handlike clusters of broad leaves, and a hollow, bamboolike trunk. They are "gap specialists," fast-growing opportunists that can fill in a gap caused by a tree fall or landslide. Their trunks are usually home to Aztec ants. **Prime Viewing:** Primary and secondary forests, rivers, and roadsides, countrywide.

Cecropia

Gumbo Limbo

Gumbo Limbo (Bursera simaruba) The bark of the gumbo limbo is its most distinguishing feature: A paper-thin red outer layer, when peeled off the tree, reveals a bright green bark. In Costa Rica the tree is called *indio desnudo* (naked Indian). In other countries it is the "tourist tree." Both names refer to its reddish, flaking outer bark. The bark is used as a remedy for gum disease; gumbo limbo–bark tea allegedly alleviates hypertension. **Prime Viewing:** Primary and secondary forests, countrywide.

Flowers & Other Plants

Costa Rica has an amazing wealth of tropical flora, including some 1,200 orchid species, and over 2,000 bromeliad species.

Guaria Morada (Cattleya skinneri) The guaria morada orchid is the national flower of Costa Rica. Sporting a purple and white flower, this plant is also called the "Easter orchid" as it tends to flower between March and April each year. **Prime Viewing:** Countrywide from sea level to 1,220m (4,000 ft.). While usually epiphytic, it also is found as a terrestrial plant.

Heliconia (Heliconia collinsiana) More than 40 of the world's species of tropical heliconia are found in Costa Rica. The flowers of this species are darkish pink in color, and the underside of the plant's large leaves are coated in white wax. **Prime Viewing:** Low to middle elevations countrywide, particularly in moist environments.

Hotlips (Psychotria poeppigiana) Related to coffee, hotlips is a forest flower that boasts thick red "lips" that resemble the Rolling Stones logo. The small white flowers (found inside the red "lips") attract a variety of butterflies and hummingbirds. **Prime Viewing:** In the undergrowth of dense forests countrywide.

Guaria Morada

Helicona

Hotlips

Red Torch Ginger

Poor Man's Umbrella

Red Torch Ginger (Nicolaia elatior) Called *bastón del emperador* (the Emperor's cane) in Costa Rica, the tall red torch ginger plant has an impressive bulbous red bract, often mistaken for the flower. The numerous, small white flowers actually emerge out of this bract. Originally a native to Indonesia, it is now quite common in Costa Rica. **Prime Viewing:** Countrywide, particularly in moist environments and gardens.

Poor Man's Umbrella (Gunnera insignis) The poor man's umbrella, a broad-leaved rainforest ground plant, is a member of the rhubarb family. The massive leaves are often used, as the colloquial name suggests, for protection during rainstorms. **Prime Viewing:** Low- to middle-elevation moist forests countrywide. Commonly seen in Poás National Park and Braulio Carrillo National Park.

SPANISH TERMS & PHRASES

C osta Rican Spanish is neither the easiest nor the most difficult dialect to understand. Ticos speak at a relatively relaxed speed and enunciate clearly, without dropping too many final consonants. The *y* and *ll* sounds are subtly, almost inaudibly, pronounced. Perhaps the most defining idiosyncrasy of Costa Rican Spanish is the way Ticos overemphasize, and almost chew, their *r*'s.

If you're looking for a more comprehensive dictionary and language resource, pick up a copy of *Frommer's Spanish Phrase Finder & Dictionary,* or *Frommer's Spanish Phrasebook and Culture Guide.* Both are excellent pocket books with a wealth of information to make your travel interactions more rewarding.

BASIC WORDS & PHRASES

English	Spanish	Pronunciation
Hello	Buenos días	***bweh*-nohss *dee*-ahss**
How are you?	¿Cómo está usted?	***koh*-moh ehss-*tah* oo-*stehd***
Very well	Muy bien	**mwee byehn**

English	Spanish	Pronunciation
Thank you	Gracias	**grah**-syahss
Goodbye	Adiós	ad-**dyohss**
Please	Por favor	pohr fah-**vohr**
Yes	Sí	see
No	No	noh
Excuse me (to get by someone)	Perdóneme	pehr-**doh**-neh-meh
Excuse me (to begin a question)	Disculpe	dees-**kool**-peh
Give me	Deme	**deh**-meh
Where is . . . ?	¿Dónde está . . . ?	**dohn**-deh ehss-**tah**
the station	la estación	la ehss-**tah**-syohn
the bus stop	la parada	la pah-**rah**-dah
a hotel	un hotel	oon oh-**tehl**
a restaurant	un restaurante	oon res-tow-**rahn**-teh
the toilet	el servicio	el ser-**vee**-syoh
To the right	A la derecha	ah lah deh-**reh**-chah
To the left	A la izquierda	ah lah ees-**kyehr**-dah
Straight ahead	Adelante	ah-deh-**lahn**-teh
I would like . . .	Quiero . . .	**kyeh**-roh
to eat	comer	ko-**mehr**
a room	una habitación	oo-nah ah-bee-tah-**syohn**
How much is it?	¿Cuánto?	**kwahn**-toh
When?	¿Cuándo?	**kwan**-doh
What?	¿Qué?	keh
Yesterday	Ayer	ah-**yehr**
Today	Hoy	oy
Tomorrow	Mañana	mah-**nyah**-nah
Breakfast	Desayuno	deh-sah-**yoo**-noh
Lunch	Almuerzo	ahl-**mwehr**-soh
Dinner	Cena	**seh**-nah
Do you speak English?	¿Habla usted inglés?	**ah**-blah oo-**stehd** een-**glehss**
I don't understand Spanish very well.	No entiendo muy bien el español.	noh ehn-tyehn-do mwee byehn el ehss-pah-nyohl

NUMBERS

English	Spanish	Pronunciation
0	cero	*ser*-oh
1	uno	*oo*-noh
2	dos	dohss
3	tres	trehss
4	cuatro	*kwah*-troh
5	cinco	*seen*-koh
6	seis	sayss
7	siete	*syeh*-teh
8	ocho	*oh*-choh
9	nueve	*nweh*-beh
10	diez	dyehss
11	once	*ohn*-seh
12	doce	*doh*-seh
13	trece	*treh*-seh
14	catorce	kah-*tohr*-seh
15	quince	*keen*-seh
16	dieciséis	dyeh-see-*sayss*
17	diecisiete	dyeh-see-*syeh*-teh
18	dieciocho	dyeh-see-*oh*-choh
19	diecinueve	dyeh-see-*nweh*-beh
20	veinte	*bayn*-teh
30	treinta	*trayn*-tah
40	cuarenta	kwah-*rehn*-tah
50	cincuenta	seen-*kwehn*-tah
60	sesenta	seh-*sehn*-tah
70	setenta	seh-*tehn*-tah
80	ochenta	oh-*chehn*-tah
90	noventa	noh-*behn*-tah
100	cien	syehn
1,000	mil	meel

DAYS OF THE WEEK

English	Spanish	Pronunciation
Monday	lunes	*loo*-nehss
Tuesday	martes	*mahr*-tehss
Wednesday	miércoles	*myehr*-koh-lehs
Thursday	jueves	*wheh*-behss
Friday	viernes	*byehr*-nehss
Saturday	sábado	*sah*-bah-doh
Sunday	domingo	doh-*meen*-goh

SOME TYPICAL TICO WORDS & PHRASES

Birra   Slang for beer.

Boca   Literally means "mouth," but also a term to describe a small appetizer served alongside a drink at many bars.

Bomba   Translates literally as "pump," but is used in Costa Rica for "gas station."

Brete   Work, or job.

Buena nota   To be good, or have a good vibe.

Casado   Literally means "married," but is the local term for a popular restaurant offering that features a main dish and various side dishes.

Chapa   Derogatory way to call someone stupid or clumsy.

Chepe   Slang term for the capital city, San José.

Choza   Slang for house or home. Also called *chante*.

Chunche   Knickknack; thing, as in "whatchamacallit."

Con mucho gusto   With pleasure.

De hoy en ocho   In 1 week's time.

Diay   An untranslatable but common linguistic punctuation, often used to begin a sentence.

Estar de chicha   To be angry.

Fria   Literally "cold," but used to mean a cold beer—*una fria, por favor.*

Fut   Short for *fútbol,* or soccer.

Goma   Hangover.

Harina   Literally "flour," but used to mean money.

La sele   Short for *la selección,* the Costa Rican national soccer team.

Limpio   Literally means "clean," but is the local term for being broke, or having no money.

Macha or **machita**   A blond woman.

Mae   Translates like "man"; used by many Costa Ricans, particularly teenagers, as frequent verbal punctuation.

Maje   A lot like *mae,* above, but with a slightly derogatory connotation.

Mala nota   Bad vibe, or bad situation.

Mala pata   Bad luck.

Mejenga   An informal, or pickup, soccer game.

Pachanga or **pelón**   Both terms are used to signify a big party or gathering.

Ponga la maría, por favor   This is how you ask taxi drivers to turn on the meter.

Pulpería   The Costa Rican version of the "corner store" or small market.

Pura paja   Pure nonsense or BS.

Pura vida   Literally, "pure life"; translates as "everything's great."

Qué torta   What a mess; what a screw-up.

Si Dios quiere   God willing; you'll hear Ticos say this all the time.

Soda   A casual diner-style restaurant serving cheap Tico meals.

Tico   Costa Rican.

Tiquicia   Costa Rica.

Tuanis   Similar in usage and meaning to *pura vida,* above.

Una teja   100 colones.

Un rojo   1,000 colones.

Un tucán   5,000 colones.

Upe!   Common shout to find out if anyone is home; used frequently since doorbells are so scarce.

Zarpe   Last drink of the night, or "one more for the road."

MENU TERMS

FISH

Almejas   Clams

Atún   Tuna

Bacalao   Cod

Calamares   Squid

Camarones   Shrimp

Cangrejo   Crab

Ceviche   Marinated seafood salad

Dorado   Dolphin or mahimahi

Langosta   Lobster

Lenguado   Sole

Mejillones   Mussels

Ostras   Oysters

Pargo   Snapper

Pulpo   Octopus

Trucha   Trout

MEATS

Albóndigas   Meatballs

Bistec   Beefsteak

Cerdo   Pork

Chicharrones   Fried pork rinds

Chorizo   Sausage

Chuleta   Literally chop, usually pork chop

Cordero   Lamb

Costillas   Ribs

Delmonico   Rib-eye

Jamón   Ham

Lengua   Tongue

Lomo   Sirloin

Lomito   Tenderloin

Pato   Duck

Pavo   Turkey

Pollo   Chicken

Salchichas   Hot dogs, but sometimes refers to any sausage

VEGETABLES

Aceitunas   Olives

Alcachofa   Artichoke

Berenjena   Eggplant

Cebolla Onion
Elote Corn on the cob
Ensalada Salad
Espinacas Spinach
Frijoles Beans
Lechuga Lettuce
Maíz Corn
Palmito Heart of palm
Papa Potato
Pepino Cucumber
Tomate Tomato
Yuca Yucca, cassava, or manioc
Zanahoria Carrot

FRUITS

Aguacate Avocado
Banano Banana
Carambola Star fruit
Cereza Cherry
Ciruela Plum
Durazno Peach
Frambuesa Raspberry
Fresa Strawberry
Granadilla Sweet passion fruit
Limón Lemon or lime
Mango Mango
Manzana Apple
Maracuya Tart passion fruit
Melón Melon
Mora Blackberry
Naranja Orange
Papaya Papaya
Piña Pineapple
Plátano Plantain
Sandía Watermelon
Toronja Grapefruit

BASICS

Aceite Oil
Ajo Garlic
Arreglado Small meat sandwich
Azúcar Sugar
Casado Plate of the day
Gallo Corn tortilla topped with meat or chicken
Gallo pinto Rice and beans

Hielo Ice
Mantequilla Butter
Miel Honey
Mostaza Mustard
Natilla Sour cream
Olla de carne Meat and vegetable soup
Pan Bread
Patacones Fried plantain chips
Picadillo Chopped vegetable side dish
Pimienta Pepper
Queso Cheese
Sal Salt
Tamal Filled cornmeal pastry
Tortilla Flat corn pancake

DRINKS

Agua purificada Purified water
Agua con gas Sparkling water
Agua sin gas Plain water
Bebida Drink
Café Coffee
Café con leche Coffee with milk
Cerveza Beer
Chocolate caliente Hot chocolate
Jugo Juice
Leche Milk
Natural Fruit juice
Natural con leche Milkshake
Refresco Soft drink
Ron Rum
Té Tea
Trago Alcoholic drink

OTHER RESTAURANT TERMS

Al grill Grilled
Al horno Oven-baked
Al vapor Steamed
Asado Roasted
Caliente Hot
Cambio or vuelto Change
Cocido Cooked
Comida Food
Congelado Frozen
Crudo Raw

El baño   Toilet
Frío   Cold
Frito   Fried
Grande   Big or large
La cuenta   The check
Medio   Medium

Medio rojo   Medium rare
Muy cocido   Well-done
Pequeño   Small
Poco cocido or **rojo**   Rare
Tres cuartos   Medium-well-done

OTHER USEFUL TERMS

HOTEL TERMS

Aire acondicionado   Air-conditioning
Almohada   Pillow
Baño   Bathroom
Baño privado   Private bathroom
Calefacción   Heating
Caja de seguridad   Safe
Cama   Bed
Cobija   Blanket
Colchón   Mattress
Cuarto or Habitación   Room
Escritorio   Desk
Habitación simple/sencilla   Single room
Habitación doble   Double room
Habitación triple   Triple room
Llave   Key
Mosquitero   Mosquito net
Sábanas   Sheets
Seguro de puerta   Door lock
Silla   Chair
Telecable   Cable TV
Ventilador   Fan

TRAVEL TERMS

Aduana   Customs
Aeropuerto   Airport
Avenida   Avenue
Avión   Airplane
Aviso   Warning
Bus   Bus
Cajero   ATM, also called *cajero automatico*
Calle   Street
Cheques viajeros   Traveler's checks
Correo   Mail, or post office
Cuadra   City block

Dinero or plata   Money
Embajada   Embassy
Embarque   Boarding
Entrada   Entrance
Equipaje   Luggage
Este   East
Frontera   Border
Lancha or bote   Boat
Norte   North
Oeste   West
Occidente   West
Oriente   East
Pasaporte   Passport
Puerta de salida or **puerta de embarque**   Boarding gate
Salida   Exit
Sur   South
Tarjeta de embarque   Boarding pass
Vuelo   Flight

EMERGENCY TERMS

¡Auxilio!   Help!
Ambulancia   Ambulance
Bomberos   Fire brigade
Clínica   Clinic or hospital
Doctor or **médico**   Doctor
Emergencia   Emergency
Enfermo/enferma   Sick
Enfermera   Nurse
Farmacia   Pharmacy
Fuego or **incendio**   Fire
Hospital   Hospital
Ladrón   Thief
Peligroso   Dangerous
Policía   Police
¡Váyase!   Go away!

Index

PHOTO CREDITS